SECOND EDITION

A History of Psychology

Main Currents in Psychological Thought

Thomas Hardy Leahey
Virginia Commonwealth University

PRENTICE-HALL, INC., Englewood Cliffs, New Jersey 07632

Library of Congress Cataloging-in-Publication Data

LEAHEY, THOMAS HARDY.
  A history of psychology.

  Bibliography
  Includes index.
  1. Psychology—History. I. Title.
BF81.L4 1987   150'.9   86–18643
ISBN 0–13–391764–9

Editorial/production supervision: Matrix Productions
Interior design: Joan Stone
Cover design: Wanda Lubelska Design
Manufacturing buyer: Barbara Kelly Kittle

© 1987 by Prentice-Hall
A Division of Simon & Schuster, Inc.
Englewood Cliffs, New Jersey 07632

Printed in the United States of America

10 9 8 7 6 5 4 3 2

ISBN   0-13-391764-9   01

Prentice-Hall International (UK) Limited, *London*
Prentice-Hall of Australia Pty. Limited, *Sydney*
Prentice-Hall Canada Inc., *Toronto*
Prentice-Hall Hispanoamericana, S.A., *Mexico*
Prentice-Hall of India Private Limited, *New Delhi*
Prentice-Hall of Japan, Inc., *Tokyo*
Prentice-Hall of Southeast Asia Pte. Ltd., *Singapore*
Editora Prentice-Hall do Brasil, Ltda., *Rio de Janeiro*

Contents

Preface to the First Edition   *vii*
Preface to the Second Edition   *xi*

I _____

BACKGROUND TO PSYCHOLOGY   1

One
Introduction   2

Understanding Psychology   *3*
Understanding Science   *4*
Psychology and Science   *24*
Understanding History   *28*
The Plan of this Book   *31*
Bibliography   *31*
References   *32*

Two
The Classical World   34

Before Philosophy   *35*
Philosophy before Plato   *37*
The Two Classic Statements of Western Philosophy   *42*
Philosophy after Aristotle   *52*
Conclusion: The Essential Tensions of Western Thought   *55*
Bibliography   *55*
References   *57*

Three
Spirituality and Individualism   58

From Classical to Medieval: The Early Middle Ages (476 1000)   *59*
The Flowering of Medieval Civilization. The High Middle Ages (1000 1300)   *67*

From Medieval to Modern: The Late Middle Ages, Renaissance, and
  Reformation (1300-1600)   73
Conclusion: The Classical-Medieval-Renaissance Outlook   83
Bibliography   84
References   86

Four
The Mechanization of the World Picture (1600-1700)   87

The Scientific Revolution   88
Remaking Philosophy   92
Philosophy, Science, and Human Affairs   98
Conclusion: The Seventeenth Century—Seeds of Change   103
Bibliography   104
References   106

Five
Reason and Reaction   107

The Skeptical Crisis   108
Philosophy, Science, and Human Nature   121
The Counter-Enlightenment   130
Conclusion: Reason and Its Discontents   133
Bibliography   135
References   137

Six
To the Threshold of Psychology   138

The World of the Nineteenth Century   139
Toward the Science of Psychology   161
Conclusions   171
Bibliography   174
References   175

II
FOUNDING PSYCHOLOGY   177

Seven
The Psychology of Consciousness   178

Wilhelm Wundt (1832-1920) and Ganzheit Psychology   179
Edward Bradford Titchener (1867-1927) and Structuralism   188
Challenges to the Analytic Psychology of Consciousness   191
Conclusion: The Fate of the Psychology of Consciousness   199
Bibliography   202
References   204

Eight
The Psychology of the Unconscious Mind   206

Background   207
Major Works   214
Conclusions   226
Bibliography   228
References   231

Nine
The Psychology of Adaptation (1855-1891)   233

The Beginnings of the Psychology of Adaptation in Britain   235
Psychology in the New World   243
Conclusion: Perception and Thinking Are Only There for Behavior's Sake   253
Bibliography   253
References   255

III
THE RISE OF BEHAVIORALISM   257

Ten
The Conspiracy of Naturalism   258

Introduction   259
*Building on the Principles: The Motor Theory of Consciousness
   (1892-1896)   268*
From Philosophy to Biology: Functional Psychology (1896-1910)   271
New Directions in Animal Psychology (1898-1909)   280
Rethinking Mind: The Consciousness Debate (1904-1912)   288
Conclusion: Behavioralism Discovered (1910-1912)   293
Bibliography   295
References   297

Eleven
Psychology Takes Off   300

Developing Behavioralism (1913-1930)   301
Major Formulations of Behavioralism (1930-1950)   311
Conclusion: We're All Behavioralists Now   325
References   326

Twelve
Psychology Takes Off   329

Applied Psychology (1896-1916)   331
Psychologists in Professional Controversy (1917-1940)   333
Psychologists in Social Controversy (1917-1940)   339
Psychology Transformed (1940-1950)   354
Conclusion   360

Bibliography   363
References   365

IV ————————————————————————————————————
PSYCHOLOGY SINCE WORLD WAR II   369

Thirteen
Eclectic Psychology (1950-1958)   370

Troubles with Behaviorism (1950-1954)   371
Are Theories of Learning Necessary? Radical Behaviorism (1938-1958)   379
The Roots of Cognitive Science (1943-1958)   389
Psychology and Society (1950-1958)   402
Bibliography   404
References   406

Fourteen
Years of Turmoil (1958-1968)   409

Challenges to Behaviorism   410
Erosion of the Foundations   417
Cognitive Psychology Asserts Itself   423
Psychology and Society   428
Conclusion: Revolt But No Revolution   435
Bibliography   438
References   439

Fifteen
Contemporary Psychology   443

Cognitive Science   444
Doubts About Cognitive Science   451
The Strange Death of Radical Behaviorism   461
Challenges to Scientific Psychology   464
Psychology and Society   472
Conclusion: The Psychological Society   478
Bibliography   480
References   483

Index   488

Preface to the First Edition

SOME WORDS TO THE STUDENT

Human beings make history—political, military, social, and scientific. In the history of science, ideas are especially important, for science is a changing collection of ideas to which short-lived human beings make contributions. This is not to deny that human personalities and institutions play a role in shaping science; but it is to say that the history of science can be written and studied in more than one way. One may choose to study the history of a science as a succession of great scientists and their major contributions to the field. Or one may study the history of a science as an institution, recording the founding of laboratories and the intellectual genealogies of the generations of scientists. Or, finally, one may study the history of a science solely as a collection of scientific concepts that evolve over time, paying relatively little attention to the personal histories of the scientists who formulate the concepts or the laboratories that put them to the test. Since historians have only limited space at their disposal, the historian cannot practice all three kinds of scientific history, no matter how desirable that might be. This book contains practically no institutional history, which is probably the least developed aspect of the history of psychology. Instead, we will focus our attention on the leading psychological *concepts* as they have evolved since the earliest days of recorded human history. To help organize our study of these concepts and how they have changed, I have chosen to consider the leading exponents of different psychological systems during each historical era. Although little will be said about the personal backgrounds of these people, concentration of them will help pull together concepts into competing viewpoints on the nature of human nature and will prevent us from diffusing our efforts.

Another important option is open to a historian of science. Older histories of the sciences were generally *internal* histories considering the development of the technical ideas of each science independent of the broader intellectual and social context in which the science operated. More recently, histories of the sciences have tended to be *external* histories considering the outside intellectual and social context and its effects on the development of the science. For the most part, this book tends to be externalistic. Psychology is a young science, with only a short history of technical concepts: Before the nineteenth century, psychological ideas were always part of some other field—philosophy, biology, or politics. Moreover, since psychology studies human nature—on which everyone has opinions—it is particularly subject to influence by larger social and intellectual currents. Such is not the case in other sciences. For example, physics has over its long history become so abstruse that society has little *intellectual* influence on it, although both physics and psychology are profoundly affected as institutions by the degree of support given by society at large.

No historian can be neutral to the subject matter. Historians must care about it enough to want to understand it and to make it come alive for others. Historians must be fair; they must weigh argument and counterargument; and finally, they must choose. Historians must choose some facts over others, for they cannot record everything. They must choose to discuss some thinkers and not others, for not all are equally great—although greatness is hard to define. Historians must choose some concepts over others, for some have survived while others have become extinct. They must choose some interpretation to put on the facts, events, people, and concepts written about, for history is an understanding of the past.

It is therefore the duty of the historian to state at the outset where he or she stands, what ideas he or she accepts or rejects. In short, the historian's point of view must be examined and communicated to the audience. What follows is an attempt to do this for myself.

I stand more in the rationalist tradition than in the empiricist. In philosophy I sympathize with Plato more than Aristotle, with the Stoics more than the atomists, with Descartes and Kant more than Locke and Hume. I came to psychology by way of Freud and later was trained as a cognitive psychologist. I admire Wundt and Piaget, Tolman and Chomsky, more than Titchener and Watson, Hull and Skinner. My views on science have been shaped by Einstein, Popper, Toulmin, Kuhn, Feyerabend, and Suppe more than by Carnap, Feigle, Mach, and Bridgmann. My approach to history has been conditioned by Hegel and Carlyle, Kendall and Cantor.

The purpose of this book and of the course for which you are using it is to give you a chance to work out your own point of view. The concepts and issues you learn about in content courses do not exist in a vacuum. They arose and existed in a particular historical context. The questions asked in today's research are the outcome of a historical process and the answer given contributes to that process. The opportunity that *history* and *systems* gives you is a chance to see the historical context and the historical process, to reflect on psychology as it is—and on your own experiences as a student of psychology.

Erik Erikson describes adolescence as a search for identity, a necessary prerequisite to a productive adult life. Identity is achieved through reflections on one's past and present and through making a decision on where to go and what to do with one's life. Your reflection on psychology's past and present state is an important part of finding your identity within psychology. You should come away from your experience not with a list of names, dates, and events, but with an understanding of what psychology is and of your own relation to it. You should not be a passive recorder of a monotonous march of years, but rather an explorer of the past and great minds. The first task is dull and bloodless; the second is an adventure and full of life.

I would also like to acknowledge the helpful, if not always agreeable comments of the usually anonymous prepublication reviewers, all professors of psychology: Dr. Richard Blanton, Vanderbilt University; Dr. James Brennen, University of Massachusetts, Boston; Dr. Darryl Bruce, Florida State University; Dr. Patrick Capretta, Miami University (Oxford, Ohio); Dr. T. S. Krawiec, Skidmore College (Saratoga Springs, New York); Dr. Richard Morris, Trent University, (Peterborough, Ontario, Canada); Dr. Barbara Ross, University of Massachusetts, Boston; Dr. E. L. Saldanha, University of Southern Maine (Portland); Dr. Anthony Walsh, Chairman of Psychology, the Newport College-Salve Regina (Newport, Rhode Island); Dr. Michael Wertheimer, University of Colorado at Boulder. It is especially important to point out that I remain solely responsible for whatever virtues and flaws are in this book.

My most important acknowledgment goes to my wife, Grace. She read every word, compiled the index, and made numerous improvements, large and small, to the writing of the book. Without her efforts the manuscript would have been awkward and unclear. She also typed several of the chapters. And above all she endured the trials of pregnancy and raising an infant through it all. My second acknowledgment is to William Brewer, my mentor in graduate school, who never demanded technical specialization to the detriment of broad philosophical and historical ideas about psychology. His own unpublished analysis of behaviorism is central to the statement of the behaviorist paradigm in Chapter 10 and 11. Two other teachers, Frederick Suppe and Don Dulany, taught me philosophy of science, and some of their ideas helped shape Chapter 1. Finally, however, the responsibility for everything in this book is mine.

Elizabeth, who came in the middle,
and
Grace, who helped through it all, twice

Preface
to the Second Edition

One of the fragments of the Greek poet Archilochus goes, "The fox knows many things, but the hedgehog knows one big thing." The distinguished historian of ideas Sir Isaiah Berlin uses this cryptic fragment to represent

> . . . one of the deepest differences which divide writers and thinkers, and it may be, human beings in general. For there exists a great chasm between those, on the one side [the hedgehogs], who relate everything to a single central vision . . . a single, universal organizing principle in terms of which alone all that they are and say has significance—and, on the other side [the foxes], those who pursue many ends, often unrelated and often contradictory, connected, if at all, only in some *de facto* way. . . .*

Dante was a hedgehog; Shakespeare a fox. Plato, who devised an ideal Republic, was a hedgehog; Socrates, the gadfly on the rump of the state, was a fox. When I wrote the first edition of this book I thought I was a hedgehog, a rationalist, albeit at times an uncomfortable one. I have found out, however, that I am a fox, and am happy to be so.

Richard Rorty, in his *Philosophy and the mirror of nature*,** distinguishes capital-P *Philosophy* from small-p *philosophy*. Capital-P Philosophers are philosophy's hedgehogs. Their ambition is to make Philosophy the first and foundational discipline for all other disciplines, providing the first principles upon which scientists and humanists build. Small-p philosophers, on the other hand, are philosophy's foxes, critically examining the ideas of their times, offering comments they hope are illuminating and instructive, but offering no foundational vision of their own, because they believe there is no foundation to be had. Plato, as a rationalist hedgehog, was a Philosopher; his teacher, Socrates the fox, was a philosopher. We might modify Rorty's division and distinguish Psychologists and psychologists. Capital-P Psychologists are the system builders, envisioning psychology unified under a single set of principles. Small-p psychologists, by contrast, believe that human life is too messy, the influences on human behavior too diverse, the dif-

The hedgehog and the fox (New York: Touchstone, c. 1954).
**(Oxford: Blackwell, 1980).

ferences between people as animal-machines and people as social-humans too great ever to be encompassed by a single point of view. The Psychologist is distressed at psychology's permanent quarrels and dreams of psychology as a genuine and accepted science. The psychologist enjoys psychology's permanent quarrels, believes they can never be resolved, and is skeptical that physchology as a whole can ever become a science. When I wrote the first edition of this book I wanted to be a Philosopher, and hoped that Psychology was possible, although I had my doubts. Having discovered I am a fox, I have become a philosopher, and think that unified, scientific psychology is a pipe dream. Becoming a fox has been liberating, for it is better to be a fox than a fox who thinks he's a hedgehog and gets depressed.

Foxes make better historians, because they attend to the daily contradictions and concrete reality of life as people live it, and are not carried away by sweeping generalities that erase the specifities of history. Hedgehog historians are wont to paint over the contradictions and grit of life with a glossy, superficial sheen of abstractions. The hedgehog, if he or she notices the messiness of history at all, is likely to be downcast by people's inconsistencies and cross-purposes, especially if he or she is a historian of science, which thinks itself a rational enterprise. The fox is at home with history's disorder and confusion, and tries to tell an instructive and entertaining tale of human life. I became a fox, a philosopher, and a psychologist by writing, with my wife, Grace, *Psychology's occult doubles: Psychology and the problem of pseudoscience**). There I set out (she was always more skeptical) to find the essence of science, believing that even if other fields are too self-contradictory to have an essence, science is not, having some central method or attitude apart from its substantive concepts. However, at the end I concluded that science is only a set of beliefs held by scientists, and that all but two beliefs have changed over the centuries. The older, dating back to the ancient Greeks, is naturalism, explaining the world without reference to supernatural entities or events. Hence "creation science" is an oxymoron, because even if creationism is true (which I don't believe), it cannot be part of science. The second belief, defining modern science, comes from Newton and says that science explains events as outcomes of timeless, universal natural *laws*. These beliefs, however, merely define science as a Western social institution; they are not essential Truths.

All of this, naturally, has affected how I have revised *A history of psychology*. The most important decision to make was, given limited time, to lightly revise everything, or to completely rework only a portion of the book. I chose the latter, deciding to properly tell parts of the story of psychology, and return to the rest in a third edition. I have almost completely rewritten the last third of the book, covering 1892 to the present. I rewrote this part for several reasons. I had come to agree with the one standard criticism of the text: That my history of twentieth-century psychology was the weakest part; it was the oldest, and reflected my graduate-student training more than any views of my own. Moreover, my current interests lay in recent psychology, especially in the foundations of cognitive science, the alleged "cognitive revolution," and the influence of psychology on society. So I went back to the sources, rereading all the major journals for psychology since 1892, at least up to World War II. After that it became impossible, since there are several hundred journals now, to "major" in psychology's proliferating subfields. You will find that the story of twentieth-century psychology is substantially different in the present edition as compared to the first.

*(Chicago: Nelson-Hall, 1983).

Having become a fox, and agreeing with Giambattista Vico that "The useful historians are not those who give general descriptions of facts and explain them by reference to general conditions, but those who go into the greatest detail and reveal the particular cause of each event," I have tried to write a more strongly narrative history than before, more chronological and less conceptually driven. Thus the great influence of Kuhn in the first edition has been largely purged. Kuhn has been used to tidy up psychological history under a tidy hedgehoggian scheme of mentalist paradigm replaced by behaviorist paradigm replaced by cognitive paradigm. I now believe that there never has been a paradigm in psychology, and to think so obliterates vital differences between thinkers lumped together in a supposed shared "paradigm." I have also expanded the coverage of twentieth-century psychology by linking changes in psychology to social changes. There is a whole new chapter on the rise of applied psychology and psychologists' involvement with social issues. I have included material on clinical psychology, because it is a major—perhaps the major—way psychology affects society.

I have also completely rewritten the first chapter to reflect both my own changed views and the changes in philosophy of science since 1980. For a while it looked like Kuhnian views might become philosophy of science orthodoxy. They have not; there is no orthodoxy.

The remaining chapters have only been slightly revised. Every chapter now has an essay-like bibliography, showing what works shaped my account of psychology's history. These bibliographies will, I hope, be able to guide interested, but perhaps novice researchers (that is, term-paper writers) through the thicket of books and articles on some subject of interest. In Chapters 2 through 9 the bibliographies also allow updates without revising. Certain other changes in Chapters 2 through 9 deserve mention. The chapter on the Middle Ages and Renaissance (Chapter 3) has been reorganized to make it more chronological. Chapters 4 and 5 on the seventeenth and eighteenth centuries, respectively, have been reorganized to reflect the death of the myth of British empiricism vs. Continental rationalism. In Chapter 4 I have corrected the commonly mistaken impression of Condillac as a radical empiricist; and in Chapter 5 I have included more material on the Counter-Enlightenment, with which I now have more sympathy.

Colleagues and students too numerous to mention have provided comments, favorable and unfavorable, on the first edition of this book, and many of them have helped me revise it. Special thanks are due to Laurence Smith and Ron Amundson. Larry kindly let me see his dissertation on the neobehaviorists before it was finished, and his outstanding historical work, especially on Clark Hull, led me to completely change my thinking about the history of behaviorism. Ron shared his philosophical analyses of Tolman and the Tolman-Hull controversies, further changing and deepening my understanding of neobehaviorism. I would also like to thank the prepublication reviewers who provided written evaluations of the first edition: Ted Jaeger and Bruce Henderson.

My greatest debt is to my wife, Grace, who edited every word of this edition as with the first, and so helped me say what I meant to say. She also offered constant intellectual stimulation and companionship, improving my insights into psychology and history. Of course, the remaining flaws in *A history of psychology* are my responsibility, and I hope you will bring them to my attention.

Thomas Hardy Leahey
Richmond, Virginia

PART I

Background to Psychology

Plato observes that philosophy begins in wonder. Science also begins in wonder, and all sciences, including psychology, were originally part of philosophy. Over the centuries, the special sciences gradually became independent of philosophy. Psychology remained part of philosophy until the nineteenth century and the founders of psychology were philosophers as well as psychologists.

Therefore, if we are to understand the history of psychology, we must understand the history of philosophy. Two philosophical questions are especially important for psychology, bearing separately upon scientific and applied psychology. Philosophers since the time of the ancient Greeks have inquired into how human beings know the world. This enterprise is called *epistemology*, from the Greek words *episteme*, knowledge, and *logos*, discourse. Since its beginnings psychologists, following philosophers, have sought to understand how people know the world, how their knowledge is organized, and how it is used. The second question psychologists have inherited from philosophers concerns the sources of human happiness. Philosophers have asked in what human happiness consists and how human happiness might best be achieved. Their inquiries have become the subject of applied psychology, concerned with human unhappiness and its cure, and with human happiness as it has been shaped by human cultures and institutions. Both of psychology's philosophical legacies have left it with awkward questions of right and wrong. Philosophy asked not only how people know, but what they should know, and not only how they might be happy, but how they should be happy. Psychologists, as scientists concerned with the world as it is, feel uncomfortable with questions about what ought to be, but are embroiled with them willy-nilly.

Psychology wedded philosophy to science to create a human science distinct from the speculation of the past. While psychologists took physics as their model, they looked to biology as a sister science, since human beings are biological creatures possessing a physiology and an evolutionary history. Human perception and thinking are physiological processes, and psychologists have often hoped to illuminate psychological processes by studying their physiological bases. More important to psychological theorizing has been evolutionary biology, which places humankind within a network of species who have evolved on earth, and whose capacities and development are rooted in the evolutionary past. To understand the history of psychology we must attend to the history of science as well as to the history of philosophy.

In Part I we will tell the story of psychology as it emerged from its inchoate roots in philosophy and science, but before it came to stand on its own as a separate institution in western civilization.

CHAPTER 1

Introduction

Psychology, Philosophy of Science, and History

UNDERSTANDING PSYCHOLOGY
UNDERSTANDING SCIENCE
    Methodological Approaches
    Naturalistic Approaches
    Neomethodological Approaches
    Realism
    Pragmatism
PSYCHOLOGY AND SCIENCE
    The Newtonian Fantasy
    Psychology as a Life Science
    Psychology and the Humanities
UNDERSTANDING HISTORY
THE PLAN OF THIS BOOK

UNDERSTANDING PSYCHOLOGY

Psychology is a large, sprawling, confusing human undertaking. Psychologists study an array of problems greater than that of any other discipline. Some psychologists study the structure and function of single nerve cells. Some psychologists try to help people overcome their personal problems. Some psychologists study how information is stored in memory. Some psychologists help construct effective advertisements. Some psychologists study group behavior. Everyone uses psychology every day. Some is borrowed from organized psychology, but most is *folk psychology*, an informal language we use to talk about ourselves and others. In folk psychology we explain human actions in terms of beliefs and desires, and by and large folk psychology works well for us. Sometimes we borrow ideas from technical psychology: Freudian terms such as "ego" and "libido," and behavioristic terms such as "conditioning" and "reflex." Within organized psychology there is widespread disagreement among psychologists about many issues. Some psychologists believe in free will, others do not. Some psychologists think it is acceptable to use mentalistic concepts in explaining behavior, others do not. Some psychologists think that all psychology ultimately will be translatable into neuroscience, others do not. Finally, psychology is socially important. Psychologists work in business and industry, in advertising, in schools, in companies that devise tests, in government, and in private practice helping people adjust to life. Even if you never consult a psychologist, psychological concepts have become part of our everyday means of understanding ourselves and others.

At the undergraduate level, only a few courses treat the full range of psychology and attempt to view the field as a whole. Introductory courses survey what psychology is doing and has discovered. The course for which you are using this book, probably called History and Systems of Psychology, takes a more analytical and synthetic approach to seeing psychology in its entirety. Our main tool in this book will be history; we will try to understand psychology as part of the history of Western civilization. Because psychology is used every day, its roots are ancient and its history reaches back to the thoughts of the most ancient of our ancestors with whom we can converse through historical records.

Like all sciences, psychology began in philosophy and then branched off from it. All sciences maintain some contact with philosophy. For example, when modern physicists discuss the nature of causality in the world of subatomic particles and quantum mechanics, they get embroiled in deep philosophical questions about the fundamental nature of reality (d'Espagnet 1979). In psychology, however, the connection with philosophy has been, and remains, more direct. Philosophers who inquire into how people know the world raise questions about human perception, thinking, and learning; and when they begin to address these questions empirically they become psychologists in practice, if not in name. Psychology, therefore, is intimately entangled with philosophy. Nor is epistemology, the study of human knowledge, the only area of philosophy involved in psychology. Psychology is also involved in ethics. Psychology is concerned with how people behave, and ethics is concerned with how people ought to behave. Understanding how people should behave cannot be entirely divorced from describing how people do behave. Prohibition failed because, despite strenuous and earnest efforts by moralists to keep people from drinking, people would not give up consciousness altering booze—a triumph of real psychology over ideal ethics. Psychology also connects with ethics and law in real life, as when murderers are found not guilty because of evidence about their psychological state at the time they committed the crime.

Psychology, then, has an intimate relationship with philosophy. It was only in the last quarter of the nineteenth century that psychology established itself as an autonomous discipline, most importantly in Germany under Wilhelm Wundt. Wundt and most of the other founders of experimental psychology sought to make psychology a science by bringing the techniques and concepts of experimental science to bear on the traditional philosophical problems of mind. They drew heavily on physiology, using techniques and concepts of nervous functioning to illumine the workings of consciousness, continuing a tradition of philosophical physiology dating back to ancient Greece. However, until physiology matured as a discipline in the nineteenth century, such efforts, however well-intended, serious, and even heroic, remained speculative. Even today, with neuroscience one of the most rapidly advancing fields in all of science, the connections between brain and mind and behavior remain remarkably murky. Therefore in our history of psychology I shall have more to say about philosophy than neuroscience.

I have spoken about history; what about systems? Psychologists, like philosophers and others in the humanities and social sciences, tend to divide themselves into ideologically definable groups based on systematically different ways of doing psychology. As we shall see, psychologists inherited their systematic viewpoints from philosophy, and systematic disagreements have produced theoretical debate and empirical research. Some observers of psychology take these disagreements seriously, dividing psychology up into systematic schools; I did so in the first edition of this text. However, I now believe that the number of deeply different psychological orientations is rather small, and that traditional systematic lines have been drawn in the wrong places. My account has become less tidy than before, but I think it is truer to psychology as it was and is.

UNDERSTANDING SCIENCE

In the nineteenth century philosopher John Stuart Mill wrote that ''the backward state of the Moral Sciences [the equivalent of today's social sciences] can only be remedied by applying to them the methods of Physical Science, duly extended and generalized.'' By Mill's time physical science in the tradition of Isaac Newton had proven itself the one reliably successful human enterprise, moving from triumph to triumph. Religion was a shambles of sects, political order dissolved into revolution, war, and tyranny, while philosophers still debated Plato's problems. Scientists, by contrast, seemed to know what they were about, solving problem after problem with increasing elegance and precision. Science alone seemed to progress. So it seemed to Mill and others that human affairs, including psychology, the study of the individual, should be subjected to the same scrutiny physical science had applied to nature. Mill's impulse gave rise to the founding of psychology as an autonomous discipline applying laboratory methods to the human mind. Although psychology today is likely to define itself as the science of behavior, it still considers itself a science on a conceptual par with the natural sciences, though not quite as developed. However, it is difficult to say exactly what science *is*.

Methodological Approaches

In speaking of "the methods of Physical Science," Mill presupposes a certain answer to the question, "What is science?" Mill assumes that there is a definable scientific method, and that it can be applied to human affairs. Such a view is popular—one often reads or hears about "the scientific method"—and deeply rooted in modern philosophy (Rorty 1980). The idea that there is a scientific method is in turn based on what Rorty calls foundational philosophy. This is the view that there is a fixed foundation to all human knowledge; that it is the job of philosophers to discover it; and that when it is revealed, everything humans do will take on the objective, progressive character of science. There have been two widely influential attempts to specify the philosophical foundation of science: logical positivism and falsificationism. Each attempts to explicate a timeless scientific method, to provide a recipe that anyone may apply to any problem and thereby become a scientist. These methodological approaches thus separate the form of science, its method, from its historical content. In their view science is a set of tools, not a set of ideas; and science derives its authority from adherence to its method, not by happening to be right in its account of nature.

Logical Positivism

In later chapters we will narrate the development of logical positivism and trace its considerable influence on psychology. At present, I will briefly describe its account of scientific method. Roughly speaking, positivism, the historical predecessor of logical positivism, which dressed positivism in fancy logic, holds that science rests upon a foundation of objective facts. Scientists collect facts without prejudice or preconception and, as facts accumulate, scientists extract generalizations—scientific laws—that apply without exception to all the facts. Thus the first step in science is *description*. Once laws are in hand, scientists can move on to *prediction*. Knowing the laws of nature, and knowing the state of a physical system at time t, it is possible to predict future events. So in the nineteenth century astronomers could precisely predict the location of a new planet, Pluto, from Newtonian laws of gravitation applied to certain peculiarities of the orbit of Neptune. If one can predict, one can *control*. So astronauts control their position in space by applying precise thrusts of rocket energy to their spacecraft. We commonly expect science to explain things; but, in the logical positivist account of science, explanation derives from prediction. To explain an event is to show how it must have occurred given the laws of nature and preceding events.

The method of science, according to positivism, is fact collection and verification. Scientists patiently accumulate facts and, because their observations are impersonal and disinterested, the facts are objective and clear to everyone. As they develop laws they carefully check the laws against new facts, seeking to *verify* the laws by checking predictions against actual occurrences. Eventually, positivists say, science will be able to account for every event, and scientific laws will be formalized into abstract, logically formulated theories.

Logical positivists were aggressive and quite certain both that science was the only human institution with any real authority and that their explication of its method was correct. Otto Neurath, one of the founders of logical positivism, wrote that "*The body of scientific propositions exhausts the sum of all meaningful state-*

ments'' (Holton 1978, emphasis in original). It is important to grasp what Neurath is saying. He is *not* just asserting that science is a true account of nature; indeed, as we shall find, positivism does not believe in truth anyway. Neurath is asserting that only scientific statements have any meaning. So, in the positivist account, all other language is meaningless: the language of poetry, of religion, of art, of drama, of philosophy, of folk psychology (''I love you'')—all are meaningless, unless such language can be turned into scientific statements of laws based on observable events. Neurath here has passed from science to *scientism,* one of the endemic attitudes of modern life. Precisely because science has been so successful, there is a temptation to think that science can solve all problems, that every field of human endeavor can and should be turned into a science, relegating those that cannot be turned into sciences to an inferior status, if not to the trash heap.

Familiar as the positivist picture of science is, logical positivism is now dead; every one of its tenets discarded (Suppe 1977). The logical positivist account of science has been shown to be philosophically flawed and historically inaccurate. Many of the arguments against logical positivism are complex, but the most basic one is simple: Science has not operated as the positivists said it should, nor can it. The basic point was effectively stated by Albert Einstein. After sketching the positivist story of science, Einstein continues:

> But a quick look at the actual development teaches us that the great steps forward in scientific knowledge originated only to a small degree in this manner. For if the researcher went about his work without any preconceived opinion, how should he be able to select out those facts from the immense abundance of the most complex experience, and just those which are simple enough to permit lawful connections to become evident? (Holton 1978)

It is quite impossible for science to be practiced in the antiseptic, inhuman way described by the positivists. As we shall see in considering naturalistic approaches to science, facts only make sense within a conceptual framework that lies, often hidden, behind the laws and theories of a given science.

Falsificationism

Like logical positivism, falsificationism arose in Vienna in the first decades of the twentieth century. As a young man Karl Popper was interested in a number of systems of thought that claimed to be scientific, including Einstein's relativistic physics and psychoanalysis, and he wondered which of them were true sciences and which were pseudosciences. Popper saw that the verificationism of positivism could not answer his question. All allegedly ''scientific'' systems, even the most obviously pseudoscientific, such as astrology, can produce facts to support their claims. Astrologers can point to prophecies fulfilled, psychoanalysts to case histories that fit their theories, and physicists to verified predictions. So, Popper concluded, mere existence of supporting data does not make a theory or system scientific.

As Popper pondered this fact he concluded that science was the exact opposite of what verificationism claimed. The failing of astrology and psychoanalysis, he came to believe, was precisely that they could explain any conceivable finding. No matter what happened, psychoanalysts or astrologers could make sense of it within their system of thought. Einstein's physics, on the other hand, said that certain things could *not* happen—for example, that light could not go straight when passing through a gravitational field. Thus, according to Popper, should light not be found to bend while passing through a gravitational field, Einstein's theory would stand refuted. In this event Einstein's theory would be wrong, but it would still be scientific. Positivist verificationism was not the key to science, Popper concluded, since both real science and pseudoscience could claim many verifications. Instead, he argued, the mark of true science is *falsifiability*. Truly scientific theories stick their necks out by forbidding certain things to occur, such as light not being bent by gravity. If Einstein is right, light will always be bent by gravity. Thus if these predictions go wrong, we would know that the theory is wrong: If light does not bend when subject to gravity, Einstein is wrong. Einstein's theory is falsifiable; we can prove it wrong. Pseudoscientific theories, on the other hand, can explain anything. No matter what the data, they can explain it. They cannot be falsified and so are not scientific at all. For Popper, scientific method is the construction of falsifiable theories and the search for data that falsifies them.

While Popper's methodological reconstruction of science avoids the philosophical difficulties of positivism, it fails on some other counts. To begin with, Popper's *demarcation criterion,* as it is called, suggests that the most scientific theories are those that are most easily falsified. So, by Popper's logic, if I claimed to be able to predict the Dow Jones average by counting the number of dead leaves in my back yard, I would have a scientific theory, since it could be so easily refuted; yet obviously my "theory" is ridiculous.

More seriously, Popper's method, like positivism, fails when compared to scientific practice. Examination of clear historical cases of pseudosciences shows that they, like Einstein, stuck their necks out (Leahey and Leahey 1983). Phrenology, for example, claimed that certain psychological traits were localized in certain areas of the brain, claims that were open to test and proven false. Yet phrenology was in its own time, and even today, regarded as a classic case of a pseudoscience. Falsifiability does not a science make. More recently, parapsychology has set out testable theories, and has systematically evaluated and tested them, eliminating some over the course of research. But it is considered a pseudoscience no matter how "scientific" its methods. Phrenology and parapsychology were rejected by the established science of their time not because they violated the alleged methodological norms of science, but because they violated the scientific dogmas of their time (Leahey and Leahey 1983). What the phrenologists, and perhaps the parapsychologists, did wrong was to *be* wrong (Hull 1973). Their method was not at fault; their content—their specific thesis—was.

Even worse for Popper's analysis is the fact that orthodox science does not practice falsification, for a single contrary fact has never been taken to refute a theory. During the nineteenth century the orbits of Neptune and Mercury were at odds with the predictions of Newtonian physics. Yet these anomalies were regarded as oddities, not as refutations of Newton's theory. Physicists were confident that some day the odd orbits would be explained within Newtonian principles. In the case of Neptune they were right; in the case of Mercury they were wrong, since only Einstein's theory could explain its peculiarities. In any event, isolated "refutations" never bring down a theory. When a chemistry student's experiment does not come out as the text says it should, no one concludes that chemistry is at fault. Rather, it is concluded that the novice chemist has done something wrong and the student, not chemical theory, is given the failing grade.

We find, in conclusion, that positivism and falsificationism share two common flaws. First of all, both methodological analyses underestimate the complex relationship between theory, method, and data. Both tend to ignore the content of scientific theories, to simplify the steps that intervene between a theory and its predictive tests, and positivism in particular ignores the way in which theories actually guide research. The point may be made by quoting Sherlock Holmes:

> Holmes then [descended] into the hollow . . . [and] stretching himself upon his face and leaning his chin upon his hands he made a careful study of the trampled mud in front of him.
> "Halloa!" said he, suddenly, "what's this?" It was a wax vesta [a sort of match], half burned, which was so coated with mud that it looked at first like a little chip of wood.
> "I cannot think how I came to overlook it," said the Inspector, with an expression of annoyance.
> "It was invisible, buried in the mud. I only saw it because I was looking for it."
> "What! You expected to find it?"
> "I thought it not unlikely."

> Sir Arthur Conan Doyle, *The Memoirs of Sherlock Holmes*

The role and value of good theory are well illustrated in the preceding passage. Theory tells the researcher what to look for. Holmes found the match because he had formed a theory of the crime that led him to expect the presence of a match, while the police—who had no theory—failed to find the match despite meticulous searching. Crude fact-gathering is never as powerful as theoretically guided research. To the fact-gatherer all facts are equally meaningless and meaningful. To the theoretically guided researcher each fact assumes its proper place in an overall framework.

Around the basic assumptions of their theories scientists construct a "protective belt" of specific, testable hypotheses. It is these hypotheses that are proposed, refined, or discarded as the research program progresses. Experimental refutations lead to modification in the protective belt, not to basic assumptions (Lakatos 1970). For example, in 1938 an important behaviorist, Clark Hull, proposed some specific mechanisms for reward learning based on drive reduction. He had to substantially modify these by 1953, but he never abandoned the assumption that all learning is based on reward and drive reduction.

From a theory, the scientist constructs a *model* of reality. Models are highly idealized, partial simulations of the world. They describe what the world would be like if the theory were completely true, if the variables found in it were the only ones involved in behavior, and if these variables act as the theory claims. The physical theory of particle mechanics, for example, describes a block sliding down an inclined plane as a system of three frictionless, dimensionless, point-masses— one each for the block, plane, and the earth. In the real world, these bodies are extended in space and there is friction between block and plane; in the model, such irrelevant or complicating factors disappear. Thus the model is a simplified, idealized version of reality, which is all a theory can cope with. It is important to realize how limited a scientific theory is. It purports to explain only some phenomena, and only some aspects of these. A scientific theory is not about the real world as we experience it, but about abstract, idealized models. The real world, unlike the model, is much too complex to be explained by a theory. To take a psychological example, a theory of paired associate learning describes an ideal learner as untroubled by neurosis or motivational factors—which of course are determinants of the memory-performance of actual subjects.

These models give science enormous power. First, they free the scientist from the impossible task of describing all of reality which, because of its infinite complexity, will never conform to theory. By using models of reality, the scientist can ignore "the *actual* counterexamples, the available data . . . [and can refuse] to be drawn into observation. He will 'lie down on his couch, shut his eyes and forget about the data.' Occasionally, of course, he will ask Nature a shrewd question: he will then be encouraged by Nature's YES, but not discouraged by its NO'' (Lakatos 1970). Scientists cannot apply their theories to the whole world, but can apply them to the model. Science does not progress by the mere accumulation of data, but by asking careful, theoretically pertinent questions of nature. Models allow the scientist to imagine how the world is, and to try out and refine theories before coping with the world. Many of the greatest experiments in physics were thought-experiments never carried out in actuality. Einstein built his theory of relativity on many such experiments.

Second, these idealized theories and models enable the scientist to make powerful and wide-ranging explanations of observed phenomena. The model embodies certain *ideals of natural order,* descriptions of an idealized world (Toulmin 1961). These descriptions, while not observed, provide the basis for explaining that which is observed.

Newton's theory, for example, provides as an ideal of natural order the idea that all natural motion of objects through space is in a straight line that continues forever. Such motion cannot be observed. Motion that does not conform to this ideal is explained as being a result of other factors. For example, a ball rolling across grass quickly comes to rest, but we say the motion would have gone on forever except for friction. The scientist does not *explain* the ideal of natural order, but rather uses it and other factors to explain phenomena that do not conform to the ideal, such as the stopping ball. Scientific explanation is always indirect and metaphorical. The scientist can only describe what the world would be like if a theory were true, and then explain why the world is not really like that.

How does the scientist go from theory and idealized model to real-world phenomena or data? The usual picture is that the scientist derives a prediction from a theory and tests it with an experiment. If the data agree with the prediction, the theory is confirmed; if they do not agree, the theory is disconfirmed. However, Lakatos's statement about the value of models has already indicated that the picture is too simple, and an example will make it clearer: Scientist A proposes a theory; Scientist B runs an experiment and finds data that appear to refute the theory. Does Scientist A say, "Boy, was I wrong! Back to the drawing board."? Almost certainly not. Scientist A will examine the experiment, not the theory, and query Scientist B's methodology. A may accuse B of using the wrong subject population, the wrong statistics, the wrong response measure, or of making incorrect inferences from the theory. The protective belt of conditions surrounding a theory is thick indeed, for it includes not only theories, but important methodological ideas as well.

The route from theory to data and back again is long and complex, not the three-step process of theory → prediction → experiment. Figure 1-1 shows the hierarchy of steps that intervene between theory, model, and observed phenomena.

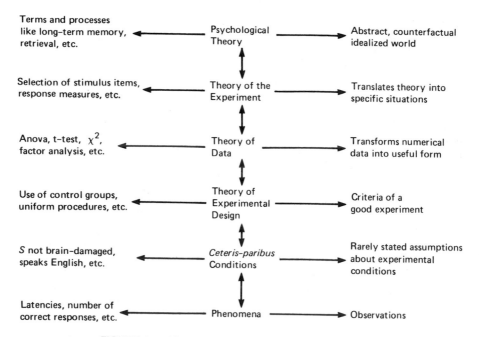

FIGURE 1-1 Hierarchy of theories (after Suppes 1962).

The center column names each step, the right-hand column describes the step in general scientific terms, and the left-hand column gives some psychological examples of each level.

At the top we have the theory itself and its associated model, which together describe the world in its idealized form. In psychology we might have a theory of memory, which will contain such theoretical terms as short-term memory, long-term memory, and rehearsal. The theory would describe an ideal memorizer (the model), untroubled by the things that trouble real subjects, such as lack of sleep, boredom with the experiment, or dislike of the experimenter. The memory model is thus idealized and counterfactual. The abstract theory must be translated into a specific situation that can be created in an experiment. The scientist must select particular items to be remembered, a measure of the subject's memory (such as trials-to-criterion), and any other pertinent variables, such as the ages of the subjects. Further, the scientist must derive specific predictions about what ought to happen in such a situation or experiment. In this way the scientist produces an empirically testable version of the idealized model derived from the theory.

The test of the theory involves deriving from the phenomena another model that as far as possible describes an idealized model based on the data. In various ways the researcher must purge from the data those variables and influences that are not part of the theory, such as motivation in the case of our memory experiment. This is done in a series of steps rising from the phenomena.

The phenomena are the actual raw observations made during an experiment, such as trials-to-criterion or response latency. The conduct of the experiment that collects these data is predicated on certain tacitly understood assumptions called *ceteris-paribus* (all other things being equal) assumptions. These are never stated by a researcher in the "method" section of a report unless some special reason compels the researcher to do so. To continue our example, it would be assumed that the subjects in the memory experiment were not brain-damaged, were not retarded, and spoke English. These assumptions will be made explicit only under special conditions. If the researcher were interested in memory in split-brain subjects, for instance, the use of such subjects would be stated.

A good experiment also must conform to the sophisticated demands of experimental design. The researcher, for example, must use appropriate control and experimental groups, uniform procedures for all subjects, and so forth. Next, the mass of raw data collected during an experiment must be analyzed by sound statistical procedures appropriate to the theory under test. Masses of data are useless until summarized and digested into a form that makes possible a test of the theory via analysis by statistical methods, such as t-tests and correlations. Finally, at all levels the theorist or researcher relies on auxiliary hypotheses that are not part of the theory under test. For instance, should the researcher pay the subjects according to the number of correct responses, it will be assumed that this reward will affect behavior in ways described by operant learning theory, which is not the theory under test, but rather an auxiliary theory used to help test the memory theory.

Each of the levels—beginning with phenomena—is designed to produce data that reflect the variables with which the theory under test is concerned, and so produce an evaluation of the theory. Theory says, "The perfect world (model) of my theory behaves just so." Experiment says, "Here is a model based on the theory's variables." The crucial question is, "Do these models act the same?" If they do, the theory is supported. If they do not, something must be changed.

The theorist may alter a theory if the data are not consistent with predictions. However, since error may occur at each step of the hierarchy, the theorist may question something else, saying, for example, that the wrong response measure was used, the wrong age subjects were run, the wrong control group used, the wrong statistical test applied, or the predictions wrongly derived from the theory. No scientific method produces truth automatically. Science is a creative enterprise. The scientist must ask nature the right questions in the right way and must carefully interpret the answers. The scientist must know when to accept disconfirming data and alter a theory, and when to reject data and retain a theory.

The second common failing of positivism and falsificationism leads to an influential alternative approach to understanding science. Both positivism and falsificationism tried to specify some timeless scientific method, but neither method is actually practiced by science. Yet, obviously, science is successful, and to understand its success historians and philosophers of science have abandoned the search for some ahistorical scientific method in favor of a close study of science in practice. The new alternative approach, because it studies science as it happens, may be termed *naturalistic*.

Naturalistic Approaches

Weltanschauungen Analyses

The most serious challenge to methodological analyses of science has been offered by a loosely knit group of historians and philosophers of science who propose one or another of what Suppe (1977) calls *Weltanschauung* analyses of science. The basic idea is that scientists' theories are not just formal axiomatic statements of scientific laws, but incorporate hidden assumptions about the nature of reality and of science, and give scientists who hold them a deep and comprehensive world view, or *Weltanschauung*. Formal models of science miss this hidden dimension of scientific practice, which can only be discovered by abandoning *a priori* accounts of scientific methodology for careful studies of real science, bringing to bear historical, sociological, and psychological viewpoints. Naturalistic approaches stress that science is a human enterprise, so that ideas taken from the social sciences will throw light on understanding science.

The fullest expression of the *Weltanschauung* approach to science was given by historian Thomas Kuhn in his *Structure of scientific revolutions* (1970). Kuhn describes the history of science as a repeating cycle of stages and provides an account of how scientific practice is shaped by deep assumptions of a world view of which working scientists may be only dimly aware. One of Kuhn's innovations was to stress the social nature of science. Science is practiced by communities of scientists, not by isolated men and women. To understand working science, then, we must understand the scientific community and its shared norms, which together constitute what Kuhn calls *normal science*.

For scientific research to be progressive, the scientific community in a particular research area must agree on certain basic issues. Its members must agree on the goals of their science, on the basic characteristics of the real world relevant to their subject, on what counts as a valid explanation of phenomena, and on permissible research methods and mathematical techniques. Given agreement on these issues, scientists can proceed to analyze nature from a collective, unified standpoint; without such agreement, each researcher would have his or her own standpoint, and there would be much fruitless discussion at cross-purposes. The traditional architectural metaphor may be modified to clarify this point. A building must be constructed according to a plan and on a firm foundation. Until the blueprints and the foundation have been decided on, there can be no construction, no progress. Only when the plans are agreed on can construction begin.

In science, the basic set of assumptions that provides the framework within which scientists work has been called a *paradigm*. A paradigm has two components: the *disciplinary matrix* and the *shared exemplars* (Kuhn 1970). The disciplinary matrix consists of a set of fundamental assumptions that are usually unstated, often unconscious, and typically not subject to empirical test. These assumptions, however, provide the basis for specific hypotheses that are subjected to empirical tests. Consider, for example, atomism, the idea that psychological behaviors can be reduced to assemblages of simple behaviors. This assumption has been part of many psychological systems. It is an untestable metaphysical concept in that it is impossible to prove that all behavior is so reducible. Once atomism is assumed, however, the scientist can explore particular, specific hypotheses about how specific complex acts are compounded out of specific simpler acts. Thus the unproved assumption of atomism makes much research possible. A disciplinary matrix is an organized structure of assumptions such as atomism.

The second component of a paradigm is a set of shared exemplars. These are models (or—as scientists ordinarily use the term—paradigms) of good research that provide agreed-upon methods for the investigation of new problems. They are examples held up to scientists in training as patterns for their own research. Consider, for instance, the standard operant-conditioning paradigm. A rat is placed in a small chamber with a bar at one end. When the rat accidentally presses the bar it is rewarded with food for doing so. After several such experiences the rat will press the bar regularly to get food. This paradigm provides a model for many other kinds of research. A psychologist trained in this (Skinnerian) tradition will approach any problem in these terms. For example, how do children learn mathematics? By assumption, it must be by the acquisition of certain "correct responses" to specific problem situations. As a result of this approach, many schools are filled today with step-by-step teaching machines and behavior modification techniques derived from the shared exemplar of the rat in the Skinner box. Each major psychological paradigm will hold up one or more shared exemplars that the psychologist trained in the paradigm will automatically apply to any research problem.

If a scientific community must, often unconsciously, agree on a paradigm, then paradigms must be learned in some way. They are rarely, if ever, specifically taught; rather a student picks up a paradigm almost by osmosis. The shared exemplars are learned by example. The student participates in research that follows the exemplars so that they become the natural approach to any problem of the student's own. The disciplinary matrix is learned by indirection. The student is exposed to theories and hypotheses that embody the assumptions, and therefore the student's thoughts come naturally to fall into certain tracks. The student learns to think in the established ways largely because these ways are embodied in everything studied and alternatives are rarely presented. The neophyte Skinnerian, for example, does not need to be told "there is no soul," for the hypothesis that there is a soul is never considered. Because paradigms are learned in such indirect ways, it is not surprising that the individual scientist is usually unaware of them.

What are the effects of a paradigm? The first effect is wholly positive. The paradigm, by answering the metaphysical questions, frees the researcher to get on with the puzzle-solving work of science. The researcher knows from the paradigm approximately what nature is like; thus, all that remains is to work out the details. For example, once we assume that learning is caused by reinforcement, we can proceed to investigate exactly *how* reinforcement works: What happens if we vary amount of reinforcement, frequency of reinforcement, or quality of reinforcement? Such specific questions cannot be thought of without the basic assumptions of a paradigm or investigated without its shared exemplars. The assumptions make possible the invention and testing of specific theories about the details of nature's workings.

It is important to understand that such experiments do not test the paradigm; rather they are attempts to answer puzzles posed by the paradigm. If a scientist fails to solve a puzzle, the failure is the scientist's, not the paradigm's. Consider what happens in your own laboratory courses. You follow all the instructions, but the "correct" results do not always occur. When you inform your instructors, they do not tear their hair and cry, "All our theories are wrong!" On the contrary, they assume that you must have erred at some point, and they give you a poor grade. This reaction is typical of what happens in "normal science," the puzzle-solving research guided by a paradigm. The scientific community recognizes certain puzzles as ripe for solution, and—except in extraordinary circumstances—when a scientist tackles one of these problems it is the scientist and his or her theories that are on trial, not the unstated paradigm.

This may seem a restrictive and unromantic view of science. Yet it is the possession of paradigms and the ensuing puzzle-solving that makes scientific progress possible. This becomes clearer if we return to our architectural metaphor. The most creative part of building is when an artist-architect makes the plans. Yet if the artist-architect and colleagues and clients get too involved in this stage in debating large issues of aesthetics and function, no progress on the building can be made. It is only when the blueprint, or paradigm, is agreed on that constructive puzzle-solving can begin. Agreement on basic assumptions is always necessary if progress is to be made.

There is a psychological consequence of acceptance of a paradigm that is also necessary for progress, but which is perhaps less fortunate. The scientist in acquiring a paradigm is learning to see the world in a certain way. The physician learns to see an X-ray correctly; the physicist must learn to read bubble chamber tracks. Neither source of data is comprehensible without training, yet once the scientist learns to interpret them, he or she will see them in those ways and no others. Thus training can act as a set of blinders, keeping the scientist from seeing things in new ways.

All observation and perception—whether scientific or not—is a matter of interpretation, as numerous psychological experiments have shown. The simple drawing of Figure 1-2a, a Necker cube, illustrates this point. If you look at it for a while, you will find that two precepts are possible, two cubes of different orientation. Your mind must give some interpretation to the figure; yet since two interpretations are available and equally valid, it vacillates between the two. At no point do you see the figure with no interpretation, for your mind naturally attempts to make sense of all it perceives.

Another example, Figure 1-2b, is even closer to what happens in scientific observation. The crucial stimulus is the last in each row. If subjects are shown the four top stimuli and then the fifth, they see the fifth as a face; if shown the bottom four stimuli first, they see the fifth as a rat. There is only one set of data in the last stimulus, but two interpretations of it; and which interpretation is adopted depends on the "training" of the subject. Paradigms have exactly this effect. The scientist learns to see in certain ways, and what he or she sees in the data depends on the paradigm the scientist has acquired. Neither face nor rat is a truer interpretation than the other; they are simply different. The stimulus, like nature, is one unchanging reality, yet the meaning and explanation of that reality depends on one's background and paradigm. It is futile to ask if it is *really* a rat or a face. One paradigm construes it as a face, another as a rat. That the meaning of the world depends on paradigms is of great consequence in disputes between paradigms. When psychics fail to perform in the laboratory, for example, the materialist sees a disconfirmation of psychic phenomena, while the believer sees the destruction of fragile psychic abilities in the cold, sterile research environment. The materialist and the spiritualist thus have a paradigm clash that cannot be resolved by the data, since each will persistently interpret the data according to his or her paradigm.

Finally, a paradigm defines limits on what science is—limits that can be crossed only if the scientist is willing to risk criticism, ostracism, and even ridicule. Such cases have occurred. Imagine a young scientist getting up before an audience of Skinnerians and attributing operant learning to the workings of a rat's immortal soul! The paper would be greeted with shouts of disbelief, because the scientist had stepped outside the acceptable bounds of psychological science. If persistent in such beliefs, the scientist would surely be exiled from the Skinnerian community. And correctly so—the builders cannot tolerate a worker who refuses to follow the blueprints. However, it remains possible for the rebel to convince others of the correctness of his or her views, and so lead a scientific revolution establishing a new paradigm, a new way of looking at the world as valid as the old.

Within normal science, research is progressive, as puzzle after puzzle is

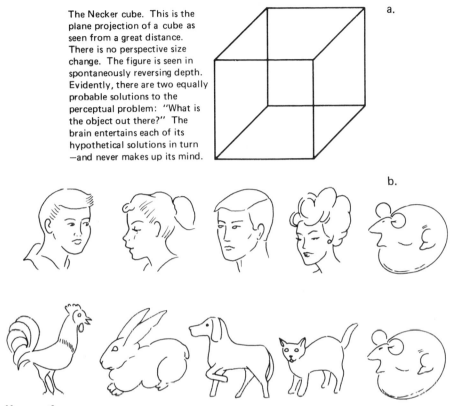

The Necker cube. This is the plane projection of a cube as seen from a great distance. There is no perspective size change. The figure is seen in spontaneously reversing depth. Evidently, there are two equally probable solutions to the perceptual problem: "What is the object out there?" The brain entertains each of its hypothetical solutions in turn —and never makes up its mind.

Man or rat?

FIGURE 1-2   (a) The Necker cube (From Gregory 1970). (b) Experience and perception (From Bugelski 1962).

solved. However, Kuhn recognizes that normal science is just one phase of scientific development. A paradigm is a specific historical achievement in which one or a few scientists establish a new scientific style based on an outstanding success in understanding nature. Paradigms also break down and get replaced when they cease to work well in guiding the research of a community. So a science's first paradigm arises out of a prescientific phase in a science's history, and paradigms are periodically replaced during scientific revolutions. This is Kuhn's cyclical model of scientific change.

Scientific change, according to Kuhn, is not always gradual and continuous. There are times when a science undergoes radical change in a short period of time— change so radical that those who were great individuals beforehand often become forgotten antiques, and concepts and issues that previously occupied scientists minds simply disappear. Such change seems to constitute revolution rather than evolution and depends on principles beyond those of variation, selection, and retention.

The cluster of concepts that change by evolution is generally in the protective belt surrounding the hard core, or paradigm, of a research program. Since much of the paradigm is unconscious, and since it is explicitly guarded by the protective belt, it will not be subject to the usual conscious processes of scientific selection. The assumptions of a paradigm are seldom debated and seldom subjected to empirical test. Indeed, many cannot be tested, for they are often metaphysical as we have seen. Paradigms then do not—indeed cannot—endure, but must be overthrown in a process similar to political revolutions.

According to this view proposed by Thomas Kuhn, any science passes through a number of distinct stages, as shown in Figure 1-3. Every science has its beginning in a prescientific period called the preparadigm period. During this time, individuals concerned with a given subject matter, protoscientists, do not all agree on a set of paradigmatic assumptions. Rather they are divided into a number of rival camps or schools, each of which attempts to impose its views on the field, to vanquish its competition. Research is undertaken as part of this competition rather than to solve puzzles posed by the paradigm, or to establish basic variables and facts on which to erect a paradigm. Taken as a whole, this kind of research is nothing but random fact-gathering, rather than a concerted attempt to understand nature. In this stage there can be no scientific progress and, indeed, no science. According to our architectural metaphor, this period would correspond to various architects squabbling over building plans, perhaps even each going off alone to build his or her own building, pausing to throw bricks at the opposition. There is no concerted, unified, and constructive effort, for energies are dissipated by infighting and random fact-gathering.

Eventually one school gains control of the field and ousts its competitors— who may be relegated to pseudoscientific status. This ushers in an era of normal science working under a paradigm, as described earlier. In our architectural metaphor, during this period the basic plans are agreed upon and building proceeds, as concrete puzzles are solved and the edifice is erected. No time is wasted in fighting with rival paradigms, for there are none.

However, scientists inevitably find problems that resist solution. In a strict sense, every research program is faced with data that are inconsistent with it, and we have seen that scientists typically do not take these data too seriously, especially if in other respects research is going well. The orbit of Mercury, for example, was never reconciled with Newtonian physics, yet this did not concern early nineteenth-

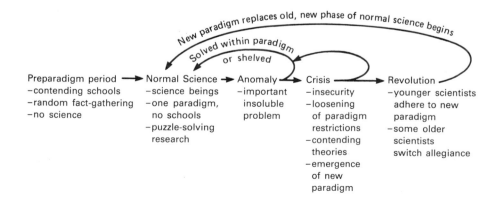

FIGURE 1-3 The revolutionary character of paradigm shifts, and the cyclical nature of science. (A schematization of Kuhn 1970).

century physicists, for otherwise Newtonian physics proceeded from success to success until the late 1800s. Such inconsistent findings are anomalies, unexplained phenomena that are not generally considered important.

Some anomalies, however, are perceived to be important, and it is on them that a research program may founder. Although Newtonian physicists were untroubled by Mercury's anomalous orbit, the late-nineteenth-century failure to find evidence of ether-drift was deeply troubling, and the ability of Einstein's theory to explain it was an important factor in its eventual acceptance. The anomaly shown in Figure 1-3 is this serious, second kind of anomaly, and it provides the opening wedge for a scientific revolution. Most anomalies, however, are eventually explained within the paradigm by making adjustments within the protective belt. It also sometimes happens that an anomalous problem resists solution and is shelved for future attention; it thus is shifted to the nonserious category of anomaly.

However, it may happen that an anomaly resists solution and is simply too important to be shelved. At this point a crisis ensues during which normal science is largely abandoned in favor of extraordinary research. The restrictions of the paradigm loosen, freeing scientists to pursue approaches otherwise forbidden. In normal science, the burden of failure to find the correct results falls on the scientist; now the burden may shift to the paradigm. Various theories are proposed to account for the anomalous findings, and these may differ more radically than the alternative hypotheses proposed during normal science. Indoctrination of young scientists into the prevailing paradigm weakens, accelerating the blurring of the paradigm and the proliferation of rival approaches. In short, it is a time of acute crisis, especially for older scientists, when scientists feel depressed and sometimes find it hard to continue.

Sometimes a crisis is resolved by solution of an anomaly within the old paradigm. However, during a crisis an alternative paradigm may emerge, usually in the work of young scientists, and if it succeeds in solving the anomaly, there may be a scientific revolution. This is an especially difficult time for a science. The effects of a paradigm are great, extending even to the observation of facts. Thus the adherents of the old paradigm and the advocates of the new frequently do not see the same things in their data. This means that the scientists talk at cross-purposes. Such paradigm clashes cannot be rationally resolved. ESP (extrasensory perception) experiments, for example, illustrate this lack of communication between paradigms. For the believer in ESP, its failure to occur in the laboratory shows merely that it cannot occur in sterile, hostile surroundings. The nonbeliever, on the other hand, sees the experiment's failure as evidence that there is no ESP. This dispute cannot be resolved, for the data mean one thing to one group, something else to the other.

A revolution is therefore won less on the basis of data than on other considerations; causes become more important than reasons. The new paradigm will be attractive to young scientists who flock to its banner. The old paradigm is left with scientists past their productive primes, some of whom may switch allegiances to the new paradigm. Eventually, the new paradigm triumphs.

After the revolution the science is radically transformed. Issues that were once important are no longer so; scientists once revered are dismissed, while previously obscure figures may gain ascendency as precursors of the new order. A new disciplinary matrix and set of shared exemplars are adopted, and a new period of normal science ensues, with scientists tackling a new set of puzzles. If the last shape in Figure 1-2b was formerly thought of as a face, it now becomes a rat.

A revolution may not entail scientific progress precisely because the puzzles change—in other words, precisely because the new paradigm is a change in point of view rather than an addition onto the old one. In terms of our architectural metaphor, the builders of a building abandon it in favor of erecting a new one. There was progress at the old site, and there will be progress at the new site, but the resulting structures may very well be merely different, neither being necessarily better than the other. The history of science in this view would resemble a landscape dotted with the ruins of previous research programs—some in an advanced state of construction, others abandoned at the foundation—while work proceeds on the most recent. There is activity; there is, or was, progress at each site; but there need be no progress when we change sites—only alterations in the approach to architecture.

Kuhn's picture of science and those of other *Weltanschauung* theorists have proven controversial. They reached their peak of influence in philosophy of science in the early 1970s, and have been waning in influence ever since (Suppe 1977). Kuhn's greatest contribution has been to direct attention to the actual history of science, rather than to idealized versions of it. However, studies of scientific history have rendered mixed judgments on the adequacy of Kuhn's model of scientific change, especially on the existence of revolutions (Gutting 1980). Some historians find little evidence that any science has ever changed in a revolutionary manner (such as Laudan 1980), and Kuhn himself has rather backed off from his revolutionary claims (Kuhn 1977). On the other hand, one of the most distinguished living historians of science, I. Bernard Cohen, has brought out *Revolution in science* (1985), in which he elaborates on Kuhn's theme through close case studies of successful, unsuccessful, real, and purported revolutions in science, and regrets that Kuhn has retracted so much. The adequacy of Kuhn's specific historical model is unresolved, though most would concede that he has shown that understanding science must incorporate historical, social, and personal influences lying outside scientific methodology.

Within philosophy, *Weltanschauung* approaches have been furiously assaulted for their apparent depiction of science as an irrational enterprise. For example, Kuhn suggests that rival paradigms cannot be rationally compared, making adherence to a paradigm more a matter of blind faith than of evidence. However, historical work and philosophical work have shown that rival viewpoints have been rationally evaluated even during times of deep crisis, using rational criteria such as simplicity, adequacy to the available evidence, and research fruitfulness. Again, Kuhn has backed away from his revolutionary claims, often saying he was misunderstood (Postscript to Kuhn 1970). But both retractions have made Kuhn's theses much less exciting and rather more conventional. There is not much left of the *Weltanschauung* thesis, except the valuable notion that scientists work in communities to which they are socialized during training, and that the values they learn shape their thinking and research. This much is enough to demolish positivism and falsificationism, but not enough to replace them.

Evolutionary Analyses

Another naturalistic account of science applies Darwin's theory of evolution to the history of science. The most complete evolutionary analysis is provided by Stephen Toulmin's (1972) *Human understanding*. Species evolve over time by the process of natural selection. Individuals possessing variant traits are produced by mutation and genetic recombination. Successful variants grow up and reproduce themselves, while unsuccessful variants die out. Given enough time, natural selection can completely alter the body and behavior of a species into something altogether new. Indeed, human beings are descended from the first single-celled animals. While the rate of evolution may vary, there are no revolutions in the history of nature.

Similarly, says Toulmin, sciences evolve by natural selection. Individual scientists seeking to improve their science propose variant concepts that they hope will be accepted by the scientific community. The community debates new ideas and subjects them to empirical tests. Concepts that win acceptance are selected, and passed to the next generation of scientists through textbooks and instruction; ideas that are not accepted become extinct. Over time, the stock of concepts accepted by a scientific community may be completely changed by this process of natural scientific selection. However, there are no scientific revolutions on the evolutionary model. There may be periods of relatively rapid conceptual evolution, but such periods are not revolutions, since the usual processes of variation, selection, and retention account for both fast and slow evolution.

Toulmin's model escapes the historical challenge that there have been no revolutions. On the other hand, of course, should Cohen's claim that science has experienced multiple revolutions prove correct, evolutionary models of science would be in trouble. Moreover, Toulmin shares with Kuhn the problem of at least seeming to claim that scientific change is irrational (Suppe 1977). For example, Toulmin is quite vague on what criteria scientists use to evaluate the fitness of variant concepts, and says almost nothing about how and why variations are produced to begin with. While the positivist and falsificationist picture of scientists as heroically unhuman calculators of predictions and weighers of data may be a myth, it seems unlikely that reasons play no role in science.

Themata

One possible problem with both Kuhn's and Toulmin's analyses of science is that they are not naturalistic enough. While each of them respects the history of science more than their methodological adversaries, each nevertheless seems to extract a methodological story from their studies. Positivism and falsificationism both offered recipes for doing science. So, in a less direct way, do Kuhn and Toulmin. Kuhn's recipe would be to get together and agree on a paradigm, define puzzles, and solve them. What Kuhn and Toulmin share with positivists and falsificationists is the conviction that at bottom science can be described as a content-free process. For the positivist it was cumulative verification of theories; for the falsificationist it was successive disconfirmation of theories; for the Kuhnian it was establishment and replacement of paradigms; for Toulmanians it was evolution of concepts. In every case the content of the concepts is irrelevant to understanding the larger process.

A truly naturalistic alternative to all these accounts would stop looking for underlying processes and look at the substantive commitments that guide scientific research. Gerald Holton (1973, 1978, 1984) has done just this with his analysis of scientific *themata*. Themata are metatheoretical, even metaphysical commitments which motivate and guide scientists' work and often come in pairs. In physics, for example, one ancient opposing pair of themata is the belief that the universe can be analyzed into a small number of discrete parts, versus the belief that there are no ultimate parts, that the universe is a continuum. Each theme can be traced back at least to ancient Greece, and neither is yet triumphant (Herbert 1985).

The concept of themata is content-based. In Holton's scheme there is no constant underlying scientific process beyond physicist Percy Bridgman's formulation: "The scientific method is doing one's damnedest, no holds barred" (Holton 1984). Rather, science is shaped by the beliefs scientists hold about the nature of the world. Holton is thus able to steer a course between Kuhn and Toulmin. Sometimes, opposing themata come into sharp conflict, and sometimes one is overwhelmingly dominant for a time, giving a picture of stable normal science punctuated by revolutions. On the other hand themata endure; so there are no real revolutions, ensuring that the science of today is entirely continuous with the science of yesterday and even of the distant past. As to rationality, science has no special method. People are rational, and try to come to reasonable understanding of each other, their political and personal arrangements, their art, and so on. Scientific reason is simply human reason applied to nature, and within science reason is guided by historical themata that commit scientists to certain ways of work.

Unfortunately, Holton's work, while well known to historians of science, has gone virtually unnoticed by philosophers of science, which makes it difficult to evaluate philosophically. Moreover, while positivism and Kuhn have had substantial impact on psychology; and falsificationism, Toulmin, and Lakatos (discussed in "Neomethodological Approaches," below) have had some influence; Holton's themata seem to have had none. One drawback I see is that Holton's approach might tempt historians or any other student of a discipline to draw up tidy lists of themata, and overlook the messiness of real science. Certainly Holton himself does not fall prey to this temptation, and the best way to follow his example would seem to be to write the history and let the themata fall where they may.

Neomethodological Approaches

Because naturalistic analyses of science seemed to impugn its rationality, some students of science tried to return to a methodological understanding of their subject. Most prominent among the reasserters of scientific method was Karl Popper's student Imre Lakatos (1970), who wrote while reviewing Toulmin's book that his (Lakatos's) goal was to again "lay down *statute law* of rational appraisal" of scientific theories (Lakatos 1976). Lakatos was distressed that Kuhn and Toulmin might legitimate the pseudoscience that Popper had fought to banish from science.

Nevertheless, Lakatos had to acknowledge that science could not properly be understood without reference to history, and he tried to set out a more rational version of Kuhn's picture of scientific change. With Kuhn, Lakatos recognized that at the center of every *research program*—Lakatos's unit of analysis—was something very like a paradigm, what he called the *hard core* of the program. The hard core contains general ideas about the nature of the universe and about the field with which the program is concerned. For example, in psychology some research programs are committed to the hard-core concept that learning does not take place unless responses are reinforced. Hard-core ideas define the program and will therefore rarely be abandoned—if they are, the program ceases to exist. Moreover, these hard core ideas cannot directly be tested by experiment; they stand behind a science and are no part of its subject matter. In our example, since the nature of reinforcement is left unspecified, there is no way to directly challenge the idea that learning depends on reinforcement.

Around the hard core of the program is a *protective belt,* containing both the methodological levels of theory testing we have already discussed as well as specific hypotheses that translate hard core concepts into testable form. To continue our example, it might be proposed that reinforcement is drive reduction, so that learning takes place only when responses are followed by drive reduction—for example, by eating food. Protective belt hypotheses are testable, in this case by seeing if animals that are not thirsty will learn when responses are followed by giving the animal access to nonnutritive sweetened water. When experimental findings are inconsistent with the research program's prediction, as they were in this case, scientists working in the program can replace their old hypothesis with a new one consistent with the program's hard core and with the available data. Such failures do not make them reject, or even question, the hard core. In our example one might propose that reinforcement results from pleasurable stimulation rather than from physiological drive reduction.

Lakatos's scheme lays down a new demarcation criterion for telling science from pseudoscience. Lakatos recognizes, contrary to Popper, that scientific status cannot be evaluated from a single prediction. Obviously, when an inconsistent finding arises, scientists can and should challenge the status of the finding rather than immediately abandon their theory. Therefore Lakatos's demarcation criterion applies to research programs over extended time. A research program that experiences a *progressive problemshift*—that is, it anticipates new findings and does not run up against too many inconsistent results—is genuinely scientific. A program that experiences a *degenerating problemshift,* one that must constantly patch itself up as inconsistent results come in, is not scientific and ought to be abandoned.

The main problem with Lakatos's proposal is that it virtually ignores everything that naturalism established; namely, that science is shaped by historical, social, and personal forces, not by impersonal methodology. For example, Lakatos (1970) claims that history of science ought primarily to be rational reconstruction. That is, the historian should tell how an achievement ought rationally to have come about, and indicate only in the footnotes how things really did go, criticizing history for its deviation from the path of true reason. To preserve scientific rationality, and, as he seems to think, Western civilization from "contemporary religious maniacs" (Lakatos 1971), Lakatos resorts to fairy-tale history, seeming to think that knowledge of the history of their discipline would turn scientists into lunatics. One of his own rational reconstructions, of Niels Bohr's early work on the atom, "is an historical parody that makes one's hair stand on end" (Holton 1978).

Realism

Are scientific theories meant to be true? Most people think that they are, while recognizing that of course a given theory may be false. This view is called *realism,* and may more precisely be stated thus: "Science aims to give us, in its theories, a literally true story of what the world is like; and acceptance of a scientific theory involves the belief that it is true" (van Frassen 1980, italics deleted). Surprisingly, perhaps, realism is a doctrine that has seldom been held by philosophers of science.

The difficulty with realism arises when we consider scientific explanation. Science attempts to account for the regularities found in nature, and to do so scientists often postulate unobserved entities. For example, modern particle physics talks about quarks, which no one has ever seen, with strange properties such as "color" and "charm." Psychologists talk about mechanisms such as intelligence and short-term memory, which similarly cannot be observed. Scientists introduce these entities into their theories because, although we cannot see them, they and the properties assigned to them seem to explain phenomena we do observe. For example, postulating a short-term memory with a very limited capacity for storing information seems to explain phenomena such as the fact that people cannot remember more than about seven numbers, and the fact that from a long list of words people remember best the early and late words.

However, are concepts such as quarks, intelligence, and short-term memory actually part of nature? Realism asserts that they are, assuming that the theories of which they are a part are true. No realist claims that our current concepts must refer to nature as it is, only that it is possible for our concepts to refer to nature as it is. Bear in mind, too, that the debate over realism concerns only unobserved entities, not observed ones. Antirealists do not doubt the reality of things that we can see, only the reality of theoretical entities we cannot see.

Modern philosophy of science was for many years dominated by the empiricist and the even more narrow positivist tradition. The basic idea of empiricism is that human knowledge begins with experience, must be continuously checked against experience, and can only be checked against experience. Hence the empiricist demands of science only that it account for what people observe, not supposed hidden secrets of nature. As a recent defender of empiricism defines his *constructive empiricism:* "Science aims to give us theories which are empirically adequate; and the acceptance of a theory involves as belief only that it is empirically adequate" (van Frassen 1980, italics deleted). Positivism was an especially narrow version of empiricism and proposed that theoretical entities be defined operationally (see Chapter 11). As positivism withered under the onslaught of the *Weltanshauung* critics, empiricism seemed to go with it, and realism experienced a resurgence (Suppe, 1977).

However, realism has been placed on the defensive again, and at least one of its stoutest defenders, philosopher Hilary Putnam, has given it up (Putnam 1978, 1981). In Putnam's current view, called internalism, theories can only be assessed against our experience, and attempts to pass beyond experience lead to incoherence. For example, on the realist account it would be possible for a theory to explain all of our experience down to the last detail and still be false, because its theoretical entities do not correspond with what is "really" there beyond observation. So, in the realist view, all of us could be brains in vats yet never know it, a possibility Putnam believes is incoherent (Putnam 1981). Evaluating the philosophical issues surrounding realism is extraordinarily difficult, and they are not yet resolved, so it might be more profitable to consider realism in two scientific contexts: physics, for many the model science, and psychology.

Quantum theory is a perfectly confirmed scientific theory. No event that has yet occurred is inconsistent with it (Herbert 1985). Quantum theory postulates unobserved particles and properties of those particles. Are they entirely real? No, say most physicists. As Niels Bohr wrote, *"There is no quantum world.* There is only an abstract quantum description" (Herbert 1985). Subatomic particles possess two kinds of attributes in quantum theory, static attributes and dynamic attributes. Static attributes define particles, and are always the same for all particles of the same class. So, for example, every electron has a mass of 1, a charge of -1, and a spin of $\frac{1}{2}$; every proton has a mass of 1836, a charge of -1, and a spin of $\frac{1}{2}$; every photon has a mass of 0, a charge of 0, and a spin of 1. The dynamic attributes of a particle vary from moment to moment; they include, for every particle, position and momentum (speed and direction of movement), while other particles have additional dynamic attributes; photons, for example, possess degrees of polarization.

Static attributes are fixed and unproblematically observable; no one doubts they are real.

Dynamic attributes, however, behave very strangely. The strangeness is perfectly described by quantum theory, but its description suggests that there is no fixed underlying reality beneath its description. Consider shooting a beam of electrons through a small hole at a phosphor screen—television, except that in a TV the beam scans the screen, whereas here the beam aims at the center. We observe a pattern of dots as electrons stimulate the phosphor dots (pixels) on the screen. To us, each electron registers as a point on the screen, and therefore has a specific location. Overall, however, the pattern looks like a wave, rather like the pattern made by the ripples caused by a stone falling into a still pond. Why is the wave pattern there? At first it seems it must be because real electrons, with definite paths of motion, are striking one another as they pass through the hole on the way to the screen, interfering with each other and creating the wave pattern. However, even if we shoot our electrons through the hole *one at a time* and record the phosphor hits on photographic paper, we still get the wave pattern, so it cannot be that the wave is created by a mob of competing electrons.

Quantum theory copes with this problem by making an astonishing move. It claims that each electron is a wave, specifically a wave of probability. Quantum theory can calculate with exquisite precision the exact probabilities governing where an electron will strike the screen, but it cannot do more. Hence, according to quantum theory, before striking the screen the electron *had no definite position*. At the moment we observed the electron, as quantum theorists put it, ''the wave packet collapsed'' and the electron assumed a fixed position. Thus, according to most quantum physicists, there is no fixed, underlying reality that we happen to observe. Reality is, in a sense, created by the act of observation. Various eminent physicists, most notably Albert Einstein, have struggled against this view; but for reasons too complicated to review, current experimental results—not theoretical speculation—seem to rule out realism about dynamic quantum states. Even worse for a naive realistic view of the universe, it now appears that any two particles that have ever interacted remain linked, so that an observation made on one at least partially and immediately determines the results of an observation made on the other—even if the particles are millions of light-years apart. So in physics, queen of the sciences, any strong realism seems to be ruled out. All quantum theory can do is describe our experience, it cannot explain the underlying reality—if any—that causes that experience.

One should finally observe that this is to some extent true even in classical physics. Newtonian physics says that an object once set in motion will travel in a straight line unless acted on by an outside force. But this claim is an ideal of natural order (Toulmin 1961)—it cannot be explained by something *deeper*. All scientific explanation stops somewhere, and where to stop is often a pragmatic rather than a principled decision.

In psychology there is a similar problem, which I will address more fully in Chapters 13 and 15. In psychology we may observe three relevant things: conscious experience, behavior, and the processes and structures of the nervous system. Yet most psychologists talk about such unobservable entities as short-term memory, superegos, and cognitive maps. Do these terms refer to anything or not? A realist would claim they do, if the theory is true. However (and this is as far as I want to push the issue now), it is not immediately clear what kind of reality these entities are supposed to possess. In the case of subatomic particles, which no one doubts exist, even if we cannot observe them we can form some notion of what kind of reality they have: subatomic *particles*. Yet it is difficult to know what kind of a *thing* short-term memory might be. It is not part of conscious experience; although it is possible there might be a "short-term memory" box in the brain, it seems unlikely; and if it just refers to such behavior as not being able to remember more than seven numbers, then it is not *real*, but merely a convenient label for such behavior. Psychological realism thus faces a special difficulty, for it must postulate a real but unobservable psychological reality lying somewhere between consciousness, behavior, and the nervous system.

Pragmatism

At the opposite extreme from realism is pragmatism, a philosophy begun by Charles S. Peirce, William James, and John Dewey, and currently upheld by Richard Rorty (1980, 1982). Pragmatism denies that there is any fixed, permanent "truth" at all. There can, therefore, be no foundationalist philosophy at all, no discipline that defines truth and the method by which we may find it. Likewise, pragmatism denies any special status to science. Since there is no truth, there is no final knowledge, and therefore there is no eternal scientific knowledge. In the pragmatist view, humans develop languages and concepts to help them cope with their experience and solve their problems. Scientific language has proven to be quite successful at helping people cope, the pragmatist admits, but its success is not due to any special method that science alone possesses. Scientific reason is ordinary human reason applied to nature. Science has worked out well, but it is no more privileged than aesthetics or ethics. In the pragmatist view humankind is living out an extended conversation over the generations, and the aim of every scientist, philosopher, artist, critic, psychologist, and citizen should be to participate in and contribute to their culture's conversation.

PSYCHOLOGY AND SCIENCE

The Newtonian Fantasy

For at least a hundred years psychology has claimed to be a science. There are three main reasons for this. First, human beings are part of the natural world, so it seems logical that natural science should encompass them. Second, by the nineteenth century, when scientific psychology was founded, scientism was ascendent, and it seemed no discipline could be respectable were it not a science. Finally, and this was especially so in the United States, scientific status was important to psychology's pretensions to social control. Only a discipline that was a science could claim to control behavior and thus contribute to social reform and practical applications. Thus while mentalists defined psychology as the science of conscious experience, and behaviorists defined it as the science of behavior, they agreed that psychology was, or at least ought to be, a science.

The science psychologists emulated was physics. Physical science had proved itself the queen of the sciences by its outstanding success. By the second half of the nineteenth century John Stuart Mill had urged the methods of physics on the moral sciences. As positivism turned into logical positivism, the preeminence of physics increased. The logical positivists based their philosophy of science on a rational reconstruction of physics, and claimed that physics was the most fundamental of sciences, to which all other sciences would eventually be reduced.

Thus psychologists developed "physics envy." Psychologists, assuming that physics was the best science, tried to apply the methods and aims of physics to their subject matter, and felt inadequate when they did not succeed. Physics envy is a hallmark of twentieth-century psychology, especially in America. Psychologists engage in a Newtonian fantasy. One day, their faith says, a Newton will arise among psychologists and propound a rigorous theory of behavior, delivering psychology unto the promised land of science. Curiously, the disappearance of logical positivism has done little to dim the Newtonian faith, changing only its terms: One day, a Newton will give psychology its paradigm, delivering psychology unto the promised land of normal science.

In Samuel Beckett's play *Waiting for Godot,* two characters wait for a third who never arrives. Psychologists have been waiting for their Newton for over a century. Will he or she ever arrive? The Newtonian fantasy assumes that a natural science of human beings is possible, and that the model of that science is physics. Both assumptions may be questioned.

Psychology as a Life Science

Although physics is psychology's ideal, its closest scientific neighbor is biology. For many years biologists, too, were in thrall to physics envy. Recently, however, some biologists have struggled free of the Newtonian fantasy and sought to find a philosophy of science appropriate to biology (Mayr 1985). Evolutionary theory has always been suspect among traditional philosophers of science, because it fits neither the verificationist nor falsificationist schemes. Specifically, evolutionary biology is able to explain the evolution of life on our planet, but it is not able to predict the future course of evolution. As a result, evolutionary biology has been derided by physicists and their epigones as a "dirty science" consisting of little more than "postage stamp collecting" (Mayr 1985).

The inability of evolutionary theory to achieve prediction and control derives from no wooly-headedness or lack of empirical rigor on the part of evolutionary biology, but from inherent properties of the living world. For example, every electron, every proton, every quark is exactly like every other electron, proton, or quark now and since the beginning of time. However, with a few exceptions, every living thing is unique, and today's species are different from yesterday's and tomorrow's. To predict future evolutionary change is, then, quite futile. Given the diversity of species and individuals, and the possibility of new forms arising through mutation and genetic combination, the effect of any given environmental change on a given species cannot be foreseen. After the fact, evolutionary theory can give a precise and rigorous account of whatever change occurred, but it cannot make predictions.

Ernst Mayr, one of the inventors of modern neo-Darwinism, argues that there are two biologies. One biology deals with *proximate causes,* that is, "with the functional processes of living organisms . . . and its most important question is how" (Mayr 1985). This biology includes genetics, the translation of genetic programs into living creatures; anatomy, the study of the structures of living organisms; and physiology, the study of the functions of an organism and its organs. The biology of proximate causation falls under the domain of traditional philosophy of science, because it is possible to predict how DNA functions and how bodily organs work. Control is also possible in the biology of proximate causes, as current work in recombinant DNA research amply demonstrates. In genetic engineering there are designer genes.

"The biology of ultimate causations deals with evolutionary biology in the broadest sense of the word. It occupies itself with the origin of new genetic programs, and its principle question is why" (Mayr 1985). The biology of ultimate causation does not fall under the domain of traditional philosophy of science. As we have seen, it explains why evolutionary developments have occurred as they have, but it cannot, and need not, predict and control evolution. Rather than dismissing evolutionary biology as not being a science, we should expand our conception of science and include sciences of ultimate causation and "why" questions alongside the sciences of proximate causation and "how" questions (Mayr 1985). If we do this, two opportunities and a challenge arise for psychology.

The first opportunity is to choose a different scientific model for scientific psychology—evolutionary biology. Interestingly, some of psychology's founders made a similar choice in taking history as the best model for psychological explanation. History and evolutionary biology are alike in having stories to tell. Biologists can tell how species evolved over time into their present forms, but cannot predict their future. Similarly, historians can tell how modern societies came to be, but cannot predict their futures. One important difference between biologist and historian is that the biologist, being a scientist, explains evolutionary change by invoking the principles of natural selection; but it is unlikely that there are any scientific principles in history. Both Wilhelm Wundt and Sigmund Freud, founders of very different psychologies, agreed that psychology should not aim at prediction and control of mental phenomena, but at the rigorous explanation of mental events after their occurrence, by showing how the events followed from the principles of psychology. If there are no laws of history, then Wundt's and Freud's proposals are more like evolutionary biology than history, their conscious model. The main difference between their conception of psychology and evolutionary biology is that they make no use of the notion of selection, the process by which individual survival determines the direction of evolution. In modern psychology, however, B. F. Skinner (1981) has drawn a distinction between sciences of causation and sciences of selection that is very like Mayr's between the two kinds of biology. In Skinner's scheme operant psychology, at least, is an individual version of Darwinian evolution, since in each case the environment selects traits or responses for retention or extinction, resulting in the slow evolution of species or behavior.

The other opportunity afforded by biology is to practice two kinds of psychology different from that practiced by most psychologists today. First, research that connects mental states and behavior with neurophysiology would furnish a proximate causal psychology that is scientific according to even traditional philosophy of science. Historically, scientific psychology has always been connected with physiology, as we shall see. However, only quite recently has neuroscience advanced to the point of allowing detailed links to be established between mind and brain. Research on the biological bases of depression, schizophrenia, and other mental conditions is now at the forefront of neuropsychology. The second new opportunity allows psychology to be approached from the ultimate causal perspective, treating human beings as products of evolution, and explaining human dispositions as the result of natural selection. Charles Darwin himself worked along these lines, but only recently have some psychologists returned to treating *Homo sapiens sapiens* within the framework of evolutionary theory. Psychologists who do so extend to humans the discipline of sociobiology, about which more will be said in Chapter 15. Attending to biology, then, offers psychology alternative models to that provided by physics, and promises to integrate psychology with the two biologies.

Doing so, however, may challenge psychology's independence as a natural science. To the extent that mind and behavior can be explained in neurophysiological terms, there would seem to be no need for a proximate causal psychology that uses psychological language, for its place will be taken by neuropsychology using the language of physiology. Treating *Homo sapiens sapiens* as one species among many subject to natural selection likewise denies psychology's autonomy, because the principles by which we then explain human traits and dispositions will be biology's, not psychology's. In each case a *natural* science of human beings will be a branch of biology, not a separate science with its own unique and special principles. Debate on both these points is a current concern of psychologists and will be taken up again in Chapter 15.

Considering the relation between psychology and biology—a recognized natural science—raises the question of whether or not psychology is a natural science at all. Clearly, neuropsychology and sociobiological psychology are natural sciences, because they are part of biology, but what of the rest of psychology?

Psychology and the Humanities

As a biological species *Homo sapiens sapiens* is part of and lives in the natural world and is therefore part of natural science. However, human beings, because they have created a world apart from nature—culture—live therefore not only in the natural world of causal forces and natural selection, but also in a humanmade social world of meaning and reason. Precisely because our cultural world is a human creation, we should not expect it to conform to the laws of natural science. Perhaps we need a different kind of science, human science, to explain humanly created forms of life.

Nineteenth-century German thinkers, following the lead of a seventeenth-century Italian thinker, Giambattista Vico, distinguished between *Naturwissenschaft* and *Geisteswissenschaft*. *Naturwissenschaft* means "natural science"; *Geisteswissenschaft* means literally "spiritual science." Ironically, the German word no longer has an adequate translation into English even though it was invented by Germans to capture the meaning of "moral science." Nowadays *Geisteswissenschaft* is usually translated as "human science" or "social science." In any event, advocates of *Geisteswissenschaft* believe that the existence of humanly created social realities demands the creation of human science. In their view, while people are part of nature, unlike animals they are not part of nature only. Unlike animals, human beings create culture and possess reason, so that a purely natural science of humans that makes no reference to culture or rationality must leave something out. Human science can have no laws, since human cultures, unlike electrons, are different from time to time and place to place. Thus human science will resemble the humanities more than natural science. In literary criticism, history, and other humanities the goal is to make sense of human behavior, not to predict or control it. In Chapter 15 we will return to debates about this *hermeneutic* approach to psychology.

UNDERSTANDING HISTORY

History is a well-developed discipline with its own professional norms and controversies. I will discuss here only those issues that bear directly on writing a history of psychology.

The most general problem in writing history, especially scientific history, is the tension between *reasons* and *causes* in explaining human action. Imagine the investigation of a murder. The police first determine the *cause* of death; that is, they must find out what physical process (for example, the ingestion of arsenic) caused the victim to die. Then investigators must determine the *reason* for the victim's death. They might discover that the victim's husband was having an affair with his secretary, had taken out an insurance policy on his wife, and had bought two air tickets to Rio—suggesting that the husband killed his wife in order to live in luxury with his mistress (who had better take care). Any given historical event may be explained in either or both of two ways, as a series of physical causes or of reasons. In our example the series of physical causes is placing arsenic in coffee, its ingestion by the victim, and its effect on the nervous system. The series of reasons, of rational acts carried out with intention and foresight, is purchasing arsenic, putting it in one's intended victim's drink, setting up an alibi, and planning an escape.

Tension arises between rational and causal accounts of human action when it is unclear how much explanatory force to attribute to each. So far in our example the causal story is relatively trivial, because we know the cause of death, and fixing the guilt seems clear. However, causal considerations may enter into our evaluations of an actor's behavior. During his first term, President Ronald Reagan was shot and wounded by a young man, John Hinckley. There was no doubt that Hinckley fired the bullet, and was thereby part of the cause of Reagan's wound, but there were serious doubts about whether Hinckley's act could be explained rationally. The reason advanced for his attack on the president was to win the love of actress Jodie Foster, but this reason seems strange, certainly stranger than murdering one's wife to run off with one's mistress. Moreover, testimony was offered by psychiatrists that Hinckley was psychotic, showing abnormal brain X-rays. Taken together, such evidence convinced the jury that Hinckley's shooting of the president had no reasons, only causes involving Hinckley's diseased brain. Thus he was found not guilty, because where there is no reason there can be no guilt. In cases such as John Hinckley's we feel the tension between rational and causal explanation at its highest pitch. We want to condemn a proven criminal, but we know we may only direct moral outrage at someone who chose to act as he or she did, who could have done otherwise. We recognize that a person with a diseased brain cannot choose what to do and so deserves no blame.

In fact, the tension between reasons and causes arises in explaining every historical action. Caesar's crossing the Rubicon may be described either as a shrewd political move or as a result of his megalomaniacal ambitions to rule the world. One may choose to major in pre-med because of a desire to help people and make money, or because of an unconscious neurotic need to show that one is just as good as one's older sibling.

In history of science the tension between reasons and causes is perennial. Science professes to be a wholly rational enterprise. Scientific theories are supposed to be proposed, tested, accepted, or rejected on rational grounds alone. Yet, as Kuhn and others have amply shown, it is absurd to exempt scientists from the causal forces that play a part in determining human behavior. Scientists crave fame, fortune, and love as much as anyone else, and they may choose one hypothesis over another, one line of research among many, because of inner personal causes or outer sociological causes that cannot be rationally defended, that may even be entirely unconscious. In every instance the historian, including the historian of science, must consider both reasons and causes, weighing both the rational merits of a scientific idea and the causes that may have contributed to its proposal, and to its acceptance or rejection.

Traditionally, history of science has tended to overestimate reasons, producing *Whig* history and *presentism*. These failings are shared by other branches of history, too, but are most tempting to the historian of science. A Whig account of history sees history as a series of progressive steps leading up to our current state of enlightenment. A Whig history of science assumes that present-day science is essentially correct, or at least superior to that of the past, and tells the story of science as how brilliant scientists discovered the truth known to us today. Error is condemned in a Whig account as an aberration of reason, and scientists whose ideas do not conform to present wisdom are either ignored or dismissed as fools.

Whig history is comforting to scientists and therefore is inevitably found in scientific textbooks. However, Whig history is fairy-tale history, and is increasingly being supplanted by more adequate history of science, at least among professional historians of science. Unfortunately, because it shows scientists as human beings and science as upon occasion irrationally influenced by social and personal causes, good history of science is sometimes seen by practicing scientists as undermining the norms of their discipline, and therefore as dangerous. I have written this book in the spirit of the new history of science, trusting, with historian of physics Stephen Brush (1974), that instead of harming science good history can help young scientists by liberating them from positivist and Whiggish dogma, making them more receptive to unusual and even radical ideas. A large-scale historical survey of the sort I am writing must be to some degree presentist; that is, concerned with how psychology got to be the way it is. This is not because I think psychology today is for the best, as a Whig historian would, but because I wish to use history to understand psychology's current condition. As we shall find, psychology could have taken other paths than it did, but it is beyond the scope of this book to explore what might have been.

An important dimension in history of science is internalism-externalism. Whig histories of science are typically internal, seeing science as a self-contained discipline solving well-defined problems by rational use of the scientific method, unaffected by whatever social changes may be occurring at the same time. An internal history of science could be written with few references to kings and presidents, wars and revolutions, economics and social structure. Recent history of science recognizes that while scientists might wish themselves free of influence by society and social change, they cannot achieve it. Science is a social institution with particular needs and goals within the larger society, and scientists are human beings socialized within a given culture and striving for success within a certain social setting. Recent history of science is therefore externalist in orientation, considering science within the larger social context of which it is a part and within which it acts. The present edition of this book is more externalist than its predecessor, as I have striven even more to place psychology—especially the formally institutional psychology of the last century—within larger social and historical patterns.

An old historical dispute, tied up with reasons vs. causes, Whig vs. New history of science, and internalism vs. externalism, is the dispute between those who see Great Men as the makers of history, and those who see history made by large impersonal forces outside human control. In the latter, *Zeitgeist* (German for "spirit of the times") view of history, people are sometimes depicted as little more than puppets.

The Great Man view was eloquently stated by the English writer Thomas Carlyle (1795–1881):

> For, as I take it, Universal History, the history of what man has accomplished in this world, is at bottom the History of the Great Men who have worked here. They were the leaders of men, these great ones; the modellers, patterns, and in a wide sense creators, of whatsoever the general mass of men contrived to do or attain; all things that we see standing accomplished in the world are properly the outer material result, the practical realisation and embodiment, of Thoughts that dwelt in the Great Men sent into the world: the soul of the world's history, it may justly be considered, were the history of these. (Carlyle 1841)

Great Man history is often stirring, for it tells of individual struggle and triumph. In science, Great Man history is the story of the research and theorizing of brilliant scientists unlocking the secrets of nature. Because Great Men are revered by later ages for their accomplishments, Great Man history is usually Whiggish and internalist, precisely because it stresses rationality and success, downplaying cultural and social causes of human thought and action.

The opposing view was essentially invented by the German philosopher Georg Wilhelm Friedrich Hegel (1770–1831):

> [O]nly the study of world history itself can show that it has proceeded rationally, that it represents the rationally necessary course of the World Spirit, the Spirit whose nature is indeed always one and the same, but whose nature unfolds in the course of the world. . . . [W]orld history goes on in the realm of the Spirit. . . . Spirit, and the course of its development, is the substance of history. (Hegel 1837)

Zeitgeist history tends to ignore the actions of human beings, because people are believed to be living preordained lives controlled by hidden forces working themselves out through historical process. In Hegel's original formulation the hidden force was the Absolute Spirit (often identified with God) developing through human history. Spirit has gone out of fashion, but *Zeitgeist* histories remain. Hegel's student Karl Marx materialized Hegel's Spirit into economics, and saw human history as the development of modes of economic production. Kuhn's model of scientific history is a *Zeitgeist* model, because it posits an entity, the paradigm, which controls the research and theorizing of working scientists.

In Hegel's or Marx's conception, *Zeitgeist* history is Whiggish. Both Hegel and Marx see human history directed toward some final end, the ultimate realization of the Spirit or God, or the ultimate achievement of socialism, the perfect economic order, and both view historical development as a rational process. Their history is not, however, internalist, because it places the determination of history outside the actions of men and women. The contribution of Hegel and Marx was inventing externalism, directing historians' attention to the larger context in which people work, discovering that the context of action shapes action in ways at best dimly seen by historical actors themselves. Taking this broad perspective, externalism provides a greater understanding of history. However, contrary to Hegel or Marx, history has no discernible direction. The history of the world, or of psychology, could have been other than it has been. We humans struggle in a semidarkness of social and personal causes, yet, as Freud observed, the still small voice of human reason, not some abstract Reason or economic plan, is finally heard.

THE PLAN OF THIS BOOK

In Part I of this book, Background to Psychology, Chapters 2 through 6, we will trace the development of psychological ideas in the centuries before anyone thought of a scientific psychology. Our survey will begin with the ancient Greeks, take us through the Middle Ages, the Scientific Revolution, the Enlightenment, and finally into the nineteenth century, when psychology as a self-consciously scientific social institution began.

In Part II, Founding Psychology, Chapers 7 through 9, the three founding psychologies will be discussed. In Germany arose a scientific psychology of consciousness closely connected to the philosophical psychology preceding it. Its founder, Wilhelm Wundt, first established psychology as an autonomous university specialty, and trained the first generation of scientific psychologists. In Vienna arose a scientific psychology of the unconscious, connected less with philosophy than with the problems of the psychiatric clinic. Its founder, Sigmund Freud, is one of the intellectual giants of the twentieth century. His influence stretches from the nursery to the artist's studio, but his influence on university psychology has been remarkably limited. In Great Britain and the United States arose a scientific psychology of adaptation. Its founders were many, but the most important were Herbert Spencer, Charles Darwin, and William James. Although the psychology of adaptation began with the new perspective on the mind given by evolution, it paid more attention to behavior than did Wundt or Freud.

In Part III, The Rise of Behavioralism, Chapters 10 through 12, we will see how the behavioral view of psychology largely supplanted the mentalistic view. During these years, which take us to World War II, psychology's center became American and psychology became behavioral and practical.

Finally, in Part IV, Psychology Since World War II, Chapters 13 through 15, we will consider the explosion and fragmentation of psychology after the war. Between World War I and World War II psychology grew steadily and became more applied, but it remained primarily an academic and scientific discipline. After World War II, with the invention of clinical psychology, the number of psychologists grew at an astonishing rate, and more and more of them were applied rather than laboratory psychologists. At the same time the influence of psychology on society grew to the point where it seemed that the United States was becoming a psychological society.

Let us now set out, carrying as few preconceptions as we can get away with, on our 2,500-year tour of psychology's fascinating zoo.

BIBLIOGRAPHY

Philosophy of science is a confusing field for the newcomer. The best introduction to philosophy of science I know of is Suppe (1977), especially Suppe's Foreword and Afterword, which clearly analyze logical positivism and its various would-be replacements. Three useful collections are Neil Bolton, ed., *Philosophical problems in psychology* (London: Methuen,

1979), giving a variety of philosophical perspectives from and on psychology; Gutting (1980), containing essays critical of Kuhn and ones applying his methods to a number of disciplines from geology to theology; and Ian Hacking, ed., *Scientific revolutions* (Oxford: Oxford University Press, 1981), containing papers from and critical of Kuhn, but also papers giving alternate approaches not discussed in my text. Two guides to post-Kuhnian philosophy of science have been written for psychologists and published in *American Psychologist:* Barry Gholson and Peter Barker evaluate Kuhn and two rivals in "Kuhn, Lakatos, and Laudan: Applications in the history of physics and psychology" (1985, *40:* 755–769); the new realistic philosophy of science is discussed by Peter T. Manicas and Paul F. Secord, "Implications for psychology of the new philosophy of science" (1983, *38:* 399–414), followed by some useful comments (1984, *39:* 917–26) by critics, with a reply from Manicas and Secord. For antirealism, see the references in the text; Herbert's (1985) book *Quantum reality* is especially fascinating. For hermeneutics and pragmatism see Richard Rorty (1980), a provocative and controversial book, but one I found well worth reading. Gary Gutting provides an elementary and highly readable discussion of these issues in "Paradigms and hermeneutics: A dialogue on Kuhn, Rorty, and the social sciences," *American Philosophical Quarterly* (1984, *21:* 1–15). One approach to science not discussed in the book, because it hasn't often been applied to psychology, is the so-called "Strong program in the sociology of science," which out-Kuhns Kuhn. David Bloor, *Knowledge and social imagery* (London: Routledge & Kegan Paul, 1976) provides a good statement of the view. Finally, I highly recommend E. A. Burtt's *The metaphysics of modern science* (Garden City, New York: Doubleday Anchor, 1932), which, while old, provides a biting alternative to positivism that anticipated much of later antipositivism.

For the origin of history as a craft, see Herbert Butterfield, *The origins of history* (New York: Basic Books, 1981). For contemporary disputes in the discipline, see Bernard Bailyn's Presidential Address to the American Historical Association, "The challenge of modern historiography," *American Historical Review* (1982, *87:* 1–24). Brush (1974) provides an outstanding discussion of the nature and challenge of history of science. For historiography of psychology, see: Robert M. Young, "Scholarship and the history of the behavioural sciences," *History of science* (1966, *5:* 1–51; and Joseph Brozek and Ludwig Pongratz, eds., *Historiography of modern psychology* (Toronto: Hogrefe, 1980), especially the essay by William Woodward, "Toward a critical historiography of psychology."

REFERENCES

Brush, S. G. (1974) Should the history of science be rated X? *Science 183:* 1164–1172.
Bugelski, B. R. and Alampay, D. A. (1962) The role of frequency in developing perceptual sets. *Canadian Journal of Psychology 15:* 205–211.
Carlyle, T. (1841/1966) *On heroes, hero-worship, and the heroic in history.* Ed. C. Niemeyer. Lincoln, Nebraska: University of Nebraska Press, A Bison Book.
Cohen, I. B. (1985) *Revolution in science.* Cambridge: The Belknap Press of Harvard University Press.
d'Espagnet, B. (1979) The quantum theory and reality. *Scientific American 241* (No. 5, November): 158–181.
Gregory, R. L. (1970) *The intelligent eye.* New York: McGraw-Hill.
Gutting, G., ed. (1980) *Paradigms and revolutions: Applications and appraisals of Thomas Kuhn's philosophy of science.* Notre Dame: University of Notre Dame Press.
Hegel, G. W. F. (1837/1953) *Reason in history: A general introduction to the philosophy of history.* Trans. R. S. Hartmann. Indianapolis: Bobbs-Merrill.
Herbert, N. (1985) *Quantum reality: Beyond the new physics.* New York: Anchor Press/Doubleday.
Holton, G. (1973) *Thematic origins of scientific thought: Kepler to Einstein.* Cambridge: Harvard University Press.

Holton, G. (1978) *The scientific imagination: Case studies.* Cambridge, England: Cambridge University Press.

Holton, G. (1984) Do scientists need a philosophy? *Times Literary Supplement* November 2: 1231–1234.

Howard, R. J. (1982) *Three faces of hermeneutics: An introduction to current theories of understanding.* Berkeley: University of California Press.

Hull, D. L. (1973) Scientific bandwagon or traveling medicine show? In M. Gregory, A. Silvers, and D. Sutch. *Sociobiology and human nature.* San Francisco: Jossey-Bass.

Kuhn, T. S. (1970) *The structure of scientific revolutions.* Enlarged ed. Chicago: University of Chicago Press.

Kuhn, T. S. (1977) Second thoughts on paradigms. In Suppe (1977).

Lakatos, I. (1970) Falsification and the methodology of scientific research programs. In I. Lakatos and A. Musgrave, eds. *Criticism and the growth of knowledge.* Cambridge, England: Cambridge University Press.

Lakatos, I. (1971) History of science and its rational reconstruction. In R. Buck and R. Cohen, eds. *Boston studies in the philosophy of science.* Dordrecht: D. Reidel.

Lakatos, I. (1976) Review of S. Toulmin's Human understanding. *Minerva 14* (Spring): 128–129.

Laudan, R. (1980) The recent revolution in geology and Kuhn's theory of scientific change. In Gutting (1980).

Leahey, T. H. and Leahey, G. E. (1983) *Psychology's occult doubles: Psychology and the problem of pseudoscience.* Chicago: Nelson-Hall.

Mayr, E. (1985) How biology differs from the physical sciences. In D. Depew and B. Weber, eds. *Evolution at a crossroads: The new biology and the new philosophy of science.* Cambridge: MIT Press.

Putnam, H. (1978) *Meaning and the moral sciences.* Boston: Routledge & Kegan Paul.

Putnam, H. (1981) *Reason, truth and history.* Cambridge, England: Cambridge University Press.

Rorty, R. (1980) *Philosophy and the mirror of nature.* Oxford: Basil Blackwell.

Rorty, R. (1982) *The consequences of pragmatism.* Minneapolis: University of Minnesota Press.

Skinner, B. F. (1981) Selection by consequences. *Science 213:* 501–504.

Suppe, F. ed. (1977) *The structure of scientific theories.* 2d ed. Urbana, Illinois: University of Illinois Press.

Suppes, P. (1962) Models of data. In E. Nagel, P. Suppes, and A. Tarski, eds. *Logic, methodology, and philosophy of science.* Stanford: Stanford University Press.

Toulmin, S. (1961) *Foresight and understanding.* New York: Harper & Row.

Toulmin, S. (1972) *Human understanding.* Princeton, New Jersey: Princeton University Press.

van Frassen, B. C. (1980) *The scientific image.* Oxford: Clarendon Press.

2

The Classical World

Origins of Philosophy, Science, and Psychology

BEFORE PHILOSOPHY
PHILOSOPHY BEFORE PLATO
    The Pre-Socratic Philosophers
    Socrates' Contemporaries
THE TWO CLASSIC STATEMENTS OF WESTERN PHILOSOPHY
    Socrates and Plato: The Philosophy of Rationalism and Being
    Aristotle: The Philosophy of Empiricism and Growth
PHILOSOPHY AFTER ARISTOTLE
    Philosophies of Happiness
    Early Christian Philosophy
CONCLUSION: THE ESSENTIAL TENSIONS OF WESTERN THOUGHT

BEFORE PHILOSOPHY

Even before human beings began to make written records of their ideas, they took a lively interest in the universe. Archeological investigations suggest that prehistoric people made records on incised bones that represented important astronomical regularities such as the phases of the moon. These systematic observations could make possible accurate calculation of eclipses and changes in the seasons. The most dramatic, but by no means the only, evidence of early humanity's astronomical sophistication is Stonehenge, which served as both observatory and calculating machine.

Stone monuments and incised bones, however, tell us nothing about our ancestors' earliest views on human nature, or psychology. For that we must consult myths, stories preserved in oral tradition for decades or centuries before being written down. Myths serve various functions. They often justify the structure of a society and its moral code, as well as meet deep human needs both for faith and for knowledge. Myths described and explained the universe before science was invented. Tales of natural events are physics-to-be; tales of human nature are psychology-to-be.

One famous pair of myths are the *Iliad* and the *Odyssey*, a collection of oral tales synthesized not long before the Golden Age of Athens and inscribed by the poet Homer. The *Iliad* and the *Odyssey* concern themselves with human action and contain the common-sense psychology of prephilosophic Greece.

The Greeks had no word corresponding to "personality," but they did have names for what we would call different components of personality. First, there was *psyche*, the "breath of life," which leaves a person at death; we may interpret *psyche* (from which "psychology" derives) as the vital principle of life that separates the organic from the inorganic. Another part of personality was *thymos*, which seems to mean a motivational principle underlying both action and feeling. Our own word "(e)motion" also expressed the idea that behavior must result from motivational arousal. Finally, there was *nous*, the psychological organ for the clear perception of truth.

A remarkable thing about the Homeric heroes was how little control they often had of the various parts of their minds. In the *Iliad* the gods often cloud a warrior's *nous* and plant madness in his *thymos*, causing him to act irresponsibly. Indeed, Agamemnon's theft from Achilles, which opens the *Iliad*, is such a divinely controlled act. The concept of personal responsibility and the attribution of behavior to entirely internal causes did not appear until approximately 500 B.C. in the works of the Greek dramatists. Consequently, we usually find it easier to appreciate Greek tragedy than the *Iliad*, for the tragic characters act out of what we recognize as deep human passions rather than at the whims of the Olympian gods.

One important philosophical distinction appears in the *Iliad* when Homer appeals to the divine knowledge of the gods who "know all things" to correct errors in his own human opinion based on "rumor." The division between truth, or reality (divine knowledge) and appearance (opinion) is a profound one in Western thought, even today. A table appears to human eyes and hands to be solid, but physics tells us it is really a swarm of infinitely small particles. Philosophers have always wrestled with the problem that appearances can be deceptive and have looked for ways humanity can know reality. We shall see that psychology, too, shares the problem of how unreliable sensory information produces our stable picture of "reality." It is the oldest problem of reflective human thought.

FIGURE 2-1 Chronology 600 B.C.–A.D. 500.

The *Iliad* and the *Odyssey* record for us the common-sense psychology and philosophy of the ancient Greeks. Common sense, however, is seldom self-critical; it engages in no attempt to improve itself. All that changed in the sixth century B.C. when philosophy was invented.

PHILOSOPHY BEFORE PLATO

The Pre-Socratic Philosophers

The Critical Tradition

It is difficult for people to accept criticism of their ideas or to reflect critically on them. Consequently, many systems of thought are *closed*—that is, they do not criticize themselves, but rather defend themselves against criticism. We frequently find closed systems of thought in religion, for believers adhere to some great revealed Truth beyond human criticism; critics are called heretics and are often persecuted. Political systems, too, may be closed. Communists often reproach each other for "deviation" from the Truth of Marx, and persecute critics as if they were religious heretics.

Closed systems, therefore, are profoundly conservative, accepting change slowly if at all. Sometimes good can result. Chinese society was largely run by intellectual Mandarins who subscribed to a uniform Confucian ideology. Consequently, China enjoyed a political stability unknown to Europe. The Mandarins' job was to preserve what they felt was a fundamentally sound society. Stability, however, can be stagnancy. Chinese science, what there was of it, made little progress under the Mandarins. The technological feats of inventing gunpowder and building the Great Wall were accomplished by artisans, not by the educated Mandarins.

In Greece, however, intellectual life took a different turn. The ancient Greek philosophers were the first thinkers to progress by employing criticism. There, beginning with Thales of Miletus (flourished* 585 B.C.), a tradition of systematic criticism whose aim was the improvement of ideas came into being. As the philosopher Karl Popper wrote (1965): "Thales was the first teacher who said to his pupils: 'This is how I see things—how I believe that things are. Try to improve upon my teaching.'" Thales did not teach his ideas as a received Truth to be conserved, but as a set of hypotheses to be improved. Thales and those who followed him sought change. They knew that ideas are rarely right, that only by making errors and then correcting them can we progress. Dogma enshrines error in concrete and makes progress impossible. The critical attitude is fundamental to both philosophy and science, but it requires overcoming intellectual laziness and the natural feeling of hostility towards critics. Founding a critical tradition was the major achievement of the Greek inventors of philosophy.

The Physicists and Naturalism

The specific problem Thales addressed was the nature of reality. Thales proposed that although the world appears to be made up of many different substances (wood, stone, air, smoke, and so forth), there is in reality only one ele-

---

*The word "flourished" will be given as fl. A person "flourishes" around age forty.

ment—water—which takes on many forms. Water can be liquid, gaseous, or solid, and was, Thales proposed, the essential constituent of all things. The name for the single element out of which all things are made was *physis,* and so those who followed Thales in searching for some such universal element were called *physicists.* Modern physics continues the search, asserting that all the substances of common experience are really composed of a few elementary particles.

Besides inaugurating a critical tradition, then, Thales also began a line of physical investigation. In doing so he moved away from religious or spiritual interpretations of the universe toward naturalistic explanations of how things are constituted and how they work. Thus Thales asserted that the world is within human understanding, for it is made up of ordinary matter and does not reflect the capricious whims of gods. Critically, he recognized that his hypothesis was fallible human opinion, but he held out hope that divine knowledge might eventually become human knowledge.

Thales' tradition continued with his student Anaximander of Miletus (fl. 560 B.C.), who accepted the concept of a *physis* but criticized Thales' hypothesis that it was water. Anaximander asked how one ordinary element could change into others. Instead, he proposed the existence of an element that was not any recognizable element, being instead something less definite that could take on many forms. He called his proposed *physis* the *apeiron,* best translated as "the Indefinite." In his turn Anaximander was challenged by his student Anaximenes of Miletus (fl. 546 B.C.), who proposed that the *physis* was air.

Anaximander also deserves notice for his shrewd observations on evolution. He argued that since human babies are fragile and require prolonged nursing, human beings' original, primeval form must have been different, sturdier, and presumably more quickly independent, as are most animal infants. Anaximander appealed to fossils of unknown creatures to support his notion of evolution. This is one of the rare instances of a Greek philosopher appealing to empirical data to buttress an opinion. As we shall see, most Greeks preferred abstract argument to empirical research.

While he was a poet rather than a philosopher, Xenophanes of Colophon (fl. 530 B.C.) broadened the critical and naturalistic traditions by his open assault on Greek religion. Xenophanes maintained that the Olympian gods were simply anthropomorphic constructions, behaving just like human beings, even lying, stealing, murdering, and philandering. Xenophanes argued that if animals had gods they too would make them in their own images, inventing lion gods, cat gods, dog gods, and so on. Xenophanes' critique is the beginning of the ancient struggle between scientific naturalism and religion that reached its greatest crisis when Darwin proposed the theory of evolution in the nineteenth century.

More directly influential on later philosophers, especially Plato, was Pythagoras of Samos (fl. 530 B.C.). Pythagoras was an enigmatic figure, both a great mathematician and a religious leader. He is most famous for the Pythagorean theorem, and he also formulated the first mathematical law of physics, expressing the harmonic ratios of vibrating strings of different lengths. Mathematics, however, was more than just a tool of science for Pythagoras. It was also a magical key to the cosmos. Pythagoras founded a secret religious sect devoted to numbers, which believed that "Everything that can be known has a number; for it is impossible to grasp anything with the mind . . . without this [number]" (Freeman 1971). The Pythagorean sect was complete with secret rites and dietary laws, and it long outlived its founder.

In psychology Pythagoras drew a sharp distinction between soul and body. Not only could the soul exist without the body, but, going further, the Pythagoreans considered the body a corrupting prison in which the soul was trapped. An important part of Pythagorean religion was directed toward purifying the flesh so the soul could more easily attain truth.

Plato was greatly influenced by the Pythagoreans. He too viewed the soul as a pure, knowing entity thrust into a corrupting body. His theory of knowledge held that sense perception, depending as it does on the corrupt body, is inherently untrustworthy. Instead, the soul's reason should seek abstract knowledge of mathematical purity.

Finally, we must mention Alcmaeon of Croton (fl. 500 B.C.), because he foreshadows the founding of psychology. Alcmaeon was a physician who practiced the first dissections. He was also interested in philosophy and directed his attention to understanding perception. He dissected the eye and traced the optic nerve to the brain. Unlike later thinkers, such as Empedocles and Aristotle, Alcmaeon correctly believed that sensation and thought occur in the brain. Alcmaeon's work hints at the founding of psychology, the attempt to answer philosophical questions about reason by using scientific methods borrowed from physiology. In most founding psychologists, including Wilhelm Wundt, Sigmund Freud, and William James, we will find the figure of Alcmaeon, the physician turned empirical philosopher.

Being vs. Becoming

An important intellectual polarity in Western thought has been, and remains, the tension between philosophies of being and of becoming. Advocates of *being* maintain that beyond the flux of the changing world there are eternal truths and values that exist apart from humanity, truths we should seek and use to guide our lives. These truths exist in a realm of pure Being; they exist changelessly apart from the changing physical world. Advocates of *becoming,* on the other hand, deny that any such truths, or realm of pure being, exist. Instead, the only constant in the universe is change; things never simply *are,* but are always *becoming* something else. For such thinkers even moral values can change as the world changes. In the pre-Socratic period the great spokesmen for becoming and being were respectively Heraclitus of Ephesus (fl. 500 B.C.) and Parmenides of Elea (fl. 475 B.C.).

Heraclitus was a difficult philosopher, known even to his contemporaries as "the Obscure." He asserted that the *physis* was fire, which has change as its most obvious characteristic. This idea led him to the conclusion that there is even less permanence in the world than there seems to be. What looks like a stone is really a condensed ball of ever-changing fire, a reality not unlike the modern physicist's swarm of particles. His most famous aphorism was that no one ever steps in the same river twice. The statement aptly sums up his philosophy, in which nothing in the universe is ever the same twice. Nevertheless, Heraclitus also believed that although change is the only constant, it is lawful rather than capricious. Regulating change is a dynamic universal harmony that keeps things in an equilibrium of balanced forces. Thus what truth philosophy and science may attain will be truth about change rather than about static things.

Although Pythagoras's worship of eternal numbers expressed a philosophy of being, his cult's secrecy limited its influence. The philosophy of being was first stated by Parmenides, like Heraclitus a difficult writer, who set his philosophy down in a poem. Parmenides sharply distinguished a Way of Seeming (ap pearances) from a Way of Truth (reality). Since, for Parmenides, Truth was eternal and unchanging, the philosopher concluded that change is an illusion based on our faulty senses. In reality there is no change. This changeless reality had to be grasped by reason and logic, and Parmenides was the first philosopher to present his arguments as logical deductions from intuitively plausible premises. Parmenides is thus the founder of rationalism.

Since the time of Parmenides the struggle between being and becoming has been fought by many thinkers. Through his admirer Plato, Parmenides' philosophy of being dominated Western thinking, although not without challenge, until modern times. Neoplatonism was the philosophical cornerstone of medieval Christian thought. It was not until the breakdown of the Middle Ages that becoming began to ascend. With Darwin's theory of evolution by random mutation and natural selection, becoming triumphed in science. This triumph is evident not only in the biological sciences, but even in physics. Thus quantum theory asserts that we can never know where a particle is with certainty, only where it might be.

There was one revealing early reaction to Parmenides in the Way of True Opinion advanced by the physician-philosopher Empedocles of Acragas (fl. 450 B.C.), who may be regarded as the founder of empiricism. Building on the ideas of Alcmaeon, Empedocles tried to develop a theory of perception that would justify our common-sense reliance on our senses. Empedocles stated that objects emit effluences that are sense-modality specific copies of themselves. Today we know that smell works this way; our noses respond to certain molecules given off by some things. Empedocles thought this true of all kinds of perception.

Unlike Alcmaeon, Empedocles believed that the effluences get in the bloodstream where they meet and mix in the heart. The agitation of the effluences in the beating of the heart, Empedocles argued, was thinking. His theory, although it sounds absurd today, was an important step for naturalism, since it proposes a purely physical basis for mental activity, which was usually attributed to a soul.

Empedocles' views are characteristically empiricist, claiming that we know reality by observing it, specifically by internalizing copies of objects. Thought can create nothing new, being able only to rearrange the atoms of experience. And Empedocles' conclusions show why empiricists have generally contributed more to psychology than rationalists have. The empiricist must show how the senses work in order to justify our using them in seeking the truth. This necessarily requires developing psychological theories of sense-functioning. The rationalist, on the other hand, simply denies the validity of sensory information, and so can ignore problems of empirical psychology as philosophically irrelevant.

Socrates' Contemporaries

The Last Physicists: Atomism

The last classical philosophers to be concerned primarily with the nature of physical reality were Leucippus of Miletus (fl. 430 B.C.) and his better-known student, Democritus of Abdera (fl. 420 B.C.). After them, philosophers turned to questions about human knowledge, morality, and happiness. As the name of their school implies, the *atomists* proposed an idea that has proven immensely fruitful in physics: that all objects are composed of infinitesimally small atoms. For physics, this has meant that the complexity of substances we find around us can be analyzed as collections of a few particles interacting in mathematically precise ways.

Atomism can be metaphorically extended to psychology, where it has proved to be the most durable of psychological assumptions. Psychological atomism says that complex ideas such as "cathedral" or "psychology" can be analyzed as collections of simpler ideas, or even of sensations, that have been associated together. This assumption has been an integral part of empiricist theories of the mind and it still, in some form, underlies all psychological systems except Gestalt psychology.

The atomists pushed their hypothesis to its limit. They supported materialism, determinism, and reductionism. A favorite motto of Democritus was that only "atoms and [the] Void exist in reality." There is no God and no soul, only material atoms in empty space. If only atoms exist, then free will must be an illusion. Leucippus said, "Nothing happens at random; everything happens out of reason and by necessity." The soul and free will are illusions that can be reduced to the mechanical functioning of our physical bodies. Democritus wrote, "We know nothing accurately in reality, but only as it changes according to the bodily condition and the constitution of those things that impinge upon [the body]" (Freeman 1971).

Like Empedocles, Democritus proposed a materialistic account of perception and thinking. Indeed, Democritus's theory is only a modification of that of Empedocles. Democritus said that every object gives off special kinds of atoms called *eidola,* which are copies of the object. When these reach our senses we perceive the object indirectly through its copy. Thus our thought processes are restricted to putting together or taking apart the *eidola*-images in our brains. Democritus did see the fatal flaw in this theory: We have no way of knowing that the *eidola* are accurate and precise copies of the objects that emit them. If they are inaccurate, our "knowledge" of real objects is in error. We will later see how this problem became a sticking point for the eighteenth-century empiricists, Locke, Berkeley, and Hume.

Democritus also maintained an ethical doctrine that came to trouble eighteenth-century ethical philosophers deeply. A consistent materialism, denying as it does God and the soul, can only offer one guide to the conduct of life: the pursuit of pleasure and the avoidance of pain. This doctrine is called hedonism. We find Democritus saying, "The best thing for man is to pass his life so as to have as much joy and as little trouble as may be" (Copleston 1962). This is the logical outcome of naturalism, for it reduces values to our natural bodily experiences of pleasure and pain. To many, however, it is morally offensive, for if an individual's pleasure is the sole criterion of the good, what right has anyone to condemn the happy and successful criminal or tyrant? Such questions were at the heart of Socrates' and Plato's thinking, and Plato once suggested burning Democritus's books. Democritus's own answer to this moral dilemma strikes most people as lame: The greatest pleasure is philosophising—greater than the obvious physical pleasures—and the happy (good) life is a philosophical one.

The Sophists: Attitudes of the Modern World

Philosophy's shift of focus from the nature of physical reality to the nature of man was expressed most forcefully by the Sophists. Their famous motto was enunciated by the greatest Sophist, Protagoras (approximately 490–420 B.C.): "Of all things the measure is man, of things that are that they are, and of things that are not that they are not" (Sprague 1972). The center of concern became man and his needs rather than the physical world or the gods.

The Sophists maintained no fixed philosophical doctrine. They were primarily teachers of rhetoric who offered—for a fee—to teach the ambitious young men of Athens how to argue well in court and in assembly. Their aim was thus the process of effective arguing, not finding true arguments. They have been likened in this respect to modern advertising agents whose first concern is to sell a product or a politician, regardless of merit.

Protagoras's motto reflects a humanistic relativism: Man is the measure of all things. This aphorism has a range of meanings. The narrowest interpretation says that one is the best judge of one's own experience. Two people may enter the same room, yet one may experience the room as warm, the other cool, if the former has been out in a blizzard and the latter downstairs stoking the furnace. Neither perception is incorrect; each is true for its perceiver. Generalizing this perceptual relativism brings us to a broader meaning of Protagoras's idea: cultural relativism. The Sophists tended to be materialists like Democritus, considering pleasure and pain to be the only guide to conduct. Pleasure and pain are individual sensory experiences, so it follows that ethically each person is the only judge of what is right for her or him. Any attempt to lay down general rules of conduct is necessarily arbitrary, for the lawgiver knows only his or her own pleasures and pains. Nevertheless, the Sophists recognized that law was necessary for the survival of human communities and accepted a cultural relativism by which any person living in one culture had to live by the rules of that culture, but should not attempt to impose that culture's rules on people from other cultures.

Finally, at its greatest level of generality, "man is the measure of all things" is a statement about the universe. There is no permanent, enduring Truth, no divinely sanctioned law, no eternal transhuman code of values. The measure of things is not God or abstract, scientific truth, but human beings, their needs, and their search for happiness. This view is central to humanism and offers a philosophy of becoming quite different from that of Heraclitus.

Like Democritus's hedonism, the Sophists' humanistic relativism is offensive to those who see in it a recipe for moral anarchy and a denial of enduring Truth. In dialogue after dialogue, Plato's Socrates defeats the Sophists, who appear as characters in many of Plato's dialogues. Out of Plato's attempt to refute relativism came a powerful philosophy of being, classical rationalism.

THE TWO CLASSIC STATEMENTS OF WESTERN PHILOSOPHY

Socrates and Plato: The Philosophy of Rationalism and Being

Socrates (470–399 B.C.) was an itinerant teacher who inquired about the meaning of such general terms as Truth, Beauty, and Justice. His greatest pupil was Plato, who provided positive answers to the provocative questions Socrates himself did not answer. Plato (428–348 B.C.) wrote dialogues in which Socrates discusses various issues with the Athenians. The early dialogues show us the early, inquiring Socrates. In the later ones Plato has Socrates propound Plato's own rationalism.

Epistemology

The Sophists and Socrates were contemporaries and antagonists. Socrates believed that the Sophists would undermine morality with their relativistic teachings. In opposition to them he sought to discover the general meaning of the Good, the Just, and the Beautiful. Plato extended the search to encompass all of knowledge.

Plato did accept, however, one aspect of Sophistic relativism: the argument that all sensations are relative to the state of the observer. Plato provided a powerful argument in support of this position, in the example of the two men from different backgrounds entering a room and therefore perceiving the room differently. You can arrange another demonstration, proposed centuries later. Take three buckets of water—one hot, one cold, one lukewarm. Place the left hand in the hot water, the right in the cold. Then plunge both hands into the lukewarm water. The left hand will feel cold, the right hot. The water, of course, is at one temperature, yet you feel it at two temperatures. Your experience of the water is relative to the state of your hands. Plato argued from this relativity that in fact you do not *know* what the temperature of the water is: You only form some opinion about it.

Plato also accepted the Heraclitean doctrine of flux, arguing that objects are constantly changing. To Plato this meant that objects cannot be known. We cannot have eternal, unchangeable knowledge—essential characteristics of knowledge for Plato—about things that are constantly changing. Plato concluded that perception gives a highly imperfect, relativistic picture of an ever-changing world of objects, a picture that cannot be called knowledge.

Plato did not question the existence of knowledge, however, but sought to show how knowledge can be achieved. If we cannot know the physical world, what can we know? Knowledge cannot be of nothing, of what does not exist, for then it would not be knowledge. Knowledge is eternally true and unchangeable, so the objects of knowledge must be eternal and unchangeable. Plato called these objects of knowledge Forms (or Ideas). There is a Form for every class of objects to which we give a general name, such as "cat," "bed," "man," "just," or "good." Plato believed that perceived objects are imperfect copies of these Forms.

The best expression of this idea comes in the metaphor of the line in Plato's *Republic*. Imagine a line (Figure 2-2) divided into four unequal sections. The line is divided into two large sections, standing for the world of perceived Appearances and opinion and the world of abstract Knowledge, the intelligible world. The former section is shorter, indicating its imperfection. The world of Appearances is further divided, in ratios equal to that of the whole line, into worlds of Imagining and of Belief. Imagining is the lowest level of cognition, dealing with mere images of concrete objects, such as images cast in water. Plato relegated art to this realm, for when we see a portrait of a man we are seeing only an image, a shadow of a shade. Plato banished art from his Utopian Republic.

Apprehension of images is the most imperfect way of knowing. We are on surer ground when we look at the objects themselves; Plato called this Belief. With the next section of the line, Thinking, we achieve knowledge, beginning with mathematical knowledge. The mathematician can prove theorems about right-angled triangles or quadratic equations without reference to actual triangles or numerical equations. The mathematician has knowledge of these things. Plato was greatly influenced by Pythagoreanism, as is evident in the stress he placed on mathematics as a form of knowledge.

	OBJECTS	STATES OF MIND
INTELLIGIBLE WORLD	The Good	Intelligence or D Knowledge
	Forms	
	Mathematical objects	C Thinking
WORLD OF APPEARANCES	Visible Things	B Belief
	Images	A Imagining

FIGURE 2-2   Plato's metaphor of the line. (From Cornford 1945).

The ideal world of geometry is very similar to that of the Forms. In geometry you might prove, for instance, that the sum of the square of the hypotenuse of a right-angled triangle is equal to the sum of the squares of the sides (Pythagorean theorem). In establishing this you might draw a right-angled triangle, yet your proof is not about that triangle, but about all right-angled triangles, or, more Platonically, the Right-Angled Triangle. Any triangle you might draw would be an inferior copy of the perfect Right-Angled Triangle, but your proof is about the Form of this Triangle. We accept this as a commonplace of mathematics and geometry, which are not about collections of numbers or drawn figures, but about ideal variables and figures. Plato, however, believed that the relation of copy to form was true of everything, not just of drawn triangle to Ideal Triangle, but also of Plymouth Rock to the Ideal Rock. This must be so in order to make knowledge of rocks (geology) possible, since perceived rocks are in flux and only relativistically experienced.

Today we might agree with Plato that mathematics is knowledge. It is rigorous, and its proofs are necessarily true. The greatest advances in modern physics have come from pursuing elementary insights with formal mathematical logic to their necessary conclusions. Yet Plato believed the highest form of knowledge, in the last section of the line (Intelligence or Knowledge in the figure), to be more than this. Mathematics, or at least the geometry of Plato's time, relied on perceived images such as triangles, circles, and squares. This reliance on images rendered geometry imperfect. More seriously, mathematics argues rigorously from certain assumptions, which it leaves unquestioned. Euclidean geometry, for example, starts with fundamental axioms and works out the consequences, but the axioms remain unproved. In the nineteenth century, forms of geometry radically different from Euclid's were discovered by altering only one or two of his axioms. Although Plato was of course unaware of this development, it would have demonstrated to him that he was right—mathematics produces knowledge within its system of assumptions, but it cannot know which assumptions are correct. Therefore mathematics is not true knowledge, for its assumptions may always be questioned.

To attain knowledge, then, we must mount still higher to the realm of the Forms themselves, not being satisfied with their mathematical replicas, their concrete replicas, or images of these replicas. We must ascend from mere assumptions to first principles, from the world of visible Appearances to the world of intelligible Forms. How is the journey to be made? How are we to attain knowledge of the Forms? On this question Plato's views evolved over the years. He always believed that we must turn away, to some extent, from sense perception and enter into philosophical dialectic out of whose give-and-take true knowledge would arise. The exact nature of his idea of dialectic, however, changed as he grew older.

In the earlier dialogues Plato believed that experience of concrete objects stimulated remembrance of the innate knowledge of the Forms acquired between incarnations. Perceived objects do resemble the Forms, although imperfectly, and so may provide an effective stimulus to awaken our knowledge of the Forms. In his middle dialogues Plato denied any valid role to sense perception and put the entire burden of learning on abstract, philosophic dialectic. Finally, in his late dialogues and unpublished lectures (which we know through Aristotle), he returned to his earlier belief in the potential value of sense perception. At the same time he elaborated his notion of dialectic into a tool for carefully classifying all things, a tool Aristotle was to perfect and make the basis for his entire philosophy. At the same time, Plato's conception of the Forms also became increasingly mathematical and Pythagorean.

The problem Plato addressed with his theory of the Forms is one that has exercised thinkers from the Middle Ages up to modern research in concept formation. For example, if one uses the term "cat," one is not referring to one's own cat, or to any particular cat, but rather to some general notion of "catness." Each physical cat is a mixture of features, some essential to its being a cat, such as meat-eating, and some not, such as the length of its fur or its color. The essential "catness" is defined by the first kind of features. This universal "catness" was for Plato the Form of the cat, and physical cats were imperfect replicas of this Form precisely because of their accidental, unessential features. This problem of general terms as opposed to specific instances came to be called the problem of universals. It is still a lively question in learning and developmental psychology. How do people, especially children, learn to separate general concepts such as "triangle," "cat," or "lie" from their experiences of specific triangles, cats, and lies? Plato believed that people had to remember these concepts as recollections of the Forms seen between incarnations.

Psychology

Plato's overriding interest in the otherworldly Forms led him to place little importance on an empirical study such as psychology. Only one dialogue, the *Timaeus,* is given over to scientific matters. Here we will glean from various dialogues Plato's opinions on a variety of psychological topics.

Nature of the Soul.   Plato divided the soul, or mind, into three parts. First there is the immortal, rational soul, located in the head. The other two parts are mortal. The spirited or courageous soul, oriented to winning honor and glory, is located in the chest, and the passionate or appetitive soul, concerned with bodily pleasure, in the belly. The rational soul is akin to the Forms and to knowledge; the perishable (mortal) souls are tied to the body and hence are only capable of opinion. It is the duty of the rational soul to control the desires of the other two, as a charioteer controls two horses. The passionate soul was viewed by Plato as particularly troublesome and requiring great restraint by reason. Centuries later we find a similar idea in Freud, who also stressed the "primacy of the reason" over instinctual drives. Plato was clearly a mind-body dualist who said that a person is defined by the rational mind, the body being a disturbing tomb in which the soul finds itself incarnated and which it operates like a puppet.

Motivation.   As might be expected, Plato, especially in his early and middle works, takes a dim view of pleasure. Seeking pleasure and avoiding pain, obvious human drives, are things of the body that serve only to debase the rational mind and hinder its contemplation of the Good. All forms of sensation, including pleasure, were seen as unavoidable evils. In his later writings, however, Plato modified this extreme view. Some pleasures, such as the aesthetic joy found in beauty, he now considered healthy; and he rejected the purely intellectual life as too limited. His view of motivation became Freudian: We have within us a stream of passionate desire which can be channeled to any of the three parts of the soul, into the pursuit of physical pleasure, honor, or philosophical knowledge and virtue. Our drives can motivate either the pursuit of transitory pleasure or the philosophical ascent to the world of the Forms.

Physiology and Perception.   Plato's physiology is quaint to our ears. He said, for instance, that the function of the liver was to display images sent by the rational soul to the passionate soul; these images were later erased by the pancreas. Since Plato distrusted perception, he said little about the empirical science of physiology. He often just records traditional Greek views. Of vision, for example, he said that we see because our eyes throw out visual rays which strike objects in our line of sight. This idea persists in modern language in such phrases as "he threw her a glance," and this theory dominated optical thinking for centuries after Plato.

Learning.   Plato was the first great nativist, for he believed that all human knowledge is innate, that is, present at birth. In his more extreme moments Plato believed that this knowledge can be revived only through dialectic and contemplation, giving no role to sense perception. Elsewhere, however, Plato proposed an account of learning—his theory of recollection—that resembles certain modern theories—for example, Noam Chomsky's nativist account of language acquisition. Perceived objects, of course, resemble the Forms they partake of, and the resemblance, especially if aided by teaching, can stimulate our rational soul to remember what the Forms are like. Put in modern terms, perceptual input arouses and develops innate cognitive mechanisms. At the same time Plato provided the basis for the doctrine of associationism, later a fundamental part of empiricist philosophy. Sensible objects remind us of the Forms either because they are similar to the Forms, or because the two objects or ideas have been frequently associated in our experience. These are two of the fundamental laws of association—resemblance and contiguity—central to many later psychological systems.

Development and Education.   Plato believed in reincarnation. At death the rational soul is separated from the body and attains a vision of the Forms. Then, depending on the degree of virtue present in one's previous life, one is reincarnated somewhere on the phylogenetic scale. When the soul is thrust into a new body full of animal sensations and desires, it becomes completely confused and must adapt. This confusion explains why knowledge of the Forms is not present in infants. It is the purpose of education to help the rational soul gain control of the body and of the other parts of the soul. Education has three phases. First, infants must be soothed and rocked to master their inner chaos. Then elementary education in gymnastics, rhetoric, and geometry gives the child mastery of the external world. Finally, for those who are capable, higher education in philosophy leads one to knowledge of the Forms. This education is especially rigorous and exacting and was meant to produce the rulers of society.

Plato's psychology is fragmentary and incomplete. The first systematic psychology was worked out by his student Aristotle, who had a higher regard for perception and empirical science than had his teacher.

Aristotle: The Philosophy of Empiricism and Growth

Aristotle was the first professor. Plato wrote dramatic dialogues in which Socrates' flashes of insight illuminated philosophical and moral problems. Aristotle wrote prosaic treatises. He was the first to systematically "review the literature" of earlier thinkers. Instead of being led by intuitive insight, he was guided by order, method, and the syllogistic logic he invented. Plato's rationalism forced him to adopt fantastic ideas, such as the Forms, which do violence to common sense. But Aristotle's careful, empirical attitude never strayed far from common sense, and his errors were usually simple and factual, such as his belief that the heart was the seat of the soul, which includes the mind. Plato created a magical world of disembodied Forms and mysterious forces of participation. Aristotle's world was one founded on common sense, in which heavy objects fall faster than light ones.

Even though Aristotle was for twenty years Plato's student, they represent outlooks so different as to be antithetical. Plato was a pure philosopher whose approach bordered on mysticism and who so distrusted sense-perception that to him the visible world was not real. Aristotle was above all else a scientist who believed in the reality of the sensible world and in the worth of sense-perception and the joy to be found in it. The body was not a tomb to Aristotle. His fundamental error was the opposite of Plato's. He believed mathematics to be useless in science because it does not deal directly with what is observed. Despite their years together, it seems that to a large extent they did not communicate. In his writings Aristotle frequently criticized Plato, but his objections were seldom telling. They only persuade those who share Aristotle's own empirical orientation, but do not touch a true Platonist.

Epistemology

Aristotle naturally rejected the doctrine of the Forms. His specific points of criticism are usually acknowledged to be weak, but his general standpoint was that the Forms do not explain anything. They are just glorified individuals—perfect, heavenly individuals, it is true—but individuals nonetheless. To introduce a new set of particulars into the universe gains nothing. In modern terms, to Aristotle Plato was rather like a child at Piaget's preoperational stage of thinking who cannot conceive of classes of objects, only particular, concrete objects. Plato attempted to answer the problem of universals by positing glorified, perfect, individual, concrete objects. Aristotle advanced to the next stage of thinking—concrete operational—characterized by class logic and exemplified by the syllogism, a form of argument Aristotle created.

What had primary existence for Aristotle was the sensible world of things. He begins his philosophy by considering "this thing here." From our experience of objects we abstract the essence of classes of things, or species. The goal of science is to understand the essence of permanent species. We begin with sensations of particular, perishable objects and ascend by the processes of the mind to knowledge of immutable species.

Universals to Aristotle are not products of the mind, however, as some later thinkers have maintained. We know universals through the mind, but we do not create them. Aristotle believed that universals exist in nature and that we discover them. There is a universal essence of what it means to be a cat, quite apart from our thinking about cats. Universals are not separate Forms, nor are they just useful labels, for they exist as the essences of naturally real species of concrete objects.

Psychology

Philosophy of Science.   For Aristotle, psychology was an empirical science, more specifically a part of biology. Hence we begin by looking at Aristotle's approach to scientific explanation.

The Four Causes. Aristotle believed that there are four kinds of natural cause—formal, final, efficient, and material. The material cause refers to the matter of which something is made. So, for example, the material cause of the Venus de Milo is marble. The efficient cause refers to an immediate source of change or motion. If you drop a vase on a concrete floor, the efficient cause of its shattering is the sharp impact of the vase on the floor. The final cause refers to the purpose of an object or of a change. For example, in response to the question, "Why did you go to the store?" you answer: "To buy this book." This answer appeals to a final cause, since it refers to the purpose of the trip. The formal cause is the essence of an object, what makes it what it is, or defines it. It refers most obviously to the shape of the object, its form. What distinguishes the Venus de Milo from other marble statues is its precise form. However, formal cause need not refer to external shape, but it always refers to the defining essence of a thing, as separate from its accidental features. Finally, it should be noted that although the causes can be discussed separately, it is possible for a single thing to function simultaneously as more than one cause. This is the case for the soul, as we shall see.

Potentiality and Actuality. Although there are various kinds of visible change recognized by Aristotle, the form of change he was most concerned with was qualitative change, an emphasis that colors his analysis of all change. How does an acorn become an oak, a child become an adult, or a ball of wool become a sweater? These questions concern qualitative change. Aristotle's answers would be that the acorn is potentially an oak, the child potentially an adult, the ball of wool potentially a sweater. This potentiality must actualize itself or be actualized—the oak is actually an oak, the adult actually an adult, the sweater actually a sweater. Qualitative change is thus explained by an appeal to *teleology*, to purpose in nature. The purpose of an acorn is to become an oak, to actualize itself as an oak. Aristotle's system is frankly and thoroughly teleological. Aristotle often said that nature does nothing to no purpose, and the scientist explains change by discovering and appealing to these purposes.

The Scala Naturae. This striving for actualization creates a grand hierarchy among all things, from perfectly unformed, neutral matter in a state of pure potentiality up to God who is pure actuality, and who moves the universe because of the universe's desire to ascend to God—to perfect actuality (hence Aristotle's God is the Unmoved Mover, Unmoved because perfect actuality cannot change or move). Of particular interest for psychology is Aristotle's scaling of living species from the simplest to the closest to God (humans). Thus, although Aristotle denied evolution, being a believer in the fixity of species, he produced something like a phylogenetic scale, his *scala naturae,* with the result that his psychology is in part a comparative psychology.

Definition and Types of Soul.

The soul is the form (or formal cause), essence, and actuality of the person. The soul is what defines an animal—a cat is a cat because it has a cat's soul and behaves like a cat. A human being is human by virtue of possessing a human soul and hence acts human. In sum, each creature is defined by its soul, and, although Aristotle is not clear on this point, each individual is defined by her or his individual soul, what we would call the self. Hence the soul is the formal cause of the person, for it defines what kind of living thing it is. The soul is thus the essence of the animal. Finally, it is the actuality of a body which potentially has life. Without soul a body is dead; with soul there is life. The potential for life in a creature, therefore, is actualized by the soul. In addition, the soul is the efficient cause of bodily movement, for it causes movement to happen. It is also the final cause, for the body serves the soul. To summarize, of any animal the material cause is the body of which the animal is made; the soul is efficient cause of motion, formal cause that defines the animal's essence, and final cause, the purpose of the body.

What is the relation of soul and body? Aristotle, a biologist, took a naturalistic view of the mind-body problem. The soul, with the exception of one part, is inseparable from the body. His view resembles what is today called the dual aspect psoition: There is only one material reality, body, but it has two aspects, physiological and mental. Soul is the form of body and can no more be separated from its material embodiment than the form of the Venus de Milo can be separated from the marble it is made of, although we can discuss them separately, considering either the marble or the shape alone. Aristotle put it this way in *De Anima:* "That is why we can wholly dismiss as unnecessary the question whether the soul and the body are one: it is as meaningless to ask whether the wax and the shape given to it by the stamp are one. . . ." Aristotle was not a dualist. He rejected Plato's dualism and would have rejected Cartesian dualism. He is not a materialist reductionist, however. Soul cannot be reduced to body, even though there is only one matter, for we can separately discuss physiological and psychological functioning.

As a teleological biologist, Aristotle asked about the soul as about any organ: What is it for? What is its purpose? He believed that the soul has several powers, such as nutrition, movement, and reason. Most philosophers call Aristotle's a faculty psychology, speaking of the faculty of reason, for example; but it would be better described as the first functional psychology, an approach congenial to a biologist. When, in the nineteenth century, American psychologists under the influence of Darwin again adopted a biological perspective, they formed a school called functionalism, emphasizing, as did Aristotle, the biological value of mental functioning.

It is obvious that not all living things exhibit the same functions, and Aristotle distinguished three levels of soul appropriate to different levels on his *scala naturae.* At the lowest level there is the *nutritive* soul, possessed by plants, serving two functions: the maintenance of the individual plant through nutrition, and the maintenance of the species through reproduction. Animals possess a more complex, *sensitive* soul, which subsumes the nutritive soul's functions while adding others. Animals, unlike plants, are aware of their surroundings. They have sensations;

hence, "sensitive soul." As a consequence of sensation, animals experience pleasure and pain, and so feel desire either to seek pleasure or to avoid pain. There are two further consequences of sensation: first, imagination and memory (since experience can be imagined or recalled); and second, in some animals, movement as a consequence of desire. Highest in the scale of souls comes the human soul, subsuming the others and adding mind, the power to think. This is the *rational* soul.

Structure of the Rational, Human Soul.

According to Aristotle, gaining knowledge is a psychological process that starts with the perception of particulars and ends with general knowledge of universals. Aristotle's analysis of the soul can be represented by a diagram showing the faculties of the soul and their interrelationships (Figure 2-3). The five primary senses send information to common sense, which unifies sensations into conscious perception and passes this processed information on to the passive mind, which is imprinted with the objects of perception. These perceptions may persist, creating images. Memory for Aristotle was a species of imagination, for our memories are always concrete images. Material passes into memory as we learn and can be recalled to consciousness later; hence, the flow of information goes both ways. Finally, the contents of the passive mind are acted on by the active mind to produce universal knowledge. We will now consider these functions in more detail.

Sense Perception.

The special senses passively receive sensations of external objects. Their power is the potential to absorb the form of external objects, actualized by reception of a sense impression. To each special sense correspond certain qualities that only it can perceive. For instance, only by vision can we sense color, only by taste, sweetness. This aspect of perception is infallible. One cannot be wrong in saying that one sees a red spot or tastes sweetness. What can be in error is perception of the "incidental sensibles," which requires judgment. What one senses as a red spot may incidentally be a lady bug. But if one says, "I see a lady bug," one may be in error, for this requires a judgment. One may be seeing a spot

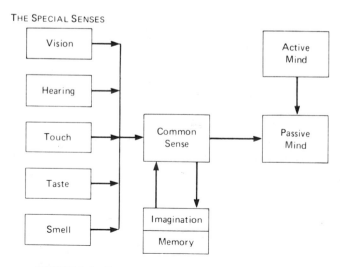

FIGURE 2-3 Structure of the soul in the *De Anima*.

of paint. There are also sense qualities that are perceivable by more than one sense. One can see that an object is moving, or one can feel it move. One can see that there are two books on the desk, or one can find this out by touch. These qualities of movement (or rest), number, shape, and size are called *common sensibles* because they are common to more than one sense.

Perception of the incidental and common sensibles is a result of common sense, which unifies data from the special senses into coherent, conscious experience. We do not live in a world of red patches or isolated sounds and tastes, but in an experienced world of objects (incidental sensibles) with important common properties (common sensibles). This apparent contradiction between what our sense organs detect and the conscious "lived experience" of which we are aware became (and remains) a vexing problem for twentieth-century psychology when the Gestalt psychologists opposed Wundt's apparent reduction of experience to bundles of sensations. Aristotle was the first to try to deal with this question by postulating this common sense that unifies color patches, touches, and other sensations into conscious experience. Common sense is also responsible for self-awareness, and it is the inactivity of common sense that causes us to lose self-awareness in sleep.

Mind.   The rational part of the soul Aristotle called *mind*. It is unique to human beings and is capable of acquiring knowledge of abstract universals, as opposed to the knowledge of individuals given in perception. As we experience different members of the same natural type, we note similarities, and so form an impression of a universal, which Aristotle believed was always an image. As one experiences a multitude of cats, one eventually forms an idea of what the essence of a cat is.

Within the mind there must be, as Aristotle believed there to be throughout nature, a difference between potentiality and actuality. The passive mind is potentiality. It has no character of its own, for it can take on the form of experienced objects. Knowledge of universals in the passive mind is actualized, or made manifest, by the operations of the active mind. The active mind is pure thought, acting on the contents of the passive mind to achieve rational knowledge of universals. This active mind is quite different from the other parts of the soul. As actuality, it is not acted upon; rather, it acts on the contents of the passive mind. For Aristotle, this meant that the active mind was unchangeable; hence, immortal, for death is a form of change. The active mind is, therefore, separable from the body and survives death, unlike the rest of the soul. However, the active mind is not a personal soul, for it is identical in all human beings. It is pure thought and carries nothing away from its sojourn on earth. Knowledge is realized only in the passive mind, which perishes.

Imagination and Memory.   Aristotle believed that thought without images was impossible, therefore we should expect considerable discussion of imagination in his works. However, there is very little. His comments on imagination describe it narrowly as the persistence of a percept after the object originally causing it has gone. He does not discuss the active use of imagination, although he seems to be aware it exists. The only place imagination is important for Aristotle is in memory. To Aristotle, the act of memory consists of having an image and being aware of it as an image of something past.

Memory as a repository consists of a set of images that represent past experi ence. Aristotle distinguishes simple memory—the recognition of an image as a representation of a past moment—from recollection, which involves a search among the memory images. Recollection is based on the fact that memory is organized, and Aristotle notes the fact (rediscovered by modern psychologists) that material inherently organized, such as mathematics, is easier to remember than that which is less organized.

This organization is based on association, as described in many modern psychological theories. Plato, as we have seen, hinted at laws of association, but Aristotle was the first systematically to exploit them. Aristotle discusses three laws of association—similarity, contiguity, and contrast. Similar images are associatively linked, images of contiguous experiences are linked, and opposite images are linked (that is, "hot" usually elicits the association "cold"). He also hints at the law of causality—causally linked experiences remind us of one another.

Motivation.   Movement is characteristic of animals and thus is a function of the sensitive soul, which can experience pleasure and pain. All action is motivated by some form of desire, which Aristotle believed involved imagination. In animals, motivation is directed by an image of what is pleasurable, and the animal seeks only present pleasure. Aristotle calls this type of motivation *appetite*. Human beings, however, are capable of reason and so can conceive of right and wrong. Therefore we can be motivated by desire for what is good or for long-term future benefits. This type of motivation is called *wish*. Animals experience simple motivational conflicts between opposing appetites, but man has in addition the problem of moral choice. Aristotle's view of motivation resembles Freud's, distinguishing between the innate, animalistic pleasure principle, which cares only for immediate pleasure, and the acquired, uniquely human reality principle, which calculates long-term gain.

PHILOSOPHY AFTER ARISTOTLE

Philosophies of Happiness

Aristotle and his one-time pupil Alexander the Great died in 323 B.C., the traditional date dividing the age of Classical Greece from the succeeding Hellenistic and Roman periods. The Hellenistic period especially was one of rapid social and political change as empires, first Alexander's short-lived one and then the more durable Roman one, replaced the small worlds of the Greek city-states. During these years intellectual life turned away from metaphysics toward reality and the problems of living in a world of uncertainty and change. Science and scholarship flourished as never before, especially at the city of Alexandria, where mathematicians, astronomers, physicians, and physicists made great strides in their fields, while the scholars of the great library gathered up the writings of the past. In the arts, sculptors and writers, painters and poets turned to realism, trying to show people as they really were in all their individuality, rather than depicting ideal forms, the goal of earlier artists.

Philosopher's aims became more modest. Plato had inaugurated the program of making philosophy the general foundation of all other knowledge, and Aristotle had continued Plato's quest, though of course the framework of knowledge he proposed was quite different. In the Hellenistic and Roman ages, however, philosophers abandoned Plato's grandiose vision (it would be revived by Descartes in the seventeenth century) and attended to the problems of human living. Specifically, Hellenistic and Roman philosophers counseled people on how to achieve happiness. In a world of woe, people sought a limited kind of happiness, *ataraxia,* which might best be translated as peace of mind or freedom from disturbance. Hellenistic men and women sought tranquility, not joy. There were many recipes for *ataraxia* offered by various schools of philosophy, and several of them have become household names.

Epicurus (341–270 B.C.) accepted atomism, though not determinism, and like Democritus he advocated hedonism. But Epicurus's formula for pleasure was not what we associate with the name of his school, epicureanism. He stressed the avoidance of pain over the active pursuit of pleasure and counseled his followers to lead quiet lives withdrawn from the strife of the outside world. His warnings strike home to an energy-conscious age: To depend on the pleasures of life is to risk pain if they are withdrawn.

The Cynics not only withdrew from the civilized world, but also attacked it. They felt that the doings of society were full of hypocrisy encompassing greed, envy, and hate. The Cynics flouted social conventions. The most famous Cynic was Diogenes (who died in 324 B.C.); he lived a life of poverty, called himself a citizen of the world, and advocated free love and communal families. It is said that Alexander the Great visited Diogenes at the cave where he lived. Standing in the entrance, Alexander asked what he could do for the renowned philosopher. "Get out of my light," was Diogenes' reply. This story epitomizes Cynicism.

Skepticism was a related but more intellectual movement, founded by Pyrrho of Elis (360–270 B.C.) and developed by several later heads of Plato's academy. Like Plato, the Skeptics distrusted sense-perception. They did not believe in any world of the Forms, however. Therefore they held that any general conclusions one might reach on the basis of experience might turn out to be wrong in the light of new experience. Since being refuted is a painful experience, the Skeptics believed we should accept no general conclusions so as to avoid the unhappiness of being wrong.

More widespread than any of these philosophies was Stoicism, which counted among its adherents both a slave (Epictetus, A.D. 50–138) and an Emperor (Marcus Aurelius, A.D. 121–180). Its founder was Zeno of Citium (333–262 B.C.), who taught at the painted collonade, or *Stoa,* in Athens. Today a Stoic is someone who accepts misfortune "philosophically"—quietly and without complaint. Ancient Stoics behaved this way because they believed that the universe was rational and good, often likening it to a living, semidivine being present in everything. The Stoics were also determinists, holding that whatever happens to a person *must* so happen because of the causal ordering of the universe. Happiness, then, lies in placing one's own reason in harmony with that of the universe, accepting one's fate as part of a greater, divinely rational whole.

The most influential happiness philosophy was Neoplatonism, whose best spokesman was Plotinus (A.D. 204–270), an Egyptian Greek. Plotinus fully developed the mystical aspect of Platonism, very nearly turning that philosophy into a religion. He described the universe as a hierarchy, beginning with a supreme and unknowable God called *the One.* The One "emanates" a knowable God called *Intelligence,* which rules over Plato's realm of the Forms. From Intelligence serially emanate more divine creatures until we reach humans, whose divine souls are imprisoned in degrading, material bodies. The physical world is an imperfect, impure copy of the divine realm.

Plotinus's concern was to turn his followers eyes away from the corrupting temptations of the flesh and toward the spiritual world of truth, goodness, and beauty in the realm of the Forms. In his *Enneads* Plotinus wrote: "Let us rise to [the] model . . . from which [the physical] world derives. . . . Over [it] presides pure Intelligence and incredible wisdom. . . . Everything there is eternal and immutable . . . [and] in a state of bliss." The last phrase makes the change from Platonic philosophy to the ecstatic vision of the religious and points toward the most successful happiness philosophy, which was a religion.

Early Christian Philosophy

The happiness philosophies gained the adherence of various Greek and Roman intellectuals. But as the Roman Empire began to disintegrate, more and more people needed something stable to believe in. The old Olympian gods were no longer plausible, and in the later Empire many religions of Eastern origin attracted Roman converts. These faiths were usually centered around followers' initiations into a religious mystery and were called *mystery religions.* There were several strong ones. *Mithraism,* for example, based on the death and rebirth of Mithras, was a complex religion with at least one temple as far away from its Persian birthplace as Roman London. It almost became the official religion of Rome. The long-run victor among these mystery religions, however, was based on the death and rebirth of an obscure Jewish teacher named Jesus. It was known as Christianity and gained many converts, including emperors. It became the Roman state religion in the fourth century A.D.

An important problem for Christian believers was how to deal with classical philosophy. Should it be condemned as pagan and necessarily heretical, as St. Jerome (345–420) contended; or should Christians accept those elements of philosophy compatible with faith, as St. Ambrose (340–430) argued? The latter position emerged victorious, and its greatest representative, one of the two greatest teachers of Catholic philosophy, was St. Augustine (354–430). Augustine is the last classic philosopher and the first Christian one, combining Stoicism, Neoplatonism, and Christian faith.

Stoicism, with its emphasis on divine wisdom and human submission, has elements that can be assimilated easily to Christian belief. Even more compatible, however, was Neoplatonism, which was a philosophy evolving into a religion. In the fourth century Christianity was a simple faith, lacking a supporting philosophy. Augustine integrated faith and philosophy into a powerful Christian world view that would dominate all aspects of medieval thought until the thirteenth century. The following passage illustrates Augustine's Christian Platonism:

> God, of course, belongs to the realm of intelligible things, and so do these mathematical symbols, though there is a great difference. Similarly the earth and light are visible, but the earth cannot be seen unless it is illumined. Anyone who knows the mathematical symbols admits that they are true without the shadow of a doubt. But he must also believe that they cannot be known unless they are illumined by something else corresponding to the sun. About this corporeal light notice three things. It exists. It shines. It illumines. So in knowing the hidden God you must observe three things. He exists. He is known. He causes other things to be known.

St. Augustine, *Soliloquies I*

Augustine assimilated a sophisticated if mystical philosophy and created basic Christian theology. In the next chapter we will look at Augustine's distinctively Christian medieval ideas, for with Augustine we have reached the beginning of the Middle Ages.

CONCLUSION: THE ESSENTIAL TENSIONS OF WESTERN THOUGHT

> I shudder when I think of the catastrophes of our time. For twenty years and more the blood of the Romans has been shed daily . . . the great cities have been sacked and pillaged and plundered by Goths . . . Huns and Vandals. . . . The Roman world is falling; yet we hold up our heads instead of bowing them.
>
> St. Jerome, "The Roman World is Falling"

The fall of Rome is dated officially as A.D. 476. All forms of culture, art, philosophy, and science went into a sharp decline around A.D. 300, a decline that began, however, about A.D. 200. There was a brief renaissance under Charlemagne in the middle of the ninth century, but European civilization did not really revive until the twelfth century. At this point, therefore, we will pause to consider the achievement of the classical world.

As the Roman Epicurean Lucretius said, the Greeks have been before us. In this chapter we have briefly inventoried some of the ideas that the classical world created and bequeathed to their intellectual successors. There are few modern concepts that cannot be traced to Greek roots. The ideas of such men as Plato, Aristotle, Democritus, and Thales are an integral part of the texture of modern intellectual life.

There are two important intellectual tensions that emerge from the Greek period and are intertwined throughout the subsequent centuries. The first tension is that between rationalism and empiricism. The rationalist, from Parmenides on, denies that true knowledge comes from perception and so turns inward to reason and innate ideas in the search for truth. The empiricist, from Empedocles on, looks outward, believing that a way of true seeming can be built on the material of sensory experience. The rationalist fears the illusions of sense; the empiricist fears the delusions of reason.

The other tension is between being and becoming. The advocate of being, often a rationalist, believes in eternal and transcendent truths and values, which exist apart from us and which we must seek. The advocate of becoming, often an empiricist, denies the existence of eternal truth and immutable being, finding in the changing flux of experience the only truth—that everything is constantly changing. The interplay and struggle between these two intellectual tensions has motivated intellectual life ever since the Classical Age.

BIBLIOGRAPHY

There are many fine books on the Classical, Hellenistic, and Roman worlds. I shall mention some of the ones I consulted and found useful. On the prehistoric roots of science Alexander Marshack's *Roots of Civilization* (New York: McGraw-Hill, 1972) is fascinating. A convenient survey of ancient Greek life and history is given by Antony Andrew in *The Greeks* (New York: Norton, 1978). On Greek psychology see G. S. Kirk, *The nature of the Greek myths* (Harmondsworth, England: Penguin, 1974); Bruno Snell, *The discovery of the mind: The Greek origins of European thought* (New York: Harper & Row, 1960); and E. R. Dodds, *The Greeks and the irrational* (Berkeley: University of California Press, 1951), which is a classic of Classical scholarship. For the Hellenistic period see F. W. Walbank, *The Hellenistic world* (Sussex, England: Harvester, 1981); and Michael Grant, *From Alexander to Cleopatra: The Hellenistic world* (New York: Scribner's, 1982); the latter is especially useful on realism, art, happiness philosophies, and mystery religions. On Rome see Donald R. Dudley, *The Romans: 850 B.C.–A.D. 337* (New York: Knopf, 1970). Although it is unavoidably out of date, Edward Gibbon's (1776) *Decline and fall of the Roman Empire* still repays study. It is beautifully written, with some biting ironic asides (Gibbon says history is "little more than the register of the crimes, follies and misfortunes of mankind"). Living before the age of professional history, Gibbon can get away with what every historian would like to, omitting, as he often does, everything that is neither "entertaining nor instructive." Penguin Books has published a fine one-volume abridgment of the original (Harmondsworth, England, 1981).

There are several valuable treatments of Classical science. An excellent short but comprehensive work, embracing both science and philosophy, is Giorgio de Santillana, *The origins of scientific thought* (New York: Mentor Books, 1961). The standard histories of science in this period are George Sarton, *A History of Science,* two vols. (New York: Norton, 1952); and Marshall Clagett, *Greek science in antiquity* (New York: Collier, 1955); Sarton set out to write a history of all science, but worked so thoroughly that he died before getting past the Hellenistic age. The major younger scholar of Greek science is G. E. R. Lloyd. His *Early Greek science: Thales to Aristotle* (New York: Norton, 1970) is a good short introduction to the field; his *Magic, reason, and experience: Studies in the origin and development of Greek science* (Cambridge, England: Cambridge University Press, 1979) and *Science, folklore, and ideology: The life sciences in ancient Greece* (Cambridge, England: Cambridge University Press, 1983) offer more specialized and technical studies. There are more general histories of science which include the Classical period. Stephan Mason's *A history of the sciences* (New York: Collier Books, 1962) is a useful one-volume history. The most erudite and comprehensive history is Lynn Thorndike's massive and magisterial *History of magic and experimental science* in eight volumes (New York: Columbia University Press, 1928–1958). Another ambitious undertaking is Richard Olson's social history of science. The first of two volumes has been published as *Science deified and science defied: The historical significance of science in Western culture 3500 B.C.–A.D. 1640* (Berkeley: Berkeley University Press, 1982).

Turning to philosophy, there are several comprehensive histories that include the Greek period. I have primarily consulted Frederick Copleston, *A history of philosophy,* nine vols. (Garden City, New York: Image Books, 1962–1977); Jacob Bronowski and Bruce Mazlish, *The western intellectual tradition* (New York: Harper & Row, 1960); and Bertrand Russell, *A history of western philosophy* (New York: Simon & Schuster, 1945). Copleston's history is comprehensive and detailed, though sometimes difficult. Bronowski and Mazlish is less detailed, but more readable. Russell's history must be used with care; it is wonderfully written, but not disinterested. As a brilliant philosopher, Russell discusses his dead colleagues from his own point of view, neglecting, and sometimes distorting, various facets of the thinkers he presents.

There are a wealth of works on the Greek philosophers. Three general works are J. Burnet, *Early Greek philosophy,* 4th ed. (New York: Collins, 1957); A. H. Armstrong, *An introduction to ancient philosophy* (London: Methuen, 1980); and W. K. C. Guthrie's multivolume *History of Greek philosophy* (Cambridge, England: Cambridge University Press), which is still being published. More specialized works follow.

The Pre-Socratics. G. Kirk and K. Raven, *The presocratic philosophers* (Cambridge, England: Cambridge University Press, 1971). Drew Hyland, *The origins of* *philosophy* (New York: Putnam, 1973). G. Kerferd, *The Sophistic movement* (Cambridge, England: Cambridge University Press, 1980). R. Sprague (1972)

Plato.   *The collected dialogues of Plato,* edited by Edith Hamilton and Huntington Cairns (New York: Pantheon, 1961, Bollingen Series LXXI). Georges Grube, *Plato's thought* (Boston: Beacon, 1958). Norman Gulley, *Plato's theory of knowledge* (London: Methuen, 1962). Erik Nis Ostenfield, *Forms, matter, and mind* (The Hague: Martinus Nijhof, 1982). J. E. Raven, *Plato's thought in the making* (Cambridge, England: Cambridge University Press, 1965). T. Robinson, *Plato's psychology* (Toronto: Toronto University Press, 1970). David Ross, *Plato's theory of ideas* (Oxford: Oxford University Press, 1951).

Aristotle.   *The basic works of Aristotle,* edited by Richard McKeon (New York: Random House, 1941). J. C. Ackrill, *Aristotle the philosopher* (Oxford: Oxford University Press, 1980). John Ferguson, *Aristotle* (New York: Twayne, 1972). G. E. R. Lloyd, ed., *Aristotle on mind and the senses* (Cambridge, England: Cambridge University Press, 1978). John H. Randall, *Aristotle* (New York: Columbia University Press, 1960). David Ross, *Aristotle* (London: Methuen, 1966). Ricahrd Sorabji, *Aristotle on memory* (Providence, Rhode Island: Brown University Press, 1972).

Hellenistic/Roman Period.   A. Long, *Hellenistic philosophy: Stoics, Epicureans, Skeptics* (London: Duckworth, 1974). Giovanni Reale, *The systems of the Hellenistic age* (Albany, New York: State University of New York Press, 1985). Emile Brehier, *The philosophy of Plotinus* (Chicago: Chicago University Press, 1958). Ramsey McMullen, *Paganism in the Roman Empire* (New Haven: Yale University Press, 1981). S. Angus, *The mystery religions* (New York: Dover, 1975). Joscelyn Godwin, *Mystery religions in the ancient world* (San Francisco: Harper & Row, 1981). R. Nash, *The light of the mind: St. Augustine's theory of knowledge* (Lexington: The University of Kentucky Press, 1969).
    Finally, there are two interesting works on Greek psychology. George Sidney Brett surveys Greek and Hellenistic psychologies in *Psychology: Ancient and modern* (New York: Cooper Square, 1963). Bennett Simon examines Greek ideas about psychopathology in *Mind and madness in ancient Greece: The classical origins of modern psychiatry* (Ithaca, New York: Cornell University Press, 1978).

REFERENCES

Copleston, F. (1962) *A history of philosophy,* V. 1., Greece and Rome. Garden City, New York: Doubleday.

Cornford, F. (1945) *The Republic of Plato.* Oxford: Oxford University Press.

Freeman, K. (1971) *Ancilla to the presocratic philosophers.* Cambridge: Harvard University Press.

Popper, K. (1965) Back to the presocratics. In *Conjectures and refutations.* New York: Harper & Row.

Sprague, R. (1972) *The older Sophists.* Columbia: University of South Carolina Press.

CHAPTER 3

Spirituality and Individualism

The Middle Ages and Renaissance

FROM CLASSICAL TO MEDIEVAL: THE EARLY MIDDLE AGES (476–1000)
  The Medieval Context
  Islamic Faculty Psychology
THE FLOWERING OF MEDIEVAL CIVILIZATION: THE HIGH MIDDLE AGES (1000–1300)
  Popular Culture
  Christian Faculty Psychology
FROM MEDIEVAL TO MODERN: THE LATE MIDDLE AGES, RENAISSANCE, AND REFORMATION (1300–1600)
  The Late Middle Ages: The Dissolution of the Medieval Synthesis
  Renaissance and Reformation
  The End of The Renaissance
CONCLUSION: THE CLASSICAL-MEDIEVAL-RENAISSANCE OUTLOOK

The Middle Ages was the crucible in which our modern world was formed, and the Renaissance was the first self-consciously modern period. The medieval period saw the beginning of constitutional democracy, romantic love, individualism, and experimental science. During the Renaissance learning and scholarship left the confines of the church to become again the property of lay society concerned with humanity's nature and needs rather than God's.

FROM CLASSICAL TO MEDIEVAL: THE EARLY MIDDLE AGES (476–1000)

The Medieval Context

The Nature of Society

Although tradition sets the date of the end of Classical civilization at A.D. 476, something like the medieval way of life began during the Roman Empire in the late third and fourth centuries. Because of economic decline, small farmers became legally tied to the land, a state which evolved into serfdom. As the control of Rome over her provinces loosened, local autonomous leadership grew, leading to feudalism. The breakdown of the Roman world was evident as barter economy began to replace the money economy of the empire, communication broke down, the imperial army became more and more a mercenary army of barbarians rather than a voluntary army of Roman citizens, populations declined, and the Eastern Empire with its own Emperor and capital at Constantinople leached treasure and resources from the European, or Western Empire to preserve its own superior way of life.

These crises were compounded by an extraordinary movement of barbarians into the empire. Early settlers had often come peacefully into the empire, but later invasions were bloody and destructive. Rome itself was sacked in Augustine's time; the Emperor Romulus Augustulus who fell in 476 was himself only a barbarian usurper. The movement of northern peoples from Goths to Vikings, which finally tore the empire asunder, continued to almost A.D. 1000.

This extended period of transition from classic to medieval times, from before 475 to about 1000, is sometimes still called the Dark Ages, but is better called the early Middle Ages. Although creative thinking declined, there were periods of intellectual development, most notably the Carolingian renaissance under Charlemagne (768–814, not to be confused with the Italian Renaissance of the fifteenth and sixteenth centuries). New political forms were developed to replace the husk of imperial government. It was even a period of technological advance. For example, the heavy plow and the modern horse-harness were invented, opening new lands for farming and improving the yield from old. Although this period saw economic, demographic, and intellectual decline, a new, creative society was arising from the imperial ashes.

The economy and population began to rise again around 1000, ushering in the high Middle Ages, which lasted to about 1300. This was an enormously creative period in Western civilization. Many Greek works, especially those of Aristotle,

	A.D. 500	
End of school at Athens		Justinian, Byzantine Emperor
	600	Last barbarian invasions
End of school at Alexandria		Mohammed dictates Koran
Byzantine iconoclasm	700	Charles Martel repels Arabs
	800	Charlemagne crowned Emperor
		Alfred the Great of England
	900	Vikings discover Greenland
	1000	European recovery begins
Ibn Sīnā		Norman conquest of England
	1100	
		St. Bernard
Abelard		Notre Dame Cathedral begun
Eleanor of Aquitaine + Courtly love	1200	
		St. Francis
Bonaventure, Aquinas		
Siger of Brabant	1300	Attempts to suppress Aristotle
Ockham		
Petrarch, Nicholas of Autrecourt		Black Death
Medieval science; Buridan, Oresme		
	1400	
Copernicus		Fall of Constantinople
Erasmus	1500	Savonarola
		Reformation
Montaigne		
		Descartes born
Hamlet, de Magnete	1600	

FIGURE 3-1 Chronology 500–1600.

were recovered, and philosophical thinking resumed in the twelfth-century renaissance. The magnificent Romanesque and Gothic churches were constructed. Modern political forms, especially in England, were developing, as was the concept of romantic love and the interest in individuality.

This fertile European culture ended between 1277 and 1350 in the rise of nationalism and in the wake of wars between the embryonic nations, the increasing dogmatism of the church, and the Black Death of 1348 to 1350, which killed no less than one-third of the population of Western Europe. Friedrich Heer calls this the "closed" Europe of the late Middle Ages, in contrast to the intellectually and politically "open" Europe of the previous period. The late Middle Ages lasted into the Renaissance, which began in Italy as early as 1300, but took about two hundred years to reach the north of Europe.

It is against this background of loss and recovery, decline and innovation that we must understand medieval thinking.

The Shape of Medieval Mentality

Reason: What, then do you want to know?
Augustine: The very things for which I have prayed.
R: Summarize them concisely.
A: I want to know God and the soul.
R: Nothing else?
A: Nothing else at all.

St. Augustine, Soliloquia

Augustine (354–430) was the last great classical philosopher and the first great Christian philosopher. His attitudes dominated medieval philosophy until about 1300. Philosophy was carried out in a context of Christian faith. Augustine wanted only to know God and the soul, and used faith to justify belief. Medieval humanity turned away form the observable world, full of pain and turmoil, and concentrated on heaven and the soul, both of which could be known through introspection.

The soul could be known by introspection by seeking within oneself that divine illumination that comes from God, so that to know the soul was to know Him. And just as the soul was the representative of God within the self, so spiritual truth could be found in all things. In Neoplatonic fashion nothing—no word, no animal, no event—was as it seemed, but had to symbolize something supernatural and beyond human experience. Just as Plato found in every class noun the symbol of a Form, medieval people found symbols in every aspect of life. The medieval thinker did not want to understand the mind or the world in its own terms, but only as clues to the invisible reality of God in heaven.

Science and philosophy as we (or the Greeks) know them are impossible in such a context. Medieval thinkers did not freely use their minds to seek the truth whatever it might be, but rather to justify what they knew to be true from faith. Few found this restriction onerous, for they did not seek to overthrow faith but to support it. Most medievals who found themselves in heresy simply concluded they had erred and rethought their views. However, as the Middle Ages progressed—especially after 1277—the boundaries of dogma became more rigid, the hand of censorship more oppressive, and the spirit of many thinkers rebelled, helping to dissolve the medieval synthesis.

The Middle Ages sought a grand synthesis of all knowledge. Since all knowledge was of God, the soul, and the spiritual world, it was believed that knowledge, tradition, and faith could be synthesized into a single grand authoritative picture of the universe. The summit of such efforts was the *Summa Theologica* of St. Thomas Aquinas (1225–1274). This belief, too, broke down after 1300.

It should be pointed out that not all Christian thinkers in whatever time have accepted the rule of reason in seeking Godly truth. Augustine had to struggle against ideas of those like Tertullian (160–230), who rejected the classical philosophers. St. Bernard (1091–1153) decried excessive "curiosity" about Christian beliefs. In the Renaissance, Savonarola (1452–1498) burned heretical books and works of art. All these people emphasized the mystical aspects of Neoplatonism, the immediate inward confrontation of man with God, either through contemplation or reading his word. They rejected natural reason as unnecessary and even dangerous. Fundamentalism and mysticism were important elements not only in Christianity, but in medieval Islam and Judaism, where they triumphed and extinguished philosophical thought. In the Christian West, the thinkers of the later Middle Ages finally drew a line between the ideas of faith and the ideas of reason and observation. This separation of science and philosophy from theology, while destroying the medieval synthesis, opened the way to independent secular thought.

Neoplatonism colored every aspect of medieval thinking. All things were symbolic of God's invisible world, and visions, prophecies, astrology, and witchcraft were everyday parts of life. The medieval mind also saw hierarchy everywhere. Just as there was a universal hierarchy from God to angels to man to animals to matter; so was the church a hierarchy from pope to archbishop to bishop to priest to layperson; as was society from king to vassal and subvassal to serf. In psychological theory, Aristotle's picture of the soul was made hierarchical, from active mind to passive mind to common sense to special sense. So all the world was doubly structured—every thing, every event was symbolic of the invisible world and found its exact place in a hierarchically structured universe.

This magical outlook was enhanced by the nature of learning in the Middle Ages. Literacy was the preserve of the church. To be literate was almost without exception to be a cleric, and the language of learning was Latin. The church forbade the translation of the Bible into vernacular language, and services were conducted in Latin. The religion of the common people, therefore, was a barely modified paganism. One of the most revolutionary developments of the later Middle Ages was unauthorized translation of the Bible and the rise of vernacular literature.

Thus medieval knowledge was priestly knowledge. The monasteries carefully preserved past learning and kept historical chronicles. Some priests became the first governmental bureaucrats, bringing order, reason, and literacy to the rule of near barbarians. The seeds of the future, however, lay in the schools attached to the cathedrals of the twelfth-century renaissance. These became the first universities, with regularly scheduled courses, lectures by masters, textbooks, and even student riots. It was also there that the most independent thinkers, such as Peter Abelard, were to be found. It was from them that the rule of reason produced heresies to be suppressed by the church, and it was from them that learning began to spread beyond the close confines of the church. One of the most important developments of the Renaissance was the increase in the numbers of literate secular people.

We must not overestimate the oppressiveness of the religious framework of thought, especially in the high Middle Ages, nor underestimate its achievement. It was the crucible of the modern mind. A modern person would be an alien in those times, but modern thought could not have developed without its medieval predecessors. Before discussing medieval achievements, however, we must consider the achievement of peoples outside Western Christendom: the Jews and Muslims.

Relations between European Christendom and its two great rival religions were, to say the least, ambiguous. It was against Muslims that the Crusades were directed, while in the early Middle Ages Islam nearly engulfed Europe. Christendom's relations with the Jews were even more unpleasant. Jews were persecuted with a ferocity rivaling that of the Nazis: They were expelled from England and France; they were forced to live in ghettos and wear distinctive clothing; they were often killed *en masse* by burning down their homes with the inhabitants inside. Yet, without Judaism, Christianity is unthinkable. Jesus was, of course, a Jew, and his teachings reflect the concerns of Jewish rabbis of the first century B.C. It was largely because of St. Paul's mission to the Gentiles that Christianity did not remain a Jewish sect.

Both Muslims and the Jews who lived among them made major contributions to the intellectual development of the West. They preserved, and later translated, the works of the ancients, forgotten in Europe. In the early Middle Ages only the *Timaeus* of Plato and the *Categories* of Aristotle (not their most representative works) were known. By 1200 much of Plato and almost all of Aristotle were available to Christian scholars. The naturalistic works of Aristotle revolutionized the thinking of the West, substituting Aristotle for Plato as *the* philosopher. Thus both the Jews and Muslims greatly enriched the knowledge of European Christendom by preserving and translating the Greek philosophers. This new knowledge was disseminated to European Christendom through Spain and Sicily, where, within Muslim culture, Jew and Muslim lived together in peace.

Both Jews and Muslims also made important philosophical contributions of their own, and their influence often rivals Aristotle's. Maimonides, the greatest Judaic philosopher, was treated with the utmost respect by Thomas Aquinas. Islamic thinkers also contributed to mathematics and science as well as philosophy. The two most important Muslims for our purposes were Ibn Sīnā, whose psychological system we will examine later, and Ibn Rushd, whose purified Aristotelianism provoked an intellectual crisis that marked the end of the high Middle Ages.

We should also note that both Judaic and Islamic philosophy failed to escape the fate so narrowly avoided in Latin Christendom. The conservatives among Jewish and Islamic leaders found the free inquiry of philosophy too dangerous to revealed "truth" to be tolerated. Philosophy and its works were prohibited, so that after the time of Ibn Rushd (died 1198) there was little independent, nontheological philosophy among Jews or Muslims. As we shall see later in this chapter, similar persecution fell upon Aristotle's teachings in thirteenth-century Europe, but was not successful in suppressing his writings. In unified, absolutist Islam, thought control could succeed; in politically diverse Europe it could not.

Islamic Faculty Psychology

He who knows his soul, knows his creator.

Proverb of the Muslim Brethren of Purity

This proverb could stand as the motto of early and high medieval psychology. Augustine, as we have seen, wanted to know God and the soul. He believed that by turning inward and inspecting the soul one could come to know God, who is present in every soul. Augustine saw a unity of Creator and Creation so that the three mental powers—memory, understanding, and will—mirror the three beings of the Holy Trinity as any three related things were thought to.

Introspective psychology characterized the earliest years of Christian philosophy. A philosopher looked inward to his own soul in order to know God—not to understand himself as a unique human being, but only as a vehicle for divine illumination. It was not until the high Middle Ages that true individualism appeared, and then largely in popular culture rather than philosophy.

However, outside of European Christendom an ultimately more fruitful naturalistic faculty psychology based on Aristotle was developing. This psychology was originally worked out in a Neoplatonic framework within which Aristotle was interpreted, and combined an elaboration of Aristotle's psychology with late Roman and Islamic medicine. Over the next two centuries, as Aristotle became better known in Europe, this naturalistic faculty psychology completely replaced the older, Augustinian Neoplatonic psychology.

In the Neoplatonic scheme of things, humans stand midway between God and matter. As a rational animal, a human being resembles God, while as a physical being a human resembles animals and other purely physical creatures. In this view, when allied with Aristotelian faculty psychology, a human's mind itself reflects this ambiguous position: The five corporeal senses are tied to the animal body, while the active intellect—pure reason—is close to God. A person is a microcosm reflecting the greater Neoplatonic macrocosm.

Various writers elaborated on Aristotle's psychology by inserting various *inward wits,* or internal senses, between the rational soul and the corporeal senses. These were thought to be the exact transition point between body and soul in the chain of being. Such a scheme appears in Islamic, Judaic, and Christian thought in the early Middle Ages. Muslims made the special contribution of placing the discussion in a physiological context. Islamic medicine carried on the Classical medical tradition, and Muslim doctors looked for brain structures that hosted the various aspects of mind discussed by philosophers. The most complete statement of the Aristotelian medical view was made by Abū Ali al-Husayn Ibn Sīnā (980–1037), known in Europe as Avicenna, who was both a doctor and a philosopher and whose works were influential in constructing high medieval philosophy and psychology.

Different lists of mental faculties had been drawn up before Ibn Sīnā. The five corporeal senses and intellect were not considered mental faculties, a status reserved for the *interior senses.* Aristotle had proposed three faculties—common sense, imagination, and memory—although the lines between them were not sharply drawn. Later writers proposed three to five faculties, but Ibn Sīnā produced a list of seven faculties that became the norm. This list presented a Neoplatonic hierarchy from the faculty closest to the senses (and the body) to the faculty closest to divine intellect, and is outlined in Figure 3-2.

Beginning with the parts of the mind closest to the body, Ibn Sīnā discusses the *vegetative soul,* common to plants, humans, and animals (which he treats as did Aristotle), saying that it is responsible for the reproduction, growth, and nourishment of all living things.

Next comes the *sensitive soul,* common to people and animals. At its lowest level it comprises the five external or *corporeal senses* (which again follows Aristotle). The second level of the sensitive soul comprises the *internal senses,* or mental faculties, which are at the border between our animal and angelic natures. They, too, are hierarchically arranged. First comes *common sense,* which (as in Aristotle)

Agent Intellect: A divine Light Creating Human Knowledge

Rational Soul { Contemplative Intellect-knows universals
Practical Intellect-manages everyday affairs

Sensitive Soul

Appetite { Approach pleasure (concupiscable appetite)
Avoid pain (irascible appetite)

Interior Senses {
Recollection-recalls intuitions from memory
Memory-stores intuitions from estimation
Estimation-intuitions about benefit and harm
Compositive human imagination-creative imagination
Compositive animal imagination-combines images
Retentive imagination-image-copies of objects
Common sense-combines the five exterior senses

Exterior Senses {
Vision
Hearing
Touch
Taste
Smell

Vegetative Soul { Reproduction
Growth
Nourishment

FIGURE 3-2   Ibn Sīnā's faculty psychology.

receives, unites, and makes conscious the various qualities of external objects perceived by the senses. These perceived qualities are retained in the mind by the second internal sense, *retentive imagination,* for further consideration or later recall. The third and fourth internal senses are the *compositive animal imagination* and the *compositive human imagination,* which are responsible for active, creative use of mental images; for they relate together (compose) the images retained by the retentive imagination into such imaginary objects as unicorns. In animals this process is simply associative, while in human beings it may be creative; hence, the distinction of two faculties. The fifth internal sense was *estimation,* a kind of natural instinct for making judgments about the "intentions" of external objects. The dog avoids the stick because it has learned the stick's punishing "intentions." The wolf seeks the sheep for it knows the sheep is edible. This power, similar to the simple conditioning of modern psychologists, "estimates" the value or harm of objects in the animal's world.

The highest internal senses are memory and recollection. Memory stores the intuitions of estimation. These intuitions are not sensible attributes of the object, but rather simple ideas of the object's essence. Recollection is the ability to recall these intuitions at a later time. The material stored by memory and recalled by recollection is thus not a copy of an object, for this function is performed by the retentive and compositive imaginations. Instead, the material is a set of simple but abstract ideas, or general conclusions, derived from experience. They are not, however, true universals, for only the human mind has the power to form universals.

Ibn Sīnā was a physician, and he tried to combine his explication of Aristotle's philosophical psychology with the traditional, though erroneous, Roman medical tradition stemming from Galen. By speculation, without resort to forbidden dissections, Ibn Sīnā and other Muslim faculty psychologists located the internal senses in different parts of the brain. His proposals became standard medical teaching until in the sixteenth century Vesalius again practiced dissection and proved Ibn Sīnā's ideas wrong.

Figure 3-3 shows a simple figure of a head from a medical textbook of about 1420, which shows the location of four internal senses. Although the figure combines some of Ibn Sīnā's senses (as he himself often did), it follows his teaching. Four "cells" of the brain are shown. The first one contains common sense, which here includes retentive imagination. The second cell contains human and animal compositive imagination. The third cell holds estimation. The fourth and rearmost cell contains memory, including recollection.

The final aspect of the sensitive soul treated by Ibn Sīnā is motivation. As Aristotle had pointed out, what sets animals apart from plants is that they move themselves. Ibn Sīnā, following Aristotle, calls this motive power *appetite*, and it has two forms. Animals sense pain or danger, and flee; this may be called avoidance. On the other hand, animals sense or anticipate pleasure and move toward it; this is approach.

The mental powers and senses so far considered by Ibn Sīnā are tied to the body and brain and are held in common by humans and animals. However, we surpass the animals in our ability to form universal concepts. This is the unique power of the human soul that alone transcends the material body and brain. Ibn Sīnā distinguished two faculties within the human soul: *practical intellect* and *contemplative intellect*. The lower practical intellect concerns itself with everyday affairs. It regulates the body, maintains good behavior, and protects the contemplative intellect so it may fulfill itself.

The fulfillment of the contemplative intellect is knowledge of universals abstracted from particular sense experiences. In this Ibn Sīnā follows Aristotle, as he does in further distinguishing active and passive intellect. The contemplative intellect of the human soul is entirely passive (Aristotle's *passive mind*) and has the potential for knowledge, which is actualized by the active intellect, or *agent intellect*. However, Ibn Sīnā sets the agent intellect outside the human soul, as Aristotle

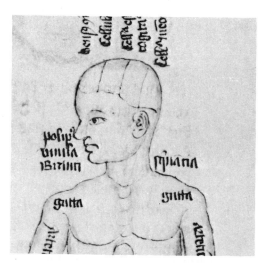

FIGURE 3-3 Head of a man from a medical textbook of about 1420 showing the locations of four internal senses. From front to back the cells contain *common sense, imagination, estimation,* and *memory.* (From Clarke and Dewhurst 1972.)

had not done. It is a kind of angelic intellect next up in the Neoplatonic hierarchy which illuminates the contemplative mind and leads it to knowledge of the Forms, as in Plato and Augustine. As we shall see, the doctrine of a separate agent intellect is un-Christian and its entry into Europe via the Muslim philosopher Ibn Rushd precipitated the intellectual part of the crisis that ended the high Middle Ages.

THE FLOWERING OF MEDIEVAL CIVILIZATION: THE HIGH MIDDLE AGES (1000–1300)

Popular Culture

The high Middle Ages saw many social developments that came to define the modern world: the primacy of law over personal rule; capitalism; the growth of cities. Two closely related developments command our attention, for they express important popular psychological attitudes that provide the setting for later theories about human motivation and society. When one speaks of "popular culture" in the medieval context, of course, nothing like the modern meaning is intended, for few people were literate outside the church. However, there was a popular vernacular literature and a common set of ideas evident in both educated clerical society and lay society that can be considered a kind of limited "popular culture."

Women, Sex, and Romantic Love

Medieval Christianity did not invent misogyny. Europe's antifeminist attitudes came from the Romans and even from Aristotle, who considered female infants as suffering from a sort of birth defect. Christianity, however, intensified the Classical disrespect for women, linking women to sexuality as the foundation of sin and temptation, and instituting a schizophrenic attitude toward good women (virgins) and ordinary women, who were at best mothers. As St. Thomas Aquinas said, "Woman was created to be man's helpmate, but her unique role is in conception . . . since for other purposes men would be better assisted by other men" (Heer 1962).

In early Christianity women were full participants in religion; they preached and often lived in chaste, mixed-sex monasteries. The early Middle Ages were full of strong female figures as capable and powerful as any man. However, as Christianity absorbed Classical culture, it absorbed Roman misogyny and Platonic aversion to sensual pleasure. Marriage was forbidden to priests; women were forbidden to preach or even approach holy relics. They were reduced to second-class status as—at best—helpers of men, as the quotation from Aquinas shows.

One especially strong source of Christian misogyny was St. Jerome (340–420), a Neoplatonist who linked womanhood to the temptation of the flesh. Medieval Christianity looked upon sex in all its manifestations as the worst sin, whether inside marriage or out; compared to the purity of Christ's body, all sexual intercourse was seen as unclean. As St. Jerome said, ". . . woman is the gate of the devil, the path of wickedness, the sting of the serpent. In a word a perilous object. . . ." (Erickson 1976). Thus the onus of sexual guilt fell much more heavily on woman than on men. Even pregnant women were viewed with distaste. A woman who had given birth bore the stigma of the "filth of sin," for a child is the product of sex. She could not return to church for thirty-three days following the birth of a son, or for sixty-six days following the birth of a daughter. Should a pregnant woman, or a woman who had recently given birth, die (as was common), she could not be buried in consecrated ground and was thought to be denied entrance to heaven.

At the same time, virginity was exalted; the immaculate Virgin Mary was contrasted with Eve the temptress. As the oppression of women grew, the cult of the Virgin spread throughout the Middle Ages until well into modern times, as is evident from the number of churches and schools named "Notre Dame." This created a schizophrenic attitude toward (and within) women. Women at their best were seen as holy vessels of God, yet most women were thought to be cesspools of corruption.

These ideas did not die out as the Renaissance approached. Boccaccio, a great early Renaissance writer, called woman "an imperfect animal, obsessed with a thousand revolting and abominable passions" (Erickson 1976).

Most medieval women lived lives of quiet desperation, but there were two important responses to their oppression. Many women became actively involved in heretical movements. Albigensianism, for example, which was more a rival religion than a heresy, put many women in positions of power and influence.

The other response was more subtle, more influential, and tied to wider developments in Christendom. It was the invention of romantic love. Medieval people certainly were not unaware of sex. It was the major topic of many folk tales, bawdy stories, and *fablioux*. It was also the main topic of the goliards, student poets and singers of the high Middle Ages. The most famous collection of their songs is *Carmina Burana,* which often presents a blasphemous glorification of the pagan goddess of love, Venus. She is described in terms such as "Rose of the World" that usually referred to the Virgin Mary. (The rose, incidently, was widely used as a symbol of both the vagina and the Virgin.) Romantic love was to have tremendous popular influence down the ages; today's popular love songs are echoes of the twelfth-century troubadors. Love is thought to form the basis of all enduring male-female relations. It is thus an important element in popular consciousness and psychology. Theories of motivation must reckon with the romantic love we think is natural, but which was invented in the Middle Ages.

Ultimately, romantic love undermined the corporate nature of medieval society, for it made the basis of relationships personal feeling rather than appointed status. Gottfried von Strasbourg, in his *Tristan and Isolde,* one of the most enduring romantic love stories, wrote about the lovers' union this way: "Man was there with Woman, Woman there with Man. What else should they be needing?" Gottfried dispenses with church, state, and society in favor of the romantic, spiritual, and carnal union of two individuals.

The Growth of Individuality

Gottfried von Strasbourg's statement in a popular thirteenth-century poem stands in total contrast to the rest of medieval society and philosophy. There was little conception of the individual in most of the Middle Ages. The concept was invented during the Middle Ages, but did not become deeply ingrained in thought until the Renaissance. This is not to say that there were no individuals in the Middle Ages, for it was full of strong and distinctive men and women. What is true is that there was no *conception* of the individual as an important object of concern or study. This lack is part of the Neoplatonic *Zeitgeist* that dictated that the human intellect knows only universals, not individuals. The rational mind of each person thus knows another only as an essence—humanness—not as an individual defined by the characteristics that make each person unique. A person's status as emperor, pope, king, or serf was far more important than status as an individual human being distinct from all others.

Medieval philosophical psychology expresses this attitude. The philosopher-psychologist was interested in *the* sensitive soul, *the* will, *the* imagination, *the* intellect; medieval theorists had no interest in, and seem to have been unaware of, individual differences in psychological makeup. This Platonic attitude has a long and durable history; it is not until the nineteenth century that we find a systematic interest in individual differences. The founder of psychology, Wundt, was himself interested only in *the* human mind. The value of studying individual differences is still debated.

Thus we cannot look for the birth of a conception of individualism in academic philosophy or theology, but must look rather in popular culture and religion, as our study of courtly love shows. The concept of the individual blossoms forth in many areas during the high Middle Ages: Biographies and autobiographies are written; portraits reflect the individual, not merely the person's status; close friendship is encouraged; and literature is increasingly concerned with individual thoughts and feelings rather than with an external narrative of action.

In two areas only does individualism make its way into academic culture—ethics and mystic religion—and even here the movement begins in popular culture. Before the twelfth century, sin was acknowledged, but not felt as something personal. Penance was a mechanical procedure for expiating sin. In the twelfth century, however, people began to weigh personal intention in judging transgressions. This attitude was formalized in Peter Abelard's (1079–1142) *voluntaristic* ethics, the motto of which was "know yourself." Abelard held, contrary to other thinkers, that sin was entirely a matter of intention, not of action. An act is not right or wrong; what is right or wrong is the intention behind the act. Intentions are, of course, intensely personal, so Abelard's ethics were part of the growth of the individual.

Mysticism begins in popular religion rather than scholastic theology. Mysticism emphasizes the personal relationship of a worshiper to God. The end result of religion, according to the mystic, should be a private, direct communion between ourselves and God; the way to God is contemplation, not ritual. St. Francis of Assisi (1182–1226), the greatest medieval popular preacher, shunned the trappings of the world in favor of communing with God through nature. St. Francis's teaching was thus individualistic and was perceived, correctly, as subversive by the Catholic church. He narrowly escaped persecution as a heretic instead of canonization as a saint. Poverty was not an ideal that a worldly rich church wished to support, while solitary contemplation threatened the complex of rituals the church claimed brought salvation. Only by absorbing St. Francis and his followers (the Franciscans) could the church avert the threat of the rising consciousness of the individual inherent in mysticism. Thus the idea of the individual, which would grow to great prominence in the Renaissance, was born in medieval popular culture.

Christian Faculty Psychology

The high Middle Ages saw an intellectual renaissance as the works of Aristotle and his Muslim commentators, such as Ibn Sīnā, and other Greek works poured into the West through Spain, Sicily, and Constantinople. Aristotle's philosophy was naturalistic and as such was restricted by the reigning Neoplatonic Augustinian establishment of the time. Aristotle brought a fresh, unreligious approach to knowledge and humanity, an approach that was reconciled with Christian faith only with difficulty. Thomas Aquinas, who synthesized faith in God's word and reason as found in Aristotle's philosophy, only narrowly escaped a charge of heresy. This union of Christ and Aristotle, impressive though it was, was relatively sterile. The future belonged to those who, like William of Ockham, divorced faith from reason and pursued only the latter. We will therefore only briefly summarize the psychology of the high Middle Ages, for it rarely surpassed Aristotle or Ibn Sīnā and was itself surpassed by fourteenth-century science.

In the twelfth and thirteenth centuries there was a great increase in education, and philosophers abounded. We will limit our consideration to the twin peaks of high medieval Christian philosophy: St. Bonaventure (1221–1274) and St. Thomas Aquinas (1225–1274). They stand for the two great medieval approaches to knowledge, humanity, and God: the Platonic-Augustinian mystical way, and the Aristotelian-Thomistic way of natural reason constrained by faith.

St. Bonaventure.   St. Bonaventure was the great voice of the conservative Platonic-Augustinian philosophy that resisted the introduction of Aristotle into Christian thinking. He took a sharply dualist, Platonic view of soul and body, as did Augustine. Although the soul is the form of body, as Aristotle maintained, to Bonaventure it was much more. The soul and body are two completely distinct substances, and the immortal soul merely uses the mortal body during its earthly existence. The essence of a person is the soul.

The soul is capable of two sorts of knowledge. First, as united with the body, it can have knowledge of the external world. Here Bonaventure follows the empiricism of Aristotle by denying innate ideas and arguing that we build up universal concepts by abstraction from experienced individual objects. However, like Aquinas, Bonaventure asserts that abstraction alone is insufficient and must be joined to the divine illumination from God for there to be any true knowledge.

The second source of knowledge belongs to the soul alone and is knowledge of the spiritual world, including God. The source of this knowledge is introspection, which discovers the image of God illuminated in the soul, and so knows him through interior reflection without recourse to sensation. The idea of God is thus innate. We should emphasize again that this Augustinian introspection is meant only indirectly to yield knowledge of self or of human nature; its goal is a vision of God, not humanity.

Bonaventure distinguishes four mental faculties: the vegetative faculties, the sensitive faculties, the intellect, and the will. However, Bonaventure speaks of other "aspects" of the soul which he refuses to call faculties, but whose inclusion makes his system resemble Ibn Sīnā's. For example, he distinguishes a "higher" aspect and a "lower" aspect to the intellect, which resembles Ibn Sīnā's contemplative and practical intellects.

Bonaventure's Platonism was destined to be overtaken and overshadowed by Aquinas's Aristotelianism, which became the official doctrine of the Catholic church. It lives on in Protestantism, however, which stresses the word of God over reason, and individual communion between each person and God over ritual.

St. Thomas Aquinas.

As Aristotle became known in the West, many thinkers struggled to reconcile his scientific naturalism with the teachings of the church. The greatest and most successful of these was St. Thomas Aquinas. He called Aristotle the Philosopher, the thinker who showed the limits of human reason, demonstrating all that could be known without the word of God. Aquinas adopted Aristotle's system and showed that it was not incompatible with Christianity. In doing so he stood Aristotle on his head. Where Aristotle stays close to nature and is silent on God, Aquinas reorients everything to depend on and reveal him.

To reconcile philosophy and theology, Aquinas distinguished sharply between them, limiting a person's reason to knowledge of the world of nature. Aquinas thus accepts Aristotle's empiricism and the consequence that reason can know only the world, not God. God can be known only indirectly, from his work in the world. This is an important moment in the evolution of Western thought. Aquinas is saying that philosophy and religion are separate, that while they are not incompatible, they do not connect. This division finally destroyed the medieval synthesis Aquinas worked so hard to achieve. However, Aquinas's philosophy and theology are, in practice if not in theory, intertwined; reason and revelation do make contact. But later thinkers pursued his division of reason and faith to its logical conclusion and destroyed theological metaphysics while giving birth to science.

Aquinas sets out to consider all topics, including psychology, philosophically; that is, independent of revelation. In his psychology he closely follows Aristotle, but also gives weight to the opinions of Islamic writers, especially Ibn Sīnā. He makes no original contribution to Aristotelian psychology, but refines and extends the classification of mental aspects given by the Philosopher and his Islamic commentators. Figure 3-4 summarizes Aquinas's picture of mind. As can be seen, most of it is similar to ideas of Aristotle and Ibn Sīnā, and most of the new points are self-explanatory. It will be necessary only to comment on a few unique points.

Aquinas, more than Aristotle or his non-Christian commentators, was concerned with distinguishing persons, who have souls, from animals. This comes out most clearly in his discussion of the faculties of estimation and appetite or motivation. Unlike Ibn Sīnā, Aquinas held that there are two kinds of estimation. First there is *estimation proper,* characteristic of animals, and not under voluntary control: The lamb *must* flee the wolf it sees to be dangerous; the cat *must* pounce on the mouse. The second kind of estimation is under rational control. Aquinas calls it *cogitava,* and it is found only in humans: We flee the wolf, or choose to approach it. One's estimative power is under the control of one's free will, for one chooses and makes judgments instead of simply responding blindly to animal instinct. Just as there are two kinds of estimation, so there are two kinds of motivation or appetite. Sensitive, animal appetite is an unfree, natural inclination to pursue pleasurable objects and avoid harmful ones, and to overcome obstacles to that pursuit. A human being, however, has intellectual appetite, or will, which seeks the general good under the guidance of reason. The animal knows only pleasure or pain; the human knows right and wrong.

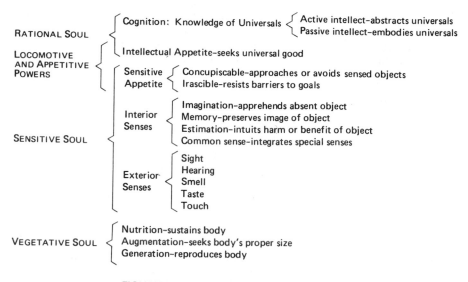

FIGURE 3-4 Aquinas's conception of mind.

Three other changes from Ibn Sīnā may be noted. First, Aquinas drops compositive imagination as unnecessary additions to retentive imagination and rational thinking. Second, by making *cogitava*—human estimation—a rationally guided faculty concerned with the outer world, the need for Ibn Sīnā's practical intellect vanishes. Finally, Aquinas makes the mind whole by returning the active intellect to the human soul. Knowledge is an active product of human thinking, not a gift of divine illumination via the agent intellect.

Despite some Neoplatonic remnants, such as the hierarchic organization of faculties, Aquinas's views are in sharp contrast to Bonaventure's. Aquinas rejects the radical dualism of soul and body of the Platonic-Augustinian tradition. The body is not a tomb, prison, or punishment; nor is it a puppet operated by the soul. A person is a whole, a mind *and* a body. Although the soul is transcendent, its natural place is in a body, which it fulfills and which fulfills it.

Aquinas also adopts a consistent empiricism. The human mind can have direct knowledge only of what was once in the senses, as there are no innate ideas. All thinking requires images. Bonaventure had upheld the Augustinian notion of direct self-knowledge through introspection, which revealed an innate image of God. Aquinas rejects this. All knowledge of the soul or God, and of all things invisible, must be indirect. Direct communion with God or with the essence of ourselves is impossible. We can know God only by examining the world, which is his work; we can know ourselves only by examining our acts, which are our work. Nothing else is possible.

Aquinas is here at a bridge point between the old medieval world view and the modern view, and he places himself in a dilemma. He said that only philosphical knowledge is possible, yet he continued to be a theologian. He acted as if his distinction between philosophy and theology had not been made. His philosophy was *not* an unfettered search for truth, but a Christian science, bound by the limits of belief. On these grounds Bertrand Russell denied that Aquinas was a philosopher.

Perhaps this criticism is true. What is important about Aquinas, however, is that his work was not only the summit of the medieval synthesis, but also a harbinger of the future, when reason and revelation became completely separated. Aquinas brought a fresh naturalism to the traditional Platonic Christian framework, but he accepted that framework and worked within it. The resulting edifice is a monument to human thought. A monument, however, commemorates the past. The future of science and psychology belonged to more radical men.

FROM MEDIEVAL TO MODERN:
THE LATE MIDDLE AGES, RENAISSANCE, AND REFORMATION
(1300 –1600)

The Late Middle Ages: The Dissolution of the Medieval Synthesis

By the fourteenth century the factors that would bring about the end of the Middle Ages had coalesced. The growth of cities, capitalism, and the nation-state eroded feudal life, which finally ended in empty playing at chivalry. A severe economic depression began. Population declined. Crime and violence increased. The death blow to the medieval synthesis was probably the Plague of 1348, which carried off about a third of Europe's population. People became cynical and pessimistic.

The church was distrusted and divided by schism, while popular preachers emphasized human sinfulness and helplessness before God. It was a period when the medieval confidence in the ability to find a total explanation of the world in unified terms was abandoned and the limits of human reason were acknowledged. We will focus on three intellectual movements that undercut the medieval world view: empiricism; its offspring analytic philosophy, which demonstrated the short-coming of human knowledge; and science, which offered an alternative to the religious conception of the universe.

The Rebirth of Empiricism

In philosophy, especially in the first half of the fourteenth century, the late Middle Ages were creative. We will briefly examine the most influential late medieval thinker, William of Ockham (1290–1349, approximately), whose contribution was to revive empiricism, opening up for psychological analysis what had previously been reserved to metaphysics.

Medieval philosophers confused psychology and ontology, the study of the nature of being or existence. As did Plato, most medieval thinkers believed that there must be something real corresponding to each mental concept. For Plato they were the Forms; for Aristotle they were real essences; for medievals they were Ideas in the mind of God.

For the Greeks and medievals the only real knowledge was knowledge of universals; indeed, it was asserted that the rational soul, or intellect, had knowledge *only* of universals, not of particular things. Following Aristotle, medievals held that the only certain knowledge was what could be deduced from universal propositions. This attitude persisted even in Aquinas. Although he described the process of abstraction as the way to universal knowledge, and although he held that the intellect knows only what is derived from the senses, he still maintained that the abstracted essences were metaphysically true, that they corresponded to holy Ideas.

Ockham changed all this by substituting psychology for metaphysics. He asserted that all knowledge begins with "intuitive cognition," direct, infallible acquaintance with some object in the world. The intellect is not restricted to knowing only abstract images; what it knows first is objects and their qualities. Intuitive cognition does not yield mere opinion, as Plato held, but yields knowledge of what is true and false. From such knowledge it may go on to "abstractive cognition" of universals. But universals exist only as mental concepts, having no existence outside the mind. These abstract concepts may be either true or false; for example, one may form the concept of a unicorn, which does not exist. Abstractive cognition is thus wholly hypothetical. The touchstone of reality and truth is intuitive cognition. Ockham discarded the metaphysical problem that bedeviled Plato, Aristotle, and the medievals—How can each individual participate in a transcendent essence or form?—and substituted the psychological question, How do we form universal concepts given that we have certain knowledge only of individuals? His answer was that the mind notes similarities among objects, and, based on the similarities, it classifies objects. Thus universals are logical terms that apply to some objects and not others and which indicate relations among objects. For Ockham, universals are a psychological problem rather than an ontological one.

Up to this point Ockham was the truest empiricist of the Middle Ages, for he made the test of knowledge become that which is revealed by intuitive cognition, or observation. However, Ockham was a Franciscan, and there is an important Augustinian element in his view of the soul. Like Bonaventure and unlike Aquinas, Ockham held that we have direct, introspective, intuitive knowledge of the soul, rather than mere reflection on our acts. The soul can know itself directly, not just indirectly.

Unlike Aquinas and other faculty psychologists, Ockham denied the distinction of soul from its faculties. According to Ockham, the soul does not *have* the faculty of Will or Intellect. Rather, what we call a faculty is simply a name for a certain kind of mental act. *Will* describes the soul in the act of willing: *Intellect* describes the soul in the act of thinking. Ockham always sought to simplify accounts as much as possible, ridding them of nonessentials, which is why we speak of "Ockham's razor," although the idea is Aristotle's. Ockham saw faculties as unnecessary reifications of mental acts into mental entities apart from the mind.

Habit was crucial to Ockham's view of the mind. For him, concepts were learned habits, ideas derived from experience. Since he rejected the world of universals, whether Platonic Forms or divine Ideas, the status of universals was reduced to habit. These habits are what make possible a person's thinking independent of actually sensed objects. We cannot think about the Forms, for they do not exist. We think instead about derived, habitual concepts; without them we would be animals, reduced to simple responses to external stimuli. Ockham was the first thinker, but not the last, to put such a burden on habit; but he was not a behaviorist, for to him habits were mental concepts, not bodily responses. Ockham drew a radical distinction, far more radical than Aquinas's, between faith and reason.

Ockham pointed out that there is no ground in experience, or intuitive cognition, for believing we have an immaterial, immortal soul. As far as reason or philosophy goes, the mind may be a perishable entity dependent on the body. It is only from faith that knowledge of the immortal soul comes. This separation of faith and reason greatly weakened theology and metaphysics, but helped bring science into being.

Analysis and the Limits of Reason

Most medieval philosophers believed, as did the Greeks, in the power of human reason to know eternal Truth. They went further in asserting that God's truth and philosophical truth were one and could be synthesized, as in Aquinas's *Summa Theologica*. The idea was rejected by some mystical clergymen, such as St. Bernard of Clairvaux, who denied that philosophy could say anything about God, who is known through faith alone. Despite the mystics, the general trend of thought before 1300 favored the Greek view.

We saw this earlier in this chapter when we touched on the problem of universals. Most medievals held to some form of *realism,* the belief that universal human concepts correspond to some enduring Form or essence, conceived by medievals as an Idea in the mind of God. This view was held by Plato, Aristotle, and Aquinas, despite their other differences. A few thinkers, called *nominalists,* maintained that universals were mere puffs of air emitted when we speak names (hence nominalism). They have no transcendent reality, being nothing more than verbal behaviors. Nominalism was held by a small minority of thinkers.

It was the analysis of the problem of universal human knowledge that led fourteenth-century philosophers to put severe limits on what man may know. The first step was taken by Peter Abelard, the greatest medieval philosopher before the high Middle Ages when Aristotle's works were recovered. Abelard saw the absurdity of the metaphysical-realist approach, predicating one thing of another thing. According to realists, to say "Socrates is a man" is to relate two things, the living Individual Socrates and the heavenly Form of man. Abelard saw that *man* should be considered a label, or better a *concept* that we apply to some individual. *Man* is a mental concept applied to Socrates, not a separate thing, or transcendent Form. For Abelard, concepts were purely mental images or labels, and when we discuss universals we are discussing these mental entities, not eternal Forms. Abelard's account of universals was thus logical and psychological rather than metaphysical. This position is best called *conceptualism,* and was a forerunner of Ockham's views discussed earlier.

An interesting point is that Abelard was attacked and ultimately convicted of heresy by St. Bernard, his contemporary, for excessive curiosity about God. Abelard thought that philosophy and theology could be harmonized, while St. Bernard saw them as necessarily separate. The irony is that the fourteenth-century analytic and scientific movements took Bernard's view, not Abelard's, even though Abelard's conceptualism and Ockham's are quite similar. Abelard's innovation lacked influence in its own time, partly because of his condemnation, but primarily because of the acceptance of Aristotle's abstractive realism by later philosophers such as Aquinas.

So, in the high Middle Ages, it was thought that human knowledge and Holy Truth were coordinate, that human universals corresponded to the divine Ideas. William of Ockham, whose psychological analysis of universals we have examined, destroyed this self-confidence. He posed a whole new set of questions about the bases of human knowledge. If universals do not reflect the divine ideas, and if they rest upon knowledge of individuals, how do we justify our knowledge and show its truth? Before Ockham's time, knowledge was taken for granted; after his time knowledge had to be justified. Philosophers now had to show how knowledge and opinion can be distinguished without reference to God or Forms.

Interestingly, it was belief in God's omnipotence that forced a skeptical attitude on fourteenth-century philosophers. Christian thinkers must believe that God is omnipotent, that he can do anything that is not self-contradictory. Therefore, if you are looking at a tree, God could destroy the tree, but maintain in you the experience of the nonexistent object. If this is so, Christian thinkers must ask how we can be certain of any perception, of any piece of knowledge.

This problem fostered a thoroughgoing critique of human knowledge by fourteenth-century philosophers. The most interesting of them was Nicholas of Autrecourt (born 1300), a follower of Ockham. Like Ockham, he did not see psychology as metaphysics, saying that there are only acts of understanding and volition, not separate faculties of Understanding and Will. Like the atomists before him (he, in fact, proposed an atomistic theory of nature) and the empiricists after him, Nicholas argued that certain knowledge lies in staying as close to appearances as possible. All we can know is what our senses tell us, so knowledge is grounded in experience, and the best knowledge is that which remains closest to experiences. To infer from sense perception to Forms, essences, or divine Ideas, he considered illegitimate.

Nicholas of Autrecourt rejected the possibility of divine intervention to maintain an illusion of perception and based knowledge on an assumption shared with Ockham: Whatever appears is true. This belief is necessary to any empiricist theory of knowledge, and Ockham held it implicitly. By making it explicit, Nicholas had to ask whether it is justified. Nicholas concluded that we cannot be certain of this assumption, only that it is probably true, since it seems more likely than the contrary assumption that whatever appears is false. Nicholas did not become a total skeptic, but he came close.

Nicholas and others worked out the complications of Ockham's psychological account of universals by close analysis of the grounds of human knowledge. The search for a justification of human knowledge of the external world has continued ever since and is a root problem for any cognitive psychology.

Ockham's new approach also had another consequence, perhaps the single most momentous revolution in human thinking since Greek rationalism. By dividing faith and reason, and by limiting human knowledge to this world, excluding it from the next, Ockham destroyed theology, which he denied was a science. No one after Ockham, save the medieval-Renaissance transition figure Nicholas of Cusa, again attempted to synthesize divine and human knowledge. Theology became an empty pursuit compared to the study of appearances, of nature; in a word, science.

The Medieval Foundations of Modern Science

We are not discussing God's miracles; what we have to do is to discuss what is natural in a natural way.

Siger of Brabant (1240–1282)

Science has displaced religion as the pivot of the modern world. Scientific knowledge is taken as the model for all knowledge. The beginnings of this trend, called *scientism,* are apparent in William of Ockham and Nicholas of Autrecourt, who tell us to study appearances rather than the divine mind. Thus began, in the Middle Ages, the scientific revolution that was to completely remake humanity's image of the self and the world.

The watershed date in ending the Middle Ages is 1277. In that year the church condemned a school of thinkers at the University of Paris led by Siger of Brabant, who went too far in accepting Aristotle's naturalism in place of Christian dogma. Some of the condemned doctrines were held by Thomas Aquinas. The church was challenged by Aristotelianism, for it was an un-Christian, naturalistic, and complete account of nature that did not depend on God's word. Aquinas struggled to reconcile the Philosopher with Christ, but the church did not accept his synthesis until it became necessary to the very survival of the church in the modern age. The church's first response was to reject Aristotle and restrict his works. It tried to do this in 1210, 1231, and 1272. Despite its attempts, however, thoroughgoing Aristotelians were to be found at the University of Paris, and the church finally could not tolerate them; they were condemned, and Siger was arrested. (He was murdered by a madman while under detention in Rome.) Naturalist philosophers were regularly attacked afterward. Nicholas of Autrecourt had to recant and burn his own books.

It was in this climate that Siger and others after him, like Ockham, began to separate the domains of faith and reason. Only by asserting that the two were separate, that one did not bear on the other, could naturalism be defended as innocuous to Christianity. It was a move that failed in Islam, where philosophy and science were stamped out after promising starts. Europe, however, with its many nations and kings, was too heterogeneous to succumb to dogmatic repression. Ockham's analysis of knowledge successfully separated Reason and Revelation. But precisely because Revelation was not something known by Reason, minds turned to study the natural world, and religion became less and less important to European intellectuals; by the Age of Enlightenment, Revelation was openly rejected and deism or atheism adopted.

The immediate result of Ockham's ideas in the fourteenth century was an increased interest in science. Scientific interests had, in fact, been present before the fourteenth century. We can trace the modern scientific attitude back to Robert Grosseteste (1168–1253) and Roger Bacon (1214–1292), both English Franciscans like William of Ockham. Grosseteste and Bacon both conducted experiments in optics because of their Platonic-Augustinian belief in the primacy of light among the world's elements. Both also stressed the role of mathematics in reaching an understanding of nature. This belief is most important, for mathematization has been the touchstone of science from Galileo through Newton to Einstein. Immanuel Kant was to deny psychology scientific status partly because he believed the mind could not be studied mathematically.

Roger Bacon is interesting for several further reasons. He ridiculed those who based ideas on authority rather than experience. In accordance with this belief Bacon venerated the vital medieval craft tradition. Even in the early Middle Ages important technical advancements were made all over the ancient world, and this technological tradition continued. Technology and craft are empirical and practical in orientation, for value is placed on what is seen to work, rather than on what authorities say is true, as in scholastic philosophy. Bacon valued this practical outlook, and based his empiricism on it. Combined with his mathematical emphasis, Bacon pointed the way to the Newtonian future, in which the universe was pictured as a divinely crafted machine, rather than a series of divine emanations. In the eighteenth century the mechanical view of the universe was applied to humanity, to be ultimately embodied in the behaviorist and information-processing theories of behavior.

Bacon also practiced alchemy. Although alchemy is often pictured as a naive and rather silly search for the ability to make gold, alchemists were the only systematic experimenters before Galileo. Alchemy was preparadigm chemistry; it is to be criticized not for its goals, but for its lack of a consistent theoretical structure. The alchemists' fundamental empirical attitude was valuable and scientific.

One attitude Grosseteste and Bacon shared that marks them as distinctly medieval was their desire to harmonize faith and science. Their researches grew from religious belief; their optics, for example, derived from metaphysical-religious beliefs about light. After Ockham, however, medieval scientists began to take the claims of religion less seriously, and to assert the claims of science more forcefully.

This new attitude emerges in Jean Buridan (approximately 1300–1358) and Nicholas Oresme (1320–1382), the greatest cleric-physicists of the fourteenth century. Both of them worked on the problem of motion, and Oresme nearly formulated the law of inertia. In this they challenged the authority of Aristotle and laid the groundwork for Galileo. They also argued that the earth rotated, contrary to the prevailing belief that the earth was motionless and circled by the stars, moon, and planets, which were each pushed by an angel. They pointed out that experience did not support the received view that the earth is stationary at the center of the universe. They believed in the power of mathematics and in the possibility of conceiving of the universe mechanically.

It was to be nearly two hundred years before Buridan and Oresme's work would bear fruit. There was a long hiatus during which science did not advance. As medieval society broke down from economic depression, the Black Death, and the end of feudalism, there was no room for science, and even Renaissance humanists did not value abstract scientific research. It remained for Galileo to found modern physics. There is also an important paradox in post-Ockham empiricism. Although Ockham argued that all general knowledge was rooted in particular experience, fourteenth-century medieval scientists did not apply their physical theories to experimental data. Rather they preferred to argue from everyday experience, from Nicholas of Autrecourt's appearances. They were, in short, *too* empiricist to do good science, for they tried to account for all aspects of the world, an impossible task, as shown in Chapter 1. Galileo took a more Platonic view of experience—he isolated crucial aspects of reality for experimental investigation. He saw, as the fourteenth-century empiricists did not, that science is built on a selective and idealized, not a comprehensive, treatment of experience.

Such is the medieval contribution to philosophy, science, and psychology. The medieval world is not one we recognize as our own, for it was deeply religious and fostered a symbolic mentality. The medieval mind was focused on God and universal truth, not on nature and individual experience. This religious-symbolic orientation began to change in the fourteenth century, inaugurating an intellectual crisis that helped bring about the consciously modern world view of the Renaissance. Because of radical thinkers such as Ockham and Nicholas of Autrecourt, and because the feudal system was no longer viable, society and the life of the mind had to reorganize on a new basis, the individualistic capitalistic world with which we are familiar.

Renaissance and Reformation

What a piece of work is man, how noble in reason,
How infinite in faculty,
In form and moving how express and admirable,
In action how like an angel,
In apprehension how like a god;
The beauty of the world, the paragon of animals.

Shakespeare, *Hamlet*, II,ii,300–303

The idea of the Middle Ages was invented by the Renaissance. Renaissance thinkers divided world history into three ages: the classical period of Greece and Rome, which was viewed as a Golden Age of philosophy and art; a Middle Age of ignorance and superstition, which was the Dark Age; and the third age, their own era. The Renaissance was a self-consciously "modern" period that saw itself breaking sharply with the past. This judgment was reaffirmed by the German historian Jakob Burkhardt, who defined the Renaissance as a special creative period crucial to the formation of contemporary society.

Ever since, historians have disputed Burkhardt's acceptance of the self-evaluation of the Renaissance. Today, continuity with the Middle Ages is stressed and historians speak of a Carolingian renaissance and a twelfth-century renaissance. It has become apparent that Western society has been renewing itself since A.D. 1000, if not earlier.

However, when all this is said, there is unquestionably something historically new, but immediately familiar about the Renaissance. One has only to compare a painting by Leonardo da Vinci or Michelangelo with any medieval work to feel the difference. One feels far more at home reading Pico della Mirandola or Michel de Montaigne than Thomas Aquinas or William of Ockham. We understand Shakespeare's works far more easily than medieval mystery plays.

The date of the Renaissance is hard to pin down. A traditional starting point is 1453, when Constantinople fell and Greek-speaking scholars fled to a West that knew only Latin. However, it would be more accurate to date the beginning of the Renaissance to around 1300 in Italy. The first Renaissance man was Francesco Petrarch (1304–1374), most famous today as a poet, but also active in the distinctive Renaissance activities of classical scholarship, education, and history. The Renaissance reached its peak in Italy around 1500, by which time it had spread to Northern Europe. Although the Renaissance is the beginning of modern history, it shares its world view with the Middle Ages, a world view that began to be weakened by the Reformation and was dissolved by the Scientific Revolution around 1600.

The nature of the Renaissance is most elusive. It contributed nothing to philosophy: There is no first-rate philosopher between Ockham (died 1348) and Descartes (born 1596). It is doubtful how much it contributed to science; for which Renaissance thinkers had little use. Its enduring achievements were in art and politics, made by such men as Shakespeare, Leonardo da Vinci, and Machiavelli.

What is most important about the Renaissance is a broad mutation of values, usually called humanism. Humanism is a word much overused in the twentieth century; today everyone from Rogers to Skinner is called a humanist. If everyone is a humanist, however, no one is. It would be better to define humanism in the present context by its secularization of life. In all spheres, thinking became more human-centered and less God-centered, although religion was never abandoned; and in the sixteenth century the Reformation dominated all else.

This secularization started modestly with the increased reclamation of the classics begun by Petrarch. *Humanism* originally meant the recovery of classical thought and its application to contemporary human problems. We have seen that the recovery of the past began in the twelfth century, but its pace accelerated in the fourteenth, and its outlook changed. The first and most obvious contribution of the humanist efforts was in the recovered works themselves. The whole of Plato became known for the first time, for example. Renaissance scholars also sought to edit the works, to separate text from commentary, to ascribe to each author the correct treatise, and to discover forgeries.

What the Renaissance scholar wanted was to understand the mind of each classical writer in itself, and in its own historical context. This is the first manifestation of the secularization of philosophy and of an important Renaissance attitude which we have not seen since the Sophists, that truth has many perspectives. Medieval philosophers held to one truth, known perfectly by God, that must be sought by humans. Although they used the classics, medieval philosophers did not want to understand Plato or Aristotle as individual thinkers. They wanted to find God's truth in the ancient writings. Accurate texts were, therefore, unimportant, as it did not matter whether the words were those of the original writer or of a later commentator, as long as God's Word could be found.

The Renaissance humanists sought human truth rather than divine truth. They wanted to converse with the ancients (to whom they wrote letters), not rummage through works in search of support for revelation.

Although the humanists believed in God and truth, they believed that truth can be seen in many ways, from many individual perspectives. During the Reformation, the northern humanist Disiderius Erasmus (1466–1536) held to this belief despite the fanaticism of Protestant and Catholic alike. He would commit himself to neither camp, despite his initial sympathy for Luther, and he found himself condemned by both sides.

The shift from God-centeredness to human-centeredness appeared in many spheres of life. The state increasingly resisted the temporal claim of the pope to a secular power. Higher education became open to laypeople, not just to clerics. Even religious movements were occasionally led by the laity; Anabaptism, a radical Protestant movement, was started by a German weaver.

What we meet in the Renaissance humanists is a figure we last met in Greece, the Sophist. Like the humanists, the Sophists were practical educators, interested in individual perspectives rather than divine truths. The most important belief of the Sophists was that humanity is the measure of all things. The humanists could not go so far without abandoning Christianity, which none did, but they came close. Shakespeare's expression of human worth is typical, found in every humanist writer. Petrarch quotes Seneca's ". . . nothing is admirable besides the mind. . . ." Pico della Mirandola (1463–1494) writes, "Who is there that does not wonder at man?" Human beings were placed at the center of God's creation, lords over nature, and in intellect like the angels and even like God himself. There is an optimism about a person's potential and a faith in a person's powers that separate the humanists from their medieval predecessors.

One might have thought that in an age which glorified humans there would have been an outpouring of psychological studies, but there was none. Authors wrote to exalt humanity, to establish humans' proper place in nature, but not to study them. Even the most scientifically oriented of all Renaissance philosophers, Sir Francis Bacon, simply modified the faculty psychologies of the Middle Ages.

Just as there was no advance in psychology in the Renaissance, there was no philosophical progress. Humanists concentrated on human needs, rather than on abstract philosophy. The other strain of Renaissance thought, Platonism, was more sympathetic to the medievals, but likewise failed to create anything new in philosophy. What the Renaissance contributes to Western thought was an attitude, humanism, not a coherent philosophy or psychology.

However, we should note three related harbingers of the post-Renaissance age. Of most relevance to psychology was the idea of physiological mechanism, the tendency to see the body as a machine. We see this clearly in Leonardo da Vinci, an acute observer of human and animal anatomy. The Renaissance was also a time of renewed medical research and dissection. As physiological knowledge grew over the years, the mechanistic attitude increased until mechanism extended naturally to the brain and, hence, to human thinking.

The second forward-looking development is what is called Renaissance *nature philosophy*. These nature philosophers revived the Greek habit of speculation about the universe. They were not scientists, but they were influenced by science, especially by Copernicus, as well as by magical and alchemical traditions. The greatest of them, Giordano Bruno (1548–1600), speculated that there were many solar systems besides our own, and that life might be found on them. These naturalistic speculations took Bruno to the stake. These men are transition figures. They are medieval because they engage in pure speculation, but they point the way to the scientific revolution by their interest in nature rather than in God.

In the works of Sir Francis Bacon (1561–1626) we find the third way the Renaissance foreshadows the modern world—the beginning of empirical science. Bacon died, characteristically, of pneumonia caught while stuffing a chicken with snow to study the effects of refrigeration. He believed that philosophy should investigate nature in a wholly naturalistic and mechanistic way, eschewing theology and teleology equally. He was the first to deny that Aristotle's final cause was legitimate. He believed that scientific study should be wholly inductive, that one should carefully collect facts unguided by any biasing hypothesis, until one could cautiously draw some simple generalization. Although science was not actually studied this way, as Galileo would show, Bacon was articulating anew the fundamental thesis on which science rests, the primacy of experience and reason over faith and dogma. Bacon died for his belief.

Although the Reformation is outside our purview, we cannot pass the sixteenth century without taking note of it. It officially began in 1517 when Martin Luther nailed his 99 Theses to the door of Wittenberg Cathedral and challenged the Catholic hierarchy. Religious unrest was already in the air, and other rebels—many socially far more radical than Luther—were active.

The Reformation pitted Augustine against Aquinas. Luther wanted a personal, intensely introspective religion, an Augustinian religion, deemphasizing ritual, priesthood, and hierarchy. The Catholic response was to make Aquinas's philosophy official Catholic dogma to which all believers must adhere.

The Reformation divided Europe into two warring camps and encouraged intolerance. Bloody wars were fought in a futile attempt to extinguish the Protestants, who fought back successfully. Both sides felt that whoever was not wholeheartedly with them must be against them, and the victim was dispassionate thought. Philosophers were caught in the middle, and in the seventeenth century charges of heresy haunted Descartes and Spinoza, and the Reformation outburst of God-centeredness undermined Renaissance humanism.

The End of the Renaissance

Tomorrow, and tomorrow, and tomorrow
Creeps in this petty pace from day to day,
To the last syllable of recorded time,
And all our yesterdays have lighted fools
The way to dusty death. Out, out, brief candle!
Life's but a walking shadow, a poor player
That struts and frets his hour upon the stage
And then is heard no more. It is a tale
Told by an idiot, full of sound and fury,
Signifying nothing.

Shakespeare, *Macbeth*, V,v,17–28

For all its creativity the Renaissance was a time of tremendous social dislocation, misery, anxiety, and superstition. Lynn White (1974) has written that the Renaissance was the "most psychically disturbed era in European history." The Hundred Years' War and later the Thirty Years' War raged, bringing destruction to much of France and Germany, as mercenary armies alternately fought each other and pillaged the countryside when they were not paid. The Black Plague that began in 1348 had by 1400 halved the population of Europe. Tremendous famines struck, beginning in the fourteenth century. Syphilis was brought back from America by Columbus and ravaged Europe. The church was corrupt, the feudal order crumbling.

Everyday life reflected the anxiety engendered by stress. Europe was obsessed with death. Picnics were held under the rotting corpses of the hanged. The image of the Grim Reaper was born. Scapegoats were sought; mobs attacked Jews and "witches." At the same time that humanity was being glorified by the humanists, human mortality and suffering were reaching new lows, and the dark side of human nature was everywhere in evidence. Intellectuals practiced the magical arts of occultism.

The later sixteenth century was a time of doubt and skepticism. Ambiguity about humanity is found dramatically in William Shakespeare (1564–1616). The quotation from Hamlet that headed the Renaissance section in this chapter sums up the optimistic humanist view of humans as noble, infinite, admirable, and godlike. Yet Hamlet goes on immediately to say, "And yet to me what is this quintessence of dust? Man delights not me. . . ." The quotation from Macbeth is a powerful statement of disdain for humankind and life in the face of mortality, a statement of the absurdity of life that would delight any existentialist. Shakespeare's dramatic genius sees both the positive side of humans stressed by the humanist and the negative side evident in history.

A more philosophical thinker also felt and articulated the limits of humanity, Michel de Montaigne (1533–1592). In stark contrast to the earlier humanists, Montaigne wrote: "Of all creatures man is the most miserable and frail, and therewithal the proudest and disdainfulest." The humanists made the human the paragon of animals with a unique and godlike intellect. Montaigne here denies the uniqueness of humans. People are not the lords of creation, they are part of it; they are not the highest of animals, they are on a par with them. Animals as well as humans have knowledge. Montaigne decries reason as a weak reed on which to base knowledge, and argues instead for experience. But he then goes on to show how deceptive and untrustworthy are the senses. In short, Montaigne topples humans from the special place given them by medieval and Renaissance thinkers. This view continued to grow, culminating in Darwin, Freud, and Skinner.

Montaigne pointed to the future, to a skeptical and naturalistic theory of humanity and the universe. Montaigne was, in fact, denying the world view that held sway in Europe from classical times. Polished and refined in the Middle Ages and Renaissance, it was ultimately to be shattered and replaced by science and an increasingly secular philosophy. We now will summarize the old world view that Montaigne challenged.

CONCLUSION:
THE CLASSICAL-MEDIEVAL-
RENAISSANCE OUTLOOK

The World's a book in Folio, printed all
With God's great works in letter Capital:
Each creature is a Page, and each Effect
A fair character, void of all defects.

du Bartas, *Divine Weeks*

The Renaissance perfected a world view implicit in classical culture and developed by the Middle Ages. Fundamental to this world view was the idea that all things in the universe are linked in a grand order that we can decipher through resemblance. So, for example, the Renaissance physician thought skull and brain damage could be cured by the administration of walnuts, for the walnut shell resembles the skull and the nut resembles the brain.

As the poet du Bartas writes, the world is like a book, any being is like a word, in that it has signs which indicate its secret meaning to what else it is linked. Nature is to be understood by deciphering these signs, not through experiment but by close observation, seeking out similarities and relationships, a practice called *hermeneutics*. Hence the medieval-Renaissance scrutiny of the classic writers: Just as the world is a book revealing nature's symbolic order, so are books collections of words, signs that should reveal universal order. This order is not the scientific order of natural law, but an order built on sympathies and analogies between things, sympathies and analogies signified by resemblance, as between walnut and brain.

The human being occupies the central place in this orderly web of analogies. Annibale Romei's seventeenth-century *Courtier's Academy:* "the body of man is no other than a little model of the sensible world, and his soul an image of the world intelligible [Plato's world of the Forms]." The human body is a summary analogy of the physical world, the mind a summary analogy of the invisible world. The human is a microcosm reflecting the natural and supernatural macrocosm. The human is at the exact midpoint of the universe. The human body is worldly flesh and the bodily passions tie humans to the animals. The human's rational soul is angelic, for angels are rational souls without bodies. In between, mediating between rational soul and worldly body, are human faculties, such as imagination and common sense. These faculties in the brain are subtle animal spirits, the purest of earthly substances, which link body and soul.

This Neoplatonic conception of humankind was a medieval and Renaissance commonplace. But it stands for a broader and deeper existence which orders the universe—sympathy and resemblance. No individual thing stood outside this natural order; some link, some resemblance could always be found. Such an existence precludes scientific specialization. The order of nature is truly universal, for the laws of resemblance in one domain are the same for all domains; there is only one universal science of order.

This world view was shattered in the seventeenth century and brushed away in the eighteenth. Montaigne pointed the way: The human is not the center of creation, but one animal among many. So also did Sir Francis Bacon: Nature is to be investigated by experiment and explained mechanistically. Soon Galileo would show that the world is to be understood not by the decipherment of signs, as in language, but by the application of mathematics, which transcends particular observation.

We conclude this chapter in 1600. In that year William Gilbert published his *de Magnete* [*On magnets*], the first systematic experimental study of any topic. Shortly after 1600 the Scientific Revolution took off under Kepler, Galileo, Newton, and others. They brought to the study of the world a new conception of the world as a great machine, understandable by simple mechanical-mathematical laws. In the nineteenth century the mechanical analogy overthrows the angelic view of human reason and mechanizes psychology. Philosophers of the seventeenth century attempted to start afresh, to ignore the teaching of the church and the old philosophers, to seek truth unencumbered by the confusion of the past.

BIBLIOGRAPHY

There are several fine introductions to medieval life and history. The briefest, but still an excellent treatment, is Denys Hay, *The medieval centuries* (New York: Harper Torchbooks, 1964). Morris Bishop, *The middle ages* (New York: American Heritage Press, 1970) is an attractive, well-written book for the general reader; also for the general reader, but more detailed, is Heer (1962). Norman Cantor, one of the outstanding students of the Middle Ages, has written two texts: *Medieval history* (New York: Macmillan, 1969), and *The meaning of the middle ages* (Boston: Allyn & Bacon, 1973). The classic scholarly work on medieval social structure is Marc Bloch, *Feudal society* (Chicago: University of Chicago Press, 1961). Finally, William Brandt, *The shape of medieval history* (New York: Schocken, 1973), provides a general intellectual history of the Middle Ages. The flavor of life in one place and one time during the Middle Ages is provided in David Howarth, *1066: The year of the Conquest* (Harmondsworth, England: Penguin, 1977). Three general surveys of medieval philosophy are Frederick Artz, *The mind of the middle ages* (Chicago: Phoenix Books, 1980); David Knowles, *The evolution of medieval thought* (New York: Vintage Books, 1962); and J. Weinberg, *A short history of medieval philosophy* (Princeton: Princeton University Press, 1964). M. Fakhry, *A history of Islamic philosophy* (New York: Columbia University Press, 1970) describes the work of medieval Islamic thinkers.

For the early Middle Ages, see W. C. Bark, *Origins of the medieval world* (Stanford: Stanford University Press, 1958); Geoffrey Barraclough, *The crucible of Europe: The ninth and tenth centuries in European history* (Berkeley: University of California Press, 1976); Michael Grant, *Dawn of the middle ages* (New York: McGraw-Hill, 1981); H. St. L. B. Moss, *The birth of the middle ages 394–814* (New York: Oxford University Press, 1964), and R. W. Southern, *The making of the middle ages: Europe 972–1204* (New Haven: Yale

University Press, 1953). For philosophy in the period, see George Bosworth, *Early medieval philosophy* (Freeport, New York: Books for Libraries Press, 1971). For psychology, see Augustine, *Confessions* (Harmondsworth, England: Penguin, 1961); Marcia Colish, *The mirror of language* (New Haven: Yale University Press, 1968), who discusses Augustine's psychology; George Mora, "Mind-body concepts in the middle ages: Part I. The classical background and its merging with the Judeo-Christian tradition in the early middle ages," *Journal of the History of the Behavioral Sciences* (1978, *14*: 344–361); and two works on medieval faculty psychology: E. Ruth Harvey, *The inward wits: Psychological theory in the middle ages and Renaissance* (London: The Warburg Institute, Survey VI, 1975), and Harry Austryn Wolfson, "The internal senses in Latin, Arabic, and Hebrew philosophical texts," *Harvard Theological Review* (1935, *28*: 69–133).

Many of the general works already cited discuss popular culture in the Middle Ages; here are some other works. Erickson (1976); Georges Duby, *The knight, the lady, and the priest: The making of modern marriage in medieval France* (New York: Pantheon, 1983); Charles Homer Haskins, *The rise of the universities* (Ithaca: Cornell University Press, 1923); Colin Morris, *The discovery of the individual 1050–1200* (New York: Harper & Row, 1972); and Jeffrey Burton Russell, *Witchcraft in the middle ages* (Ithaca: Cornell University Press, 1972). For psychology in the high Middle Ages, see the works by Harvey and Wolfson already cited; Charles A. Hart, *The Thomistic conception of mental faculty* (Doctoral dissertation, Catholic University, Washington, D.C., 1930); and George Mora, "Mind-body concepts in the middle ages: Part II. The Moslem influence, the great theological systems, and cultural attitudes toward the mentally ill in the late middle ages," *Journal of the History of the Behavioral Sciences* (1980, *16*: 58–72).

The late Middle Ages, grim as they are, are nevertheless fascinating. The pivotal century was the fourteenth, admirably captured by Barbara W. Tuchman, *A distant mirror: The calamitous fourteenth century* (New York: Knopf, 1978). The classic work on the period is J. Huizinga, *The waning of the middle ages* (Garden City, New York: Doubleday Anchor, 1954). The intellectual history of the period is told by Gordon Leff, *The dissolution of the medieval outlook* (New York: Harper & Row, 1976). The most important thinker of the late Middle Ages was William of Ockham, a selection of whose works is in *Philosophical writings: A selection* (Indianapolis: Library of Liberal Arts, 1964); his biographer is Gordon Leff, *William of Ockham* (Manchester: Manchester University Press, 1975). Ockham's skeptical follower was Nicholas of Autrecourt, *The universal treatise* (Milwaukee: Marquette University Press, 1971). The folk thought of the late Middle Ages has received much attention from historians since the first edition of this book. The most important finding has been how little the Christian Neoplatonic outlook penetrated the thought of uneducated men and women. The best known of these revisionist works is Emmanuel Le Roy Ladurie, *Montaillou: The promised land of error* (New York: George Braziller, 1978), which examines the daily life of an un-Christian village in southern France. A similar book on Italy is Carlo Ginzburg, *The cheese and the worms: The cosmos of a sixteenth century miller* (London: Routledge & Kegan Paul, 1980). A related and more general work, which tries to describe the characteristic mentality of the late Middle Ages is Le Roy Ladurie's *Love, death, and money in the Pays d'Oc* (New York: George Braziller, 1982). A useful commentary on the mentality works is H. C. Erik Midelfort, "Madness and the problems of psychological history in the sixteenth century," *Sixteenth Century Journal* (1981, *12*: 5–12).

It is now clear that scientific thought began in the Middle Ages, not the Renaissance, as is usually thought. Important works on medieval science include R. Dales, *The scientific achievement of the middle ages* (Philadelphia: University of Philadelphia Press, 1973), Edward Grant, "Scientific thought in fourteenth century Paris: Jean Buridan and Nicole Oresme," in M. P. Cosman and B. Chandler, eds., *Machaut's world: Science and art in the fourteenth century* (New York: New York Academy of Sciences, 1978); E. Moody, *Studies in medieval philosophy, science, and logic* (Berkeley: University of California Press, 1975); Tina Stiefel, "The heresy of science: A twelfth century conceptual revolution," *Isis* (1977, *68*: 347–362); Nicholas H. Steneck, *Science and creation in the middle ages* (Notre Dame: University of Notre Dame Press, 1975), K. Wallace, *Francis Bacon on the nature of man*

(Urbana: University of Illinois Press, 1967; and Lynn White, *Medieval technology and social change* (London: Oxford University Press, 1962).

On the Renaissance: The classic work is Jakob Burkhardt, *The civilization of the Renaissance in Italy* (New York: Mentor, 1862/1960); more recent works include J. R. Hale, *Renaissance Europe* (Berkeley: University of California Press, 1971); Denys Hay, *The Italian Renaissance in its historical background* (Cambridge, England: Cambridge University Press, 1961); Lacey Baldwin Smith, *The Elizabethan world* (Boston: Houghton Mifflin, 1972). For the Reformation, see Roland Bainton, *The Reformation of the sixteenth century* (Boston: Beacon Books, 1956). On Renaissance thought, see E. Cassirer, P. O. Kristeller, and J. H. Randall, eds., *Renaissance philosophy of man* (Chicago: University of Chicago Press, 1948); Paul Kristeller, *Renaissance thought* (New York: Harper & Row, 1961); D. Wilcox, *In search of God and self: Renaissance and Reformation thought* (Boston: Houghton Mifflin, 1975); and, for a work emphasizing the continuity rather than the break between the Middle Ages and the Renaissance, Walter Ullman, *Medieval foundations of Renaissance humanism* (Ithaca: Cornell University Press, 1977).

For the medieval and Renaissance world views, see Erickson (1976), and E. M. W. Tillyard, *The Elizabethan world-picture* (New York: Vintage Books, n.d.).

REFERENCES

Clark, E. C. and Dewhurst, K. (1972) *An illustrated history of brain function.* Berkeley: University of California Press.

Erickson, C. (1976) *The medieval vision.* New York: Oxford University Press.

Heer, F. (1962) *The medieval world.* New York: Mentor.

Spencer, T. (1966) *Shakespeare and the nature of man.* New York: Collier Books.

White, L. (1974) Death and the Devil. In D. S. Kinsman, ed. *The darker vision of the Renaissance.* Berkeley: University of California Press.

The Mechanization of the World Picture (1600–1700)

THE SCIENTIFIC REVOLUTION
REMAKING PHILOSOPHY
   Truth from Doubt: René Descartes (1596–1650)
   Human Understanding: John Locke (1632–1704)
PHILOSOPHY, SCIENCE, AND HUMAN AFFAIRS
   The Laws of Social Life: Thomas Hobbes (1588–1679)
   The Heart has its Reasons which the Reason does not
   Understand: Blaise Pascal (1623–1662)
   Determinism Extended: Baruch Spinoza (1652–1677)
   Levels of Consciousness: Gottfried Wilhelm Leibniz
   (1646–1716)
CONCLUSION: THE SEVENTEENTH CENTURY—SEEDS OF
CHANGE

The two centuries after 1600 were literally revolutionary. The period begins with the Scientific Revolution of the seventeenth century and closes with political revolutions in colonial America and monarchical France. The scientific and philosophical revolutions laid the basis for the political. In broad historical terms these centuries witnessed the crystallization of the Western world we know today. The nascent nation-states of the Renaissance began to be consolidated by tyrants of more or less enlightened dispositions such as Louis XIV (1638–1715) of France and Frederick the Great (1712–1786) of Prussia. Ideologies of liberty and revolution, so much a part of modern politics, were first articulated by Age of Enlightenment philosophers. The modern economies of industry and capitalism were born in the Industrial Revolution of late eighteenth-century England.

One general trend, which has enormous import for psychology, may be extracted from all these changes. To the medieval and Renaissance thinker the world was a somewhat mysterious place, organized in a grand hierarchy from God to human to material world, in which each event had a special meaning. The world was profoundly spiritual. In the seventeenth century this view was attacked and replaced by another one: scientific, mathematical, and mechanical. Natural scientists demonstrated the mechanical nature of heavenly and earthly phenomena and then of the bodies of animals. Finally, the mechanical approach was extended to humanity itself. Thus the study of humankind, from politics to psychology, could be subjected to the scientific method, and laws of nature could be sought in the human mind as well as in the heavens. By 1800 both the universe and humanity were believed by most to be machines subject to natural law. In the process, the older view of the world and its relation to humankind as a pattern of mystically meaningful symbols disappeared.

We will divide our study of this period in two parts. The first runs from about 1600 to 1700 and sees the establishment of modern science and the reconstruction of philosophy on new (yet familiar) lines. The second period, from 1700 to 1800, is commonly known as the Enlightenment. In this era the principles of science and reason were applied to human affairs, including the study of human mind and behavior.

THE SCIENTIFIC REVOLUTION

> The Scientific Revolution outshines everything since the rise of Christianity and reduces the Renaissance and Reformation to the rank of mere episodes, mere internal displacements, within the system of medieval Christendom. (Butterfield 1965)

The importance of science in the modern world cannot be doubted, and the Scientific Revolution can be passed over by no history of the West—especially a history of a science—although psychology was not part of the revolution. The outcome of that revolution is unquestioned. It displaced the earth from the center of the universe and made of the universe a grand machine quite independent of human feelings and needs. It overthrew the philosophic attitudes of scholasticism and the secretive magical attitudes of alchemy, substituting a public search for precise mathematical regularities confirmable by experiment. It also proposed that people could improve their lot by the application of reason and experiment rather than prayer and devotion (Rossi 1975). However, the roots of the scientific revolution

Francis Bacon	1600	Bruno burned as heretic
Galileo		
		Settlement at Jamestown
Harvey discovers circulation of the blood		
		First newspaper (London)
	1625	
		Settlement in Massachusetts
Descartes's *Discourse*		Harvard founded
		Charles I beheaded
	1650	
Hobbes's *Leviathan*		Louis XIV takes power
Pascal		English Restoration
Spinoza		
		Milton
	1675	
		Ice cream popular
		Dodo becomes extinct
Leibniz		
Principia mathematica		England's Glorious Revolution
Locke's *Essay* published		
	1700	First daily newspaper (London)
Berkeley		Last execution for witchcraft
		Louis XIV dies
		Bach's Brandenburg concertos
	1725	American Philosophical Society
Hume's *Treatise*		Pope's "Essay on Man"
La Mettrie's *L'Homme*		Frederick the Great takes power
Hartley's *Observations*		
	1750	First New York theater
Reid		Mozart born
Condillac's *Treatise*		Mason-Dixon line drawn
		First public restaurant (Paris)
Electrical nature of nerves discovered		
Hume's *Inquiry*	1775	American Revolution
Kant's *Critique*		
		Frederick the Great dies
		French Revolution
Stewart's *Philosophy of the mind*		
	1800	Jefferson elected president

FIGURE 4-1   Chronology 1600–1800.

and its means of progress are monstrously confused, becoming more so with each new piece of historical research.

It is all too easy—and used to be traditional—to write the early history of science as if it were an unrelenting step-by-step progression to modern science, in which prototypical materialist scientists rejected superstition and alchemy for mathematics, experiment, and mechanism. However, this comfortable story is no longer tenable. Far from rejecting alchemy, Newton spent more time on it than on physics (Westfall 1975). Some fathers of the Catholic church saw mechanism as vindicating God, the creator of the perfect world-machine. Galileo was greatly influenced (as was Newton) by Renaissance Neoplatonism, and he drew on medieval philosophers for a number of his scientific ideas.

Francis Bacon may be taken as a convenient figure to represent the swirls of controversy over the formation of modern science. Bacon is conventionally taken to be one of the great figures of early science because of his rejection of scholasticism, Aristotle, mystical Neoplatonism, and other forms of received and preconceived authority. In their place Bacon urged the authority of observation against all hypotheses, anticipating Newton's later disregard for speculation. Bacon was also important for calling attention to the value of craft and technology. Craftsmen work directly on the world and have no room for superfluous hypotheses, so their wisdom may serve as a model for science and a means to humanity's improvement. Bacon is therefore modern in calling for observation and application as basic parts of science.

However, Bacon was sometimes a rather Aristotelian conservative. He did not accept Copernicus's sun-centered world system because it was too hypothetical and mathematical. Similarly, he rejected Galileo's physics, for Galileo studied movement by restricting himself to a few mathematically treated variables. Like Aristotle and the medieval scientists, Bacon distrusted mathematics and wanted to explain all aspects of every phenomenon. It has also been argued that despite his attacks on magic and alchemy, Bacon's desire that science be useful derives from alchemy's practical goals; that is, the transmutation of lead into gold (Rattansi 1972). Finally, Thomas Kuhn (1976) has argued that Bacon was outside the Scientific Revolution altogether. The only sciences revolutionized during the seventeenth century were the "classic," already mathematicized sciences of astronomy and physics in which Bacon was uninterested. Instead, Bacon stands at the head of more purely empirical "Baconian" sciences, such as chemistry, which were not mathematicized until the nineteenth century.

Today's historical scholarship has demonstrated that not only Bacon, but every figure in the Scientific Revolution, can be made to look modern or medieval, and—with a few exceptions—crucial or trivial.

We must conclude that the Scientific Revolution took a long time, and no single figure was a thoroughgoing spokesman for modern science. The revolution may be said to have begun in 1453 with the publication of Nicholas Copernicus's *Revolution of the heavenly orbs,* which proposed that the sun, not the earth, was the center of the solar system. However, Copernicus's physics was Aristotelian, and his system was no better supported by the data than the old Ptolemaic one, although some found its simplicity attractive. Galileo Galilei (1564–1642) was the most effective spokesman for the new system, supporting it with his new physics, which helped make sense of the sun-centered proposal, and producing telescopic evidence that the moon and other celestial bodies were no more "heavenly" than the earth. However, Galileo, like Copernicus, could not shake the old Greek assumption that the motion of the planets had to be circular, even though his friend Johann Kepler

(1571–1630) showed planetary orbits to be elliptical. The final unity of celestial and earthly physics, and the ultimate victory of the new world view of science, came from Isaac Newton's *Principia mathematica,* published in 1687.

Newton's laws of motion put the capstone on the idea that the universe was a grand machine. The machine analogy was proposed by Galileo and René Descartes, and quickly became a popular view of the universe. Originally, it was put forward as a support for religion against magic and alchemy: God the master engineer constructed a perfect machine and left it running. The only operative principles are, therefore, mechanical, not occult; magical machinations cannot affect machines. However, implicit in the mechanical view is the possibility that God is dead and has left behind a cold, impersonal universe. Newton himself seems to have suspected this, for in his own mechanical world there are various imperfections, requiring God to be ever-present, ever-vigilant, and ever-active to keep things running smoothly. Unfortunately for God, the image of him as a cosmic tinkerer flitting about keeping the planets steady is demeaning. The more consistent mechanism of Descartes and Galileo triumphed, supported by Newton's physics. The view was deadly to the old medieval conception of God as an ever-present being who manifested himself in signs and portents.

Two important views of knowledge became separated in the seventeenth century, with important later implications for psychology. Should science be pure and abstract, or applied and useful? The old Platonist tradition upheld the former view: In the words of Platonist Henry More, the value of science is not to be measured by "what help it can procure for ye back, bed, and board" (Rattansi 1972). Wundt and Titchener upheld this view for psychology. In the seventeenth century, however, a tradition that science should be useful arose, expounded most forcefully by Bacon, although whether its inspiration came from magic, the craft tradition, or the Puritan zeal for good works is unclear. By the eighteenth century the latter tradition was well established in England and America, and was drifting toward anti-intellectualism. The English entrepreneur Richard Arkwright wrote: "It is well known that the most useful discoveries that have been made in every branch of art and manufactures have not been made by speculative philosophers in their closets, but by ingenious mechanics . . . practically acquainted with the subject matter of their discoveries" (Bronowski and Mazlish 1960). William James upheld this tradition for psychology.

An important epistemological distinction emerged during the Scientific Revolution, reviving an old atomist idea. Some sensory qualities of objects are readily measurable: their number, weight, size, shape, and motion. Others are not: color, texture, smell, taste, sound. If science is to be a quantitative, mathematical undertaking (as Galileo and Newton desired), then it could only deal with the former sorts of qualities, called *primary qualities,* which the atomists had attributed to atoms themselves. These objective qualities are to be contrasted with the subjective *secondary qualities,* which exist only in human perception and are the subjective outcome of atoms striking the senses. So, for example, color is a secondary property, for totally color-blind people see only greys. Color is a property of vision's response to light waves, it is not really in a colored object.

Psychology was founded as the study of consciousness, and therefore included all sensory properties. However, when the behaviorists revolted against introspective psychology, they deliberately modeled themselves on physics and took the subject matter of psychology to be behavior, an organism's motion in space. Behavior as motion is an objective, primary quality. Such primary qualities, so the behaviorists believed following Newton and Galileo, were the only suitable data for science. Subjectivity was banished first from physics in the seventeenth century, and from psychology in the twentieth.

The change in world view wrought by the Scientific Revolution cannot be underestimated. Science provides the basis for almost all thinking in the twentieth century, from political science to philosophy to physics. It has given us a powerful technology that has changed the face of the earth and taken men and women into space. Psychology, as a science, came to the revolution late, but was nonetheless affected by its assumptions of mechanism, technological progress, and objectivity. It is because of the Scientific Revolution that the medieval-Renaissance world view is so alien to us. A distinguished philosopher, E. A. Burtt (1954), contrasts the two views this way:

> The scholastic scientist looked out upon the world of nature, and it appeared to him a quite sociable and human world. It was finite in extent. It was made to serve his needs. It was clearly and fully intelligible, being immediately present to the rational powers of his mind; it was composed fundamentally of, and was intelligible through, those qualities which were most vivid and intense in his own immediate experience—colour, sound, beauty, joy, heat, cold, fragrance and its plasticity to purpose and ideal. Now the world is an infinite and monotonous mathematical machine. Not only is his high place in a cosmic teleology lost, but all these things which were the very substance of the physical world to the scholastic—the thing that made it alive and lovely and spiritual—are lumped together and crowded into the small fluctuating and temporary positions of extension which we call human nervous . . . systems. . . . It was simply an incalculable change in the viewpoint of the world held by intelligent opinion in Europe.

REMAKING PHILOSOPHY

The Renaissance worshiped the classical writers, even claiming at times that the modern world would never attain the perfection of the classical world, so mighty did the ancients seem. Modern science, however, showed that the ancients were not perfect. Furthermore, the sixteenth-century voyages of exploration had discovered strange and wonderful things unknown to the ancients. In 1636 Tomasso Campanella wrote, "The exploration of the globe having resulted in discoveries that have destroyed many of the data on which ancient philosophy reposed, a new conception of things will inevitably be called for" (Hazard 1963). Although familiar themes continued, two avowedly new philosophical conceptions were shortly to be provided.

Truth from Doubt: René Descartes (1596–1650)

Descartes was a Renaissance man: soldier, tutor, scientist, mathematician, philosopher, speculative psychologist. In three areas his influence has been deep and lasting: in his reformulation of rationalism, in his mechanical concept of the world, and in his dualist concept of humans. We shall examine each in turn.

As it was for Plato's rationalism, the immediate philosophical background for Descartes's program was skepticism. The late Renaissance had produced a herd of skeptics, such as Montaigne. Like the Sophists, they were uncertain that humans could attain absolute Truth. Unlike the Sophists, Renaissance skeptics did not consider humanity to be the measure of all things, however. On the contrary, human senses were considered so weak, human reason so frail, that people needed faith in God to achieve anything. Like Plato, Descartes did not accept either the skeptics' belief in the unattainability of knowledge or their low estimation of human reason. For Descartes, proper use of the divinely implanted light of reason was the way to truth.

While serving in the army of the Emperor of Germany, Descartes spent one day in a stove-heated room meditating on his own thoughts and formulated the basic principles of his philosophy. Setting aside the ancients as hopelessly confused, and taking a leaf from the skeptics, he resolved to systematically doubt everything until he found something so self-evidently true that it could not be doubted. Descartes found he could doubt the existence of God, the validity of his sensations, the existence of his body. He continued in this way until he found one thing he could not doubt, his own existence as a self-conscious, thinking being. One cannot doubt that one doubts, for in doing so, one realizes the very action supposedly in doubt. Doubting is an act of thinking, and Descartes expressed his first indubitable truth as the famous *"Cogito, ergo sum"*: I think, therefore I am. Descartes then erected his philosophy on this simple truth. From his own existence Descartes established the existence of God by arguments whose validity, cogency, and even sincerity have been doubted since he first stated them. Having established God, the rest was plain sailing. Descartes established the existence of the world and his own body, and the general accuracy of perception.

We will sidestep the vexing questions of Cartesian metaphysics to look at important features of the philosopher's approach. In the first place Descartes firmly believed that the correct method of reasoning can discover and prove what is true. Descartes's first published philosophical work was *Rules for the Direction of the Mind, on the Method of Rightly Conducting The Reason and Seeking for Truth in the Sciences* (1637). Descartes held that there is but one proper way to search for the truth: namely, the discovery by reason of intuitively obvious truths, and the deduction from them of other truths. This method is the opposite of Bacon's method of induction, for it is a rationalist method. Descartes's faith in reason was to have long-lasting and revolutionary consequences. Many later thinkers decided Descartes erred in his specific conclusions, but respected his method of accepting as true only what was evident to reason, cutting through sophistry, superstition, prejudice, propaganda, and the divine right of kings. While Descartes professed to believe in God and the church, his sword of reason served the cause of freethinkers everywhere. It should also be pointed out that in elevating reason, Descartes did not wholly condemn the senses as Plato did. Part of his method involved collecting all observations relevant to a question at hand. Descartes simply insisted that facts were of little value until rightly ordered by reason. Certainly Descartes did not value facts as ends in themselves, but as aids to finding more general truth.

Descartes was not the first to prove his own existence from mental activity. St. Augustine had said, "If I am deceived, I exist" and Parmenides had said, "For it is the same thing to think and to be." So we may place Descartes in the introspective rationalist tradition: Truth is primarily evident in me, in my self-consciousness, my thinking. After Descartes, however, introspection became the major philosophical tool of rationalist and empiricist alike. Philosophers differed about what they found in the mind, but they all looked to it for truth. After Descartes, therefore, philosophy became increasingly psychological, seeking to know the mind through introspection, until in the nineteenth century psychology was founded as the *scientific*, rather than armchair-philosophical, study of consciousness known through introspection.

The method was more widely revolutionary as well. No longer was philosophy to be practiced by pouring over ancient texts, whether the *Republic,* the *de Anima,* or the Bible. Instead, philosophers begin with an analysis of mind, or experience, or will, as they understand them. This is a decisive break with the scholastic and Renaissance tradition of studying texts and marks a return to the more freely speculative philosophizing of the Greeks. The break is underlined by noting that by and large the modern philosophers were not academic professors; Descartes, for example, supported himself for a time by soldiering. Furthermore, these philosophers abandoned Latin in favor of their native tongues as vehicles for writing and publication. Increasingly, philosophers did not care to persuade established scholastic academics, but sought the wider audience of all literate people. Philosophy and science gradually escaped the control of church and state by publishing widely in the vernacular.

Finally, Cartesian philosophy is rationalist in its nativism. Plato had thought knowledge of the Forms innate in the human soul. For the Forms, Descartes substituted clear and distinct ideas we immediately know are true; moreover, these ideas come not from the senses but from "certain germs˙ of truth which exist naturally in our souls." Thus the indubitable, principle truths are innate. As for Plato, they are potential ideas only, requiring activation by experience. Descartes held the idea of God to be innate (certainly we never see God), but obviously infants do not have the idea yet. Descartes draws an analogy with certain inherited diseases: They are not present at birth, but the disposition to develop them is. Descartes also speaks of innate ideas in another sense, not as concepts, such as the concept of God, but as certain innate ways of thinking. For example, we know that if A = B and B = C, then A = C. We did not learn this through experience, so it must be innate. It is an innate way of thinking, and so our minds are thus disposed naturally to conceive things in certain set ways. This kind of nativism will be developed with great force by Immanuel Kant; rejection of the first kind was the beginning of Locke's empiricism.

Descartes's first work was in science, not philosophy, but his account of it, *The World,* he suppressed upon hearing of Galileo's condemnation by the church in 1632. Some of his scientific ideas were later published in 1644 in the *Principles of Philosophy.* In its details Descartes's physics is reminiscent of the pre-Socratics. His description of the world is largely speculative, founded sometimes on out-of-date information and ignorant of current developments, such as Kepler's laws of planetary motions. It relies more on abstract argument than on empirical proof, as one might expect from a rationalist. If its details were wrong, however, its basic conception was triumphant. With Newton's help it has given us our modern view of the world. Descartes was from his earliest education impressed with mathematics, and his world view became mathematical. He conceived the world, the entire material universe, to be one complex machine obeying deterministic, mathematical laws knowable to the mind. In the material world there was nothing but extended matter; there were no colors, no tastes, no angels, no demons. God had created the perfect machine and set it running. Human reason could understand the natural laws and use them to its advantage, but they are fixed and remorseless. Descartes's own account of the world machine was unsatisfactory, his speculative nature playing loose with the facts. It remained for Newton to truly grasp the machinery of physics.

His success and Descartes's vision have guided science ever since. To a large extent the subsequent history of all the sciences has been to formulate each in mechanical terms, beginning with physics, then chemistry, and in our own times, biology. Nor has man escaped Descartes's vision, which brings us to his psychology.

If the material world as it objectively exists possesses the single primary property of extension, it is obvious that the world as we subjectively experience it possesses many other secondary properties—color, smell, taste, sound, joy, pain, fear. There is therefore, in addition to a material world which includes the body, a subjective world of consciousness and mind. Perhaps this second world is spiritual as well, for God and the soul are not material. In any case, as far as human knowledge is concerned there are two worlds, an objective, scientifically knowable, mechanical-material world—the world as it really is—and a subjective world of human consciousness known through introspection—the world of a person as a thinking being.

Thus Descartes proposed a dualism of mind and body seen as quite distinct entities, one physical (the body), the other nonphysical (the mind). These two entities interact: The mind acquires information about the material world through the senses; the desires of the body are felt in consciousness, while the mind may direct the actions of the body. The exact nature of Descartes's dualism has been long debated. To many of his contemporaries Descartes seemed to have eliminated the Christian soul, for the only property he definitely assigned it was consciousness or thinking, not immortality. Moreover, his proofs of God seemed weak. Descartes himself asserted his orthodoxy, but his own suppression of his first scientific works indicates heterodoxy. The question is unsettled. Some argue that Descartes was a sincere Christian whose system contained seeds of materialistic atheism. Others contend that Descartes was himself a thoroughgoing mechanist who believed subjective consciousness to be only a brain process, but that he tried to conceal his true beliefs from the authorities of church and state.

In any event, the most important consequence of his psychology was its mechanism. As a material entity, Descartes conceived the body as a machine, and he gave detailed mechanical accounts of how sensation and action occurred as body and mind interacted through the pineal gland, the seat of the mind. As with his physics, Descartes's physiology was speculative and incompatible with already existing information on the nervous system. What is important is Descartes's view of the human body as a machine incorporating many faculties previously assigned to the soul. Like Aristotle and the medieval faculty psychologists, Descartes wrote about memory, imagination, and common sense. However, unlike them, Descartes assigned these faculties to the body, implying that although they appear to be mental activities, they may be explained as bodily activities. Therefore Descartes sought to account for as much of the mind as possible on materialist, mechanical terms within the sphere of science, reserving only self-consciousness at most to philosophy. Hence, whether or not he intended to give a completely materialist and mechanical account of human mental activity, Descartes gave great impetus to the assimilation of mind to mechanical science. In the eighteenth century we will find complete mechanistic psychologies.

Descartes also suggested the possibility of comparing human and animal minds. Descartes looked on animals as nothing but mechanical automata lacking self-conscious souls, using the uniqueness of human language to support his view. Human beings, no matter how otherwise unintelligent, possess a creative language capable of expressing reflective rational thought. Animals, in contrast, possess at best vocal signals that indicate simple bodily states such as fear. In the 1950s language became a special problem for psychology, and at least one linguist would follow Descartes in treating language as an innate, uniquely human ability.

Descartes is finally a paradoxical figure. In his emphases on reason as opposed to perception, on innate ideas as opposed to experience, on absolute truth as opposed to relativism, he is a rationalist. However, in his mechanical view of the world and the human body, his psychology would ultimately support empiricism and behaviorism.

Human Understanding:
John Locke (1632–1704)

John Locke was a friend of the scientists Isaac Newton and Robert Boyle (in whose laboratory he assisted), a member of the Royal Society, adviser and tutor to noble politicians, and at times a practicing physician. As we might expect, therefore, Locke brought a practical and empirical bent to his philosophy. His major work was *An Essay Concerning Human Understanding* (1690), which he started writing in 1671. Unlike the rationalist Descartes, who sought ultimate Platonic Truth, Locke wanted to understand how the human mind actually works—the sources of its ideas, and the limitations of human knowledge. Thus Locke's epistemology is really a psychology, for his emphasis is on *how* the mind knows rather than on *what* it knows. Locke thus brought the scientific spirit to philosophy, shearing off metaphysics, to say what can be empirically known about the human mind. In the history of psychology, then, Locke is an important turning point. Now the inspection of the human mind itself becomes important, replacing metaphysical speculation on what cannot be known.

What, then, may humans know? Locke stated: "Since the Mind, in all its thoughts and Reasonings, hath no other immediate Object but its own *Ideas* . . . it is evident, that our Knowledge is only conversant about them." The mind does not know Forms or Essences, but its own ideas only. Where do our ideas come from? Locke wrote: "To this I answer, in one word, From *Experience:* In that, all our knowledge is founded and derived itself. Our Observation employed either about *external, sensible objects; or about the internal Operations of our Minds . . . is that which supplies our Understandings with all the materials of thinking.* These two are the Fountains of Knowledge, from whence all the *Ideas* we have, or can naturally have, do spring."

Locke thus states the empiricist principle that knowledge derives from experience alone. Elsewhere, he uses the famous simile for the mind of the *tabula rasa*, or piece of white paper, on which experience writes ideas. However, we must note some important qualifications to Locke's thesis, for he was not a radical empiricist. To begin with, experience is of two types: sensation of external objects and reflection on the working of our minds. Thus we may know about both the external world and our own inner, mental world. Direct knowledge about the mind is therefore possible through introspection. Furthermore, Locke does not say that the operations of mind are acquired through experience. The powers of thinking, memory, perception are all innate, as they were for Descartes. Locke's later followers reject both these theses.

It is well known that Locke attacked innate ideas, spending the first book of his *Essay* arguing against them. However, he was not attacking Descartes, as is usually assumed. What Locke opposed were a large number of English writers who believed in innate *moral principles,* seeing in them the foundation of Christian morality. Thus they could say that it was God's law implanted in the soul that a person should believe in him; anyone who did not believe was depraved and as much a moral monster as a three-legged baby would be a physical monster. Indeed, Locke himself was widely denounced as a dangerous atheist for denying innate moral truths. Locke attacked them because he believed the idea of innate moral and metaphysical truths to be pillars of dogmatism. The schools of his day used maxims as the basis of teaching. Students were to accept them and then prove them. Locke advocated a discovery principle. Students should keep open minds, discovering truth through experience and following their own talents, instead of being forced into the straitjacket of scholastic maxims. To see in Locke, as many do, the father of structured education, is wrong.

Locke's arguments against innate ideas make no headway against Descartes's or Leibniz's nativism, as he recognized. They believed in innate ideas activated by experience, which Locke believed was only trivially different from his own doctrine of innate mental abilities. In fact, one finds a great deal of innate active mental machinery in Locke's "empty mind." Like Descartes, Locke indicates that language is a human, species-specific trait. He wrote in *Essay:* "God having designed Man for a sociable Creature . . . furnished him also with language. . . . Parrots, and general other Birds, may be taught to make articulate sounds distinct enough, which yet, by no means, are capable of Language." Only humans can use articulate sounds to represent ideas. In his work on education, Locke holds that much of a child's personality and abilities are innate. Man's basic motives, to seek happiness and avoid misery, are likewise "innate practical principles," although of course having nothing to do with truth.

For Locke the mind was not merely an empty room to be furnished by experience, but was rather a complex information-processing device prepared to convert the materials of experience into organized human knowledge. Direct experience provides us with simple ideas, which are then elaborated and combined by the mental machinery into complex ideas. Knowledge comes about as we inspect our ideas, and see how they agree or disagree. The bedrock of knowledge for Locke, as for Descartes, was intuitively self-evident propositions, although for Locke they are self-evidently experienced truths instead of truths found in the soul. For example, you know directly and intuitively, without possibility of error, that the colors black and white are not the same (they "disagree"). More complex forms of knowledge arise as we deduce consequences from self-evident propositions. Like Descartes, Locke believed that in this way all human knowledge, even ethics and aesthetics, could be geometrically systematized.

We may conclude that the differences between Locke and Descartes were primarily differences of emphasis. Both wanted to transcend sterile scholastic philosophy; both tried to do so by examining the human mind. Descartes was more the captive of the past, still searching with pure reason for transcendent truth. Locke points more to the empirical future. He recognized the limits of human knowledge and reason; indeed one reason for writing the *Essay* was to show what humanity could hope to know so that only fruitful questions might be pursued.

Locke was usually a very clear and common-sensical writer. However, on one crucial point he was ambiguous. As we have seen, Locke states that human knowledge is only about ideas. However, what is an idea? Two interpretations are possible. The first was adopted by Locke's first commentator, Bishop Berkeley, with radical implications we will come to in the next chapter. According to this view, ideas are mental objects, furniture of the mind, and our knowledge is limited to them. So when one says, "A snowball is white," one is referring only to the mental picture of a snowball. Although it is clear Locke believed ideas to correspond to things in the world, Berkeley showed that this cannot be proven, so we have no guarantee that our knowledge is "real" knowledge. Skepticism results. On the other hand, most, but not all, modern commentators follow the Scottish philosopher Reid and reject Berkeley's interpretation. They hold that Locke meant *idea* to be a kind of mental act, specifically an act of perception by which the mind contacts the outside world. Thus when one says, "A snowball is white," one is referring not to some mental image, but to real snowballs.

This dispute affects how we place Locke in the history of psychology. In the nineteenth century there were two major European academic psychologies, each of which is compatible with one interpretation of Locke's *idea*. One was the psychology of content, whose best spokesman was E. B. Titchener. In this psychology, sensations were believed to be irreducible atomic constituents of consciousness—the elementary content, or furniture, of the mind. This account follows Berkeley. The other psychology, whose spokesman was Franz Brentano, was the psychology of *act,* in which any mental event was construed as a mental act referring to something in the outside world. This account follows Reid. Titchener saw that here are two rival ways of viewing the mind. Locke's ambiguous use of "idea" can be related to either system.

In any case, what is most important about Locke is his empirical attitude regarding the mind. Locke wanted to know how it works, and this is a psychological question unencumbered by metaphysics. Locke did not practice a scientific psychology, collecting data and designing research programs; he believed the mind could know itself through reflection. But he opened the way for a science of mind.

PHILOSOPHY, SCIENCE, AND HUMAN AFFAIRS

In the wake of the scientific revolution it became clear that humanity's place in nature would have to be reevaluated. As religion began to lose its authority, and science began to assume its own authority, new answers to the traditional questions of philosophy, psychology, politics, and values were demanded. The task of reworking human self-understanding and human life within the framework of science is an enterprise in which psychology is intimately involved, and it is one that continues in our own day still. Science raises important questions about the springs of human conduct, about the place of values in a world of facts, about moral responsibility, about the proper forms of human government, and about the place of feelings in world views founded on scientific reason. In the seventeenth century philosophers began to wrestle with these problems, and began to offer solutions that still inspire or infuriate us today.

The Laws of Social Life:
Thomas Hobbes (1588–1679)

Hobbes's importance derives from being the first to comprehend and express the new scientific view of humans and their place in the universe. Hobbes wrote: "For seeing life is but a motion of limbs . . . why may we not say, that all *automata* . . . have an artificial life? For what is the *heart*, but a spring; and the *nerves*, but so many strings; and the joints, but so many *wheels*, giving motion to the whole body" (Bronowski and Mazlish 1960). Hobbes's contemporary, Descartes, believed animals, but not humans, to be entirely machines. Hobbes went considerably further, claiming that spiritual substance is a meaningless idea. Only matter exists, and the actions of people, no less than those of animals, are fully determined.

On one point Hobbes and Descartes agreed, that philosophy should be constructed after the model of geometry. Indeed, it was Hobbes's accidental exposure, at age forty, to the elegant proofs of Euclid that led him to philosophize. Hobbes believed that all knowledge is ultimately rooted in sense-perception. He upheld extreme nominalism, seeing in universals no more than convenient names grouping remembered sense-perceptions. He dismissed arguments over metaphysics as scholastic wrangling about meaningless concepts. He rigidly separated philosophy, which is rational and meaningful, from theology, which is irrational and meaningless. His most interesting psychological doctrine is that language and thinking are closely related, perhaps even identical. In his major work, *Leviathan* (1651), Hobbes wrote: "Understanding is nothing else but conception caused by speech." Further, he states that "Children are not endowed with reason at all, till they have attained the use of speech." Hobbes was the first in the long, and still living, line of British philosophers who equate right thinking with right use of language. For psychology, this is an old and unresolved issue: whether thinking is overt or covert speech, or whether speech merely dresses up abstract concepts. Hobbes clearly argued the former.

However, Hobbes's real interest was political science, which he claimed to have invented. Hobbes believed that if human beings are deterministic machines like the stars and planets, then a science of human affairs ought to be as attainable as astronomy and physics.

As one who had endured the English civil war, he desired to put government on a sound rational footing to avoid such horrors in the future. In *Leviathan* Hobbes begins with a commonplace of modern liberalism, that persons are created roughly equal in physical and mental powers. However, were there no government, each person would seek his or her own interest against fellow humans. Outside of organized society, Hobbes wrote: "*There is always war of every one against every one* . . . and the life of man is solitary, nasty, brutish, and short." The solution is for people to recognize that their rational self-interest lies in a regulated state which will provide security, the fruits of industry, and other benefits. This means recognizing the existence of Laws of Nature—for example, that each person should give up the total liberty and equal right to all things that breeds war, and "be contented with so much liberty against other men, as he would allow other men against himself." The best state for securing such liberties, Hobbes went on to argue, is an absolute despotism, in which all members of society contract their rights and powers to a sovereign, whether king or parliament, who will then rule and protect them, uniting their many wills into one will.

Hobbes's idea that Natural Law would apply to people is of considerable importance to psychology. He said that there are regulations inherent in nature, existing apart from humanity's recognition of them, that govern everything from the planetary machine of the solar system to the biological machines of the animals, including humans. Hobbes's attitude however, is not fully scientific, for he says that we rationally consent to follow Natural Laws. Only in times of security must we follow them; they may be broken should government or other persons try to compel anyone to personal ruin. The planets cannot choose to obey or not obey Newton's laws of motion, and in this respect Hobbes's Natural Laws are not like the laws of physics. As time passes, other thinkers would make them more similar.

The Heart has its Reasons which the Reason does not Understand: Blaise Pascal (1623–1662)

If Descartes prefigures the confident rationalist of the Enlightenment, Pascal prefigures the anguished existentialist of recent times. For Descartes, doubt led to the triumphant certainty of reason; for Pascal, doubt led to worse doubt. Wrote Pascal: I am "engulfed in the infinite immensity of spaces whereof I know nothing and which know nothing of me, I am terrified. . . ." (Bronowski and Mazlish 1960). Pascal detested Descartes's excessive rationalism and derived solace and truth from his faith in God. For Pascal what is essential in humans is not natural reason, but will and the capacity for faith, that is, the heart. Pascal thus resembles earlier Christian skeptics such as Montaigne. But Pascal is Cartesian in the value he places on self-consciousness, as shown by his statement in the *Pensées:* "Man knows that he is wretched. He is wretched, then, because he is wretched; but he is great, because he knows it. . . . Man is only a reed, the frailest thing in nature; but he is a thinking reed." Pascal doubted a person's capacity to fathom nature or to understand self—humanity is wretched. Yet a human's unique self-consciousness lifts her or him above nature and the animals, offering salvation through faith in the Christian God. Pascal's anguish and need for faith echoes through all modern existentialists, not excepting atheists such as Sartre.

Pascal was also a scientist and mathematician who investigated the vacuum and helped found probability theory. As a mathematician he was a child prodigy. At nineteen he constructed the first mechanical calculators, some of which still exist. Although its purpose was humble—to help his father, a tax official, do calculations—its implication was profound. Pascal wrote: "The arithmetical machine produces effects which approach nearer to thought than all the actions of animals." (Bronowski and Mazlish 1960). Pascal was the first to sense that the human mind could be conceived as an information-processer capable of being mimicked by a machine, a concept central to contemporary cognitive psychology. In Pascal's time, and to someone with his sensibilities, the implication was frightening, for it meant that reason—which Descartes exempted from his mechanical system—could not be so exempted. Perhaps animals, wholly mechanical creatures according to Descartes, *do* reason. Pascal then declared that a human's free will, not reason, is what distinguishes humans from animals. It is the heart, not the brain, that makes a human being human.

Determinism Extended: Baruch Spinoza (1652–1677)

Spinoza was a thinker out of step with his own time. Born a Jew, but excommunicated for his disbelief in Yahweh, he articulated a philosophy that identified God with nature, and saw the state as merely a revocable social agreement. He was spurned by the people of his birth, denounced by Christians, and his works were suppressed even in the liberal state of Holland where he lived. In the Enlightenment he was admired for his independence but rejected for his pantheistic philosophy. Later, the romanitics venerated his apparent mysticism, while scientists saw in him a naturalist.

Spinoza's philosophy begins with metaphysics and ends with a radical reconstruction of human nature. Spinoza argued that God is essentially nature. Without the existing natural world, nothing would exist, so that God (nature) is the supporter and creator of all things. But God is not a separate being apart from nature; all things are a part of God without exception, and God is no more than the totality of the universe. Hence Spinoza was thought to be an atheist. Furthermore, nature is entirely deterministic. Spinoza argued that to understand anything means to unravel its efficient causes. Spinoza denied the existence of final causes, believing teleology to be a projection of humanity's feelings of purpose onto nature, applied only to events we cannot explain with efficient, that is, deterministic causes.

Spinoza extended his deterministic analysis to human nature. Mind is not something separate from body, but is produced by brain processes. Mind and body are one, but may be viewed from two aspects, as physiological brain processes or as mental events—thoughts. Spinoza did not deny that mind exists, but did see it as one aspect of a fundamentally material nature. Thus for Spinoza mental activity is as deterministic as bodily activity. Spinoza rejected Cartesian dualism, and so for him there is no problem of interaction. We feel we are free, but this is only an illusion. If we properly understood the causes of human behavior and thinking we would see we are not free. Just as no blame may be attached to the river that floods and destroys a town, so no blame can be attached to a multiple murderer. Society may act to control the river or the killer to prevent future devastation, but this is a pragmatic consideration rather than a moral one. Spinoza's account of responsibility thus calls for a psychological science to unravel the causes of human behavior, and bears a striking resemblance to B. F. Skinner's. Spinoza's account of memory, which says that ideas experienced together become mechanically linked, also resembles later conditioning theories which associate stimulus and response.

Spinoza, however, went on to describe an ethics of self-control that transcends materialistic determinism, and which to some degree conflicts with the rest of his thought. He argued that right action and thinking depend on the control of bodily emotions by reason. The wise person is one who follows the dictates of reason rather than the dictates of the momentary and conflicting passions arising from the body. Reason will lead one to act out of enlightened self-interest—helping others as one would want to be helped. Spinoza's ethics and his view of humanity are quite Stoic. The physical universe is beyond our control, but our passions are not. Thus wisdom is rational self-control, rather than a futile effort to control nature, or God. Spinoza also argued that states should allow freedom of thought, conscience, and speech, for each person should be free to order his or her mind as he or she sees fit. For all this, Spinoza was reviled even by the most advanced thinkers of his day.

Levels of Consciousness:
Gottfried Wilhelm Leibniz
(1646–1716)

Leibniz was a mathematician, logician, and metaphysician. He independently invented calculus, and dreamed of a formal conceptual calculus that would do for verbal reasoning what mathematics had done for the sciences. His metaphysics is extremely difficult. Briefly, he conceived of the universe as composed of an infinity of geometrical-point entities called *monads,* each of which is to some extent living and possesses some degree of consciousness. Animals and people are made up of monads that subserve a most conscious, and hence most dominant, monad. Thus, unlike Descartes, Leibniz ascribed souls to animals.

Leibniz's theory of monads led to a solution to the mind-body problem that became increasingly popular over the next two centuries. Descartes had said that mind and body interact. However, it was unclear how spirit could act on matter and vice versa, leading to a view called *occasionalism* in which God saw to it that when a bodily event occurred, so did a mental event and vice versa. This, too, has its difficulties, with God running around keeping mind and body coordinated. Leibniz proposed an answer which has since been called mind-body (or psychophysical) *parallelism.* Leibniz argued that God had created the universe (the infinitude of monads) such that there is a preestablished harmony between the monads. Leibniz used an analogy of two clocks. Imagine two identical and perfect clocks, both set to the same time and started at the same moment. From then on the clocks would always agree with, and mirror, one another, but they would not be causally connected. Each would run identical but parallel—not interacting—courses of development. Just so mind and body. Consciousness (mind) mirrors exactly what happens in the body, but only because of God's preestablished harmony, not because of a causal connection. In fact, Leibniz extended this scheme to the whole universe, holding the monads never interact but stay coordinated in their pictures of the universe because of God's perfect harmony. Although the metaphysical basis of psychophysical parallelism was dropped later, the doctrine itself caught on as physiological knowledge of the body and the growth of physics rendered both interactionism and occasionalism implausible.

Leibniz reintroduced final causes into philosophy. The material world is governed by efficient causes, as Spinoza argued; but since Leibniz believed in his immaterial monads, a second kind of causation was needed. Leibniz postulated that monads have a tendency to perfect themselves, to actualize their potentiality, a view that recalls Aristotle. In fact, since monads do not interact, the only way they can change (and so reflect changes in the universe) is through inner development. Thus monads are purposeful and develop toward an end: their own perfection. This development is natural and spontaneous; it is not caused by anything outside the monad. Again, with the metaphysics dropped the idea has been influential, especially in developmental psychology. Some developmental psychologists, notably Jean Piaget, believe child development to be a spontaneous, natural progression relatively unaffected by the environment. This is, of course, in contrast to empiricist views, which see the child as being extensively molded by the environment.

Also in contrast to empiricists, Leibniz upheld innate ideas. Like Descartes, Leibniz believed many ideas, such as God and mathematical truths, were impossible to derive from experience for they are too abstract. Such ideas must be innate. Leibniz expressed his conception by his famous statue metaphor. The mind at birth is likened to a block of marble. Marble is veined, and it may be that the veins outline the form of Hercules in the marble, for example. Certain activities are required to bring out the statue, but in a sense Hercules is "innate" in the marble. Similarly, an infant's innate dispositions to certain kinds of knowledge must be activated, either by experience or by the infant's own reflection on mental life.

Finally, we will consider Leibniz's account of perception, for here Leibniz laid the ground for both psychophysics and Wundt's founding psychology (McRae 1976). First, Leibniz distinguished *petite perception* from *perception. Petite per-*

ception is a stimulus event (to borrow a modern term) so weak it is not perceived. To use Leibniz's most usual metaphor, one does not hear the sound of a single drop of water hitting a beach; this is a *petite perception*. Yet a wave crashing on the beach is but thousands of drops hitting the beach, and this we do hear. Thus our perception of the wave's crash is made up of many *petite perceptions* each too small to be heard, but together making a conscious experience. This doctrine points the way to psychophysics, the systematic study of the quantitative relation between stimulus intensity and experience, which we will discuss in Chapter 6. Leibniz's account also implies the existence of the unconscious, or as Leibniz writes, "changes in the soul itself of which we are not conscious." As modified in the nineteenth century and adopted by Freud, the concept of the unconscious had momentous impact on psychology.

Leibniz also distinguished perception from *sensation*. A perception is a raw, confused idea, not really conscious, which animals, as well as humans, may possess. However, a person can refine and sharpen perceptions, and become reflectively aware of them in consciousness. They then become sensations.* This refining process is called *apperception*. Apperception also seems to be involved in uniting *petite perceptions* to become perceptions. This uniting process, stressed Leibniz, is not a process of mere aggregation. Perceptions, rather, are emergent properties coming from masses of *petite perceptions*. If we combine blue and yellow lights, for example, we do not experience separately blue and yellow but instead green, an emergent experience not present in the simpler constituent lights.

Attention is the major component of apperception for Leibniz, and he distinguished two types, passive and active. If you are absorbed in some activity, you may not notice another stimulus, such as a friend speaking to you, until that stimulus grows so strong that it automatically draws your attention. Here the shift in attention is passive, for the new stimulus captures attention. Attention may also be voluntary, as when you focus it on one person at a party to the exclusion of others. Sometimes Leibniz tied apperception closely to voluntary attention, for he saw apperception as an act of will. This is also how Wundt used the term apperception.

Memory is also involved in attention, for when we attend to something it must be fixed in the mind by memory. Leibniz cites a simple example used in twentieth-century research on echoic memory and attention. If a friend speaks to you while you are otherwise absorbed, it sometimes happens that your first response is "What?" but that you can then answer your friend's question. This shows that the question was at first unattended, but somehow stored in memory so you could attend to it subsequently; similarly, once your attention is caught, you can usually remember having heard a noise earlier, if only dimly.

We will later see all these ideas refined and elaborated in Wundt's theory of apperception.

CONCLUSION: THE SEVENTEENTH CENTURY— SEEDS OF CHANGE

The seventeenth century laid the foundations for the Enlightenment of the eighteenth. The Newtonian-Cartesian mechanical universe rationalized God, world, and

---

*Leibniz's usage is roughly the opposite of modern psychological usage. Today, a sensation refers to a sensory receptor process, while a perception is a central brain or mental event.

humankind. It had no room for miracles, oracles, visions, and metaphysical dogmatism. It proposed theories of humanity, society, and ethics that discounted the heavenly nature of humans but held out hope of happiness here on earth. In the seventeenth century Locke abandoned metaphysics for psychology, and Leibniz proposed ideas basic to later scientific psychology. In the eighteenth century these seeds would come to fruition as science and reason replaced religion as the chief intellectual institution of modern society. Human beings would be proclaimed soulless machines, and societies would be overthrown in the name of material happiness.

By 1700 the medieval world order was finished. Three dates seem especially portentous. In 1686 a popular French writer, Fontenelle, brought science to the literate public of France, dazzling his readers. Although humans were reduced to a mechanical speck in a mechanical universe, knowing this secret was uplifting. Science and mathematics became all the rage. In 1687 Newton's *Principia Mathematica Philosophiae Naturalis* appeared, the triumph of the mathematical view of the world-machine. Soon Natural Law would be extended to human beings and governments with revolutionary impact. In 1688 came England's Glorious Revolution, the peaceful deposition of James II and the installation of William of Orange. In this revolution was born the modern liberal state: Kings are not divinely appointed agents whose will is absolute law. They are instruments of the people, replaceable at the people's will. The revolution was philosophically justified by John Locke in terms that were similar to the American Declaration of Independence ninety years later. Reason had prevailed over tradition and faith.

The triumph of reason in the Age of Reason was at hand. Yet, a different undercurrent lurked just below the surface. The voyages of discovery had found strange primitive cultures. To Hobbes and Locke these wild men represented humanity in an uncivilized and unhappy state of Nature. Locke wrote in his *Second Treatise on Government:* "In the beginning all the world was America." Yet were the Indians unhappy? They lived close to nature, unfettered by artifice, living according to natural instinct. Perhaps happiness lies in giving up reason, with its abstract, artificial ways, and returning to the instinct of the happy savage. A reaction against reason was about to set in. The poet Chalieu wrote in 1708 that reason is an "inexhaustible source of errors, poison that corrupts the natural feelings." Jean Rousseau wrote that reason "feeds our mad pride . . . continually masking us from ourselves." Asked Rousseau: "Which is the least barbarous . . . reason which leads you astray, or instinct which guides [the Indian] truly?" Chalieu said he came "to destroy the altars which have been raised to thee [Reason]." Here the seed is sown for the Romantic Rebellion against reason and for the concept of the Noble Savage. The tension between the individual and society, so poignantly felt by Sigmund Freud, was increasing as reason demanded more and more of men and women.

BIBLIOGRAPHY

The seventeenth century is recognized by historians as critical in Western history, because it was during this century that the modern world of science and nations was created. It was a period of incredible ferment in philosophy, political thought, and religion. The most distinguished historian of the century is Christopher Hill, who aptly titles his text on the seventeenth century *The century of revolution: 1603–1714* (New York: Norton, 1966). As a Marxist, Hill has been concerned to show how deeply seventeenth-century thinkers challenged the shibboleths of their time. His main work along this line is *The world turned upside down: Radical ideas during the English revolution* (Harmondsworth, England: Pelican, 1972); whether or not one agrees with Hill's politics (I don't), his works amply repay reading, casting new and revealing light on our attempts to understand ourselves. Paul Hazard, *The European mind 1680–1715* (New York: New American Library, 1963) suggested that Europe experienced a "general crisis" during the seventeenth century, and his thesis has generated controversy ever since he proposed it in 1935. Theodore K. Rabb, *The struggle for stability in early modern Europe* (New York: Oxford, 1975) updates Hazard's thesis; and G. Parker and L. M. Smith, eds., *The general crisis of the seventeenth century* (London: Routledge & Kegan Paul, 1978) provide a symposium on the thesis. Finally, Basil Willey, *The seventeenth century background* (Garden City, New York: Doubleday, 1953) provides a general survey of society and politics in the century.

The most important event of the seventeenth century was, of course, the scientific revolution. Here are some general histories: Vern Bullough, ed., *The scientific revolution* (New York: Holt, Rinehart, & Winston, 1970); Herbert Butterfield (1965), the standard history; I. Bernard Cohen, *The Newtonian Revolution* (Cambridge, England: Cambridge University Press, 1980); A Rupert Hall, *The scientific revolution 1500–1800: The formation of the modern scientific attitude,* 2d ed. (Boston: Beacon Press, 1962), another standard history; Hugh Kearney, *Science and change 1500–1700* (New York: McGraw-Hill, 1971), a recent book incorporating some of the occult vs. reason debate in the newest history of science; and Richard S. Westfall, *The construction of modern science: Mechanisms and mechanics* (Cambridge, England: Cambridge University Press, 1971).

Scientists have always fancied that science is a self-contained, rational enterprise, relatively free from philosophical and social influence. As we saw in Chapter 1, this assumption has come under sharp questioning, and has set off historical debates on the roots of the scientific revolution. Burtt (1954) was the first to challenge science's philosophical purity, and is, in consequence, much cited today. Richard Westfall, "Newton and the fudge factor," *Science* (1973, *179:* 751–758), shows how Newton's psychological commitment to his theory led him to bend data to suit it; see also Westfall's biography of Newton, *Never at rest* (Cambridge, England: Cambridge University Press, 1980). The most violent debates among historians of science have been over the degree to which the scientific revolution was influenced by the deep occultism of the Renaissance and seventeenth century. The claim that science was indebted to the occult is often known as "the Yates thesis" after historian Francis Yates—for example, her chapter on "The hermetic tradition in Renaissance science" in C. S. Singleton, ed., *Art, science, and history in the Renaissance* (Baltimore: Johns Hopkins University Press, 1968). A good collection favoring the occult connections of science is M. L. Righini Bonelli and W. R. Shea, eds., *Reason, experiment, and mysticism in the scientific revolution* (New York: Science History Publications, 1975). The sides of reason and occult influence are respectively upheld in a debate between Mary Hesse, "Reasons and evolutions in the history of science," and P. M. Rattansi, "Some evaluations of reason in sixteenth- and seventeenth-century natural philosophy," both in M. Teich and R. Young, eds., *Changing perspectives in the history of science* (London: Heinemann, 1973). The most recent symposium on the topic is B. Vickers, ed., *Occult and scientific mentalities in the Renaissance* (New York: Cambridge University Press, 1984); see also G. A. J. Rogers, "The basis of belief: Philosphy, science, and religion in seventeenth century England," *History of European Ideas* (1985, *6:* 19–39). For a case study on the influence of occult ideas on one scientist see Betty Jo Teeter Dobbs, *The foundations of Newton's alchemy* (Cambridge, England: Cambridge University Press, 1983).

For seventeenth-century philosophy see Bronowski and Mazlish (1963); and, with special reference to France, Edward John Kearns, *Ideas in seventeenth century France* (Manchester, England: Manchester University Press, 1983). For a comparative study of Descartes's and Locke's psychologies, see David E. Leary, "The intentions and heritage of Descartes and Locke: Toward a recognition of the moral basis of modern psychology," *Journal of General Psychology* (1980, *102:* 283–310). For the individual philosophers see the following.

Descartes. René Descartes, *The philosophical works of Descartes,* 2 vols. (Cambridge, England: Cambridge University Press, 1972); *Descartes: His moral philosophy and psychology* (New York: New York University Press, 1978); Richard B. Carter, *Descartes' medical philosophy: The organic solution to the mind-body problem* (Baltimore: Johns Hopkins University Press, 1983); Desmond M. Clarke, *Descartes' philosophy of science* (University Park: The Pennsylvania State University Press, 1984); Bernard Williams, *Descartes: The project of pure inquiry* (Harmondsworth, England: Pelican, 1978).

Locke. Locke (1975); *The Locke reader,* J. W. Yolton, compiler (Cambridge, England: Cambridge University Press, 1977); I. C. Tipton, ed., *Locke on human understanding* (Oxford: Oxford University Press, 1977); John Yolton, *Locke and the compass of human understanding* (Cambridge, England: Cambridge University Press, 1970). The intimate connection between the thinking of Locke and Newton is detailed in G. A. J. Rogers, "The system of Locke and Newton," in Z. Bechler, ed., *Contemporary Newtonian research* (Dordrecht, Holland: D. Reidel, 1982).

Hobbes. Hobbes (1962).

Pascal. Blaise Pascal, *Pensées* (New York: Washington Square Press, 1965).

Spinoza. Baruch Spinoza, *The works of Spinoza,* 2 vols. (New York: Dover Books, 1955); Stuart Hampshire, *Spinoza* (Harmondsworth, England: Pelican, 1962).

Leibniz. G. W. Leibniz, *Leibniz: Selections* (New York: Scribner's, 1951); Robert D. Brandom, "Leibniz and degrees of perception," *Journal of the History of Philosophy* (1981, *19:* 447–479); McRae (1976).

REFERENCES

Bronowski, J. and Mazlish, B. (1960) *The western intellectual tradition.* New York: Harper & Row.

Burtt, E. A. (1954) *The metaphysical foundations of modern science.* Garden City, New York: Doubleday.

Butterfield, H. (1965) *The origins of modern science 1300–1800.* New York: The Free Press.

Hazard, P. (1963) *The European mind 1680–1715.* New York: New American Library.

Hobbes, T. *(1962) Leviathan.* New York: Collier Books.

Kuhn, T. (1976) Mathematical vs. experimental traditions in the development of physical science. *The Journal of Interdisciplinary History 7:* 1–31.

Locke, J. (1975) *An essay concerning human understanding* (Variorum edition). Peter Nidditch, ed. Oxford: Clarendon Press.

McRae, R. (1976) *Leibniz: Perception, apperception, and thought.* Toronto: University of Toronto Press.

Rattansi, R. (1972) The social interpretation of science in the seventeenth century. In P. Mathias (ed.) *Science and Society 1600–1900.* Cambridge: Cambridge University Press.

Rossi, P. (1975) Hermeticism, rationality, and the scientific revolution. In M. Bonelli and W. Shea, eds., *Reason, experiment and mysticism in the scientific revolution.* New York: Science History Publications.

Westfall, R. (1975) The role of alchemy in Newton's career. In M. Bonelli and W. Shea, eds. *Reason, experiment and mysticism in the scientific revolution.* New York: Science History Publications.

CHAPTER 5

Reason and Reaction

The Eighteenth-Century Enlightenment

THE SKEPTICAL CRISIS
    Mind over Matter: Bishop George Berkeley (1685–1753)
    Habit over Reason: David Hume (1711–1776)
    The Reassertion of Common Sense: The Scottish School
    The Reassertion of Metaphysics: Immanuel Kant
    (1724–1804)
PHILOSOPHY, SCIENCE, AND HUMAN NATURE
    British Associationism and Economics
    French Naturalism
    The Enlightenment in Germany
THE COUNTER-ENLIGHTENMENT
    The Criterion and Rule of Truth Is to Have Made It:
    Giambattista Vico (1668–1704)
    We Live in a World We Ourselves Create:
    Johann Gottfried Herder (1744–1803)
    Nature vs. Civilization: Jean-Jacques Rousseau
    (1712–1778)
CONCLUSION: REASON AND ITS DISCONTENTS

The seeds of the Enlightenment were planted in the seventeenth century. The most important sources were Newton and Locke. Newton was the hero of the new age. He showed that restrained empirical enquiry, shorn of unprofitable speculation, could work wonders in understanding and controlling nature. Locke, who by his own statement was Newton's "under laborer," brought the empirical approach to the human mind, considering it without speculation and with due regard for facts. In his efforts Locke had many followers who wanted to be Newtons of the mind. Psychology replaced metaphysics as the central philosophical concern of the eighteenth century, with questions about the mind's power to know replacing speculation about ultimate truth.

Newton and Locke also sowed the seeds of revolution. Newton showed that if Nature could be understood, we could hope to bend it to our will, as Bacon had foreseen. In denying innate ideas, and therefore innate depravity, Locke asserted that people may be educated and perfected and, consequently, society may be enlightened and perfected. So the Scientific Revolution, and what we may call Locke's psychological revolution, implied social and political revolution.

Locke himself participated in the first and mildest revolution, the Glorious Revolution of 1688, and partly laid the philosophic foundation for the second bloody, but not vicious revolution—the American Revolution of 1776. The Enlightenment may be said to have ended with the third, bloody, vicious, and finally unsuccessful revolution, the French Revolution of 1789.

THE SKEPTICAL CRISIS

As the philosophers of the eighteenth century extended scientific reason to understanding the human mind, they ran into the same problem that had bedeviled the naturalistic philosophers of the Middle Ages, Ockham and Autrecourt. If we rely only on the evidence of the senses and on human logic, rejecting or at least setting aside the claims of religious faith, is it possible to justify human knowledge at all? The great irony of the scientific revolution is that it began as a triumph of unaided human reason, but ended by doubting the very possibility of human knowledge. Newton's physics proclaimed the victory of reason over nature, his physics seeming to penetrate the very heart of nature. Yet in Newton's wake came philosopher-psychologists who examined the human mind and human nature in the light of Newtonian reason, and concluded that no human opinion was free from the possibility of error, and that the very existence of the physical world was open to doubt. These were the conclusions of the British philosophers David Hume and George Berkeley, and they were, unsurprisingly, stoutly resisted by philosophers loath to give up the possibility of secure human knowledge. Against the skepticism of Hume the Scottish followers of Thomas Reid asserted common-sense faith in human cognition and religious faith in God, who made men and women so that they might know God's word. In Germany Immanuel Kant responded to Hume's skepticism by asserting the old claim of metaphysics to be science's true foundation, restoring faith in Newtonian science as the final description of natural truth.

Mind over Matter: Bishop George Berkeley (1685–1753)

Like Locke and Descartes, Berkeley as a philosopher wanted to refute skepticism, while as a deeply religious man he wanted to refute the Newtonian materialism that imperiled faith in God. He admired Locke deeply, and felt Locke had taken the correct road toward both knowledge and religion. However, he took Locke to say that our knowledge is about ideas ultimately rooted in sensation. Berkeley, interpreting and agreeing with Locke that ideas are mental objects, not acts, saw an opening for skepticism. Locke believed in the existence of "real" objects that exist beyond our perception and which have unobservable properties. But the skeptic may ask, if *ideas* are the objects of our knowledge, if in fact what we perceive are ideas of objects, how can we be sure our ideas truly correspond to the "real" material objects? In Berkeley's view, Locke was helpless to refute the skeptic.

Berkeley saw the problem to be Locke's belief in matter as something apart from perception. For example, as I am sitting here writing, I know my pen exists because I sense it. But when I lay it down and leave the room, what grounds have I for asserting that it still exists? All I can say is that if I went back I would see it, or if someone else looks for it, he or she will see it. Ultimately then, I know the pen exists only because I see it. And in fact, said Berkeley, the pen exists when it is perceived. Berkeley's famous motto is "Esse est percipi": To exist is to be perceived. Berkeley thus refuted skepticism by an astoundingly simple assertion. As Locke said, all we know are our ideas, but Berkeley adds that there is no permanent material reality apart from our perceptions. The question of how ideas correspond to "real objects" does not arise if there are no "real objects" at all. Furthermore, Berkeley's philosophy refutes atheism, for God may now be introduced as the omniscient perceiver who sees all things and so continues their existence.

The arguments Berkeley adduced to support his immaterialism or idealism (the view that there is no matter and that only ideas are real) are complex and controversial. What is psychologically important about Berkeley is that as part of his arguments he gave a persuasive empiricist account of perception—especially vision—that was widely accepted until the twentieth century.

Berkeley focused on the problem of distance perception. We see the world in three dimensions, yet the retinal image—the immediate (or "proper") object of vision—is only two-dimensional, lacking depth. So, for example, as a friend walks away from you, you see him or her getting farther and farther away, but if we examine your retinal image, we would find only that the image of the friend gets smaller and smaller. Of course, you may observe that indeed your friend looks smaller, but your subjective experience is that he or she is getting farther away. So the problem arises, how does one perceive three dimensions when all one can see (on the retina) are two dimensions?

Berkeley's answer was that other sensations are available which do give cues about distance. For example, as an object approaches, you move your eyes close together as you follow it; as it recedes, you move them apart. Thus there is a regular association between an object's distance, and the degree to which you cross your eyes to focus on it. (Berkeley and others found many additional distance cues.) So far, Berkeley's analysis of how we see depth is uncontroversial, and is the foundation of modern analyses. However, Berkeley goes on to make the empiricist claim that the association must be *learned*. The infant would not know that a person was receding as the person walked away; the infant would simply see the figure shrink. Berkeley's claim that depth perception must be learned was countered later by Immanuel Kant, who asserted depth perception to be innate. Although the controversy between the nativist and empiricist views continued for decades, it was not until the 1960s that experiments with infants showed Kant to be reasonably correct (Bower 1974).

The real force of Berkeley's argument becomes clear if we generalize the problem to all visual experience. You hold a blue book at right angles to your eyes. What do you see? The naive answer is to say a book, yet as Berkeley would argue, all you really see is a rectangular patch of blue, the retinal image. You rotate the book to a 45-degree angle. What do you see now? Again, you want to say "a book," and in fact you would still believe the book to be a rectangle. But Berkeley would say that what you are really seeing is a blue patch which now has the shape of a truncated pyramid. Berkeley's argument is that all anyone ever sees is a collection of colored patches on one's retina. One must *learn* to "see" them as books, people, cats, cars, and so on. One must *learn* to believe one is still seeing a rectangular book when in fact one is seeing a truncated-pyramid blue patch.

Berkeley's analysis of vision supports his idealism. One's sensory and ideational world is just a collection of sensations, and one believes in the permanence of objects only because certain collections of sensations are regularly associated. Belief in matter is therefore a learned inference only, for matter is not directly perceived. For Berkeley, if something, even matter, cannot be directly perceived it is a metaphysical fiction to be eliminated.

Two important psychological systems branch off from Berkeley's psychological analysis of vision and his philosophy. Berkeley constantly appeals to introspection as evidence for his conclusions and implies that we should try to describe conscious experience without making inferences. That is, psychology should strive to describe only color-patches and shapes, the true objects of perception. This is later the approach of E. B. Titchener's structuralism. He taught his subjects to report their experiences only as sets of sensations, the basic Berkeleyan building blocks of experience. Titchener also tried to show how we learn to associate stimuli together into complex ideas, such as a book or a person, in line with Berkeley's associative psychology. Berkeley thus set Titchener's empirical problems.

The second problem, the radical behaviorism of B. F. Skinner, appears at first wholly unrelated to Berkeley, and it is certainly hostile to structuralism. Yet Berkeley asserted the fundamental tenet of the positivism that underlies radical behaviorism: If something cannot be perceived, it is a metaphysical relic to be expunged from science. Berkeley said that substance is only inferred from experience, and so is unreal. Skinner says that mind is likewise an inference from experience, but that we never perceive mind itself. It, too, is a metaphysical, unobservable entity to be expunged from science. Of course, Skinner is a materialist, not an idealist. The fundamental similarity between Berkeley and Skinner is in restricting inquiry to that which is immediately perceived.

Habit over Reason: David Hume (1711–1776)

It is evident that all the sciences have a relation, greater or less, to human nature. . . . To explain the principles of human nature, we in effect propose a complete system of the sciences, built on a foundation almost entirely new, and the only one upon which they can stand with any security . . . and the only solid foundation we can give to this science itself must be laid on experience and observation.

So Hume wrote in his *Treatise of Human Nature.* Locke began the attempt to replace metaphysics with psychology as the foundation for the other sciences, and Hume carried out the task in a rigorously Newtonian manner. Hume analyzed human nature as he found it in his own introspection and in the behavior of others. As with Locke, Hume's intention was to fix the limits of human knowledge, to sort out the knowable from the unknowable so that inquiry could be profitably fixed on the former. Precisely because science is a human enterprise, psychology, not speculative metaphysics, is the foundation for all science.

Hume began his inquiry into human nature by categorizing the contents of our minds somewhat as Locke had. Locke had spoken of the contents of our minds as "ideas" for which Hume, following the Scottish moral philosopher Francis Hutcheson (1694–1746), substituted "perceptions." Perceptions are then divided into two types, *impressions* and *ideas.* Impressions are essentially what we today call *sensations,* and ideas were for Hume less vivid copies of impressions. Thus you have an immediate impression of the book before you, an impression you may recall later on as an idea, a pale copy of the actual experience. Both impressions and ideas come either through sensation of external objects, or through reflection, by which Hume meant our emotional experiences (or what Hume also called the *passions*). Passions are of two sorts: the violent passions, such as love and hate and the other emotions we ordinarily call passions. However, Hume also included *calm passions,* such as aesthetic and moral feelings. Figure 5-1 summarizes Hume's categories; remember, however, that the distinctions under *impressions* apply also to *ideas.*

Finally, Hume distinguished *simple* and *complex* perceptions. An impression is a single, unanalyzable sensation, such as a blue spot of ink. Most impressions are complex, since our senses are usually exposed to many simple sensations at once. Simple ideas are copies of simple impressions, and complex ideas are aggregates of simple ideas. This means that complex ideas may not exactly correspond to some

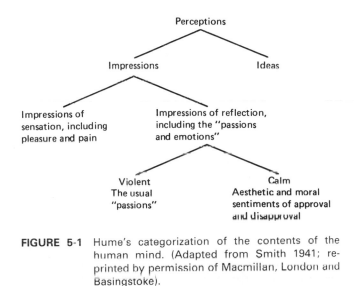

FIGURE 5-1 Hume's categorization of the contents of the human mind. (Adapted from Smith 1941; reprinted by permission of Macmillan, London and Basingstoke).

complex impression. So, you may imagine a unicorn, which of course you have never seen. However, complex ideas may always be broken down into simple ideas which are copies of simple impressions. So, your complex idea of a unicorn simply combines the impression or idea of a horse with the impression or idea of a horn, both of which you have experienced. Before considering how complex perceptions are formed, two important conclusions may already be drawn from Hume's category of mental content. First, Hume gave priority to impressions over ideas. Impressions bring us directly in touch with reality by perception, while ideas may be false, corresponding to nothing (such as the unicorn). The truth is to be determined by tracing ideas to impressions, and whatever ideas are found to have no empirical content, such as the ideas of metaphysics and theology, are to be expunged. Thus Hume asserted a positivism—the claim that all meaningful ideas must be reducible to something observable. The second important conclusion is that Hume assigned priority to simple perceptions over complex ones. All complex perceptions are built up from our experiences of simple ones and may be completely analyzed into simple components. Thus Hume was a psychological atomist, holding that complex ideas are built up out of simple sensations.

When we turn to how complex perceptions are built up out of elementary ones, we come to what Hume himself thought was his central contribution to the science of human nature: his doctrine of the association of ideas. The concept of association was not new with Hume. We find it in Hobbes, Spinoza, and Berkeley; the phrase "association of ideas" was coined by Locke. However, they had used it in only a limited way—Locke, for example, seeing in association an obstacle to clear thinking and sound education. What Hume prized was his use of association to inquire into fundamental philosophical and psychological questions. It was the chief theoretical tool of his new science.

Hume wrote in his essay *An Inquiry Concerning Human Understanding* (Hume 1962), "To me there appear to be only three principles of connection among ideas, namely, *Resemblance, Contiguity* in time or place, and *Cause* [and] *Effect.*" In his *Abstract of a Treatise of Human Nature* (Hume 1962), Hume exemplified each: " 'resemblance'—a [portrait] naturally makes us think of the man it was drawn for; contiguity—when St. Denis is mentioned, the idea of Paris naturally occurs; 'causation'—when we think of the son we are likely to carry our attention to the father . . . [T]hese are the only links that bind the parts of the universe together or connect us with any person or object exterior to ourselves. . . ." At least, said Hume, "so far as regards the mind."

The influence of Newton is strong here. Gravity is the attractive force that binds the atomic parts of the universe together. For Hume association "is a kind of *attraction* which in the mental world will be found to have as extraordinary effects as in the natural" (Hume 1817), and the laws of association "are really *to us* the cement of the universe" as experienced. Thus for Hume complex human experience (complex ideas) is at root simple ideas (derived from impressions) united together by the principle of association. As Newton did with gravity, Hume thus made association into an ultimate principle that could not be reduced further.

Hume then proceeded to investigate human knowledge in light of these three (soon to be two) laws. Cause and effect is the most important law, underlying most everyday reasoning. You will lift your arm; it rises. You knock one billiard ball into another; the second one moves. You turn off a light switch; the light goes out. Moreover, cause and effect even lies at root of the inference that, contrary to Berkeley, a material world exists; for one assumes the world acts on the senses so as to cause one to perceive it. However, whence comes our knowledge of causation? Causes are never directly perceived. Rather we perceive a regular conjoining of two events: the feeling of intention with the subsequent movement of the hand; the flipping of the switch with the subsequent extinguishing of the light; the motion of one ball with the subsequent motion of the second; the opening of the eyes with the appearance of things. Furthermore, no rational argument can be produced to prove causation. Hume argued that belief in causes is learned through experience. As a child experiences many regular conjunctions of events, a "propensity" of the child's mind leads to the firm conviction that the first event caused the second. This propensity also brings along a feeling of necessity. Causation is not simply correlation for Hume, it is a *feeling* of necessity between two events. This means, of course, that cause-and-effect is not a basic principle of association, since it is reducible to contiguity plus the feeling of necessity.

Hume generalized his argument to all generalizations. When one claims "All swans are white," it is on the basis of experiencing a number of swans, all of which were white; so one assumes that future swans in one's experience will also be white and one therefore draws the conclusion. It is quite like assuming—based on past experiences—the light will go out when one flips the switch. In neither case, however, can the generalizations be given a rational justification, for they are based on experience, not on reason. No principle of reason underlies empirical generalizations. But we do make them and Hume wanted to explain how we do so, in order to have a complete theory of human nature.

The principle Hume employed is the principle of *custom* or *habit*. In *Inquiry* (Hume 1962) Hume wrote: "For whenever the repetition of any particular act or operation produces a propensity to renew the same act or operation without being impelled by any reasoning or process of the understanding, we always say that this propensity is the effect of *custom*. . . . All inferences from experience . . . are effects of custom [habit], not of reasoning."

It was, and is, frequently assumed by Hume's readers that by reducing causation and inductive generalization to habit he is denying their validity, and that he must have been a total skeptic, surprised each morning to find that the sun had risen. This is wrong (Smith 1941). Hume was only trying to find out *how* we reach causal and inductive conclusions; he was not concerned with validity. He discovered that reason is not involved; but he did not therefore have to deny the validity of causation and induction. In fact, Hume wrote (1962), "as this operation from the mind, by which we infer effects from causes, and *vice versa* is so essential to the subsistence of all human creatures, it is not probable that it could be trusted to the fallacious deductions of our reason, which is slow . . . appears not, in any degree, during . . . infancy, and, at best, is . . . extremely liable to error and mistake." Further, the "wisdom of nature" has implanted in us this "instinct or mechanical tendency" that is "infallible in its operation" and appears at birth. Thus the ability to form general conclusions, or habits, is founded on association, on our propensity to generalize from limited instances, and on our propensity to feel causes necessarily linked to effects. This ability to generalize is innate, "infallible," and of its operations we are "ignorant." Habit is a surer guide to the world than reason.

In support of this Hume noted that the same generalizing tendency is present in animals, whose practical knowledge of the world is nearly faultless, yet who do not possess reason. Animals learn habits, and according to Hume (1962) "any theory by which we explain the operations of the understanding . . . in man will acquire additional authority if we find the same theory is requisite to explain the same phenomenon in other animals.'' Other philosophers had stressed man's unique-ness, but Hume here stressed man's similarity to animals, implying the value of a comparative approach to human and animal mind.

As a consequence of his views, Hume made a statement that seems startling coming from a philosopher in the Age of Reason. He writes in *A Treatise of Human Nature:* ''Reason is, and ought only to be the slave of the passions, and can never pretend to any other office than to serve and obey them.'' This is quite natural, given Hume's position. Reason is helpless to know reality, it must serve experience and the instinct for generalization, which reflect the world as it is. For Hume, morality is a matter of feeling (passion). We approve and disapprove the actions of ourselves and others according to how we feel about them and reason must thus serve our moral sentiments.

Hume thus resisted skepticism by relying on human nature. As he and others pointed out, the most extreme skeptic never behaves according to his beliefs; he always assumes there will be a tomorrow. Hume wrote in his *Inquiry* (1962): ''[N]o durable good can ever result from *excessive* skepticism,'' nor can it hope that ''its influence will be beneficial to society.'' Hume preferred a moderate skepticism, which accepts the limits of reason, properly values animal nature, and knows that general conclusions may be false (after all, there *are* black swans). Such a skep-ticism is practical (for it does not doubt the accumulated wisdom of experience) and useful (for it preaches toleration and provides a science of human nature for the proper founding of the other sciences).

In Hume's work we see the first glimmerings of the psychology of adaptation. At bottom, human knowledge is habit, whether mental as with Hume, or behav-ioral, as with the behaviorists. Hume stressed the practical knowledge of the every-day world that lets us adapt to our environment, as would post-Darwinian American and British psychologists. Hume appealed to human continuity with animals, as would psychologists after Darwin, especially the behaviorists. Hume viewed feel-ing—the passions—as an essential part of human nature. A person is not pure rational soul locked in a material, passionate body. So, too, would Freud and the behaviorists stress the emotional, or motivational, side of humans. Finally, in preferring one theory to another because of its social and practical utility, Hume also anticipated those American psychologists for whom one defect of structuralism was its avowed practical inutility.

Although Hume's philosophy was not widely read (his history of England was), he roused two important responses to his apparent radical skepticism. One response became the common-sense psychology of American colleges; the other was the critical philosophy of Immanuel Kant.

The Reassertion of Common Sense: The Scottish School

Although Hume endorsed only a limited skepticism, many who read him thought he was a radical skeptic—and a hypocrite to boot—since he did not live as a skeptic. Hume himself, along with Adam Smith, the economist, was a Scot, and it was some of his fellow Scots who reacted most strongly to his apparent skepticism. These philosophers asserted the claims of the common person against the abstruse speculations of philosophy. ''I despise philosophy, and renounce its guidance—let my soul dwell with Common Sense,'' wrote Thomas Reid, the founder and best philosopher of the movement. In addition to Reid (1710–1796), other members of the Scottish School were James Beattie (1735–1803), popularizer and polemicist against Hume, and Reid's student, Dugald Stewart (1753–1828).

As we have seen, Locke's "Way of Ideas" is subject to two interpretations, as act or content. Reid found the latter view in both Locke and Hume, and traced it to Descartes. According to Reid, Locke claimed there were four elements to any perceptual act: the perceiver, the act of perception, the idea that is the immediate object of perception, and the real object the idea represents. Reid claimed that Hume had simply worked out the skepticism inherent in Locke's account, driving his skeptical wedge between object and idea.

Reid found Hume's conclusion offensive to common sense, as simply too absurd to be believed. We all have secure knowledge of our world and never become skeptical unless prodded by abstruse philosophy. Reid adopted common-sense beliefs as his philosophy. He explicated common sense by an analysis of the ordinary language that embodies it. This approach is similar to that of modern ordinary-language philosophy. For our purposes, two points of Reid's common-sense philosophy are important.

First, Reid repudiated the way of ideas, or as he called it, idealism, and supported common-sense realism, arguing that perceived objects are real. He maintained that there are only three elements in perception: the perceiver, the act of perception, and the real object. Our perceptual acts made direct contact with objects, not with just their representative ideas. We know the world in a direct, unmediated way, consistent with what each of us believes common sensically. Reid formulated the *act psychology* version of Lock's "idea." In the nineteenth century act psychology was the chief European rival to Wundt's and Titchener's psychology of content. Reid stated the fundamental tenet of act psychology, that perceptions imply something seen and known directly: "I cannot see, without seeing something." The founder of act psychology, Franz Brentano, would call this principle *intentionality.*

Reid also anticipated two related ideas that grew out of act psychology and are later found in the Gestalt movement. First, Reid said, experience is not a compound of simple sensations. Our primary experience is of complex impressions, to use Hume's term. Reid acknowledged that one can analyze complex impressions into simple ones, but denied that the complex ideas are formed by learned associations. As the Gestalt psychologists would say, a triangle is composed of three lines, but we always experience it as an organized whole—the triangle. Reid derived from this observation the conclusion that perception is always meaningful. Concepts are mental symbols that stand for something real. Perception is thus like language. As believed the medievals, Reid said we get knowledge by reading the "book of the world," which tells us the meaning of reality as surely as reading a book tells us its meaning. Complex experience cannot be reduced to atomic sensations without robbing it of something vital—its meaning.

The second general point central to Reid's philosophy, and it will also be found in Gestalt psychology, is his nativism. According to Reid, we are naturally endowed with certain innate faculties and principles of mind which allow us to know the world accurately and which furnish us with essential moral truths as well. Reid wrote: "Such original and natural judgments are, therefore, a part of that furniture which Nature had given to the human understanding. They are the inspiration of the Almighty . . . they serve to direct us in the common affairs of life, where our reasoning faculty would leave us in the dark . . . and all the discoveries of reason are grounded upon them. They make up what is called *the common sense of mankind.* . . . When a man suffers himself to be reasoned out of the principles of common sense, by metaphysical arguments, we may call this *metaphysical lunacy.* . . .'' (Reid 1975). Thus knowledge of the world is secure because of our innate constitution which delivers it. We are so constructed as to know. Reid's claims for the existence of innate mental faculties sometimes cause his school to be called faculty psychology; but they clearly did not invent the concept, they only popularized it.

What Reid said really only restated what Hume actually argued, and Hume never took Reid seriously. We have seen how Hume, too, subordinated reason to innate powers of association and propensities to generalize. Reid exceeded Hume in the number of principles he believed are built into the human constitution, including such moral "first principles" as the worship of God.

The root difference between them was religious. A curious aspect of the nativism-empiricism debates of the eighteenth century often escapes the modern eye. We today assume that native constitution is the arbitrary product of natural selection. Our ability to see depth is basically a genetic accident based on a favorable mutation in some early creature. However, most philosophers before Darwin believed in God, and assumed that since God made human beings, whatever ideas or principles he implanted must be *true,* unless God is a deceiver. Thus, Locke, staunch opponent of innate truths, never used the best counter-claim to so-called innate principles—namely, to show that they may not be true—for Locke assumed that whatever God did implant must be true. Hume, however, was an agnostic (if not an atheist) and his moderate skepticism was an inevitable result. Our faculties, not being God-given, may err. Reid, however, avoided any skepticism whatsoever by dogmatically asserting that the Almighty implanted in us first principles, necessarily valid because of their source. Thomas Reid was a clergyman—perhaps a clergyman first and a philosopher second.

We may ask if he was a psychologist. Reid, like Hume, wanted a science of human nature conducted along Newtonian lines. However, his extensive nativism coupled to his claim that the God-given first principles cannot be revised, puts his system outside psychology as a science. The hypotheses of any science must be open to proof, test, and revision. They cannot be enshrined as God's immutable truth. A similar criticism may be directed at Hume. By replacing metaphysics with psychology, he made psychology into a metaphysics, a set of necessary principles underlying the other sciences. Again, there could be no revision; Hume opened no paths for scientific investigation. Both Reid and Hume elevated psychology to a central place among human concerns; both enunciated general principles and embodied certain attitudes that shaped psychology later; but neither was really a psychologist. Both used psychology to pursue philosophy, their first concern.

Among the Scots, a step toward psychology was taken by Reid's student, Dugald Stewart. Stewart was more reconciled to Hume than was Reid, abandoning the term *common sense* and using association extensively. His basic work, *Philosophy of the Human Mind* (1792), reads like an introductory psychology text based on everyday experience instead of laboratory experiments. There are sections on attention, association (learning), memory, imagination, and dreaming. Stewart wrote charmingly about magicians, jugglers, and acrobats to illustrate his points. His discussions of attention and memory have a contemporary air about them, with Stewart making some distinctions found in modern information-processing psychology, citing everyday experiences to support them. Stewart followed Reid in dissecting the mind into component faculties, each of which is assigned its role in mental life and knowledge. Stewart spent sixty-two pages showing the practical value of the study of psychology.

In all, Stewart's work is engaging and attractive. Through Stewart especially, Scottish philosophy became quite influential in some places. It was especially important in America. Some of America's earliest college founders were adherents of the Scottish School, as were some important college presidents in the nineteenth century. In the hands of later writers (beginning with Stewart), Scottish philosophy became a readily acceptable psychology, intuitively appealing and consistent with Christianity. Most American colleges were (and many still are) religious, and in the nineteenth century Scottish faculty psychology was part of the "moral sciences" taught to their students.

The Reassertion of Metaphysics: Immanuel Kant (1724–1804)

Kant himself tells us that Hume's skeptical arguments roused him from his "dogmatic slumbers." Before reading Hume, Kant had been a follower of Leibniz through his teacher Christian Wolff (1679–1754), though Kant was not without originality. However, Hume upset Kant's Leibnizian "dogmatism" by his psychological analysis of human knowledge. Kant saw Hume's conclusions as undermining certain knowledge and as threatening the absolute achievement of Newton's physics. As a result, Kant tried to rescue metaphysics. He realized that the old speculative metaphysics about God and humankind's spiritual substance was dead, and in fact Kant proved that it had always been an illusion. However, Kant could not accept Hume's merely psychological analysis of knowledge, for it only said we have a tendency to form general conclusions based on association. Kant wanted to prove the validity of human knowledge quite apart from any empirical facts about human habit formation. He thus reasserted the claim of philosophical metaphysics over psychology to be the foundation of the other sciences.

Kant's answer to Hume bears a strong resemblance to Reid's. What we have knowledge of, in Kant's term, is *phenomena*. The objects of science, such as planets or balls rolling down inclined planes, are found in human experience. Kant argued that experience is organized by the inherent nature of human perception and thinking. For example, in our experience every event has a cause. Why? According to Hume, belief in causation is something learned, primarily by association. But for Kant, Hume's account undermined the absolute truth of causation; a mere habit cannot be absolutely true, as required by the Newtonian physics Kant took as his model of human knowledge. Belief in causation therefore cannot derive from habit, but from something inherent in human thinking. The world as we experience it, phenomena, *must* be such that every event has a cause, for this is the only way we can conceive the world. Our experience will never violate causality because we are so constructed that every experienced event has a cause. The Newtonian assumption of universal causality can never be falsified, and it is therefore absolutely and necessarily true—at least as regards phenomena.

Behind phenomena are what Kant called *noumena,* or things-as-they-are. In the noumenal world there may be uncaused events, and in fact Kant assigned human moral freedom to the noumenal realm. However, as noumena affect us to produce phenomena, all events are perceived to be caused. Thus, according to science, all behavior is caused, for science rests on phenomena; but people may very well be noumenally free—in fact must be free if moral responsibility is to have any meaning. Kant built in many inherent principles of understanding which structure our phenomena—from time and space as preconditions of sensation to concepts of causality and existence.

Previous empiricist philosophers assumed that humans have knowledge because objects impose themselves on understanding, which conforms itself to them. Hume's philosophy is the end point of this assumption. For Hume, events in the real world are regular because of the laws of nature, and these regularities register themselves in our mind as habits. But Hume's view leads to at least moderate, if not total, skepticism, which Kant (like so many others) found appalling. So Kant advanced a startling assumption—that objects conform themselves to our understanding. The following example may help clarify Kant's view (Copleston 1964). If a person wears red glasses, every object of his or her understanding will be red. Now the person will probably assume, if he or she has worn them all his or her life, that all objects are red, that is, that understanding conforms itself to objects. However, it is possible (and in fact true in this instance) that objects have many colors, but that something about the perceiver (the glasses) imposes redness on all objects of knowledge, and for the wearer it is phenomenally true to say, "Everything is red." Kant argued that something like this is true of human knowledge as it is. We are endowed with certain qualities of perception and thinking which impose themselves on experience to create the objects of knowledge about which science makes true statements. For the empiricist, the mind is passive in registering the qualities of objects; but for Kant the mind actively structures experience into an organized, knowable shape. Only thus can human knowledge be rescued from skepticism. Of course, only phenomena are rescued from skepticism; noumena may or may not be always caused or always organized in time and space. Illusory metaphysics arises when human reason applies its inherent concepts to noumena, to which they do not apply. Thus attempts to prove the existence of God are futile, for God is never known phenomenally, and so the empirical, if innate, concept of "existence" simply cannot apply to God. Of course, God cannot be proved not to exist either.

Kant's philosophy is extremely difficult, and its influence in pure philosophy has been very great. However, from the psychological standpoint we may question whether Kant departs in any essential way from Hume or Reid. Hume gave a psychological analysis of knowledge as founded on our propensity to form habits. Reid proposed an involved nativism in which common-sense beliefs are implanted by God and therefore correspond to the material world. Kant also proposed that human innate principles so structure experience that knowledge is necessarily true of phenomena, though not of noumena. Kant thought he had *proved* the transcendental validity of his innate concepts, but from a modern perspective these concepts, if they exist, are evolutionary accidents, and Kant's explanation is just as psychological as Hume's or as physiological as Reid's. In other words, what applied to Reid as against Hume applies to Kant as well. The major difference between Hume, on the one hand, and Reid and Kant on the other, is the amount and nature of innate equipment humans come with. The verdict of history is mixed on this score. Kant has been supported by findings that perception of three-dimensional space is innate, but has been undermined by modern quantum physics (in which not all events have causes) and the construction of non-Euclidean geometrics (which Kant implied were inconceivable).

Given his disdain for Hume's psychological account of knowledge, Kant cared little for psychology. Kant believed that psychology, defined as the introspective study of the mind, could not be a science. It is usually said that Kant said this because he believed psychology could not be mathematicized, but that is only a part of the reason. According to Kant, any science has two parts—the empirical part, involving observation and research, and the rational or metaphysical part, comprising the philosophical foundations that justify the empirical science's claim to produce knowledge. Kant believed that he had provided the metaphysical grounding of physical science in his account of human experience, the *Critique of Pure Reason*. There he showed that the basic assumptions of physics, such as universal causality, were necessarily true of human experience. Hence physics is a complete science.

Kant argued, however, that rational psychology is an illusion. The object of rational psychology is the thinking substance, or soul—Descartes's "I think." According to Kant, the soul is pure thinking; it has no content, and there can be no science without a subject matter. Kant held that since our experience is unitary—we do not experience disjuncted sensations—we assume that there is a self or ego, the soul, behind this unity. However, we do not experience the soul—or what Kant called the *Transcendental Ego*—directly; for it has no content, being pure thought, and has only noumenal, not phenomenal, existence. To apply our inherent empirical categories of understanding to the ego—for example, to say that it exists and that it has a spatial location—is illusion and bad metaphysics. There is an empirical ego, however, the sum total of our sensations or mental content, and of course we can study it through introspection. However, this empirical psychology, unlike empirical physics, cannot be a science for it lacks its rational counterpart, and so Kant thinks little of it.

Nevertheless, Kant believed in a science, or at least a discipline, concerned with humanity; he called it anthropology, the study (*logos*) of humans (*anthropos*). As Kant practiced anthropology, however, it bears much greater resemblance to psychology than to anthropology as we know it. Kant's anthropology studied human intellectual faculties, human appetite, and human character, but was not the cross-cultural study of societies. Kant delivered a very popular series of lectures published as *Anthropology from a Pragmatic Point of View*. If Kant's philosophy is similar to Reid's, his *Anthropology* is similar to Stewart's psychology, complete with an enumeration of faculties. Kant's lectures are accessible, full of shrewd observations of everyday behavior, charming and even funny anecdotes, and popular prejudice. In short, *Anthropology* is Kant's common-sense psychology, and bears some attention.

Kant distinguished physiological anthropology, concerned with the body and its effect on mind, and pragmatic anthropology, concerned with the person as a morally free agent and citizen of the world. The goal of pragmatic anthropology was to improve human behavior and so was grounded not in the metaphysics of experience, but in the metaphysics of morals. Pragmatic anthropology's methods were many. First, we have some introspective knowledge of our own minds, and by extension, of other's minds. Kant was aware of the pitfalls of introspection, however. When we introspect we change the state of our minds, so what we find is unnatural and of limited value; the same holds for trying to observe our own behavior. Kant even went so far as to say that excessive reflection on one's own mind may drive one insane. Similarly, when we observe others, they will act unnaturally if they know we are watching. Anthropology must be an interdisciplinary study embracing these methods—but using them with care—and also calling on history, biography, and literature for information about human nature.

Anthropology is a rich work. Kant discusses everything from insanity (which he felt was innate), to the nature of women (they are weaker but more civilized than men), to how to give a dinner party for philosophers (Kant wrote: "Dinner music . . . is the most tasteless absurdity that debauchery could have devised," because it prevents conversation). Just one of Kant's many topics will be presented here, however, for it occurs in Wundt's psychology in much the same form.

Kant discussed "ideas that we have without being aware of them." If we examine our awareness, we will find that some perceptions are clear—the ones we are attending to—while others are obscure. As Kant put it, "our mind is like an immense map, with only a few places illuminated." This view of consciousness as a field with clear and obscure areas is identical to Wundt's, as we will find later. The obscure ideas are those we are not clearly aware of, so obviously Kant's doctrine is not Freud's view of repression into the unconscious. However, Kant does say we can be subtly affected by obscure ideas. He observes that we often unthinkingly judge persons by their clothes without directing conscious attention to them. Kant also offers pragmatic advice to writers: Make your ideas a little obscure so that when a reader clarifies them you will make him feel clever.

In addition to his conception of consciousness, many other ideas of Kant's influenced Wundt, the founder of the psychology of consciousness. By Wundt's time, ways to experiment on and quantify mind had become available, and so Wundt was able to show that a scientific empirical psychology was possible without a rational companion. Wundt thus could abandon the Transcendental Ego altogether. However, it still lived in Wundt's system in modified form. Wundt emphasized how apperception gives unity to conscious experience, a role Kant assigned to the Transcendental Ego. In addition, Wundt put thinking beyond the reach of introspection, as did Kant, holding that it could be investigated only indirectly through a study of people in society, similar to Kant's *Anthropology*. Wundt's psychology had two parts: the laboratory study of experience via introspection (Kant's empirical psychology made into a science despite him), and the study of the higher mental processes via the comparative study of culture similar to Kant's *Anthropology* (although Wundt did not use the label). Wundt also modified Kant's view of introspection. Wundt said good, scientific introspection was not the intense scrutiny of the soul Kant found dangerous, but only the self-observations of one's experience, which even Kant said was possible.

We have noted here only some of Kant's influence on Wundt, but Kant's overall influence on Western thinking was profound. He is frequently viewed as the greatest thinker since Plato, and all philosophy after him was shaped by his philosophy—either through elaboration on his system or by provoking alternative answers to the problems he raised. His thought thus influences psychology directly (as in Wundt's case) or indirectly (as in behaviorism, which discarded the ego altogether), for it emerged out of philosophy. His most direct intellectual successors were the German speculative idealists Johann Fichte (1762–1814), Friedrich Schelling (1775–1854), Arthur Schopenhauer (1788–1860), and G. W. F. Hegel (1770–1831), who all in one way or another dispensed with the things-in-themselves so that the Transcendental Ego, or alternatively the World-Spirit, constitutes the world via its own ideas. In America, Kant's transcendental philosophy was a vital influence on transcendentalism, an important intellectual movement in the first part of the nineteenth century. The value of Kant's influence is much debated. True empiricsts, such as Bertrand Russell in his *History of Philosophy*, maintain that Kant is refutable by Hume, and that through his influence on Hegel, he is responsible for modern totalitarian governments that purport to serve transcendent truth. Others claim that Kant's influence on psychology was a disaster, because of its exclusive emphasis on introspection and a radical dualism between self and world (Wolman 1968). It may be replied, however, that Kant did not invent introspection, and indeed warned against it, and that the dualism of self and world has been part of Western thought at least since Plato. It is true that the categories of human understanding he thought necessarily true have proven unnecessary, but Kant was trying to reconcile human nature—including morality and the concept of freedom that it requires—to the mechanical Newtonian-Cartesian world view that seemed about to engulf and alienate humanity.

PHILOSOPHY, SCIENCE, AND HUMAN NATURE

The eighteenth century swarmed with would-be Newtons of the mind. Few of them had such long-term effects on Western thought as to rival the major philosophers, but they are admirable barometers of the general current of psychological thinking during the Enlightenment, when the possibility of a scientific psychology was first seen and debated.

British Associationism and Economics

The association of ideas was not new in the eighteenth century. We have found it in Plato and Aristotle, and later in Locke. What was new in the eighteenth century was the extensive use to which the idea was put. Hume considered his widespread employment of association to be his main achievement, while others as diverse as Spinoza, Reid, and Kant recognized association as a force in human thinking. However, in the hands of the great philosophers it was used philosophically, either as a key to human knowledge or as an example of bad thinking.

Associationism as a distinct psychological program was founded by a British physician, David Hartley (1705–1757), whose major work was *Observations on Man* (1749). He worked out a complete associationistic account of human mind *and* behavior from simple sensation to sexual activity. Although Hartley's work appeared some years after Hume's *Treatise on Man*, Hartley had been working at his system for many years, and Hume was not one of his sources.

Hartley acknowledged his debt to John Gay (1699–1745), a clergyman who developed a moral associationism, inspiring Hartley's more extensive work. Hartley, like so many protopsychologists, was a physician, and one of Hartley's aims was to establish the physiological basis of association. Hartley's greatest influence, however, as with the other "Newtons of the mind," was naturally Isaac Newton. Hartley attempted to follow Newton's methodological rules, indulging in no hypotheses and attempting to deduce phenomena from propositions already rooted in observation. In good Newtonian fashion Hartley at one point admitted his proposed physiological laws of association were probably fictions, but were valuable because they explained so much. Additionally, unlike Hume, Hartley also adopted some of Newton's ideas on the physiological operation of sensation as given in Newton's *Opticks*.

Hartley believed in a close correspondence between mind and brain, and he proposed parallel laws of association for both. He was not a parallelist like Leibniz, however, for he made clear that mental events causally depend on neural events, although he could not explain how. The door to later parallelistic associationism remained open, nevertheless.

Beginning with the mental sphere, Hartley built up the mind from simple atomic units of sensation, as did Hume. Our sensory contact with a perceivable quality (what Hartley called an *impression*) causes a *sensation* (similar to Hume's impression) to arise in the mind. If the mind copies the sensation, this constitutes a simple *idea of sensation* (comparable to Hume's simple ideas) which may be compounded via association to form complex *intellectual ideas* (comparable to Hume's complex ideas). Like everyone else we have looked at so far, Hartley assumed the mind possessed certain faculties that could transform mental elements, although association remained the basic mental operation.

Turning to the physiological substrate of elements, Hartley adopted Newton's theory of nervous vibrations, which said that the nerves contain submicroscopic particles whose vibrations pass along through the nerves and constitute neural activity. An impression started the sensory nerve-substance vibrating and this vibration passed to the lower brain where it brought a sensation to the mind. Repeated occurrence created a tendency in the cortex to permanently copy this vibration as a smaller vibration, or *vibratiuncle,* corresponding to an idea. Thus vibratiuncles are weak copies of vibrations, and ideas of sensations are weak copies of impressions, just as in Hume's account.

Hartley distinguished two fundamental forms of association: successive and simultaneous. Successive associations are built up when trains of ideas regularly follow one another and so get bound up together. For example, a sentence could be analyzed as a string of words associated together in sequence. We will see the same kind of view in the work of James Mill and then in that of John B. Watson, founder of behaviorism. Simultaneous associations are bonds built up between ideas that regularly occur together at the same time. So, for example, a child's face is made up of many atomic features, all of which naturally occur together in consciousness. The elements become united by association so that if you see only a few features, you mentally fill in the rest of the face. Hartley stated only one law of association, that of contiguity. Sensations, and their consequent ideas, occur either in regular temporal order or together at once, and are associated by sheer closeness in time, that is, by contiguity. Hartley went on to apply these principles to the whole of the mind and also to behavior, claiming that motor responses, too, could be associated together and with ideas. This is one of the rare attempts to include actual behavior in a philosophical system.

Hartley's associationism was quite popular. It was propounded to the public and defended against critics by Joseph Priestley (1733–1804), a great chemist and codiscoverer of oxygen. Because Hartley said pleasure and pain accompanied sensations and so affected thought and action, it worked its way into utilitarianism, which we will consider in the next chapter. It was also quite influential in artistic and literary circles, deeply affecting the critical sensibility of turn-of-the-century artists, especially the romantics. Coleridge named his eldest son David Hartley. And of course in the long-run, associationism eventually gave rise to analysis of behavior in terms of associated habits.

Among the many later eighteenth-century associationists, Thomas Brown (1778–1820) deserves mention. Brown was a pupil of Dugald Stewart, and is often accounted a member of the common-sense school. However, he was severely critical of Reid, noting that Reid failed to differ from Hume. Brown also was much more an associationist than Reid or even Stewart. He also seems to have been

influenced by Kant, for Brown discarded Hartley's physiological substrate of association, and possibly even its dependence on real-world regularities, in favor of a
purely phenomenal account of association. Brown preferred to call association
suggestion on the rather Humean grounds that *association* implies an unobservable
bond between ideas. According to Brown, one idea simply suggests another, but
there is no substantive link between them.

Brown offered three laws of suggestion which he felt were variations on the
basic principle of proximity: resemblance (compare with Hume), contrast (*white*
suggests *black*), and nearness in time and space (essentially contiguity). Brown took
a step toward a more fruitful, empirical associationism with his enumeration of
secondary laws of suggestion. They are nine in all and represent specific conditions
which affect the operation of the basic law or laws. So, for example, memory of
associated events is facilitated by long duration of the original ideas, liveliness of
ideas, frequency of association, and closeness of ideas in time. Other secondary
laws cover learned and constitutional individual differences in memory and associa-
tion-formation. The step forward here is that these secondary laws suggest obvious
experiments: What are the exact effects of frequency, of duration, of contiguity? It
would be some years before anyone would actually do the experiments, but Brown
points the way to an empirical and experimental psychology of mind.

By the middle of the eighteenth century associationism was surely an idea
whose time had come. What started with Locke as a modest suggestion for how the
mind errs in thinking became to various thinkers the real key to the science of
human nature. So far the British associationists were not radical associationists,
leaving other mental forces in their theories, such as Hartley's faculties. When we
turn our attention to the French philosophes however, we shall meet thinkers in
whom Locke's empiricism and association of ideas took a more extreme form.

1776 saw not only the birth of a new nation, but of a new social science—
economics—with the publication of Adam Smith's (1723–1790) *Wealth of Nations.* Smith's economics was perhaps the first fruit of Hume's science of human
nature, for Smith put economics on a scientific basis. Smith extended to human
economy the idea of natural law, and in particular the law of self-interest. Each
person naturally seeks his or her own self-interest, and out of everyone's interactions general benefit will accrue. Smith described nature as an "invisible hand"
which promotes the general interest out of each person's desire for personal benefit.
It follows that a good political economy will be one that helps the "invisible hand"
as much as possible.

One interesting point of Smith's theory is its anticipation of Darwin's theory
of natural selection. In economics, according to Smith, each individual seeks his or
her own good, but nevertheless the general good of society is served by the competition of interests. According to Darwinian biology, each member of a species seeks
only its own survival, but the good of the species is served as the weak are weeded
out by individual competition.

French Naturalism

The Enlightenment was led by a diverse collection of thinkers called philosophes; as the name implies, they were largely French. Few philosophes were
academic philosophers, except in Germany. Their interests were eclectic, and they
debated among themselves every topic of human knowledge. What united them was
hostility to the established church and the feudal governments it supported. They

believed that the Christian religion was founded on superstition and myth, and that by enforcing belief in theological dogma it robbed man of intellectual freedom. When we speak of the Age of Reason, reason should be understood to be in contrast to Christian faith and revelation, rather than in contrast to emotions. The great enterprise of the French philosophes was Denis Diderot's *Encyclopedia,* meant to be a compendium of human knowledge and achievement, declaring to the world man's independence from God. The *Encyclopedia* embodied reason; the Bible embodied revelation. The philosophes wanted to be able to inquire freely into all matters without censorship or the threat of condemnation.

Although the philosophes opposed Christianity, few were atheists. Most followed Voltaire in believing in a Supreme Creator, while rejecting the ritual and accumulated dogma of Christianity.

The philosophes tried to reconstruct society and philosophy on a new and natural basis, inspired by Newton's physics. For medieval and even Renaissance thought, the natural and human worlds were given meaning by God: God created the world and everything was ultimately related to him through the Great Chain of Being. In particular, human beings were spiritual creatures, possessing an immortal soul. However, as the medieval world view collapsed, it became necessary to give a new account. Newton's physics seemed to accomplish this task for the physical universe. Newton gave a complete account of the material world based only on the application of reason and observation. The philosophes, rejecting Christianity, wanted to complete Newton's work, that is, to provide a rational account of humankind and its relations to the world. We may call the philosophes' orientation *naturalism,* an understanding of people in natural rather than supernatural terms. People were conceived to be part of nature, not forever outside it in a spiritual world of God, angels, and souls.

There were two major sources for the philosophes' naturalism (Vartanian 1953). One was John Locke's empirical psychology. In eighteenth-century France there was a mania for things English, especially Newton's science and Locke's psychology. The supreme philosophe, Voltaire, wrote in his *Philosophical Letters:* "So many philosophers having written the romance of the soul, a sage has arrived who has modestly written its history. Locke set forth human reason just as an excellent anatomist explains the parts of the human body. He everywhere takes the light of Newton's physics for his guide." The other source of naturalism was native to France, Descartes's speculative physiology. As there were so many philosophes, major and minor, sometimes anonymous, we will focus our attention on two representatives of each tradition, beginning with the Cartesian.

Immediately after Descartes proposed that animals are simply machines (the beast-machine), but that humans were not machines by virtue of their souls, many of his religious opponents saw the trap he had set. For if animals, which behave in such diverse and often sophisticated ways, are but machines, is not the next logical step to say that a person, too, is but a machine (the *human*-machine)? They believed that Descartes was a secret materialist who only intimated what he hoped others might later say openly. They also spotted an interesting flaw in his *cogito.* If I know I exist as a thinking, spiritual substance only through introspection, how may I know other people are not machines and myself the only soul? Of course Descartes replied that language was the sign of the soul in other people, but his opponents countered that one can certainly imagine language produced by some clever mechanical device. The religionists said these things to ridicule Descartes's system as subversive of faith; but in the irreligious eighteenth century there were those who said them in earnest, proclaiming materialism.

Although materialists can be found at least as far back as the seventeenth century (for example, Pierre Gassendi [1592–1655]), their number multiplied in the eighteenth century. They spoke up first in anonymous pamphlets, fearing persecution, but they soon grew bolder. The most outspoken and complete extension of Descartes's beast-machine into the human-machine was made by Julien Offray de La Mettrie (1709–1751), whose major work was *L'Homme Machine* (*The Man-Machine*) of 1748. Interestingly, La Mettrie, too, thought Descartes was a secret materialist, but praised him for it. La Mettrie wrote: "He was the first to prove completely animals are pure machines," a discovery of such importance that one must "pardon all his errors." La Mettrie takes the step feared by religionists: "Let us boldly conclude that man is a machine," that the soul is but an empty word.

La Mettrie was a physician, and stated that only a physician may speak on human nature, for only a physician knows the mechanism of the body. La Mettrie went into some detail to show how the state of the body necessarily affects the mind, for example in the effects of drugs, disease, and fatigue. Against Descartes's insistence on the uniqueness of human language, La Mettrie suggested that apes might be made into "little gentlemen" by teaching them language the way the deaf are taught. In the 1960s La Mettrie's proposal of teaching apes language was carried out with some success. La Mettrie remained a Cartesian, however, in asserting that language is what makes a person human. He only denies that language is innate, claiming that we can make the ape human, too, via language.

In general La Mettrie gives the impression not of lowering humans to the level of animals, but of raising animals to near-human status. This emerges most clearly in his discussion of natural moral law. La Mettrie argued that animals share moral sentiments such as grief and regret with humans, so that morality is inherent in the natural biological order. Having said this, however, La Mettrie leaves the door open to sheer hedonism by stating that the point of living is to be happy.

La Mettrie adopts an uncompromisingly scientific, anti-Aristotelian attitude to his subject. He denies finalism or any Godly act of intentional creation. For example, the animal eye was not made to see, but is a natural outcome of physical law. La Mettrie here was stating a doctrine called transformism, increasingly popular in the later eighteenth century, which marks the beginning of evolutionary thought. According to transformism, the universe was not created by God, but emerged from primordial matter as a result of the action of natural law. The development of the physical and, La Mettrie implies, biological universe is a necessary consequence of the way nature is organized. Voltaire's Creator is no more necessary than the Christian God.

However, La Mettrie looked at the universe differently from Newton, Descartes, or the atomists and Epicureans. For them matter was dead, incapable of spontaneous action. Hence Descartes's dualism of dead matter and living but immaterial soul. However, La Mettrie advocated a new doctrine, just then coming into prominence in biology, that is later called *vitalism*. He thought biological matter at least to be capable of self-generation and motion. La Mettrie cited recent physiological research to prove his point. Polyps cut in two regenerate their missing halves; muscles of a dead animal still move when stimulated; the heart may beat after removal from the body. Matter is alive; it is vital, not dead; and it is precisely this natural vitality that made La Mettrie's human-machine plausible. In the twentieth century vitalism became the great enemy of scientific biologists, but it was a necessary step in the founding of biology as a coherent field apart from physics. La Mettrie's vitalism again attests that his materialism was not meant to degrade humanity, to make of a human being a cold, metallic machine (the image we have today of the machine), but rather to make of a human a vital, living, dynamic machine, an integral part of a living nature.

We should conclude this summary as La Mettrie did his book. Like a good philosophe, and like B. F. Skinner today, La Mettrie urged the progressive nature and moral goodness of accepting materialism, of giving up vain speculation and religious superstition to live pleasurable lives. Recognizing ourselves to be part of nature, we can then revere, honor, and never destroy nature. Our behavior to others will improve. Wrote La Mettrie: "Full of humanity we will love human character even in our enemies . . . in our eyes they will be but mismade men . . . we will not mistreat our kind. . . . Following the natural law given to all animals we will not wish to do to others what we would not wish them to do to us. . . . Such is my system, or rather the truth, unless I am much deceived. It is short and simple. Dispute it now who will." Thus La Mettrie closed *L'Homme Machine.* Although his "truth" was not acceptable to all philosophes in its extreme form, and of course Christians hotly disputed it, materialism was a growing doctrine. It was reluctantly and partially accepted by Voltaire himself, by Denis Diderot, conceiver of the *Encyclopedia,* and espoused in extreme form by Baron Paul d'Holbach (1723–1789), who worked out its deterministic and atheistic implications. Its deeper implications we will see shortly.

The other route to naturalism was from Locke's empiricism. We have already seen how Hartley derived naturalistic psychology from Locke, Newton, and associationism. In France, too, there were *soi-disant* "Newtons of the mind." The general tendency of their thought was toward *sensationism,* deriving the mind entirely from sensations, denying the existence of the autonomous mental faculties and the power of reflection found in Locke's psychology. The French commentators thought they were improving on Locke.

The outstanding French Lockean was Etienne Bonnot de Condillac (1715–1780). Although he knew and influenced the philosophes, he was never one himself. He shied away from the controversy they reveled in; he was a Catholic priest, albeit inactive, in the midst of anti-Christians.

Condillac dismissed everyone but Locke: "Immediately after Aristotle comes Locke. . . ." and he subtitled his first book, *An Essay on the Origin of Human Knowledge* (1746), "Being a Supplement to Mr. Locke's Essay on the Human Understanding." Like Berkeley, Condillac believed Locke had not pursued his own empiricism far enough, but in his *Essay* he followed Locke closely. It is only in a later work, *Treatise on Sensations* (1754), that Condillac really fulfilled his earlier promise to "reduce to a single principle whatever relates to the human understanding." That principle is sensation.

Locke had allowed the mind certain autonomous powers: the power of reflection on itself, and mental faculties or acts, such as attention and memory. Condillac strove to see the mind in a more purely empiricist way. He denied the existence of reflection, and tried to derive all mental faculties from simple sensation. His motto might have been, "I sense, therefore I am." Condillac asks us to imagine a statue which we will endow with each sense in turn, starting with smell. Condillac then endeavors to build up complex mental activity from these senses. For example, memory arises when a sensation is experienced for a second time and recognized.

We should observe that here Condillac cheats, for he assumed an inner power or faculty to store the first sensation, an innate power indistinguishable from memory. Attention is reduced to the strength of one sensation to dominate the mind over other weaker sensations. In his *Essay* Condillac had followed Locke and said attention was a mental act (as will Wundt a century later); but in the *Treatise* his sensationism is consistent, and he anticipates Titchener's identical sensationist revision of Wundt's theory.

In short, Condillac attempted to work out an empiricist theory of mind, leaving as innate only the senses, the passions, reason, and (implicitly) memory. Or so Condillac is, and was, typically interpreted. It is true that he tried to show that the usual mental faculties need not be innate but might be learned, but the conclusion he drew from his hypothetical statue are, and were, typically ignored. In the end, having acquired every mental faculty and every human sense, the statue still lacked the essential human trait: It could not speak. It could not speak, Condillac said, because it lacked reason. Its mind was passive, not active, lacking the power of thought. In Condillac's scheme, the statue and animals are set off from human beings. The former possess sensation and the various mental faculties, but are bereft of reason and language, which are reserved for human beings alone. Condillac was a Christian, and although he pointed the way to empiricist theories of mind, he did not strip human beings of their soul, the seat of reason. That task was taken up by more radical men, more willing to embrace La Mettrie's materialism and to work out its consequences.

Stripping away the immaterial soul was performed by Claude Helvetius (1715–1771), who accepted Condillac's empiricism and a mechanical version of La Mettrie's materialism. Helvetius consequently proclaimed a complete environmentalism, in which humans have neither a divine soul nor a complex biological structure. The human possesses only senses, a passive mind able to receive sensations, and a body capable of certain actions. This mind is passively built up through watching the effects of a person's own and others' actions and observing the ways of the world. For Helvetius, then, the mind at birth is both blank and powerless; everything a person becomes is the result of the environment. Helvetius found cause for optimism in the malleability of the mind, holding out the hope that improved education can lead to improved people. In this he presaged the radical behaviorists, who believe human behavior is similarly malleable. Such beliefs, however, have a negative potential as well—the possibility that an effective dictatorship can be founded on brainwashing.

Helvetius also presents the crucial problem of the Enlightenment: If we are going to conceive of humans as part of the natural world, on what basis can we erect a system of ethics? Ethics depend on rational control of passions, and the philosophes, far from glorifying reason, reduced it to the slave of the passions. La Mettrie said pleasure is the natural cause for our existence; nature made us to pursue pleasure. Condillac, too, reduced reason to desire, or need. If each sensation produces pleasure or pain, then our thinking, built up out of our sensations by association, is determined by their affective quality and directed by our momentary, animal needs. Hence empiricism undercuts the autonomy of reason. For the rationalist reason is prior to, and independent of, sensation, so hedonism is only a temptation to be overcome. The empiricist, however, constructing reason out of affectively charged sensations, makes hedonism the directing force behind all thought.

Condillac tried to elude the obvious hedonism in such a view by appealing to God and his transcendental moral order, but Helvetius, the materialist, did not. Like

Freud, Helvetius postulated a pleasure principle as our fundamental drive, and he reduced all feelings, including love and altruism, to the egotistical pursuit of pleasure or avoidance of pain. La Mettrie maintained much the same position. Helvetius, however, differed in asserting that this pleasure principle could be harnessed through education, a position La Mettrie did not accept.

Here we see the fundamental crisis of naturalism, first confronted by the philosophes, and which became acute after Darwin. If we are only machines, destined to pursue pleasure and avoid pain, what can be the ground of moral value and of meaning in our lives? The early philosophes assumed, as humanists, that the world was made for humans by a beneficient, if non-Christian, Creator. As the century progressed, however, it became evident that this optimism was unjustified. The great Lisbon earthquake of midcentury, for example, blotted out thousands of lives. Newton's universe seemed to be a machine indifferent to human life, which was a mere speck of no consequence. Moreover, the extension of materialism, determinism, and hedonism to human beings, while intellectually persuasive, was hard to accept emotionally. Diderot, for example, wrote in a letter, "I am maddened at being entangled in a devilish philosophy that my mind can't help approving and my heart refuting" (Knight 1968). The whole dilemma thus comes down to a question of our feelings—our feelings of freedom and dignity versus our natural desire to seek pleasure and avoid pain.

But how can life be given meaning by the hedonistic pursuit of pleasure? One solution was given by romanticism, which glorified the emotions, especially love. Another solution was to make pleasure and pain reasonable and prudent, to seek general happiness rather than personal happiness. This was the way of English utilitarianism, already implicit in Hume and Hartley. It tried to found society on a naturalistic ethic of calculating pleasure rationally and balancing diverging needs. Both these solutions become important in the nineteenth century.

However, one darker solution was offered at once. There is a remarkably existentialist sentence in La Mettrie's *L'Homme Machine:* "Who can be sure that the reason for man's existence is not simply the fact that he exists?" He continued: "Perhaps he was thrown by chance on some spot on the earth's surface, nobody knows how or why, but simply that he must live and die, like the mushrooms which appear from day to day. . . ." La Mettrie states the possibility of a meaningless world, the abyss of moral nihilism that every philosophe saw and tried to avoid.

However, one man cheerfully jumped into that abyss, proclaiming the autonomy of pleasure, the illusion of morals, and the rule of the strong. The Marquis de Sade (1740–1814) wrote in *History of Juliette:*

> The weak is then right when, trying to recover his usurped possessions, he purposely attacks the strong and obliges him to make restitution; the only wrong he can have is to depart from the character of weakness that nature imprinted in him: she created him to be poor and a slave, he doesn't want to submit to it, that is his wrong; and the strong, lacking this wrong, since he preserves his character and acts only according to it, is equally right when he tries to despoil the weak and obtain pleasure at his expense. Let both now look for a moment into their hearts; the weak, in deciding to attack the strong, whatever his rights may be, will experience a slight struggle; and this resistance to satisfying himself comes from his trespassing against the laws of nature by assuming a character which is not his; the strong, on the contrary, in despoiling the weak, that is to say in enjoying all the rights he has received from nature, in giving them the greatest possible extension, finds pleasure in proportion to this extension. The more atrociously he harms the weak, the more voluptuously he is thrilled; injustice

is his delectation, he enjoys the tears that his oppression snatches from the unfortunate wretch; the more he grieves him, the more he oppresses him, the happier he is. . . . Besides, this necessary gratification which is born from the comparison that the happy man makes between the wretch and himself, this truly delicious gratification never establishes itself better for the fortunate man than when the misery he produces is complete. The more he crushes that wretch, the more he intensifies the comparison and consequently the more he nourishes his voluptuousness. He has then two very real pleasures in the wrongs he inflicts upon the weak: both the increase of his physical resources, and the moral enjoyment of the comparisons which he makes all the more voluptuous in proportion as his injuries weaken the unfortunate wretch. Let him pillage then, let him burn, let him ravage, let him not leave the wretch more than the breath to prolong a life whose existence is necessary for the oppressor to establish his laws of comparison; whatever he does will be in nature, whatever he invents will be only the active use of the forces which he has received from her, and the more he exercises his forces, the more he will experience pleasure, the better he will use his faculties, and the better, consequently, he will have served nature.*

If the only goal in life that naturalism can find is pleasure, then we should each seek it uninhibited by morals or the opinions of society, according to Sade. In doing so, we will be fulfilling natural law. The strong must triumph over the weak. Sade extended comparative psychology to morals. The animals prey upon one another without compunction; they have no moral law. Since we are animals we should act in the same way. Moral law is a metaphysical illusion. The philosophes first struggled with the problem of a world ruled only by efficient causes and hedonism and tried to avoid Sade's logical extrapolation of naturalism. In the twentieth century the problem remains unsolved, and in our own time we have seen moral nihilism proclaimed again, while modern existential humanists seek to restore man's dignity. The problem became acute in the nineteenth century when Darwin cut away all reason for believing that humans transcend nature. In Darwin's universe, too, the strong destroy the weak. And Sade was a harbinger of the moral nihilism that would stare every Victorian in the face.

The Enlightenment in Germany

The Enlightenment took a different turn in Germany than in France or England. German thinkers were generally academic philosophers rather than amateur philosophes; the movement failed to widely penetrate German consciousness. It was here too that a counter-movement arose against the Age of Reason.

The German Enlightenment may be said to start with the philosopher Christian Thomasius (1655–1728). Thomasius valued French more than German philosophy, believed philosophy should be useful, and rejected metaphysics for empiricism, all Enlightenment beliefs. Most interestingly, Thomasius seems to have conducted the first empirical psychological research of all time (McReynolds and Ludwig, 1977). Thomasius used a four-dimensional rating scale to define individual personalities. He did not conduct experiments, but based his ratings on conversations with his subjects, plus background information on occupation and personal habits. Thomasius even used multiple raters to increase his scales' reliability. In his attention to individual differences Thomasius was out of step with the Platonic tradition of German psychology we will see in Wundt, and Thomasius's pioneering

*Quoted and translated by Lester Crocker, *An Age of Crisis,* Baltimore: Johns Hopkins University Press, 1959, 212–213.

researches appear to have exerted no influence on the history of psychology. The time was not yet ripe for empirical, scientific psychology.

With Christian Wolff (1679–1754) German philosophy returned to rationalist Leibnizian metaphysics. Wolff propounded a systematic metaphysical philosophy that dominated German thinking for many years, keeping out more empiricist Anglo-French thinking. So it was that Kant was slumbering in Wolff's dogmatism when he was aroused by Hume's radical empiricism. After Wolff there were a number of philosophe-like "popular philosophers" of limited influence.

More important for psychology was Johann Nikolaus Tetens (1736–1807), the first German to propose a systematic empirical psychology. Like Hume, Tetens wrote an essay on human nature, but his approach was different. Tetens rejected the empiricist view, manifested most clearly in Condillac's sensationism, that the mind was no more than a collection of sensations. Following a more rationalist line, Tetens maintained that the mind was active and autonomous, uniting sensations by its own activity, not merely registering passively regularities in sensation. The mind to Tetens did not rest content with empirical generalizations, but actively sought scientific and aesthetic ideals. Psychology, then, should not study only the content of the mind, to which an empiricist would be limited, but also the energetic activities of the mind that unify and process sensations.

THE COUNTER-ENLIGHTENMENT

Newton had applied human reason, logic, and mathematics to nature, and had showed that the human mind could encompass nature's laws and bend nature to human will. The vision of the philosophes of the Enlightenment was that Newtonian reason could be applied to human affairs, to psychology, ethics, and politics. In the Newtonian scheme of the philosophes scientific reason would banish superstition, religious revelation, and historical tradition, setting in their place laws of human conduct whose use by enlightened despots could create the perfect human society. The philosophes were intolerant of cultural diversity, because cultural traditions are not products of reason, so that all existing cultures fall short of the rational ideal. The philosophes were scornful of history, regarding it as no more than gossip from the past, entirely irrelevant to understanding contemporary society and to the task of reconstructing society in the light of reason.

The philosophes' imperialism of reason and science provoked a reaction from diverse thinkers who found it horrifyingly unhuman. Against the imperialism of natural science they set the autonomy of culture, and against the excesses of reason they set the feelings of the heart. The most important spokesmen for this Counter-Enlightenment were Giambattista Vico, a voice crying in the wilderness, and Johann Gottfried Herder, who established German Romanticism.

The Criterion and Rule of Truth Is to Have Made It: Giambattista Vico (1668–1704)

Vico began with the astonishing assertion that knowledge of nature is inferior, secondhand knowledge compared to knowledge of society and history. Vico's criterion of knowledge derived from the scholastics of the Middle Ages, who held that one cannot really know something unless one has made it. In the case of nature, only God can really know the natural world, because he made it. To us humans, nature is a given, a brute fact, something we can only observe from the outside, never from the inside. People, however, make their societies in the historical process of creation. We can see our own lives from the inside and, through sympathetic understanding, we can understand the lives of men and women in other cultures and other historical times.

For Vico, then, history is the greatest science; for through history we come to know how our society, or any society we choose to study, was created. History is not gossip, said Vico, but the process of human self-creation. The Enlightenment philosophes claimed there was a universal, timeless human nature that could be known to science, and upon which we could build a perfect society. But according to Vico human beings make themselves through history, so there is no eternal human nature, and each culture must be respected for the human creation it is. We understand cultures by studying what they create, especially myths and language. Myths express the soul of a culture at a certain point of development, and its language shapes and expresses the thoughts of its members. To understand another time's or place's myths and language is thus to understand how men and women thought and felt then and there.

Vico anticipates a distinction that is clearer in Herder, and clearer still in nineteenth-century German historians, the distinction between *Naturwissenschaft* and *Geisteswissenschaft*. *Naturwissenschaft* is natural science, built upon the observation of nature from the outside, noting regularities in events and summarizing them in scientific laws. *Geisteswissenschaft* is much harder to translate, meaning literally "spiritual science," but more often rendered today as "human science." Human science studies the human creations of history and society. Its method is not observation from without, but sympathetic understanding from within.

It is apparent that psychology straddles the divide between the two sciences. People are part of nature—things—and as such are subject in part to natural science. But people live in human cultures, and as such are subject to human science. In Wundt's psychology the division remains, between his experimental, "physiological" psychology of human conscious experience on the one hand, and his *Völkerpsychologie*—the study, as Vico recommended, of human myth, custom, and language, which penetrated from the surface of consciousness to the inner thought processes. The distinction between natural and social sciences begun by Vico had its primary impact on nineteenth century German intellectuals, including Wundt. Outside Germany the division was largely unknown, and psychology was assimilated, as the philosophes would have wished, to natural science and the search for universal laws of human behavior.

We Live in a World We Ourselves Create: Johann Gottfried Herder (1744–1803)

Vico was little read outside his own circle in Italy. However, his ideas reappeared, independently asserted, in the works of Herder, who rejected the Enlightenment's worship of reason and universal truth, for romanticism's trust in the human heart, and a historical reverence for many human truths. Herder's views are remarkably similar to Vico's, although they were formed in ignorance of Vico's works. His motto, "We live in a world we ourselves create," could have been said by Vico. Herder, too, stressed the absolute uniqueness of each living or historical culture. We should strive to fulfill ourselves and our own culture, not slavishly follow classical styles and attitudes of a bygone age. Herder is modern in his belief that each person should try to fulfill his or her potential as a total person instead of being an alienated collection of roles. Herder even opposed faculty psychology for its fragmentation of the human personality. For both the individual and the individual's culture, Herder stressed organic development.

Because each culture is unique, Herder opposed any attempt to impose one culture's values on any other. He detested the tendency of the philosophes to caricature the past and hold out their own times as a universal model for humanity. Herder even went so far as to imply the degeneracy of the Age of Reason. It was artificial; it aped the Greeks and Romans; it was too reasonable and insufficiently spiritual.

Herder's views were highly influential, especially in Germany. The intellectual framework in which Wundt founded psychology was permeated by the idea of the unique historical development of each cultural group, or *Volk*. The contrast of "degenerate" Anglo-French Enlightenment "civilization" with vital German *Kultur* was also popular, as was an opposition to mechanism and a belief in organic development. Half of Wundt's psychology, his *Völkerpsychologie,* was an attempt to grasp humans' inner nature through the study of history and human cultural products, such as language and myth, both of which Herder valued highly. Also like Herder, Wundt stressed the organic unity of the human mind against the faculty psychologists. We should note in passing that the authoritarian, militant German nationalism in Wundt's milieu would have been rejected by Herder himself, although it partly grew out of his philosophy.

More generally, Herder helped lay the foundation for romanticism. He passionately opposed the mock-classical art of his time, calling modern critics "masters of dead learning." Instead he advocated "Heart! Warmth! Blood! Humanity! Life!" Descartes had said, "I think, therefore I am. " Condillac implied, "I sense, therefore I am." Herder wrote "I feel! I am!" Thus ended the rule of abstract reason, the geometric spirit, and reasonable emotion. Instead, organic development led by emphatic emotion was the base of the new romanticism.

Nature vs. Civilization: Jean-Jacques Rousseau (1712–1778)

To place Rousseau outside the Enlightenment may seem unusual, since he, along with Voltaire, is popularly thought of as a paradigmatic philosophe. However, in significant ways Rousseau, like Herder, rebelled against the Age of Reason. Rousseau is best known as the incipient revolutionary. In *Social Contract* he wrote: "Man is born free, and everywhere he is in chains." When Marx and Engels wrote, "The proletariat have nothing to lose but their chains," their call to revolution echoed Rousseau's *Social Contract*. Rousseau is also famous for his concept of the Noble Savage, a picture of humans before the coming of the society that put people in chains. It is, however, an image we have met before, inspired by the voyages of discovery.

In many ways Rousseau's complaints about the Enlightenment parallel Herder's, although Rousseau was less conscious of history than was Herder. Rousseau said, "To exist is to feel" and "the first impulses of the heart are always right," sentiments that recall Herder and point to romanticism. Like Herder, he rejected mechanism because it cannot explain human free will. Both Rousseau and Herder felt that language is what makes man unique in the world.

Rousseau became famous—not to say notorious—with his first works, which, in opposition to the Enlightenment spirit, denied that humanity has benefited from scientific and technological advances. Like Herder, Rousseau felt contemporary French civilization was artificial and excessively rational; it had put humans in chains. Rousseau's invented Noble Savage was not intended to describe a primitive Eden to which we ought to return, but to reveal human nature. Rousseau believed that people are inherently sociable and that primitive isolation is neither desirable nor possible. Still, Rousseau argued that the present state of society corrupted and degraded human nature. Instead of a return to primitivism, Rousseau advocated building a new, less alienating society, and it is in this that his revolutionary potential lay.

He was a friend of Condillac and was similarly empiricistic and interested in education. His greatest influence has been on educational psychology. Rousseau described his ideal educational program in *Emile,* in which a child and his tutor retire from corrupt civilization and return to nature for education. After his education is complete, Emile returns to society. Rousseau advocated a kind of nondirectional education, believing that a child should be allowed to express his or her native talents, and that a good education is one that cultivates the natural growth of these talents. The tutor should not impose views on the student. Nevertheless, behind the apparent freedom is firm control. At one point Rousseau described what we would call open education: "It is rarely your business to suggest what he ought to learn; it is for him to want to learn." However, earlier, he had written: 'Let him always think he is master while you are really master. There is no subjection so complete as that which preserves the forms of freedom. . . ." For Rousseau the empiricist, the corrupt state of civilization may be overcome by a proper education which perfects the potentialities of each person. Herder believed in self-fulfillment, but was less individualistic, seeing fulfillment in the larger context of the person's culture, which the person helped perfect while perfecting self.

Rousseau's influence has been wide. His affinities with romanticism and political revolutionaries have been alluded to. In education he inspires those who support open education of the "whole child" against those who prefer highly structured teaching of separate basic skills. He is also behind those who want to reform society through education. In his belief in human malleability and perfectability, he foreshadows B. F. Skinner, who advocates a carefully controlled society whose goal is human happiness, although Skinner openly disbelieves in human freedom.

CONCLUSION: REASON AND ITS DISCONTENTS

The major theme of the period between 1600 and 1800 was the triumph of science, in particular Newtonian science, over the old medieval theological world view. In the seventeenth century Galileo, Kepler, Descartes, and Newton demonstrated the power of a new kind of understanding of nature. The new scientific view substituted the idea of universal mathematical order for the older idea of universal meaning in nature. Humanity's view of nature changed greatly. Nature had been a book of signs revealing the invisible world beyond. Now it became an indifferent machine that could be known only in a limited way, via mathematics. Nature lost its meaningfulness, but humanity gained power over it from mathematically precise predictions.

The viewpoint of science was something fundamentally new in human history. Heretofore, thinkers had merely speculated about the nature of reality—speculations that were comprehensive in scope but lacking in detail. Newtonian science substituted detailed analysis of concrete cases for vast speculations about cosmic order. Since Newton's time, of course, science has grown in comprehensiveness until for many it has entirely supplanted religion as a world picture.

No sooner had Newton propounded the new antimetaphysical science of physics, than philosophers began to see the possibility of extending it to human nature. The enterprise began with Locke, and occupied almost every eighteenth-century thinker. The keynote was sounded by Hume in his call for a science of human nature to be as fundamental to science as metaphysics had been thought to be. Of course it has emerged that natural science can get along quite well without psychology, and the average physicist would laugh at Hume's proposal. Still, the eighteenth century did move significantly toward creating a science of human nature. The philosophes believed in Hume's science, but showed no more unanimity on the nature of human nature than psychology shows today.

There is no doubt that the Enlightenment finally marks the beginning of modern times. The philosophes wrestled with the problem of understanding human nature apart from God and faith. They generally agreed that humanity could be improved, but they did not agree on what was beneath the social veneer. Their optimistic hopes seemed upheld by the American Revolution, which seemed to put the new world view into motion in the new world. The French Revolution was greeted at first as the triumph of reason over feudal oppression. But the new triumph quickly went sour. The change may be marked in one revolutionist, Robespierre, who began as a foe of capital punishment and upholder of democracy, and ended as a tyrant who executed the entire family of one girl suspected of thinking about assassinating him. It is easy for persons who believe they know human nature to go on to think they know what "the people" want better than the people do themselves. So the modern world witnesses despotism in the name of liberty and murder in the name of enlightenment. The Reign of Terror in France seemed to show that Sade's vicious ideas were right, and we still have not resolved the crisis of naturalism.

A poet, Alexander Pope (1688–1744), caught the spirit of the age in his *Essay on Man*. In the following lines he begins in good Enlightenment fashion by telling humanity to study people, not God, but ends by despairing of the possibility of such knowledge:

Know then thyself, presume not God to scan;
The proper study of Mankind is Man.
Placed on this isthmus of a middle state,
A being darkly wise, and rudely great:
With too much knowledge for the Sceptic side,
With too much weakness for the Stoic's pride,
He hangs between; in doubt to act, or rest,

In doubt to deem himself a God, or Beast,
In doubt his Mind or Body to prefer,
Born but to die, and reas'ning but to err;
Alike in ignorance, his reason such,
Whether he thinks too little, or too much:
Chaos of Thought and Passion, all confused;
Still by himself abused, or disabused;
Created half to rise, and half to fall;
Great lord of all things, yet a prey to all;
Sole judge of Truth, in endless Error hurled:
The glory, jest, and riddle of the world!

Go, wondrous creature! mount where Science guides,
Go, measure earth, weigh air, and state the tides;
Instruct the planets in what orbs to run,
Correct old Time, and regulate the Sun;
Go, soar with Plato to th' empyreal sphere,
To the first good, first perfect, and first fair;
Or tread the maze round his follow'rs trod,
And quitting sense call imitating God;
As Eastern priests in giddy circles run,
And turn their heads to imitate the Sun.
Go, teach Eternal Wisdom how to rule—
Then drop into thyself, and be a fool!

BIBLIOGRAPHY

A general history of the centuries culminating in the eighteenth is Fernand Braudel's three-volume history, *Civilization & capitalism 15th–18th century* (New York: Harper and Row, 1981, 1982, 1984): vol. 1, *The structures of everyday life: The limits of the possible;* vol. 2, *The wheels of commerce;* and vol. 3, *The perspective of the world.* Braudel aims to write "total history" reaching from everyday life at the base of society to the total world economy. Braudel is very difficult, but widely influential. On the Enlightenment itself, a fine treatment is given by Peter Gay in his two-volume *The Enlightenment: An interpretation* (New York: Knopf, 1966, 1969). Of special interest to the history of psychology is the second volume, subtitled *The science of freedom,* which covers the Newtons of the mind. A selection of the philosophes' major writings has been assembled by Gay in *The Enlightenment: A comprehensive anthology* (New York: Simon and Schuster, 1973). A somewhat older book that stresses the darker side of the Enlightenment is Crocker (1959). A recent book that does for the eighteenth century what Christopher Hill did for the seventeenth in his *World turned upside down* is Margaret C. Jacob, *The radical enlightenment: Pantheists, Freemasons and Republicans* (London: Allen & Unwin, 1981). The revolutionary consequences of the Enlightenment are discussed by Norman Hampson, *The first European revolution 1776–1815* (New York: Norton, 1969); in this connection see also James H. Billington, *Fire in the minds of men: Origins of the revolutionary faith* (New York: Basic Books, 1980). For science in the period see Thomas L. Hankins, *Science and the Enlightenment* (Cambridge, England: Cambridge University Press, 1985). Finally, for social histories of the period see Richard Sennett, *The fall of public man* (New York: Vintage, 1978); Lawrence Stone, *The family, sex, and marriage in England 1500–1800* (New York: Harper & Row, 1982); and Neil McKendrick, John Brewer, and J. H. Plumb, *The birth of a consumer society: The commercialization of eighteenth century England* (New Haven: Yale University Press, 1982), especially the last chapter by Plumb on how people responded to modernity.

In discussing the philosophy of the eighteenth century, a paper by David Fate Norton

"The myth of 'British empiricism,' " *History of European Ideas* (1981, *1*: 331–344), caused me to reorganize the present and preceding chapters. Norton shows that neither rationalism nor empiricism are the fixed traditions they are taken to be; Thomas Reid started the idea of empiricism vs. rationalism, and his myth has been enshrined by teachers ever since. A survey of the philosophy of the period is in S. C. Brown, ed., *Philosophers of the Enlightenment* (Sussex, England: Harvester Press, 1985). Two books by John Yolton discuss the central psychological ideas of the eighteenth-century philosophers: *Thinking matter,* on materialism, and *Perceptual acquaintance from Descartes to Locke,* on perception (both Minneapolis: University of Minnesota Press, 1983 and 1984, respectively).

Works on the specific philosophers follow, omitting works cited in the text.

Berkeley. Berkeley's major philosophical works are *Three dialogues between Hylas and Philonus* and *A treatise concerning the principles of human knowledge* (Indianapolis: Hackett, 1979 and 1982, respectively). His analysis of perception is in *Works on vision* (Indianapolis: Bobbs-Merrill, 1963). For commentary on Berkeley, see Ian C. Tipton, *Berkeley: The philosophy of immaterialism* (London: Methuen, 1974); J. O. Urmson, *Berkeley* (Oxford: Oxford University Press, 1982); or G. J. Stock, *Berkeley's analysis of perception* (The Hague: Mouton, 1972).

Hume. David Hume, *An inquiry concerning the principles of morals* (Indianapolis: Hackett, 1983). For commentary, David Fate Norton, *David Hume: Common sense moralist, sceptical metaphysician* (Princeton: Princeton University Press, 1982), John Passmore, *Hume's intentions* (New York: Basic Books, 1968), or John P. Wright, *The skeptical realism of David Hume* (Manchester, England: Manchester University Press, 1980).

The Scots. Dugald Stewart, *Elements of the philosophy of the human mind* (London: A. Strahan & T. Caddell, 1792). For a broad view of the Scottish Enlightenment, see R. H. Campbell, ed., *The origins and nature of the Scottish Enlightenment* (Edinburgh: John Donald, 1982).

Kant. Kant's most important book is *Critique of pure reason* (New York: St. Martin's Press, 1929), but it is extraordinarily difficult; more accessible, and deliberately so, is *Prologomena to any future metaphysics that will be able to come forward as science* (Indianapolis: Hackett, 1977). There is also a large amount of Kant commentary. A useful short introduction is S. Körner, *Kant* (Harmondsworth, England: Pelican, 1955). Karl Ameriks discusses *Kant's theory of mind* (Oxford: Clarendon Press of Oxford University Press, 1982).

French Naturalism. The account of French naturalism is based largely on the cited works and on the general treatments of the period listed above, especially Gay. See also Robert J. Richards, "Influence of sensationalist tradition on early theories of the evolution of behavior," *Journal of History of Ideas* (1979, *40*: 85–105). That Condillac has long been misrepresented has been demonstrated by Hans Aarslef, *From Locke to Saussure: Essays on the study of language and intellectual history* (Minneapolis: University of Minneapolis Press, 1982).

British Associationism and Economics. David Hartley, *Observations on man* (New York: Garland, 1971); Thomas Brown, *Sketch of a system of philosophy of the human mind* (Edinburgh: Bell & Bradfute, Manners & Miller, 1820); Adam Smith, *The wealth of nations* (New York: The Modern Library, 1937). For commentary, again see the general works listed above. On Hartley, see also Corinna Deleskamp, "Medicine, science, and moral philosophy," *The Journal of Medicine and Philosophy* (1977, *2*: 162–176).

Enlightenment in Germany. Again, see the general sources. Also Robert J. Richards, "Christian Wolff's prolegomena to empirical and rational psychology: Translation and commentary,'' *Proceedings of the American Philosophical Society* (1980, *124:* 227–239).

The Counter-Enlightenment.   Without doubt, the outstanding modern student of the Counter-Enlightenment is Isaiah Berlin. For Vico and Herder, see his *Vico and Herder: Two studies in the history of ideas* (New York: Vintage, 1977). Several essays in his *Against the current* (Harmondsworth, England: Penguin, 1982) touch on the Counter-Enlightenment, especially ''The Counter Enlightenment,'' which briefly but insightfully reviews the major spokesmen of the movement. Vico, in particular, has experienced a revival in interest; see G. Tagliacozzo and D. P. Verene, eds., *Giambattista Vico's science of humanity* (Baltimore: Johns Hopkins University Press, 1976).

REFERENCES

Bower, T. G. R. (1974) *Development in infancy.* San Francisco: W. H. Freeman.

Condillac, E. B. de (1974) *An essay on the origin of human knowledge.* New York: AMS Press.

Copleston, F. (1964) *A History of Philosophy.* V. 5. Garden City, New York: Image Books.

Crocker, L. (1959) *An age of crisis.* Baltimore: Johns Hopkins University Press.

Hume, D. (1817) *A treatise of human nature.* London: Thomas and Joseph Allman.

Hume, D. (1962) *David Hume on human nature and the understanding.* Anthony Flew, ed. New York: Collier Books.

Kant, I. (1974) *Anthropology from a pragmatic point of view.* M. J. Gregor, trans. The Hague: Martinus Nijhoff.

Knight, I. F. (1968) *The geometric spirit: the Abbe Condillac and the French Enlightenment.* New Haven: Yale University Press.

La Mettrie, J. O. de (1961) *Man a machine.* La Salle, Illinois: Open Court.

McReynolds, P. and Ludwig, K. (1977) Psychometrics in the seventeenth century: the personology of Christian Thomasius. Paper presented at the annual meeting of CHEIRON, Boulder, Colorado.

Reid, T. (1975) *Thomas Reid's Inquiry and Essays.* K. Lehrer and R. Beanblossom, eds. Indianapolis: Bobbs-Merrill.

Rousseau, J. (1974) *Emile.* New York: Dutton.

Smith, N. K. (1941) *The philosophy of David Hume.* London: Macmillan.

Vartanian, A. (1953) *Diderot and Descartes: A study of naturalism in the Enlightenment.* Princeton: Princeton University Press.

Wolman, B. (1968) Immanual Kant and his impact on psychology. In B. Wolman, ed. *Historical roots of contemporary psychology.* New York: Harper & Row.

CHAPTER 6

To the Threshold of Psychology

The Nineteenth Century

THE WORLD OF THE NINETEENTH CENTURY
    The Reassertion of the Transcendental:
    The Romantic Revolt
    The New Enlightenment
    Heraclitus Triumphant: The Darwinian Revolution
    On the Fringes of Science and the *Fin de Siècle*
TOWARD THE SCIENCE OF PSYCHOLOGY
    Progress outside Psychology
    Progress in Philosophy
CONCLUSIONS
    The Nineteenth-Century Crisis
    Founding Psychology

THE WORLD OF THE
NINETEENTH CENTURY

The Enlightenment consensus ended with the French Revolution, which was at first welcomed as the dawn of a greater Age of Reason, but later feared and hated for its Reign of Terror. The real implications of the geometric spirit became clear, and nineteenth-century thinkers had to come to grips with naturalism. This task was made more pressing by Darwin's theory of evolution, which not only made man into an ape but also took all purpose and progress out of natural history. Throughout this period, then, the problem of human nature was considered by many philosophers, physiologists, writers, and revolutionaries. The second half of the century saw the founding of scientific psychology and the formulation of its three variants: the study of consciousness, of the unconscious, and of adaptation.

A student of the nineteenth century, Franklin Baumer (1977), has suggested a useful conceptual division of the period, finding it too complex for chronological treatment. He proposes four nineteenth-century worlds, which we will roughly follow here. The first is the romantic world, which reacted strongly against the naturalism of the philosophes. The second world is the New Enlightenment, which carried on, in somewhat altered form, the program of the philosophes. The third is the world of Darwinism and evolution. The fourth world Baumer calls the *fin de siècle* (end of the century), a world of anxiety born of despair over nature, humanity, and the future.

The Reassertion of the Transcendental: The Romantic Revolt

Although we usually think of romanticism as a movement in the arts that emphasized human feeling, it was much more. It established a general revolt against the Cartesian-Newtonian world view. The first romantic poet, William Blake (1757–1827), in the hope that humanity could escape the scientific outlook, wrote: "May God us keep/ From Single vision and Newton's sleep."* Where the Enlightenment writers had valued mild and moral "passions," the romantics were inclined to worship all strong emotions—even violent and destructive ones. Above all, the romantics wanted there to be something more in the universe than atoms and the void. In a certain sense, romanticism reasserted a rationalist belief in something transcending material appearance.

It is appropriate, then, that the romantic movement, at least in philosophy, began with Kant. We have already noted how his idealist successors made material reality the expression of something spiritual that manifested itself in appearances. The romantic poet Coleridge adapted and elaborated Kant's distinction of *Verstand*, the limited process of understanding described by Locke, and *Vernuft*, an intuitive faculty capable of transcending appearances and grasping noumenal truth.

Several concepts important for psychology are evident in romanticism. One was the unconscious. Conscious, discursive thought was the tool of the Enlightenment in both art and philosophy. Romanticism, however, in its search for the

---

*Blake taunted the philosophes: "Mock on, Mock on, Voltaire, Rousseau:/ Mock on Mock on: 'tis all in vain!" As did other romantics, Blake detested the Industrial Revolution, whose "dark Satanic Mills" defiled "England's mountains green."

Lamarck	1780	Serfdom abolished in Hungary
Mesmer		U.S. Constitution
Bentham's *Principles of Morals*		French Revolution
	1790	
Gall's *Functions of the Brain*		Lavoisier executed
Malthus's *Essay*		
	1800	Jefferson elected president
		Beethoven's "Eroica" Symphony
	1810	
		War of 1812
Herbart		
		Jane Austen dies
Magendie–Bell law	1820	
		First U.S. Utopian community (New Harmony)
James Mill's *Analysis*	1830	Faraday's research on magnetism
Transcendentalism		Darwin sails on Beagle
Comte, Donders		Victoria becomes Queen
	1840	
Stuart Mill's *Logic*		First telegraph line
	1850	1848 Year of Revolutions
Spencer's *Principles*		Thoreau's *Walden*
Origin of Species		
Fechner's *Psychophysics*	1860	Civil War in U.S. begins
		U.S. slavery abolished
Taine's *On Intelligence*	1870	Franco-Prussian War
Bain founds *Mind*		Telephone invented
Peirce launches pragmatism		Wundt founds laboratory
	1880	
Galton's *Inquiries*		Twain's *Huckleberry Finn*
American Journal of Psychology		Hitler born
Eugenics movement	1890	
Dewey's "Reflex arc"		X-rays, radio discovered
Freud's *Dreams*	1900	
Myer's *Survival of Death*		Victoria dies
Angell's "Province"		General Motors founded
	1910	South Pole reached
Watson's "Behaviorist"		World War I
	1920	Russian Revolution

FIGURE 6-1 Chronology 1780–1920.

infinite, held the unconscious to be more important. Poets, for example, hoped to write automatically in an ecstatic transport so that the Infinite was recorded directly on paper. In philosophy, Schopenhauer posited Will as the noumenal reality behind appearances. Schopenhauer's Will, specifically the will to live, pushes humanity on to endless, futile striving for something better. This description of the Will foreshadows Freud's id. Schopenhauer wrote in *Parerga*, "In the heart of every man there lives a wild beast." Intelligence tries to control the Will, but its raging inflicts pain on the self and others. Also prefiguring Freud were those writers who saw in dreams the language of the unconscious needing only to be decoded to reveal the secrets of the Infinite.

In Schopenhauer's Will (the core of mental life) we find another important and complex romantic concept—that of mental activity and freedom. The Will is a wild beast, but while that wildness implies pain, it also implies freedom of choice. Schopenhauer's philosophy thus was voluntaristic, a romantic reaction against Enlightened materialistic determinism. Generally, this led the romantics to worship heroes, geniuses, and artists—those who asserted their Wills and did not bow to the way of the world. Thomas Carlyle, for instance, revered heroes who ranged from Odin to Shakespeare to Napolean. Psychologically speaking, this new form of voluntarism did away with the *tabula rasa*. Such a willful mind as the romantics envisioned would hardly be a mere passive receptacle for external stimuli. Coleridge, for instance, likened the mind to a lamp that casts intellectual light. Schopenhauer's effect is also evident in Wundt's psychology of consciousness, for Wundt lays great stress on the mind's ability to organize its own content, a form of voluntarism that contrasts sharply with the passivity of associationism.

Not only did the romantics reject the idea that a person is a machine, they also rejected the idea that the universe is a machine. They were vitalists and teleologists for whom nature was not dead matter—mere atoms in the void—but something organic, growing, improving itself with time. Biology, not physics, should be the model for thinking about things, the romantics said. Herder expressed this sentiment in Germany. In England, it was forcefully stated by the conservative thinker Edmund Burke (1729–1797), who said that human nature and society develop slowly over the course of centuries. He decried the attempt of the French Revolutionists to erect a society based only on pure, geometric reason, ignoring the wisdom of history. This romantic conception of nature was progressive and optimistic, but was soon to be shattered by Darwin's theory of natural selection. The romantics already believed in evolution, but it was not the randomly directed process of Darwinism.

Romantic vitalism meant that although we may see in romanticism a reassertion of the rationalist search for transcendent Truth, the romantics were not advocates of Being. Carlyle, for instance, insisted that Truth is always becoming, it never simply is. Truth is not a static collection of Forms, but something alive, something always perfecting itself. This belief, at least, would be quite compatible with Darwinian evolution.

There was one Enlightenment concept that inspired the romantics, and which they enriched. Hartley's associationism was an important part of romantic critical theory. Classical poetry was full of capitalized abstractions such as "Beauty," but the romantics wrote about the concrete, individual beautiful things out of which we form our idea of Beauty. In associationism, aesthetic and moral judgments are sentiments, subjective emotional reactions relatively separate from discursive reason. The romantics elevated the subjective and passionate and sought to use the associative analysis of mind as a way to evoke emotional responses in their readers. They enriched associationism by stressing the concept of coalescence, that is, the active imagination may synthesize atomic elements into a creation that is more than the sum of the atomic units themselves, as when elementary colors are mixed to make a qualitatively different one. Wundt made much of the power of the mind to synthesize mental elements, while the Gestalt psychologists became even more holistic.

We may conclude by saying that the romantics opposed mechanism in every field and promoted rival concepts such as individual freedom, voluntarism, holism, vitalism, and teleology. Although romanticism was subdued by subsequent developments in science, especially Darwinism, it played a role in forming psychology—especially in its birthplace, Germany—and in one form or another, romanticism has always appealed to those discomfited by the geometric spirit and its products.

The New Enlightenment

Of course, not everyone was disenchanted by naturalism. Many important thinkers carried on the spirit and ambitions of the Enlightenment, especially in England and France. Several movements in the New Enlightenment are important to psychology.

Utilitarianism and Associationism

Utilitarianism and associationism are inextricably intertwined doctrines. *Utilitarianism* describes the motivational dynamics of mind; *associationism* describes the cognitive structure of mind. Utilitarianism was implicit in the teachings of the eighteenth-century associationists from Hume onward who said that sensations are either pleasant, which we desire to repeat, or unpleasant, which we desire to avoid. Utilitarianism simply tried to apply this motivational system to society as a whole.

The motivational doctrine of utilitarianism was most completely worked out by the English reformer Jeremy Bentham (1748–1832). He opened his *Introduction to the Principles of Moral Legislation* (1789) with a forceful statement of utilitarian hedonism: "Nature has placed mankind under the governance of two sovereign masters, *pain* and *pleasure*. It is for them alone to point out what we ought to do, as well as to determine what we shall do. . . . They govern us in all we do, in all we say, in all we think." Individuals should conduct their lives, therefore, by choosing those courses of action that will maximize personal pleasure and minimize pain; this is the only scientific ethics. The legislature—Bentham's target as a reformer—should follow the same standard, seeking to promote the greatest happiness of the greatest number in all acts of government. Bentham saw government as naturally oppressive; he assumed, as did the first economist, Adam Smith, that minimal government would let each individual seek his or her own happiness.

The laws of Bentham's principle of pleasure resemble the laws of association proposed by Hume, Hartley, and Brown. The value of pleasure and pain is determined by the intensity, duration, certainty, and propinquity of the corresponding sensation. Bentham sought to quantify both pleasure and pain, so that moral decisions could be made by summing up the net pleasure or pain to be expected to follow from a selection of possible acts and choosing that which satisfied the principle of utility. Also following the associationists, Bentham distinguished simple pleasures or pains and their compounds, complex pleasures and pains. He goes on to give an elaborate enumeration of the kinds of pleasure, giving a much longer list than a post-Freudian modern would expect. There are sensual pleasures and pains, to be sure, but there are also the pleasures of wealth, power, piety, and benevolence, to name only a few. Bentham also discussed individual and racial characteristics that modify the workings of the utility principle according to personal disposition. His major effort was then to devise a program of good government based solely on the rational principle of utility, disregarding any considerations of historical context or human rights. It was an exercise in the geometric spirit and the mechanistic philosophy to make Edmund Burke or any romantic shudder.

One of Bentham's most enthusiastic followers was James Mill (1773–1836), a politician turned philosopher. He ardently expounded Benthamism, but is best known in psychology for his mechanistic associationism. In no way did Mill really add to associationism; rather he represented its ultimate form. He follows Hume and Hartley in distinguishing sensations and their copies—ideas—and follows Condillac in trying to reduce all mental activity to association. Mill adopts what one might call the tinker-toy theory of mind. In this view the mind is a passive, blank slate, receptive to simple sensations (the tinker-toy nodes) out of which complex sensations or ideas are compounded by forming associative links (the sticks linking the nodes) between atomic units. Associative links are built in two ways. Some sensations always occur together, or *synchronously,* and become linked. Smelling a rose suggests its other attributes with which the smell is regularly associated in our experience. Other sensations regularly occur in sequence, or *successively,* and Mill follows Hume in reducing causation to regular associative trains. Mill analyzes speech as a train of associated atomic words, wholly ignoring a sentence's meaning's control of discourse. His mechanical associationism is widely taken as a *reductio ad absurdum* of the associative psychology. For example, in *Analysis of the Phenomena of the Human Mind* Mill describes the idea of a house as compounded out of a huge number of simpler units such as nails, boards, and pieces of glass. He then concludes: "How many more [ideas make up] the idea called Every Thing?" One imagines the mind filled with a colossal and unwieldy tinker-toy arrangement.

Mill's associationism dispenses with the mental faculties retained by Hartley and other associationists. Combined with utilitarian hedonism, the result is a completely mechanical picture of mind in which idea follows idea automatically with no room left for voluntary control. The exercise of will is an illusion, Mill maintained. Reasoning is no more than the associative compounding of the ideas contained in syllogisms. Attention is no more than the fact that the mind is preoccupied with whichever ideas are particularly pleasurable or painful. The mind does not direct attention; its attention is mechanically directed by the principle of utility. Like Bentham and many others who wrote on the mind, Mill expounded his psychology for purposes of reform. He was not a psychologist. Influenced by Helvetius, as Bentham also was, Mill was especially interested in education. If the person is entirely passive at birth, it is the duty of education to correctly mold the person's mind. Mill put his ideas into practice by the rigorous education he gave his son, teaching him ancient Greek at three and Latin at eight. This son wrote a history of Roman law at ten.

The son, John Stuart Mill (1806–1873), did not become the perfect utilitarian his father had expected, however. Although an early adherent of Benthamism, he experienced a nervous breakdown during which he came to find Benthamism sterile, narrow, and excessively calculating. He even went so far as to call Bentham's program "evil." He eventually tempered Bentham's hedonistic principles with Wordsworth's romantic vision of nature and human feeling. He even endorsed the romantic preference for the grown or natural over the manufactured, and denied that the human being is a machine. He saw people as living things whose autonomous development and growth should be nurtured.

J. S. Mill's version of associationism was tempered by the romantic penchant for synthesis. This combination led to his idea of mental chemistry. Earlier associationists, including his father, had recognized that certain associative links became so strong that the linked ideas appeared inseparable. J. S. Mill went further, maintaining that elementary ideas could fuse into a whole idea not reducible to its elements. The elements generate the new idea, they do not merely compose it. He offered colors as an example of such a process. Spin a wheel divided into wedges, each colored with a primary color, and at a certain speed the experience will be of whiteness, not of spinning colors. The atomic colors on the wheel are generating a new color, a different kind of experience.

We must emphasize, however, that although Mill tempered his father's associationistic Benthamism with the broader conceptions of romanticism, he still sought to improve utilitarianism and empiricism, not to refute them. He always detested the mystic intuitionism of Coleridge, Carlyle, and the other romantics. He returned to Berkeley's analysis of matter, although without God, allowing for no noumenal reality beyond appearances. Matter is no more than the permanent possibility of sensation for J. S. Mill. The pen in one's room, for example, exists only because it always may be perceived, whether or not it is being perceived at the moment. Nor did Mill accept romantic voluntarism. His mental chemistry, although it recognized the possible coalescence of sensations and ideas, remained a passive description of mind. It is not the mind's autonomous activity that brings about the qualitative chemical change, but the way the sensations are associated in experience: One does choose to see the white spinning disc, because the experience is forced on one's perception by the conditions of the experiment.

John Stuart Mill was the last great philosophical associationist. His associationism arose in the context of logical and metaphysical—not purely psychological—discussions. Mill did believe in the possibility of Hume's science of human nature and in fact tried to contribute to its methodology. Later associationists became more distinctly psychological; therefore we will postpone them to a later section.

Positivism

We have already met philosophers such as Berkeley, Hume, and Newton who are at least partially positivistic, favoring an epistemology that restricts human knowledge to what is immediately observable. However, as natural science and technology marched from success to success, a general attitude called *scientism* spread through Europe, a faith in the ability of science to answer all questions, to solve all problems. It was natural then for science, based since Newton and Bacon on a positivist epistemology, to be elevated to a new religion—a world view intended to supplant already embattled Christianity. Such was the undertaking of Auguste Comte (1798–1857). Comte named *positivism,* which embraced an epistemology, philosophies of science and history, and a religion.

As an epistemology, positivism adopted a radical empiricism. Metaphysical speculation and explanations of nature in terms of unobservable entities were to be abandoned. Instead, human knowledge would confine itself to collecting and correlating facts to yield an accurate description of the world. Such was the method and proper philosophy of science, according to Comte. With the ability to predict nature comes the ability to control nature. Hence, when a science of humanity emerges, society and individuals will likewise be subject to control.

Comte gave a sweeping picture of history as inevitable upward progress in three broad stages. The first step is the theological, in which humanity explains natural events by positing invisible gods and spirits responsible for them. The second stage is the metaphysical, in which the gods and spirits become abstractions or other unobservable causes thought to explain nature. The third stage is the scientific, in which explanation is given up for description, prediction, and control, and in which the Religion of Humanity supplants Christianity. Comte gives elaborate descriptions of his new religion. It is complete with a scientific elite of priests, a revolutionary manifesto for the scientific control of society, and a flag. Some of Comte's views are quaintly Victorian—for instance, his belief that worship of Woman was the first part of worship of humanity.

Comte's interest was not in science as such, but in how science might be used to improve humanity. His epistemology and his philosophies of science and history are all subordinate to the construction of a new scientific society. His real audience was composed of women and working people, whom Comte believed were oppressed by the vested interests then ruling society. He believed it was through their efforts that the positivist revolution would come about. Although a scientific elite would rule the new society, Comte wanted first to persuade the masses.

Comte's views on psychology are unusual. He lists a hierarchy of sciences, from most basic (and first developed) to most comprehensive (and last to develop). This hierarchy is mathematics, astronomy, physics, chemistry, physiology and biology, and sociology. He is usually credited with being one of the founders of sociology, which was to be the science that would make his new, scientifically managed world possible. Psychology, however, does not appear on the list. Comte disapproved of introspective psychology, which he regarded as muddled and metaphysical. He held out some hope for phrenology, which tried to tie personality traits to distinct areas of the brain. Hence he divided psychology in two, destroying it as a coherent field. The study of the individual he assigned to physiology and biology, as in phrenological psychology. The study of the human being as a social animal belonged to sociology. Moreover, Comte seems to have found contemporary philosophical psychology too intellectual. He emphasized over and over that human beings are creatures of feeling first and intellect second.

Comte's positivism and his Religion of Humanity inspired many people all over Europe. Some tried to carry on his religious-revolutionary program, founding positivist societies and even opening positivist churches. More serious thinkers, however, found Comte's religion distasteful, preferring instead his epistemology. Such, for example, was the attitude of John Stuart Mill, who carried on extensive correspondence with Comte. Consequently, positivism increasingly became a purely philosophical movement, and finally a philosophy of science. Two figures deserve recognition in this connection: Claude Bernard (1813–1878) and Ernst Mach (1838–1916).

Bernard was a French physiologist who wrote an influential work in the philosophy of science, *Introduction to the Study of Experimental Medicine* (1865).

Although he rejected Comte's system and religion for displaying the same vices as other metaphysical systems and religions, his account of science is eminently positivistic. Only the rigorous testing of objective scientific hypotheses with objective methods could yield knowledge. Any question not subject to such treatment is regarded as meaningless. The world is to be viewed as a perfectly deterministic system, for only on such a view is science possible. The first goal of science is prediction and control.

Ernst Mach was a great German physicist who put forward a radical version of positivism as a philosophy of science in an attempt to explicate the true foundations of science. He admired Berkeley, and like Berkeley he saw human consciousness as a collection of sensations beyond which we cannot penetrate without committing the crime of metaphysics. The goal of science is the economical ordering of sensations and nothing more. So, for example, Mach refused to believe in the existence of atoms because no one had ever seen one. Theory was to be avoided except insofar as it correlated experiences and was useful for making predictions. Knowledge for Mach ultimately served a pragmatic, biological function. Organizing our experience helps us to adapt to our environment; it penetrates no reality beyond appearance. Mach also introduced a critical, historical method to the study of science. He believed that many scientific concepts had incorporated metaphysical accretions in the course of their development, and that the best way to strip off the accretions and reduce the concepts to their sensory base was to study the development of the concepts. Echoing Comte, Mach noted that early science had grown up in the theological atmosphere of the seventeenth century and, consequently, concepts such as force had acquired "divine" attributes as something transcending mere experience.

The influence of positivism in one form or another was very great, embracing physicists and realistic novelists alike. In psychology it affected the English and American schools more than the European schools. Wundt, for example, was very critical of Comte. Although his individual psychology in some ways resembled Mach's science in that both were analyses of immediate experience, Wundt postulated unperceived mental processes to explain experienced mental events. Mach's philosophy had more influence on Wundt's English student Titchener, who took science to be a descriptive, not explanatory, enterprise, and on the Gestalt psychologists who studied objects as given immediately to experience. Freud's explanation of the unconscious, which is unobservable by definition, is certainly not positivistic, giving another example of the German's relative immunity to this view of science.

In America, however, the influence of positivism was great. William James was a great admirer of Mach, whose concept of knowledge as a practical adaptation to life is quite consistent with James's pragmatism. Mach was a source of inspiration to the twentieth-century logical positivists who had considerable influence on behaviorism. The clearest influence of positivism is on B. F. Skinner. Although Mach's psychology was introspective, that is, a psychology of the subject, once behaviorists decided to treat human beings as objects of observation, Mach's philosophy led directly to radical behaviorism. Skinner maintains that the single goal of science is to find lawful relations between independent and dependent variables, leading to prediction and control. Reference to unobservable "mental" processes is as much illegitimate metaphysics to Skinner as it was to Mach. Furthermore, Skinner's call for a scientifically managed, nondemocratic utopia is secular Comtism. Both believe in the perfectability of human beings through scientific control.

Marxism

It is impossible to pass over the thought of Karl Marx (1818–1883) in any account of the nineteenth century. Marxism, in one form or another (many of which Marx would have disowned) has been one of the most important philosophies of modern times. Furthermore, Marx erected his system not just on considerations of economic history, but also on a particular view of humanity. Marx maintained that, although human consciousness is determined by the economic structure of a given era, there is a real underlying human nature whose needs are stifled by all historically existing forms of society. Hence people are alienated from their true selves, and this alienation is the motive force for human improvement and political revolution. Only in a genuine communist society (nowhere achieved in Marx's or our own time) would humans no longer be alienated from their true selves.

Given Marx's fame and general influence, it is remarkable how little impact his thought has had on psychology outside the Soviet Union, where it is, of course, official dogma. We must suspect the reason for his lack of influence is political. After 1848 communism was a specter haunting Europe, a specter rendered frighteningly concrete in the Russian Revolution of 1917, and in subsequent revolutions.

In the early days of psychology Marxism was probably a dangerous philosophy to study, let alone espouse, and neglecting this theory could be rationalized by its apparent irrelevance to psychology. Few Western psychologists are sympathetic to Marx; of those who are, most prominent are the humanist psychologist Erich Fromm and the developmental psychologist Klaus Riegel, both of whom are widely viewed within psychology as distinctly eccentric. Yet Marx's thought is perfectly compatible with other accepted influences on psychology. His stage view of history and his revolutionary call to the masses resemble Comte. He accepted naturalism and materialism. He studied the influence of the environment on the human personality, yet held a rather humanistic view of human nature. However, the other revolutionary thinker of the nineteenth century was quieter, happily bourgeois, and much more influential.

Heraclitus Triumphant: The Darwinian Revolution

Background

The Newtonian-Cartesian mechanical world was changeless. God, or some Creator, had constructed a marvelous machine perfect in conception and endless in time. Each object, each biological species, was fixed for eternity, changelessly perfect in obedience to fixed natural laws. Such a world view was equally consistent with Plato's Forms, Aristotle's essences, and Christian theology. On this view, change was something unusual in nature. Even the geological doctrine of uniformitarianism, which helped Darwin invent his theory of evolution, was antievolutionary in tracing the continuum of natural forces back over millions of years. In biology the Aristotelian belief that species were fixed and immutable was a dogma supported by the highest scientific authorities right up until Darwin's time. Given the Cartesian-Newtonian concept that matter is inert, incapable of acting, and passive only, and that spontaneous change is the origin of new species, the mutation of old seemed impossible. Once the supreme Intelligence had acted creatively, dead matter could effect nothing new.

In the atmosphere of progress characteristic of the Enlightenment, however, this static view of nature began to change. Evolutionary ideas go back at least to Anaximander (see Chapter 2), but in the eighteenth century they really began to take hold. One old Aristotelian-theological concept that helped evolution along was the Great Chain of Being, or Aristotle's *scala naturae*. The Chain was viewed by medievals as a measure of a creature's nearness to God and consequently its degree of spiritual perfection. To the naturalistic thinkers, on the other hand, it became a record of the ascent of living things toward nature's crowning perfection, humankind.

To accomplish the change from a stable but perfect universe to a changing, striving one, a different view of matter was needed; dead, stupid matter can neither change nor strive. In the eighteenth century precisely the necessary conception arose. Matter—for some thinkers, even inorganic matter—was now endowed with vitality and a tendency to progress. It was thus possible for many writers to assert that the universe had evolved from simple beginnings, and that species had changed and progressed since the beginning of time and could go on changing and progressing forever. This view was embodied in one form or another in French transformism and German nature philosophy. It certainly does not abandon naturalism, for it enables one to eliminate God altogether and give a thoroughly natural account of the origin of the earth and its inhabitants. This concept of evolution is not mechanical, however, for it endows matter with godlike attributes. For the Newtonian, stupid matter was set in mechanical motion by an intelligent, purposeful Creator. For the vitalist, matter itself is intelligent and purposeful. Vitalism is thus a romantic view of Nature—self-perfecting and self-directing, progressively unfolding itself throughout time.

Charles Darwin's signal contribution to the concept of evolution was to mechanize it, to deromanticize nature and capture evolution for the Newtonian world view. However, before examining Darwin's theory, we should first consider the major romantic alternative whose appeal is strong even today—and which even Darwin himself could not entirely resist—the evolutionary theory of Jean-Baptiste Lemarck (1744–1829). Lamarck, being a naturalist well-known for his work in taxonomy, was the most scientific exponent of the romantic-progressive view of evolution. There were two important aspects of Lamarck's theory. The first said that organic matter is fundamentally different from inorganic, that each living species possesses an innate drive to perfect itself. Each organism strives to adapt itself to its surroundings and changes itself as it does so, developing various muscles, acquiring various habits. The second part of his theory claimed that these acquired characteristics could be passed on to an animal's offspring. Thus each individual's striving for perfection was recorded and passed on, and over generations species of plants and animals would improve themselves, fulfilling their drives for perfection. Modern genetics has destroyed Lamarck's vision. Organic matter is now said to be merely complexly arranged inorganic molecules; DNA is a collection of amino acids. The DNA chain is unchanged by modifications to an individual's body. (Certain external influences, such as drugs or radiation, can affect genetic information, but that is not what Lamarck meant.) In the absence of genetics, however, the inheritance of acquired characteristics is plausible and even Darwin from time to time accepted it, although he never accepted the vitalist view of matter. Later, both Wundt and Freud believed that acquired habits and experiences were capable of being passed through heredity.

So, by Darwin's time, evolution was a widespread concept, disbelieved only by firm religionists and the biological establishment, which still accepted the fixity of species. A naturalistic but romantic conception of evolution was in place. The phrase "survival of the fittest" had already been coined in 1852 by Herbert Spencer, an English Lamarckian. And in 1849, a decade before the publication of Darwin's *Origin of Species,* Alfred, Lord Tennyson wrote in his greatest poem, *In Memorium,* lines that foreshadowed the new view of evolution, in which the individual sacrifices for the species in the struggle for survival, a view of which Tennyson disapproved:

> Are God and Nature then at strife,
> That Nature lends such evil dreams?
> So careful of the type [species] she seems,
> So careless of the single life.

Later in the poem, in a widely quoted line, Tennyson calls nature "red in tooth and claw."

The Victorian Revolutionary: Charles Darwin (1809–1882)

Evolution could not long remain a poetic effusion, although Darwin's own grandfather, Erasmus Darwin, anticipated his grandson's theory in a scientific poem, *Zoonomia.* Nor could it remain a romantic fancy, inspiring but finally implausible. Darwin's achievement was to make evolution into a scientific theory by providing a mechanism—natural selection. Then a campaign to convince scientists and the public of the fact of evolution was needed. Darwin never campaigned himself. He was something of a hypochondriac—one biographer (Irvine 1959) called him "the perfect patient"—and after his trip on the *Beagle* he became a recluse, rarely leaving his country home. The struggle for the survival of natural selection was carried on by others, most spectacularly by Thomas Henry Huxley (1825–1895), "Darwin's bulldog."

Darwin was a young naturalist who had the good fortune to be included on a round-the-world scientific voyage aboard *HMS Beagle* from 1831 to 1836. Darwin was impressed, especially in South America, by the tremendous variation within and between species. Darwin noted there are innumerable distinct natural forms, each of which is peculiarly suited to its particular habitat. It was easy to imagine that each subspecies had descended from a common ancestor, and that each subspecies had been selected to fit some part of the environment.

Then, sometime after his return to England, Darwin began to collect data on species, their variation and origin. In his *Autobiography* he said that he collected facts "on a wholesale scale," on "true Baconian principles." Part of his investigation centered on artificial selection, that is, on how breeders of plants and animals improve their stocks. Darwin talked with pigeon fanciers and horticulturalists and read their pamphlets. One pamphlet he read, "The Art of Improving the Breeds of Domestic Animals," written in 1809 by John Sebright, indicated that nature, too, selected some traits and rejected others, just as breeders did: "A severe winter, or a scarcity of food, by destroying the weak and unhealthful, has all the good effects of the most skillful selection" (Ruse 1975). So, by the 1830s, Darwin already had a rudimentary theory of natural selection: Nature produces innumerable variations among living things, and some of these variations are selected for perpetuation. Over time, isolated populations become adapted to their surroundings. What was entirely unclear was what maintained the system of selection. Why should there be improvement in species? In the case of artificial selection, the answer is clear. Selection is made by the breeder to produce a desirable kind of plant or animal. But what force in nature parallels the breeder's ideal? Darwin could not accept Lamarck's innate drive to perfection. The cause of selection must reside outside the organism, he insisted, but where?

Darwin got his answer in 1838 while reading Thomas Malthus's (1766–1834) *Essay on the Principle of Population as it Affects the Future Improvement of Society* (1798). Malthus attacked the utopian fantasies of certain writers by arguing that population growth necessarily exceeds growth in the food supply, with the consequence that life is a struggle of too many people for too few resources. The mass of humanity is necessarily kept at a subsistence level economy, at best. In his *Autobiography* Darwin stated he had at last "got a theory on which he could work." It was the struggle for survival that motivated natural selection. Too many creatures struggled over too few resources, and those who were "weak and unhealthful" could not support themselves and died without offspring. The strong and healthy survived and procreated. In this way favorable variations were preserved and unfavorable ones eliminated. Struggle for survival was the engine of evolution.

Darwin need not have gone to Malthus for the concept of individual struggle for survival. As William Irvine (1959) points out, "In her evolutionary aspects nature is almost tritely mid-Victorian." Darwin's theory "delighted . . . mid-century optimists" who learned that "nature moved forward on the sound business principles of laissez-faire." Natural selection may have offended the pious, but not the Victorian businessman of the industrial revolution, who knew that life was a constant struggle that rewarded failure with poverty and disgrace. The improvement of the species from the struggle of individuals was merely Adam Smith's "invisible hand" all over again.

Darwin had formulated the essentials of his theory by 1842, at which time he first set them on paper with no thought of publication. His theory may be summarized as a logical argument (Vorzimmer 1970). First, from Malthus, Darwin holds that there is a constant struggle for existence resulting from the tendency of animals to outgrow their food sources. Second, nature constantly produces variant forms within and between species. Some variants are better adapted to the struggle for survival than others. Consequently, organisms possessing unfavorable traits will not reproduce, causing their traits to disappear. Finally, as small adaptive change follows small adaptive change over eons, species will differentiate from a common stock as each form adapts to its peculiar environment. Furthermore, environments will change, selecting new traits for perpetuation, and as environment succeeds environment, species will diverge ever more from their parent forms. Thus the observed diversity of nature can be explained as the result of a few mechanical principles operating over millions of years, as species evolve from species.

The theory as it stands is deficient. Without our knowledge of genetics, the origin of variations and the nature of their transmission could not be explained. Darwin was never able to overcome these difficulties and was in fact pushed closer and closer to Lamarckism as he defended his theories against critics. It is an irony of history that while Darwin was writing and defending his *Origin of Species,* an obscure Polish monk, Gregor Mendel (1822–1884), was doing the work on heredity that eventually supplied the answer to Darwin's difficulties. It was not until 1900 that Mendel's work, published and ignored in 1865, was rediscovered and hailed as the foundation of modern genetics. By the time Darwin died he had earned burial in

Westminster Abbey, and his thought had revolutionized the Western world view, but it was not until the twentieth century that evolution seriously affected biology, following the synthesis of genetics and natural selection into modern neo-Darwinian theory in the 1930's.

Darwin set his ideas down in 1842, but he did not publish his *Origin of Species* until 1859. Why? It appears that even for its discoverer, evolution was too threatening a thought. In a letter Darwin said that admitting that species are not fixed "is like confessing a murder" (Irvine 1959). It has been suggested that Darwin's hypochondria and various physical symptoms resulted from a neurotic crisis over the enormity of the idea of natural selection. In any event, Darwin pursued other things, spending eight years, for example, studying barnacles. Then, on June 18, 1858, Darwin was shocked to discover that someone was about to publish his theory. Evolution was truly in the air. Alfred Russell Wallace (1823–1913) had also been to South America, had been impressed by natural variation, and had read Malthus. Younger than Darwin, he was less hesitant to publish his conclusions. In fact, in later years Wallace was faithful to natural selection after Darwin retreated to Lamarckism.

It was arranged that Darwin and Wallace would each write a paper on natural selection. These were read on July 1, 1858, in their absence, to the Linnean Society of London, thus establishing Darwin and Wallace as codiscoverers of natural selection. Darwin rushed through a short version of his projected work on evolution, which appeared in 1859 as *The Origin of Species by Means of Natural Selection or the Preservation of Favored Races in the Struggle for Life*. It presented his theory backed by a mass of supporting detail. It was revised until its sixth edition in 1872, as Darwin tried to answer his scientific critics—unsuccessfully, as it turned out—in ignorance of genetics. Darwin wrote numerous other works, including two on the descent of humans and the expression of emotion in humans and the animals. The latter two works form part of the founding of the psychology of adaptation, and therefore will be considered in Chapter 9.

Reception and Influence

The world was well prepared for Darwin's theory. The idea of evolution was already around well before 1859, and when the *Origin* was published it was taken seriously by learned men in all quarters. Biologists and naturalists greeted the work with varying degrees of criticism. Part of Darwin's thesis, that all living things descend from one common ancestor in the remote past, was scarcely novel and was widely accepted. Great difficulties were seen with the theory of natural selection, however, and it was still easy for scientists to hang on to some form of Lamarckism, to see the hand of God in progressive evolution (as did Charles Lyell, the great geologist, even though he was a powerful proponent of Darwin's ideas), or to exempt man from natural selection (as did nearly everyone).

If the reception of the *Origin* was so calm, how can we speak of a Darwinian revolution? To begin with, an appearance of revolution is given by the vituperative reception given evolution by Christian fundamentalists. Beginning with Bishop Wilberforce and continuing with William Jennings Bryan, defenders of the Bible attacked evolution, only to be crushed by such powerful personalities as T. H. Huxley and Clarence Darrow. Such clashes are the stuff of drama and give an appearance of revolution to the situation. The biblical literalists, however, were already well behind the times. The Bible had received two hundred years of histor ical scrutiny and had been found wanting as a historical document. Even the Catholic *Dublin Review* was not shocked by Darwin's ideas.

To consider Darwinism as an intellectual revolution we must distinguish Darwinism as a scientific hypothesis and Darwinism as the fulfillment of Enlightenment naturalism. Darwin himself cared only for the first, his intellectual child, but was alive to the possibilities of the second. Darwinism as a naturalistic metaphysics was the creation of others. Herbert Spencer, who had believed in the survival of the fittest before Darwin and applied it ruthlessly to man and society, was one forceful proponent of metaphysical Darwinism. Another was T. H. Huxley, who used evolution to batter the Bible, miracles, and the church generally.

Huxley did much to popularize Darwinism as a naturalistic, even scientistic metaphysics. Darwin's theory did not begin the modern crisis of conscience. Profound doubts about the existence of God and about the meaning of life go back to the eighteenth century. Darwinism was not the beginning of the scientific challenge to the old medieval-Renaissance world view. It was the culmination of this challenge, making it most difficult to exempt human beings from immutable, determinate natural law. In *Man's Place in Nature,* Huxley carefully related mankind to the living apes, lower animals, and fossil ancestors, showing that we did indeed evolve from lower forms of life, that no Creation was needed. In the hands of people like Huxley, science then became not just the destroyer of illusions, but also a new metaphysics offering a new kind of salvation through science itself. Huxley wrote that:

> This new nature begotten by science upon fact . . . [constitutes] the foundation of our wealth and the condition of our safety . . . it is the bond which unites into a solid whole, regions larger than any empire of antiquity; it secures us from the recurrence of pestilences and famines of former times; it is the source of endless comforts and conveniences, which are not mere luxuries, but conduce to physical and moral well being.

More effusively, Winwood Reade wrote in *The Martyrdom of Man:* "The God of Light, the Spirit of Knowledge, the Divine Intellect is gradually spreading over the planet . . . Hunger and starvation will then be unknown . . . Disease will be extirpated . . . immortality will be invented . . . Man will then be perfect . . . he will therefore be what the vulgar worship as a God" (Houghton 1957). This hope is similar to Comte's positivism, which Huxley called "Catholicism *minus* Christianity." Clearly for some, the new religion of scientific humanity was at hand. Huxley also boasted of sciences' practical fruits: "Every chemically pure substance employed in manufacture, every abnormally fertile race of plants, or rapidly growing and fattening breed of animals . . ." This immediately brings to mind today's cancerous chemicals, tasteless tomatoes, and steroid-stuffed steers.

Darwinism did not instigate modern doubt, but it did intensify it. Darwin effected a Newtonian revolution in biology, robbing nature of her romantic capital *N,* reducing evolution to random variation and happenstance victory in the struggle for survival. The beginning of the reduction of biological nature to chemical nature that was completed with the discovery of DNA had begun. In psychology Darwinism leads to the psychology of adaptation. Assuming evolution, one may ask how mind and behavior, as distinct from bodily organs, help each creature adapt to its surroundings. Behaviorism is the ultimate heir to Darwinism in psychology; Skinner carefully modeled his account of animal learning on Darwinian variation, selection, and retention. Darwinism contributed also to the mechanization of human nature. In one of his more effusive moments, Huxley proclaimed that he would willingly be a clockwork mechanism if it were set to think and act correctly. Just such an image becomes the justification for Skinner's projection of a scientific Utopia.

Many, however, could not accept naturalism or were depressed by it. Huxley himself in his last writings said that man was unique among animals, for by his intelligence he could lift himself out of the natural Cosmic Process and transcend organic evolution. Sentiments such as this were not at all uncommon among both scientists and laymen, and help account for the popularity both before and after Darwin's time of various semi- or pseudoscientific trends based on the uniqueness of man.

On the Fringes of Science and the *Fin de Siècle*

We now come to three movements that at first seem unrelated: *mesmerism,* the belief that an imponderable fluid permeating the universe can be manipulated to cure certain illnesses; *phrenology,* the belief that bumps on the head correspond to well-developed mental faculties manifested as highly developed parts of the brain; and *spiritualism,* the belief that there is a plane of existence apart from material appearances that can be known through certain occult experiences and practices. In fact, however, these three beliefs are historically interconnected; adherents of one were frequently adherents of the others. They were presented in various combinations in nineteenth-century popular self-help psychology. Two of these movements, mesmerism and phrenology, ultimately contributed substantially to psychology; and the third, spiritualism, was taken seriously by many men of science, notably William James. All three are intimately related to the way science gradually filled the popular void left by the weakening of religion. Faith in science was replacing faith in the church. At the same time all three, but most particularly spiritualism, often consoled those who were distressed by naturalistic materialism. This distress intensified after 1859 in the *fin de siècle* period, and thoughtful people, among them philosophers and scientists, turned to the occult for spiritual comfort.

Mesmerism: The First Popular Science

The term *mesmerism* comes from the name of the movement's founder, Franz Anton Mesmer (1734–1815), a Viennese physician who attributed numerous bodily diseases to an impalpable fluid penetrating the entire universe. Mesmer believed that this fluid was vital to the nervous activity of the body and that physicians could cure various diseases by manipulating the fluid in a patient's body. Mesmer began by using magnets to draw the fluid away from the afflicted areas, but soon decided that the fluid was really susceptible to animal magnetism rather than to mineral magnetism. Mesmer devised a complicated and outré therapy for his patients involving, among other things, striking the diseased parts of the body with his hands or a magic wand, tubs of water with iron rods focused on a patient's symptoms, and a "crisis room" lined with mattresses in which Mesmer's cures were effected during a kind of seizure. He specialized in what we now call "functional" illnesses, those that come from purely psychological causes. Although it was suggested at the time that at least some of the cures were a result of the patient's suggestibility,

Mesmer firmly resisted any such hypothesis, insisting on his theory of animal fluids.

No single element of mesmerism was new. The curing of apparently physical diseases by inspired individuals goes back at least as far as the time of Jesus. It was also practiced by such contemporaries of Mesmer as Valentine Greatraks in England and Johann Gassner in Germany, Greatraks's speciality was scrofula, or the King's Evil, so-called because the touch of the monarch was said to cure it. If Mesmer's practice was not new, neither was the hypothesis of an ineffable universal fluid. Central to Newton's universe was the *ether,* a subtle fluid that carried electromagnetic waves and defined absolute space. A whole line of alchemical doctors had believed in a universal fluid essential to health, and even such a modern chemist as Robert Boyle attributed Greatraks's cures to invisible particles passing from doctor to patient. Gassner was a German priest who allegedly cast out demons. Mesmer himself investigated Gassner, concluding that Gassner's cures resulted from the natural use of animal magnetism, not religious exorcism.

Mesmer's novel approach was to try to put such cures and theorizing on a scientific basis. He attempted to convince medical establishments, first in Vienna and later in Paris, that his cures were genuine and that animal magnetism was real. Over and over again physicians admitted that Mesmer had seemingly effected great cures, but they found his methods too bizarre, his theory unscientific. Some even intimated that he was a fraud. Mesmerism was too close to the occult—using trances, magical passes, and the trappings of the seance—to satisfy any Newtonian doctors. Mesmer was eventually worn down by these repeated rebuffs and by what he felt were betrayals by some of his followers, and in 1784 he left Paris to live the rest of his life detached from the movement he had started.

That movement was enormously popular. In the years before the French Revolution it was an absolute mania, garnering far more attention from the French public than the issues of the Revolution. Mesmeric lodges sprang up all over France in the 1780s. Mesmer enlisted the Marquis de Lafayette as a patron and corresponded briefly with George Washington. Mesmer and mesmerism seemed to fill perfectly a gap left by religion's receding influence. Science was all the rage in the late eighteenth century, and its influence grew in the nineteenth. People were hungry for a new set of certainties to replace the old. Mesmer offered at least the trappings of science—a reasoned theory about why his cures worked, an explanation that also covered the ancient miracle workers. Yet at the same time Mesmer's practice was served up in mystical and magical dress, more interesting than the austere rationalism of Newton's science. In short, Mesmer offered exactly the right pseudoscience to appeal to the times. It was scientific enough to appeal to the new rationalism, but spiritual enough to appeal to latent religious needs as well. Whether or not Mesmer himself was a charlatan is an extremely difficult question. Certainly he demanded absolute obedience from his followers, lest they betray his invention. But so did Freud. His treatment sessions were lurid seances, with Mesmer attired in mystic robes and wielding an iron wand. Moreover, Mesmer drifted into genuine occultism, using animal magnetism to explain clairvoyance, telepathy, and precognition. Yet Mesmer always tried to convince the medical establishment, even when it brought him nothing but ridicule. Mesmer was at once a magician and a pioneer in abnormal psychology.

There was at the center of mesmerism a useful tool for the treatment of neuroses. Mesmer did cure many people of a great range of hysterical symptoms, from hysterical blindness to mysterious pains. He obscured the sources of his cures with the trappings of the seance and the theory of the universal fluid. What was central to Mesmer's cures, however, was the trance he could induce in his patients. In this trance he could command their actions and effect a cure. Although Mesmer attributed the trance to animal magnetism, it became apparent even to some of his followers that something simpler was involved. The trance was due to the psychological control of one person over another rather the passing of an invisible fluid from one body to another.

Once this insight was obtained, it became possible to extract the mesmeric trance from the mystical context Mesmer had given it and make it into a tool for the ordinary physician. Mesmerism was transformed into hypnotism.

This transformation occurred in France, scene of Mesmer's greatest successes and greatest denunciations, and in England, little touched by Mesmeric mania. In 1825 the French Royal Academy of Sciences decided to look into animal magnetism again, and their report, delivered in 1831, was far more favorable than any Mesmer had received in his lifetime. Without Mesmer's abrasive personality and occult theory, the magnetic trance could be viewed more objectively as an unusual but real mental state of possible use to doctors and meriting further investigation.

In the late 1830s animal magnetism was brought to England by the Baron Dupotet de Sennevoy who conducted a series of magnetic demonstrations. They caught the attention of a young, radical, and innovative physician named John Elliotson (1791–1868). He began to use magnetism both as a cure for various diseases and as an anesthetic drug during surgery. Like Mesmer, Elliotson was eventually drummed out of established medicine for his beliefs. He founded a journal devoted to animal magnetism and phrenology and encouraged other physicians to use magnetism in their practices. James Esdaile (1808–1859) was another persecuted English physician who tried to use mesmerism, especially as an anesthetic. Despite his popularity with the natives of India where he worked, the government denied support for his mesmeric hospital. In one respect, Esdaile stayed too close to Mesmer, maintaining in *Natural and Mesmeric Clairvoyance* that "the essential condition of the mesmeric state is the transmission of foreign nervous matter [according to Esdaile, a fluid] to the brain of the patient from the brain of the agent." Mesmer's old fluid theory, however, was becoming less and less plausible in the mid-nineteenth century, as the electrical nature of nervous conduction became known.

The transformation of mesmerism was completed by James Braid (1795–1860), who named it neuro-hypnotism, or more briefly hypnotism, derived from the Greek *hypnos,* meaning sleep. Braid considered the hypnotic state to be "nervous sleep." He began as a skeptic of mesmerism, but his own investigations convinced him that the phenomena were real enough, but that the theory of animal magnetism was incorrect. In *Neurypnology,* Braid wrote: "The phenomena of mesmerism were to be accounted for on the principle of a derangement of the state of the cerebrospinal center . . . induced by a fixed state, absolute repose of the body, [and] fixed attention . . ." The hypnotic state, Braid wrote, depends "on the physical and psychical [mental] condition of the patient . . . not at all on the volition or passes of the operator, throwing out a magnetic fluid, or exciting into activity some mystical universal fluid or medium." Braid rescued hypnotism from the occult surroundings of mesmerism and gave it to scientific medicine. But Braid himself encountered resistance from the medical establishment. The development of chemical anesthetics rendered the use of hypnosis in surgery unnecessary, and even today hypnotism has not completely shed its occult image.

In France hypnotism advanced as a treatment for hysteria. In this connection two theories arose as to the nature of the hypnotic trance. A. A. Liebeault (1823–1904) began one school of thought in Nancy, France, which was carried on by his student Hippolyte Bernheim (1837–1919). The Nancy school held that the hypnotic state was an intensification of certain tendencies in ordinary sleep or wakefulness. Some actions, even sophisticated ones, are automatic: We all respond impulsively to some suggestions; we all hallucinate in dreams. According to the Nancy school, in hypnosis the conscious will loses its usual close control over perception and action, and the orders of the hypnotist pass immediately and unconsciously into action or hallucinatory perception. The rival school of the Salpêtrière hospital in Paris maintained that since hypnotic suggestion could be used to remove hysteric symptoms, the hypnotic state must be a completely abnormal one, found in hysteric patients only. Hypnosis and hysteria were both seen as evidence of a pathological nervous system. The leading spokesman for the Salpêtrière school was Jean Martin Charcot (1825–1893), under whom Freud studied for several months. With the coming of Freud, the study of hypnotism became part of the psychology of the unconscious, for Freud used hypnosis in his early activities as a psychotherapist. It may be maintained that subsequent developments have supported the Nancy school's concept of hypnosis, but that today the exact nature of the hypnotic state, including its existence is a distinct mental state, still remains unclear.

If we return to Braid, we find hypnotism linked to another of our three fringe sciences—phrenology. Braid practiced what he called phreno-hypnosis, believing that in a hypnotic trance one could differentially manipulate the various mental faculties located, according to phrenology, in the different parts of the brain.

The First Physiological Psychology: Phrenology

So far in treating the history of psychology we have found it to be part of philosophy. Even the occasional physician-psychologists generally founded their psychologies on philosophical, not physiological, principles. Hartley is a case in point. He erected his psychology on the principles of associationist philosophy and only buttressed it with Newton's speculative account of nerve function. The separation of the physiological and philosophical portions of Hartley's psychology was so complete that his follower Priestley could issue an edition of Hartley's *Observations on Man* that omitted all the physiology. Hartley wanted to create a psychology that combined philosophy and physiology, but philosophy clearly came first.

Franz Joseph Gall (1758–1828) reversed this relationship. Gall was unusual because he took seriously the idea that the brain is the seat of the soul. The idea was hardly new: Plato believed it; the Hellenistic scientists of Alexandria demonstrated it; the medieval faculty psychologists located each faculty in a different portion of the brain. However, beyond encouraging materialism, the concept had little effect on psychological thought. The locations assigned to the medieval faculties were based on prior analysis of mind, not brain, and philosophical psychology had done nothing to change this. Gall, however, stated that the brain was the specific organ of mental activity, in the same way that the stomach is the organ of digestion and the lungs the organ of respiration. Therefore the study of human nature should begin with those functions of the brain that give rise to thought and action, rather than with abstract and introspective inquiries into mind.

The philosophical background of Gall's work was French empiricism, especially Condillac's sensationism. Gall offered several reproaches to the philosophical approach to psychology (Young 1970). To begin with, the empiricists claimed that experience was the proper basis of science, yet their own psychology, Hume's science of human nature, was wholly speculative, having no reference to objective behavior or to the brain that controls it. Furthermore, the categories of analysis used by the philosophes were "mere abstractions." None of the faculties listed by philosophers—such as memory, attention, and imagination—were specific enough to explain actual human behavior and concrete individual differences. In *On the Functions of the Brain,* Gall wrote: "How are we to explain, by sensation in general, by attention [etc.] . . . the origin and exercise of the principle of propagation; that of the love of offspring, of the instinct of attachment? How explain by all these generalities, the talents for music, for mechanics, for a sense of the relations of space, for painting, poetry, etc." The philosophers' faculties exist but "they are not applicable to the detailed study of a species, or an individual. Every man, except an idiot, enjoys all these faculties. Yet all men have not the same intellectual or moral character. We need faculties, the different distribution of which shall determine the different species of animals, and the different proportions of which explain the differences in individuals" (Young 1970). In short, the philosophers' concepts are useless for the specific empirical investigations that science requires.

Gall's ideas brought him into conflict with empiricist philosophers in a final way. Condillac had attempted to derive every faculty of mind from sensation. Gall, however, believing the brain to be the organ of the mind, went on to conclude that each of his faculties was innate, based in a particular region of the brain. Gall's approach also implies a comparative psychology. Since the brains of species differ up and down the Great Chain of Being (Gall wrote before Darwin), so should the corresponding faculties differ. In fact, Gall and his followers carried out comparative studies to support this argument.

The problem for Gall, then, was to correlate specific behavioral functions with particular regions of the brain. Although he carried out detailed anatomical studies of the brain and nervous system, he found the techniques of his time too crude to answer the questions he posed, and he had moral scruples about experimenting on living but "martyrized" animals. Gall's method, therefore, was different. He assumed that well-developed faculties would correspond to well-developed parts of the brain. Those "organs" corresponding to the well-developed faculties in the brain would be larger than those organs corresponding to less developed faculties, and their relative size would be registered on the skull as bumps overlying the developed organ. Empirically, then, Gall's method was to show that people possessing certain striking traits would possess skulls with bumps over the corresponding organs of the brain, and that weak traits would go with undeveloped brain-organs and skull-regions. Although Gall's specific hypothesis was new, the idea that personality traits reveal themselves in physique and face was as old as antiquity.

Gall's theory has been schematized by Young (1970), as in Figure 6-2.

Thus Gall could observe an individual's unique behaviors and correlate them with cranial prominences. On the basis of such observations Gall drew up a long list of faculties, including such faculties as destructiveness, friendship, and language, each located in a particular region of the brain. Destructiveness, for example, was located just above the ear. Later followers of Gall expanded his list to include such faculties as veneration, whose existence was believed to show that God must exist to be the object of veneration.

Certain conceptual features of Gall's approach have been mentioned: it was

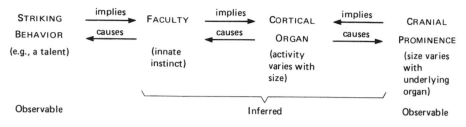

FIGURE 6-2   Gall's theory of mind, brain and behavior. (Adapted from Young.

nativistic; it compared humans with other animals; it was materialistic, although Gall himself struggled against this tendency. Gall's psychology was also behavioristic rather than introspectionistic. His system rested on the observation of behaviors, and of bumps on the skull rather than on the introspection of his own mind. Gall's psychology was therefore the first objective, rather than subjective, psychology. More broadly, Gall's was a functional psychology concerned with how the mind and its organ, the brain, actually adapt a person or animal to everyday demands. Philosophical psychology was more concerned with grand problems of epistemology. Finally, Gall's psychology was a psychology of individual differences. He explicitly rejected the study of the generalized adult mind in favor of a study of how people differ.

Gall's conception points in two directions, one scientific and one occult. Scientifically, it inspired more experimentally minded physiologists to investigate the localization of behavioral functions in particular parts of the brain. At the hands of these men Gall's system suffered badly. His specific locations were found to be faulty. Worse, the basic assumptions that size of brain organ corresponds to strength of faculty and that bumps on the skull conform to the shape of the brain, were found to be without foundation. The entire system was violently rejected as a pseudoscience, appealing like astrology only to the credulous lay society.

The appeal to the lay society was the other direction—occult direction— taken by Gall's ideas. His close associate Johann Caspar Spurzheim (1776–1832), who coined the term *phrenology* that Gall refused to accept, popularized the concept by turning it into a general and optimistic philosophy of life. In Spurzheim's hands phrenology became the new popular psychology, and Spurzheim aimed to reform education, religion, and penology. His missionary activities carried him to the United States, where the ground was most fertile for phrenology. He died shortly after arriving, but his work was carried on by the English phrenologist George Combe. The story of phrenology in the United States belongs to the chapter on the psychology of adaptation, where we will find that precisely those features in phrenology that appealed to ordinary Americans were also those that ensured the success of evolutionary psychology in America.

Revolt Against Materialism: Spiritualism and Psychic Research

The doctrine of materialism and the religion of positivism may have inspired enthusiasts of scientism, but many people were unsettled and even repelled by them. The crisis of naturalism got worse after Huxley proclaimed humans to be only well-developed apes. Religion seemed dead; the prospect of the immortal soul annihilated. So, especially after 1859, many thoughtful people, including well-known scientists, turned to science itself for assurance that there was more to human life than the bodily and cerebral machines.

"The discovery that there was a life in man independent of blood and brain would be a cardinal, a dominating fact in all science and in all philosophy." So wrote Frederic Myers (1843–1901), the leading psychical researcher of the nineteenth century. Myers was horrified even as a child with the thought of not living forever. This fear was intensified when, like many Victorians, he lost his religious faith during his education. He met the philosopher Henry Sidgwick, who encouraged Myers to search scientifically for evidence of immortality. Sidgwick, too, had lost his faith, but deeply believed that ethics required personal immortality for the rectification of evil on earth. Myers took up Sidgwick's challenge and gathered an enormous amount of relevant data. Sidgwick and Myers founded the Society for Psychical Research, and in 1882 their journal published Myers's findings. These were also published posthumously in two volumes in 1903.

Simply as a catalogue of unusual psychological phenomena, Myers's *Human Personality and Its Survival of Bodily Death* won the respect of no less a psychologist than William James, himself once president of the Society for Psychical Research. Although from its title one might expect a collection of ghost stories, Myers in fact surveys the whole realm of abnormal psychology, from sleep and hysteria to messages from departed spirits. Myers's approach to his problem is psychological. He was the first English writer to disseminate Freud's early studies of hysteria. Hysteria was an important phenomenon for Myers, for it demonstrated the power of purely mental activity over the body when physical symptoms are caused by psychological disturbances (see Chapter 8).

Indeed, Myers fixed on exactly what Freud found most instructive in his early cases, that a hysteric's symptoms express unconscious desires that the patient does not want to admit to consciousness. Like Freud, Myers formulated a theory of the unconscious, which Myers called the *subliminal self*. In Freud's hands the unconscious was an affront to human pride, revealing the irrational, impulsive, frightening depths that underly rational, discursive conscious thought. Myers's conception of the subliminal self, however, was romantic, Platonic, optimistic, and progressive. True, the subliminal self is irrational, said Myers, but it enables us to communicate with a spiritual world that transcends the material one. The existence of the subliminal self demonstrated for Myers the separability of soul and matter. It opened up the prospect of not just material evolution, in which the individual plays a brief part, but also of spiritual, cosmic evolution, in which each soul perfects itself forever, actualizing mental powers hindered by our animal bodies. We must conclude that although Myers scientifically investigated spiritualistic phenomena—and he was as skeptical of mediums as anyone could wish—his scientific searching was really guided by a Neoplatonic and occult view of the cosmos.

Myers could sound like a Huxleyan naturalist, as when he wrote: "The authority of creeds and Churches will be replaced by the authority of observation and experiment." Psychical research, however, was not well received in Huxley's circle. Huxley (1871) himself was sarcastic, likening "the talk in the spiritual world" to "the chatter of old women and curates," saying of both, "They do not interest me." Despite this hostility, the intellectuals of the Society for Psychical Research carried on, and at the popular level spiritualism approached a mania around the turn of the century. As quickly as debunkers, such as the magicians Harry Houdini and John Maskelyne, exposed fake mediums, new ones sprang up.

The dialectic of paranormal claim and skeptical counter-claim continues today, as illustrated by the controversy over persons such as Uri Geller. Psychical research, now called parapsychology, continues in scholarly journals and research programs today, while college courses in the subject proliferate. Nevertheless, it is an even more suspect subject than hypnotism, and its very mention makes most psychologists uncomfortable. Its existence and appeal, however, are undeniable.

Disquiet at the End of the Century

It is unsurprising that the three movements we have examined belong together. Each has something of science about it—mesmerism as a medical tool; phrenology as a chart of brain faculties; psychical research as a study of abnormal mental states. At the same time, each has something of religion about it: Mesmerism duplicated the ecstatic trance of the saint or mystic; phrenology offered a guide to moral life; mediums offered proof of a life beyond the physical. In 1852 an anonymous writer linked the three movements with homeopathy, vegetarianism, and hydropathy as ''Physical Puritanism'' in an ''age of physiological reformers.'' Science offered a new morality. Nothing could better illustrate the weak state of orthodox religion and the effect of science in the nineteenth century than these occult movements. Atheistic materialism was too great a burden for most people. They feared Sade's amoral abyss and the meaningless world of the existentialist. They reached out, therefore, to science for reassurance upon matters about which Christianity was no longer plausible (Webb 1974).

That all three movements could exist together in an eminent Victorian and renowned scientist is proved by Alfred Russell Wallace, codiscoverer of evolution. As a young man Wallace had been exposed to phrenology and mesmerism. Later he used phrenology to argue that humankind's evolution was no longer physical, but was now mental. He also thought phrenology would be the psychology of the twentieth century. Wallace practiced mesmerism, which he believed enhanced telepathic and clairvoyant powers. Around 1865 Wallace attended a seance and was converted to spiritualism, writing a series of books reporting his investigations of mediums and promulgating a new philosophy of life. He finally concluded that a godlike mind was directing evolution, a conclusion that left Huxleyans wondering about Wallace's mental health.

Wallace was not alone in the dismay he felt at the new world of naturalism. Myers (1903) summed up the feelings of many around the turn of the century when he spoke of ''the deep disquiet of our times. Never, perhaps, did man's spiritual satisfaction bear a smaller proportion to his needs. The old world sustenance, however earnestly administered, is too unsubstantial for the modern craving.'' There is, said Myers, an ''underlying *Welt-Schmerz*, the decline of any real belief in the dignity, the meaning, the endlessness of life.'' Both occult movements and aggressive socialism were responses to the crisis. A particular variety of psychology was strengthened by the late nineteenth-century malaise, the psychologies of the irrational. The dark side of human nature became apparent to philosophers, sociologists, and psychologists. We therefore owe the origins and popularity of psychoanalysis, the psychology of the unconscious, to the same feelings that made people fasten onto mesmerism, phrenology, and spiritualism. Like these movements, psychoanalysis offered insight into the human unknown, practical advice, and hope of salvation—at least in this world.

TOWARD THE SCIENCE OF PSYCHOLOGY

Within the general intellectual climate of the nineteenth century, certain specific developments in various areas made important contributions to the nascent science of psychology.

Progress outside Philosophy

A Contribution from Astronomy: Chronometric Analysis of Mental Processes

An important function of astronomy is to precisely map the stars. Until the advent of modern mechanical and photographic methods in which an astronomer rarely looks through a telescope, accurately locating stars depended on the ability of an astronomer to note the exact moment when a star passed directly overhead, marked by a single cross-hair in the telescope's field of vision. In one common early method the astronomer noted the exact time on a clock as the star entered the field of vision, and then counted as the clock beat seconds until the star crossed the cross-hair. Accurately noting the exact moment of transit was critical, for slight errors would be translated into immense interstellar distances in calculating the exact positions of stars in the galaxy.

In 1795 an assistant astronomer at Greenwich observatory lost his job when his superior discovered that his own transit-times were about 0.5 seconds faster than his assistant's. Of course, the head astronomer assumed his own times to be correct and his assistant's in error. Years later, this event came to the attention of the German astronomer F. W. Bessel (1784–1846), who began systematically to compare the transit-times of different astronomers. Bessel discovered that all astronomers differed in the speed with which they reported transits. To correct this grave situation, Bessel constructed "personal equations" so that the differences between astronomers could be canceled out in astronomical calculations. For example, the "personal equation" of the two Greenwich astronomers would be Junior − Superior = 0.5 sec. The observations of any pair of astronomers could be compared by these equations reflecting their personal reaction times, and calculations of star positions could be corrected accordingly. Unfortunately for astronomers, use of the personal equations assumed that individual differences were stable, which proved to be false. Indeed, experiments with artificial stars with known transit-times, showed that sometimes observers "saw" the star intersect the cross-hair before it occurred. Only the increasing automation of observation was able to eliminate these problems.

Meanwhile, the reaction-time experiment had been independently invented by the great German physicist Hermann von Helmholtz in response to a very different problem, the speed of nerve conduction. In 1850 Helmholtz stimulated the motor nerve of a frog's leg at points near and far from the muscle itself, measuring the time it took for the muscle to respond. Before Helmholtz's investigation, it had been widely assumed that nerve impulses traveled at infinite or at least immeasurably fast speeds. Helmholtz estimated the speed to be only 26 meters per second.

These two lines of research on reaction time came together in the work of F.

C. Donders (1818–1889), a Dutch physiologist. Donders saw that the time between a stimulus and its response could be used to objectively quantify the speed of mental processes. Helmholtz had measured the simplest sort of stimulus-response (S-R) reaction, while astronomers had, for another purpose, investigated mental processes such as judgment. It was Donder's especial contribution to use reaction time to infer the action of complex mental processes. So, for example, one could measure a person's simple key-press response to a single stimulus—a mild shock to the foot. This is *simple reaction time*. However, one might ask the subject to press a key with the left hand when the left foot is shocked and with the right hand when the right is shocked. Obviously, a simple reaction is involved, but in addition the subject must discriminate which foot is shocked and choose which response to make. If simple reaction takes, for example, 150 msec to complete, and the discrimination and choice experiment takes 230 msec to complete, Donders reasoned then that the mental actions of choice and discrimination inserted into the simple reaction must take 230 msec − 150 msec, or 80 msec. This seemed to offer an objective way of measuring physiological and mental processes and was called mental chronometry.

The method was early taken up by Wundt and extensively used by the early mentalistic psychologists. Precisely because it was a quantitative method, it helped assure the scientific stature of experimental psychology as apart from qualitative philosophical psychology. It took the mind out of the armchair and into the laboratory. Unfortunately, numerous difficulties in the application of mental chronometry cropped up, and it ran into a dead end early in the twentieth century. One of the difficulties was implicit in its original discovery by astronomers—the problem of individual differences. They troubled Wundt, the psychologist of the general mind, but fascinated his American student, J. M. Cattell. With the advent of behaviorism, psychologists largely turned away from reaction time experiments in their attention to learning. However, when cognitive psychology arose in the 1960s, mental chronometry was reborn, for cognitivists wanted ways to infer the temporal nature of inferred mental processes such as judgment, reasoning, memory, and pattern matching.

Psychophysics: Psychology's First Research Program

The dean of historians of psychology, E. G. Boring, dates the founding of experimental psychology to 1860, the year in which a book called *Elements of Psychophysics* was published, written by a retired physicist, Gustav Theodore Fechner (1801–1887). Boring's claim rests on the fact that Fechner conceived and carried out the first systematic research in experimental psychology—research, moreover, that produced mathematical laws. Before Fechner, philosophers had widely assumed, following Kant, that the mind can neither be experimented on nor subjected to mathematical scrutiny. Fechner showed these assumptions to be false. The difficulties do at first seem to be immense. In physics we can manipulate objects and observe what they do, and we can measure their position and momentum, writing mathematical laws interrelating these variables (such as Newton's inverse-square law of gravitation). However, minds are private, and no instruments can be applied to conscious experiences.

Fechner's greatness was to overcome these problems. He saw that the content of consciousness can be manipulated by controlling the stimuli to which a person is exposed. This control makes mental experiment possible. We can have a person lift objects of known weight, listen to tones of known pitch and volume, and so on. Even so, how do we measure the resulting conscious experiences, or sensations? We can assign no number to a tone or weight sensation. Fechner perceived the difficulty and got around it by quantifying sensations indirectly. We can ask a subject to say which of two weights is heavier, which of two tones is louder. By systematically varying both the absolute values of the pairs of stimuli and the difference between them, and by observing when subjects can and cannot distinguish the pairs, sensation can be indirectly quantified. Hence we can mathematically relate stimulus magnitude (R) with the resulting strength of sensation (S). One might expect that sensation would vary directly with stimulus, but Fechner found it did not. Instead, he found that $S = k \log R$ (where k is a constant). That is, stimulus differences are easier to detect when both stimuli are of moderate absolute intensity than of high absolute intensity (for example, it would be easier to distinguish a 10-ounce weight from an 11-ounce weight than a 10-pound weight from a 10-pound, 1-ounce weight).

Fechner's approach was not without antecedents. The basic method of asking subjects to distinguish stimulus differences had been pioneered by the physiologist, E. H. Weber (1795–1878). The concept of treating sensations as quantitatively varying conscious states goes back to Leibniz's monads and his doctrines of *petite perception* and *apperception*. This line of thinking had been developed further by the German philosopher, Herbart (see the section on Progress in Philosophy). Fechner followed both in admitting the existence of unconscious or, as he called them, negative sensations, which do not cross the threshold of consciousness. The immediate motivation of Fechner's work was the mind-body problem. Fechner held a dual aspect position, believing that mind and brain were simply two aspects of the same underlying reality, and therefore that physical stimuli and subjective sensations ought to be functionally related. Fechner hoped his psychophysics would solve the mind-body problem.

Fechner is not the founder of the science of psychology because, unlike Wundt, he carved out no societally recognized role for psychologists to take. Nevertheless, Fechner founded experimental psychology, for his methods, broadened to encompass more than sensations, were basic to Wundt's experimental psychology of consciousness. In Wundt's experiments antecedent stimulus conditions were controlled, as in Fechner's, and data were provided as subjects reported the resulting conscious content. It was not Wundt's only method, but it was an important one, and it was the one most of his students carried away with them from his laboratory.

Physiology Approaches Psychology: The Functions of the Brain

Gall, in his system of phrenology, had been the first to take seriously the idea that the brain is the organ of the mind. He therefore investigated the detailed relationship of brain organ and mental faculty. Gall's researches raised a storm of controversy in physiology, helping to push physiologists to experiment on the brain to discover exactly how it works and what it does. These experiments first led away from phrenology and then back to a "new phrenology" as physiologists discounted, and then discovered, the localization of brain functions.

Gall's major critic was a leading French physiologist, Jean-Pierre-Marie

Flourens (1794–1867), a pioneer in experimental brain research. Flourens discovered the functions of the various lower parts of the brain, but when it came to the cerebral hemispheres he parted company with Gall. Flourens ridiculed phrenology and argued on the basis of his own researches—which involved lesioning or ablating parts of the brain—that the cerebral hemispheres act as a unit, containing no specialized organs for special mental faculties. In his conclusions Flourens was more dominated by philosophical ideas than Gall was. Flourens was a Cartesian dualist who viewed the soul as residing in the cerebral hemispheres, and since the soul is unitary, the action of the hemispheres must be so too. He believed there was no organic connection between the sensory and motor functions of the lower parts of the brain and the cerebrum. Flourens's stature assured the success of his attack on Gall, and his view of the unitary action of the cerebrum remained orthodox dogma for decades.

In 1822 a discovery of momentous long-term implications was announced by Francois Magendie (1783–1855). Earlier, on the basis of postmortem dissections, the English physiologist Charles Bell (1774–1842) had distinguished two sets of nerves at the base of the spinal column. Bell suggested that one set carried information to the brain (sensory nerves) while the other carried information from the brain to the muscles (motor nerves). Previously, it had been thought that nerves work in both directions. Magendie discovered the same thing independently and more conclusively, because he demonstrated the different functions of the nerves in the spinal column by direct experiment on living animals. The next decade in brain physiology saw the extension of the sensorimotor distinctions up the spinal column and into the cerebrum. Magendie, however, did not take this step. Like Flourens, his views on the functions of the cerebral hemispheres were controlled by a philosophy—in Magendie's case by a modified sensationism. For Magendie, all faculties were just modifications of perception, and he saw no role for the hemispheres in the direct control of behavior. The empiricist philosophy traces sensations and their associations as concepts are formed by the understanding, but says little or nothing about human action. Magendie, therefore, went no further in his physiology.

Another breakthrough in the study of the functions of the cerebrum suggested that Gall was at least correct in asserting that different parts of the brain have specific behavioral functions. This discovery was made by Pierre Paul Broca (1824–1880), who observed that patients with speech disorders showed, when autopsied, damage to the same area of the left frontal lobe of the brain. Broca, who rejected the study of bumps on the head, viewed his finding as limited support for Gall, although the faculty of language had not been found where Gall had predicted.

Meanwhile, other researchers had been extending the distinction between sensory and motor nerves up the spine and into the cranium. Young (1970) reports that, in 1845 one English physician wrote, "The brain . . . is subject to the laws of reflex action, and that, in this respect it does not differ from the other ganglia of the nervous system . . . [and] must necessarily be regulated . . . by laws identical with those governing the spinal ganglia and their analogues in the lower animals." That is, it was known that the involuntary reflexes of the lower nervous system work by sensory-motor reflex, and it is suggested here that the cerebrum works the same way.

Against this view was the observation that the cerebral hemispheres seemed insensitive. They had been poked, prodded, pressed, and pricked, but no movement resulted in living animals. This supported Flourens's view that the hemispheres were not involved in action. However, in 1870 two German researchers announced that electrical excitation of the cerebrum can elicit movement and that different parts of the brain, when stimulated, seem to regulate different movements.

This finding encouraged others to map out the brain, locating each sensory and motor function. Today such maps are remarkably precise and allow tumors to be located with great accuracy. A "new phrenology" was thus born, in which each part of the brain was assigned a discrete sensory or behavioral function. But the new localizations were different from Gall's, for they resulted from an extension of the sensorimotor nerve distinction to the cerebrum. Some parts of the brain receive sensations, others govern specific actions, and the association of sensation and action produces behavior. In this view, the brain is a complex reflex machine. It should be pointed out here that not all neurophysiologists accepted then, or accept now, the localization of brain functions. Some maintain that the brain acts at least in some respects as a unit and that information present in one part of the brain is at least potentially present in others.

The formulation of the brain as a reflex device associating sensory input with motor action made possible the integration of British associationism with physiology and the extension of associationism and empiricism to action as well as understanding. This integration was the work of Alexander Bain.

Progress in Philosophy

England: Alexander Bain (1818–1903) and Association Psychology

In 1851 Bain wrote to his friend and colleague, John Stuart Mill, "There is nothing I wish more than so to unite psychology and physiology that physiologists may be made to appreciate the true ends and drift of their researches into the nervous system." Bain fulfilled his desire in two massive volumes, *The Senses and the Intellect* (1855) and *The Emotions and the Will* (1859), a comprehensive survey of psychology from the standpoints of associationism and physiology and embracing every psychological topic from simple sensation to esthetics and ethics.

Bain offers few new ideas. His associationism derives from Hartley and the Mills. His physiology was drawn from leading texts and lectures of his time. Even the idea of uniting physiology and philosophical psychology was Hartley's. Bain's physiology, however, was based on experimental research, not on Newton's speculations. Bain's wish to unite psychology and physiology probably came from his early exposure to phrenology, which he later rejected in favor of Mill's associationism and Flourens's physiology.

What is most important about Bain is the attitude he adopted toward his material. The aim of the earlier associationists was to give an adequate empiricist epistemology. Bain, however, wrote as a psychologist. He assumed the associationist epistemology and inquired instead into how to account for human action, not just conception. Bain was not concerned to justify human knowledge, but to explain human thinking and behavior.

To this end Bain adopted the sensorimotor physiology of the German physiologist, Johannes Müller (1801–1858). In his *Elements of Physiology* (1842), Müller had already proposed that the role of the brain is to associate incoming sensory information with appropriate motor responses. Bain knew the *Elements* and incorporated Müller's conception of the role of the brain into his psychology. Thus Bain united the philosophy of associationism with sensorimotor physiology to give a unified human psychology. Even today most general psychology texts are organized like Bain's, beginning with simple nerve function in sensation and working up to thinking and social relations. Bain's integration was quite influential. He wrote before the functions of the cerebrum were known, and his uncompromising associative view of physiology guided later English investigators to press their studies into the mysterious cerebral hemispheres.

Thus Bain had a considerable effect on psychology. The journal *Mind*, which he founded in 1874, is still in existence as an organ of philosophical psychology. He was, however, too philosophical in his outlook; his conception of mind was soon out of date. Despite his use of physiological data, he did no experiments, and while he recognized the importance of Darwin's work, his associationism remained preevolutionary. The future of association psychology lay more in its integration with evolution than with physiology.

France: Ideology, Spiritualism, and Positivism

During and after the French Revolution, French philosophical psychology was carried on by the "ideologists," named by their founder, Destutt de Tracy (1754–1836). *Ideology* means here the study of ideas and of their origin, and it continued the Enlightenment tradition of French empiricism. De Tracy returned to a conventional faculty psychology consistent with Locke. As heirs to the Enlightenment, the real goal of the ideologists was social reform. They favored a moderate democracy based on personal property and were particularly interested in improving education as the foundation for the new society.

The best known of the ideologists is Pierre Jean Georges Cabanis (1757–1808), a physician who is sometimes called the father of physiological psychology. Cabanis is the epitome of Enlightenment empiricism and materialism. Stating what could have been Condillac's motto, Cabanis said, "We sense; we are." He compared the function of the brain to the function of the stomach. Wrote Cabanis (1824): "The brain digests the impressions; [and] organically produces the secretion of thought." Although Cabanis detested the Reign of Terror—when ideologists had been imprisoned—he used the "experiments" of the guillotine to argue that mental activity and action are multileveled: the body may twitch after the head is severed, but this is simply unconscious reflex activity. Consciousness resides in the brain and disappears at the moment of execution. Cabanis never performed physiological researches and avoided any precise speculation on the relation of nervous activity to mind, although he was clearly a materialist. Consequently, his ideas remain more philosophical than those of Gall or the later experimental physiologists, although he does tend in their direction.

One interesting figure began as an ideologist, but then swam against the prevailing empiricist-materialist stream toward Catholicism. He was François-Pierre Maine de Biran (1766–1824). Although Maine de Biran was not afraid to take a physiological approach to the study of the mind—and always insisted that psychology should study the whole person—he felt that there was more to human nature than mere matter. He possessed an intensely introspective disposition and argued that the fundamental method of psychology should be reflection, or the scrutiny of one's own mind. Maine de Biran called this enterprise "experimental psychology." Upon such reflection, the central psychological fact he discovered was will, or the feeling of effort we experience as we carry out a voluntary action. Like Wundt, Maine de Biran was a voluntarist, with the important distinction that Maine de Biran's "experimental psychology" used an intense Cartesian form of introspection rather than Wundt's simple self-observation. Maine de Biran's one direct influence on psychology was on Freud, who knew of Maine de Biran's belief that many important influences on mental life are marginally conscious at best and that only careful reflection could reveal them. As Maine de Biran grew older, he moved further still from French naturalism and toward religion. He finally believed in a separate immortal soul whose relation to God needed investigation. This last direction of his thinking helped found the later French school of spiritualism, which opposed materialism and insisted on humankind's spiritual nature, but did not involve psychic phenomena. Maine de Biran completed his retreat from the naturalism of ideology by dying a Catholic. He represents an attempt, ultimately unsuccessful, to reassert the reflective Platonic-Cartesian rationalist psychology against the rising tide of naturalism and positivism.

The last French philosophical psychologist, Hippolyte-Adolphe Taine (1828–1893), expounded these new positions. Although most of his works are on history and literature, he was most proud of his psychological book, *On Intelligence* (1870), which William James used as his text when he first taught psychology at Harvard. In *On Intelligence* Taine presents an integration of association psychology similar to Bain's, arguing that all ideas, no matter how apparently abstract, may be reduced to a collection of sensations associated with the idea's name. The business of psychology is thus similar to chemistry's—"to decompose [compounds] into their elements to show the different groupings these elements are capable of, and to construct different compounds with them" (Taine 1875). Following Leibniz, Taine proposed that conscious sensations are simply aggregates of weaker, more fleeting sensations that are only marginally conscious at best. Thus Taine, like so many others in the nineteenth century, believed in the unconscious.

Taine then discussed the physiological substrate of sensation. He maintained a dual aspect psychophysical parallelism, holding that every event in consciousness has a corresponding neural event. According to Taine, the reverse is not true, for some neural events give rise only to unconscious sensations. Taine's neurophysiology presents the brain as an unspecialized organ associating stimulus and response: "The brain, then, is the *repeater* of the sensory centers. . . ." That is, the brain simply copies incoming neural information, as mental images copy sensations. Mind and brain are both seen in terms similar to Hume's or Hartley's.

Taine, then, may be regarded as a French Bain, although he had less systematic effect on later psychology than Bain since his later writings abandoned psychology. Nevertheless, he integrated physiology and philosophical association psychology and is followed historically by the earliest French psychologists. In his philosophy he even pointed beyond Bain toward behaviorism. His approach to science resembled that of the later logical positivists. In this view the first task of a science is to gather firm observational data from which simple generalizations are drawn. Then, a logically organized, deductive, theoretical edifice is to be erected on the observational foundation. Finally, new phenomena may be predicted from the theoretical system and these predictions checked against observation. Biran had tried to return French psychology to reflective rationalism, but Taine put it back on course as an objective, empiricistic science integrated with biology.

Germany: Struggle Toward Science

As we have seen, the dominant philosophical system in Germany after Kant's time was idealism in one form or another. Certain concepts of the idealists found a place in early German psychology. Wundt studied individual consciousness, proposed a historical, genetic approach to the investigation of the higher mental processes, and stressed human will as the unifying force in mental life. All of these ideas are part of idealist philosophy. Freud, too, was influenced by Schopenhauer's concept of unconscious primitive forces lurking in the personality. Nevertheless, the German idealists, following Kant, took a dim view of psychology as a would-be science. Psychology studies only a concrete individual, or a set of individuals, whereas what the idealists sought was transcendent Platonic knowledge of a godlike Absolute Spirit, which they took to be the noumenal reality behind physical appearances and the individual mind. Although Wundt retained a bias toward the study of the general human mind, he did not believe in an Absolute Mind. Empirical research seems trivial in the idealist context, and the idealists—most forcefully Hegel—actively opposed the development of empirical psychology (Leary 1978b).

However, there were those in Germany who did seek a scientific psychology, taking Kant's negative analysis of psychology as a challenge (Leary 1978a). The most important of them was Johann Friedrich Herbart (1776–1841), who attempted to mathematicize psychology. Herbart viewed psychology as applied metaphysics. His extremely complex psychological system formed only a small part of an even more complex metaphysics, developed largely out of Leibniz's monadology.

Herbart pictured the mind as a collection of elementary ideas of varying intensity. Some ideas are strong enough to cross the threshold of consciousness; others reside in unconsciousness. In fact, Herbart prefigured Freud by maintaining that no idea is ever completely destroyed. Ideas struggle with one another for access to consciousness, as dissonant ideas repel one another and associated ideas help pull each other into consciousness or drag each other down into unconsciousness. Herbart's real aim was to formulate a Newtonian mathematics of the mind. Just as Newton described the mathematically exact interaction of objects in space, so Herbart tried to describe the mathematically exact interaction of ideas in the mind. In equation after equation Herbart proposed exact formulas for the mechanics of ideas entering and leaving consciousness.

The difficulty of Herbart's system was that there was no way to connect it to empirical reality. To begin with, Herbart himself argued that the mind could not be subject to experiment because each mind is unique and can shed no light on general mental functioning. Furthermore, he admitted that his calculations were wholly fictional, based on hypothetical assumptions incapable of proof. Finally, Herbart said that in his psychology for an idea to be "in consciousness" doesn't mean that its possessor is conscious of it! This seems to cut Herbart's psychology off from science as ordinarily understood, and Wundt continually attacked Herbart's metaphysical, unscientific psychology. It was a common criticism of Herbart that he failed to measure mind, as Fechner was able to do later.

We must bear in mind, however, that mental measurement and experiment were not Herbart's aim. It is best to view him as proposing a mental algebra or geometry in Plato's realm of mathematics. When you solve the quadratic equation or prove the Pythagorean theorem you are concerned wholly with abstract entities. Algebra and Euclidean geometry are, like Herbart's psychology, hypothetical systems based on *a priori* rules for manipulating symbols, rules that may be changed to create a different system (such as non-Euclidean geometry). Algebra can be used to compute the price of apples or the force of gravity; geometry can be used to survey roads or map the stars. Each is also an autonomous study in its own right. So, Herbart would have thought his laws of the rise and fall of ideas could be applied equally to dissonant musical notes or dissonant Oedipal attitudes toward one's father.

Viewed this way, Herbart resembles the modern psychological school of structuralism, associated with Chomsky and Piaget. Piaget, for example, treats thinking as an abstract activity which can be described in the language of formal logic. *What* a child thinks about is less important to Piaget than the logical *structure* of his thinking. The Western child may think about classifying sports cars, the African child about classifying species of antelope, but the logic of classification is universal. Herbart seems to have held the same position. Each person's mind is absolutely unique, for the experiences giving us our ideas are unique; but common to all people are the mathematics of how ideas are related.

Herbart's direct influence was small, for he had no devoted students. His idea that ideas continuously vary in intensity helped Fechner formulate psychophysics, using a version of Leibniz's concept of apperception which was greatly stressed by Wundt. He contributed to the idea of the unconscious and, against the idealists, proclaimed psychology a science. Yet Wundt, Fechner, and all experimental psychologists repudiated Herbart's metaphysical, vaguely introspective, fictional mathematics of mind. They had to if they were to establish psychology as an independent science. Herbart was much interested in pedagogy, and several decades after his death "Herbartianism" enjoyed a vogue in educational circles. But Herbartianism was more the creation of others who picked up and reshaped Herbart's ideas, and even in modified form it exerted no long-term influence. Herbart's most lasting effect was his determination to make psychology a science despite the strictures of Kant and the opposition of the idealists.

Another important German philosophical psychologist was Hermann Lotze (1817–1881). Before he turned to philosophy, Lotze received his M.D., and he was Fechner's friend and physician. In one respect Lotze appears to be German psychology's Bain or Taine. In his *Outlines of Psychology* (1881) Lotze proposed an empiricist view of consciousness, saying that depth perception is learned, not innate, and experience is compounded out of simple ideas. This empiricism he integrated with the growing sensorimotor concept of brain function.

However, Lotze was not wholly dedicated to empiricism and naturalism. He insisted that although physiology offered a valid approach to the material aspects of mind and behavior, human beings and the animals each possessed divinely given souls. As was typical of German philosophers, Lotze (and Herbart) emphatically rejected materialism in favor of Cartesian dualism. By insisting on the human spiritual nature, Lotze earned the admiration of English-speaking psychologists dissatisfied with the associationistic and reductive psychologies they found around them. Among them were James Ward, the English psychologist who bitterly attacked naturalism, and William James, the tender-minded psychologist who took part in psychical research.

A more eminent and consistent exponent of naturalism and empiricism was

Hermann von Helmholtz (1821–1894), probably the greatest natural scientist of the nineteenth century. For much of his career he was occupied with physiology. We have already learned of his measurement of the speed of nerve conduction; he also conducted definitive studies of physiological optics and acoustics. But he was also a leading physicist, formulating the law of conservation of energy when he was only twenty-six.

Helmholtz's approach to the mind is essentially that of a Lockean empiricism in which ideas are interpreted as mental content. Helmholtz argued that all we know for certain are our ideas, or images of the world gathered by experience. He strikes a pragmatic note by acknowledging that we cannot know if our ideas are true, but argues that this does not matter as long as they lead to effective action in the real world. Science was an example of such effective action. Although he followed Kant in holding causality to be an innate principle, Helmholtz, like the empiricists, maintained that the other Kantian categories of knowledge are acquired.

Of particular interest to psychology is Helmholtz's theory of unconscious inference. If, for example, visual perception of space is not an innate intuition, then in the course of development we must learn to calculate the distance of objects from us, as Berkeley proposed. Yet we are not aware of performing such calculations. Helmholtz theorized that these kinds of calculations, or inferences, must be unconscious and moreover must be unconsciously learned, as happens in language acquisition. Like words, ideas (including sensations) are mental contents which represent reality. Just as children learn language spontaneously and with no direct instruction, so too they spontaneously and unconsciously learn the meanings of ideas. Helmholtz's theory of the unconscious differs from other views. For Herbart the unconscious was just a place where ideas reside when they are not conscious. For the romantics it was a repository of ancient and irrational forces. For Helmholtz it was an agency autonomous of consciousness, but essentially rational; unconscious inferences were of the same form as conscious ones.

As we would expect of a physicist and physiologist, Helmholtz was a forceful advocate of the natural sciences. He welcomed their growth in the German universities and heaped scorn on the idealist philosophers for whom natural science was the trivial study of physical reality, which was of no consequence compared to the spirit behind physical reality. Furthermore, Helmholtz's own researches supported materialism. His physiological studies of sensation established the dependence of perception on mere fleshly matter. His theory of conservation of energy inspired some young physiologists to swear, as Helmholtz's friend Emil du Bois-Reymond put it in a letter, "a solemn oath to put in effect this truth: no other forces than the common physical-chemical ones are active within the organism" (Kahl 1971). This attitude encouraged the young Freud to compose his first systematic psychology, one that was entirely materialistic.

Helmholtz, however, was aware of the dangers of too much materialism when he wrote in "Thought in Medicine": "Our generation has had to suffer under the tyranny of spiritualistic metaphysics; the younger generation will probably have to guard against materialistic metaphysics." He continues, "Please do not forget that materialism is a metaphysical hypothesis . . . If one forgets this, materialism becomes a dogma [compare this to the "solemn oath" above] which hinders the progress of science and, like all dogmas, leads to violent intolerance." While he could not accept spiritualism or vitalism, neither could he accept extreme materialism. He preferred to maintain an open mind and let the facts decide.

CONCLUSIONS

The Nineteenth-Century Crisis

The nineteenth century was a century of conflict and its conflicts are our conflicts. It saw the Industrial Revolution bring unparalleled material progress and tremendous urban poverty. It witnessed widespread religious revival, while the foundations of belief were steadily eroded by science. It inculcated in its people acute and ferocious sexual morality, while allowing—or causing—prostitution and crime to be endemic. The sciences and humanities flourished as never before, but the practical businessman sneered at the ivory tower intellectual. Pessimism and optimism mixed in the same mind. Wrote Carlyle: "Deep and sad as is our feeling that we stand yet in the bodeful night; equally deep, indestructible is our assurance that the morning also will not fail" (Houghton 1957).

To summarize the specific ideas of nineteenth-century thinkers would be merely confusing. It will be more useful to note that one conflict underlies all the others: the conflict between the new scientific naturalism and the older beliefs in a transcendent spiritual reality.

Naturalism, product of the Enlightenment, occasioned both hope and despair. It held out the hope of perpetual progress, of the perfectability of humanity, of useful and profound knowledge of the universe. Yet it challenged every prejudice from naive beliefs about physics to faith in God and in his highest creation, the human being. Science also threatened to dehumanize humans, reducing the individual to a collection of chemicals laboring in a vast industrial machine. It seemed to strip the world of meaning and each person of freedom and dignity.

Proponents of naturalism, of course, did not see the conflicts. They believed that technical, scientific solutions could be found for every human problem. Their problem was to convince society of their sincerity and efficacy. Science became scientism, a new religion, most clearly seen in Comte's positivism, but also present in popularizing scientists such as Huxley. The naturalists benefited from being united in a single Newtonian conception of nature, differing among themselves only in detail. Forceful, optimistic, successful, natural science came to dominate the intellectual world.

Arrayed against the naturalists were a motley group of people who felt poignantly the conflicts precipitated by naturalism. Their answers were diverse. Some clung to traditional religion; there was a significant Catholic revival in Protestant England, for example, and Maine de Biran died a Catholic. Some, like Wallace, found a faith in a divine intelligence guiding evolution. Some sought assurance of immortality through psychical research into the spirit world. Still others embraced philosophical idealism, transforming God into Hegel's Absolute Spirit.

Against united science, believers in these varied transcendental ideas could not prevail. But neither were they conquered. Science is today's orthodox belief, but the occult maintains an underground existence. Every newspaper has its astrologer. Every bookstore has its occult section, where one may find a bewildering variety of "secret" doctrines published in both cheap paperbacks and expensive hardbacks. Science has prevailed in that every doctrine wants to call itself a science, but it has failed in that popular science is pseudoscience ranging from mesmerism and phrenology to the *Chariots of the Gods*. The concept of God as an alien astronaut epitomizes the Victorian conflict of religion and science and shows us that it is our conflict still.

Psychology was, and is, caught in the middle. Nothing is harder for most to believe than that we are no more than chemical machines devoid not only of spirit but also of free will. Consequently, psychology became a battleground contested by the materialists who could believe it and by the many who could not. Bentham, Cabanis, and Darwin stood on one side; Herbart, Lotze, Maine de Biran, and Myers stood on the other. Nor is the conflict over. Victorian conflicts are very much with us.

Founding Psychology

Out of the nineteenth century emerged the three founding forms of psychology. Wundt founded the psychology of consciousness. Freud founded the psychology of the unconscious. And various evolutionary psychologists founded the psychology of adaptation. All the concepts for each were in place, awaiting only the creative minds and forceful personalities needed to weld them into coherent psychological programs. Since we will explore the immediate background of each psychology in detail in later chapters, we need only briefly summarize them now.

The Psychology of Consciousness

The ground was well prepared for the founding of experimental psychology by Wundt. Physiology and philosophy had been mated many times and with increasing frequency in the mid-nineteenth century. Wundt, too, made the journey from physiologist to philosopher, but he alone established psychology as an independent, experimental science.

The first component of Wundt's system, the experimental study of the individual consciousness, had already begun with Fechner and Donders. The definition of psychology as the study of conscious experience was virtually unanimous in the nineteenth century. Fechner and Donders showed that consciousness could be manipulated through experiment, and Wundt extended their techniques and invented others to furnish the raw data of an experimental, mentalistic psychology. Wundt's central concept, that of the voluntary control of mind through apperception, was present in thinkers as diverse as Leibniz, Maine de Biran, and Schopenhauer.

The other part of Wundt's psychology, the comparative historical approach to the development of mind and to the higher mental processes, was also ready to hand. Vico, Herder, and the German idealist philosophers put great stress on studying the historical development of anything, and Wundt tried to do just that for the mind. Wundt held that laboratory experiment was helpless to reveal deep mental processes and hoped to reach them indirectly through their social and historical products, particularly language and myth. Only by combining the experimental and historical methods, Wundt believed, could a complete picture of the human mind be obtained.

The Psychology of the Unconscious

It is sometimes said that if Freud had died in infancy, psychoanalysis would have been invented anyway. This acknowledges the strong historical trend toward a psychology of the unconscious. Like Wundt, Freud began his work in medicine and physiology. However, he came to consider psychological questions because of his clinical experience treating hysterics, rather than because of a desire to find scientific answers to philosophical questions. Psychoanalysis has always been strongly set off from academic psychology, finding its home in the clinic, not the laboratory.

The idea of the unconscious was present in much of European thought. Scarcely anyone denied its existence, although it took different forms in different philosophies. For Helmholtz it was a rational calculator of sense-data. For Herbart it was a repository of ideas. For the romantics it was a wild, untamed force. Freud combined Herbart's conception with that of the romantics, and added the mechanism of repression to create the psychoanalytic unconscious.

The other cornerstone of psychoanalysis, Freud's theory of motivation, was also available. Hedonism as our basic need was proposed by the utilitarians; the pleasure principle was nothing new. Wedded to the romantic unconscious it produced the psychoanalytic id, repository of irrational but vital forces motivating all activity and opposing the constraints of civilization.

The Psychology of Adaptation

From Plato to Wundt, the aim of psychology was epistemological: How does *the* human mind arrive at general knowledge? Whatever particular answer was given, empiricist or rationalist, individual differences and the demands of the environment were viewed as mere nuisances. The focus was clearly on the abstract universal mind as it sought abstract, universal truths. This rather Platonic psychology was especially strong in Germany and created an intellectual gulf between Wundt and his Anglo-American students.

Once a theory of evolution is available, however, different kinds of questions arise. What is mind good for in the evolutionary scheme of things? How does mind help the individual creature adapt to his or her individual environment? The focus shifts from what the mind contains to how it works. Whether evolution is conceived in Lamarckian or Darwinian terms, these questions are natural ones to an evolution-minded thinker. The Darwinian theory also demands the scrutiny of individual differences in mental function, for such differences are the grist for the mill of natural selection. As evolutionary thinking penetrated European philosophy, especially in England and America, a new psychology concerned with how the individual adjusts to his environment naturally arose. Later, coupled to radical materialism and an aggressive positivism, the psychology of adaptation would become behavioralism. In one form or another, it was a psychology destined to dominate academic psychology for much of the twentieth century.

One logical question suggested by evolution was seldom raised, however. If the brain is the organ of the mind, it is reasonable to ask how evolutionary pressures have shaped that organ. What aspects of human thinking and behavior are innate? Although the question is reasonable, other forces eclipsed it until very recently. Both the association psychology, with its attendant empiricism, and the sensorimotor model of the brain naturally minimized the native structure of the mind, reducing it to a *tabula rasa*. Associationism sees the mind, and sensorimotor physiology sees the brain, as simply a device for linking incoming stimuli with outgoing responses. The only innate differences between individuals and species are in the number of possible connections, which still makes the environment responsible for qualitative differences. Given this conception of mind and brain, it is no surprise that the question of evolution's impact on the structure of the species' mind did not arise.

BIBLIOGRAPHY

The literature on the nineteenth century is understandably vast. For social history, at least in Victorian England, see Houghton (1957); W. J. Reader, *Life in Victorian England* (New York: Capricorn, 1964); or G. M. Young, *Victorian England: Portrait of an age* (New York: Oxford University Press, 1953); and, for the late nineteenth and early twentieth centuries, Samuel Hynes, *The Edwardian turn of mind* (Princeton: Princeton University Press, 1968). For intellectual history, see Owen Chadwick, *The secularization of the European mind in the nineteenth century* (Cambridge, England: Cambridge University Press 1975); Elie Halevy, *The growth of philosophical radicalism* (Boston: Beacon Press, 1955); Maurice Mandlebaum, *History, man, and reason: A study in nineteenth century thought* (Baltimore: Johns Hopkins University Press, 1971); John Passmore, *A hundred years of philosophy*, rev. ed. (New York: Basic Books, 1966); W. M. Simon, *European positivism in the nineteenth century* (Ithaca: Cornell University Press, 1963); D. C. Somerville, *English thought in the nineteenth century* (New York: David McKay, 1929); Patrick L. Gardiner, ed., *Nineteenth century philosophy* (New York: The Free Press, 1969) collects important writings by the major philosophers.

The worlds of the nineteenth century are well covered in the general sources and the references. Some additional useful sources are the following. As a spokesman for romanticism, Edmund Burke resembles Vico and Herder; see L. Bredvold and G. Ross, eds., *The philosophy of Edmund Burke* (Ann Arbor: University of Michigan Press, 1960). For a biography of the Mills, see Bruce Mazlish, *James and John Stuart Mill* (New York: Basic Books, 1975). Auguste Comte's own *A general view of positivism* (New York: Robert Speller & Sons, 1975) provides a starting point for understanding the movement. Ernst Mach's most important philosophical-psychological work is *The analysis of sensations* (New York: Dover, 1959); a recent biography is John Blackmore, *Ernst Mach* (Berkeley: University of California Press, 1972). Karl Marx, of course, is much written about. L. S. Feuer, ed., *Marx and Engels: Basic writings on politics and philosophy* (Garden City, New York; Doubleday, 1959) samples the major works. Erich Fromm discusses *Marx's concept of man* (New York: Ungar, 1966), and includes translations of Marx's young writings on human nature; you should know that Fromm is deeply committed to Marx's ideas. A standard biography is Isaiah Berlin, *Karl Marx: His life and environment*, 4th ed. (Oxford: Oxford University Press, 1978). Finally, a beautifully lucid and balanced assessment of Marx and his legacy may be found in Robert L. Heilbroner, *Marxism: For and against* (New York: Norton, 1980). For the occult movements of the nineteenth century, see Thomas H. Leahey and Grace Evans Leahey, *Psychology's occult doubles: Psychology and the problem of pseudoscience* (Chicago: Nelson-Hall, 1983); the references and bibliography therein are fairly exhaustive. An important work subsequently published is Roger Cooter, *The cultural meaning of popular science: Phrenology and the organization of consent in the nineteenth century* (Cambridge England: Cambridge University Press, 1984). Deserving special mention is Robert Darnton, *Mesmerism and the end of the Enlightnment in France* (New York: Schocken Books, 1968), a model of intellectual and social history.

Works on Darwin flourish. To read the first formulations of the theory by Darwin and Wallace see their *Evolution by natural selection* (Cambridge, England: Cambridge University Press, 1958). For the background in biology, see William Coleman, *Biology in the nineteenth century: Problems of form, function, and transformation* (Cambridge, England: Cambridge University Press, 1977); or Ernst Mayr's authoritative *The growth of biological thought* (Cambridge: Harvard University Press, 1984). For the specific background to Darwin's work, see Loren Eiseley, *Darwin's century* (Garden City, New York: Doubleday, 1958), a beautifully written standard introduction to evolution. Eiseley has also drawn attention to a previously unknown forerunner and influence on Darwin in his *Darwin and the mysterious Mr. X: New light on the evolutionists* (New York: Dutton, 1979). Another very readable account of the rise of evolutionary theory is John C. Greene, *The death of Adam: Evolution and its impact on Western thought* (Ames: Iowa State University Press, 1959). Two interesting but more technical works are B. Glass, O. Temkin, and W. Straus, eds. *Forerunners of*

Darwin: 1745–1859 (Baltimore: Johns Hopkins University Press, 1959), and Peter J. Bowler, *Fossils and Progress: Paleontology and the idea of progressive evolution in the nineteenth century* (New York: Science History Publications, 1976). Works focusing on Darwin's thinking include P. Bamler, "Malthus, Darwin, and the concept of struggle," *Journal of the History of Ideas* (1976, *37:* 631–650); Michael Ghiselin, *The triumph of the Darwinian method* (Berkeley: Berkeley University Press, 1969); and Dov Ospovat, *The development of Darwin's theory: Natural history, natural theology, and natural selection 1838–1859* (New York: Cambridge University Press, 1981). Works concentrating on the reception of evolution include Tess Cosslett, ed., *Science and religion in the nineteenth century* (Cambridge, England: Cambridge University Press, 1984) reprints major works by nineteenth-century debaters of the subject, including Darwin himself; Gertrude Himmelfarb, *Darwin and the Darwinian revolution* (New York: Norton, 1959); D. R. Oldroyd, *Darwinian impacts: An introduction to the Darwinian revolution* (Milton Keynes, England: The Open University Press, 1980); Michael Ruse, *The Darwinian revolution: Science red in tooth and claw* (Chicago: Chicago University Press, 1979), who, with Himmelfarb and Oldroyd, set the Darwinian revolution in broad perspective; Peter J. Bowler, *The eclipse of Darwinism* (Baltimore: Johns Hopkins University Press, 1983); David Hull, *Darwin and his critics* (Cambridge: Harvard University Press, 1973); and Cynthia Eagle Russett *Darwin in America: The intellectual response 1865–1912* (San Francisco: W. H. Freeman, 1976) focus on the more scientific aspects of Darwin's reception. J. W. Burrow, *Evolution and society: A study in Victorian social theory* (Cambridge, England: Cambridge University Press, 1966) discusses the effect of evolution on social thought and on the nascent sciences of anthropology and sociology. In a short but far-ranging paper, D. P. Crook considers "Darwinism—The political implications," *History of European Ideas* (1981, *2:* 19–34). Finally, for the state of evolutionary theory today, see D. S. Bendall, ed. *Evolution from molecules to men* (Cambridge, England: Cambridge University Press, 1983).

Works by some of the important transitional figures to psychology include A. Bain, *Mental science* (New York: D. Appleton, 1868); F. C. Donders, "On the speed of mental processes," *Attention and performance II, Acta Psychologica* (1969, *30:* 412–431), G. T. Fechner, *Elements of psychophysics,* vol. 1 (New York: Holt, Rinehart & Winston, 1966); H. Helmholtz, *A treatise on physiological optics,* partially reprinted in T. Shipley, ed., *Classics in psychology* (New York: Philosophical Library, 1961); J. F. Herbart, *A textbook of psychology* (New York: D. Appleton & Co., 1891) [see also H. B. Dunkel, *Herbart and Herbartism* (Chicago: University of Chicago Press, 1970)]; and H. Lotze, *Outlines of psychology* (Boston: Ginn & Co., 1886). Young (1970) is the standard history of neuroscience in the nineteenth century. L. Hearnshaw, *A short history of British psychology 1840–1940* (New York: Barnes & Noble, 1964) covers nineteenth-century British philosophical psychology. Two papers by David Leary discuss the situation in Germany: "Philosophical development of the conception of psychology in Germany, 1780–1850," *Journal of the History of the Behavioral Sciences,* (1978, *14:* 113–21), and "German idealism and the development of psychology in the nineteenth century," *Journal of the History of Philosophy* (1980, *18:* 299–317). See also several papers in the Woodword & Ash collection in the bibliography of Chapter 7.

REFERENCES

Baumer, F. (1977) *Modern European thought.* New York: Macmillan.

Bentham, J. (1789/1973) *Principles of Morals and Legislation.* Reprinted in *The Utilitarians.* Garden City, New York: Doubleday.

Braid, J. (1843) *Neurypnology.* London: John Churchill.

Cabanis, P. (1974) Relations between the body and the mind of man (1824). Partially reprinted in S. Diamond, ed., *The roots of psychology.* New York: Basic Books.

Darwin, C. (1958) *The autobiography of Charles Darwin and selected letters.* F. Darwin, ed. New York: Dover.

Darwin, C. (1959) *The origin of species.* New York: Mentor.

Esdaile, J. (1852) *Natural and mesmeric clairvoyance.* London: Hippolyte Bailliere.

Helmholtz, H. (1971) Thought in medicine. Reprinted in R. Kahl, ed., *Selected writings of Hermann von Helmholtz.* Middletown; Connecticut: Wesleyan University Press.

Houghton, W. E. (1957) *The Victorian frame of mind.* New Haven: Yale University Press.

Huxley, T. H. (1871) Letter. In London Dialectical Society, eds., *Report on Spiritualism.* London: Longmans, Green, Reader & Dyer.

Huxley, T. H. (1954) *Man's place in nature.* Ann Arbor: The University of Michigan Press.

Irvine, W. (1959) *Apes, angels, and Victorians.* Cleveland: Meridian Books.

Kahl, R. K. (1971) ed. *Selected writings of Hermann von Helmholtz.* Middletown, Connecticut: Wesleyan University Press.

Leary, D. E. (1978a) The philosophical development of the conception of psychology in Germany, 1750–1850. *Journal of the History of the Behavioral Sciences 14:* 113–121.

Leary, D. E. (1978b) German idealism and the development of psychology in the nineteenth century. Unpublished manuscript, University of New Hampshire.

Mill, James. (1964) Analysis of the phenomena of the human mind. Partially reprinted in J. M. Mandler and G. Mandler, eds. *Thinking: From Association to Gestalt.* New York: John Wiley.

Myers, F. (1903) *Human personality and its survival of bodily death,* 2 vols. London: Longmans, Green & Co.

Ruse, M. (1975) Charles Darwin and artificial selection. *Journal of the History of Ideas 36:* 339–350.

Taine, H. (1875) *On intelligence.* New York: Holt.

Vorzimmer, P. (1970) *Charles Darwin: The years of controversy.* Philadelphia: Temple University Press.

Webb, J. (1974) *The occult underground.* LaSalle, Illinois: Open Court.

Young, D. (1970) *Mind, brain, and adaptation in the nineteenth century.* Oxford: Clarendon Press.

PART *II*

Although psychologists traditionally revere one man, Wilhelm Wundt, as the founder of psychology, and one date, 1879, as the founding year of psychology, their faith is misleadingly simple. Wundt's long-term importance for psychology has proven to be institutional, for it was he who created a socially recognized and independent science and a new social role for its practitioners. Conceptually, psychology was founded three times, each founding giving rise to a distinctive way of thinking about psychology's problems. Each founding took place in the late nineteenth century.

The most traditional founding psychology was the psychology of consciousness, the introspective study of the normal, adult human mind. This psychology directly continued traditional philosophical psychology and made it more rigorous. Wundt stands at the head of this tradition, although many others took part. The most important rival psychology of consciousness was Gestalt psychology, which rejected many of Wundt's premises and drifted into a kind of science of behavior. The psychology of consciousness proved to be the least durable form of psychology, notwithstanding Wundt's unique and momentous creation of institutional psychology.

The most famous, and in its own time notorious, founding psychology was Sigmund Freud's psychology of the unconscious. Freud attempted to plumb the hidden and threatening dark side of human nature, and what he found there offended some and inspired others. Freud's psychology of the unconscious is less a rival to Wundt's psychology than it is its complement. It has, however, been much more influential and durable than Wundt's psychology. Freud's ideas have profoundly affected Western thought in the twentieth century, and Freud's psychotherapy—psychoanalysis—has spawned innumerable variants into our own time.

Among academic psychologists, the most important founding psychology has been the psychology of adaptation. Its founding was the work of many hands, first among them being William James. The psychology of adaptation does not see the problem of psychology to be the philosophically motivated dissection of consciousness, or the therapeutic exploration of the unconscious, but sees it to be the biological study of the evolutionary utility of mind and behavior. The psychology of adaptation began as an introspective study of mental activity, but soon became the study of activity itself, that is, behavior.

In the next three chapters we will describe each founding psychology in turn.

CHAPTER 7

The Psychology of Consciousness

WILHELM WUNDT (1832–1920) AND GANZHEIT PSYCHOLOGY
  Background
  Wundt's Psychology
EDWARD BRADFORD TITCHENER (1867–1927) AND STRUCTURALISM
  Background
  Structural Psychology
CHALLENGES TO THE ANALYTIC PSYCHOLOGY OF CONSCIOUSNESS
  The Psychology of Thinking: The Würzburg School (1901–1909)
  Against Atomism: The Gestalt Movement
  Act Psychology: Franz Brentano (1878–1917)
CONCLUSION: THE FATE OF THE PSYCHOLOGY OF CONSCIOUSNESS

WILHELM WUNDT (1832–1920) AND GANZHEIT PSYCHOLOGY

Although Wilhelm Maximilian Wundt is revered as the founder of scientific psychology, he is the most misunderstood of all psychology's major figures. His system is usually considered to be dualistic, atomistic, associationistic, purely introspective, and concerned only with describing the conscious contents of the normal adult mind viewed as the passive recipient of sense perception. It was none of these things. It is, however, often confused with E. B. Titchener's system, which had all these characteristics except dualism. Titchener was Wundt's student, but he made Wundt's voluntaristic psychology into an experimental British associationism, abandoning along the way many Wundtian essentials. This alteration is one reason for Wundt's distorted image today. Another reason is that his psychology was swamped in the later behaviorist movement. Thus Wundt is remembered primarily as a ponderous old German introspectionist of no importance save as psychology's founder.

Contemporary scholars, however, have begun to demonstrate that Wundt's system was very different from the way it usually presented and that it has contemporary relevance. Today, cognitive psychologists are returning to the study of the mind, if not of consciousness, and are rediscovering many of the basic mental phenomena first discovered by Wundt. They are also returning to topics, such as attention, that preoccupied him. Wundt's psychology and its fate provide a valuable lesson for both history and psychology.

Background

Wilhelm Maximilian Wundt was born on August 16, 1832, in Neckarau, Baden, Germany—the fourth child of a minister, Maximilian Wundt, and his wife Marie Frederike. Many ancestors on both sides of Wundt's family were intellectuals, scientists, professors, government officials, and physicians. At the age of thirteen Wundt began his formal education at a Catholic *gymnasium*.* He disliked school and failed, but transferred to a school in Heidelberg from which he graduated in 1851. Wundt decided to go into medicine and, after an initially poor start, he applied himself and excelled in his studies. His scientific interests emerged in physiological research. He got his M.D. in 1855, *summa cum laude,* and after some study with the physiologist Johannes Müller received in 1857 the second doctorate German universities required of lecturers. He immediately gave his first course in experimental physiology—to four students in his mother's apartment in Heidelberg.** These courses were interrupted by an acute illness from which he almost died.

During his convalescence Wundt applied for and received an assistantship with Hermann von Helmholtz. Although Wundt admired Helmholtz they were

---

*The German gymnasium was a college-preparatory high school; entrance was generally restricted to the sons of middle-class intellectuals.

**The German university system in the nineteenth century was very different from the modern American system. One had to obtain the usual doctorate and then a second, higher-level doctorate before one could teach—and even then one had no regular salary and could only give private, fee-supported courses. Only after years of private teaching and a life of relative poverty could one obtain a salaried professorship.

	A.D. 1879	Einstein born
Wundt founds laboratory		
Galton's *Inquiries*		Marx dies, Keynes born
American Journal of Psychology		Jack the Ripper
James' *Principles*	1890	
Dewey's "Reflex Arc"		"Adventures of Sherlock Holmes"
		Safety razor invented
Titchener's "Structural Psychology"		Trans-Siberian Railroad
Freud's *Dreams*	1900	
Pavlov's Nobel Prize		Wright Brothers fly
Angell's "Province"		Special Relativity proposed
	1910	China abolishes slavery
Start of *Gestalt* School		
Watson's "Behaviorist"		Titanic sinks
		World War I
Final revisions of Freud's theory	1920	
		Immigration to U.S. restricted
Beginning of Neobehaviorism		Hirohito becomes Emperor of Japan
	1930	Stock market crash
		F.D. Roosevelt elected president
		Hitler comes to power
Skinner's *Behavior of Organisms*		Hindenburg disaster
	1940	World War II
Hull's *Behavior System*		Atom bomb dropped
Tolman's "Cognitive Maps"		
Conference on Learning Theory	1950	McCarthy attacks "Reds"
A Study of Thinking		Korean War
		Civil Rights movement starts
Chomsky reviews Skinner		First commercial jets
	1960	John Kennedy elected president
Kuhn's *Scientific Revolutions*		
Collins & Quillian		U.S. troops sent to Vietnam
Skinner's *Beyond Freedom*	1970	Moon landing
		Watergate
		Communists win in Vietnam
Simon's Nobel Prize		Jimmy Carter elected president
		Ronald Reagan elected president
	1980	

FIGURE 7-1 Chronology 1879–1980.

never close, and Wundt rejected Helmholtz's materialism. While with Helmholtz, Wundt gave his first course in "Psychology as a Natural Science" in 1862, and his first important writings began to appear.

He worked his way up the academic ladder at Heidelberg while dabbling in politics, for the first and last time, as an idealistic socialist. He got married in 1872. His publications continued, including the first edition of his fundamental work, *Grundzüge der Physiologischen Psychologie,* in 1873 and 1874. This work in its many editions propounded the central tenets of his experimental psychology.

After a year in a "waiting room" position in Zürich, Wundt received a chair in philosophy at Leipzig, where he taught from 1875 to 1917. It was at Leipzig that Wundt won a degree of independence for psychology by founding his Psychological Institute. Beginning as a purely private institute in 1879, it was supported out of his own pocket until 1881. Finally, in 1885 it was officially recognized by the university and listed in the catalog. It began as a primitive, one-room affair and expanded over the years; in 1897 it moved to its own specially designed building, later destroyed during World War II.

During the years at Leipzig, Wundt continued his extraordinary output— supervising at least two hundred dissertations, teaching over 24,000 students, and writing or revising volume after volume, as well as overseeing and writing for the psychological journal he founded, *Philosophische Studien.* He trained the first generation of psychologists, many of them Americans.

In 1900 he began a massive undertaking, the publication of his *Völkerpsychologie,* which was completed only in 1920, the year of his death. In it Wundt developed what he believed was the other half of psychology, the study of man in society as opposed to man as an individual in the laboratory. Wundt's work continued to the last. His final undertaking was his reminiscences, *Erlebtes und Erkanntes,* which he completed only a few days before he died on August 31, 1920, at the age of eighty-eight.

During World War I Wundt, like almost all German intellectuals, was fervently nationalistic. He, like many other "patriots of the lectern," wrote violently anti-English and anti-American tracts that can be read only with embarrassment today. They are interesting, however, as they reveal the gulf between the German and the Anglo-French-American world views. For Wundt and other German intellectuals the English were—in the words of Werner Sombart—mere "traders" who regarded "the whole existence of man on earth as a sum of commercial transactions which everyone makes as favorably as possible for himself" (Ringer 1969). The English were excoriated by Wundt for their "egotistic utilitarianism," "materialism," "positivism," and "pragmatism" (Ringer 1969). The German ideal, on the other hand, was "the hero," a warrior whose ideals were "sacrifice, faithfulness, openness, respect, courage, religiosity, charity and willingness to obey" (Ringer 1969). The goal of the Englishman was seen as personal comfort while that of the German was seen as sacrifice and service. Germans also had a long-standing contempt for French "civilization," which they considered a superficial veneer of manners as opposed to the true German, organic "culture."

Such polemics illustrate the German intellectual climate in the nineteenth century. The Germans as a whole, and despite Kant, followed Herder in openly rejecting the Enlightenment. They were romantic intellectuals who valued things of the heart, spirit, and soil rather than things of the cold intellect. They saw Germany as midway between the intellectualism of the countries west of the Rhine, and the anti-intellectual, religious culture of Holy Mother Russia to the east. They rejected the atomism and utilitarianism of British philosophy and were anti-individualistic. In place of atomism the German intellectuals constantly sought synthesis, to reconcile opposites into a higher truth. Thus "psychological synthesis" was a key element in Wundt's psychology. Wundt and the other elitist intellectuals of the German "Mandarin" tradition perceived, maintained, and strengthened an immense intellectual gulf between themselves and the West (Ringer 1969). Wundt held himself to be the heir of Kant, Fichte, and Hegel, and rejected the philosophies of Locke, the Mills, Spencer, and William James.

Underneath all this we can once more detect the division between rationalism and empiricism. The West was empiricist: associationistic, atomistic, utilitarian, and concerned with individual rights and happiness. Germany was nationalistic and romantic, rejecting the narrow utilitarian rationalism of the West in favor of a spiritual romantic rationalism. Since Plato, there has always been a mystic, anti-individualistic aspect to rationalism. Ascent to the Forms is a sort of mystical union. People existed to serve Plato's Republic, not vice versa; rationalism easily tends toward totalitarianism. Hence German thinkers were rationalists: anti-associationistic, searching for synthesis, avowedly impractical (the universities cultivated unworldly fields like philosophy and refused to recognize such practical fields as engineering), and statist (the individual is seen as the servant of the state).

Wundt's psychology shares this Mandarin tradition. It rejects association of static ideas and the tinker-toy theory of mind. It rejects atomism and reductionism in favor of psychological synthesis and an analysis of consciousness. It seeks no practical results, although it does not exclude them. Finally, it rejects the study of individual differences in favor of an almost Platonic investigation of *the* human mind.

This rationalism explains not only certain essential features of Wundt's system, but also its failure to gain a foothold in America. It was too alien. Wundt's American students happily got their degrees in Leipzig, but pursued a thoroughly American psychology, functionalism, when they returned home; thus psychology quickly became an American science. In Germany Wundt was attacked as an atomist by the even more "synthetic" Gestalt psychologists and, along with the rest of the German intellectual community, his ideas perished under the pressures of the Nazis and World War II.

All this tells us something of Wundt's background, but how did he come to found psychology? Psychology is a hybrid offspring of physiology and philosophy. Alcmaeon won the title of the first psychologist because he was a physician-philosopher. Bain and Lotze also combined physiology and philosophy. Yet none of them founded psychology. Wundt is the founder because he wedded physiology to philosophy and made the resulting offspring independent. He brought the empirical methods of physiology to the questions of philosophy and also created a new, identifiable role—that of the psychologist, separate from the roles of philosopher, physiologist, or physician. This was Wundt's professional achievement, but there were personal reasons as well as philosophical ones, behind it.

In the mid-nineteenth century physiology came into its own as a science. It expanded rapidly, with new opportunities arising for individual advancement all over Germany. At the same time, philosophy was a nonexpansive field in which advancement was difficult. Wundt entered physiology during the boom period. Beginning as early as 1860, and certainly by 1870, however, the growth of physiology slowed down and competition for the existing positions became fierce. In philosophy, a period of growth began about 1860.

Thus, to an ambitious academic with the right interests, philosophy in the 1860s became an attractive field; and in accepting the Zürich and Leipzig posts in philosophy, Wundt switched from a closed to an open discipline. However, at the same time, the relative prestige of physiology was greater than that of philosophy, a situation which naturally placed Wundt in a state of cognitive dissonance. A resolution was possible by innovation—invent a new role, that of scientific psychologist, derived at least in part from the higher-status field of physiology, but investigating the questions of philosophy (Ben-David and Collins 1966).

Wundt's stature as a historical figure lies in this innovation. Others had combined philosophical and physiological interests, but it remained for Wundt to create something new and enduring, the hybrid science of experimental psychology.

Wundt's Psychology

General Standpoint

Wundt never gave a name to his school of psychology. As the founder, what he did was simply *psychology* without qualification. Later, his student Titchener, who opposed (and named) American functionalism, called his own system "structuralism," and this label became erroneously attached to Wundt's psychology. Wundt's German students who carried on his tradition later called it *Ganzheit* psychology, which means essentially "holistic" psychology. Although holism describes Wundtian psychology, the label became attached to subsequent movements unrelated to Wundt, so we shall retain the German term Ganzheit psychology.

For Wundt, psychology was the scientific study of immediate experience— and thus the study of human consciousness or the mind, as long as mind is understood as the totality of conscious experience at a given moment and not as a mental substance. The natural sciences are also based on experience, but of a kind Wundt called *mediate* experience, because the experience is regarded as dependent on external objects and all subjective elements are removed. Psychology studies all experience—including subjective elements such as feelings—directly as it is given in consciousness, and as dependent on the psychological state of the observer.

Wundt thus proposed an introspective psychology, but with important qualifications. According to Wundt, it is unnecessary to postulate a special inner sense to observe one's consciousness. One simply *has* experiences and can describe them; one does not have to observe the experiences happening. Wundt specifically rejected Locke's idea of reflection as a source of ideas. To Wundt, *all* experience is direct experience. A second way in which Wundt's psychology differed from philosophical introspective psychologies was that in the study of individual experience the method was to be *experimental*. To Wundt, the ordinary act of introspection is untrustworthy because it disturbs experience and because it applies only to some unique experience that has already passed. For this unreliable form of introspection, used in part by Titchener and the Würzburg psychologists, Wundt substituted a host of objective procedures involving measures of reaction time, emotional states, and other variables.

This kind of psychology was what Wundt (1896) meant by *physiological psychology:*

> In psychology we find that only those mental phenomena which are directly accessible to physical influences can be made the subject matter of experiment. We cannot

experiment upon mind itself, but only upon its outworks, the organs of sense and movement which are functionally related to mental processes. So that every psychological experiment is at the same time physiological. . . .

Physiological psychology was thus just the experimental psychology of the individual, and was physiological only in that the experimental approach was borrowed from Wundt's original field, physiology.

The final distinction between Wundt and other introspective psychologists and philosophers is that his work was not limited to experimental psychology. He considered the development of mind an important topic, which could be addressed partially by child and animal (comparative) psychology, but above all by the study of the historical development of the human species. Life is short, so our own experience is limited; but we can draw on the historical experience of humanity as written and preserved in existing cultures at different levels of development. This collective experience enables us to study the inner recesses of consciousness, those well removed from sensorimotor responses and hence not amenable, in Wundt's view, to experimental study. He called this his *Völkerpsychologie* (ethnic or folk psychology), embracing especially the study of language, myth, and custom.

Wundt was as antimetaphysical as any modern experimental psychologist. He rejected all forms of speculative psychology, both dualistic and materialistic. He refused to postulate the existence of a separate spiritual or mental substance as Descartes had done. To do so, he thought, would be inconsistent with modern science and unnecessary—psychology studies experience given in consciousness, not a separate, substantial mind. On the other hand, he rejected materialistic reductionism. He recognized that all mental phenomena have a bodily substrate, but thought that experience and physiology can be studied independently. Further, he believed conscious experience and physiological events to be so different that they cannot be causally related. This separation of the mental and physical into connected but separate realms, each with its own laws of causality, Wundt called the principle of psychophysical parallelism. It is not, however, the same parallelism we have come across before. What Wundt perceived as parallel was not a body-substance and a mind-substance, but only bodily events and mental events. To Wundt, there is only one reality, but it can be examined from two points of view: the mental and the physical. His position is less a form of parallelism than it is a form of the dual aspect theory.

Wundt resisted any attempt to materialize the mind. Hence he rejected the view of the British associationists and Herbart that ideas are little billiard balls (Wundt used this phrase) connected by association that bounce in and out of consciousness; in short, he rejected the tinker-toy model of the mind. For Wundt ideas were active *processes,* not passive elements interacting via mechanical laws. Each experience is an *event,* not a *thing* appearing in consciousness and disappearing into unconsciousness. Memory is not the resurrection of a previous idea—which Wundt held to be impossible since consciousness is ever-changing—but is instead the use of rules for the reconstruction of previous experience.

For Wundt mind was active in even its simplest aspects, a doctrine he referred to awkwardly as the *actuality* of mind. Wundt also called his system *voluntaristic,* to underline its emphasis on mental activity and the important role in mental events it assigned to feeling and will. In line with this Wundt replaced atomistic reductionism with a doctrine of mental synthesis. Complex mental events are based on simpler ones, but according to Wundt the relation is one of active synthesis of elements into a higher unity rather than a reduction of the complex to the simple.

Experimental Psychology of Consciousness

A good way to begin to understand Ganzheit psychology is by looking at one of Wundt's most important experiments. His psychology was the study of consciousness, so a natural question is, "How many ideas may be present in consciousness at a given moment?" Simple introspection cannot answer this question. How many ideas do you have in consciousness right now? It is futile to try to hold for analysis a moment in the stream of consciousness in order to answer the question.

Therefore an experiment is called for, one that complements and perfects introspection and will yield quantitative results. The following is an updated and simplified version of Wundt's experiment. Imagine sitting in a darkened room facing a projection screen. For an instant, about 0.09 sec, a stimulus is flashed on the screen. This stimulus is a 4-column by 4-row array of randomly chosen letters, and your task is to recall as many letters as possible. What is recalled provides a measure of how many simple ideas can be grasped in an instant of time, and so may give an answer to the original question. Wundt found that unpracticed subjects could recall about four letters; subjects who have practiced could recall up to six but no more. These figures agree remarkably well with modern results on the capacity of short-term memory.

Two further important phenomena can be observed in this experiment. First, imagine an experiment in which each line of four letters forms a word, for example, *work, many, room, idea*. Under these conditions one could probably recall all four words, or at least three, for a total of 12 to 16 letters. Similarly, one could quickly read and recall the word "miscellaneousness" which contains 17 letters. Letters as isolated elements quickly fill up consciousness so that only four to six can be perceived in a given moment, but if these elements are organized many more can be grasped. In Wundt's term the letter-elements are *synthesized* into a greater whole, which is understood as a single complex idea and grasped as one new element.

This phenomenon shows in what sense Wundt was an atomist and in what sense he was not. The word *work* is in fact made up of four simpler elementary idea-processes, *w, o, r,* and *k,* but it cannot be reduced to these elements. The word is a *synthesis* of the elements and the whole word functions as an element. Complex ideas derive from elements; they are not compounded out of them or reducible to them. Wundt rejected the atomism of the British associationists, including the mental chemistry of J. S. Mill.

A second phenomenon can be observed in this memory experiment. The subject in the original experiment very easily notices that some letters—the ones the subject names—are perceived clearly and distinctly, but that other letters are only dimly and hazily perceived. Consciousness seems to be a large field populated with ideational elements. One area of this field is in the focus of *attention,* and the ideas within it are clearly perceived. The elements lying outside the focal area are only faintly felt as present and cannot be identified.

Attention, like synthesis, played a key role in Wundt's theory. In fact, attention was the process that could actively synthesize elements into larger units. Wundt's ideas on attention were derived from Leibniz, and Wundt used Leibniz's terms. An idea that enters the large field of consciousness was said to be *apprehended,* and one that enters the focal area of attention was said to be *apperceived.*

Apperception was especially important in Wundt's system. Not only was it responsible for the active synthesis of elements into wholes, but it also accounted for the higher mental activities of analysis (revealing the parts of a whole) and of judgment. It was responsible for the activities of relating and comparing, which are simpler forms of synthesis and analysis. Synthesis itself took two forms: imagination and understanding. Apperception was the basis for all higher forms of thought, such as reasoning and use of language, and so was central to Ganzheit psychology.

Finally, Wundt's emphasis on apperception displays the *voluntaristic* nature of his system. Since neither *mind* nor *self* referred to a special substance for Wundt, to what did he attribute our sense of self and the feeling that we have a mind? It is this *feeling* that provides the answer. Apperception is a voluntary act of the will by which we control and give synthetic unity to our mind. It is the feeling of activity, control, and unity that defined the self. Wundt wrote: "What we call our 'self' is simply the unity of volition plus the universal control of our mental life which it renders possible."

Wundt did not neglect feelings and emotions, for they are an obvious part of our conscious experience. He often used introspectively reported feelings as clues to what processes were going on in the mind at a given moment. Apperception, for instance, he thought to be marked by a feeling of mental effort. He also studied feelings and emotions in their own right, and his tridimensional theory of feeling became a source of controversy, especially with Titchener. Wundt proposed that feelings could be defined along three dimensions: pleasant vs. unpleasant, high vs. low arousal, and concentrated vs. relaxed attention. He conducted a long series of studies designed to establish a physiological basis for each dimension, but the results were inconclusive, and other laboratories produced conflicting findings. Recent factor-analyses of affect, however, have arrived at similar three-dimensional systems (Blumenthal 1975). While Wundt emphasized the active, synthesizing power of apperception, he recognized the existence of passive processes as well, which he classified as various forms of association or "passive" apperception. There were, for example, *assimilations,* in which a current sensation is associated to an older element. When one looks at a chair, one knows immediately what it is by assimilation, for the current image of the perceived chair is immediately associated with the older universal element *chair.* Recognition is a form of assimilation, stretched out into two steps—a vague feeling of familiarity followed by the act of recognition proper. Recollection, on the other hand, was for Wundt, as for some contemporary psychologists, an act of reconstruction rather than reactivation of old elements. One cannot reexperience an earlier event, for ideas are not permanent. Rather one reconstructs it from current cues and certain general rules.

Finally, Wundt did not fail to notice abnormal states of consciousness. He discussed hallucinations, depressions, hypnosis, and dreams. Of particular interest was his discussion of what we now call *schizophrenia.* He observed that this disease involves a breakdown in attentional processes. The schizophrenic loses the apperceptive control of thoughts characteristic of normal consciousness and surrenders instead to passive associative processes, so that thought becomes a simple train of associations rather than coordinated processes directed by volition. This theory was developed by Wundt's student and friend, the great psychiatrist Emil Kraepelin, and has been revived by modern students of schizophrenia and autism.

Völkerpsychologie

Wundt believed that experimental individual psychology could not be a complete psychology. The minds of living individuals are the products of a long course of species development of which each person is ignorant. Therefore, to understand the development of the mind, we must have recourse to history. The study of animals and children is limited by their inability to introspect. History expands the range of the individual consciousness. In particular, the range of existing human cultures represents the various stages in cultural and mental evolution, from primitive, tribal to civilized, national man. *Völkerpsycholgie* is thus the study of the products of collective life—especially of language, myth, and custom—that provide clues to the higher operations of mind. Wundt said the experimental psychology penetrates only the "outworks" of the mind; *Völkerpsychologie* reaches deeper.

Emphasis on historical development, a legacy from Vico and Herder, was typical of German intellectuals in the nineteenth century. In the German view every individual springs from, and has an organic relationship with, his or her natal culture. Further, cultures have complex histories which determine their forms and contents. Thus it was generally believed that history could be used as a method for arriving at an intuitive understanding of human psychology.

Wundt's remarks on myth and custom are unexceptional. He saw history as going through a series of stages from primitive tribes to an age of heroes and then to the formation of states, culminating in a world state based on the concept of humanity as a whole. It was, however, in the study of language (which early in his career Wundt almost pursued instead of psychology) that he made his most substantial contribution, articulating a theory of psycholinguistics that reaches conclusions being rediscovered today. Language was a part of *Völkerpsychologie* for Wundt because, like myth and custom, it is a product of collective life.

Wundt divided language into two aspects: *outer phenomena*, consisting of actually produced or perceived utterances, and *inner phenomena*, the cognitive processes that underlie the outer string of words. This division of psychological phenomena into inner and outer aspects is central to Ganzheit psychology and has come up before in the contrast between the "outworks" of the mind that can be reached by experimentation and the deeper processes that cannot. The distinction between inner and outer phenomena is easiest to understand with regard to language. It is possible to describe language as an organized, associated system of sounds which we speak or hear; this constitutes the outer form of language. However, this outer form is the surface expression of deeper cognitive processes that organize a speaker's thoughts and prepare them for utterance and enable the listener to extract meaning from what she or he hears. These cognitive processes constitute the inner mental form of speech.

Sentence production, according to Wundt, begins with a unified idea which one wishes to express, the *Gesamtvorstellung*, or whole mental configuration.* The analytic function of apperception prepares the unified idea for speech, for it must be analyzed into component parts and a structure that retains the relationship between

---

Gesamtvorstellung was misleadingly translated by Titchener, Wundt's leading translator, as "aggregate idea" but Blumenthal (1970) has shown Titchener's error and proposed the phrase used here: "whole mental configuration." The mistranslation reveals Titchener's misperception of Ganzheit psychology.

the parts and the whole. Consider the simple sentence, "The cat is orange." The basic structural division in such a sentence is between the subject and predicate, and can be represented with the *tree-diagram* introduced by Wundt. If we let G = *Gesamtvorstellung*, S = subject, and P = predicate, then we have

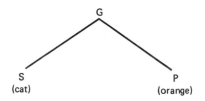

The idea of an orange cat has now been divided into its two fundamental ideas, and can be expressed verbally as "the cat is orange" with the addition of the function words (*the, is*) required in our particular language. More complex ideas require more analysis and must be represented by more complex diagrams. The entire process in all cases can be described as the transformation of an unexpressible organized whole thought into an expressible sequential structure of words organized in a sentence.

The process is reversed in comprehension of speech. Here, the synthesizing rather than the analytic function of apperception is called on. The words and grammatical structure in a heard sentence must be used by the hearer to reconstruct in his or her own mind the whole mental configuration that the speaker is attempting to communicate. Wundt supported his view of comprehension by pointing out that we remember the gist of what we hear, but only rarely the surface (outer) form, which tends to disappear in the process of constructing the *Gesamtvorstellung*.

We have touched on only a small portion of Wundt's discussion of language. He also wrote on gesture-language; the origin of language from involuntary, expressive sounds; primitive language (based more on association than on apperception); phonology; and meaning-change. Wundt has a fair claim to be the founder of psycholinguistics as well as psychology. His ideas about how language works were central to Wundt's views and, as we shall see, are remarkably similar to many aspects of contemporary psycholinguistics.

EDWARD BRADFORD TITCHENER (1867–1927) AND STRUCTURALISM

Edward Bradford Titchener was an Englishman who brought German psychology to America. He thus played an important role in the founding of American psychology, for he was the foe of both functionalism and behaviorism, while on the European front he was the enemy of act psychology and of imageless thought. In this chapter we will examine his system, structuralism, and its relation to Wundt's Ganzheit psychology.*

*Titchener adopted the label "structural psychology" to distinguish his position from functionalism (which he also named in the same paper). He later came to prefer the label "existentialism," but this term now stands for a very different approach to philosophy and psychology associated with people such as Sartre and Heidegger.

Titchener has usually been taken by historians to be a faithful reflection of Wundt, the two systems being seen as identical. A recent history of psychology says this: "Titchener's system was so close to Wundt's and so much easier to describe, that we shall not here dwell on . . . Wundt. . . ." (Keller 1973). This attitude naturally led American psychologists who rejected Titchener's system to reject Wundt's at the same time. We shall see to what degree this identification and simultaneous rejection was justified. Given the complexity of Ganzheit psychology, however, we should be suspicious of substituting Titchener for Wundt because the former is "so much easier." Much is bound to be left out.

Background

E. B. Titchener was born in 1867 at Chichester, England. His ancestors included a mayor of Chichester, a school headmaster, and a distinguished lawyer. He attended a prestigious secondary school and went to Oxford from 1885 to 1890. His educational record was outstanding. During his Oxford years his interests shifted from classics and philosophy to physiology. The conjunction of interests in philosophy and physiology naturally predisposed Titchener to psychology, and while at Oxford he translated the third edition of Wundt's massive *Principles of Physiological Psychology*. Titchener could find no one in England to train him in psychology, so in 1890 he went to Leipzig, taking his doctorate in 1892. Titchener was impressed by Wundt, but they were never close.

We must remember that as an Englishman Titchener arrived in Leipzig from the other side of the intellectual gulf separating Germany from the West. He was thoroughly versed in philosophy and was much impressed by James Mill, remarking that Mill's speculations could be empirically demonstrated. In his first systematic book, *An Outline of Psychology* (1897), he wrote: "The general standpoint of [my] book is that of the traditional English psychology." It is reasonable to expect, therefore, that Titchener may well have assimilated Wundt's German Ganzheit psychology into the "traditional English psychology" that Wundt rejected. Titchener's personality was reputedly "German," but his psychology is more a mixture of German and English.

After a short stint as a lecturer in biology in England—a country long unreceptive to psychology—Titchener left for America to teach at Cornell, replacing his Leipzig friend, Frank Angell, who was going to Stanford. He remained at Cornell until his death in 1927. He transformed Cornell into a bastion of mentalistic psychology, even as America's focus went first functionalist and, after 1913, behaviorist. Titchener never compromised with these movements, despite his friendships with the functionalist J. R. Angell and with Watson, the founder of behaviorism. He published almost exclusively in the *American Journal of Psychology,* which he edited, shunning rival journals like *Psychological Review* and *Journal of Experimental Psychology*. He did not participate actively in the American Psychological Association, even when it met at Cornell, preferring instead his own group, the Experimental Psychologists, which he kept true to his version of psychology. It was clear that structuralism depended upon one man, Titchener, and when he unexpectedly died in 1927 the school collapsed.

Structural Psychology

Titchener apparently possessed a mind in which everything had imaginal-sensational character. His mind even had an image for such an abstract word as *meaning*. Titchener (1909) wrote: "I see meaning as the blue-grey tip of a kind of scoop, which has a bit of yellow above it . . . and which is just digging into a dank mass of . . . plastic material." Even though he recognized that not everyone had an imaginal mind as he called it, he built his psychology on the premise that the mind was made up of sensations or images of sensation and *nothing else*. This led to his rejection of various Wundtian concepts such as apperception, which is not directly observed. Titchener's system was thus explicitly sensationistic as opposed to Wundt's, which was voluntaristic.

The first task of Titchener's sensationistic psychology was the discovery of the basic sensation-elements to which all complex processes could be reduced. As early as 1897 he drew up a catalog of elements found in the different sense-departments. There were, for instance, 30,500 visual elements, four taste elements, and three sensations in the alimentary canal.

Elements were defined by Titchener as the simplest sensations to be found in experience. They were to be discovered through the systematic dissection by introspection of the contents of consciousness; when an experience could not be dissected into parts it was declared *elemental*. Titchener's method of introspection was much more elaborate than Wundt's, for it was not a simple report of an experience but a complicated retrospective analysis of that experience. Wrote Titchener (1909): "Be as attentive as possible to the object or process which gives rise to the sensation, and, when the object is removed or the process completed, recall the sensation by an act of memory as vividly and completely as you can." Persistant application of this method would in Titchener's view eventually produce a complete description of the elements of human experience. It was an unfinished (and, as many thought, unfinishable) task when Titchener died.

The second task of Titchener's sensationistic approach was to determine how the elementary sensations are connected together to form complex perceptions, ideas, and images. These connections were not all associations, because for Titchener an association was a connection of elements that persisted even when the original conditions for the connection no longer could be obtained. Titchener rejected the label of associationism, not only for this reason but also because the associationists spoke of association of meaningful ideas, not of simple meaningless sensations, which was all that concerned Titchener.

The third task of Titchener's psychology was to explain the workings of mind. Introspection, according to Titchener, could yield only a description of mind. At least until about 1925, he believed that a scientific psychology required more than mere description. Explanation for Titchener was to be sought in physiology, which would explain why the sensory elements arise and become connected. Titchener rejected Wundt's attempt to psychologically explain the operation of the mind. According to Titchener's system, all that can be found in experience are sensory elements rather than processes such as attention. Appeal to such an unobservable entity as apperception was illegitimate in Titchener's eyes, and betrays his positivism. He therefore sought to explain mind by reference to observable nerve-physiology.

How did Titchener treat a process such as attention that was so central to Ganzheit psychology? He rejected as wholly unnecessary the term *apperception,* which in Wundt's psychology gave rise to attention. Attention itself Titchener reduced to sensation. One obvious attribute of any sensation is clarity, and Titchener said that "attended" sensations are simply the clearest ones. Attention was not for him a mental process, but simply an attribute of sensation—clearness—produced by certain nerve-processes. What of the mental effort that Wundt says goes along with attention? This, too, is reduced to sensation. Wrote Titchener in *Experimental Psychology: A Manual of Laboratory Practice:* "When I am trying to attend I . . . find myself frowning, wrinkling my forehead etc. All such . . . bodily sets and movements give rise to characteristic . . . sensations. Why should not these sensations be what we call 'attention.'"

Was Titchener a more comprehensible, English-speaking double for Wundt, as is so often assumed? We must conclude not: Titchener is "so much easier" than Wundt because Titchener discounted so much of his teacher's teaching. He took the complex voluntaristic psychology of Wundt and filtered it through his own positivism and atomism to produce a reductive sensationism for which mind is nothing but complexes of elements found in experience. He had nothing similar to Wundt's *Völkerpsychologie*. Wundt's Ganzheit psychology has many resonances with modern cognitive psychology; Titchener's structuralism has none. However, as we will see, it does have resonances with the most extreme form of behaviorism—B. F. Skinner's descriptive behaviorism.

A word should be said about the direction Titchener's thought was taking at his death. His last work was *Systematic Psychology: Prologemena*, which appeared posthumously in 1929. In this book he was becoming even more positivistic than before. He abandoned explanation as a goal of science in favor of pure description. He abandoned the notion of analytically discovered sensory elements in favor of phenomenologically described dimensions of sensory attributes. He departed even farther from Wundt's attempt to penetrate the hidden mental processes underneath the outer, sensory phenomena.

CHALLENGES TO THE ANALYTIC PSYCHOLOGY OF CONSCIOUSNESS

Three assumptions were important to Wundt's analytic study of human consciousness. The first was that all the elements of consciousness derived directly or indirectly from sensation or bodily feelings; all the contents of thought were *images* of some sort. The second assumption was that all complex ideas were associative or apperceptive combinations of simpler elements, even when emergent properties resulted from the combination. The third assumption was methodological, that the higher mental processes, such as thinking, were too unstable, too subject to individual differences, and too far removed from outer mental phenomena to be studied in the laboratory. Wundt's *Völkerpsychologie* was intended to remedy this shortcoming. These fundamental assumptions did not escape criticism by other psychologists of consciousness.

The Psychology of Thinking: The Würzburg School (1901–1909)

One of Wundt's most outstanding and successful students was Oswald Külpe (1862–1915). Although his early psychology was even more conservative than Wundt's, during his brief professorial tenure at the University of Würzburg, he helped develop a new approach to psychological experiment, one which claimed that thinking could be studied experimentally. Two important sets of results emerged from this research. The first indicated, contrary to Wundt, that some thoughts are imageless, while the second undermined associationism as an account of thinking.

Wundt's exclusion of the higher mental processes from the laboratory turned out to be merely a dogmatic prejudice. As early as 1879 Hermann Ebbinghaus undertook to study the higher process of memory, his results appearing in 1885. Shortly after leaving Wundt, Külpe seems to have decided that the highest mental process of all, thinking, could be experimentally studied and could be introspected—if only Wundt's methods were changed. Wundt's experiments were quite simple, involving little more than reaction to, or a brief description of, a stimulus. Fechner's psychophysics, Donder's mental chronometry, and Wundt's apperception experiments are examples of this procedure. Under Külpe (who never published an experiment from his Würzburg days but participated in others' experiments) the tasks were made more difficult and the job of introspection more elaborate.

During the years of the Würzburg school, the complexity of the experimental tasks increased from giving free associations to stimulus words to agreeing or disagreeing with difficult metaphysical theses or Nietzche's aphorisms. These tasks, whether simple or difficult, required thinking, whereas Wundtian tasks did not. Subjects had to respond to the problem and then describe the thought-processes leading to the response. As the method developed, the subject would be asked to concentrate introspective attention on different parts of the subjective experience, that is, the subjects would focus on their mental state while awaiting the stimulus word, or on the appearance of the answer in consciousness. In these experiments the Würzburgers hoped to directly observe thinking as it happened.

The first results were a shock to almost all psychologists: Thoughts can be imageless. This finding emerged in the first Würzburg paper by A. M. Mayer and J. Orth, published in 1901. In this experiment the subject was instructed to respond with the first word that came to mind after hearing a stimulus word. The experimenter gave a ready signal, called out the stimulus word, and started a stopwatch; the subject gave a response and the experimenter stopped the watch. The subject then described the thinking process. Mayer and Orth reported that most thinking involved definite images or feelings associated with acts of will. However, wrote Mayer and Orth (1901), ''apart from these two classes of conscious processes, we must introduce a third group . . . The subjects very frequently reported that they experienced certain conscious processes which they could describe neither as definite images nor as acts of will.'' For example, while serving as a subject, Mayer ''made the observation that following the stimulus word 'meter' there occurred a peculiar conscious process, not further definable, which was followed by the spoken word 'trochee.' '' So Wundt was wrong, according to Mayer and Orth; nonimaginal events in consciousness had been found.

The Würzburgers refined their methods over the years, but the results remained: There are imageless thoughts. Moreover, the finding was made independently in Paris by Alfred Binet in his studies of children's thinking, and in New York by Robert Woodworth. Both studies were reported in 1903, but the investigators did not know the Würzburg work. In fact, Binet later claimed that the new method should be called the ''method of Paris.'' In any event, the finding of imageless thought was a challenge to psychological orthodoxy and provoked a controversy that aided and abetted the birth of behaviorism.

What was to be made of imageless thought? The Würzburger's own interpretation changed during the life of the school. Mayer and Orth did no more than discover imageless thoughts—vague, impalpable, almost indescribable "conscious states." Later on they were identified simply as "thoughts" themselves. The final interpretation was that thought is actually an unconscious process, reducing the imageless thought elements to conscious indicators of thinking rather than thinking itself. However, on both sides of the Atlantic many psychologists found the Würzburg methods, results, and interpretations to be unacceptable or at least suspect.

Writing in 1907, Wundt tried to falsify the Würzburg results by attacking the method. He argued that the Würzburg experiments were sham experiments, merely reversions to unreliable armchair introspection that happened to be conducted in a laboratory. According to Wundt, experimental control was entirely lacking in the thought experiments. The subject did not know exactly what task would be set. The ensuing mental process would vary from subject to subject and from trial to trial, so the results could not be replicated. Finally, said Wundt, it is difficult if not impossible for a subject to both think about the set problem and to watch that process at the same time. Consequently, Wundt said, the so-called findings of imageless thought are invalid. Properly conducted experiments would show that, properly analyzed, "imageless" content was imaginal after all.

Titchener undertook the experimental refutation of the Würzburg findings. Methodologically, Titchener echoed Wundt by claiming that subjects' reports of "imageless" thought were not descriptions of consciousness at all, but fabrications based on beliefs about how one would solve the problems set in the experiments. Experimentally, Titchener's students performed thought experiments and reported that they could find no evidence of imageless thought elements; they successfully traced all conscious content to sensations or feelings (Clark 1911). Titchener concluded that the Würzburgers had failed as introspectors by declining to analyze a mental content and then calling it "imageless thought."

Other commentators offered alternative interpretations of the Würzburg results. It was suggested by some that certain types of minds possess imageless thought while others do not, reducing the Titchener-Külpe controversy to one of individual differences. This hypothesis was criticized as unparsimonious; why should nature create two types of mind to attain the same end—accurate thinking? The hypothesis of unconscious thinking was rejected on the grounds that what is not conscious is not mental but physiological, and therefore not a part of psychology. A similar criticism greeted Freud's hypothesis of the unconscious.

Perhaps the most important consequence of the debate about imageless thought was the suspicion that introspection was a fragile and unreliable tool, easily prejudiced by theoretical expectations. The Würzburg subjects believed in imageless thought, and they found it. Titchener's subjects believed only in sensations and feelings, and they found only those. R. M. Ogden, an American suporter of imageless thought, wrote (1911a) that if Wundt's and Titchener's criticisms of the Würzburg methods were valid, "may we not carry the point a step farther and deny the value of *all* introspection. Indeed, in a recent discussion among psychologists, this position was vigorously maintained by two among those present." Ogden himself suggested that the differential results from Cornell and Würzburg betray "unconscious bias" based on different training (Ogden 1911b). The imageless thought controversy revealed difficulties with the introspective method and by 1911, the year of Ogden's papers, we find some psychologists ready to discard it altogether. Two years later Watson, the founder of behaviorism, included this controversy in his indictment of mentalism.

The imageless thought results represent a budding anomaly for certain forms of mentalism. Woodworth wrote as late as 1938 that "the whole question may well be shelved as permanently debatable and insoluble." This is one fate of anomalies, according to Kuhn. The debate over imageless thought showed signs of developing into a Kuhnian paradigm clash. In 1911 J. R. Angell wrote: "One feels that the differences which divide certain of the writers are largely those of mutual misunderstanding as to the precise phenomenon under discussion. . . ." However, the anomaly and paradigm clash were incipient only; their development was cut short by the advent of behaviorism. Woodworth found the problem being shelved in 1938 not because the problem had been exhausted, but because no one cared anymore. By the second (1954) edition of Woodworth's *Experimental Psychology*, this controversy which had occupied many pages in the 1938 edition had shriveled to four paragraphs.

The Würzburgers' second shock for the psychological establishment arose when they studied the process of thinking. Their results led them to reject traditional associationsism as an adequate account of mind. Their problem was this: What makes one idea rather than another follow a given idea? For free association, as in Mayer's and Orth's experiment, associationism has a plausible answer. If the stimulus word is "bird" the subject may respond "canary," then the associationist can say simply that the bird-canary bond was the strongest in the subject's associative network. However, this situation is complicated if we use a method of constrained association, as Henry J. Watt did in 1905. In this method we set a specific task for the subject to carry out, such as "give a subordinate category" or "give a superordinate category." To the former task the subject may still reply "canary." To the second task the correct response cannot be "canary," but instead should be "animal." However, these tasks are no longer free associations, but rather are acts of directed thinking that produce propositions that may be true or false—unlike free association. So the simple associative bond, bird-canary, is overridden in directed thinking.

The Würzburgers argued that associationism fails to explain thinking, for something must direct thought along the proper lines in the associative network in order for a subject to respond correctly to such tasks as Watt's. The Würzburgers proposed that it was the task itself that directed thinking. In their later terminology they said that the task establishes a mental set—or determining tendency—in the mind that properly directs the subject's use of his or her associative network. It was these experiments that suggested unconscious thinking, for subjects found that given the task "Give superordinate to canary," the response "bird" popped into their heads with little experienced mental activity. The Würzburgers concluded that the mental set accomplishes thinking even before the problem is given; the subject is so prepared to give a superordinate that the actual response occurs automatically.

Their investigations of the process of thinking took the Würzburg psychologists toward a psychology of function instead of content. They found that laboratory work could reveal something about how the mind functions in addition to what it contains. We will find that American psychology was predominantly functional, and the reception of the idea of the mental set was much more favorable in America than the reception given imageless thought. While the discussion of imageless thought in Woodworth's authoritative *Experimental Psychology* shrank between 1938 and 1954, index references to *set* increased from 19 to 35, with more extended discussions. The concept of set made sense to American functional psychologists interested in mental operations, and the behaviorists found that they could reinterpret *set* as establishing determining tendencies in behavior instead of in mind.

Although Würzburg-inspired work was continued after 1909 (especially by Otto Selz, who had worked there), the school essentially dissolved when Külpe left for the University of Bonn. No systematic theory based on the Würzburg studies was ever published, although there is evidence Külpe was working on such a theory when he died. It is puzzling that from 1909 until his death Külpe said almost nothing about the dramatic Würzburg results. Therefore no alternative psychology arose from the Würzburg school. Their methods were innovative, their findings stimulating and anomalous, and in the concept of the mental set they made a permanent contribution. But the Würzburg school remained a school, a research program cut off prematurely. The other challenge to traditional psychology was more sustained, systematic, and memorable.

Against Atomism: The Gestalt Movement

Atomism is a useful dimension on which to classify psychologists. The most atomistic psychology was James Mill's tinker-toy theory, and Titchener's catalog of sensory atoms is not much different. Moving toward holism, we find John Stuart Mill's mental chemistry and Wundt's theory of apperceptive synthesis. Both recognized the emergence of new properties as mental elements combine, but both still believed psychology should analyze complexes into elements, just as chemists do. More holistic still was Thomas Reid, who maintained that complex ideas are not built up out of elements by any process, but are immediately given in experience as meaningful wholes. Introspection can break them down into elements, but this is artificial and does not imply that the mind starts with atoms and forms wholes; according to Reid the wholes are there from the beginning.

The *Gestalt* psychologists went even further, arguing that decomposing wholes into parts is not only artificial, but pointless and scientifically sterile, revealing nothing about the mind whatsoever. The philosophical root of their protest was *phenomenology,* whose proponents argued that experience should be simply described as given, never analyzed. Presented with a triangle, a good Titchenerian introspector would report, "I see three lines"; the report would contain only meaningless sensory atoms. The phenomenologist would say, "I see a triangle," reporting a meaningful mental whole transcending the atomic elements.

Even some elementalists were moving in this direction. Christian Ehrenfels (1859–1932) discussed "Gestalt qualities" in 1890. Ehrenfels wanted to know how certain experiences maintain their character despite sensory changes. This is most apparent in hearing tunes. Despite transposition of keys, and thus its sensory elements, we always hear the same tune as the same. Ehrenfels was dealing with the problem of organized perceptions, not elements, and arguing for a new mental element. A tune is made up of sensory elements—its specific notes—but it possesses in addition a Gestalt (or form) quality that represents the organization. Similarly, in the case of the triangle it is made up of three sensory elements, the lines, plus a form-quality element of triangularity. Ehrenfels's former teacher, the philosopher Alexius Meinong (1853–1920), tried to specify the source of the form-quality. Sensory elements are given by experience, and then the mind in a mental act adds the structuring form-quality. This theory of an additional mental act derived from the act psychology of Franz Brentano, whom we shall consider next. Both Ehrenfels's and Meinong's theories remained elementalistic, merely adding a mental element of organization to the accepted list of sensory elements.

Both atomistic elementalism and the act interpretation of form-qualities were rejected by the phenomenologically oriented Gestalt psychologists, as is shown by the following Gestalt experiment. A subject is seated in a darkened room and two spots of light are flashed off and on alternately. When the interval between flashes is more than 0.2 sec, the subject sees two flashing lights; but when the interval is less than 0.2 sec the subject sees one light in continuous motion. The subject perceives apparent motion where in fact there is none. This phenomenon underlies our experience of movies, which are actually a rapidly displayed series of still photographs. Such experiments indicated that more than a mental element was needed. Such apparent motion undermines the atomistic account of consciousness, for sensational "atoms" given on the retina are not perceived, but instead give rise to a qualitatively different experience. Apparent motion is an experience that emerges from simple sensations but cannot plausibly be reduced to them. It is, in short, a perceptual whole (*Gestalt*, in German), given immediately to consciousness and deserving direct study. The Gestalt psychologists advocated a holistic psychology based on the mind's perception of complete forms.

This experimental demonstration (called the *phi phenomenon*), which shows that conscious experience is not usefully reducible to bundles of discrete sensations, was the starting point of the Gestalt movement. Its inspiration, however, had deeper and more general sources. We have already seen how German culture rejected the tide of associationism, atomism, and mechanism that flowed from traditional British and French philosophies. Wundt's psychology was a partial reaction to this tide, but the young men of the next generation reacted even more strongly. Even more than Wundt they looked for wholeness and transcendence as a way out of the post World War I crisis of German culture. They fought against all philosophies or sciences that saw creatures or cultures as machines, as no more than collections of simpler parts.

The leader of this movement in psychology was Max Wertheimer (1880–1943), who carried out the phi phenomena research in 1912 using the other two great Gestalt psychologists, Wolfgang Köhler (1887–1967) and Kurt Koffka (1887–1941), as the main subjects. Wertheimer was by nature a prophet for whom the idea of the Gestalt was "not only a theory of perception or of thinking, or a theory of psychology, or even an entire philosophy; it was, rather, a *Weltanschauung*, indeed an all encompassing religion. The core of this religion is the hope that the world is a sensible coherent whole, that reality is organized into meaningful parts, that natural units have their own structure" (Wertheimer 1978).

The phi phenomenon demonstrated a faith that Wertheimer held before 1912. Despite being a Jew, he received an education "typical of the elite of his day" including studies with von Ehrenfels at Prague and Külpe at Würzburg (Wertheimer, 1978). In all his studies he was immersed in the reaction against traditional atomism and traditional psychology, but Wertheimer moved in a more holistic direction than either of his teachers. His Gestalt ideas appeared first in a 1910 paper on the primitive music of a Ceylonese tribe, in which he concluded that their compositions were organized by "*Gestalten* that are rhythmically and melodically strict" (Wertheimer 1978).

Central to the Gestalt movement was the "Gestalt vision," Wertheimer's holistic *Weltanschauung*. In 1924 Wertheimer declared that "Gestalt theory is neither more nor less'' than the belief that ''there are wholes, the behavior of which is not determined by that of their individual elements, but where the part processes are themselves determined by the intrinsic nature of the whole. It is the hope of Gestalt theory to determine the nature of such wholes.'' So Wundt's half-way holism in which wholes are constructed by the mind was unacceptable. Wertheimer condemned traditional—Wundtian—psychology for containing what he called (1925) an abundance of ''things arid, poor and inessential'' and for having ''alien, wooden, monstrous'' implications. He argued that traditional psychology rested on two erroneous assumptions. The first is *''the mosaic or bundle hypothesis,''* which is Wertheimer's term for sensationism. The second is *''the association hypothesis,''* by which Wertheimer means the tinker-toy theory. Nor could Wertheimer accept Wundt's idea that the mind's power of apperception unites elements into greater wholes, for this still concedes the fundamental status of sensational elements. Wrote Wertheimer (1922): ''Gestalten'' are not ''the sums of aggregated contents erected subjectively upon primarily given pieces. . . . Instead, we are dealing with wholes and whole-processes possessed of inner intrinsic laws. 'Elements' are determined as parts by the intrinsic conditions of their wholes and are to be understood 'as parts' relative to such wholes.'' This is the central formula of Gestalt psychology.

Two important new concepts were used by the Gestalt psychologists to put their formula into practice. The first is the concept of the psychological field, consciously borrowed from field theory in physics. Gestaltists deny that experience is like a mosaic, a collection of inert, noninteracting, discrete units, or sensations. Instead, they see experience as a field of dynamically interacting parts. In the phi phenomenon the ''parts'' of the field, the two flashing lights, interact to give rise to the perception of motion. Thus a visual illusion such as the Müller-Lyer is produced by interactions among the visual elements. The central lines are the same size, but because of the context in which they are viewed (the arrowheads) they seem to be different lengths.

The Gestalt psychologists extended the field concept to refer not only to the phenomenal field of immediate experience involved in the phi phenomenon or illusions, but to the behavioral field in which our actions take place. For the Gestalt psychologists, a problem to be solved defined a behavioral field in stress. An animal or child, for example, might be prevented from reaching visible food by a barrier. The ''stress'' in such a field is obvious. The problem is resolved when the field is reorganized by ''insight,'' that is, when the subject sees that the barrier may be walked around. The solution allows access to the food and relieves the stress in the behavioral field; the problem no longer exists. An important implication is that the subject must be aware of all elements in a problem situation before a real psychological problem exists. Should the subject not be able to see the food, no problem would exist, for no psychological field-stress would exist, even if the subject were hungry. For this reason the Gestalt psychologists criticized animal-learning experiments, such as E. L. Thorndike's, in which the animal could not perceive all elements of the situation. How can an animal exhibit its intelligence unless the relevant factors are available for intelligence to consider? According to Gestaltists, animals are reduced to trial-and-error conditioning if this is the only kind of behavior allowed in an experiment.

The field concept proved capable of indefinite extension to psychological problems. Not only could it be applied to simple visual experiences and problem solving, but was also applied to creativity (by Wertheimer himself) and social psychology (by Kurt Lewin, 1890–1947). However, the concept of the experiential field was insufficient. The two flashing lights do not by themselves create apparent motion; it is a psychological phenomenon. Problems do not solve themselves, they only pose themselves. The Gestalt psychologists, however, were unwilling to posit an active mind "which is able to grasp intrinsic relations and utilize such understanding," just as they did not recognize active apperception as a unifying force behind the creation of whole ideas. In their view this alternative would lead to "vitalistic or spiritualistic dualism which we . . . have refused to accept." (Koffka 1935). Instead, he said, "the dynamics of the process (of perceiving or thinking) are determined by the intrinsic properties of the data."

These "intrinsic properties" must act on the organism to produce experience or behavior. If there is no mind to act on, the action must be directly on the nervous system. This leads us to the second important concept of Gestalt psychology, the principle of *isomorphism*. This principle has given rise to numerous misconceptions. The Gestalt psychologists held that the brain is not the sensorimotor association machine that most believed it to be, but instead is a complex electrical field. The idea of isomorphism is that the structural relationships in the behavioral field create in the individual who experiences them a pattern of brain-fields isomorphic to themselves. So in the phi phenomenon the flashing lights create two brain-fields that overlap and create the experience of motion. In a problem situation, the stresses in the behavioral field are represented in the brain as stresses in its electrical field. Insight is the resolution of the brain-field stresses that leads to resolution of the real problem.

The concept of isomorphism is difficult to grasp. A good analogy was suggested by Woodworth (1938). Functional isomorphism exists between the United States and a map of the United States. The two things are not the same, but structural relations in the former are directly related to structural relations in the latter. So, the problem of driving from Chicago to Los Angeles can be experienced and solved through the map. The "stresses" of the trip can be seen and resolved on the map. But Woodworth's analogy is simplified. The Gestalt psychologists did not maintain that a picture of the behavioral-field exists in the brain. Exactly what they did mean remains obscure; it is only certain that they maintained a functional isomorphism between behavioral and brain-fields. It was only through isomorphism and the electric field picture of the brain that the Gestalt psychologists could uphold their holistic dynamic-field explanations of experience and behavior without falling into dualism.

The Gestalt movement thus attempted to avoid both atomism and dualism by considering people as perceiving organisms that respond to whole perceptual fields. The Gestalt experiments uncovered several interesting quirks of perception, such as the phi phenomenon, that had to be included in any later perceptual psychology. The Gestalt psychologists' almost mystical theory, however, did not travel well. It was far too German to do well in England and America, where psychology has been most studied since World War II.

Act Psychology: Franz Brentano
(1878–1917)

By and large, all the psychologies we have considered so far may be regarded primarily as psychologies of content. That is, they are concerned to discover and describe the contents of consciousness. The imageless thought debate, for example, is a controversy about mental content: Do sensations, feeling, and images exhaustively describe all possible mental contents, or must we add "conscious states" to the list?

Franz Brentano, however, insisted that what is most important and characteristic of the mind is that it *acts*. Mental acts are directed at contents, Brentano said, but more important than the content is the act. Brentano divided mental acts into three classes: *ideating* (I see, I hear, I imagine), *judging* (I reject, I believe, I recall), and *loving-hating* (I wish, I intend, I desire). Acts are always directed at mental contents, and here arises Brentano's most significant concept, *intentionality*, as the criterion of mind. Rather than advocating a Cartesian dualism of substances, Brentano argued that only mental states—his "acts"—possess intentionality. Mental states are always directed at, or represent, something. So my idea of my cat Freya is directed at, is about, Freya; I possess a mental representation of her. The direction of thought on object Brentano called intentionality, and should not be confused with the idea of purpose, for it is much broader. Purposes possess intentionality, for they are directed at something, a goal. However, Brentano said that all mental states are directed, even those that are purely cognitive. Intentionality separates mind from brain because only mental states are intentional. A neuron can never refer to, be about, intend anything, because it is mere matter, and can no more refer to something outside itself than can a rock.

In his own time Brentano's influence on psychology was limited. He was sympathetic to experimental psychology, and tried, but failed, to establish an experimental laboratory at the University of Vienna. Psychologists, among them Titchener, tended to regard him as an armchair functional psychologist, and paid little heed to his doctrine of intentionality. His influence was much greater in philosophy, especially through his student Edward Husserl's phenomenology. Today, however, his impact on psychology is greater than in his own time. For today Brentano's separation of mind and brain via intentionality as the criterion of the mental looms as a serious challenge to cognitive science's goal of creating intelligence in a computer.

CONCLUSION:
THE FATE OF THE
PSYCHOLOGY OF
CONSCIOUSNESS

What happened to the psychology of consciousness? Wundt and Titchener are no more cited by modern psychologists than are Aristotle and Newton by modern physicists. Wundt and Titchener died only about fifty years ago, yet little trace of them remains but the memory of one as founder of psychology the other as a faithful pupil. This question has two sets of answers, for Wundt and Titchener proposed different systems and worked in different contexts.

Ganzheit psychology suffered a number of blows. American students crossed the divide from the English world to the German to take their degrees and become psychologists, but without really assimilating Wundt's system. They returned to America and pursued their "completely American" questions. In Germany, Wundt was abandoned by one of his best students, Oswald Külpe, who found things in the mind Wundt would not admit to, thereby altering the scope and theory of experimental psychology. At the same time Wundt's position was rejected by other Germans even more holistic than he, the Gestalt psychologists. In America Titchener promulgated a vastly simplified form of Ganzheit psychology that was modified from Wundt's. Structuralism became a straw man for the attacks of functionalists such as William James and behaviorists such as Watson. The *coup de grace* to German psychology was delivered by the Nazis, who destroyed the German intellectual community by expulsion, fear, and intimidation, as well as the general destruction of World War II that they brought down on Germany.

There is, moreover, a deeper reason for the disappearance of Ganzheit psychology. It is often said that nothing is more powerful than an idea whose time has come. Psychoanalysis succeeded for just this reason, but Ganzheit psychology failed because it was an idea whose time had passed.

Wundt and the psychological system he fathered were products of the German Mandarin culture described earlier, a culture that experienced a devastating crisis in the years between 1890 and 1930. It was simply too elitist, too rationalist, too romantic, and too fragile to withstand the rising tide of socialism and democracy, positivism and pragmatism, as well as defeat in World War I and the coming of the Nazis. The rational psychology of consciousness could not compete with the psychology of the irrational and the unconscious of which Freud was only a part. The aloof, arcane, and subjective method of introspection could not compete with the objective study of behavior that held out the promise of Utopia. Americans in particular were deadened and depressed by working with Wundt (Steffens 1938). As Ganzheit psychology could not compete, it became an unsuccessful variant in the struggle for scientific existence. It carved out an academic niche which was then more successfully occupied by rival psychologies. The birth of psychology was historically inevitable, but Ganzheit psychology was obsolete at birth—the product of a culture that could not last.

What of structuralism? Titchener took Wundt's Ganzheit psychology and reduced it to a sterile sensationism. He threw away Wundt's explanatory psychology in favor of an introspective dissection of consciousness that never completed its initial task of cataloguing the elements of consciousness. At the end, Titchener and his students produced almost grotesque descriptions of sensations like "the glassy sensation," utterly alien to anything in ordinary awareness. This baroque elaboration of introspection repelled even some of Titchener's students (Washburn 1961). When he died there was no one to carry on, and structuralism vanished.

Turning to those who revolted against Wundt and Titchener, we find that the Würzburg school simply faded away after Külpe left Würzburg, and was gone by the time he died. The fate of Gestalt psychology is more complex. The usual view is to agree with E. G. Boring that Gestalt psychology was simply absorbed into an increasingly eclectic mainstream psychology. There is some support for this view. The Gestalt psychologists completely changed the field of perception. It made the field turn from atomistic sensationism of a Berkeleyan type, to examining, as Koffka (1935) put it, "why things look as they do" in our everyday, unanalyzed experience. They paid attention to problem-solving and other complex behaviors while the behaviorists were running rats in mazes. In both these areas Gestalt demonstrations are a standard part of every textbook, even today. Some direct influence on others is also evident. For example, E. C. Tolman looked at maze learning as a process by which a rat constructs a holistic map of its environment, and he even incorporated the term *Gestalt* into his technical vocabulary.

On the other hand survivors of the Gestalt movement disagree with Boring's conclusion. If we look at Germany, we find that "by the end of World War II, the first generation of young Gestalt psychologists was essentially wiped out," either by death, immigration, or adoption of a different kind of work (Henle 1977). Koffka came to America in 1927 at the invitation of Americans interested in the Gestalt movement. He was followed in the 1930s by Wertheimer and Köhler, who were fleeing the Nazis.

Therefore the center of Gestalt psychology shifted to America, where it suffered two handicaps. The first was that all three founders obtained academic posts at institutions that gave no graduate degrees, so a new generation of professors and scientists could not be raised. More important, however, was the intellectual gulf between "trader" and "hero" that weakened Wundt's influence. Unlike Wundt, Gestalt psychologists were able to speak for themselves in America; but, although they earned respect, their influence was limited. In 1935 Koffka acknowledged not only the difference in intellectual climate, but also noted that when Gestalt psychology was introduced to America, its most German interest (namely the stress on moral values) "was kept in the background." American psychology, moreover, was in the grip of behaviorism, which the Gestaltists saw as fundamentally similar to mentalistic associationism.

As a result the Gestalt psychologists were holistic prophets of theoretical psychology in an atomistic, relatively atheoretical wilderness. While their demonstrations were impressive, many found their theory obscure. The general American reaction is described by Gordon Bower: "There were always several features to their writings—an experimental or demonstrational part . . . and then a polemical, almost philosophical part in which the ancient elementarism of Titchener's (or Watson's) analyses was flogged to death and some relatively incomprehensible 'field theory' . . . would be advanced" (Hilgard and Bower 1975). Americans respected good data, but found the German "Gestalt vision" completely unacceptable—when it could be understood at all. What revolutionized the study of perception were the new questions and demonstrations proposed by the Gestaltists, not their theory of perception. The same holds true in thinking. Their other work—in memory, association, and so on—was generally ignored, while their whole theory was distorted into an easily criticized straw man. Despite the enduring fame of the Gestalt psychologists, their systems could no better cross the Atlantic than Wundt's. But they did at least provide a continuing criticism of behaviorism that modern cognitive psychologists appreciate, even if they do not always agree with it.

So in 1959 we find Wolfgang Köhler, in his presidential address to the American Psychological Association, continuing to hold out hope of fruitful collaboration between Americans and Gestalt psychology, while despairing that it would occur. He found Americans to be over-cautious and over-critical, daring nothing, while the promise of mechanical behaviorism caused "in the present speaker a mild, incredulous horror." In 1975 A. S. Luchins, an old Gestaltist, decried the increasing misunderstanding of Gestalt psychology and ignorance of what it had accomplished. He observed that while certain Gestalt terms have been adopted by contemporary psychologists, they fail to see "the main thrust of Gestalt psychology." And in 1977 Mary Henle, a student of Köhler, concluded that Gestalt ideas have not "been given a real hearing." Like Köhler, she expressed hope of a hearing, but doubted it would occur.

BIBLIOGRAPHY

This is the chapter I most regret not having time to revise. Largely because of psychology's centennial celebration in 1979, a great deal has been written about psychology's founding, the psychology of consciousness, and about Wundt and his psychology in particular. In this bibliography I will indicate only some of the new literature on Wundt and the founding of psychology, trying to highlight the more important and accessible new work.

First, several edited volumes on psychology's beginnings have appeared recently. I will list them here, and refer more specifically to them later:

1. Wolfgang Bringmann and Ryan D. Tweney, eds., *Wundt studies* (Toronto: C. J. Hogrefe, 1980).

2. Jozef Brozek and Ludwig Pongratz, eds., *Historiography of modern psychology* (Toronto: C. J. Hogrefe, 1980).

3. C. Buxton, ed., *Points of view on the history of psychology* (New York: Academic Press, 1986).

4. Eliot Hearst, ed., *The first century of experimental psychology* (Hillsdale, New Jersey: Erlbaum, 1979).

5. Sigmund Koch and David Leary, eds., *A century of psychology as science* (New York: McGraw–Hill, 1985).

6. R. W. Rieber, ed., *Wilhelm Wundt and the making of a scientific psychology* (New York: Plenum, 1980).

7. William W. Woodward and Mitchell G. Ash, eds., *The problematic science: Psychology in nineteenth century thought* (New York: Praeger, 1982).

An excellent introduction to the intellectual climate in nineteenth-century Germany is provided by Ringer (1969). Three papers discuss the conditions of psychology's founding. Richard Littman provides a general account of psychology's emergence as a discipline in "Social and intellectual origins of experimental psychology," in Hearst (1979). Mitchell G. Ash, "Academic politics in the history of science: Experimental psychology in Germany, 1879–1941," *Central European History* (1981, *13*: 255–186), concentrates on the struggle by psychologists to gain acceptance in the rigidly centralized German academic system. Kurt Danziger, "Historical construction of social roles in the psychological experiment," Paper presented at the annual meeting of the American Psychological Association, 1981, uses sociological techniques to analyze the emergence of the human psychology experiment. Finally, an older but still useful account of psychology's beginnings, written just after it happened is found in J. Mark Baldwin, "Sketch of the history of psychology," *Psychological Review* (1905, *12:* 144–165).

A great deal of work has been done on Wundt and his psychology. Besides Wundt (1896), the following works of his are available in English: *Outlines of psychology* (1897; reprinted St. Clair Shores, Michigan Scholarly Press, 1969); *Principles of physiological psychology*, vol. 1, 5th ed. (New York: Macmillan, 1910); *An introduction to psychology* (1912; reprinted New York: Arno, 1973); *Elements of folk psychology* (London: Allen & Unwin, 1916); and *The language of gestures*, an excerpt from his *Völkerpsychologie* of 1900–1920 (The Hague: Mouton, 1973). For Wundt's biography see Wolfgang Bringmann, William Balance, and Rand Evans, "Wilhelm Wundt, 1832–1920: A brief biographical sketch," *Journal of the History of the Behavioral Sciences* (1975, *11:* 287–297; Wolfgang Bringmann, Norma J. Bringmann, and William Balance, "Wilhelm Maximilian Wundt

1832–1874: The formative years," in Bringmann and Tweney (1980); and Solomon Diamond, "Wundt before Leipzig," in Rieber (1980).

Both the Rieber and Bringmann and Tweney volumes contain many papers on the origins of Wundt's ideas, the nature of his system, and its reception; they both also reprint some contemporary critiques of Wundt; and, in Rieber's case, some important short pieces from Wundt himself. One issue arises several times: How consistent was Wundt's psychology over the years? William James said that Wundt's system had no vital center, but changed so constantly one couldn't seize hold of it. Commentators today usually maintain that while Wundt's system did undergo much change, there were constant guiding ideas; see, for example, Willem van Horn and Thom Verhave, "Wundt's changing conceptions of a general and theoretical psychology," in Bringmann and Tweney (1980). Solomon Diamond, however, upholds James's contention, and argues that Wundt created two radically different psychologies. The first one, which fired the minds of would-be psychologists around the world, was more physiological in the modern sense than the second one, which was more purely mentalistic. The later system is described by most modern rehabilitators of Wundt and the chapter you have just read. Diamond buttresses his claim by translating (in Rieber [1980]) the opening section of the *Principles of physiological psychology* from every edition from first (1873) to last (1908–1911), showing how drastically Wundt changed his description of "The task of psychology."

Other sources on Wundt include Joseph Jastrow "Experimental psychology in Leipzig," *Science* (1886, 7 (198, Supplement): 459–462), which describes in detail a few of Wundt's experiments, some of which are startlingly similar to current work in cognitive psychology. These parallels are discussed in my own "Something old, something new: Attention in Wundt and modern cognitive psychology," *Journal of the History of the Behavioral Sciences* (1979, 15: 242–252). Theodore Mischel discusses "Wundt and the conceptual foundations of psychology," *Philosophical and Phenomenological Research* (1970, 31: 1–26). William R. Woodward, "Wundt's program for the new psychology: Vicissitudes of experiment, theory, and system" (in Woodward and Ash, 1982), presents Wundt as a typical German intellectual with a Will to System. Two papers by Kurt Danziger correct errors in the older picture of Wundt and examine his fate in Germany: "The positivist repudiation of Wundt," *Journal of the History of the Behavioral Sciences* (1979, 15: 205–230) and "The history of introspection reconsidered," *Journal of the History of the Behavioral Sciences* (1979, 16: 241–262). Arthur Blumenthal (in Buxton, above) provides a good general orientation to Wundt's psychology in "Wilhelm Wundt: Psychology as the propaedeutic science."

Titchener was a prolific writer. Important works in addition to those cited in the chapter include *Experimental psychology: A manual of laboratory practice* (New York: Macmillan, 1901–1905); *Lectures on the elementary psychology of feeling and attention* (New York: Macmillan, 1908); "The past decade in experimental psychology," *American Journal of Psychology* (1910, 21: 404–421); "The scheme of introspection," *American Journal of Psychology* (1912, 23: 485–508; "Experimental psychology: A retrospect." *American Journal of Psychology* (1925, 36: 313–323); and *A text-book of psychology* (New York: Macmillan, 1913). In my article "The mistaken mirror: On Wundt's and Titchener's psychologies," *Journal of the History of the Behavioral Sciences* (1981, 17: 273–282), I show that Titchener was not, as is usually assumed, a simple follower of Wundt faithfully reflecting the master's views.

Some of the Würzburg school's papers are translated and excerpted in George and Jean Mandler, eds., *The psychology of thinking: From association to Gestalt* (New York: Wiley, 1964). Besides the references in the text, there were two important contemporary discussions of imageless thought: J. R. Angell, "Imageless thought," *Psychological Review* (1911, 18: 295–323); and Robert S. Woodworth, "Imageless thought," *Journal of Philosophy, Psychology, and Scientific Methods* (1906, 3: 701–708). A recent discussion is David Lindenfield, "Oswald Külpe and the Wurzburg school," *Journal of the History of the Behavioral Sciences* (1978, 14: 132–141). George Humphrey, in part of his *Thinking* (New York: Science Editions, 1963) discusses the Würzburg findings, though he overestimates their damage to Wundt's psychology.

Gestalt psychology. Besides the references, Köhler's important works include, *The mentality of apes* (New York: Liveright, 1938); *The place of value in a world of facts* (New York: Liveright, 1938); *Dynamics in psychology* (New York: Liveright, 1940); *Gestalt psychology* (New York: Mentor, 1947); and *Selected papers of Wolfgang Köhler* (New York: Liveright, 1971); by Wertheimer, *Productive thinking* (New York: Harper & Row, 1959); Mary Henle has edited a selection of papers by the Gestaltists, *Documents of Gestalt psychology* (Berkeley: University of California Press, 1961); the most influential Gestalt psychologist in the United States was Kurt Lewin, who for some time affected social, personality, and, to a lesser extent, learning, psychology; for example, his *Principles of topological psychology* (New York: McGraw-Hill, 1936). Julian Hochberg, "Organization and the Gestalt tradition," in E. Carterette and M. Friedman, eds., *Handbook of perception,* vol. 1: *Historical and philosophical roots of perception* (New York: Academic Press, 1974) discusses their influence on perception. Mary Henle tries to explain isomorphism in "Isomorphism: Setting the record straight," *Psychological research* (1984, *46:* 317–327. The roots of Wertheimer's ideas are discussed in Abraham S. and Edith H. Luchins, "An introduction to the origins of Wertheimer's Gestalt Psychologie, *Gestalt Theory* (1982, *4:* 145–171). In a massive doctoral dissertation, Mitchell Graham Ash thoroughly documents and discusses the origin and development of Gestalt psychology in Germany in *The emergence of Gestalt theory: Experimental psychology in Germany 1890–1920,* unpublished doctoral dissertation, (Harvard University, 1982). The reception of Gestalt psychology in the United States is discussed by Michael Sokal, "The Gestalt psychologists in behaviorist America," *American Historical Review,* 1984, 89, 1240–1263.

Brentano's basic work is *Psychology from an empirical standpoint* (New York: The Humanities Press, 1973). For discussions of Brentano, see L. McAlister, ed., *The philosophy of Brentano* (Atlantic Highlands, New Jersey: Humanities Press, 1976).

REFERENCES

Ben-David, J. and Collins, R. (1966) Social factors in the origin of a new science: The case of psychology. *American Sociological Review 31:* 451–465.
Wundt, W. (1896) *Lectures on human and animal psychology.* New York: Macmillan.
Blumenthal, A. L. (1970) *Language and psychology: Historical aspects of psycholinguistics.* New York: John Wiley.
Blumenthal, A. L. (1975) A reappraisal of Wilhelm Wundt. *American Psychologist 30:* 1081–1088.
Clark, H. M. (1911) Conscious attitudes. *American Journal of Psychology 22:* 214–249.
Henle, M. (1977) The influence of Gestalt psychology in America. *Annals of the New York Academy of Sciences 291:* 3–12.
Hilgard, E. R. and Bower, G. (1975) *Theories of learning.* 4th ed. Englewood Cliffs, New Jersey: Prentice-Hall.
Keller, F. S. (1973) *The definition of psychology.* New York: Prentice-Hall.
Koffka, K. (1922) Perception: An introduction to Gestalt Theorie. *Psychological Bulletin 19:* 531–585.
Koffka, K. (1935/1963) *Principles of gestalt psychology.* New York: Harcourt Brace Jovanovich.
Luchins, A. S. (1975) The place of gestalt theory in American psyhology. In S. Ertel, L. Kemmler, and M. Stadler, eds. *Gestalt-theorie in der modernen psychologie.* Darmstadt, Germany: Dietrich Steinkopf Verlag.
Mayer, A. and Orth, J. (1901/1964) Experimental studies of association. Partially reprinted in G. Mandler and J. Mandler, Eds. *The psychology of thinking: From association to Gestalt.* New York: John Wiley.
Ogden, R. M. (1911a) Imageless thought. *Psychological Bulletin 8:* 183–197.

Ogden, R. M. (1911b) The unconscious bias of laboratories. *Psychological Bulletin 8:* 330–331.

Ringer, F. K. (1969) *The decline of the German Mandarins: The German academic community 1890–1933.* Cambridge: Harvard University Press.

Steffens, L. (1938) *The letters of Lincoln Steffens.* New York: Harcourt, Brace.

Titchener, E. B. (1897) *An outline of psychology.* New York: Macmillan.

Titchener, E. B. (1901–1905) *Experimental psychology: A manual of laboratory practice.* 4 vols. New York: Macmillan.

Titchener, E. B. (1904) *Lectures on the experimental psychology of the thought processes.* New York: Macmillan.

Titchener, E. B. (1972) *Systematic psychology: Prologemena.* Ithaca: Cornell University Press.

Washburn, M. F. (1961) Some recollections. In *History of psychology in autobiography.* V. 2 C. Murchison, ed. New York: Russell & Russell.

Wertheimer, M. (1922/1938) The general theoretical situation. Reprinted in W. D. Ellis, ed. *A sourcebook of Gestalt psychology.* London: Routledge & Kegan Paul.

Wertheimer, M. (1925/1938) Gestalt theory. Reprinted in W. D. Ellis, ed. *A sourcebook of Gestalt psychology.* London: Routledge & Kegan Paul.

Wertheimer, Michael. (1978) Max Wertheimer: Gestalt prophet. Presidential address to Division 26, annual meeting of the American Psychological Association, Toronto, Ontario, August 31.

Woodworth, R. S. (1938) *Experimental psychology.* New York: Holt, Rinehart & Winston.

Woodworth, R. S. and Schlosberg, H. (1954) *Experimental psychology.* 2d ed. New York: Holt, Rinehart & Winston.

Wundt, W. M. (1896) *Lectures on human and animal psychology.* New York: Macmillan.

CHAPTER 8

The Psychology of the Unconscious Mind

Sigmund Freud and Psychoanalysis

BACKGROUND
  Freud and Academic Psychology
  Intellectual Antecedents
  Social Context
  Freud's Life (1856–1939)
MAJOR WORKS
  Laying the Foundations (1895–1899)
  Defining Psychoanalysis (1900–1920)
  Revision, Systematization, and Cultural Analysis
  (1920–1939)
CONCLUSIONS
  Freud and Psychoanalysis
  The Reception of Psychoanalysis

If greatness may be measured by scope of influence, then Sigmund Freud is without doubt the greatest of psychologists. Scarcely any inquiry into human nature has not felt his touch. His work affected—and affects—literature, philosophy, theology, ethics, aesthetics, political science, sociology, and popular psychology. He revolutionized our thinking about sex. "Freudian slip" is a household word. The modish belief that we all have secret selves with which we must get in touch through the aid of some therapy or belief-system comes from Freud—although he would scorn most such enterprises, for they stress a person's feelings, and Freud valued reason above all else.

Freud, along with Darwin and Marx, is one of the great fathers of twentieth-century Western thought. Freud saw himself as a revolutionary, fighting alone against a condemning world. He explicitly placed himself in the line of Copernicus and Darwin, as one of those who challenged humanity's childish egocentrism and pushed it toward self-sufficient maturity. He was pessimistic about human nature and the dangers of the future, yet his pessimism was hopeful. He wanted us to understand our unconscious, darker nature so that we might subject it to the rule of reason.

BACKGROUND

Freud and Academic Psychology

For all Freud's influence on Western culture, the relations between psychoanalysis and academic psychology have been ambivalent. No psychologist can be ignorant of psychoanalysis, and its concepts are discussed even in texts that call them wrong. Academic psychologists have been critical of and even hostile to Freud's ideas (when they have not ignored them), and psychoanalysts have generally remained aloof from experimental psychology.

In Freud's own time and place the major source of disagreement was over the unconscious. Belief in unconscious mental processes is the cornerstone of any "depth" psychology; but for Wundt and other mentalistic psychologists, psychology was the science of consciousness. One can hardly introspect the unconscious, so Wundt dismissed it as a metaphysical "myth." On his side, Freud marshaled clinical evidence in support of his concept of the unconscious and believed that those who refused to accept the unconscious did so on metaphysical rather than scientific grounds. Sometimes Freud read academic psychologists, but he was rarely influenced by them. For example, he cites Wundt several times in *The Interpretation of Dreams,* but never thereafter, for he had less and less use for academic psychologists as psychoanalysis grew and built on itself.

Early American psychology shared some of the European prejudice against psychoanalysis, but it was more willing to listen to Freud. His first public recognition was his 1909 trip to Massachusetts to deliver a series of anniversary lectures at Clark University. But William James, the founding American psychologist, shared Wundt's view of the unconscious; and later on behaviorism rejected both consciousness and the unconscious as useless myths. If the acceptance of psychoanalysis had depended on academic psychology, psychoanalysis would have vanished long ago. But psychoanalysis found its support in psychiatry and clinical psychology, where it began; it also found support and acceptance by many in the humanities and the educated public.

Intellectual Antecedents

Freud is the most analyzed of psychologists. Because of his wide influence Freud's writings have been scrutinized by everyone from biologists to literary critics. We have available not only Freud's massive published output, but his unpublished drafts, letters revealing his personal and intellectual development, and the recollections of friends, associates, and patients. This mass of material has been attacked by a small industry of Freud scholars; Freud's concepts have been dissected and traced to their roots.

We now know that little Freud said was entirely original, rather it was his synthesis and use of old ideas that was original. For example, his idea of sexual energy—libido—was a combination of Victorian morality and physics. The everyday concept of sex in Victorian times was that a man had allotted him a limited amount of sexual energy to "spend" and that "profligacy" would lead to illness and a rundown nervous system. We find that Freud's sexual theory is replete with economic imagery and he viewed libido as fixed in amount. From the concept of conservation of energy in physics, Freud derived the conservation of libido. Sexual energy may be converted from one form to another, but cannot be created or destroyed. For example, persons who devote themselves to science will engage in sexual activity less frequently than others, for scientists have less libido to spend. Freud's hypothesis appears innocuous, but Freud used it to argue that civilized people are inevitably unhappy because civilization demands that we give up instinctual pleasures, which directly produce pleasure, in order to pursue more civilized ends. Freud's concept of libido thus was not original, but the implications he drew from it are profound.

We will now examine the sources of two of Freud's major concepts: the unconscious and the theory of sexuality.

The Unconscious

We have already met the concept of unconscious ideas or sensations in the works of Leibniz, Herbart, and Fechner. In the nineteenth century there was a popular book called *The Psychology of the Unconscious* by Eduard von Hartmann (1842–1906). So, in arguing the existence of unconscious ideas, Freud was saying nothing new. In fact, Freud was not alone among late nineteenth-century thinkers in assigning to irrational factors beyond our awareness a greater role in human behavior than had been allowed by earlier nineteenth-century social science.

We must distinguish, however, the hypothesis of unconscious ideas from the hypothesis of the unconscious. It is obvious that one is unconscious of one's phone number until the occasion to use it arises. But does the idea continue to exist unseen in a mental place called the unconscious, or is it no longer a mental entity at all, having disappeared into the neural network? Freud followed von Hartmann and Herbart in positing a mental place called the *unconscious* where ideas reside when they are not conscious and from which they can affect behavior without our awareness. Leibniz's and Fechner's conceptions were more purely descriptive, saying that some ideas are conscious and others are not-in-consciousness, or are unconscious. For them there is no place called "the unconscious"; when an idea is unconscious it exists only physiologically, as a brain trace, not psychologically. Wundt and William James differed on much else, but they both accepted the

Leibniz-Fechner description of "unconsciousness" and rejected Herbart's concept of a mental place called "unconsciousness."

In considering the concept of the unconscious, it is also important to distinguish different kinds of unconscious material. Theorists of unconsciousness before Freud, whether they reified the unconscious or not, saw unconsciousness as a state readily overcome, for unconscious ideas are weak. An increase in attention can make an unconscious idea conscious, or an increase in sensation can make a *petite perception* an apperception. Freud, however, distinguished two—and later three—kinds of unconscious material. Freud assigned unconscious but not repressed material to the *preconscious,* indicating that such material, although descriptively unconscious, could easily become conscious. He reserved the term *unconscious* for a more innovative concept, the repository of a second kind of unconscious material that does not have ready access to consciousness because it is *repressed.* This concept is also called the *dynamic unconscious.* Truly unconscious ideas are so unacceptable to consciousness that we deliberately keep them unconscious; we defend our egos against them. However, such ideas remain strong and constantly try to enter consciousness so that repression must be a continuing activity. Freud found the source of dreams, neuroses, behavioral errors, and resistances to therapy in repressed ideas.

This concept was unlike earlier psychological views of the unconscious, but it can be found in German philosophy. Schopenhauer, for example, speaks of the opposition of our Will to "repellent" ideas, whose breakthrough into consciousness may cause insanity. Freud again combined several current ideas into a new synthesis. Freud claimed that some ideas are not just too weak to enter consciousness, but are too threatening to be allowed to enter consciousness. Repressed ideas are not weak; on the contrary, they are strong but repulsive ideas that must be forcibly repressed. This concept also implies the concept of the unconscious as a mental place. Repressed ideas are active, forcing themselves to our attention in dreams and other phenomena. Therefore they must continue to exist and seek expression from some secret place in the mind. The hypothesis of the repressed is a cornerstone of psychoanalysis. Without it the whole system would fall apart, for Freud traced nearly all behavior and mental life to unconscious determinants. Freud's distinctions of conscious, preconscious, and unconscious concern the topography of mind. Another essential concept describes the energy that drives behavior and mental activity.

The Instincts

Freud believed that all behavior is motivated by one or more innate, physiological instincts. Some behaviors directly satisfy instincts, while others do so only indirectly. In either case Freud's model is always one of drive reduction, for all behavior must somehow reduce a physiological tension. As is well known, Freud put special emphasis on the sexual instinct, particularly before 1920. At no time did he forget other needs such as hunger and thirst, but he did not find them implicated in neuroses or other human problems. In 1920 Freud placed a death instinct alongside the sexual, or life, instincts; but, in his characteristically pessimistic way, Freud never believed in any uniquely human instinct that might separate humans from the animals. Humans have no inherent "higher nature"; whatever in humans is "higher" is the product of cultural repression or reason. In setting humans on the side of the apes, Freud was heir to Darwin.

Antecedents to Freud's views are easily found in nineteenth-century German philosophy. Arthur Schopenhauer shared Freud's pessimistic view of humans' essential nature. Friedrich Nietzsche (1844–1900) even more closely resembled Freud. Both believed that each person has an animal nature of which he or she tries to remain unconscious to satisfy the demands of civilization. Nietzsche always believed in natural human aggression, a view Freud came to share late in life. Both also saw the cultural side of humans as a transformation, or *sublimation,* of their baser nature, setting civilization at war with human animal instinct. In contrast to Freud, however, Nietzsche's answer to this conflict was to transcend civilization.

Schopenhauer and Nietzsche were sources Freud sometimes acknowledged, but some of Freud's ideas on sex can be traced to less obvious, unacknowledged sources. David Bakan has argued that Freud was influenced by the Jewish mystical tradition in theology. For example, an esoteric Jewish book, the Cabala, presents sex as a powerful force present in both human beings and God. Sex and knowledge are closely identified by the Cabala—similarly, the biblical word for sexual intercourse is "know." This indicates that sexual energy may be sublimated to intellectual pursuits. Popular Victorian ideas about sex were also an unacknowledged influence on Freud. Victorian pornography, for example, represents female sexuality as a deeply repressed animal nature to be awakened by the right seducer. In his *Three Essays on the Theory of Sexuality,* Freud says almost exactly the same thing about the "average uncultivated woman." Further, Victorians were horrified by masturbation and strove mightily to detect it and stamp it out in their children. Again, in *Three Essays,* Freud says that abandonment of masturbation is part of "the course of development laid down for civilized men." In many ways Freud was thoroughly Victorian. Intellectually, he tried to free himself from repressive Victorian views; but as he says in a letter, "I stand for an infinitely freer sexual life, although I myself have made very little use of such freedom" (Freud 1960). Freud prescribed sexual liberation for the world at large, but could not follow his own advice.

The aspect of Freud's sexual theories that contemporaries found most shocking was his belief in childhood sexuality. The hypothesis that children are sexual creatures would not have shocked medievals, who were merely amused by children's sexual play. By the nineteenth century, however, greater privacy had enabled the middle and upper classes to avoid knowledge of it. How Freud arrived at his hypothesis that children have sexual desires is controversial. All agree that Freud always believed in the importance of sexual needs in the causation of neurosis, as his early correspondence makes clear. What is less clear is how he came upon the hypothesis of *infantile* sexuality as the basis for neurosis.

The "orthodox" account of his discovery of childhood sexuality, put forward by Freud and his major biographers, is as follows. Freud found that many of his early patients reported being seduced as children, usually by servants. The patients naturally found the seductions traumatic, and Freud believed their later neuroses originated in the traumatic event and its repression. However, as more data came in, Freud found these events to have an air of unreality about them, and he also found that some non-neurotics had been seduced as children. He was slowly forced to the conclusion that the seductions were fantasies, reflecting the patient's childhood desire to sleep with mother (or father), and that the fantasy was repressed just as a real traumatic seduction might be. This formulation requires that children have sexual feelings that motivate the fantasies. This conclusion contradicted his earlier belief that children had no sexual feelings and that seductions gave them traumatic sexual feelings. Freud was so reluctant to accept this conclusion and admit his seduction error that years passed between private and public changes of view.

The orthodox story has been vigorously challenged, especially by Frank Cioffi. He asks why Freud's patients should tell us of seductions in childhood. Even during the period when he believed in the seductions, Freud wrote that his patients did not believe in them, so that he later concluded that the stories were invented "screen memories" concealing fantasies of incestuous desires for the patients. The first difficulty Cioffi raises is that in his early cases Freud reported no seductions by parents. The second difficulty concerns motivation. Freud held that the stories were fabricated to hide incestuous, Oedipal wishes, yet is it really more acceptable to "remember" sexual abuse during childhood than to "remember" childhood sexual desires? Cioffi suggests that the seduction stories came not from his patients, but from Freud himself. Freud was already convinced of the role of sexuality in the neuroses and simply pushed his patients until they "recalled," or accepted from the analyst, a story of a childhood seduction. In *Studies in Hysteria,* a book that preceded the seduction theory period, Freud wrote that the analyst must *insist* that a patient recall the cause of a symptom. The analyst's technique will cause "thoughts to emerge which the patient never recognizes as his own, which he never remembers!" Cioffi argues that Freud's patients simply made up stories to satisfy Freud's demands.

There is also evidence of a cover-up, intentional or unintentional, regarding the seduction error. When he finally confessed the error, Freud justified the change in view by saying that some non-neurotics had also been seduced, so that such trauma cannot cause neurosis, and he asserted that at the time of the seduction error he did not know this fact. However, Freud clearly states in one of the original papers that he did know. Finally, if it is asked where Freud could have got the idea of childhood sexuality in a prudish world, we need look to no crank but to one of the most eminent psychiatrists of the nineteenth century, Richard von Krafft-Ebbing, who wrote in 1886 that any physician familiar with neuroses is aware that the "sexual instinct may occur in very young children."

Cioffi then asks how Freud got himself into such a difficult situation. Freud had to defend his clinical method of scientific investigation—a method in which a patient's unconscious is plumbed by free association by an analyst who knows the patient's mind better than does the patient. The analyst interprets symptoms and, by his superior knowledge, leads the patient to a cure. But the seduction episode raised an ominous possibility. If no seductions took place, then what patients tell their analysts is untrustworthy and cannot be an accurate guide to the unconscious. The obvious alternative to Freud's defense of the seduction error was to believe that the recollections were fabricated to please Freud or were interpolated events forced on the patient by the therapist. Freud consistently maintained that a therapist should be authoritarian, so it is plausible that such interpolation could easily occur. This account undercuts Freud's method as a scientific tool, for if true, it means the therapist is learning nothing about the patient's past or unconscious. Freud resolved this dilemma by saying that the seduction memories were not true childhood memories but were true childhood fantasies, preserving the psychological, if not the historical, accuracy of clinical recollection.

The criticism that Freud's method could lead to false results because of therapists' suggestions was made very early, and the seduction error seemed to confirm it. Freud, however, publicly denied making such suggestions, and the orthodox account of the genesis of the hypothesis of childhood sexuality argues that Freud successfully overcame the seduction error. Cioffi's view holds that Freud fooled himself as well as his patients into believing the suggested seduction stories, whether they are believed to be truth or fantasy, producing confirmation of the sexuality hypothesis and of the Oedipus complex by simply demanding such evidence from patients. Which account of Freud's discovery of childhood sexuality is correct remains debatable, but certain doubts remain about the scientific, if not the therapeutic, value of the psychoanalytic method.

Social Context

Since Freud's experience was in the clinic treating real human problems, his theory, more than those of experimental psychologists, is erected on social foundations. We therefore need to consider certain social and personal attitudes of Victorian people. "Where should we find that reverence for the female sex, that tenderness towards their feelings, that deep devotion of the heart to them, which is the beautiful and purifying part of love? Is it not certain that all of the delicate, the chivalric which still pervades our sentiments, may be traced to the *repressed,* and therefore hallowed and elevated passion?" So wrote W. R. Greg in 1850. The Victorians did not accept the animal part of their nature, whether sexual or simply sensual. Wrote Greg: "Smoking . . . is liked because it gives agreeable sensations. Now it is a positive objection to a thing that it gives agreeable sensations. An earnest man will expressly avoid what gives agreeable sensations" (Houghton 1957). (Earnestness was a cardinal virtue to Victorians.) Victorian culture and religion thundered against pleasure, especially sexual pleasure, and Victorians were burdened by an oppressive sense of guilt. Like a medieval saint, British Liberal Prime Minister William Gladstone recorded his least sin and grieved over it. Guilt was heightened by constant temptation. Prostitution was rampant; men and women, boys and girls—all could be had for a price. The anonymous author of *My Secret Life,* a sexual autobiography, supposedly seduced over two thousand people of all ages and sexual orientations and engaged in every vice. Boys at the finest private schools were sexually abused. The Victorians were caught between stern conscience and compelling temptation; it is no wonder that so many were neurotic.

These two sides of Victorian life emerged in their attitudes toward women, which resemble the medieval attitudes we explored in Chapter 3. Wives and mothers were "angels"—unhuman, holy voices of God, as described by Tennyson in *The Princess:*

> No angel, but a dearer being, all dipt
> In angel instincts, breathing Paradise . . .
> On tiptoe seem'd to touch upon a sphere
> Too gross to tread, and all male minds perforce
> Sway'd to her from their orbits . . .
> Happy he
> With such a mother! faith in womankind
> Beats with his blood. . . .
> He shall not blind his soul with clay.

Too feel lust for such a one would obviously bring disgust and repression. Thus it is easy to see why Freud discovered an Oedipus complex. It certainly fit the society he knew, even if it was not as universal as he claimed.

Woman was the guardian of the home, protector of the hearth from the harsh outside world. Emancipation therefore could only degrade, not liberate. Freud himself wrote the following in a letter to his fiancée (Freud 1960). He is commenting on J. S. Mill's "Emancipation of Women," one of the best feminist tracts of the nineteenth century.

> It seems a completely unrealistic notion to send women into the struggle for existence in the same way as men. Am I to think of my delicate, sweet girl as a competitor? . . . Women's delicate natures . . . are so much in need of protection. [Emancipation would take away] the most lovely thing the world has to offer us: our ideal of womanhood . . . the position of woman cannot be other than what it is: to be an adored sweetheart in youth and a beloved wife in maturity.

Freud was very Victorian.

As in the Middle Ages, on the dark side of the Good Woman and Mother was the Bad Woman. Victorian men went to prostitutes for the sexual pleasure they often could not get, and almost certainly did not want to get, at home. Prostitutes gave pleasure, but for that very reason were not respected; they were fallen women, good only for satiating animal lust. The price was high for the Good Woman who strayed. Lady Ward is a case in point. Her husband did not sleep with her, preferring merely to stare at her naked except for her jewelry. She took a lover, and got pregnant. Both her husband and father threw her out, and she died soon after. No one blamed her husband or her parents (Plumb 1972). A similar belief in the Bad Woman is betrayed in Freud's comment on the "uncultivated" woman, mentioned earlier, who he said was awaiting the right seducer.

There was, however, one Victorian trait Freud rejected, and its rejection is the essence of Freud's revolution. He was not a hypocrite. Victorian men and women knew about sex and pleasure, but tried to cover it up in public—just as they covered "indecent" piano legs and tried, often desperately, to repress sexuality in their private lives. What Freud did was call on people to not hide from instincts but rather to face them openly, to confront their darkest secrets and conquer them through reason. Freud told his colleagues that he sought to lift repression—not to liberate sexuality, but to rationally suppress it. Like the Victorians Freud did not want to liberate lust; but unlike them he faced its temptation and power directly.

Freud's Life (1856–1939)

The story of Freud's life has been told many times by many hands. It would be pointless to add to this list of biographical studies. We will here only comment on his relation to German culture and let him describe his character himself. Freud was an outsider to German and Austrian intellectual life. He was an intellectual but no Mandarin, as was Wundt. In his *Future of an Illusion* Freud wrote: "I scorn to distinguish culture and civilization." He prized being an outsider, often judging the correctness of his ideas by how much they offended society. He formed a tightly knit group of analysts bound to a single faith and embarked on a crusade from which heretics were expelled. He identified with Moses and valued his Jewishness. Although he was irreligious, he felt a bond with his Jewish brethren who were much persecuted in Vienna, as well as a bond with the historic experience of Judaism. He felt himself to be beyond nationalistic claims because he was a Jew. When the Nazis seized Austria, Freud and his family narrowly escaped arrest with the help of outsiders. In Nazi Germany Freudian psychoanalysis and Einsteinian physics were both condemned as "Jewish science."

We may let Freud himself describe his character. The following letter (Freud 1960) was written in 1886 to his fiancée, while Freud was under the influence of cocaine, which he used as a young man. The letter reveals Freud's state of mind shortly before he began the self-analysis that led to *The Interpretation of Dreams,* his masterpiece.

> There was a time when I was all ambition and eager to learn, when day after day I felt aggrieved that nature had not, in one of her benevolent moods, stamped my face with that mark of genius which now and again she bestows on men. Now for a long time I have known that I am not a genius and cannot understand how I ever could have wanted to be one. I am not even very gifted; my whole capacity for work probably springs from my character and from the absence of outstanding intellectual weaknesses. But I know that this combination is very conducive to slow success, and that given favorable conditions I could achieve more than Nothnagel, to whom I consider myself superior, and might possibly reach the level of Charcot. . . . Breuer told me he had discovered that hidden under the surface of timidity there lay in me an extremely daring and fearless human being. I had always thought so, but never dared tell anyone. I have often felt as though I had inherited all the defiance and all the passions with which our ancestors defended their Temple and could gladly sacrifice my life for one great moment in history. . . .

MAJOR WORKS

Trying to present Freud's thought is an enormous task, for his writings span almost fifty years and cover everything from memory lapses to neurosis to the nature of civilization. To give a summary of psychoanalysis as a system obscures the tremendous changes Freud made as his thinking advanced. It also takes one far from what Freud said about specific topics or theoretical problems. Here, we will discuss several specific major works in chronological order, to remain close to Freud's concepts as they evolved from 1895 to 1939.

Laying the Foundations
(1895–1899)

Studies in Hysteria (1895)

Freud started out doing neurological research, but circumstances forced him to become a practicing physician specializing in "neurological" disorders, what today we would recognize as a psychiatrist. The most widespread psychological disorder of Freud's time (it is much rarer now) was *hysteria,* in which some mental disturbance manifests itself as a physical symptom that has no physiological basis. The name *hysteria* comes from the Greek word for womb, for the Greek physicians blamed the ailment on a diseased uterus. In Freud's time it was still widely believed that only women could become hysterical, since the overwhelming majority of hysterical patients were women.

In 1885 Freud briefly studied hysteria at the clinic of Jean Martin Charcot in Paris. Charcot believed, as did many other physicians, in a close relationship between hysteria and the hypnotic state, since hysteria-like symptoms could be induced by hypnosis, and hypnotic suggestion could be used to remove a hysteric's symptoms. Most important for Freud was Charcot's hypothesis that hysteria was *ideogenic,* that its causation lay in a disturbed mental state that acted on an underlying, inherited predisposition to hysteria. Freud would later abandon hypnotic therapy and minimize the constitutional basis of hysteria while emphasizing its origin in a disturbed mind.

In Vienna Freud went into practice with Joseph Breuer (1842–1925). Together they developed a new kind of cathartic hypnotic treatment of hysteria, which they presented in *Studies in Hysteria* (1895). At this point Freud's work was not yet psychoanalytic, but contained the germs of many psychoanalytic ideas.

The book begins with a journal article Breuer and Freud published in 1893 describing their new method. They argued that the cause of hysteria is a traumatic experience in which the generated emotion is not adequately discharged. Then, because the experience was unpleasant, the event and its affect are *repressed,* that is, not allowed into consciousness or remembered. However, the affect is still present, and its undischarged or "strangulated" tension gives rise to the hysterical symptoms. As Breuer and Freud put it: "Hysterics suffer mainly from reminiscences." But these are *unconscious* reminiscences; the patient is aware only of his or her symptoms, not of the precipitating event, which is repressed. Breuer and Freud reported that they had been able to cure each hysterical symptom in their patients by hypnotizing them and having them remember the traumatic episode and discharge the pent-up affect. They called this discharge *abreaction* and considered it the key to successful therapy. Remembering the event alone is insufficient; the patient must emotionally *relive* the event to be cured.

In *Studies* Breuer and Freud went on to support their views with a series of case histories, the most famous of which was Breuer's case of Anna O. (treated between 1880 and 1882), which furnished Freud with much food for thought. Anna O. was a young Austrian woman with a rich array of hysterical symptoms, from paralysis to disorders of vision and hearing to occasional inability to speak anything but English. Her symptoms generally centered around her feelings for her father, and Breuer methodically eliminated each symptom by letting her (under hypnosis) talk about and abreact the events that gave rise to them. Anna called this procedure the "talking cure," a label that has stayed with psychotherapy ever since. The cure went well until Breuer announced he was taking a vacation, whereupon Anna manifested a hysterical pregnancy with a child "fathered" by Breuer himself. Breuer panicked, dropped the case, and left Vienna for two years. Breuer did not report these events in his case history, but says only that Anna was restored to health.

By 1895 Breuer and Freud had some differences over the etiology and treatment of hysteria; *Studies* concludes with separate chapters by each author. Breuer contributed a long chapter on the theory of hysteria, which elaborated the preliminary theory of 1893 and went on to argue that the precipitating events of hysterical symptoms are experienced during "hypnoid states," which accounts for their unconsciousness and curability by hypnosis; Freud eventually rejected this theory. Freud contributed a chapter on therapy in which he abandoned Breuer's hypnotic method for a method that is closer to classical psychoanalysis. Freud found that, since not all patients could be hypnotized, the usefulness of Breuer's method was limited. Freud therefore insisted that his patients free associate to their symptoms and report anything that entered their minds, no matter how seemingly trivial or irrelevant. Thoughts were not to be censored or arranged in any way, but simply reported. In this way Freud effected cures by uncovering the ideas underlying the hysteria, but without using hypnosis. Freud saw that in the physician-patient relation lay a key to successful therapy. Breuer had been alarmed by his stormy relationship with Anna O., but Freud instead made it the basis of therapy, saying that the source of the healer's strength lay in the affection the patient has for the therapist. In this way the therapist gains influence and power and effects the cure by insisting on the patient's cooperation. Freud made two more important points. First, he argued that the underlying problem in hysteria is always sexual, as in Anna's feelings for her father—Freud and Breuer broke over this hypothesis. Second, Freud found that hysterics *resist* their cures. They do not want to know, or reexperience, the events that precipitated their symptoms. They are not simply ignorant of the cause; they resist knowing it. Therapeutic success is thus a matter of overcoming resistances by exploiting the therapist's power over the patient.

Although *Studies in Hysteria* is really a prepsychoanalytic work, we find in it some foundation stones of psychoanalysis. Most important is the claim that hysterics, and probably everyone else, have within them motives that they cannot accept and therefore repress. These motives do not lose their force, however, but manifest themselves as symptoms (or—in Freud's later work—dreams, slips of the tongue, myths, and the like). The key to mental health is to make these unacceptable ideas conscious and deal with them rationally. The first great theme of psychoanalysis is this existence within each person of unconscious, irrational forces that must be conquered by conscious reason. The second great theme announced in *Studies* is the nature of the irrational force. In *Studies,* and until about 1920, Freud saw the irrational force as sex; later he proposed a death wish as an even darker force, controlled by reason, civilization, and sexuality.

In *Studies* we also find the beginnings of psychoanalysis as a therapy. Charcot had cured hysterics by giving hypnotic commands that their symptoms disappear. Breuer made his patients hypnotically relive traumatic, precipitating events. Freud inaugurated a real "talking cure" in which his patients talked about their problems, feelings, and experiences, while the therapist guided, interpreted, and sometimes commanded compliance. Eventually, patients would unravel their own troubles by reflecting on them and discovering their cure. It was a lengthy procedure that Freud much later said could never really end.

Finally, a recurrent personal theme is evident in *Studies,* namely, Freud's pessimism. Freud tells us that he could not treat anyone who struck him as "low-minded" or "repellent"; later he would say that most people are "worthless." Freud never had a high opinion of the human race. He was also pessimistic about the limitations of therapy. In his last paragraph he notes an objection made by many patients: Why should I endure this arduous course of cure if you cannot alter the circumstances of life that make me unhappy? Freud replies: "You will be able to convince yourself that much will be gained if we succeed in transforming your hysterical misery into common unhappiness. With a mental life that has been restored to health you will be better armed against that unhappiness." Freud never believed that therapy could bring about human happiness. All it could do was to prepare a person to endure the inevitable hardships of living.

Project for a Scientific Psychology

As quoted above, at the end of *Studies in Hysteria* Freud spoke of restoring a patient's "mental life" to health. It is significant that in editions before 1925 Freud used the phrase "nervous system," not "mental life." Early in his career Freud, trained as a neurologist, was strongly committed to materialistic reductionism, to the view that human behavior was to be scientifically explained by reference only to brain processes. Shortly after *Studies* appeared, in 1895, Freud (1950) wrote a manuscript "to furnish a psychology that shall be a material science, that is, to represent psychical processes as quantitatively determinate states of specifiable material particles." Freud never published the manuscript; in fact he tried to prevent its publication late in his life, and it only appeared posthumously, as "Project for a scientific psychology."

Because Freud did not wish to publish his "Project," it would be wrong to consider it a proper part of psychoanalysis. But it does contain, in primitive and broad form, a number of important psychoanalytic concepts. The first of these concepts was Freud's quantitative approach to mental functioning. Unlike academic psychologists, Freud was first of all concerned with human motivation, which he believed comes from the organism's desire to lower its states of tension. According to Freud's quantitative conception, the goal of all mental and behavioral functioning is to discharge built-up quantities of nervous tension, felt as "unpleasure." The need for discharge Freud called the "unpleasure" principle, later changed to the "pleasure principle," an important psychoanalytic concept. The former name is more accurate, for Freud's view of motivation, like Plato's, was negative. What we call pleasure is in fact the discharge of built-up unpleasure—not something desired in its own right.

We also find here Freud's characteristic division of the mind into separate components whose conflicts, demands, and regulations underlie human behavior and thinking. In the "Project" Freud proposed three neurological systems based on different modes of synaptic functioning. There is, first, a perceptual system of neurons; second, an unconscious system, within which most of our mental life takes place; and third, a system giving rise to consciousness which regulates behavior by distinguishing real perceptions from hallucinations. Although these systems are not exact forerunners of the id, ego, and superego, we do find in them evidence of Freud's analytic approach of dividing the mind into independent entities.

Freud also made an important functional distinction that does persist, with modifications, into psychoanalysis. Freud wrote of a *primary process* of nervous functioning whose goal is immediate and complete discharge of unpleasurable tension. However, this system is unrealistic, for it seeks its goal through wish-fulfilling fantasy. There is therefore a need for a more realistic mode of functioning, one that operates in accord with reality; Freud called this the *secondary process*. It was also believed to modify primary functioning by seeking to lower tension to a manageable, but not a nonexistent, level. The residual tension provided the rational self with a pool of energy on which it could draw to fuel its own activities.

Finally, both in the "Project" and later, Freud stressed the role of endogenous stimulation in determining mental life. Academic psychologists on the other hand were concerned more with perception of the outside world. Wundt for instance, wanted to understand how we attend to and understand the world. Kant had set this problem by his contention that psychology should study how consciousness imposes organization on the unknowable noumena. What made Freud special was his attempt to understand how consciousness deals with internal sensation, especially innate instincts, which operate in a confused, unconscious world (later called the *id*) that we sense only indirectly. Wundt looked at the external world through human consciousness; Freud sought to fathom our unconscious inner world. Both the noumena and the unconscious are primordial and formless; Wundt chose to study the former, Freud the latter.

After the "Project," Freud cast his theory in mental, not physiological terms, as the change in the passage from *Studies in Hysteria* shows. However, he never seems to have abandoned the hope of a psychology that would be purely materialistic, positing nothing beyond atoms and the void. The "Project" was a premature attempt along these lines. However, it indicates the direction of Freud's thinking as he began to write his masterpiece, *The Interpretation of Dreams*.

Defining Psychoanalysis
(1900–1920)

In the years after the *Studies* and the "Project," Freud worked out the system he called psychoanalysis in a long series of writings. He did this largely alone, based on his analysis of patients and his own self-analysis. We will examine now the only two works Freud considered worthy of constant revision as psychoanalysis evolved, *The Interpretation of Dreams* and *Three Essays on the Theory of Sexuality*.

The Interpretation of Dreams (1900)

Of all his works, Freud himself believed *The Interpretation of Dreams* to be his greatest. In a letter to Fliess (Freud 1960) he hoped that a plaque would be erected some day saying, "In this House on July 24, 1895 the Secret of Dreams was revealed to Dr. Sigmund Freud." The insight Freud valued so highly was that a dream is not the meaningless collection of images it appears to be, but is "the royal road to the unconscious": a clue to the innermost recesses of the personality. That dreams have meaning was not a new idea, as Freud acknowledged, but it was out of step with the received academic opinion of his times. Most thinkers, including Wundt, assigned little importance to dreams, believing them to be only confused nighttime versions of waking mental processes. Freud sided instead with supposedly disreputable philosophers and ancient religions in valuing dreams as symbolic statements of a reality unavailable to waking experience.

Freud's basic idea is simple, but its details and ramifications are complex and far-ranging: All of us, whether neurotic or not, carry within us desires that we cannot accept consciously. In fact we deliberately keep these desires unconscious, or *repress* them. Nevertheless, they remain active, precisely because they are repressed and not subject to conscious scrutiny and memory-decay. They constantly press for access to awareness, and hence the control of behavior. in our waking life our *ego,* or conscious self, represses these wishes; but during sleep consciousness lapses and repression weakens. If our repressed desires ever completely eluded repression, we would awaken and reassert control. Dreaming is a compromise that protects sleep, for dreams are hallucinatory, disguised expressions of repressed ideas. They give partial satisfaction of unacceptable wishes, but in such a way that consciousness and sleep are rarely disturbed.

Freud summarized his view by saying that every dream is a *wish-fulfillment,* that is, a disguised expression (fulfillment) of some unconscious desire, or wish. It is this characteristic of dreams that makes them the royal road to the unconscious: If we can decipher a dream and retrieve its hidden meaning, we will have recovered a piece of our unconscious mental life and be able to subject it to the light of reason. Dreams and hysteria thus have the same origin, for both are symbolic representations of unconscious needs, and both can be understood by tracing them back to their sources. The existence of dreams shows that no sharp line can be drawn between neurotic and normal mental lives. Everyone has needs of which they are unaware and whose realization they would find distrubing. In neurotics, however, the usual means of defense have broken down, and symptoms have taken their place.

The method of decoding is also the same in both hysteria and dreams—the method of free association. Just as hysterical patients were asked to freely talk about their symptoms, so we may understand dreams by free associating to each element of the dream. Freud's assumption was that free association would reverse the process that produced the dream and bring one at last to the unconscious idea embodied in it. In both symptom analysis and dream analysis the goal is the same: to reach rational self-understanding of the irrational unconscious, a step toward mental health.

Freud introduced technical terms as part of his theory of dreams. The actually experienced dream he called the *manifest content* of the dream. The true meaning of the dream, the repressed unconscious desires symbolized by the dream, he called the *latent content*. The process of transformation of latent to manifest content is the *dream work*, performed because of the demands of the *endopsychic censor*, which is the psychic agency which refuses direct expression to anxiety-producing desires.

The last chapter of *The Interpretation of Dreams* is a theoretical account of dream production, which appears to be an informal mentalistic version of parts of the "Project." Freud pictured the mind as a complex structure comprising several independent but related systems. Closest to the world is the *perceptual system* that receives impressions from the environment and conveys them inward, where they leave behind a series of memory-traces. At the other end of this chain of reflexes (for Freud said that all mental processes are ultimately reflexes) is the *motor system*, which produces overt behavior. The motor system is governed by the *preconscious* and its rational *secondary process* thought, which guides realistic action. In the deepest level of the mind resides the *unconscious,* the home of repressed wishes and of the irrational *primary process.* Freud located consciousness in two places. One was the preconscious, for part of it is at any time conscious since it contains only rational and acceptable chains of thought. Consciousness is then the ultimate governor of behavior. We are also conscious of what we perceive, so consciousness is also found in the perceptual system. In the normal course of events, sensations enter the perceptual system, lay down memory-traces, and eventually progress to the preconscious, where they may be acted on in the conduct of behavior.

Dreams, however, are regressive. Unacceptable wishes, which live forever in the unconscious, seek expression but are blocked by repression during the waking hours. This control weakens during sleep, and the impulses gain strength. Sleep, however, blocks all motor activity, so these impulses cannot become behavior. Instead, they move toward the perceptual system, where they can find hallucinatory fulfillment as mock-perceptions distorted to preserve sleep.

We cannot leave *The Interpretation of Dreams* without discussing Freud's introduction of his most famous, or infamous, concept: the *Oedipus complex.* Freud described a kind of "typical dream," which expresses certain infantile wishes regarding one's parents. These wishes are repressed and persist in the unconscious to later provide latent content for dreams. This infantile complex of wishes is made up of the child's sexual desire for the cross-sex parent and of the child's consequent desire that the same-sex parent, the child's rival, be eliminated. This set of feelings Freud considered universal, and named it the Oedipus complex after the mythical Greek king who unwittingly killed his father and married his mother.

Oedipal feelings are powerful ones, subject to repression, and consequently fertile ground for the formation of neuroses. Indeed, Freud puts the blame on the parents of neurotics for their child's later sickness. If they react badly to the trying Oedipal period, neurosis or even psychosis will ensure. If the storm is weathered, the child will attain a sound personality.

It was said earlier that Freud revised the *Interpretation of Dreams* as his system evolved. The major change was in the means by which dreams may be decoded. In the early editions of the book, the only method was free association; but because of the work of a follower, Wilhelm Stekel, Freud came to believe that dreams could also be interpreted according to a more-or-less uniform set of symbols. That is, in most cases certain objects or experiences could be shown to stand for the same unconscious ideas in everyone's dreams. So, for example, walking up a flight of stairs symbolizes sexual intercourse, a suitcase stands for the vagina, and a hat for the penis.

Such an approach of course simplified the process of dream interpretation. It also made possible a wider application of Freud's insight, namely the interpretation of myths, legends, and works of art. Freud had already engaged in such an analysis in the early versions of the work, treating Sophocles' *Oedipus Rex* and Shakespeare's *Hamlet* as Oedipal stories, and he and other psychoanalysts would go on to do many such analyses. Psychoanalysis was never limited to a mere psychotherapy, but was increasingly used as a general tool for understanding all of human culture. Myth, legend, and religion were seen as disguised expressions of hidden cultural conflicts; art was seen as the expression of the artist's personal conflicts: all share the same mechanism with dreams. The symbol-system helped justify and make possible this extension of psychoanalysis. We cannot put Sophocles, Shakespeare, or a whole culture on the analytic couch and ask them to free associate, but we can search their products for universal clues to the universal human unconscious.

Throughout *The Interpretation of Dreams,* Freud makes clear that all the repressed wishes that we find in dreams have an infantile character, as in the Oedipus complex. It is during childhood that the repressions form that produce the latent material for the dreams of adulthood. The roots of personality should be sought in childhood and especially in the development of the sexual instinct during the early years of life. This brings us to Freud's other classic work, *Three Essays on the Theory of Sexuality.*

Three Essays on the Theory of Sexuality (1905)

In the popular mind, Freud is best remembered for saying that sexual motivation is the major cause of human behavior. There is no denying that Freud's most revolutionary impact has been on our willingness, in contrast to the Victorians, to accept sexuality as an essential part of being human. It is ironic, therefore, that it is in his theory of sexuality that Freud is most Victorian. As was shown earlier, there are great similarities between Freud's views on sex and the ordinary Victorian view. The virtue of Freud's discussions lies not in the details of his theory, which are anachronistic and culture-bound, but in his lack of shocked hypocrisy. By drawing attention to sexuality, he provoked the research and the culture change that transscended his own concepts.

As the title of the book says, the text consists of three short essays on different aspects of sex: "The Sexual Aberrations," "Infantile Sexuality," and "The Transformations of Puberty." Far more than *The Interpretations of Dreams,* his *Three Essays*—especially the last two—were revised after 1905 as Freud developed his later libido theory.

Freud made two important general points in the first essay, on sexual aberrations. First: "There is indeed something innate lying behind the perversions but . . . it is something innate in *everyone.*" What society calls "perverse" is only a development of one component of the sexual instinct, an activity centering on an erotogenic zone other than the genitals, a zone that plays its part in "normal" sexual activity in foreplay. The second point was that *"neuroses are, so to say, the negative of perversions."* That is, all neuroses have a sexual basis, and arise out of the patient's inability to deal with some aspect of his or her sexuality. Freud went so far as to say that a neurotic's symptoms *are* his or her sex life. The neurotic has symptoms rather than perversions or healthy sexuality.

Freud's second essay, on infantile sexuality, was the most revolutionary. When Freud said that the neurotic has difficulty with sexual needs, he meant that this difficulty began with the child's confrontation with sexual feelings in the first five years of life. Freud's basic claim was that children have sexual feelings. This shocked the Victorians, who looked on childhood as a time free of sexual demands, a view Freud himself had echoed at one point in *The Interpretation of Dreams.*

Freud, however, believed that the child's sexual feelings are different from the adult's in that they are egocentric, or to use his term, a child is *narcissistic.* Children primarily get pleasure from the several *erotogenic zones* distributed about the human body: the mouth, the anus, and the genitals—although Freud believed the entire skin surface could be erotogenic. Pleasure from self-manipulation is narcissistic because the child chooses no other person as the object of desires but gives self-pleasure, as in masturbation or thumb-sucking. Nevertheless, these powerful feelings should later play their part in foreplay as part of adult, other-directed sexuality. The way in which the child and the parents handle these feelings early on has much to do with adult personality.

Why, Freud asked, do we usually have so little memory of our infantile sexual feelings, or indeed of any experiences before we are about six years old? Freud said that early sexual desires are strongly inhibited, or repressed, so that we do not recall them. This repression is so strong that it spreads to all early experiences and brings on a period of sexual latency, during which sexual desires are dormant, to be later activated at puberty. Freud put great value on this *primal repression* and the ensuing period of latency, for he believed them to be essential to civilization. He was, however, rather obscure as to the reason for the first repression. Although he did not deny that the most obvious source—a culture's moral teachings—may play a role, he seems to have put most emphasis on inherited "digust" at "perverse" sexual activities and went so far as to claim that many moral taboos are inherited. Freud maintained this position throughout his life, but it was vehemently rejected by almost every later thinker, in or out of the psychoanalytic school.

We also find in the central essay Freud's most notorious error, the concept of *penis envy* and the related *castration complex*. Freud believed that children are curious about the facts of sex and form many peculiar theories as a result of their researches—Victorian parents being loathe to reveal the truth. According to Freud, the most significant of these childish ideas is that girls are castrated boys. In boys this theory leads to fear of castration as a punishment for Oedipal desires and helps bring on latency. Girls, however, are overcome by desire for a penis and wish to be boys themselves. Research has not supported the universality of these notions. It is an interesting example of Freud's Victorianism, for it was then a common belief that women had hidden penises. As a physician Freud knew better, but his own male Victorian valuation of the penis caused him to view female clitoral orgasm as just childish imitations of male orgasm. He believed women should put away their hopeless emulation and locate their sexual feelings in their vaginas.

In the last essay Freud turned to adult sexuality, which begins in puberty when maturational changes reawaken and transmute the dormant sexual instincts. At this time in the healthy person, sexual desire is directed to another person of the opposite sex, and reproductive genital intercourse becomes the goal; the instincts of childhood sexuality now serve genital drives through the kissing and caressing of foreplay that create the arousal necessary to actual coitus. In perverse individuals the pleasure associated with some infantile instinct is great enough to replace genital activity altogether. The neurotic is overcome by adult sexual demands and converts his or her sexual needs into symptoms.

In 1915 Freud introduced an important theoretical concept, *libido*. He believed that all behavior must be motivated by some instinct, and before 1920 he thought that the most important of these was the sexual instinct—which produces a form of mental energy called libido. Libido cannot be destroyed but can only be expressed directly in sexual behavior, or repressed, or indirectly expressed (*displaced*) as a dream, a neurotic symptom, or some other nonsexual behavior. The concept of libido and its displacement allowed Freud to retain the simple tension-reduction model of motivation formulated as early as the "Project," while being able to explain almost any behavior as an outgrowth of the sexual impulses. It was the libido theory that led critics to assert that Freud saw sex everywhere.

At various places in *Three Essays,* but especially in the conclusion, Freud introduced a concept that was central to the analysis of culture that occupied his later years. This was the concept of *sublimation,* the most important form of displacement. We may express our sexual desires directly; we may repress them, in which case they may find expression in dreams or neurotic symptoms; or we may employ sexual energy to motivate higher cultural activities, such as art, science, and philosophy. This last process is sublimation, and it diverts animalistic drives to the service of civilization. In *Three Essays* Freud only discussed sublimation as an option for a person with a constitutionally strong sexual disposition: but in his later works the alternatives of satisfying direct sexual expression, on the one hand, and repression, sublimation, and consequent residual tension on the other, were to pose a dilemma for Freud and—as he saw it—for civilization itself.

Throughout *Three Essays* only one human drive, sex, is discussed, and it is assigned the central role in determining behavior. However, Freud became dissatisfied with this formulation and began to feel that some other drive was present in humanity besides sex and its associated pleasure principle (the tendency to seek pleasure and avoid pain). His doubts grew and in 1920 crystallized in the aptly named *Beyond the Pleasure Principle.*

Revision, Systematization, and Cultural Analysis (1920–1939)

Beyond the Pleasure Principle (1920)

Freud always represented mental life as a field of battle. Conflict between unacceptable memories or drives, and the ego (or self) produces neurotic symptoms or dreams. This conflict arises from people's incompatible instinctual needs. In his earliest formulation Freud distinguished between sexual impulses unacceptable to the ego and the ego's own instincts for self-preservation. In this approach ego-instincts provide the ego with energy to repress sexual instincts.

Freud altered his view on the nature of instinctual conflict without ever abandoning the thesis of conflict itself. As he pointed out many times, the theory of instincts and their conflicts was the essence of psychoanalysis. In *Beyond the Pleasure Principle* Freud put forward his final views on instinctual conflict.

Freud pictured the instincts as basically conservative. Their goal is always the restoration of some earlier state of affairs—the reduction of tension to a tension-free state, a view that goes back to the "Project." In the development of life the starting point was inorganic matter. Thus the ultimate possible "earlier state of affairs" for a living creature is the nonliving state, or as Freud starkly stated: "*The aim of all life is death.*" There are thus instincts within each being whose aim is death, the return to nonliving, inorganic matter and the *dissolution* of life. Freud called these the *death instincts*.

The sexual instincts, on the other hand, aim at the reproduction and the continuation of life, and Freud argued that in addition they tend to keep the organism whole and functional. Freud now wrote of an expanded sexual instinct, *eros,* the preserver of life, or the life instincts. In this new account of our mental life, conflict arises out of the struggle within each person between the forces of life and death, on seeking a "return" to death, the other seeking longevity and immortality in our offspring.

In *Beyond the Pleasure Principle* Freud raised an issue that has been debated again in recent years: the origin of human aggression. He traced sexual aggression and sadism to displacements of the death instincts, and in *The Ego and the Id* he stated that all forms of aggression have the same origins. Aggression, then, is an inherent part of human nature. This pessimistic belief is typical of Freud, and it is found, although in a different form, in several modern thinkers, particularly some ethologists such as Konrad Lorenz. Many others, for example the anthropologist M. F. Ashley Montague, share Freud's earlier view that aggression is a perversion of a loving and life-preserving human nature. Thus the debate between the early and late Freud is still with us.

In addition to his revisions of the instinct theory, Freud modified his concepts of the conscious and the unconscious in *Beyond the Pleasure Principle.* Heretofore the repressing agency, the ego, had been loosely equated with consciousness. Unconscious impulses were unacceptable to consciousness, the ego, and so it repressed them. Now, however, Freud remarked that much of the ego is unconscious. This heralds Freud's complete reexamination of his theory of the unconscious and the conscious and his presentation of an entirely new map of the mind. This change occupied Freud's last major theoretical work, which gave final shape to the mind as seen by Freud.

The Ego and the Id (1923)

The unconscious is by its very nature unobservable, and in consequence presents problems for any science. The terms *unconsciousness* and *unconscious* may be used in three different senses, which Freud disentangles and reformulates in *The Ego and the Id,* a further development of *Beyond the Pleasure Principle.*

Two senses of "unconscious" have already been distinguished: the *descriptive* and the *dynamic.* We can describe as unconscious any idea or sensation of which we are not aware (as did Leibniz, Herbart, or Fechner). What was of greater importance for Freud was the body of ideas or desires that are unconscious because they are repressed; these are dynamically unconscious. They are unconscious because we have a positive aversion to them, not just because they are too weak to cross the threshold of consciousness; indeed, they are powerful, threatening ideas. Reflecting this distinction, Freud distinguished the preconscious—containing ideas readily accessible to consciousness, but not now conscious—from the unconscious, the dynamic unconscious. The distinction was present from Freud's earliest work.

All along, however, Freud tended to use unconscious in a more theoretical sense, designating an active mental system in opposition to the system of consciousness. It is this *systematic* notion of the unconscious that comes to the fore in this work as the id, and Freud herein remarks that the old conscious/unconscious dichotomy "begins to lose significance." On the remains of the old system of unconscious-preconscious-conscious, Freud now builds a new system of id-ego-superego.

The primal system is the *id,* wholly unconscious, irrational, home of the pleasure principle and the great reservoir of instinctual energy. During the early months of a child's life the id directs energy at (*cathects*) objects in the environment, especially the parents and particularly the mother. Because the child thus gets to know these objects, they are incorporated into the child's personality and form the nucleus of the ego, the representative of mental life. The *ego* is rational and follows the reality principle, withholding tension reduction until pleasure is realistically attainable. The ego's energy, with which it manages the id and conducts rational thought, is derived from the id. The ego identifies with, and so tries to be like, the objects the id has chosen for libidinal cathexis, the parents. By becoming like them the ego itself is cathected by the id, and so it gains energy from the id. Freud calls this state *narcissism,* love of self or ego. It is important to the growth of a healthy personality, for the ego must become strong in order to control the other two systems, to adapt to reality, and to engage in science, art, philosophy, and humanity's other civilized pursuits.

One component of personality remains to be developed: the *superego,* or the inner moral agency. It is formed during the Oedipal period when the child must renounce desire for the cross-sex parent under moral strictures laid down by the parents, especially the father. The fear and rivalry felt by the child creates a new kind of identification with the parents that is moral in nature: the child accepts moral rules enunciated by the parents. These rules now act as an ideal by which the ego is expected to conduct itself, and repression is carried out by the ego at the behest of the superego. Repression sets the stage for neurosis, dreams, slips of the tongue, and other evidences of our unconscious mental life. The Oedipus complex is part of what is repressed, and consequently the superego is itself unconscious. It is also irrational, like the id, except that it is irrational in its moral rather than in its instinctual demands.

In another way, too, the superego is more like the id than the ego, for part of it is innate. This aspect of the superego reveals a Lamarckian side of Freud's thought. It is one of Freud's more controversial beliefs that experience could become part of one's "archaic heritage" inherited through the genes. Wrote Freud: "Thus, in the id, which is capable of being inherited, are harbored residues of the existence of countless egos; and, when the ego forms the superego out of the id, it may perhaps only be reviving shapes of former egos and bringing them to resurrection." The superego is, then, the internal voice not only of the parents, but of ancient moral experiences as well.

It is the interaction of these three systems, whose relations can become complex indeed, that gives rise to conscious mental life and behavior. The id desires and commands the ego to satisfy it; the superego prohibits and commands the ego to repress the id; the ego must compromise these sets of command and also attend to the world and execute realistic actions. Should it fail in its task, mental illness ensues, and psychoanalytic therapy must teach the ego to conquer the id.

A final topic, sublimation, also occupied Freud's attention in *The Ego and the Id*. Sublimation is the conversion of sexual libido into neutral mental energy and is carried out by the child's narcissism. This unbound energy allows the ego to function, but it is an energy that serves both eros and the death instincts. On the one hand, the ego is adaptive and hence enables the person to live; but on the other hand it opposes the id's pleasure principle, as do the death instincts. Thus a dilemma is raised for civilization. Civilized life makes increasing demands on the ego to control the immoral id, and to pursue civilized activities rather than simple animal pleasures. Yet such demands aid death and oppose pleasures, making happiness harder to achieve. The problem of civilization occupied Freud more and more as the years went by and he no longer had to establish psychoanalysis as a movement. In the next two works, Freud analyzed religion, a major carrier of moral demands, and this analysis carried him on to civilization itself.

The Problem of Civilization

The Future of an Illusion (1927).   The nineteenth century appears to us to be a religiously secure age. In public, people professed strong belief in religion, holding it to be the bulwark of civilization. However, in private these same believers were often tormented by grave doubts about the validity of what they professed. They wanted to believe, they tried to believe, they yearned for the simple untroubled faith of their childhoods—but the doubts remained. Doubt was especially frightening precisely because it appeared to be a crack in the bulwark of civilization.

Freud, however, had no doubts; *The Future of an Illusion* is Freud's most polemical and assured work. He said simply that religion *is* an illusion, a massive attempt at wish-fulfillment. Religion is based on nothing more than our infantile feelings of helplessness and the consequent desire to be protected by an all-powerful parent who becomes God. Moreover, to Freud religion is a dangerous illusion, for its dogmatic teachings stunt the intellect, keeping humankind in a childish state. Religion is something to be outgrown as humans develop scientific resources and can stand on their own. The secret religious doubters are people who have outgrown religion but do not know it, and it was to them Freud addressed his work. His goal was, as ever, to assert the "primacy of the intellect" over infantile wishes and emotional needs.

Before turning to religion, Freud made some startlingly pessimistic statements that he took up in *Civilization and Its Discontents,* companion to *Future of an Illusion.* He wrote: "Every individual is virtually an enemy of civilization . . ." and people "feel as a heavy burden the sacrifices which civilization expects of them to make a communal life possible." In a phrase, the topic of *Civilization and its Discontents* is the unhappiness of civilized people.

Civilization and its Discontents (1930).

Wrote Freud: "The sense of guilt [is] the most important problem in the development of civilization and . . . the price we pay for our advance in civilization is a loss of happiness through the heightening of a sense of guilt." Each person seeks happiness, and according to Freud the strongest feelings of happiness come from direct satisfaction of our instinctual, especially sexual, desires. Civilization, however, demands that we renounce to large degree such direct gratification and substitute cultural activities in their stead. Such sublimated drives provide us less pleasure than direct gratification. To add to our discontents we also internalize the demands of civilization as harsh superegos, burdening us with guilt for immoral thoughts as well as deeds. Civilized people are consequently less happy than their primitive counterparts; and as civilization grows, happiness diminishes.

On the other hand, civilization has its rewards, and is necessary to human social life. Along with Hobbes, Freud feared that without a means of restraining aggression, society would dissolve into a war of all against all. Civilization is therefore necessary for the survival of all but the strongest, and at least partly serves eros. Moreover, in return for repression, civilization gives us not only security but also art, science, philosophy, and a more comfortable life through technology.

Civilization thus presents a dilemma from which Freud saw no way out. On the one hand civilization is the protector and benefactor of mankind. On the other hand it demands unhappiness and even neurosis as payment for its benefactions. Near the end of the book Freud hinted that civilizations may vary in the degree of unhappiness they produce—a question he left for others to consider.

This question has been taken up by many thinkers, for *Civilization and its Discontents* has proven to be one of Freud's most provocative works. Some writers such as Erich Fromm, have argued that Western civilization is neurotic and they anoint some utopia as savior, as Fromm does socialism. Others, such as Norman O. Brown, believe the only way out of Freud's dilemma is renunciation of civilization itself and a return to the simple physical pleasures of childhood. Whatever the validity of these claims, Freud's dilemma remains and is acutely felt today when the rebellion against inhibition and guilt that Freud saw beginning in his own time has achieved such large dimensions.

CONCLUSIONS

Freud and Psychoanalysis

Freud did not lack followers—disciples in his own time and apostles after his death. He succeeded in founding a self-conscious psychological and psychotherapeutic movement that lives today in psychoanalytic associations and psychoanalytic journals that have never merged with general psychological associations and publications.

Freud kept psychoanalysis close to his concepts while he lived. He had a firm idea of what normal-science psychoanalytic research and theory should look like, and in true Kuhnian fashion (although Freud's model was Moses) he was intolerant of any analyst who violated the paradigm. However, original minds were attracted to psychoanalysis, and original minds challenge established concepts. Freud valued intelligence, and consequently a series of bright people were welcomed to psychoanalysis only to be expelled later on.

As a result, even during Freud's lifetime psychoanalysis experienced schism after schism. Beginning with Alfred Adler (1870–1936), various analysts broke with Freud or were expelled from psychoanalytic circles because of disagreement with the master. The loss Freud felt most deeply was that of Carl Gustav Jung (1875–1961), who rejected Freud's insistence on the primacy of the sexual instinct. Freud prized Jung's discipleship, for he was an established psychiatrist and a gentile, which meant that Jung's arrival was the first sign of recognition from the medical establishment and the non-Jewish world. Freud valued his own Jewishness, and most of the early analysts were Jewish, but Freud wanted his movement to escape the stigma of being an exclusively Jewish science. So Jung was welcomed, at least by Freud, with open arms and became something of a crown prince to Freud's patriarchal father-figure. There were neurotic elements in their relationship, at least on Freud's side. Once, for example, Freud fainted when Jung challenged him on a scientific point. Such challenges were inevitable, since Jung had his own ideas about the mind even before joining Freud. For a time Jung was groomed to succeed Freud, but in the end he too had to leave Freud's circle to found his own school, analytic psychology.

Psychotherapy had existed before Freud and after his time the number of therapies multiplied greatly. Many of these new movements, like Adler's individual psychology and Jung's analytic psychology, grew out of psychoanalysis; other arose in opposition to it. Today the number of therapies available to the neurotic, or even to the healthy seeker after self-improvement, is bewilderingly large but still includes orthodox psychoanalysis. Each therapy has its own concepts and methods, but few have had significant impact on Western culture or on the human goal of scientific self-understanding, even if they have improved individual lives. We will therefore have little to say about these therapies in future chapters. It should be remembered, however, when we discuss the behaviorist revolution and its dominance of academic psychology, that outside the academy there existed and exists a large, independent movement committed to mentalistic psychology.

The Reception of Psychoanalysis

Freud liked to measure the worth of his ideas against the resistance they met in the outside world. He reasoned that if resistance hides truth in the neurotic, so it must in society at large. Freud was, therefore, in the interesting position of being able to count as evidence for his concepts their rejection by others. Freud liked to see himself as a lone battler against a hostile world, and Freud's self-image, embodied in friendly biographies, has been widely accepted.

However, recent research has shown that the reaction to psychoanalysis was not uniformly hostile. We must look at two levels of reception, among psychological professionals and among popular writers and the press. At the professional level Freud's theory received a mixed response (Cioffi 1973). Some writers were horrified, especially at the emphasis on sex. One review of *Three Essays* called it "pornography gone to seed; and a well-known American psychiatrist, whom Freud respected, burned a book of Freud's because it was "filthy." On the other hand, when *Studies in Hysteria* was reviewed by *Brain*, it was seen as nothing new, only the reviving of the old theory of the origin of hysteria in sexual disorders. A distinguished biologist, W. M. Wheeler, compared psychoanalysis favorably to academic psychology on the grounds that it recognized our animal inheritance.

At the popular level Freud's works were well received, although the complaint was sometimes heard that Freud said nothing poets had not said better. This evaluation Freud would have at least partly accepted. *The Interpretation of Dreams* received almost unanimous praise in the German popular press. Freud's visit to America received favorable coverage in the newspapers. New York society women, who had five hundred analysts to choose from by 1916, found psychoanalysis an interesting diversion: "It became an absorbing game to play with oneself, reading one's motives, trying to understand the symbols by which the soul expresses itself" (Cioffi 1973).

The two levels of response to Freud accounts for the peculiar fact that psychoanalysis has had much more impact on general cultural values and beliefs than on mainstream academic psychology. Since its appearance, psychoanalysis has been subjected to relentless criticism by academic psychology—when it has not been altogether ignored. Behaviorism, the dominant psychological movement since the 1920s, has had little use for Freud's mentalistic system. Aside from a brief attempt in the 1940s and early 1950s by some neobehaviorists to behaviorize psychoanalysis, Freud's theories have been either dismissed as a myth or attacked as a failure.

At the popular level, however, few thinkers have had as much influence on modern Western civilization as Sigmund Freud. The common person's intuitive psychology and child-rearing methods would today be very different had there been no psychoanalysis. This is entirely consistent with Freud's own character. He viewed himself not as a genius or even a scientist, but as a conquerer, overcoming cultural resistance to his profound insights. He sought less to persuade the world than to take it by storm. He failed to persuade the professional scientific psychologist, but he did conquer the popular mind.

When Freud's concepts are discussed today, they may be called "wrong," but it is a measure of his enduring influence that his "wrong" ideas must be discussed at all. Freud's scientific hypotheses have not always fared well at the hands of researchers. It is therefore best to see Freud not as a doctor, or a scientist, but ultimately as a philosopher. As a philosopher he is a modern Stoic, a man who could remain calm in the face of the irrational—confident that a rational order could be found. His commitment to determinism was less a faith in efficient neural causation than a faith in the *logos* of the universe. Like the Stoics, Freud bids us to abandon repressive civilization not to surrender to the simple joys of the id, but rather to substitute rational self-control for unconscious repression. Freud asks us to face the unconscious in order to conquer it in the name of reason.

BIBLIOGRAPHY

The best general introduction to Freud's psychoanalysis are his sets of lectures, *A general introduction to psychoanalysis* (1924; New York: Washington Square Press, 1952), and their sequel *New introductory lectures on psychoanalysis* (1933; New York: Norton, 1965).

Freud's complete works are assembled in J. Strachey, ed., *The standard edition of the complete psychological works of Sigmund Freud*, 24 vols. (London: Hogarth Press, 1966–1974), to which there is an abstract: C. R. Rothgeb, ed., *Abstracts of the standard edition of the complete psychological works of Sigmund Freud* (New York: International Universities Press, 1973). Some of Freud's letters have been published, though often in expurgated form. Only two complete sets have been published, W. McGuire, ed., *The Freud/Jung letters* (Princeton: Princeton University Press, 1974); and Jeffrey M. Masson, ed., *The complete letters of Sigmund Freud to Wilhelm Fliess* (Cambridge: Harvard University Press, 1985). The Freud/Fliess correspondence is especially important, as the letters were written to Freud's closest friend during the formative years of psychoanalysis. An incomplete set of letters was published earlier (with more explanatory apparatus) as Sigmund Freud, *The origins of psychoanalysis: Letters to Wilhelm Fliess* (New York: Basic Books, 1977).

The standard biography of Freud is Ernest Jones's three-volume *The life and work of Sigmund Freud*, available in a one-volume abridgement (New York: Basic Books, 1961). Freud, of course, has had many biographers, and I will mention only two more recent ones: Ronald William Clarke, *Freud: The man and the cause* (New York: Random House, 1980), and Richard Wollheim, *Sigmund Freud* (New York: Viking, 1971). For Freud's circle, see Paul Roazen, *Freud and his followers* (New York: Meridian, 1976).

Understanding Freud requires understanding Victorian sexuality, a topic that has been much written about recently. The traditional view is that Victorians—especially women—were intensely repressed and deeply ashamed about sex, the view followed in the text. Standard sources here include Stephen Marcus, *The other Victorians* (New York. Meridian, 1964), a work I relied on; Vern and Bonnie Bullough, *Sin, sickness, and sanity: A history of sexual attitudes* (New York: Meridian, 1977), which covers periods before and after the Victorian; G. J. Barker-Benfield, *The horrors of the half-known life: tale attitudes toward women and sexuality in nineteenth-century America* (New York: Harper Colophon, 1976), which takes a feminist perspective; Ronald Pearsall, *The worm in the bud: The world of Victorian sexuality* (Harmondsworth, England: Penguin, 1983), a social history of Victorian sexuality; John S. and Robin M. Haller, *The physician and sexuality in Victorian America* (Champaign: University of Illinois Press, 1974), a fascinating study of physician's ideas about sex, and how they were translated into popular and professional "cures" for alleged sexual disorder; and Jeffrey Weeks, *Sex, politics and society: The regulation of sexuality since 1800* (New York: Longman, 1981). Victorians were especially alarmed by masturbation: see Arthur N. Gilbert, "Masturbation and insanity: Henry Maudsley and the ideology of sexual repression," *Albion* (1980, *12*: 268–282). However, revisionist historians have begun to assert that the traditional view of repressed Victorian sexuality is seriously mistaken. For example, a recently discovered unpublished sex survey—the first ever—of women who had grown up in the Victorian period suggests that they may have had orgasms with the same frequency as today's "liberated" women: Clelia Duel Mosher, *The Mosher survey: Sexual attitudes of Victorian women* (New York: Arno, 1980). Peter Gay, *The bourgeois experience—Victoria to Freud*, vol. 1: *The education of the senses* (Oxford: Oxford University Press, 1984) has used the Mosher survey, a diary by a sexually active young American woman, and other sources to try to debunk the "myth" of the asexual Victorian; see also Cyril Pearl, *The girl with the Swansdown seat: An informal report on some aspects of mid-Victorian morality* (London: Robin Clark, 1980), and Edmund Leites, *The puritan conscience and human sexuality* (New Haven: Yale University Press, 1986). How far the revisionist picture is accurate, however, is still open to question. For an evaluation, see Carol Zisowitz Sterns, "Victorian sexuality: Can historians do it better?," *Journal of Social History* (1985, *18*: 625–634). Freud himself was an advocate of sexual reform. See John W. Boyer, "Freud, marriage, and late Viennese liberalism: A commentary from 1905," *Journal of Modern History* (1978, *50*: 72–102), which contains a transcript with translation of Freud's reply to a query from a commission looking into the laws regulating marriage in Austria in 1905; and Timothy McCarthy, "Freud and the problem of sexuality," *Journal of the History of the Behavioral and Social Sciences* (1981, *17*: 332–339). Other important rebels against Victorian sexual repression, assuming it existed, are described by Paul Robinson, *The modernization of sex: Havelock Ellis, Alfred Kinsey, William Masters and Virginia Johnson* (New York: Harper Colophon, 1977).

The unconscious before Freud has been written about by Henri F. Ellenberger, *The discovery of the unconscious* (New York: Basic Books, 1970), the standard work; and D. B. Klein, *The unconscious: Invention or discovery?* (Santa Monica, California: Goodyear, 1977), which is more critical. Other important works on the background include the following: For the cultural milieu, and a wonderful book, Carl E. Schorske, *Fin de Siècle Vienna: Politics and culture* (New York: Knopf, 1979); for the intellectual setting in Europe, in which many thinkers were discovering irrational sources of human action, H. Stuart Hughes, *Consciousness and Society* (New York: Vintage, 1962), and Stephen G. Brush, "Scientific revolutionaries of 1905: Einstein, Rutherford, Chamberlin, Wilson, Stevens, Binet, Freud," in M. Bunge and W. R. Shea, eds., *Rutherford and physics at the turn of the century* (New York: Dawson & Science History Publications, 1979); for Freud's background as a Jew, David Bakan, *Sigmund Freud and the Jewish mystical tradition* (Princeton: D. van Nostrand, 1958), and for the concept of neurosis, Jose M. Lopez Piñero, *Historical origins of the concept of neurosis* (Cambridge, England: Cambridge University Press, 1983).

Freud's seduction mistake is much in the news again. Jeffrey Moussaieff Masson, *The assault on truth: Freud's suppression of the seduction theory* (New York: Farrar, Straus, & Giroux, 1984), argues, on the basis of some new Freud/Fliess letters (see above), that Freud was right to begin with, and abandoned the seduction theory to coverup his friend Fliess's surgical incompetence; a short version of the thesis appeared as "Freud and the seduction theory" in *The Atlantic Monthly* (February 1984: 33–60). Masson's ideas caused a huge blow-up among the keepers of Freud's letters, into whose circle Masson entered to edit the Freud/Fliess correspondence. The whole affair has been deliciously told by Janet Malcolm, "Annals of scholarship: Trouble in the archives," in *The New Yorker* (December 5, 1983: 59–152, and December 12: 60–119), and as a book, *In the Freud archives* (New York: Random House, 1985). Along with most reviewers I find Masson's thesis implausible; an interesting review is by Freud skeptic Frank Cioffi, "The cradle of neurosis", *Times Literary Supplement* (July 6, 1984: 743–744), in which he attacks Masson, but advances again his own assault on Freud's honesty.

Freud's creation, psychoanalysis, has been much examined, both philosophically and empirically. The chief philosophical question is whether or not psychoanalysis is, as Freud claimed, a science. Heated claims have been made, ranging from the assertion that psycho-analysis is a pseudoscience, to the assertion that it is just as scientific as physics. Four books consider the debate: Sidney Hook, ed., *Psychoanalysis, scientific method, and philosophy* (New York: New York University Press, 1959); B. A. Farrell, *The standing of psycho-analysis* (Oxford: Oxford University Press, 1981); Adolf Grünbaum, *The foundations of psychoanalysis: A philosophical critique* (Berkeley: University of California Press, 1984); and Louis Breger, *Freud's unfinished journey* (Boston: Routledge & Kegan Paul, 1981). Two books summarize the empirical work on the adequacy of psychoanalysis as science and as therapy: Seymour Fisher and Roger Greenberg, *The scientific credibility of Freud's theory and therapy*, 2d ed. (New York: Columbia University Press, 1985); and Paul Kline, *Fact and fantasy in Freudian therapy*, 2d ed. (London: Methuen, 1981).

On the reception of psychoanalysis, see the following: Hannah S. Decker, "The interpretation of dreams: Early reception by the educated German public," *Journal of the History of the Behavioral Sciences* (1975: *11*: 129–141); Hannah S. Decker, *Freud in Germany: Revolution and reaction in science, 1893–1907* (New York: International Univer-sities Press. 1977); *Psychological Issues Monographs 11* (31), Monograph 41; Nathan Hale, *Freud and the Americans* (New York: Oxford University Press, 1971); and David Shakow, *The influence of Freud on American psychology* (New York: International Universities Press, 1964).

As a great thinker and writer, Freud may be interpreted many ways. There is the traditional view of Freud as the inventor of a unique science, psychoanalysis, and as a therapist. However, other views have been offered. He may be seen as a cognitive psychologist: Karl H. Pribram and Merton Gill, *Freud's "Project" re-assessed: preface to contemporary cognitive theory and neuropsychology* (New York: Basic Books, 1976), or Matthew Hugh Erdelyi, *Psychoanalysis: Freud's cognitive psychology* (San Francisco: W. H. Freeman, 1985). He may be seen as a humanist: Philip Rieff, *Freud: The mind of the moralist*, 3d ed. (Chicago: Chicago University Press, 1979); or Bruno Bettelheim, *Freud and man's soul* (New York: Vintage, 1984). Another way of placing Freud among the humanities is to treat him as a hermeneutic writer, concerned with interpreting meaning, not predicting and controlling behavior. This view arose in Europe, especially in the work of Paul Ricouer, *Freud and philosophy: An essay on interpretation* (New Haven: Yale University Press, 1970); the approach has recently exerted influence here, for example, Charles D. Axelrod, *Studies in intellectual breakthrough, Freud, Simmel, and Buber* (Amherst: University of Massachusetts Press, 1970); or Samuel Weber, *The legend of Freud* (Minneapolis: University of Minnesota Press, 1982), who applies the latest trendy figure in hermeneutics, Jacques Derrida, to Freud. He has been integrated with Marxism by the so-called Frankfurt School of social thought: for example, Richard Lichtman, *The production of desire: The integration of psychoanalysis into Marxist theory* (New York: Free Press, 1982). He may be taken to be a philosopher: for example, Richard Wollheim, ed., *Freud: A collection of critical essays* (Garden City, New York; Doubleday, 1974); or Richard Wollheim and J. Hopkins, eds, *Philosophical essays on Freud* (Cambridge, England: Cambridge University Press, 1982). Finally (though I may have missed a viewpoint), Frank Sulloway, *Freud, Biologist of the mind: Beyond the psychoanalytic legend* (New York: Basic Books, 1979) sees Freud as a Darwinian biologist. My own favorites among the above works are Rieff's and Sulloway's. Rieff reads Freud with sympathy and depth, and relates his thought both to his times and ours. Sulloway masterfully demonstrates the pervasive influence of evolutionary thought on Freud, and, in the last part of the book, deftly dismantles the standard view of Freud the pure psychologist.

Freud's influence has been very great in fields other than psychiatry and psychology. A nice collection that is especially useful for a beginner in Freud is Jonathan Miller, ed., *Freud: The man, his world, his influence* (Boston: Little, Brown, 1972), because it contains essays on Freud and his time, and then a set on Freud's influence in various fields. Books on specific areas of influence follow. Art: Ellen H. Spitz, *Art and Psyche: A study in psychoanalysis and aesthetics* (New Haven: Yale University Press, 1985). The social sciences, including anthropology, sociology, and political science: Arthur Berliner, *Psychoanalysis and society* (Washington, D.C.: University Press of America, 1982); Peter Bocock, *Freud and modern society: An outline of Freud's sociology* (Sunbury on Thames, England: Nelson, 1976); Paul Roazen, *Freud: Political and social thought* (New York: Knopf, 1968); H. M. Ruitenbeek, ed., *Psychoanalysis and social science* (New York: Dutton, 1962); Melford Spiro, *Oedipus in the Trobriands* (Chicago: University of Chicago Press, 1983); and Edwin R. Wallace, *Freud and anthropology* (New York: International Universities Press, 1983). One controversial offspring of psychoanalysis is psychohistory, which is discussed and critically examined in David E. Stannard, *Shrinking history: On Freud and the failure of psychohistory* (New York: Oxford University Press, 1980).

Finally, for a general account of the psychoanalytic movement as a whole, including the many post-Freudian theorists up to recent times, see Reuben Fine, *A history of psychoanalysis* (New York: Columbia University Press, 1979).

REFERENCES

Cioffi, F. (1972) Wollheim on Freud. *Inquiry 15:* 172–186.
Cioffi, F. (1973) Introduction. In F. Cioffi, ed. *Freud: Modern judgments*. London: Macmillian.
Cioffi, F. (n.d.) Was Freud a Liar? British Broadcasting Corporation Radio 3.

Freud, E. (1960) *The letters of Sigmund Freud.* New York: Basic Books.
Freud, S. (1950) Project for a scientific psychology. In *Standard edition of the complete psychological works of Sigmund Freud.* V. 1. London: Hogarth Press.
Freud, S. (1960) *The ego and the id.* New York: Norton.
Freud, S. (1961a) *Beyond the pleasure principle.* New York: Norton.
Freud, S. (1961b) *The future of an illusion.* New York: Norton.
Freud, S. (1961c) *Civilization and its discontents.* New York: Norton.
Freud, S. (1962) *Three essays on the theory of sexuality.* New York: Avon.
Freud, S. (1968) *The interpretation of dreams.* New York: Avon.
Freud, S. and Breuer, J. (1966) *Studies in hysteria.* New York: Avon.
Houghton, W. E. (1957) *The Victorian frame of mind.* New Haven: Yale University Press.
Plumb, J. H. (1972) The Victorians unbuttoned. In *In the light of history.* New York: Delta/Dell.

CHAPTER 9

The Psychology of Adaptation (1855–1891)

THE BEGINNINGS OF THE PSYCHOLOGY OF ADAPTATION IN BRITAIN
  Lamarckian Psychology: Herbert Spencer (1820–1903)
  Darwinian Psychology
PSYCHOLOGY IN THE NEW WORLD
  Background
  America's Native Philosophy: Pragmatism
  The New Psychology
CONCLUSION: PERCEPTION AND THINKING ARE ONLY THERE FOR BEHAVIOR'S SAKE

The last founding psychology we will examine has proved the most durable and influential in academic psychology. Wundt's psychology of consciousness was an anachronistic product of nineteenth-century German thought, and it survived neither transplantation to other countries nor the destruction of its intellectual ecology by the Nazis and World War II. The same is largely true of Gestalt psychology. Psychoanalysis is a living tradition, having adapted to conditions outside nineteenth-century Vienna, and its influence on modern culture has been greater than that of any other psychology. Nevertheless, psychoanalysis remains primarily a branch of medical psychiatry, and its relations with academic psychology have been ambivalent from Freud's time to our own.

The approach that academic psychologists—first in England and later in America—have found most attractive and useful is a psychology based on evolution, Lamarckian or Darwinian. With the ascendance of American psychology in the twentieth century, the psychology of adaptation in one form or another has dominated academic psychology.

Any theory of evolution raises two questions that can engender psychological research programs. The first we may call the *species question*. If the body and brain are products of organic evolution, then we may ask in what ways this inheritance shapes the thought and behavior of organisms. This question leads to comparative psychology, ethology, and sociobiology, which study species differences in mental and behavioral capacities—differences presumably created by evolution. The second psychological question raised by evolution we may call the *individual question*. As the individual creature grows up it can be seen as adapting psychologically to the environment in a way analogous to organic evolution. This question leads to the study of learning, research designed to uncover how the individual adjusts to the environment.

The species question and the individual question are interrelated. If species differences are great, then different psychologies of individual adaptation will be needed for different species. If, on the other hand, species differences are small, then the same laws of individual learning will apply to all individuals, regardless of species. In this chapter we will trace the development of the psychology of adaptation and will soon discover that its proponents adopt the latter line of thought. Gall's phrenology had implied a comparative psychology that looked for species differences in the possession of mental faculties. To a phrenologist, structural differences in the brain meant structural differences in mind. However, by the middle of the nineteenth century the sensorimotor concept of the brain had vanquished phrenology among scientists, while associationism was displacing faculty psychology among philosopher-psychologists. The view of the brain as an intially formless associative machine, and the view of the mind as a *tabula rasa* awaiting associations, combined to cause psychologists to focus on the individual question and minimize species differences.

THE BEGINNINGS OF
THE PSYCHOLOGY
OF ADAPTATION IN BRITAIN

Lamarckian Psychology: Herbert
Spencer (1820–1903)

In the summer of 1854 Herbert Spencer began to write a psychology whose "lines of thought had scarcely anything in common with lines of thought previously pursued" (Spencer 1904). His work appeared the following year, 1855, as *Principles of Psychology*. This book gives Spencer a good claim to be the founder of the psychology of adaptation. Bain had integrated associationism and the sensorimotor conception of brain function; but, although he acknowledged the validity of Darwinian evolution, his psychology remained part of classical, pre-evolutionary associationism. Writing before Darwin, Spencer integrated not only associationism and sensorimotor physiology, but also Lamarckian evolution. Consequently, he anticipated the psychology of adaptation. Furthermore, not only did he raise the two evolutionary questions, but he also answered them in the ways basic to Anglo-American psychology ever since.

Spencer's *Principles of Psychology* was just one part of his all-embracing *synthetic philosophy*. Spencer was the greatest systematizer since Aquinas, although Spencer thought of himself as the new Newton. Another part of his system was the *Principles of Sociology*, and Spencer is regarded as a founder of that field, too. Aquinas organized all philosophy around the Christian God. Spencer organized it around Lamarckian evolution, in which he believed as early as 1852. He referred all questions, metaphysical or otherwise, to the principle of evolution and presented it as a cosmic process, embracing not only organic evolution but also the evolution of mind and societies.

In 1854 Spencer wrote, "If the doctrine of Evolution is true, the inevitable implication is that Mind can be understood only by observing how Mind is evolved." Here is the starting point of the psychology of adaptation. Spencer proceeded to discuss both evolutionary psychological questions. Considering the individual, Spencer viewed development as a process by which the connections between ideas come to mirror accurately the connections between events prevailing in the environment. The connections between ideas are built up by contiguity. Wrote Spencer (1897): "The growth of intelligence at large depends upon the law, that when any two psychical states occur in immediate succession, an effect is produced such that if the first subsequently recurs there is a certain tendency for the second to follow it." This tendency is strengthened as ideas are more frequently associated together. Like Bain, Spencer attempted to "deduce" the laws of mental association from the sensorimotor constitution of the nervous system and brain. In general, then, Spencer's analysis of the individual mind is that of atomistic associationism. He carried out the "successive decomposition of the more complex phenomena of intelligence into simpler ones . . . down to the simplest . . . element." What Spencer adds to Bain is the evolutionary conception, viewing the development of the mind as an adaptive adjustment to environmental conditions.

Spencer pictured the brain as a sensorimotor associational device, stating (1897) that "the human brain is an organized register of infinitely numerous experiences." His view has two important consequences. Given the Lamarckian idea of the heritability of acquired characteristics, instinct can be made acceptable to associationists and empiricists. Following the passage just quoted, Spencer described how the brain accumulates experiences "during the evolution of that series of organisms through which the human organism has been reached." Thus innate reflexes and instincts are simply associative habits so well learned they became part of a species' genetic legacy. Such habits may not be acquired during an individual's life, but they are still acquired following the laws of association in the life of the species. Innate ideas need no longer terrify the empiricist.

The second consequence of Spencer's integration of evolution and the sensorimotor concept of nervous function is more portentous: Differences in the mental processes of different species reduce to the number of associations the brains are able to make. All brains work the same way, by association, and differ only quantitatively in the richness of their associations. As Spencer (1897) put it, "The impressions received by inferior intelligences, even down to the very lowest, are dealt with after a like model." Thus his answer to the species question is to deny qualitative differences between species and admit only quantitative, associational differences. This idea extends to differences within, as well as between, species; the "European inherits from twenty to thirty cubic inches more brain than the Papuan," he said. This implies that the "civilized man has also a more complex or heterogeneous nervous system than the uncivilized man," as he wrote in *First Principles*.

Spencer's conclusions are of tremendous importance for the development of the psychology of adaptation. Given his framework, comparative psychology would be directed toward studying species differences in simple associative learning, studies aimed at quantifying a single dimension of "intelligence" along which species can be arranged. Moreover, such studies could be performed in the laboratory, ignoring an organism's native environment. If the brain is no more than an initially empty stimulus-response associating mechanism, then it is irrelevant whether the associations are natural or contrived; in fact, the laboratory offers greater control of the process than naturalistic observation.

It also follows that, if all organisms learn the same way, then the results of studies of simple animal learning, with their precision, replicability, and rigor can be extended without serious modification to human learning. We will find that all of these conclusions are of fundamental importance to behavioralism, the twentieth-century psychology of adaptation. Behavioralists seek laws of learning valid for at least all mammals and assume the extension of animal findings to human psychology—often without supporting data.

Finally, the quantitative conception of associative mental function would help develop intelligence testing, which purports to assign a number to a person's intelligence. Although it is not demanded by the theory, the connection of associational ability with brain mass and complexity of association would push mental testing in a racist direction. We have already seen Spencer denegrate "uncivilized" people for having low brain mass and a simple nervous system, and in *First Principles* he implies that the "lower human races" are children: "In the infant European we see sundry resemblances to the lower human races."

One application of the theory of evolution to human society is to see it as an arena for the struggle for existence. This attitude is called *social Darwinism,* although it began before Darwin with Herbert Spencer. Spencer argued that natural selection should be allowed to take its course on the human species. Government should do nothing to save the poor, weak, and helpless. In nature poor, weak, helpless animals, and their poor hereditary traits, are weeded out by natural selection. This should be the way in human society as well, said Spencer. Government should leave the cosmic process alone, for it will perfect humanity by the selection of the fittest. To help human failures will only serve to degrade the species by allowing them to have children and thus pass on their hereditary tendency to fail.

When Spencer toured America in 1882 he was lionized. Social Darwinism had great appeal in a *laissez-faire* capitalist society where it could justify even cut-throat competition on the grounds that such competition perfected humanity. Although it promised eventual perfection of the species, social Darwinism was profoundly conservative, for all reform was seen as tampering with nature's laws. The American social Darwinist Edward Youmans complained bitterly about the evils of the robber barons, but when asked what he proposed to do about them replied, "Nothing" (Hofstadter 1955). Only centuries of evolution could relieve human problems.

Darwinian Psychology

Spencer's general principles, while inspired by Lamarck, are not inconsistent with Darwin's theory of natural selection. The only new assumption needed is that natural selection has produced the sensorimotor nervous system believed to exist in all animals, which justifies an associationist theory of mind, or later of behavior. Many naturalistic thinkers, including Darwin himself, consciously or unconsciously adhered to the Lamarckian view of progressive evolution, however, and sometimes even accepted the heritability of acquired characteristics. Thus Spencer's Lamarckian psychology shades insensibly into a Darwinian psychology.

Darwin on Humans

The central challenge of Darwin's *Origin of Species* concerned what Huxley called man's place in nature. In the comprehensive, naturalistic scheme of evolution, humanity was made part of nature, no longer a being who transcended it. Everyone saw this implication immediately whether they agreed with it or not. Yet *Origin* itself contains very little on human psychology. We know that in his early notebooks, dating back to the 1830s, Darwin was concerned with these topics, but he seems to have set them aside from his initial publication as too troublesome. All his life Darwin projected, but never completed, a master work on evolution in all its facets. In any event, it was not until 1871 that he finally published *The Descent of Man*, which brings human nature within the scope of natural selection.

Darwin's aim in *The Descent of Man* is to show that "man is descended from some lowly organized form," a conclusion that he regretted would "be highly distasteful to many." He broadly compared human and animal behavior and concluded that "the difference in mind between man and the higher animals, great as it is, is certainly one of degree and not of kind. We have seen that the senses and intuitions, the various emotions and faculties, such as love, memory, attention, curiosity, imitation, reason, etc., of which man boasts may be found in an incipient, or even sometimes in a well-developed condition, in lower animals." Even "[t]he ennobling belief in God is not universal with man."

Descent is not primarily a work of psychology; it mainly attempts to incorporate humans fully into nature. Darwin felt that Spencer had already laid the foundations for an evolutionary psychology. Yet Darwin's work contrasts importantly with Spencer's *Principles*. Darwin followed philosophical faculty psychology, relegat ing association to a secondary factor in thought. Partly as a consequence, Darwin was concerned almost exclusively with the species question, for he assumed that evolution shaped the faculties. He also allowed great scope to the effects of heredity, sounding at times like an extreme nativist: Both virtue and crime may be heritable tendencies; woman is genetically inferior to man in "whatever he takes up." On the other hand Darwin agreed with Spencer that the nature of species differences is quantitative rather than qualitative and that well-learned habits can become innate reflexes. Lamarckian psychology and Darwinian psychology differ only in emphasis, not in content. The major difference is that Darwin's psychology is only a part of a materialistic, evolutionary biology. Spencer's psychology, in contrast, was part of a grand metaphysics that tended toward dualism and postulated an "Unknowable" forever beyond the reach of science. Darwin sheared off this metaphysical growth from the psychology of adaptation.

The Spirit of Darwinian Psychology: Sir Francis Galton (1822–1911)

Galton was the most outstanding of that distinct Victorian type, the gentleman dilettante. Independently wealthy, he was able to turn his inventive mind to whatever he chose. He traveled over most of Africa and wrote an unsurpassed manual for travelers in wild lands. He empirically investigated the efficacy of prayer. He pioneered the use of fingerprints for personal identification. He invented composite photographic portraiture. Many of his wide-ranging investigations were psychological or sociological. He once tried to understand paranoia by suspecting everyone he met of evil intentions. He canvassed the female beauties of Great Britain trying to ascertain which county had the most beautiful women in it. He measured boredom at scientific lectures. He applied anthropomorphic tests to thousands of individuals visiting a fair in Kensington. However, Galton's researches were so eclectic that they do not add up to a research program. Consequently, Galton cannot be considered a psychologist in the same sense as Wundt, Titchener, or Freud.

Nevertheless, Galton made important contributions to the growing psychology of adaptation. He broadened psychology to encompass topics excluded by Wundt. In his *Inquires into the Human Faculty* (1883) he wrote: "No professor of . . . psychology . . . can claim to know the elements of what he teaches, unless he is acquainted with the ordinary phenomena of idiocy, madness, and epilepsy. He must study the manifestations of disease and congenital folly, as well as those of high intellect" (Galton 1907). Wundt wanted to understand only the normal, adult mind. Galton inquired into any human mind.

Galton devised a number of important methods used by the psychology of adaptation. He was the first to systematically apply statistics to psychological data, and he invented the correlation coefficient. He studied twins to sort out the contributions of nature and nurture to human character, intellect, and behavior. He tried to use indirect behavioral measures (rate of fidgeting) to measure a mental state (boredom). He invented the free-association technique of interrogating memory. He used questionnaires to collect data on mental processes such as mental imagery. He tried to use a psychophysical method (lifting weights) to measure acuteness of perception, and thus—he though—intelligence. He tried to directly introspect his higher mental processes, which Wundt had said was impossible. All these techniques found a place in English and American psychology.

Spencer began the psychology of adaptation, but Galton epitomized it. His eclectic attitude concerning both method and subject matter, and his use of statistics, would strongly characterize Darwinian psychology from this point on. Above all, his interest in individual differences points to the future: In German rationalist fashion Wundt had wanted to describe the transcendent human mind; he quite literally found the study of individual differences to be foreign. Galton, however, was interested in concrete individuals and in all those factors that make people different. The study of individual differences is an essential part of Darwinian science, for without variation there can be no differential selection and no evolutionary improvement of the species.

Improvement of the human species was precisely Galton's aim. Underlying his various investigations was not a research program, but rather "religious duty." He was convinced that the most important individual differences, including those of morals, character, and intellect, are not acquired. His great aim was to demonstrate that these characteristics were innate and then to measure them so that they could inform the procreative behavior of mankind. Eugenics is the selective breeding of human beings to improve the species.

In his *Hereditary Genius* of 1869 Galton "propose[d] to show that a man's natural abilities are derived by inheritance, under exactly the same limitations as are the form and physical features of the whole organic world. Consequently, as it is easy, not withstanding these limitations, to obtain by careful selection of permanent breed of dogs or horses gifted with peculiar powers of running, or of doing anything else, so it would be quite practicable to produce a highly gifted race of men by judicious marriages during several consecutive generations" (Galton 1925). In this work Galton endeavored to show that abilities as different as those required to be a good judge or a good wrestler are innate and heritable, which would make a eugenics program feasible. Galton, like Darwin, was primarily interested in the species question. Galton, however, cared about the improvement of man and thought selective breeding would improve humanity faster than improved education. Galton's program for selective human breeding was a form of positive eugenics, attempting to get especially "fit" individuals to marry one another. Galton proposed that examinations be used to discover the ten most talented men and women in Great Britain. At a public ceremony recognizing their talent, each would be offered £5,000—a staggering sum in days when a moderately frugal person might live on a pound or so a week—as a wedding present should they choose to marry one another.

Galton's proposals gained few adherents when he first set it forth in 1869. Just after the turn of the century, however, Britons were more disposed to listen. In the wake of their near defeat in the Boer War for South Africa, and the gradual recession of their empire, Britons began to worry that they were degenerating as a nation. In 1902 the Army reported that 60 percent of Englishmen were unfit for military service, setting off a furious public debate on the physical deterioration (after the name of the Army report) of the British people. In this atmosphere worriers of all political stripes were excited by Galton's eugenic program for race improvement.

In 1901 Karl Pearson, an intimate of Galton's who had extended and perfected Galton's statistical approach to biology, pressed Galton to reenter the fray for eugenics. Pearson was a socialist who opposed conservative, *laissez-faire* social Darwinism, and hoped to replace it with planned, politically enforced programs of eugenics. Galton agreed, despite his advance age, again to take up the cause, and in that year gave a public lecture on eugenics and began to work for the establishment of eugenics policies. In 1904 he gave £1,500 to establish a research fellowship in eugenics and a eugenics record office at the University of London. In 1907 he helped found the Eugenics Education Society, which began to publish a journal, *Eugenics Review*. Eugenics appealed to people all across the political spectrum. Conservative, establishment leaders used alleged "laws of heredity and development" to support their crusade for moral, especially sexual, reform. Social radicals could press eugenics into service as part of their programs for political and social reform. Eugenics was much talked about in the first decade of the twentieth century in Britain.

Despite the attention it received British eugenics, in contrast to American eugenics, enjoyed only limited success in affecting public policy. Galton's program of rewards was never seriously considered. Some attention was given to laws enforcing negative eugenics—attempts to regulate the reproduction of the alleged "unfit"—but these were relatively mild measures that placed the socially incapacitated in institutions where they could receive care. British eugenicists were themselves divided on the need for government eugenics programs, the social radical eugenicists in particular urging education and voluntary control instead of legal compulsion. British eugenics was never fueled, as American eugenics was, by racism and race hysteria. British eugenicists were more concerned to encourage the reproduction of the middle and upper classes, whose birthrate had long been in decline, than to restrict spitefully the reproduction of allegedly inferior races. While eugenics began in Britain, it was mostly practiced in America, as we shall see.

The Rise of Comparative Psychology

It is clear that a psychology based on evolution should call forth research aimed at comparing the various abilities of different species of animals. Simple comparison of human and animal abilities goes back to Aristotle, and both Descartes and Hume buttressed their philosophies with such considerations. The Scottish faculty psychologists argued that humans' moral faculty distinguished them from animals. Galton studied animals and people to discover the special mental faculties of each species. The theory of evolution, however, gave comparative psychology a powerful impetus, placing it in a wider biological context and giving it a specific rationale. In the later nineteenth century comparative psychology grew in strength, until in the twentieth century learning theorists studied animals in preference to humans.

Modern comparative psychology may be said to have begun in 1872 with the publication of Darwin's *The Expression of the Emotions in Man and Animals* (Darwin 1965). The new appraoch is heralded by Darwin's statement early in the book: "No doubt as long as man and all other animals are viewed as independent creations, an effectual stop is put to our natural desire to investigate as far as possible the causes of Expression." However, he who admits "that the structure and habits of all animals have been gradually evolved, will look at the whole subject in a new and interesting light." In the rest of his book Darwin surveyed the means of emotional expression possessed by humans and animals, noting the continuity between them, and demonstrating their universality among the races of humanity. Darwin's theory is very Lamarckian, it may be noted: "Actions, which were at first voluntary, soon become habitual, and at last hereditary, and may then be performed even in opposition to the will." Darwin's theory was that our involuntary emotive expressions have gone through this development.

Darwin's early work in comparative psychology was systematically carried on by his friend George John Romanes (1848–1894). In *Animal Intelligence* (1883) Romanes surveyed the mental abilities of animals from protozoa to apes. In later works, such as *Mental Evolution in Man* (1889), Romanes attempted to trace the gradual evolution of mind down the millennia. Romanes died before he could complete his comparative psychology. His literary executor was C. Lloyd Morgan (1852–1936), who in his own *Introduction to Comparative Psychology* (1894) objected to Romanes's overestimation of animal intelligence. Romanes had quite freely attributed complex thinking to animals from analogy to his own thinking. Morgan, in formulating what has since been called *Morgan's canon,* argued that inferences of animal thinking should be no more than absolutely necessary to explain some observed behavior. The last British comparative psychologist was the philosopher Leonard T. Hobhouse (1864–1928), who used the data of comparative psychology to construct a general evolutionary metaphysics. He also carried out some experiments on animal behavior that in some respects anticipated Gestalt work on animal insight and were designed to undermine the artificiality of behaviorist animal experiments.

These comparative psychologists combined faculty psychology with associationism in their theories of development and collected some interesting facts. The paradigm that informed their efforts was less important than their method, however. What Romanes consciously introduced to psychology was an objective, behavioral method in contrast to the subjective method of introspection since we cannot observe the minds of animals, only their behavior. Nevertheless, the theoretical goal of the British animal psychologists was never merely to describe behavior. Rather they wanted to explain the workings of animal minds, and therefore they attempted to infer mental processes from behavior. The problems involved in this research program importantly affected the development of behavioralism, which was founded by American comparative psychologists.

Methodologically, comparative psychology began with Romanes's *anecdotal method.* He collected vignettes of animal behavior from many correspondents and sifted through them for plausible and reliable information from which to reconstruct the animal mind. The anecdotal method became an object of derision among the experimentally oriented Americans, especially E. L. Thorndike. The method lacked the control available in the laboratory and was felt to overestimate animal intelligence. The anecdotal method did have the virtue, largely unappreciated at the time, of observing animals in natural, uncontrived situations. We will find that animal psychology runs into real difficulties in the 1960s because of its exclusive reliance on controlled laboratory methods that overlook the animals' ecological histories.

Theoretically, inferring mental processes from behavior presented difficulties. It is altogether too easy to attribute to animals complex mental processes they may not possess—any simple behavior can be explained (incorrectly) as the result of complex reasoning. Anyone who today reads Romanes's *Animal Intelligence* will feel that he frequently committed this error. Morgan's canon was an attempt to deal with this problem by requiring conservative inferences.

In his own treatment of animal mind Morgan (1886) contributed a distinction that unfortunately was less known and less influential than his famous canon of simplicity. Morgan distinguished objective inferences from subjective   or, as he called them in the philosophical jargon of his time, ejective—inferences from animal behavior to animal mind. Imagine watching a dog sitting at a street corner at 3:30 one afternoon. As a school bus approaches the dog gets up, wags its tail, and watches the bus slow down and then stop. The dog looks at the children getting off the bus and, when one boy gets off, it jumps on him, licks his face, and together the boy and the dog walk off down the street. Objectively, Morgan would say, we may infer certain mental powers possessed by the dog. It must possess sufficient perceptual skills to pick one child out from the crowd getting off the bus, and it must possess at least recognition memory, as it responds differently to one child than all the others. Such inferences are objective, because they posit certain internal cognitive processes that may be further investigated by, for example, testing dogs' discriminative learning capacities. On the other hand, we are tempted to attribute a subjective mental state, happiness, to the dog on analogy with our own happiness when we greet a loved one who has been absent. Such inferences by analogy to our own subjective mental-states are Morgan's subjective inferences. Objective inferences are legitimate in science, Morgan held, because they do not depend on analogy, are not emotional, and are susceptible to later verification by experiment. Subjective inferences are not scientifically legitimate because they result from projecting our own feelings into an animal, and may not be more objectively assessed. Morgan did not claim that animals do not have feelings, only that their feelings, whatever they may be, fall outside the domain of scientific psychology.

Morgan's distinction is important, but it was neglected by later comparative psychologists. When Romanes's methods of anecdote and inference were challenged by American animal psychologists in the 1890s, the absurdities of subjective inference—calling rats "happy" and "carefree"—led to wholesale rejection of any discussion of animal mind. Had Morgan's distinction between objective and subjective inference been heeded, however, it might have been seen that although subjective inferences are scientifically worthless, objective inferences are perfectly respectable.

However, no matter how conservatively and carefully mind might be reconstructed from behavior, it remained possible for the skeptic to doubt. As Romanes (1883) put it: "Skepticism of this kind is logically bound to deny evidence of mind, not only in the case of lower animals, but also in that of the higher, and even in that of men other than the skeptic himself. For all objections which could apply to the use of [inference] . . . would apply with equal force to the evidence of any mind other than that of the individual objector." Such skepticism constitutes the essence of the behaviorist revolution. The behaviorist may admit that she or he possesses consciousness, if not mind, but refuses to use mental activity to explain the behavior of animals, or of other human beings.

The psychology of adaptation began in England, where the modern theory of evolution was born. However, it found more fertile ground in one of Britain's former colonies: the United States. There it became the only psychology; and, as the United States came to dominate psychology, so did the psychology of adaptation.

PSYCHOLOGY IN THE
NEW WORLD

Background

General Intellectual and Social Environment

America was new. Its original inhabitants were seen as savages, noble or brutish, who revealed original human nature untouched by civilization. The first settlers confidently expected to displace the Indians, replacing their primitive state with farms, villages, and churches. The wilderness found by the settlers opened up possibilities of erecting a new civilization in the new world. The Puritans came to establish a "city on a hill," a perfect Christian society and example to be looked up to by the rest of the world. In America there was no feudal hierarchy, no established church, no ancient universities. Instead, each person could make his or her own way in the wilderness.

This is not to say that the European settlers brought no intellectual baggage. They did, and two traditions are particularly important: evangelical religion and Enlightenment philosophy. America was initially settled by Protestants, not Catholics. In fact, when Catholics first came to America in large numbers they were forced to remain outside the maninstream of American life. Catholics were seen as agents of a dangerous foreign power, the pope, and anti-Catholic riots and the burning of Catholic churches were not unknown in nineteenth-century America. What emerged most strongly from the dominant American Protestantism was evangelical Christianity. This form of Christianity has little or no theological content, looking instead to the salvation of the individual soul in an emotional conversion experience when the person accepts the will of God.

An important part of the European reaction to the excessive geometric spirit of the Enlightenment was romanticism. In America, however, the reaction against the Age of Reason was religious. America experienced revivals in the colonial period, and another took place shortly after the French Revolution. Romanticism touched America only briefly, in the transcendental movement. Henry David Thoreau, for example, decried industry's encroachment on romantic nature. However, more important for most people was evangelical Christianity, which rejected the anti-religious skepticism of the Enlightenment.

It is no accident that many early American psychologists, including John B. Watson, the founder of behaviorism, were early intended for the church. The stock in trade of the evangelical preacher is conversion, playing on an audience's emotions to change people from sinners to saints, modifying both soul and behavior. The goal of many American psychologists in both the functional and behavioal periods has been to modify behavior, to make the person of today into the new person of tomorrow. The evangelical preachers wrote about the ways to change souls through preaching; the psychologists wrote about the ways to change behavior through conditioning.

The importance of evangelical Christianity in the developing intellectual life of the United States should not be underestimated. America's tradition of freedom of religion may suggest that the founders did not care especially about religion. The contrary is true. Freedom of religion came into existence because of the demands of evangelical sects afraid of the power of established churches. Evangelical Christianity acted as a filter for Enlightenment thought, keeping out the radical skepticism and antireligious attitudes of the late Englitenment that were unacceptable to most Americans.

In the period before 1800 America did possess some genuine philosophes. There was Benjamin Franklin, whose experiments on electricity were admired in Europe, who charmed France as the "natural man" of the new world, and who was enshrined as one of the leading figures of the Enlightenment, ranking even with Voltaire. Thomas Jefferson, another philosophe, is perhaps the best example of the geometric spirit in America. Jefferson attempted to apply numerical calculation to every subject from crop rotation to human happiness. His Newtonian mechanism even blinded him to biological facts: Arguing against the possiblity of Noah's flood, he "proved" from physical calculations that in any flood the waters cannot rise more than about fifty feet above sea level, and that consequently the fossil sea shells found in the American Appalachian mountains were just unusual rock growths (Wills 1978). Jefferson, who was skeptical of the claims of Christianity, was probably a Voltairian deist.

Ideas such as these were anathema to evangelical religion, however, and only certain moderate elements of Enlightenment thought became important in America. Foremost among these acceptable ideas were those of the Scottish Enlightenment, which in fact exerted more influence in Jefferson than is commonly supposed. As we have seen, Reid's common-sense philosophy was perfectly compatible with religion. In America's religious colleges, which were the vast majority of American colleges, Scottish philosophy became the established curriculum, dominating every aspect of higher education from ethics to psychology. Scottish philosophy became the established curriculum, dominating every aspect of higher education from ethics to psychology. Scottish philosophy was American orthodoxy.

In considering the intellectual climate of the United States, to the influences of evangelical Christianity and a moderate Enlightenment must be added a third element, business, which interacted with the other two in important ways. America came to be a nation of business unlike any other nation on earth. There was no feudal aristocracy, no established church, and only a distant king. What remained was individual enterprise, and the individual's struggle to survive in confrontation with the wilderness and in competition with other businessmen. The business of America was indeed business.

Out of this unique American mix of ideas, combined with a growing national chauvinism, several important ideas emerged. One was the supreme value placed on useful knowledge. The Enlightenment certainly held that knowledge should serve human needs, should be practical rather than metaphysical. American Protestants came to think of inventions as glorifying the ingenuity of God in creating the clever human mind. *Technology* was an American word. An unfortunate consequence of this attitude was anti-intellectualism. Abstract science was scorned as something European and degenerate. What counted was practical accomplishment that at once enriched the businessman, revealed God's principles, and advanced the American dream. The businessman valued the same hard-headed "common sense" taught in the colleges. Common-sense philosophy told the ordinary person that his or her untutored ideas were basically right, which tended to increase American anti-intellectualism.

In "businessman" the word *man* ought to be stressed. It was the men who struggled for survival in the world of business and who valued clearheaded common sense and practical achievement. Feeling and sentiment were the special province of women, who in the nineteenth century were increasingly removed from the world of work, as such formerly domestic activities as baking, brewing, cheese making, spinning, and weaving became industrialized. This change left women with little economic importance, leaving only the realm of the emotions to female rule. In America emotions were not romantically inspiring, but were instead taken to be feminine and weak.

Americans also tended to be radical environmentalists, greatly preferring to believe that peoples' circumstances, not their genes, were the primary cause of human characteristics and achievements. They believed that, contrary to the prejudices of Europeans, the American environment was the best in the world and would produce geniuses to surpass Newton. This belief reflects the empiricism of the Enlightenment and the flexible beliefs of the businessman. There would be no bounds on the perfectibility of humans in the new world, no bounds on the achievement of the free individual. Progress was the order of the day. There was even a cult of self-improvement from the early days of the American republic. In the 1830s there was a monthly magazine called *The Cultivator,* "designed to improve the soil and the mind." Not only could a man improve his farm business, but he could improve his mind as well. In fact, it was expected that the good Christian would be a successful businessman or farmer.

All these attitudes—religious, Enlightened, and commercial—are nicely epitomized in the American attitude to the machine: the product of human ingenuity, improver of the world, and enricher of its maker. The builder of a machine became Newton's God, and the machine was made divine by association with the celestial mechanism. A writer named John Pendleton Kennedy visited an early American factory and recorded his reactions (Miller 1965):

> When I look upon this vast enginery, this infinite complication of wheels, this exquisitely delicate adjustment of parts, and this sure, steady and invariable result shown in the operation of the perfect machine . . . I am lost in admiration of the genius that masters the whole.

One observer of the early American scene recognized these American trends. Alexis de Tocqueville wrote in *Democracy in America* following his visit to America during 1831 and 1832: "The longer a nation is democratic, enlightened and free, the greater will be the number of these interested promoters of scientific genius, and the more will discoveries immediately applicable to productive industry confer gain, fame and even power." However, Tocqueville worried that "in a community thus organized . . . the human mind may be led insensibly to the neglect of theory." Aristocracies, on the other hand, "facilitate the natural impulse of the highest regions of thought." Tocqueville foresaw well. American psychology since its founding has neglected theory, even being openly hostile to theory at times. While Europeans such as Jean Piaget construct grand, almost metaphysical theories, B. F. Skinner argues that theories of learning are unnecessary.

Pre-Darwinian Background in Philosophical Psychology

The Puritans brought medieval faculty psychology with them to America. It perished in the early eighteenth century, however, when America's first great philosopher, Jonathan Edwards (1703–1758), read Locke. His enthusiasm for empiricism was such that his genius carried him independently in the direction of Berkeley and Hume. Like Berkeley, he denied the distinction between primary and secondary qualities and concluded that the mind knows only its perceptions, not the external world. Like Hume, he expanded the role of associations in the operation of the mind, finding as Hume had that contiguity, resemblance, and cause and effect are the laws of association (Jones 1958). Finally, like Hume, he was driven toward skepticism through his recognition that generalizations about cause cannot be rationally justified, and that emotion, not reason, is the true spring of human action (Blight 1978). Edwards, however, remained a Christian, as Hume did not, and he may be regarded as more medieval than modern in this respect (Gay 1969).

Edwards's stress on emotion as the basis of religious conversion helped pave the way for the American form of romanticism and idealism: transcendentalism. Transcendentalism was a New England revolt against what had become a comfortable, stuffy, and dry form of Puritanism. The transcendentalists wanted to return to the lively, emotional religion of Edwards's time, and to the direct, passionate encounter with God that Edwards had believed in. Such an attitude was compatible with both romanticism and post-Kantian idealism. The former prized individual feeling and communion with nature, similar to Thoreau's report of an extended, solitary sojourn in the wilderness in *Walden*. The latter believed Kant's transcendent noumena were knowable; similarly, George Ripley, a leading transcendentalist, wrote in *A Letter Addressed to the Congressional Church in Purchase Street*. that they "believe in an order of truths which transcend the sphere of the external senses" (White 1972). Thus, in some respects, transcendentalism was in tune with European romanticism and idealism.

In other respects, however, transcendentalism appears very American. It supported, for example, an evangelical, emotional Christianity that put the individual's feelings and conscience above hierarchical authority. Ralph Waldo Emerson preached "self-reliance," always an American ideal. He derided the radical empiricists as "negative and poisonous." Whether European or American in tone, however, transcendentalism's effect on mainstream American thought was limited. Like romanticism, its chief products were artistic rather than philosophical, and even its great art, such as Melville's *Moby Dick,* was much less popular than other works totally forgotten today. The American intellectual establishment of the colleges viewed transcendentalism, Kant, and idealism with horror, so that budding scientists and philosophers had little contact with the movement.

Instead of any romantic revolt, Scottish common-sense philosophy maintained its grip on American thought. Americans, too, began to produce faculty psychology texts at an accelerating rate as the nineteenth century progressed. There were at least two attempts to integrate German and American psychology. Frederick Rauch (1806–1841) tried to Americanize Hegel in his *Psychology* (1841), only the second book to use *psychology* in its title. The theologian Laurens Perseus Hickock (1798–1888) followed both Wolff and Kant, writing a *Rational Psychology* (c. 1848) and an *Empirical Psychology* (1882). Both reveal the American tendency to make psychology serve religion by "improving" the mind. Rauch concluded his text with a discussion of religion, while Hickock appealed to Christian faith as the source of the noumenal knowledge that Kant thought unattainable. Scottish faculty psychology was so well entrenched, however, that it either overrode or assimilated outside influences.

Academic faculty psychology in America did not add anything original to European faculty psychology. The Americans simply used the Europeans' ideas to improve and indoctrinate students into proper American and religious ways of thinking. More revealing of the American temperament is the popularity of phrenology, or popular faculty psychology. Phrenology enjoyed some popularity in Europe, especially in England; but in America, where it was put on a sound business basis and decked out in the trappings of vaudeville, it became a mania.

Early in the nineteenth century Gall's colleague Spurzheim started on a triumphal tour of the United States, whose rigors took his life after only a few weeks. Spurzheim was followed by the British phrenologist George Combe, who was well received by educators and college presidents. These lectures were too theoretical for American audiences, however, and phrenology fell into the hands of two industrious and businesslike brothers, Orson and Lorenzo Fowler. They minimized the scientific content of phrenology and maximized the practical applications. They set up an office in New York where clients could have their characters read for a fee. They wrote endlessly of the benefits of phrenology and published a phrenological journal that endured from the 1840s to 1911. They traveled around the country, concentrating on the frontiers, giving lectures and challenging skeptics. Like the great magician Houdini, they accepted any kind of test of their abilities, including blindfolded examinations of volunteers' skulls.

What made the Fowler's phrenology so popular was its appeal to the American character. It eschewed metaphysics for practical application. It pretended to tell employers what people to hire and to tell men which wives to take. It was thus the first mental testing movement in America and was Galtonian in its scrutiny of individual differences. Furthermore, it was progressive and reformist. Gall had believed the brain's faculties to be set by heredity. The Fowlers, however, said that weak faculties could be improved by practice and overly strong ones controlled by efforts of will. Many people sought out the Fowlers for advice on how to lead their lives; the Fowlers were the first guidance counselors. They also held out the hope that the nation and the world could be improved if only every person would be "phrenologized." Finally, the Fowlers believed they served religion and morality. They encouraged their clients to improve their moral faculties and believed that the existence of the faculty of veneration demonstrated the existence of God, because the existence of the faculty implies the existence of its object.

Mesmeric magnetism also flourished in America, and spiritualism began there as well. On his tour of America in the 1840s George Combe reported that mediums ran a flourishing business in New York. in the early twentieth century spirtualism was so widespread that both *Scientific American* and the United States Congress appointed committees to investigate the claims of spiritualism. Animal magnetism arrived in the United States as a music hall turn and then was assimilated to phrenology in phrenomagnetism, which joined phrenology in the business of selling advice. No one could better look out for Number One than the possessor of *Instantaneous Personal Magnetism,* a system that included diets and physical exercises to build the "magnetic mind" capable of outstanding business success.

America's Native Philosophy: Pragmatism

In 1871 and 1872 a group of young, Harvard-educated, well-to-do Bostonians—"the very topmost cream of Boston manhood," William James called them—met as the Metaphysical Club to discuss philosophy in the age of Darwin. Among the members of the club were Oliver Wendell Holmes, destined to become perhaps the United States' most distinguished jurist; and, more important for the history of psychology, Chauncey Wright (1830–1875), Charles S. Peirce (1839–1914), and William James (1842–1910). All three were important to the founding of psychology in America. Wright articulated an early stimulus-response theory of behavior, Peirce carried out the first psychological experiments in the new world, and James laid the foundations of American psychology with his book *Principles of Psychology* (1890). The immediate fruit of the Metaphysical Club was America's only homegrown philosophy, pragmatism, a hybrid of Bain, Darwin, and Kant. The club opposed the regnant Scottish philosophy, dualistic and closely connected to religion and creationism, and proposed a new naturalistic theory of mind.

From Bain they took the idea that beliefs were dispositions to behave; Bain defined belief as "that upon which a man is prepared to act." From Darwin they, like most intellectuals of the day, learned to treat mind as part of nature, not a gift from God. More important—this was Wright's contribution—they took the survival of the fittest as a model by which to understand mind. Wright combined Bain's definition with Darwin's theory of natural selection, and proposed that a person's beliefs evolve just as species do. As one matures, one's beliefs compete for acceptance, so that adequate beliefs emerge "from the survival of the fittest among our original . . . beliefs." This is the essential idea of the individual approach to the psychology of adaptation—and, if we substitute "behaviors" for "beliefs," it states the central thesis of B. F. Skinner's radical behaviorism. Wright also tried to show how self-consciousness, far from being a mystery to naturalism, evolved from sensorimotor habits. A habit, Wright held, was a relation between a class of stimuli and some response or responses. The cognition needed to link stimulus and response was rudimentary, involving recalled images of past experiences. Self-consciousness arose when one—or people, as compared with the animals—became aware of the connection between stimulus and response. Wright's ideas go a long way to making mind part of nature, and point to the behavioral emphasis of American psychology, in which beliefs are important only insofar as they produce behavior.

Charles S. Peirce summed up the conclusions of the Metaphysical Club, and in so doing invented pragmatism. Kant had, as a foundational philosopher, sought the foundation of certain knowledge. Nevertheless, he recognized that men and women must act upon beliefs that are not certain; a physician, for example, may not be absolutely certain of a diagnosis, but must nevertheless proceed believing the diagnosis is correct. Kant called "such contingent belief which still forms the basis of the actual use of means for the attainment of certain ends, *pragmatic belief.*" The upshot of the meditations of the Metaphysical Club was that beliefs could never be certain. The best that humans could hope for were beliefs that led to successful action in the world, natural selection operating to strengthen certain beliefs and weaken others as beliefs struggled for acceptance. Darwin had shown that species were not fixed, and the Metaphysical Club concluded that truth, contrary to Kant, could not be fixed either. All that remained to epistemology, then, was Kant's pragmatic belief, which Peirce refined into "the pragmatic maxim," reflecting the conclusions of the club.

In 1878 Peirce published these conclusions in a paper, "How to make our ideas clear," first read to the Metaphysical Club at the end of its life. Peirce (1878/1966) wrote that "the whole function of thought is to produce habits of action", and that what we call beliefs are "a rule of action, or, say for short, a *habit.*" "The essence of belief," Peirce argued, "is the establishment of a habit, and different beliefs are distinguished by the different modes of action to which they give rise." Habits must have a practical significance if they are to be meaningful, Peirce went on. "Now the identity of a habit depends on how it might lead us to act. . . . Thus we come down to what is tangible and conceivably practical as the root of every real distinction of thought . . . there is no distinction so fine as to consist in anything but a possible difference in practice." In conclusion, "the rule for attaining [clear ideas] is as follows: consider what effects, which might conceivably have practical bearings, we conceive the object of our conceptions to have. Then, our conception of these effects is the whole of our conception of the object." Or, as Peirce put it more succinctly in 1905, the truth of a belief "lies exclusively in its conceivable bearing upon the conduct of life."

Peirce's pragmatic maxim is revolutionary, because it abandons the old Platonic aim of a foundational philosophy. It admits with Heraclitus that nothing can ever be certain, and draws from Darwin the idea that the best beliefs are those that work in adapting us to our changing environment. The pragmatic maxim is also consistent with scientific practice. Peirce had been a working physicist, and learned that a scientific concept was useless and meaningless if it could not be translated into some observable phenomenon; thus Peirce's pragmatic maxim anticipates the positivist concept of operational definition. Later, when William James allowed emotional and ethical considerations to weigh in deciding whether a belief works, Peirce, the hardheaded physicist, refused to go along. In psychology, pragmatism represents a clear articulation of the individual question approach to the psychology of adaptation. It takes, as B. F. Skinner later would, Darwin's account of species' evolution as a model by which to understand individual learning. The pragmatic maxim also anticipates the behavioral turn in American psychology, because it says that beliefs are always (if meaningful) manifested in behavior, so that reflection upon consciousness for its own sake is idle.

While Peirce never became a psychologist, he did aid its development in the United States. He read some of Wundt's researches in 1862, and campaigned against the continued reign of Scottish common-sense psychology and for the establishment of experimental psychology in U.S. universities. In 1877 he published a psychophysical study of color, the first experimental work to come from America. A student of his, Joseph Jastrow, became one of the leading American psychologists in the first part of the twentieth century, and a president of the American Psychological Association. In 1887 Peirce asked the central question of modern cognitive science: Can a machine think like a human being? Despite all this, his influence remained remarkably limited. He was an extraordinarily difficult man to get along with. Despite the best efforts of William James, he never could hold a permanent position at Harvard, and lived most of his life as a near penniless recluse. He wrote badly, and most of his papers were not published during his lifetime. Pragmatism's great influence on philosophy and psychology came from his associate, William James.

James began to work out his own version of pragmatism in the 1870s and 1880s. At first he advanced his philosophy timidly, as psychology rather than philosophy. In 1878 he contracted with the publisher Henry Holt to write a textbook on psychology; and during the 1880s James published a series of articles that formed the core of his new psychology and philosophy, and were incorporated into the book *Principles of psychology*. Its publication in 1890 marks a watershed in the history of American psychology, for it inspired American students as neither the Scots nor Wundt could, and it set the tone for American psychology from 1890 to

1913. James combined the usual interests of a founding psychologist, physiology and philosophy. He began his academic career with an M.D. and held a variety of posts at Harvard. Beginning as an instructor of physiology, he next saw to the establishment for himself of a Chair in Psychology; he spent his last years as a professor of philosophy. It was in the *Principles* that James began to develop his pragmatic philosophy.

"Psychology is the Science of Mental Life," James told his readers. Its primary method is ordinary introspection, accompanied by the "diabolical cunning" of German experimentalism and by comparative studies of men, animals, and savages. James rejected sensationistic atomism, the billiard-ball theory also rejected by Wundt. According to James, this theory takes the discernable parts of objects to be enduring objects of experience, falsely chopping up the flow of experience. Wrote James: "Consciousness . . . does not appear to itself chopped up in bits. Such words as 'chain' or 'train' do not describe it fitly, as it presents itself in the first instance. It is nothing jointed; it flows. A 'river' or a 'stream' are the metaphors by which it is most naturally described. *In talking of it hereafter let us call it the stream of thought, of consciousness, or of subjective life.*"

In Darwinian fashion, James found that what consciousness contains is less important than what it does; it is function, not content, that counts. The primary function of consciousness is to choose. He wrote (1890): "*It is always interested more in one part of its object than in another, and welcomes and rejects, or chooses, all the while it thinks.*" Consciousness creates and serves the ends of the organism, the first of which is survival through adaptation to the environment. For James, however, adaptation is never passive. Consciousness chooses, acting always toward some end. The ceaseless flow of choices affects perception as well as conduct: "The mind, in short, works on the data it receives very much as a sculptor works on his block of stone." James's mind is not the passive blank slate of the sensationists. It is a "fighter for ends," actively engaged with a practical world of experience.

Although James said psychology is the Science of Mental Life, it must simultaneously be "cerebralist." It is a fundamental assumption that "the brain is the one immediate bodily condition of the mental operation," and the *Principles,* all 1,377 pages of it, is "more or less of a proof that the postulate is correct." James applies the cerebralist approach throughout his text, and intensifies it in his *Brief Course* (1892). He applauds Hartley's attempt to show that the laws of association are cerebral laws, "and so far as association stands for a *cause,* it is between *processes in the brain. . . .*"

This seems to involve James in a contradiction; the brain-machine must make choices. He has said that consciousness plays a positive role in human and animal life and explicitly rejected mechanism, or what he called the "automaton theory." For James an evolutionary naturalism demands consciousness. A dumb machine knows no direction, it is like "dice thrown forever on a table . . . what chance is there that the highest number will turn up oftener than the lowest?" James argued that consciousness increases the efficiency of the cerebral machine by "loading its dice." Wrote James (*Principles of Psychology*): "Loading its dice would bring constant pressure to bear in favor of *those* of its performances" that serve the "interests of the brain's owner." Consciousness transforms survival from "mere hypothesis" into an "imperative decree. Survival *shall* occur and therefore organs *must* so work. . . . Every actually existing consciousness seems to itself at any rate to be a *fighter for ends*. . . . Consciousness thus possesses survival value. Association may depend on cerebral laws, but our will can, through emphasis and reinforcement, direct chains of association to serve our interests, and their direction is "all that the most eager advocate of free will need demand," for by directing association it directs thinking, and hence action, wrote James.

Although James has here proclaimed the efficacy of consciousness and will, the central doctrine of the *Principles*, on which American psychologists built for thirty years, was the "motor theory of consciousness." James's famous theory of emotion, the James-Lange theory, aptly illustrates the motor theory. On common understanding, if I see a bear in the woods, I feel afraid, and as a consequence I run away. On James's motor account of consciousness, however, I see the bear, begin to run away, and then, finding myself fleeing, feel scared. More generally, James said that mental states have two sorts of bodily effects. First, unless some inhibition is present, the thought of an act automatically leads to the execution of the act. Second, mental states cause internal bodily changes, including covert motor responses, changes in heart rate, glandular secretions, and perhaps "processes more subtle still." Therefore, James argued, "it will be safe to lay down the general law that *no mental modifaction ever occurs which is not accompanied or followed by a bodily change.*" The contents of consciousness are thus determined not only by sensations coming in from outside, but by kinesthetic feedback (as we call it today) from the body's motor activity. "Our psychology must therefore take account not only of the conditions antecedent to mental states, but of their resultant consequences as well. . . . The whole neural organism [is] . . . but a machine for converting stimuli into reactions; and the intellectual part of our life is knit up with but the middle or 'central' part of the machine's operations."

James found himself caught in the same dilemma felt by Diderot and other philosophes, between the heart's feeling of freedom and the intellect's scientific declaration of determinism. James was deeply committed to free will from personal experience. As a young man he pulled himself out of a black depression by literally willing himself to live again, and, dogged by depression his whole life, made human will the center of his philosophy. However, in his psychology, committed to cerebralism, he found himself almost forced to accept determinism as the only scientifically acceptable view of behavior. He stoutly resisted the conclusion, denouncing mechanistic conceptions of human conduct and, as we have seen, proclaiming that consciousness decreed survival and commanded the body. After writing *Principles*, James abandoned psychology for philosophy, and developed his own brand of pragmatism. There he tried to resolve the struggle between the head and the heart by setting the feelings of the heart on an equal footing with the cognitions of the head. Nevertheless, the conflict remained, and the influence of *Principles* was to lead American psychologists away from consciousness and toward behavior, and so away from James's own definition of psychology as the science of mental life.

The New Psychology

In the United States experimental psychology was called the "new psychology," to distinguish it from the "old psychology" of the Scottish common-sense realists. The great majority of American colleges were controlled by Protestant denominations, and in the 1820s the Scottish system was installed as a safeguard against what religious leaders took to be the skeptical and atheistic tendencies of British empiricism as described by Reid. The works of Locke, Berkeley, and

Hume—and, later, the German idealists—were banished from the classroom and replaced with texts by Reid, Dugald Stewart, or their American followers. Common-sense psychology was taught as a pillar of religion and Christian behavior. For the American followers of the Scots, psychology "is the science of the soul," and its method, ordinary introspection, reveals "the soul as an emanation from the Divine, and as made in the image of God" (Dunton, 1895). "Mental science, or psychology, will therefore, be [foundational] for moral science. . . . The province of psychology will . . . be to show what the faculties are; that of moral philosophy to show how they should be used for the attainment of their end" (Mark Hopkins 1870, quoted by Evans 1984). Unsurprisingly, with few exceptions adherents of the old psychology looked askance at the new psychology which brought the mind into a laboratory and investigated the connection of mental states to nervous processes.

Nevertheless, as higher education became more secular after the Civil War, the intellectual tide turned in favor of the naturalism of the New Psychology. In 1875 William James established an informal psychological laboratory at Harvard in connection with a graduate course in the department of natural history called "The relations between physiology and psychology." In 1887 he began to offer a course called "Psychology" in the philosophy department; and in 1885 he obtained recognition and funds from Harvard for his laboratory, establishing the first official psychology laboratory in America (Cadwallader 1980). At Yale the old psychology of the president, Noah Porter, yielded to George Trumball Ladd (1842–1921) who, though a Congregationalist minister and a psychological conservative, respected Wundt's experimental psychology, incorporating it into an influential text, *Elements of physiological psychology* (1887). At Princeton the president, James McCosh, was a staunch Scot, but recognized that "the tendency of the day is certainly towards physiology" (Evans 1984) and taught Wundt's psychology to his students.

Harvard minted its first Ph.D. philosopher in 1878, G. Stanley Hall (1842–1924). A student of James's Hall was really a psychologist. He went to Johns Hopkins University—the United States' first graduate university—where he established a laboratory and a series of courses in the new psychology. Hall's psychology went well beyond Wundt, however, including, in typically American eclectic fashion, experimental studies of the higher mental processes, anthropology, and abnormal psychology, or "morbid phenomena." Hall also vigorously pursued developmental psychology, launched the child study movement, and coined the term "adolescence." Hall led the institutionalization of American psychology, starting the *American Journal of Psychology* in 1887, and organizing the founding of the American Psychological Association in 1892. One of Hall's students was James McKeen Cattell (1860–1944), who later studied with Wundt, and returned to the United States to establish laboratories at the University of Pennsylvania (1887) and Columbia University (1891).

As historians have often pointed out, however, while Americans got the methods of experimental psychology from Wundt, their ideas and theories came from elsewhere. When Cattell was in Leipzig, he proposed to study individual differences in reaction time, but Wundt disapprovingly called the subject "*ganz Amerikanisch*" (completely American). After Leipzig, Cattell studied with Francis Galton, and E. G. Boring (1950) explains American psychologists' departure from Wundtian ideals by saying "the apparatus was Wundt's, but the inspiration was Galton's." Rand Evans (1984) locates the source of American inspiration in the continuing influence of Scottish psychology. The Scots had always emphasized mind in use, mental activity, more than mental content. Their faculty psychology was, like Aristotle's, implicitly a psychology of function. And as Aristotle's was a biological psychology, the Scot's psychology of mental function, despite its religious connection, was ultimately compatible with modern Darwinian biology, as McCosh himself saw. Experiment was new in American psychology, but American psychologists have retained to the present day the Scots' concern with mental activity and with making psychology servicable to society and the individual.

CONCLUSION: PERCEPTION AND THINKING ARE ONLY THERE FOR BEHAVIOR'S SAKE

By 1892 psychology in America was well launched. In Europe, scientific psychology was making slow headway even in Germany, the country of its birth. In the United States, by contrast, psychology expanded rapidly. In 1892 there were fourteen laboratories, including one as far west as Kansas. Half of them had been founded independently of philosophy or any other discipline. Psychology would soon be what it largely remains, an American science.

But psychology in America would not be the traditional psychology of consciousness. Once psychology met evolution, the tendency to study behavior instead of consciousness became overwhelming. Traditionally, philosophers had been concerned with human knowledge, with how we form ideas and how we know they are true or false. Action resulting from ideas formed only a tiny part of their concern. However, in a biological, evolutionary context, ideas matter only if they lead to effective action. The Metaphysical Club realized this, and created the pragmatic maxim. The struggle for existence is won by successful action, and any organism "sicklied o'er with the pale cast of thought," no matter how profound, is doomed to failure. The essence of the psychology of adaptation was the idea that mind matters to evolution because it leads to successful action, and so is adaptive. As James said, "if it ever should happen that [thought] led to no active measures, it would fail of its essential function, and would have to be considered either pathological or abortive. The current of life which runs in at our eyes or ears is meant to run out at our hands, feet, or lips. . . . perception and thinking are only for behavior's sake" (Kuklick 1977).

The psychology of adaptation from Spencer to James remained nevertheless the science of mental life, not the science of behavior. However, much consciousness was tied up with behavior; no matter that it was merely a way station between stimulus and response, it was real and deserved serious study, because it was a vital way station. James said consciousness decreed survival, that it commanded the body to behave adaptively. Underneath the main current of mentalism, however, ran an undercurrent that headed toward the study of behavior instead of the study of consciousness, and in time the undercurrent became the main current, and finally a flood tide, virtually erasing the Science of Mental Life.

BIBLIOGRAPHY

Samuel Hynes, *The Edwardian turn of mind* (Princeton: Princeton University Press, 1968) provides a social history of turn-of-century Britain; he describes the impact of the Army's Physical Deterioration Report, treating it as the dividing point between the Victorian and post-Victorian eras. The changes in psychology during these years are discussed by Reba N. Soffer, *Ethics and society in England: The revolution in the social sciences 1870–1914* (Berkeley: University of California Press, 1978). Spencer's biographer is J. Peel *Herbert Spencer* (New York: Basic Books, 1971). Howard Gruber insightfully discusses *Darwin on man: A psychological study of scientific creativity,* 2d. ed. (Chicago: Chicago University Press, 1981). On Galton see F. Forest, *Francis Galton* (New York: Taplinger, 1974). For Galton and British eugenics see Ruth Schwartz Cowan, "Nature and nurture: The interplay of biology and politics in the work of Francis Galton," in W. Coleman and C. Limoges, eds., *Studies in the History of Biology* vol. 1, 133–208 (Baltimore: Johns Hopkins University Press, 1977); Robert C. Bannister, *Social Darwinism: Science and myth in Anglo-American social thought* (Philadelphia: Temple University Press, 1979); and Daniel Kevles, *In the name of eugenics: Genetics and the uses of human heredity* (New York: Knopf, 1985). Greta Jones, *Social Darwinism in English thought: The interaction between biological and social theory* (Sussex, England: The Harvester Press, 1980) discusses both social Darwinism and eugenics during the period. In addition to the cited work an important book by Romanes is *Mental evolution in man* (New York: D. Appleton, 1889); the only biography of Romanes is Ethel Romanes, *The life and letters of George John Romanes* (New York: Longmans, Green & Co., 1898), but Frank Miller Turner, "George John Romanes, From faith to faith," in Turner, *Between science and religion: The reaction to scientific naturalism in late Victorian England* (New Haven: Yale University Press, 1974), provides a fine short discussion of Romanes, focusing on his part in the Victorian crisis of conscience. Morgan's major work is *An introduction to comparative psychology* (London: Walter Scott, 1894).

For a comprehensive treatment of American life in the years before 1890, see Bernard Bailyn, "Shaping the Republic to 1760," Gordon S. Wood, "Framing the Republic 1760–1820," David Brion Davis, "Expanding the Republic 1820–1860," and David Herbert Donald, "Uniting the Republic 1860–1890," in B. Bailyn, D. B. Davis, D. H. Donald, J. L. Thomas, R. H. Wiebe, and G. S. Wood *The great Republic: A history of the American people* (Boston: Little, Brown, 1977). Daniel Boorstin concentrates on intellectual and social history during the same years in *The Americans: The colonial experience* (New York: Vintage, 1958) and *The Americans: The national experience* (New York: Vintage, 1965); both are wonderfully readable and exciting books. The best book on the American character is still Tocqueville (1969); reporter Richard Reeves, *In search of America* (New York: Simon & Schuster, 1982) retraced Tocqueville's itinerary, and his insights do not surpass Tocqueville's. A valuable general intellectual history of thought in the United States is Morton White, *Science and sentiment in America: Philosophical thought from Jonathan Edwards to John Dewey* (New York: Oxford University Press, 1972). Intellectual life in the early colonial and postrevolutionary periods is discussed by Henry Steele Commager, *The empire of reason: How Europe imagined and America realized the Enlightenment* (Garden City, New York: Doubleday, 1978); Henry May, *The Enlightenment in America* (New York: Oxford University Press, 1976); and Perry Miller, *Errand into the wilderness* (New York: Harper & Row, 1956).

For specific relevant movements of the nineteenth century, see A. Douglas, *The feminization of American culture* (New York: Knopf, 1977); Richard Hofstadter, *Anti-intellectualism in American life* (New York: Vintage, 1962); and R. B. Nye, *Society and culture in America 1830–1860* (New York: Harper & Row, 1974); and for American phrenology see Thomas H. and Grace E. Leahey, *Psychology's occult doubles* (Chicago: Nelson-Hall, 1983). For American philosophy see A. L. Jones, *Early American philosophers* (New York: Ungar, 1958); Herbert W. Schneider, *History of American philosophy* (New York: Columbia University Press, 1963); and, especially for the post-Civil War period, Kuklick, from which all quotes in the Metaphysical Club section are drawn, unless otherwise indicated. The standard biography of Jonathan Edwards is Perry Miller, *Jonathan Edwards* (New York: Meridian, 1959). On Wright see Edward H. Madden, "Chauncy Wright's functionalism," *Journal of the History of the Behavior Sciences,* (1974 *10*: 281–290). For the early philosophy of pragmatism and its influences, see Philip P. Wiener, *Evolution and the founders of pragmatism* (Cambridge: Harvard University Press, 1949); J. K. Feibleman, *An introduction* to the philosophy of Charles S. Peirce (Cambridge: MIT Press, 1946); and Thomas S. Knight, *Charles Peirce* (New York: Twayne, 1965). For Peirce as psychologist see Thomas Cadwallader, Charles S. Peirce: The first American experimental psychologist," *Journal of the History of the Behavioral Sciences* (1974, *10:* 191–198). The standard biography of William James is Ralph Barton Perry, *The thought and character of William James,* 2 vols. (Boston: Little, Brown, 1935); Perry's biography, while still the standard, suffers somewhat from Perry's attempt to make James into a realist like himself. A recent biography is Gay Wilson Allen, *William James* (Minneapolis: University of Minnesota Press, 1970). For James's lasting influence, see Don S. Browning, *Pluralism and personality: William James and some contemporary cultures of psychology* (Lewisburg, Pennsylvania: Bucknell University Press, 1980).

The only comprehensive source for the establishment of American psychology is Evans (1984); related is R. Dolby, "The transmission of two new scientific disciplines from Europe to North America in the late nineteenth century," *Annals of Science* (1977, *34:* 287–310). For psychology before the new psychology see J. W. Fay, *American psychology before William James* (New York: Octagon Books, 1966); J. R. Fulcher, "Puritans and the passions: The faculty psychology in American Puritanism," *Journal of the History of the Behavioral Sciences* (1973, *9:* 123–139) and E. Harms, "America's first major psychologist: Laurens Perseus Hickock," *Journal of the History of the Behavioral Sciences* (1972, *8:* 120–123). Two overlapping collections edited by Robert W. Rieber and Kurt Salzinger treat American psychology primarily in the Old and New periods, but also after: *The roots of American psychology: Historical influences and implications for the future* (New York: New York Academy of Sciences, *Annals of the New York Academy of Sciences* vol. 291, 1977), and *Psychology: Theoretical-historical perspectives* (New York: Academic, 1980). Josef Brozek, ed., *Explorations in the history of psychology in the United States* (Lewisburg, Pennsylvania: Bucknell University Press, 1984) contains articles on both the old and the new psychologies. On the early psychologists mentioned in the text: Eugene S. Miller, *G. T. Ladd: Pioneer american psychologist* (Cleveland: Press of Case Western Reserve University, 1969); Dorothy Ross *G. Stanley Hall: Psychologist as prophet* (Chicago: University of Chicago Press, 1972); Michael Sokal has spent his career writing about James McKeen Cattell, and expects to publish a biography shortly. Meanwhile, two works by Sokal may be consulted among his many: "The unpublished autobiography of James McKeen Cattell," *American Psychologist* (1971, *26:* 626–635) and *An education in psychology: James McKeen Cattell's journal and letters from Germany and England, 1880–1888* (Cambridge: MIT Press, 1980).

One of the landmark articles in the introduction of the new psycholology to the United States is John Dewey, "The new psychology," *Andover Review* (1884, *2:* 278–289); the background and influence of the piece is discussed in Morton White, *The origin of Dewey's instrumentalism* (New York: Octagon Books, 1964). Two other contemporary or near-contemporary articles are useful for the history of the early laboratories in the United States: Anonymous, "Psychology in American universities," *American Journal of Psychology* (1892, *3:* 275–286); and Christian A. Ruckmich "The history and status of psychology in the United States," *American Journal of Psychology* (1912, *23:* 517–531). J. Mark Baldwin provides a more general account, with more background, in his "Sketch of the history of psychology," *Psychological Review* (1905, *12:* 144–165).

REFERENCES

Bartlett, F. C. (1932) *Remembering*. Cambridge, England: Cambridge University Press.
Blight, J. G. (1978) The position of Jonathan Edwards in the history of psychology. Paper presented at the annual meeting of the American Psychological Association, Toronto, Ontario, September 1.

Boring, E. G. (1950) *A history of experimental psychology.* Englewood Cliffs, New Jersey: Prentice-Hall.

Cadwallader, T. C. (1980) William James' Harvard psychology laboratory reconsidered. Paper presented at the annual meeting of the American Psychological Association, Montreal, Canada, September.

Darwin, C. (1896) *The descent of man and selection in relation to sex.* New York: Appleton & Co.

Darwin, C. (1965). *The expression of emotion in man and animals.* Chicago: Chicago University Press.

Dunton, L. (1895) The old psychology and the new. In L. Dunton, H. Münsterberg, W. T. Harris, and G. Stanley Hall. *The old psychology and the new: Addresses before the Massachusetts Schoolmaster's Club, April 27, 1895.* Boston: New England Publishing Co.

Emerson, R. W. (1950) *Selected prose and poetry.* New York: Holt, Rinehart & Winston.

Evans, R. (1984) The origins of American academic psychology. In J. Brozek, ed. *Explorations in the history of psychology in the United States.* Lewisburg, Pennsylvania: Bucknell University Press.

Galton, F. (1907) *Inquiries into the human faculty and its development.* London: J. M. Dent.

Galton, F. (1925) *Hereditary genius.* London: Macmillian.

Gay, P. (1969) The obsolete Puritanism of Jonathan Edwards. Reprinted in J. Opie, ed. *Jonathan Edwards and the Enlightenment.* Lexington, Massachusetts: D. C. Heath.

Hofstadter, R. (1955) *Social Darwinism in American thought,* rev. ed. Boston: Beacon.

Hopkins, M. (1870) *Lectures on moral science.* Boston: Gould & Lincoln.

James, W. (1890) *Principles of psychology.* 2 vols. New York: Dove.

Jones, A. L. (1958) *Early American philosophers.* New York: Ungar.

Kuklick, B. (1977) *The rise of American philosophy: Cambridge, Massachusetts 1860–1930,* New Haven: Yale University Press.

Miller, P. (1965) *The life of the mind in America.* New York: Harcourt, Brace & World.

Morgan, C. L. (1886) On the study of animal intelligence. *Mind 11:* 174–185.

Murray, D. J. (1976) Research on memory in the nineteenth century. *Canadian Journal of Psychology, 30:* 201–220.

Peirce, C. S. (1878/1966) How to make our ideas clear. Partially reprinted in A. Rorty, ed. *Pragmatic Philosophy.* Garden City. New York: Anchor Books.

Peirce, C. S. (1887) Logical machines. *American Journal of Psychology 1:* 165–170.

Romanes, G. (1883) *Animal intelligence.* New York: Appleton & Co.

Spencer, H. (1897) *The principles of psychology.* 3d ed. New York: Appleton & Co.

Spencer, H. (1904) *An autobiography.* 2 vols. London: Williams & Norgate.

Spencer, H. (1945) *First principles.* London: Watts & Co.

Tocqueville, A. de (1969) *Democracy in America.* New York: Anchor.

White, L. (1972) *Science and sentiment in America.* London: Oxford University Press.

Wills, G. (1978) *Inventing America: Jefferson's Declaration of Independence.* Garden City, New York: Doubleday.

III

The Rise of Behavioralism

The founders of psychology took psychology to be the science of mental life. For Wundt and James psychology was the study of consciousness; for Freud it was the study of both consciousness and the unconscious. Scientific psychologists in the twentieth century, however, have little use for conscious experience and little tolerance for Freud's cauldron of the id; instead, they take psychology to be the study of behavior. How psychology was transformed from mentalism to behavioralism, and how behavioralism became entrenched, will occupy us in the next three chapters.

Part of the reason for psychologists' increasing interest in behavior and flagging interest in introspection was their desire to be practical and succeed in business, industry, government, and among other professional providers of services such as physicians and lawyers. During World War I psychologists established their social usefulness, and after the war psychologists became involved in applied activities and in such social issues as eugenics and remaking the family. The trend toward applied psychology nearly tore institutional psychology apart, but the demands of World War II reunited psychologists at least temporarily. In the chapters to come we will see how social forces helped shape psychology into a behavioral science and how psychologists in turn helped shape society.

On the scientific side, the major development of the years just before and then between the world wars was the articulation and development of behaviorism. Behaviorism is a movement that has been much misunderstood by historians of psychology, primarily because their thinking has been controlled by behaviorism's own myths of origin. Behaviorism is usually seen as a dramatic break with the past largely created by one man, John B. Watson; in fact, behaviorism was part of the larger trend toward behavioralism—defining psychology as the science of behavior—with roots in the 1890s. Behaviorism is similarly seen as a reasonably coherent movement, marked by theoretical disagreements to be sure but held together by shared assumptions about the nature of science and psychology; in fact, the disagreements among behaviorists are profound, so profound that in some cases they were invisible to the behaviorists themselves and have remained so to many historians.

10

The Conspiracy of Naturalism

From Consciousness to Behavior (1892–1912)

INTRODUCTION
>   Mentalism and Behavioralism
>   Psychology and Society
>   James and Pragmatism
BUILDING ON *THE PRINCIPLES:* THE MOTOR THEORY OF CONSCIOUSNESS (1892–1896)
>   Hugo Münsterberg and Action Theory
>   John Dewey and the Reflex Arc
FROM PHILOSOPHY TO BIOLOGY: FUNCTIONAL PSYCHOLOGY (1896–1910)
>   Experiments Become Functional
>   Functional Psychology Defined
>   From Undercurrent to Main Current
NEW DIRECTIONS IN ANIMAL PSYCHOLOGY (1898–1909)
>   From Anecdote to Experiment
>   The Problem of Animal Mind
RETHINKING MIND: THE CONSCIOUSNESS DEBATE (1904–1912)
>   Does Consciousness Exist? Radical Empiricism
>   The Relational Theory of Consciousness: Neo-Realism
>   The Functional Theory of Consciousness: Instrumentalism
CONCLUSION: BEHAVIORALISM DISCOVERED (1910–1912)

INTRODUCTION

In April 1913 the philosopher Warner Fite reviewed—anonymously, as was the custom at *The Nation*—three books on "The Science of Man." One was a text on genetics, but the other two were by psychologists: Hugo Münsterberg's *Psychology and Industrial Efficiency* and Maurice Parmellee's *The Science of Human Behavior*. Fite observed that psychology in 1913 seemed little concerned with consciousness; Münsterberg explicitly stated that the psychological "way of ordinary life, in which we try to understand our neighbor by entering into his mental functions . . . is not psychological analysis." Fite went on to conclude:

> Precisely. True "psychological analysis" ignores all personal experience of mentality. The science of psychology is, then, the finished result of what we may call the conspiracy of naturalism, in which each investigator has bound himself by a strange oath to obtain all his knowledge from observation of the actions of his fellows—"as a naturalist studies the chemical elements or the stars" [Münsterberg]—and never under any circumstances to conceive them in the light of his own experience of his living. Even the psychologist's "mental states" or "objects of consciousness" are only so many hypothetical entities read from without. . . . [W]hat is to be expected from a science of humanity which ignores all that is most distinctive of man?

Clearly, psychology had changed since we left it in 1897. Wundt and James had created a science of mental life, the study of consciousness as such; Freud used introspection and inference to enter his patients' minds, both conscious and unconscious. But by 1913 Fite found a psychology aimed at behavior, not consciousness, based on treating people as things, not as conscious agents.

In twenty years a new kind of psychology had arisen, which we will call *behavioralism*. While one might imagine that a scientific revolution had occurred, there was instead an inevitable, steady—if rapid—evolution of psychology from the science of consciousness to the science of behavior. To discuss these watershed decades we need some new terms to appreciate the major historical forces at work transforming mentalism into behavioralism.

Mentalism and Behavioralism

Traditionally (as in the first edition of this book), psychology is described as having changed from mentalism—the study of the mind—to behaviorism. However, "behaviorism" as it is usually used is becoming useless as a philosophical category and unworkable as a historical entity. While it has always been recognized that the various behaviorists disagreed on certain points, it has only recently been shown how many and how deep these disagreements were. As we shall see in the next chapter, it is futile to lump all of the usual behaviorists into one narrowly defined camp. Compounding this difficulty is the tendency nowadays to identify behaviorism with B. F. Skinner—and, worse, attributing to him a confused mishmash of his distinctive ideas mixed up with those of traditional 1930s behaviorists. A final motivation for redefining our usual terms is that the new and growing field of cognitive science shares many affinities with behaviorism; but simply calling it behaviorism without qualification would obscure its novel features and further distort the meaning of "behaviorism."

A new umbrella term, *behavioralism*, will denote the new psychology described by Fite. It contrasts with *mentalism*, defined in the old way as the science of consciousness as such, whose method was introspection or self-observation, augmented by objective measures of reaction times and certain other behaviors. The essential feature of mentalism is that it is aimed at studying *consciousness;* even when behavior, human or animal, is brought in, the aim is always to describe, explicate, or explain what happens in consciousness.

Behavioralism turns mentalism upside down. The behavioralist seeks to predict, control, explain, or model behavior, and to do so he may or may not refer to conscious or unconscious mental processes. Behavioralism is aimed at behavior; consciousness—the mind—is not the object of study, although it may be called upon to explain behavior.

Our present approach differs from an older distinction made by behaviorists and philosophers. Traditionally, two kinds of behaviorism have been distinguished, methodological behaviorism and metaphysical (or radical) behaviorism. Methodological behaviorists say that consciousness is not a fit subject for science, however real it may be; scientific *method* demands that scientists limit themselves to what is publicly observable—that is, behavior. Metaphysical behaviorists contend that mind is just a myth, to be banished from any proper understanding of the world, along with angels, demons, and spirits.

Although valuable in identifying the sorts of arguments actually made on behalf of a behavioral approach to psychology, these two categories obscure some important features of behavioralism. Methodological behaviorists refused to have anything to do with consciousness as hopelessly unscientific, but they nevertheless postulated intervening variables and hypothetical constructs: unobserved entities or processes within the organism supposed to produce behavior. Metaphysical behaviorists, on the other hand, although denying that the mind is real, nevertheless admit private, conscious events (toothaches, for example) to their science of behavior.

There is a more useful way to capture the difference between these two sets of "behaviorists." Some behavioralists, including methodological behaviorists and cognitive scientists, are willing to hypothesize the existence and functioning of largely unconscious faculties and processes as determiners of behavior. While a given theorist of this camp may or may not be willing to call these faculties and processes "mental," they are seen as internal, causal agencies that produce behavior. These behavioralists have little to say about consciousness. Other behavioralists are true *behaviorists,* unwilling to consider any nonobservable influence on behavior or to talk about any but manifest, observable behavior. However, any influence that is observed—even if to only one person, as with a toothache—may be legitimately invoked in explaining behavior.

Psychology and Society

It is appropriate to begin the history of modern psychology in 1892, because in that year the American Psychological Association (APA) was founded, largely due to the activities of G. Stanley Hall. Our attention from now on will be fixed on American psychology, for although Germany granted the earliest degrees in psychology, it was in America that psychology became a profession; the German equivalent of the APA was not founded until 1904 (Danziger 1979). For better or worse, and for sometimes extraneous reasons, modern psychology is essentially American psychology. American movements and theories have been adopted overseas—so much so that in 1980 a German text in social psychology was filled with American references and made no mention of Wundt or *Völkerpsychologie.*

Society today is so professionalized—even beauticians need a state license in many states—that we may overlook the impact of professionalization on the content and shape of a discipline. Until now we have happily called "psychologist" people whose aims, ideas, and circumstances were quite different: Plato and Freud; Aristotle and Descartes; Leibniz and Galton. But professionalization brings self-consciousness about the definition of a field and control over who may call himself or herself a member of it. To establish an organization such as the APA means to establish criteria for membership, to allow some to call themselves "psychologists," to forbid the name to others. The state is then induced to enforce the rules, issuing licenses to applicants who meet the criteria for "psychologist," and prosecuting those who falsely practice psychology.

The founding of the APA took place early in a period of important change in American life, in which the professionalization of academic and practical disciplines played a part. The years between 1890 and World War I are generally recognized as critical ones in U.S. history. America in the 1880s was, in Robert Wiebe's phrase, a nation of "island communities" scattered across the immense ocean of rural America. In these small, isolated communities people lived lives enclosed in a web of family relations and familiar neighbors; the world outside was psychologically distant and did not—indeed, could not—intrude very often. By 1920 all this had changed. The United States had become a nation-state, united by technology and forming a common culture.

Part of the change was urbanization. In 1880 only 25 percent of the population lived in cities; by 1900, 40 percent did so. The trend has continued apace until the last few years. A city is not an island community—it is a huge collection of strangers, especially when immigration—both from our own farms and abroad—every day brings new hundreds to the metropolis. Changing from farm or village-dweller to urban citizen effects psychological changes and demands new psychological skills.

Changing from island community to nation-state has, as Daniel Boorstin (1974) argues, deeply affected daily lives, widening personal horizons, narrowing the range of immediate experience, and introducing a constant flow of change with which people must keep up. The railroad could take the rural immigrant to the big city. It could also bring to farmers and villagers the products of the city: frozen meat and vegetables, canned food, and above all the wonders of the Ward's and Sears-Roebuck catalogues. Previously, most men and women lived out their lives in the small radius of a few hours walking. Now the train took them immense distances occasionally, and the trolley took them downtown every day to work and shop at the new department stores. All this freed people from what could be the stultifying confines of small-town life. It also homogenized experience. Today we can all watch the same television programs and news, buy the same brands of foods and clothes, and travel from coast to coast, staying in the same Holiday Inn motel room and eating the same McDonald's hamburger.

Psychology, as the study of people, has not been untouched by these events. As we move through this and future chapters we will see professional psychologists—no longer mere speculators about the mind—defining their job and role in society with respect to the new American scene. [As the twentieth century wears on, psychology will become deeply enmeshed in American life.]

The years 1892 to 1896, standing as they did at the beginning of the modern era, were especially chaotic and disquieting. The Panic of 1893 started a four-year depression of major proportions, bringing in its wake not only unemployment but riot and insurrection. The "Année terrible" of 1894 to 1895 witnessed 1,394 strikes and a march on Washington by Coxey's Army of unemployed, dispersed by troops and rumors of revolution. It all culminated in the crisis and election of 1896. One candidate, William Jennings Bryan, was the voice of Populism—and to established leaders he was also a leftist revolutionary, leader of "hideous and repulsive vipers." His opponent was William McKinley, a dull, solid, Republican. Far from being a Marxist, Bryan was really the voice of the rural, small-town, pietistic past, a preacher of religious morality. McKinley represented the immediate future: urban, pragmatic, the voice of big business and big labor. McKinley narrowly won and revolution was averted; reform, efficiency, and progress became the watchwords of the day. After 1896 psychology would participate strongly in all three noble goals.

Read against this background of chaos and crisis, professional discussions in the APA's early years appear parochial and tedious. Nevertheless, one important theme of the times does emerge—the last defenses of the old psychology against the new. For it was in these years that the new psychology finally overthrew the old.

Ladd—who had done much to introduce the new psychology to America— rejected what it was becoming. He rejected the physiological, natural science conception of psychology he found in James and defended spiritualistic dualism (Ladd 1892). In his APA presidential address he decried the replacement of introspection by experiment and objective measurement as "absurd" and pointed out that objective experimentation was incompetent to say anything about important parts of human psychology, including the religious sentiments. Other adherents of the old psychology, such as Larkin Dunton (before the Massachusetts School Masters' Club 1895), defended the old psychology as "the science of the soul," "an emanation of the Divine," furnishing the key "to moral education."

Like Bryan, Ladd, Dunton, and the old psychology represented the passing world of rural, village America, based on traditional religious truths. The Scottish common-sense psychology had been created to defend religion and would continue to do so as fundamentalists clung to it against the tide of modernism. The old psychology had a soul and taught the old moral values of an American culture that were being overtaken by progress.

For the 1890s was the "age of the news"—the new education, the new ethics, the new woman, and the new psychology. The future belonged to aggressive new psychologists, professionalizers of psychology who looked to its future. Chief among them was Wundt's *ganz Amerikanisch* student Cattell, fourth president of the APA. Cattell (1896) described the new psychology as a rapidly advancing quantitative science. Moreover—and this would be a key part of professional psychology in the years to come—he claimed for experimental psychology "wide reaching practical applications" in education, medicine, the fine arts, political economy, and, indeed, in the whole conduct of life." The new psychology, not the old, was in step with the times: self-confident, self-consciously new and scientific, ready to face the challenges of urbanization, industrialization, and the unceasing ever-changing flow of American life.

Reform, efficiency, and progress were the actuating values of the major social and political movement following the crisis of 1896, Progressivism. In Chapter 6 we saw how the English middle class sought to tame both the decadent aristocracy and the unruly working class by imposing on both their own values of frugality, self-control, and hard work. Progressivism filled the same role in America, with of course distinctive American touches. Progressives were middle-class professionals—including the new psychologists—who aimed to reign in the rapacious American aristocracy—the Robber Barons—and the disorderly masses of urban immigrants. Not only did the Robber Barons prey on Americans through business, but they were turning their riches to the control of politics and the living of opulent but empty lives, captured by F. Scott Fitzgerald in *The Great Gatsby*. Progressives saw the urban masses as victims exploited by corrupt political machines, which traded votes for favors and indispensable services to hopeful immigrants building new lives in a strange but opportunity-filled land.

In place of what they defined as the greedy self-interest of the moneyed class, and the opportunistic self-interest of the political bosses, the Progressives sought to establish disinterested, expert, professional government, that is, government by themselves. There can be no doubt that, especially in the cities, living conditions were often appalling as the waves of immigrants stretched American cities beyond their old bounds and beyond their ability to cope. Urban political machines were an organic, adaptive response to urban ills, providing bewildered immigrants with a helpful intermediary between them and their new society. But because the machines' help was bought with votes, rational, middle-class Progressives, led by academics, saw only corruption and manipulation of helpless victims by self-serving politicians. The Progressives replaced corruption with the scientific management principles of the great corporations.

The philosopher of Progressivism and the prophet of twentieth-century liberalism was John Dewey, elected president of the APA for the last year of the old century. In his presidential address, "Psychology and Social Practice," Dewey examined psychology's role in modern society by focusing on the reform of education.

Educational reform was one of the central concerns of Progressivism, and John Dewey was the founder of Progressive education. Education as it stood was ill-suited to the needs of urban, industrial America. G. Stanley Hall had begun the reform of education with his child study movement and the idea that schools should be child-centered institutions. Nevertheless, more reforms were urgently needed, as Dewey and others recognized. Immigrants were perforce bringing with them alien customs and alien tongues; they, and especially their children, needed to be Americanized. Immigrants from the farm also needed to be educated in the habits appropriate to industrial work and in new skills unknown on the farm. Above all, the schools had to become the child's new community. America's island communities were disappearing, and immigrants had left their home communities. The school had to be a community for the child and then reform the American community through the adult it produced.

"The school is an especially favorable place in which to study the availability of psychology for social practice," Dewey told the assembled psychologists. Sounding the themes of the psychology of adaptation, Dewey argued that "mind [is] fundamentally an instrument of adaptation" to be improved by school experience, and that for "psychology to become a working hypothesis"—that is, to meet the pragmatic test—it would have to involve itself with the education of America's young minds.

Once we involve ourselves with education, Dewey continued, psychologists would inevitably be led to society at large. Above all schools must teach values, and these values must be the values of social growth and community solidarity, the values of pragmatism and urban life. Finally, these values are not just the school's values but must become the values of every social institution; and so pychologists must naturally become engaged in the great enterprise of Progressive social reform.

Progressivism was the American New Enlightenment and as such condemned custom and replaced it with rational calculation. Dewey recognized that the island communities' values were maintained through custom, but that once values "are in any way divorced from habit and tradition" they must be "consciously proclaimed" and must find "some substitute for custom as an organ of their execution." Consequently, psychology, the study of mental adaptation, plays a special role in the reconstruction of society:

> The fact that conscious, as distinct from customary, morality and psychology have a historic parallel march, is just the concrete recognition of the necessary equivalence between ends consciously conceived, and interest in the means upon which the ends depend. . . . So long as custom reigns, as tradition prevails, so long as social values are determined by instinct and habit, there is no conscious question . . . and hence no need of psychology. . . . But when once the values come to consciousness . . . then the machinery by which ethical ideals are projected and manifested, comes to consciousness also. Psychology must needs be born as soon as morality becomes reflective.

Psychology, then, is a social analogue to consciousness. According to James, consciousness arises in the individual when adaptation to new circumstances is imperative. American society faced imperative changes, Dewey said, and psychology was arising to meet them. Only psychology offers an "alternative to an arbitrary and class view of society, to an aristocratic view" that would deny to some their full realization as human beings. Echoing the philosophes of the French Enlightenment, Dewey said that "we are ceasing to take existing social forms as final and unquestioned. The application of psychology to social institutions is . . . just the recognition of the principle of sufficient reason in the large matters of social life." The arrangements that exist among people are the results of the working of scientific laws of human behavior, and once psychologists understand these laws they will be able to construct a more perfect society by substituting rational planning for haphazard growth.

Individual personality would be blended into the social whole. "To save personality in all, we must all serve alike" by reducing personality to lawful scientific mechanism. "To affirm personality independent of mechanism is to restrict its full meaning to a few [the lucky aristocracy]. . . . " "The entire problem," Dewey concluded, "is one of the development of science, and of its applications to life." For the capricious freedom of aristocratic society, we should look forward to a scientific society, anticipating "no other outcome than increasing control in the ethical sphere." In the new society psychology will "enable human effort to expend itself sanely, rationally, and with assurance."

In his address Dewey touched all the themes of Progressivism, and he deepened and developed them over the course of a long career as a public philosopher. He gave Progressivism its voice; as one Progressive said, "We were all Deweyites before we read Dewey." For not only was Progressivism the politics of the moment and of the future, it reflected America's deepest traditions: distrust of aristocrats—hereditary, moneyed, or elected—and a commitment to equal treatment of all.

Where Progressivism and Dewey broke new ground were in their conceptions of the ends to be reached by society and by the means to be used to reach them. As de Tocqueville had observed, Americans distrusted intellect, which they associated with aristocracy, and still did nearly a century later. *The Saturday Evening Post* in 1912 attacked colleges for encouraging "that most un-American thing called class and culture. . . . There should be no such thing [in America] as a superior mind. . . . " Yet Progressivism called for government rule by a scientifically trained managerial elite. In a Progressively reformed city, the political authority of the mayor was replaced by the expertise of a university-trained city manager, whose job description was taken from big business. Progressives were obsessed by social control, the imposing of order on the disordered mass of turn-of-the-century American citizens. Progressivism's permanent legacy is government bureaucracy. The "corrupt" politicians of the urban machine knew their constituents as individuals, to be helped or harmed insofar as they supported the machine. Bureaucracy in contrast is rational and impersonal—rule by the expert. Questing for fairness, it imposes anonymity; people become numbers, the poor become case files, to be scientifically managed and manipulated to ensure the good of the whole.

The goal of society in the Progressive vision was the cultivation of the individual within a supportive community that nurtures him or her. Permanent achievements were replaced by growth. As Dewey later wrote, "The process of growth, of improvement and progress, rather than . . . the result, becomes the significant thing. . . . Not perfection as a final goal, but the ever-enduring process of perfecting, maturing, refining is the aim in living. . . . Growth itself is the only moral end" (Dewey 1957). Progressivism's novel goal is Darwinian. Since there is no end to evolution, there should be no end to personal growth. Darwin had abolished God, but Dewey defined a new sin; as a Progressive enthusiast wrote: "The long disputed sin against the holy ghost has been found . . . the refusal to cooperate with the vital principle of betterment."

Were the goal of self-cultivation and the means of scientific social control at odds? By no means. In Dewey's view individuals acquire their personality and thought from society. There is, in reality, no individual who preexists society, nor is society a collection of atomic individuals. Although the island communities were going, Americans still craved community, and Progressives offered a new kind of rationally planned community. A leading Progressive, Randolph Bourne, argued that in the new order of things nothing was as important as a "glowing personality"; self-cultivation "becomes almost a duty if one wants to be effective toward the great end" of reforming society.

So, despite its resonance with certain American values, Progressivism was at odds with America's individualistic, libertarian past. The scientific view of people and the scientific management of society on psychological principles had no room for individual freedom, for of course to a scientist there is no freedom. The individual should be cultivated but in the interests of the whole:

> Social control cannot be individually determined, but must proceed from a controlled environment which provides the individual with a uniform and constant source of stimuli. . . . The counter plea of "interference with individual liberty" should have no weight in court, for individuals have no liberties in opposition to a scientifically controlled society but find all their legitimate freedom in conformity to and furtherance of such social function. (Bernard 1911)

The Progressive vision was not, of course, confined to psychology but was remaking all the social sciences along similar lines. The inevitable direction was behavioral, because ultimately social control is control of behavior. And to acheive social control psychologists would have to give up the arcane procedure of introspection for the study of how behavior is controlled by its circumstances, and finally for how conrol of the environment gives managers control of behavior. As the twentieth century went on, psychologists would fulfill Dewey's hopes. Psychologists would increasingly move out into society, remaking its misfits, its children, its schools, its government, its businesses, its very psyche. Psychology in the twentieth century would profoundly alter our conceptions of ourselves, our needs, our loved ones, and our neighbors. John Dewey, philosopher and psychologist, more than any other single person drew the blueprint of the twentieth-century American mind.

James and Pragmatism

For all its influence on psychology, James's *Principles* was for him just a diversion. In 1892 he brought out a one-volume *Briefer Course* more suitable as a text but pronounced himself weary of psychology. In that same year he secured a successor to himself as Harvard's experimental psychologist and resumed his career as a philosopher, making 1892 a doubly significant year for psychology.

In response to Ladd's attack on psychology as a natural science—that is, on the new psychology—James (1892) agreed that psychology was not then a science, but "is a mass of phenomenal description, gossip and myth." He wrote the *Principles,* he said, wishing "by treating Psychology *like* a natural science to help her become one."

James correctly set out the new psychology's theme as a natural science. The cerebralist, reflex-action theory is invaluable because, by treating people as reaction tendencies, it works toward the "practical prediction and control" that is the aim of all natural sciences. Psychology should no longer be regarded as part of philosophy but as "a branch of biology." Finally, what is needed, said James, is a practical psychology that tells people how to act, that makes a difference to life. "The kind of psychology which could cure a case of melancholy, or charm a chronic insane delusion away, ought certainly to be preferred to the most seraphic insight into the nature of the soul."

Psychology should be practical, should make a difference. James not only voiced the growing desire of American psychologists as they organized and professionalized but announced his own touchstone of truth: True ideas make a real difference to life. James's next task was, then, the full development of the characteristically American philosophy, pragmatism.

By the mid-1890s the outlines of a new psychology, distinctively American in character, were emerging. The interest of American psychologists was shifting away from what consciousness contains toward what consciousness does and how it aids an organism, human or animal, in its adaptation to a changing environment. In short, mental content was becoming less important than mental function. This new functional psychology was a natural offspring of Darwinism and the new American experience. Mind, consciousness, would not exist, James had said in the *Principles,* unless it served the adaptive needs of its host; in the America of the 1890s it was clear that consciousness' prime function was to guide adjustment to the rapid flow of change engulfing immigrant and farmer, worker and professional. In a world of constant change, ancient truths—mental content, fixed doctrines—became uncouth every day. Heraclitus's universe had at last become true, and people no longer believed in Plato's eternal Forms. In the Heraclitean flux the only eternal constant was change, and therefore the only reality of experience—psychology's subject matter—is adjustment to change.

In both philosophy and psychology America was ready to produce new doctrines to meet the challenge of the modern American experience. In philosophy, William James expanded Peirce's narrow scientific pragmatism into a broad method capable of guiding one in the flux of modern experience: pragmatism. In psychology a new generation of young American psychologists, inspired by James's *Principles,* built a psychology of mental adjustment: functionalism.

Pragmatism had begun with the practical, scientific attitude of C. S. Peirce as a way of determining if concepts had any empirical reality. But Peirce's conception was too narrow and dry to meet fully the demands of a post-Darwinian, Heraclitean world. Virtually every nineteenth-century philosophy—romanticism, Darwinism, Hegelian idealism, Marxism—pictured a universe of change. It had become clear that there were no Platonic permanent truths; yet people will not live without some certainty, some fixed star to steer by. James found in Peirce's pragmatism a fixed star of a new sort. James offered a method for making, rather than finding, truths.

In a series of works beginning in 1895 and culminating in *Pragmatism* (1907), James developed a comprehensive pragmatic approach to the problems of science, philosophy, and life. James argued that ideas were worthless or, more precisely, meaningless, unless they *mattered* to our lives. An idea with no consequences was pointless and meaningless. As he wrote in *Pragmatism:*

> True ideas are those that we can assimilate, validate, corroborate and verify. False ideas are those that we can not. That is the practical difference it makes for us to have true ideas. . . . The truth of an idea is not a stagnant property inherent in it. Truth happens to an idea. It becomes true, is made true by events. Its verity is in fact an event, a process. . . . (italics deleted)

So far, this sounds like Peirce: a hardheaded, Darwinian approach to truth. James went beyond Peirce, however, when he said that the truth of an idea should be tested against its agreement with all of one's experience, "nothing being omitted." When Peirce had said we weigh ideas against experience, he meant experience in a narrow, cognitive sense: the scientist's apprehension of the physical world. James, however, saw no reason to value one kind of experience above another. Noncognitive experience—hopes, fears, loves, ambitions—were just as much part of a person's living reality as sensations of number, hardness, or mass. "Ideas," James said, "(which themselves are but parts of our experience) become true just in so far as they help us get into satisfactory relations with other parts of our experience . . . " (James 1907, italics deleted). James's criterion of truth was thus much broader than Peirce's and could apply to any concept, no matter how seemingly fanciful or metaphysical. To the tough-minded empiricist the ideas of God or of free will were empty, meaningless, since they were devoid of sensory content. But to James these ideas could make a difference in the way we conduct our lives. If the idea of free will and its corollary, moral responsibility, leads men and women to live better, happier lives than if they believed in the automaton theory, then free will was true; or, more exactly, it was made true in the lives and experience of the people who accepted it.

James's pragmatism held no metaphysical prejudices, unlike traditional Rationalism and Empiricism. "Rationalism sticks to logic and the empyrean. Empiricism sticks to the external senses. Pragmatism is willing to take anything, to follow either logic or the senses and to count the humblest and most personal experiences. She will count mystical experiences if they have practical consequences'' (James 1907). Against the cold intellectual positivism of Peirce's pragmatism, James asserted the claims of the heart, so congenial to Americans since the time of Jonathan Edwards. As James recognized, his pragmatism was anti-intellectual in setting heart and head as equals in the search for truth. Functional psychologists and their heirs, the behaviorists, would likewise depreciate the intellect. Learning and problem solving, as we shall see, would soon be explained in terms of blind trial and error and resulting reward and punishment, not in terms of directed cognitive activity.

Pragmatism was a functional philosophy, a method, not a doctrine. It provided a way of coping with the Heraclitean flux of experience no matter what the challenge, no matter what the topic. In the fields of theology and physics, politics and ethics, philosophy and psychology, it offered a star to navigate by. While one could not hope to find a fixed, final truth about God or matter, society or morality, metaphysics or the mind, one could at least know what questions to ask: Does this concept matter, does it make a difference to me, to my society, to my science? Pragmatism promised that even though there were no final solutions to any problem, at least there was a method of concretely resolving problems here and now.

Heretofore philosophers had searched for first principles, indubitable ideas upon which to erect a philosophical system and a philosophy of science. James's pragmatism gives up the quest for first principles, recognizing that after Darwin no truth could be fixed. Instead, James offered a philosophy that *worked* by turning away from content—fixed truths, and toward function—what ideas do for us. As James did this, psychologists were quietly developing a psychology of function, studying not the ideas a mind contained but how the mind worked in adapting its organism to a changing environment. At the same time they hoped that psychological science would work in the modern world, meeting the challenges of immigration and education, madness and feeblemindedness, business and politics.

BUILDING ON *THE PRINCIPLES:* THE MOTOR THEORY OF CONSCIOUSNESS (1892–1896)

The spirit of the new psychology in America was that of James's *Principles of Psychology:* Cattell said it "has breathed the breath of life into the dust of psychology." James himself detested the professional, even commercial, attitudes overcoming academia and harbored doubts about scientific psychology. Nevertheless, it was upon his text that American psychology built itself for years to come.

Hugo Münsterberg and Action Theory

By 1892, James was weary of psychology and eager to move on to philosophy. He looked for someone to replace him as Harvard's experimental psychologist, and his attention was drawn to Hugo Münsterberg, a promising student of Wundt's, who nevertheless disagreed with his teacher in a way that attracted James to him.

We have already discussed James's ideo-motor theory of voluntary behavior and contrasted it to Wundt's. Münsterberg's "action theory" developed a more thoroughgoing motor theory of consciousness that did away with will altogether (a step James could never take) and reduced consciousness to sensation and behavior.

Anyone who, like Wundt, was a voluntarist and assigned to will an active, determining role in mind and behavior must see consciousness as deciding on actions. Information, or stimuli, are attended to, a decision is made, and behavior follows, roughly:

$$S \longleftrightarrow \text{Consciousness} \longrightarrow R$$

(the double arrow following S reflects the role of active apperception in determining what we experience).

Now will is a tricky concept for psychology as a natural science. It seems to fly in the face of causality and determinism. It is also unphysiological—there seems no room for will in the reflex concept of the brain, then coming to full development. After the work of Fritsch and Hitzig there seemed no place to put will: the brain produced behavior simply by associating incoming stimulus nerves with outgoing response nerves. As far as physiology went, there was no need for consciousness at all.

$$S \longrightarrow \text{Physiological Process} \longrightarrow R$$

Reflex theory seemed now to be a tenable conception of how behavior is produced. As Münsterberg wrote, "For the preservation of the individual, it is obviously irrelevant whether a purposeful motion is accompanied by contents of consciousness or not" (Hale 1980).

However, there *are* conscious contents (the traditional subject matter of psychology) to explain: Why do we believe we have an effective will? With James, but more consistently, Münsterberg located the source in behavior—"our ideas are the product of our readiness to act," "our actions shape our knowledge" (quoted by Kuklick 1977). Our feeling of will, the motor theory explains, comes about because we are aware of our behavior and our incipient tendencies to behave. Thus I might announce that I'm going to stand up from my chair, not because I've reached a decision to stand but because the motor processes of standing have just begun and have entered consciousness. I feel my "will" to be effective because generally the incipient tendencies to act are followed by real action, and the former trigger memories of the latter. Because the covert tendencies have usually in fact preceded overt behavior, I believe my "will" is usually carried out.

We may summarize the Motor Theory of Consciousness (MTC) this way:

The contents of consciousness are determined by stimuli impinging upon us, by our overt behaviors, and by peripheral changes in muscles and glands produced by the physiological processes linking stimulus and response. As Münsterberg argued, in this account consciousness is no more than an epiphenomenon, playing no role in causing behavior. Psychology, moreover, had to be physiological in a reductive sense, explaining consciousness in terms of underlying physiological processes, especially at the periphery. Practical, applied psychology, a field in which Münsterberg was quite active, would perforce be behavioral, explaining human action as the outcome of human circumstances.

The MTC was not confined to James or Münsterberg. In one form or another, it grew in influence. We have before us now the central philosophical-psychological theme of these two decades: What, if anything, does consciousness *do?* This question surfaces over and over in place after place. In the MTC we see a good reason for the rise of behavioralism. If the theory is true, consciousness in fact does nothing. So why, except from faith in the old definition of psychology as the study of consciousness, should we study it?

John Dewey and the Reflex Arc

After 1890, following James's *Principles,* John Dewey moved away from his earlier Hegelian idealism and began to develop what he later called instrumentalism, becoming the most influential of all American philosophers. In the mid-1890s he wrote a series of important but tediously written papers that, taking the *Principles* as the footings, laid the foundations of his lifelong attempt to bring together philosophy, psychology, and ethics in a harmonious whole. These papers also furnished the central conceptions of America's native psychology, functionalism.

The most influential of these papers was "The Reflex Arc Concept in Psychology" (1896). He criticized the traditional associatonist reflex arc concept, S ⟶ Idea ⟶ R, as artifically breaking up behavior into disjoint parts. He does not deny that stimulus, sensation (idea), and response exist. He does, however, deny that they may be regarded as separately occurring events. Instead Dewey considered stimulus, idea, and response to be divisions of labor in an overall coordination of action—the reflex arc—as the organism adjusts to its environment.

Developing his own motor theory of mind, Dewey regarded sensation not as the passive registration of an impression but as itself an act conditioned by other behaviors occurring at the same time. So, to a soldier anxiously awaiting contact with the enemy, the sound of a twig snapping has one significance; to a hiker in a peaceful woods it has quite another. Indeed, the hiker may not even notice the snapping sound at all.

Dewey made here a decisive move whose significance, buried in his dry, abstract prose, is not immediately apparent. We might, with Wundt and even James, naively attribute the differences in apperception of the twig's snapping to willfully focused attention. The soldier is actively listening for sounds of approach, the hiker is attending to the songs of birds. But Dewey's motor theory, like Münsterberg's, dispenses with the individual ego and its will. It is the *current behavior,* claimed Dewey, that gives a sensation its significance, or even determines if a stimulus becomes a sensation at all. A stimulus counts as a sensation, and takes on value, only if it has a relationship with our current behavior.

James had advanced a cerebralist approach to mind but had not fully examined the implications of this view. Dewey saw that behavior often runs off by itself, occasioning no sensations or ideas in any significant sense of the term. It is only when behavior needs to be newly coordinated to reality—that is, needs to be adjusted—that sensation and emotion arise. The hiker's behavior need not be adjusted to the snap of a twig, and his walking continues uninterrupted. The soldier urgently needs to coordinate his behavior to the snap of a twig and its sound thus looms large in consciousness. Moreover, the soldier's emotion, fear, apprehension, and perhaps anger at the enemy are felt, Dewey argued, only because his behavior is in check; his emotions arise from feedback from his thwarted action tendencies. Emotion, said Dewey, is a sign of conflicting dispositions to act; in the soldier's case, to fight or flee. Could he do either immediately and wholeheartedly, he would feel nothing, Dewey said.

Dewey's formulation was centrally important for later American psychology; in 1943 the reflex arc paper was chosen as one of the most important articles ever published in *Psychological Review*. Dewey showed that psychology could do away with the central willing self of Wundt and James, a mysterious and unscientific being. Rather than assigning the control of perception and decision to an inaccessible ego, it became possible to account for them in terms of coordinated, ever-changing, adaptive behaviors. So hearing was one sort of behavior, attending another, and responding a third. All were coordinated toward the end of survival in a constant, fluid stream of behavior ever in motion, not unlike the daily lives of contemporary Americans. Dewey's ideas became the commonplaces of functionalism.

The new psychology had eliminated the soul, but a self, and ego, remained. The new motor theories—which, it should be emphasized again, were logical developments out of cerebralism and James's *Principles*—also promised to eliminate the ego. What remained were consciousness and behavior, the latter controlling the former. Soon the existence of consciousness, too, would become problematic.

FROM PHILOSOPHY TO BIOLOGY: FUNCTIONAL PSYCHOLOGY (1896–1910)

Experiments Become Functional

In keeping with epistemological aims, traditional philosophy had been concerned with the ideas the mind contains and whether or not they are true. Of course, philosophers did not ignore or even neglect mental processes, but nevertheless their first concern was with mental content, that is, putative knowledge. Traditional psychology of consciousness, while naturally investigating mental processes such as apperception, retained an emphasis on conscious content as the subject matter of psychology; its primary novelty was subjecting consciousness to experimental control in order to capture psychology for science. However, as we saw in the last chapter, William James, in his *Principles of Psychology*, shifted the interest of psychology from content to process. As he pictured the mind, mental contents were evanescent, fleeting things, seen once, never to return; what endured in the mind was function, especially the function of choosing. James's new emphasis was reinforced by the new American experience of the 1890s—old truths replaced by new ones, familiar scenes by strange ones. What remained constant was the process of adjusting to the new.

The development of the motor theory of consciousness continued the process of depreciating mental content and, by implication, the method used to access it, introspection. In the motor theory conscious content was a result of sensation and incipient motor response and seemed to play little, if any, role in actually producing behavior. While of course it remained possible to introspect and report conscious content—as Münsterberg continued to do in his laboratory—it could easily be seen as pointless, even irresponsible. American psychologists agreed with James: What was needed was a psychology that met the pragmatic test by being effective. Awash in change, Americans needed a psychology that did something to cope with the new. Introspection only revealed what *was*; Americans needed to prepare for what *is to be*. James, Münsterberg, and Dewey were preparing for the new functional psychology by turning their attention from content to adaptive process.

At the same time experimental psychologists were shifting their interest from introspective report of conscious content to an objective determination of the correlation between stimulus and response. As developed by Wundt, the experimental method had two aspects. A standardized, controlled stimulus was presented to a subject who responded to it in some way, reporting at the same time the contents of his experience. Wundt, as a mentalist, was interested in the experience produced by given conditions and used objective results as clues to the processes that produced conscious content. However, in the hands of American psychologists, emphasis shifted from conscious experience to the determination of responses by stimulus conditions.

As an example, we may take an experiment on how people locate an object in space on the basis of sound (Angell 1903). In this experiment a blindfolded observer—in this case, one of them was John B. Watson, the founder of behaviorism—was seated in a chair at the center of a circular device that could display a sound at any point around the observer. After setting the sound generator at a given point, the experimenter made it produce a tone, and the observer pointed to where he believed the sound was coming from. Then the observer provided an introspective report of the conscious experience concomitant with the experimental procedure. Watson reported seeing a mental image of the apparatus surrounding him, with the sound generator located where he pointed. Now one could, as a true mentalist would, focus on the introspective report as the data of interest, aiming to describe and explain this bit of mental content. On the other hand, one could focus on the accuracy of the pointing response, correlating the position of the sound generator with the observer's indicated position.

In the present case, although both objective data—the correlation of stimulus position with the observer's response—and introspective reports were discussed, the latter were given secondary importance. The objective findings were highlighted and extensively discussed; the introspective findings were briefly mentioned at the end of the article. In the Motor Theory of Consciousness introspection was becoming less important, since consciousness played no causal role in determining behavior. The same attitude is also found in the experiments of the time, such as Angell's. For him, too, introspective report was less important than the determination of behavior by the environment, and in the experiments of this entire period one finds, with the exception of reports from Titchener's laboratory, introspective reports being first isolated from the primary objective results and then shortened or removed altogether.

In addressing how behavior is adjusted to stimulus, American psychologists were turning from the study of mental content to the study of adaptive mental functions. Another experiment, Bryan and Harter (1897), reveals a second sense in which American psychology was becoming functional—socially functional. Bryan, an experimental psychologist, and Harter, a former railroad telegrapher turned graduate student in psychology, investigated the acquisition of telegraphic skills by new railroad telegraphers. Their report contained no introspective reports at all but instead charted the students' gradual improvement over months of practice and telegraphic work. This completely objective study was socially significant because Bryan and Harter were studying an important skill learned by people who were assuming an important role in industrialized America. As the railroads expanded and knit together the island communities of formerly rural America, railroad telegraphers were vital: They kept track of what goods were sent where, of what trains were going to what places; in short, they were the communication links that made the whole railroad system function. Their significance may be judged from the fact that Ward began his mail order business (soon rivaled by Sears') as a railroad telegrapher picking up unwanted merchandise shipped west and then selling it by advertising up and down the railroad telegraph line. Bryan and Harter, then, were bringing psychological research to bear on a topic of real social value.

Their study is significant in another respect as well. It foreshadowed the central problem of experimental psychology in the twentieth century: learning. The traditional psychology of consciousness, mentalism, had primarily investigated perception and its allied functions, because it was these that produced introspectible mental contents. But in the post-Darwinian psychology of James and his followers, consciousness was important for what it does, especially the adjustment of the organism to its environment. Gradual adjustment over time is learning—finding out about the environment and then behaving in accord with it. Bryan and Harter plotted learning curves and discussed how the novice telegraphers gradually adjusted to the demands of their jobs. In its objectivism, in its concern with a socially useful problem, and in its choice of learning as subject matter, Bryan and Harter's paper was a sign of things to come. It is no wonder, therefore, that in 1943 it was voted by leading American psychologists as the most important experimental study yet published in the *Psychological Review* and one of the five most important papers of any kind. Even today it is cited in important texts in introductory psychology.

By 1904 it was clear that the "objective" method, in which responses were correlated with stimuli, was at least as important as the introspective analysis of consciousness. Speaking before the International Congress of Arts and Science, Cattell, the American pioneer in psychology, said, "I am not convinced that psychology should be limited to the study of consciousness as such," which of course had been the definition of psychology for James and Wundt. His own work, Cattell said, "is nearly as independent of introspection as work in physics or in zoology." While introspection and experiment should "continually cooperate," it was obvious from "the brute argument of accomplished fact" that much of psychology now existed "apart from introspection." Although Cattell seemed to place introspection and objective measurement on an equal footing, it is clear from his tone, and from his later call for applied psychology, that the objective, behavioral approach to psychology was on the rise.

Functional Psychology Defined

In both theory and research, then, American psychology was moving away from the traditional psychology of conscious content and toward a psychology of mental adjustment inspired by evolutionary theory. Interestingly, it was not an American psychologist who spotted and identified this new trend but the staunchest defender of a pure psychology of content, E. B. Titchener. In his "Postulate of a Structural Psychology" (1898) Titchener cogently distinguished several kinds of psychology; and while others may have disagreed about which kind of psychology was best, his terminology endured.

Titchener drew a broad analogy between three kinds of biology and three kinds of psychology:

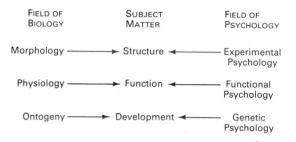

FIELD OF BIOLOGY	SUBJECT MATTER	FIELD OF PSYCHOLOGY
Morphology ⟶	Structure ⟵	Experimental Psychology
Physiology ⟶	Function ⟵	Functional Psychology
Ontogeny ⟶	Development ⟵	Genetic Psychology

In biology the anatomist, the student of morphology, carefully dissects the body to discover the organs that compose it, revealing the body's structure. Once an organ is isolated and described, it is the job of the physiologist to figure out its function, what it does. Finally, one might study how an organ develops in the course of embryogenesis and postnatal development and how the organ came into being in the course of evolution; these studies constitute developmental biology, the study of the origin and path of change of an organ in the history of the species and of the individual.

Similarly, in psychology, the experimental psychologist—by which Titchener meant himself—dissects consciousness into its component parts; this anatomy of the mind defines structural psychology. What the revealed structures do is the province of the psychological physiologist—functional psychology. The development of mental structures and functions is the subject matter of genetic psychology, which investigates the course of individual and phylogenetic development.

In Titchener's estimation structural psychology logically preceded functional psychology, since only after mental structures had been isolated and described could their functions be ascertained. At the same time Titchener noted the appeal of functional psychology. Its roots were ancient, its analysis of mind hewed close to common sense, as it employed faculty concepts such as "memory," "imagination," and "judgment," and it seemed to promise immediate practical application. Citing Dewey's reflex arc paper, Titchener also acknowledged that functional psychology was growing in influence. Nevertheless, Titchener urged psychologists to avoid the comfortable spaces of functional psychology and to stick to the tough, scientific job of experimental introspective psychology. Genetic psychology, while logically possible and indeed already on the scene (Baldwin 1895, Wozniak 1982), remained a yet more distant prospect for Titchener.

From Undercurrent to Main Current

In the decade following Titchener's "Postulates," it became apparent that other psychologists found his analysis basically correct but his priorities reversed. In his December 1900 presidential address to the American Psychological Association, Peirce's one-time collaborator explored "Some Currents and Undercurrents in

Psychology'' (Jastrow 1901). He declared that for him psychology is ''the science of mental function,'' not content. The functional approach arose out of evolution; it ''at once cast a blinding light'' upon dark areas of psychology long held by ''dogmatism, misconception and neglect'' and ''breathed a new life'' into ''the dry bones'' of psychology. Jastrow correctly observed that although functional psychology pervaded current research, it did not act as the central subject of investigation but rather gave a distinctive ''color tone'' to American psychology. Jastrow saw functional psychology as an accepted undercurrent, which he wanted to bring forward as a ''main current.'' Functional psychology is more catholic than structural psychology. It welcomes to psychology the previously excluded topics of comparative psychology, abnormal psychology, mental testing, the study of the average person, and even psychical research, although this last clearly troubled him. Jastrow predicted that functional psychology would prove of more value to practical affairs than structural psychology. Finally, he noted, as we have, that all these trends are characteristically American, and he prophesied that the future would belong to functional, not structural, psychology.

A ''revision'' of the traditional central topic of mentalistic psychology, perception, from the functional-biological viewpoint was worked out by Thaddeus Bolton (1902). Bolton integrated theoretical developments in psychology since James, including the motor theory of consciousness and Dewey's account of the reflex arc, into a theory of perception embodying the coming behavioralist psychology. The ''common view of perception held by most psychologists,'' according to Bolton, was Titchenerian: A percept is a complex of ''all the different sensations'' it produces. While not denying the reality of directly produced sensations, Bolton asserted that much more important to our perception of an object were sensations resulting from the actions provoked by that object, what Bolton, following James, called ''the backstroke'' in perception. We also see here the influence of Dewey (also cited by Bolton), whose reflex arc paper also pictured consciousness as largely determined by bodily response.

Perception, then, is more than a complex of sensations, argued Bolton; it is ''an attitude,'' or, more strongly, ''an act,'' so that ''the study of perception becomes synonymous with a study of animal activity.'' While Bolton did not discuss introspection, his theory naturally implies that introspection is not psychology's necessary method. If perception is to be identified with a particular adjustive response to a stimulus, as Bolton argued, then introspection is not necessary, because we can determine an organism's perceptions by observing what it does. ''Only those objects . . . [that] are acted towards . . . are perceived.'' The only biologically significant percepts are those that enter into an organism's behavior; those conscious contents that are ''without functional importance'' are ''epiphenomenal'' and can be ''left out of consideration.'' In Bolton's scheme of things, therefore, mind is not private: Anyone can determine the contents of anyone else's consciousness simply by watching them behave—no special introspective method is necessary. As he put it, ''What [an] object means, then, may be stated by describing the activity of the animal.''

Consistent with his Darwinian biological orientation, Bolton stressed the continuity between humans and other ''lower'' animals. Humans are especially discriminating perceivers, not because of any special qualities of intellect but because we possess ''an enormous variety of bodily responses'' provided by language. We are able to associate with virtually any sensation some distinct motor response, or word; it is not our brains that make us unique among animals—not some central mental process—but our speech musculature. Thinking, Bolton implied, is just behavior: "Mind is to be regarded as an outgrowth of conduct, a superior and more direct means of adjusting the organism to the environment."

James Rowland Angell (1869–1949), who was about to publish a textbook written from the functional standpoint (*Psychology*, published in 1904), contrasted an admittedly inchoate functional psychology with structural psychology, while asserting the priorty of the latter over the former. Unlike bodily organs, the structuralists' mental elements were not permanent, enduring objects but existed only at the moment of perception. That is, "the functions produce the structures," the reverse of biology, in which a given organ performs a distinct function that would not exist without it. Angell also alleged that structural psychology was socially pointless and biologically irrelevant. It studied consciousness removed from "life conditions" and could therefore tell us nothing useful about how mind works in the real world. Moreover, structuralist reductionism made of consciousness an irrelevant epiphenomenon. Functional psychology, in contrast, reveals consciousness to be "an efficient agent in the furtherance of the life activities of the organism," that is, as biologically useful and quite in accord, as Titchener himself had said, with common sense.

In several papers published in 1903 and 1904, the pragmatist philosopher H. Heath Bawden set out the new functional view of consciousness, a view that was coming to be commonly held by psychologists. Mental life, Bawden said, "is simply a name for the orderly functioning of an organism under conditions of tension in adaptation." As long as habits meet the needs of life, there is no consciousness. Consciousness only arises when there is a challenge, some novel circumstance calling for a novel behavior. Consciousness is a product of the tension produced by the need to adjust: "Consciousness never arises without a certain tension," and when new habits are devised, consciousness disappears again. In Bawden's view, like Bolton's, consciousness and behavior are closely connected: "The most fundamental statement we can make about consciousness is that it is action"; "consciousness is not another realm or reality; it is simply the one world we know in its process of reconstruction."

Angell, Bawden, and Bolton were advancing James's conception of consciousness toward behavioralism. Conscious content, as such, is not very important in their functional theory of mind. For them, mind is a process whose biological value lies in its ability to be summoned forth genie like when its organism finds itself faced with a new situation. It is not needed when instincts are adequate to the stimuli at hand, nor when previously learned habits are functioning smoothly. Consciousness is a sometime thing, needed only occasionally, and it would not be long before psychologists were able to go beyond Bolton and Bawden and dispense with mind altogether. As Frank Thilly (1905) pointed out, the functional view of consciousness retained James's fatal flaw. Along with just about everyone else, James and the functional psychologists following him held to mind-body parallelism while at the same time arguing that consciousness actively intervenes in the adjustive activities of the organism. Bolton was aware of the problem and tried to maintain that although consciousness does not affect nervous processes, it somehow plays a role in learning. This was not a happy position for functional psychologists to be in, and they would be rescued—or replaced—by the bolder behaviorists ready to chuck consciousness completely out of psychology. After all, if one can see conscious content in behavior, as Bolton maintained, why not just stick to talking about behavior?

By 1905 it was clear to contemporary psychologists that the functional tide was in. Edward Franklin Buchner, who for some years wrote for *Psychological Bulletin* an annual history of the year's "Psychological Progress," observed "the widespread acceptance and defense of the 'functional' as over against the 'structural' view" of psychology. The replacement of the older system by a new one did have the unfortunate effect, Buchner noted, of starting the development of the field all over again, undoing cumulative progress. In the same volume Felix Arnold raised "the great cry" of current psychologists: "WHAT IS IT GOOD FOR?" He praised functionalists for giving up the old view of perception Bolton had attacked, and replacing it with perception conceived "as a motor process . . . determining serial reactions toward [an] object."

In the same year Mary Calkins took the opportunity of her APA presidential address to advance her self-psychology as a way to reconcile structural and functional psychologies. If psychology is conceived as the study of a real psychological self possessing both conscious content and mental functions, each system could be viewed as contributing part of the total psychological picture. Although Calkins aggressively pushed her self-psychology over the years in every forum she could find, it seems to have found few followers. For the time of compromise had passed. In 1907 Buchner wrote that in 1906 "the functional point of view seem[ed] to have almost completely won out"—so much so that psychology's " 'older' (and almost consecrated) terms" were about finished. Buchner awaited the framing "of a new vocabulary of psychology for the new twentieth century."

Angell seized the occasion of his APA presidential address to codify "The Province of Functional Psychology." Angell's address (given in December 1906 and published the next year) was a milestone on the road to behavioralism. In it we can see that functionalism was mainly a bridge between mentalism and behavioralism, a way-station rather than an enduring movement in its own right. As Angell conceded at the outset, functional psychology was "little more than a program" and a "protest" against the sterilities of structural psychology. Functional psychology was also not new, being found in Aristotle, in Spencer, in Darwin, and in pragmatism.

Angell repeated the already familiar distinction: Structural psychology was concerned with mental "*contents,*" functionalism with mental "*operations.*" Functionalism studies mental process as it is in the actual life of an organism; structuralism studies how mind "appears" in a "merely postmortem analysis." To this end, "modern investigations . . . dispense with the usual direct form of introspection and concern themselves . . . with a determination of what work is accomplished and what the conditions are under which it is acheived." Angell here acknowledges the trend we earlier found in his and others' research and defines the point of view of behavioralist experimentation. Repeating his argument of 1903, Angell justified this new research emphasis by quite correctly asserting that unlike physical organs dissected by the anatomist, "mental contents are evanescent and fleeting." What endures over time are mental functions: Contents come and go, but attention, memory, judgment—the mental faculties of the old psychology rehabilitated—"persist."

Functional psychology also brings with it a change in psychology's institutional relationships. Structural, mentalistic psychology grew out of philosophy and remained closely allied to it. In contrast, functional psychology "brings the psychologist cheek by jowl with the general biologist," because both study the "sum total" of an organism's "organic activities," the psychologist concentrating on the "accommodatory service" of consciousness. This new biological orientation will bring with it practical benefits as well, Angell averred. "Pedagogy and mental hygiene . . . await the quickening and guiding counsel" of functional psychology. Animal psychology—"the most pregnant" movement of "our generation"—finds its "rejuvenation" in the new movement, because it is becoming "experimental . . . wherever possible" and "conservatively . . . non-anthropomorphic," trends we will examine in the next section. Genetic psychology and abnormal psychology—the former barely mentioned and the latter completely ignored by Titchener (1898)—will likewise be inspired by a functional approach.

Angell endorsed the view set forth by Bawden that consciousness "supervenes on certain occasions" in the life of an organism, describing the adjustment theory as "the position now held by all psychologists of repute." But he went farther than Bawden or Bolton in claiming that consciousness "is no indispensable feature of the accommodatory process." Although in a footnote Angell still held that accommodation to "the novel" is "the field of conscious activity," we may still sense here a further step toward behavioralism in its suggestion that learning may take place without conscious intervention.

In conclusion, functional psychology is "functional" in a triple sense. First, it considers mind to have a distinct biological function selected by Darwinian evolution: It adapts its organism to novel circumstances. Second, it describes consciousness as itself a result of the physiological functioning of the organism: Mind, in its view, is itself a biological function. Third, functional psychology promises to be socially useful in improving education, mental hygiene, and abnormal states: Psychology will become functional in twentieth-century life. In 1906 Angell stood at a hinge in the development of modern psychology. His continued concern with consciousness, however interpreted, still links functional psychology with the mentalism of the past. But at the same time his emphasis on biology, on adaptation, and on applied psychology link functional psychology as a "new-old movement" whose time will someday pass with "some worthier successor [to] fill its place."

By 1907, then, functional psychology had by and large replaced structural psychology as the dominant approach to the field. However, it never became more than a program and a protest. It was finally too inconsistent to survive, clinging to a definition of psychology as the study of consciousness, while at the same time putting forth theories of perception and learning that made consciousness less and less necessary as a concept for scientific psychology. Functional theory reflects very nicely the historical forces of the time pushing psychology ever toward the study of behavior, and it helped psychologists change their fundamental conceptions of their profession without quite realizing that they were doing anything extraordinary.

While functional psychology was strongest in America, psychologies that could be identified with functionalism also arose in Europe. Brentano's psychology, because it was labled an "act" psychology, was often assimilated to the functional viewpoint. Similarly, the Würzburg school could be called "functional" because of its concern with and investigations of mental processes, and its discovery of contentless (imageless) thought.

In Britain, home of modern evolutionism, functional psychology found its William James in James Ward (1843–1975), sometimes called the "father of modern British psychology" (Turner 1974). He was for a time a minister, but after a crisis of faith turned first to physiology, then psychology, and finally philosophy, exactly as James had done. His tremendous influence in British psychology comes from his article on psychology in the *Encyclopaedia Brittanica's* ninth edition of 1886. It was the first article by that name in the *Encyclopaedia,* and Ward reworked it later into a text. Ward settled at Cambridge University, where he was active in attempts to establish a psychological laboratory.

Like James, Ward rejected atomistic analysis of the continuum of consciousness. Instead of a sensationistic atomism, Ward advocated a functional view of consciousness, the brain, and the whole organism. Ward wrote (1904): "Functionally regarded, the organism is from first to last a continuous whole . . . the growing complexity of psychical life is only parodied by treating it as mental chemistry." To Ward perception is not the passive reception of sensation, but active grasping of the environment. In a passage that resembles James, Ward (1904) wrote that "not mere receptivity but creative or selective activity is the essence of subjective reality. . . ." He struck a Darwinian note when he said (1920): "Psychologically regarded, then, the sole function of perception and intellection is, it is contended, to guide action and subserve volition—more generally to promote self-conservation and betterment."

Ward is clearly expounding the same kind of pragmatic, or functional, psychology that James did. For both men consciousness is an active, choosing entity that adjusts the organism to the environment and so serves the struggle for survival. Ward resembles James in one more way—his *fin de siècle* concern with defending religion against the rising tide of Huxlean naturalism. Ward devoted his last great works to the refutation of naturalism and the support of Christianity.

Ward's influence endured for many years in English psychology. Britain retained a functionalist psychology that provided an orienting point for later cognitive psychology. Ward's anti-atomism also endured, to be picked up by later anti associationists. The Cambridge psychologist Frederick Bartlett, for example, explicitly rejected the attempt to study memory as the acquisition of discrete "bits" of information such as the nonsense syllables used in most memory experiments. Instead, Bartlett studied memory of everyday paragraphs. He argued that running prose is not a set of atomistic ideas, but is rather an embodiment of a larger meaning, which he called a *schema*. Bartlett (1932) showed, for example, that different cultures possess different schemas for organizing their experience, and that consequently systematic distortions are introduced into one culture's member's memory of another culture's stories. In exploring alternatives to behaviorism in the 1960s, Bartlett's schema theory was revived and refined.

Of greater influence on later psychology was Hermann Ebbinghaus's (1850–1909) study of memory. Ebbinghaus was a young doctor of philosophy unattached to any university when he came across a copy of Fechner's *Elements Psychophysics* in a secondhand bookstore. He admired the scientific precision of Fechner's work on perception and resolved to tackle the "higher mental processes" that Wundt had excluded from experimental treatment. Using himself as his only subject, Ebbinghaus set out in 1879 to demonstrate Wundt's error. The result was his *Memory* of 1885, which was hailed as a first-rate contribution to psychology and which helped win him a professorship at the prestigious University of Berlin.

Memory represents a necessarily small-scale but well-thought-out research program. Ebbinghaus decided to investigate the formation of associations by learning serial lists of nonsense syllables, meaningless combinations of three letters invented by Ebbinghaus for the purpose. In electing to memorize nonsense syllables, Ebbinghaus reveals the functionalist cast of his thought. He chose nonsense syllables because they are meaningless, because the sameness of their content would not differentially affect the process of learning. He wanted to isolate and study memory as the pure *function* of learning, abstracting away any effects of content.

Ebbinghaus remained an eclectic rather than a systematic thinker, and his influence derives from his work on memory rather than from any theoretical views. But that influence was wide. In Germany memory studies were carried on by G. E. Müller and his associates, whose distinctions, new procedures, and theories anticipated modern cognitive psychology. In America James praised Ebbinghaus's work in *Principles*, and in 1896 Mary Calkins augmented Ebbinghaus's serial learning method with a paired-associate procedure in which the subject learns specific pairs of words or nonsense syllables. More broadly, Ebbinghaus's *Memory* prefigures the style of twentieth-century psychology. Its subject is learning, the favorite topic of functionalists, behaviorists, and cognitive psychologists. The book minimizes theory while multiplying facts and looking for systematic effects on behavior of independent variables, such as list length. Ebbinghaus strove to quantify his data and apply statistical methods. In short, Ebbinghaus is the empirical, atheoretical, research-oriented, eclectic modern psychologist.

NEW DIRECTIONS IN ANIMAL PSYCHOLOGY (1898–1909)

Animal psychology, as it had been begun by Romanes, used two methods: the anecdotal method to collect data, and the method of inference to interpret it. While both methods had been challenged, discussed, and defended from their inception, they came under special scrutiny and criticism among American psychologists in the late nineteenth and early twentieth centuries. Anecdote was replaced by experiment, particularly by the techniques of E. L. Thorndike and I. P. Pavlov. Inference was gradually given up, at least by some animal psychologists, as it became clear that Descartes's problem of other minds had no empirical solution.

From Anecdote to Experiment

Beginning in 1898 animal psychology experienced a surge in activity and a quickening of interest. But in the new animal psychology laboratory experiment replaced anecdotes and informal, naturalistic experiments, as psychologists investigated the behavior of species ranging from protozoa to monkeys. The aim of animal psychology, as of psychology in general, was to produce a natural science, and the young men in the field felt that gentlemanly anecdote was not the path to science; as E. L. Thorndike (1898) wrote: "Salvation does not come from such a source." While there were many psychologists now experimenting on animal mind and behavior, two research programs deserve special attention, because their methods became enduring ones, and their theoretical conceptions embraced the whole of psychology. These programs arose at almost the same time, but in very different places and circumstances: in William James's Cambridge basement, where a young graduate student employed his mentor's children as his research assistants, and in the sophisticated laboratories of a distinguished Russian physiologist already on his way to a Nobel Prize.

The Connectionism of Edward Lee Thorndike (1874–1949)

Thorndike was attracted to psychology when he read James's *Principles* for a prize competition at his undergraduate school, Wesleyan (Connecticut). When Thorndike went to Harvard for graduate study he eagerly signed up for courses with James and eventually majored in psychology. His first research interest was children and pedagogy but, no child subjects being available, Thorndike took up the study of learning in animals. James gave him a place to work in his basement after Thorndike failed to secure official research space from Harvard. Before completing his work at Harvard, Thorndike was invited to go to Columbia by Cattell; at Columbia he pursued his animal research. Upon graduation Thorndike returned to his first love, educational psychology, which—along with psychometrics—he made his field of study. Thorndike's importance for us is in his methodological and theoretical approach to animal learning and in his formulation of an S-R psychology he called connectionism.

Thorndike's animal researches are summarized in *Animal Intelligence,* which appeared in 1911. It includes his most important work, the report on his graduate studies, "Animal Intelligence: An Experimental Study of the Associative Processes in Animals," published in 1898. In the introduction to his monograph Thorndike (1911) adopts the usual problem of animal psychology, "to learn the development of mental life down through the phylum, to trace in particular the origin of the human faculty." However, he deprecated the value of previous research, for it relied on the anecdotal method, which Thorndike argued focused only on unusual animal performances, not on the typical. As a substitute Thorndike argued that the experimental approach is the only way to completely control the animal's situation. Thorndike's goal was by experiment to catch animals "using their minds."

Thorndike placed an animal in one of many "puzzle boxes," each of which could be opened by the animal in a different way. When the animal escaped it was fed. Thorndike's subjects included cats, chicks, and dogs. Thorndike's setup is an example of what would later be called *operant conditioning* or *learning·* An animal makes some response, and if it is rewarded—in Thorndike's case with escape and food—the response is learned. If the response is not rewarded, it gradually disappears.

Thorndike's results led him to heap scorn on the older view of the anecdotal psychologists that animals reason; animals learn, he said, solely by trial and error, reward and punishment. In a passage that foreshadowed the future, Thorndike wrote that animals may have no ideas at all, no ideas to associate. There is association, but (maybe) not of ideas. Wrote Thorndike (1911): "The effective part of the association [is] a direct bond between the situation and the impulse." In 1898 Thorndike could not quite accept this radical thesis, although he acknowledged its plausibility.

Thorndike's scorn for the old animal psychology did not escape sharp replies. Wesley Mills, America's senior animal psychologist, attacked Thorndike for having swept away "almost the entire fabric of comparative psychology" and for regarding his predecessors as "insane." Mills argued that animals could only be properly investigated in their natural settings, not in the artificial confines of the laboratory. Directly addressing Thorndike's studies, Mills turned sarcastic: Thorndike "placed cats in boxes only 20 × 15 × 12 inches, and then expected them to act naturally. As well enclose a living man in a coffin, lower him, against his will, into the earth, and attempt to deduce normal psychology from his behavior" (Mills 1899). By 1904, however, Mills had to concede the ascendancy of "the laboratory school," led by Thorndike, "the chief agnostic of this school." They denied that animals reason, or plan, or imitate. But Mills, and Wolfgang Köhler, maintained that animals seemed not to reason in the laboratory because their situations did not permit it. Köhler (1925) said that animals were forced into blind trial and error by the construction of Thorndike's puzzle boxes. Since the penned-up subject could not see how the escape mechanism worked, it simply could not reason its way out; without all the relevant information, insight cannot be acheived. So instead, the poor animal is thrown back on the primitive strategy of trial and error. The method, as Flourens had said of his ablation technique, gives the results. Thorndike's method only permitted random trial and error, so that is what he found. But to go on to claim that all an animal is capable of is mere association is entirely unjustified.

Such considerations did not deter Thorndike from developing his radically simplified theory of learning. In 1911 he wrote in the introduction to *Animal Intelligence:* Any "of the lower animals is . . . obviously a bundle of original and acquired connections between situation and response." He argued that we should try to study animal behavior, not animal consciousness, because the former problem is easier. He contended that this objective method could be extended to human beings, for we can study mental states as behavior. He criticized the structuralists for fabricating a wholly artificial and imaginary picture of human consciousness. He argued that the purpose of psychology should be the control of behavior: "There can be no moral warrant for studying man's nature unless the study will enable us to control his acts." He concluded his introduction by prophesying that psychology would become the study of behavior.

Thorndike proposed two laws of human and animal behavior. The first was the law of effect: "Of several responses made to the same situation, those which are accompanied or closely followed by satisfaction to the animal will, other things being equal, be more firmly connected with the situation, so that, when it recurs, they will be more likely to recur." Punishment, on the other hand, reduces the strength of the connection. Further, the greater the reward or punishment, the greater the change in the connection. Later, Thorndike abandoned the punishment part of the law of effect, retaining only reward. The law of effect is the basic law of operant conditioning, accepted in some form by most learning theorists. Thorndike's second law is the law of exercise: "Any response to a situation will, all other things being equal, be more strongly connected with the situation in proportion to the number of times it has been connected with that situation, and to the average vigor and duration of the connections."

Thorndike contended that these two laws can account for all behavior, no matter how complex: It is possible to reduce "the processes of abstraction, association by similarity and selective thinking to mere secondary consequences of the laws of exercise and effect." He analyzed language as a set of vocal responses learned because parents reward some of a child's sounds but not others. The rewarded ones are acquired and the nonrewarded ones are unlearned, following the law of effect.

Thorndike applied his connectionism to human behavior in *Human Learning,* a series of lectures delivered at Cornell in 1928 and 1929. He presented an elaborate S-R psychology in which many stimuli are connected to many responses in hierarchies of S-R associations. Thorndike asserted that each S-R link could be assigned a probability that S will elicit R. For example, the probability that food will elicit salivation is very near 1.00, while before conditioning the probability that a tone will elicit salivation is near 0. Learning is increasing S-R probabilities; forgetting is lowering them. Just as animal learning is automatic, unmediated by an awareness of the contingency between response and reward, so, Thorndike argues, is human learning also unconscious. One person may learn an operant response without being aware that one is doing so. As he did for animals, Thorndike reduced human reasoning to automatism, custom, and habit. Thorndike held out the promise of scientific utopia, founded on eugenics and scientifically managed education.

Thorndike recognized a number of difficulties that frequently troubled later critics of behaviorism. For example, he admitted that the objective psychologist, who stresses how the environment determines behavior, has a difficult time defining the situation in which an animal acts. Are all stimuli equally relevant to an act? When I am asked, for example, "What is the cube root of sixty-four?" many other stimuli are acting on me at the same time as this question. Defining the response is equally difficult. I may respond "four," but many other behaviors (such as breathing) are also occurring. How do we know what S is connected with what R without recourse to subjective, nonphysical meaning? Thorndike admitted that such questions were reasonable and that answers would have to be given eventually. About reading and listening, Thorndike wrote (1911): "In the hearing or reading of a paragraph, the connections from the words somehow cooperate to give certain total meanings." That "somehow" conceals a mystery only partially acknowledged. He realized the complexity of language when he said that the number of connections necessary to understand a simple sentence may be well over 100,000, and he conceded that organized language is "far beyond any description given by associationist psychology."

Was Thorndike a behaviorist? His biographer (Joncich 1968) says he was, and can cite in support such statements as this: "Our reasons for believing in the existence of other people's minds are our experiences of their physical actions." He did formulate the basic law of operant learning, the law of effect, and the doctrine that consciousness is unnecessary for learning. Unlike Pavlov, he practiced a purely behavioral psychology without reference to physiology. On the other hand, he proposed a principle of "belongingness" that violates a basic principle of classical conditioning, that those elements most closely associated in space and time will be connected in learning. The sentences "John is a butcher, Harry is a carpenter, Jim is a doctor," presented in a list like this, would make *butcher-Harry* a stronger bond than *butcher-John* if the classical conditioning contiguity theory were correct. However, this is clearly not the case. *John* and *butcher* "belong" together (because of the structure of the sentences) and so will be associated, and recalled, together. This principle of belongingness resembled Gestalt psychology rather than behaviorism.

Historically, Thorndike is hard to place. He did not found behaviorism, though he practiced it in his animal researches. His devotion to educational psychology quickly took him outside of the mainstream of academic experimental psychology in which behaviorism developed. It might best be concluded that Thorndike was a practicing behaviorist but not a wholehearted one.

The Neuroscience of I. P. Pavlov (1849–1936).

The other most important new experimental approach to animal psychology grew from Russian objective psychology, an uncompromisingly materialistic and mechanistic conception of biology. The founder of modern Russian physiology was Ivan Michailovich Sechenov (1829–1905), who studied in some of the best physiological laboratories in Europe, including Helmholtz's, and who brought back their methods and ideas to Russia. Sechenov believed that psychology, which was known to him only as a branch of philosophy, could be scientific only if it were completely taken over by physiology and adopted physiology's objective methods. Introspective psychology he dismissed as akin to primitive superstition. Sechenov (1973) wrote:

> Physiology will begin by separating psychological reality from the mass of psychological fiction which even now fills the human mind. Strictly adhering to the principle of induction, physiology will begin with a detailed study of the more simple aspects of psychical life and will not rush at once into the sphere of the highest psychological phenomena. Its progress will therefore lose in rapidity, but it will gain in reliability. As an experimental science, physiology will not raise to the rank of incontrovertible truth anything that cannot be confirmed by exact experiments; this will draw a sharp boundary-line between hypotheses and positive knowledge. Psychology will thereby lose its brilliant universal theories; there will appear tremendous gaps in its supply of scientific data; many explanations will give place to a laconic "we do not know"; the essence of the psychical phenomena manifested in consciousness (and, for the matter of that, the essence of all other phenomena of nature) will remain an inexplicable enigma in all cases without exception. And yet, psychology will gain enormously, for it will be based on scientifically verifiable facts instead of the deceptive suggestions of the voice of our consciousness. Its generalizations and conclusions will be limited to actually existing analogies, they will not be subject to the influence of the personal preferences of the investigator which have so often led psychology to absurd transcendentalism, and they sill thereby become really objective scientific hypotheses. The subjective, the arbitrary and the fantastic will give way to a nearer or more remote approach to truth. In a word, *psychology will become a positive science. Only physiology can do all this, for only physiology holds the key to the scientific analysis of psychical phenomena.*

Sechenov, like American functionalists, abandoned mentalism. Psychology is to be positive, concerned with objective, public facts. Starting with the simple it will proceed to the more complex, being cautious and unspeculative. It will ignore consciousness.

Sechenov's great work was *Reflexes of the Brain* (1863), in which he wrote: "All the external manifestations of brain activity can be attributed to muscular movement. . . . Billions of diverse phenomena, having seemingly no relationship to each other, can be reduced to the activity of several dozen muscles. . . ." Watson's peripheralism is found in Sechenov (1863): "Thought is generally believed to be the cause of behavior . . . [but this is] the greatest of falsehoods: [for] the initial cause of all behavior always lies, not in thought, but in external sensory stimulation. . . ." He also stated that all conscious, voluntary movements are reflexes. Elsewhere, he too adopted the model of language as a chain of vocal responses.

Sechenov's objectivism was popularized by Vladimir Michailovitch Bechterev (1867–1927), who called his system *reflexology,* a name that accurately describes its character. However, the greatest of Sechenov's followers, though not his student, was Ivan Petrovich Pavlov (1849–1936), one of psychology's few household names. Pavlov was a physiologist whose studies of digestion won him the Nobel Prize in 1904. In the course of this work he discovered that stimuli other than food may produce salivation, and this led him to the study of psychology, especially to the concept of the conditioned reflex and its exhaustive investigation.

Pavlov's general attitude was uncompromisingly objective and materialistic. He had the positivist's faith in objective method as the touchstone of natural science, and consequently rejected reference to mind. Pavlov (1957) wrote: "For the naturalist everything lies in the method, in the chance of obtaining an unshakable, lasting truth; and solely from this point of view . . . the soul . . . is not only unnecessary but even harmful to his work.'' Pavlov rejected any appeal to an active inner agency, or mind, in favor of an analysis of the environment: It is possible to explain behavior without reference to a ''fantastic internal world,'' referring only to ''the influence of external stimuli, their summation, etc.'' His analysis of thinking was atomistic, and reflexive. ''The entire mechanism of thinking consists in the elaboration of elementary associations and in the subsequent formation of chains of associations.'' His criticism of nonatomistic psychology was unremitting. He carried out replications of Köhler's ape experiments in order to show that ''association is knowledge, . . . thinking . . . [and] insight,'' and devoted many meetings of his weekly Wednesday discussion group to unfriendly analyses of Gestalt concepts. He viewed the Gestaltists as dualists who ''did not understand anything'' of their own experiments.

Pavlov's technical contribution to the psychology of learning was considerable. He discovered classical conditioning and inaugurated a systematic research program to discover all its mechanisms and situational determinants. In the course of his Nobel Prize–winning investigation of canine salivation, Pavlov observed that salivation could later be elicited by stimuli present at the time food was presented to an animal. He originally called these learned reactions *psychical secretions* because they were elicited by noninnate stimuli, but later he substituted the term *conditioned response*.*

Following the fully refined paradigm of classical conditioning, one begins with a reflex elicited by some innate stimulus, as salivation is elicited by presentation of food. This connection is between an *unconditioned stimulus* (US) and an *unconditioned response* (UR). Then, while presenting the US, one presents some other stimulus that does not elicit the reflex, such as the sound of a metronome. This stimulus is called the *conditioned stimulus* (CS), for after several pairings with the US it will come to elicit the same response (UR), now called the *conditioned response* (CR). It is also possible, although more difficult, to establish a new CS-CR relationship starting with a previously learned CS-CR relationship (for example, pairing a tone with the metronome sound to get the tone to elicit salivation). Such a procedure is known as *higher-order conditioning*.

Pavlov systematically investigated conditioned reflexes. He found that conditioned responses will occur to stimuli similar to the original CS; this is called *generalization*. Similarly, Watson found that little Albert's fear spread to objects resembling the rat, the original CS. Further, Pavlov found that one could require that an animal make a CR to one stimulus but not another; this is called *discrimination*. If too-fine discriminations are required of an animal, it displays neurotic like symptoms. Pavlov also studied how to inhibit conditioned reflexes. If one repeatedly presents the CS without the US, eventually the CR will disappear; this is called *extinction*. However, if one leaves the animal alone for a while, the CS will again elicit the CR; this is called *spontaneous recovery*. There is also *conditioned inhibition*, in which one presents the CS and some new CS together without the US, although the old CS is still occasionally paired with the US. After a while the new combination will fail to elicit the CR. Pavlov's researches were meticulous and detailed, one of the best examples in psychology of a research program in Lakatos's sense.

*This is the English term. However, a more accurate rendering of *ooslouny* would have been *conditional response*.

Between them, Thorndike and Pavlov contributed important methods to psychology, methods that were to become the shared exemplars of behaviorism. At the same time, each questioned the need for psychologists and biologists to talk about animal mind. Thorndike found only blind association forming in his animals, denying that animals reason or even imitate. Pavlov, following Sechenov, proposed to substitute physiology for psychology, eliminating talk about the mind for talk about the brain. La Mettrie's vision seemed about to be fulfilled.

The Problem of Animal Mind

The trouble with animal psychology, said E. C. Sanford in his 1902 presidential address to the APA, is that it "tempts us beyond the bounds of introspection," as do the other growing elements of comparative psychology, the studies of children, the retarded, and the abnormal. But, Sanford asked, should we be "content with a purely objective science of animal or child or idiot behavior?" Sanford thought not and spelled out why, recognizing, with Romanes, the logical conclusion of an objective psychology:

> I doubt if anyone has ever seriously contemplated [a purely objective psychology] in the case of the higher animals, or could carry it to fruitful results if he should undertake it. Nor would anyone seriously propose to treat the behavior of his fellow men in the same way, i.e. to refuse to credit them with conscious experience in the main like his own, though this would seem to be required logically. . . . (Sanford 1903)

However, comparative psychologists still faced Descartes's problem: If they were going to infer mental processes in animals, they had to come up with some criterion of the mental. Just which behaviors could be explained as due to mechanism alone, and which ones reflected mental processes? Descartes had had a simple answer, suited to the Age of Reason: The soul, not the body, thinks; so language—the expression of thought—is the mark of the mental. Things were not so simple for comparative psychologists, though. Accepting phylogenetic continuity and having disposed of the soul, Descartes's criterion was no longer plausible. It seemed clear that the higher animals possess minds and that paramecia do not (though a few animal psychologists thought they did possess very low-grade intelligence), but exactly where to draw the line was intensely problematic.

They wrestled with the problem and proposed numerous criteria, thoughtfully reviewed by Robert Yerkes (1876–1956), a leading animal psychologist, in 1905. Like Sanford, Romanes, and others, Yerkes knew the problem was important for human psychology, too, since we know other human minds just as much by inference as we know animal minds. Indeed, "human psychology stands or falls with comparative psychology. If the study of the mental life of lower animals is not legitimate, no more is the study of human consciousness" (Yerkes 1905b).

As Yerkes saw it, proposed "criteria of the psychic" could be divided into two broad categories. First, there are the structural criteria: An animal might be said to have a mind if it had a sufficiently sophisticated nervous system. More important were the functional criteria, behaviors that indicated presence of mind. Among the possible functional criteria, Yerkes found that most workers took learning to be the mark of the mind, and arranged their experiments to see if a given species could learn. Such a criterion was consistent with James's Darwinian psychology and with contemporary developments in functional psychology. As we have seen, functionalists, following James, viewed consciousness as above all an adjustive agency, so naturally they looked for signs of adjustment in their subjects. An animal that could not learn would be regarded as a mere automaton.

Yerkes thought the search for a single criterion too simple, and proposed three grades, or levels, of consciousness, corresponding to three classes of behavior. At the lowest level there was *discriminative* consciousness, indicated by the ability to discriminate one stimulus from another; even a sea anemone had this grade of consciousness. Next, Yerkes proposed a grade of *intelligent* consciousness, whose sign was learning. Finally, there is *rational* consciousness, which initiates behaviors rather than just responding, however flexibly, to environmental challenges.

At least one young psychologist was coming to find the whole problem a hopeless mare's nest. John B. Watson was a graduate student of Angell's at the University of Chicago, stronghold of Dewey's intstrumentalism and psychological functionalism. Watson disliked introspection and took up animal psychology. His dissertation, "Animal Education," which was cowritten by Angell, had very little mentalism in it, and was mostly an attempt to find a physiological basis for learning. As a promising animal psychologist, Watson was one of the main reviewers of the literature in animal psychology for *Psychological Bulletin,* and there we find him becoming bored by the controversy over the criterion of the mental. In 1907 he called it "the *bête noir* of the student of behavior," and asserted, "The whole contention is tedious." However, he was still at Chicago under Angell's eye, and defended a psychology of animal mind. Mind could not be eliminated from psychology, as long as mind-body parallelism was its working hypothesis.

In the fall of 1908 Watson obtained a position at Johns Hopkins University; away from Angell and on his own, he became bolder. At a talk before the Scientific Association of Johns Hopkins, the newly arrived professor said that the study of animal behavior could be carried out purely objectively, producing facts on a par with the other natural sciences; no reference to animal mind was made (Swartz 1908).

On December 31 of that same year Watson spelled out "A Point of View in Animal Psychology" for the Southern Society for Philosophy and Psychology, then meeting at Hopkins. Watson reviewed the controversy surrounding the criteria of consciousness in animals, and stated (quoting E. F. Buchner, the society's secretary) "that these criteria are impossible of application and . . . have been valueless to the science" of animal behavior. Watson argued that the "facts of behavior" are valuable in themselves, and do not have to be "grounded in any criteria of the psychic." Human psychology too, Watson said, is coming to be more objective, seeming to abandon the use of introspection and "the speech reaction." These trends away from introspection will lead psychology toward "the perfection of technique of the physical sciences." As "criteria of the psychic . . . disappear" from psychology, it will study the whole "process of adjustment" in "all of its broad biological aspects" rather than focusing narrowly on a few elements caught in a moment of introspection. While Watson would not proclaim behaviorism as such until 1913, it is clear that the "viewpoint" he described that afternoon in McCoy Hall was behaviorism in all but name. For Watson, criteria of the mental were useless in animal psychology. Grasping the nettle of the logic of his argument, he had concluded that criteria of the mental were useless in human psychology, too.

RETHINKING MIND:
THE CONSCIOUSNESS
DEBATE (1904–1912)

Mind's place in nature was being fundamentally revised by functional psychologists and by their colleagues in animal psychology. Mind was becoming problematic, reduced to a problem-solving genie in later functional psychology, and slowly disappearing altogether in animal psychology. In 1904 philosophers, too, began to reexamine consciousness.

Does Consciousness Exist? Radical Empiricism

Pragmatism was a method for finding the truth, not a substantive philosophical position. James, nearing the end of his life, turned to the problems of metaphysics, and worked out a system he called "radical empiricism," beginning in 1904 with a paper called "Does Consciousness Exist?" As always, James was provocative, setting off a debate among philosophers and a few psychologists that reshaped their conceptions of mind.

James argued that consciousness did not exist as a distinct, separate thing apart from experience. There simply *is* experience: hardness, redness, tones, tastes, smells. There is nothing above and beyond them called "consciousness" that possesses them and knows them. Pure experience is the stuff of which the world is made, James held. Rather than being a thing, consciousness is a function, a certain kind of relationship among portions of pure experience.

James's position is complex and difficult to grasp, involving a novel form of idealism (experience is the stuff of reality) and panpsychism (everything in the world, even a desk, is conscious). For psychology, what was important was the debate James began, because out of it arose two new conceptions of consciousness that supported behavioralism. James had said that consciousness was a function holding between two appropriately related bits of experience. From this, two distinct concepts of consciousness arose, the relational theory of consciousness and the functional theory of consciousness.

The Relational Theory of Consciousness: Neo-Realism

To some extent, the important place of consciousness in psychology and philosophy derived from the copy theory of knowledge. The copy theory asserts, as James put it, a "radical dualism" of object and knower. For the copy theory, consciousness is a distinct entity that contains representations and knows them. It follows, then, that consciousness is something that can be studied—since it is a distinct thing; and should be studied—since it is our contact with the world. Of course, the copy theory had been challenged before, and James was challenging it again. In James's wake a group of young American philosophers proposed a new form of realism that owed nothing to the old Scottish realists.

They called themselves neorealists, and asserted what they took to be a scientific theory of mind. There is a world of physical objects that we know directly, without the mediation of internal representations. Now while this theory is epistemological in aim—asserting the knowability of a real external physical world—it carries interesting implications for psychology. For in this realist view consciousness is not a special, inner world to be reported on by introspection. Rather, consciousness is a relationship between self and world, the relationship of knowing. This is the basic idea of the relational theory of consciousness, and it was developed in these years by Ralph Barton Perry (1876–1957), James's biographer and teacher of E. C. Tolman; by Edwin Bissel Holt (1873–1946), with Perry at Harvard, and Münsterberg's successor as Harvard's experimental psychologist; and by Edgar Singer (1873–1954), whose papers on mind would later be regarded by many as the first and best statements of behaviorism.

The development of the neorealist theory of mind begins with Perry's analysis of the allegedly privileged nature of introspection. Since Descartes, philosophers had supposed that consciousness was a private, inward possession, known only to itself; upon this idea much of the radical dualism of world and mind rested. In the traditional view, introspection was a special sort of observation of a special place, quite different from the usual sort of observation of external objects, including the behavior of people and animals. Mentalistic psychology accepted the radical dualism of mind and object, and enshrined introspection as the observational technique peculiar to the study of consciousness. Perry argued that introspection was special only in a trivial way, and that the "mind within" of introspection was in no essential way different from the "mind without" exhibited in everyday behavior.

Asking me to introspect is certainly an easy way to enter my mind, Perry conceded. Only I have my memories, and only I know to what I am attending at any given moment. But in these instances introspection is not specially privileged, nor is mind a private place. What I experienced in the past could in principle be determined by other observers present when memories were laid down; careful observation of my current behavior will reveal to what I am paying attention. In short, these contents of consciousness are not exclusively my own: Anyone else may discover them. Indeed, such is the method of animal psychology, said Perry: We discover animal mind by attending to animal behavior, reading an animal's intentions and mental content by observing the way it behaves toward the objects in its environment. As Bolton had argued, an object perceived is an object acted toward, so an animal's percepts are revealed by its conduct.

Another kind of knowledge that seems to make self-consciousness and introspection special sources of knowledge is knowledge of the states of one's own body. Clearly, no one else has *my* headache. Of course, in this sense introspection is privileged. But Perry refused to see any momentous conclusion to be drawn from this circumstance. In the first place, although one does not have direct awareness of another's inner bodily states, one can easily know about them from one's own analogous states; while you do not have my headache, you do know what a headache is. Second, inner bodily processes could be better known by a properly equipped outsider. "Who is so familiar with farming as the farmer?" Perry asked. Obviously, no one; but nonetheless an expert, scientifically trained, may be able to tell the farmer how to grow more efficiently. Similarly, inner bodily processes are not one's exclusive possession, being open to physiological study. Finally, to assert special introspective access to bodily states is a very trivial defense of introspective psychology, because such contents are hardly the essence of mind.

If we follow Perry we must conclude that mentalistic psychology is misguided. Consciousness is not a private thing known only to myself and shareable only through introspection. Rather, my consciousness is a collection of sensations derived from the external world or from my own body; with James, Perry maintains there is no entity "consciousness" apart from these sensations. But since these sensations may be known by anyone else who takes the trouble, my mind is, in fact, an open book, a public object open to scientific study. Introspection remains pragmatically useful of course, since no one has as ready access to my sensations, past and present, as I have; so the psychologist who wishes to open my mind should simply ask me to look within and report what I find. In Perry's view, however, introspection is not the unique road to the mind, since mind is always on view as behavior. In principle, then, psychology can be conducted as a purely behavioral enterprise, engaging its subjects' self-awareness when expedient, but otherwise attending only to behavior. Perry's philosophical analysis of mind coincides ultimately with the view being developed in animal psychology: Mind and behavior are, functionally, the same, and both animal and human psychology rest on the same basis—the study of behavior.

Perry claimed anyone's consciousness could be known by a sufficiently well-informed outside observer. E. B. Holt took consciousness out of a person's head and put it in the environment with his theory of *specific response*. Holt argued that the contents of consciousness were just a cross section of the objects of the universe, past or present, distant or near, to which a person is responding. To clarify his proposal Holt offered an analogy: Consciousness is like a flashlight's beam at any given time, and these are the things we see. Similarly, at any given moment we are reacting only to some of the objects in the universe, and these are the ones of which we are conscious. So consciousness is not inside a person at all, but is "out there wherever the things specifically responded to are." Even memory is treated the same way; memory is not the recovery of some past idea stored away and recalled, but is simply present to an absent object.

Holt's view, like Perry's, rejects the alleged privacy of mind. If consciousness is no more than specific response, and its contents no more than an inventory of the objects controlling my current behavior, then anyone who turns the flashlight of consciousness on the same objects as mine will immediately know my mind. Behavior, Holt argued, is always controlled by or directed toward some real object—that is, a goal—and behavior is to be explained by discovering the acted-toward objects. So to do psychology we need not ask our subjects to introspect, though of course we may. We may understand their minds by examining their behavior and the circumstances in which it occurs, abandoning mentalistic for behavioralistic psychology.

Although he was not formally a neorealist, E. A. Singer proposed a behavioral concept of mind consistent with Perry's or Holt's. Singer applied the pragmatic test of truth to the problem of other minds: Does it matter, does it make a difference in our conduct? Singer argued that pragmatically the other minds problem is meaningless, because it cannot be resolved. It had been debated by philosophers and psychologists since Descartes with no sign of progress. So we should conclude that it is only a pseudoproblem incapable of solution: it doesn't matter.

Singer then considers a possible pragmatic objection that consciousness in others does deeply matter to our everyday behavior. James once asked us to consider the "automatic sweetheart." Suppose you are deeply in love: Every adoring glance, every gentle caress, every tender sigh you will take as signs of your sweetheart's love for you; everything she does will bespeak a love for you like yours for her. Then, one day, you discover she is only a machine, cleverly constructed to exhibit tokens of love for you; but she is not conscious, being but a machine, a simulacrum of a sweetheart. Do you love her still? James thought one could not;

that vital to love is not just the glances, caresses, and sighs but the conviction that behind them is a mental state called love, a subjective condition of fondness, affection, and commitment like one's own. In short, belief in other minds passes the pragmatic test, James concluded, for we will feel very differently about and of course act very differently toward a creature depending on whether or not we think it possesses a mind.

Singer tries to refute James's argument. He asks how terms such as "mind" or "soul" or "soulless" are really used. They are, of course, inferences from behaviors, constructions we erect out of another's conduct. Of course, these constructions may be wrong, and we discover our error when our expectations about a person's behavior are not fulfilled. In the case of the automatic sweetheart, Singer argued, discovering that she is "soulless" only means that you now fear that her behavior in the future will not be like her behavior in the past; that is, that you have just misunderstood her, and that falling out of love with her is not due to her not having a mind, but because you no longer know how she will act.

Singer goes on to argue that mind is an observable object. "Consciousness is not something inferred from behavior, it is behavior. Or, more accurately, our belief in consciousness is an expectation of probable behavior based on observation of actual behavior, a belief to be confirmed or refuted by more observation. . . ." We believe in a separate entity called consciousness only because of deeply ingrained habits of thought, most important, the tendency to analyze things into component parts, some of which may prove not to be a part at all. So, for example, in the past people were tempted to think of a hot rock as a rock + heat, or of a living thing as a body + life. In these cases we have reified into a separate entity something that merely describes behavior. Heat is not a thing, but a certain behavior; life is not a thing added to a body (for example, the Greek psyche), but the behavior of the body. Similarly, Singer maintains, "mind" is not something separate from behavior, it *is* behavior, falsely reified by us. In Singer's view, then, there is no mind for anyone to investigate: mentalistic psychology was a delusion from the start. Psychology should abandon mind, then, and study what is real: behavior.

Whether or not you find Singer's position plausible (I don't), his debate with James raised an issue probably more important today than in their day. For we can now build machines that appear to think, as James's automatic sweetheart appeared to love. Do they really think? And James's own creation has been brought to life in the writings of science-fiction novelists. Can a machine, an android, love? In our age of computers and genetic engineering these are not idle questions, and we shall meet them again in the new field of cognitive science.

Neorealism did not last long as a philosophical movement. Its primary failing was epistemological, accounting for the problem of error. If we know objects directly and without mediation by ideas, how is it that we make mistaken perceptions? With the copy theory error is easy to account for, by saying that copies may not be accurate. Realism finds error difficult to account for. Realism did, however, have lasting influence. The neorealists professionalized philosophy. The older generations of philosophers such as James and Royce wrote for a wide audience of interested readers, and their names were well known to educated Americans. The neorealists, however, modeled their philosophy after science, making it technical and inaccessible to nonphilosophers (Kuklick 1977). In psychology their relational theory of consciousness aided the development of behavioralism and behaviorism, by reworking the mentalistic concept of consciousness into something knowable from behavior, and perhaps even something identical with behavior, in which case the concept of mind need play no role in scientific psychology, however important it might remain outside the profession.

The Functional Theory of Consciousness: Instrumentalism

The neorealists developed the relational conception of mind suggested by James (1904). Dewey and his followers developed the functional conception. Dewey's emerging philosophy was called *instrumentalism,* because of his emphasis on mind as an effective actor in the world, and on knowledge as an instrument for first understanding and then changing the world. Dewey's conception of mind was thus more active than the neorealists, who still adhered to what Dewey called the ''spectator theory of mind.'' Copy theories are spectator theories, because the world impresses itself (to use Hume's term) on a passive mind, which then simply copies the impression over into an idea. Although the neorealists rejected the copy theory, they had not, in Dewey's view, gotten away from the spectator theory, because in the relational theory consciousness is still fully determined by the objects to which one is responding. So mind is still a spectator passively viewing the world, only directly rather than through the spectacles of ideas.

Dewey got rid of the spectator theory, but retained a representational theory of mind. He described mind as a function of the biological organism, adapting actively to the environment, a view going back to his 1896 reflex arc paper. As he developed his instrumentalism, Dewey became more specific about what mind actually does. Mind, he proposed, is ''the presence and operations of meanings, ideas,'' or, more specifically, is ''the ability to anticipate future consequences and to respond to them as stimuli to present behavior.'' So mind is a set of representations of the world that function instrumentally to adaptively guide the organism in its dealings with its environment. Echoing Brentano, Dewey claimed that what makes something mental rather than physical is that it points to something else, that is, has meaning. Postulation of meanings does not require postulation of a separate realm of mind, for ideas are to be conceived as neurophysiological functions, whose total functioning we conveniently designate ''mind.''

Dewey also stressed the social nature of mind, even coming at times to deny that animals had minds, a change from the 1896 paper. Dewey was impressed by Watson's claim (to be described later) that thinking is just speech, or, more strongly, that vocalization is all thinking consists in, whether such vocalization is out loud or covert. Interestingly, this returns Dewey to Descartes's old view, seemingly rejected by functional psychologists, that animals do not think because they do not talk. Dewey has reversed Descartes's priorities, though. For Descartes, thinking comes first and is only expressed in speech; for Dewey, learning to speak creates the ability to think. Descartes was an individualist, endowing each human with an innately given self-consciousness endowed with thought, but forever isolated from other consciousnesses.

Dewey was, generally speaking, a socialist. Humans do not possess some *a priori* consciousness; since language—speech—is acquired through social interaction, it follows that thinking, perhaps all of mind, is a social construction rather than a private possession. When we think inwardly we just talk to ourselves rather than out loud, adjustively using our socially given speech-reactions. Dewey, the philosopher of Progressivism, always aimed at reconstructing philosophy and society on a social basis, breaking down individualism and substituting for it group-consciousness and a submerging of the individual into the greater whole. By conceiving of mind as a social construction, the Cartesian privacy of the individual mind was erased. Instead, the truly mindful entity was society itself, the larger organism of which each person was a cooperative part.

CONCLUSION: BEHAVIORALISM DISCOVERED (1910–1912)

By 1910 all the forces moving psychology from mentalism to behavioralism were well engaged. Philosophical idealism, which made the study of consciousness so important, had been replaced by pragmatism, realism, and instrumentalism, all of which denied consciousness a special, privileged place in the universe. The concept of consciousness had been reworked, becoming successively motor response, relation, and function, and could no longer be clearly differentiated from behavior. Animal psychologists were finding mind to be a problematic, even an unnecessary concept in their field. Psychology as a whole, especially in America, was shifting its concern from the structural study of mental content to the functional study of mental processes, at the same time shifting the focus of experimental technique from the introspective ascertaining of mental states to the objective determination of the influence of stimulus on behavior. Lurking behind all these changes was the desire of psychologists to be socially useful, implying the study of behavior—what people do in society—rather than the socially useless study of sensory contents. The shift from mentalism to behavioralism was inevitable, and it only needed to be discovered to be a *fait accompli*.

Change was in the air. Surveying the year 1910, E. F. Buchner confessed that "some of us are still struggling at initial clearness as to what psychology was about." A signal event of the year was Yerkes's discovery of the "low esteem" in which psychology was held by biologists, whom most psychologists now considered their closest disciplinary colleagues. Surveying leading biologists, Yerkes found that most of them were simply ignorant of psychology, or convinced it would soon disappear into biology. Yerkes concluded that "few, if any, sciences are in worse plight than psychology," attributing its "sad plight" to a lack of self-confidence, an absence of agreed-upon principles, poor training of psychologists in physical science, and a failure to teach psychology as anything more than a set of bizarre facts or as a branch of philosophy, instead of as a natural science. Yerkes's survey was widely discussed, and clearly troubled psychologists, who had labored long and hard to make of psychology a dignified scientific profession.

Psychologists were casting about for a new central concept around which to organize their science, perhaps rendering it more securely a natural science. Bawden, who was continuing to push his own program of interpreting mind "in terms of hands and feet," observed that recently psychologists, without "being clearly conscious of what was happening," had begun to look at mind afresh, in terms of muscle movement, physiology, and "behavior." In any case, psychology needed a general shift in methods and attitudes away from philosophical conceptions and toward biological ones.

The APA convention that year was dominated by discussion of the place of consciousness in psychology, according to an observer, M. E. Haggerty (1911). He noted with some surprise that *no one* at the convention defended the traditional definition of psychology as the study of self-consciousness. Speaking in a symposium on "Philosophical and Psychological Uses of the Terms Mind, Consciousness, and Soul," Angell put his finger on the change from mentalism to behavioralism. Soul, of course, had ceased as a psychological concept when the new psychology replaced the old. But mind, too, Angell noted, was now in "a highly precarious position," and consciousness "is likewise in danger of extinction." Angell defined behavioralism as we did at the beginning of the chapter:

> There is unquestionably a movement on foot in which interest is centered in the *results* of conscious process, rather than in the *processes* themselves. This is peculiarly true in animal psychology; it is only less true in human psychology. In these cases interest is in what may for lack of a better term be called "behavior"; and the analysis of consciousness is primarily justified by the light it throws on behavior, rather than vice-versa.

If this movement should go forward, Angell concluded, psychology would become "a general science of behavior," exactly the definition of the field being offered in the latest textbooks of psychology, Parmelee's (1913), C. H. Judd's (1910), and McDougall's (1912).

The year 1912 proved to be pivotal. Buchner observed further confusion about the definition of mind, and noted the philosophers and their psychological allies who wanted to identify mind with behavior. Knight Dunlap, Watson's older colleague at Johns Hopkins, used the new relational theory of consciousness to make "the case against introspection." Introspection had value only under a copy theory of mind, Dunlap said, because introspection describes the privileged contents of consciousness. But on a relational view of mind, introspection loses its special character, becoming no more than a description of a real object under special conditions of attention. Introspection is thus not the reporting of an internal object, but merely the reporting of the stimulus currently controlling behavior. The term "introspection," Dunlap concluded, should be restricted to the reporting of internal stimuli, which can be gotten at no other way. Introspection was not the central method of psychology.

Elliot Frost reported on European physiologists who were taking a radical new view of consciousness. These physiologists, who included Jacques Loeb, an influence on Watson at Chicago, pronounced psychological concepts "superstitions" and found no room for animal consciousness in the explanation of animal behavior. Frost tried to refute these challenges with a functional view of mind as adaptive "consciousizing" behavior.

More important for us are the reductionistic claims of these European physiologists and certain psychologists then and soon to come. Mind may be eliminated from psychology in two ways that are distinct, and must be kept separate. The program of the physiologists Frost reviewed, including Pavlov, and of psychologists such as Max Meyer, another influence on Watson, called for the reduction of mental concepts to underlying neurophysiological processes thought to cause them. Mental concepts could be eliminated from science as we learn the material causes the mentalistic terms designate. The other program for eliminating mind was inchoate as yet, and would be often mixed up with reductionism for years to come. It claims that mental concepts are to be replaced by behavioral ones, which themselves may not be reducible to mechanical underlying physiological laws. We can see something of this view, perfected later by B. F. Skinner, in the relational theories of mind, especially Singer's; but it is not in 1912 a distinct psychological system. The historical importance of the reductionists reviewed by Frost remains— the validity of consciousness and mind as central concepts in psychology was under increasing assault from every quarter.

The December 1912 meeting of the APA in Cleveland marked the final transition of psychology, with only a few holdouts, from mentalism to behavioralism. Angell identified the behavioral view in "Behavior as a Category of Psychology" (Angell 1913). Angell began by recalling his own prophecy, made at the 1910 APA meeting, that the study of behavior was overshadowing the study of consciousness. Just two years later, consciousness had become a "victim marked for slaughter," as behavior was poised to completely replace mental life as the subject matter of psychology. In philosophy the consciousness debate questioned consciousness' very existence. In animal psychology researchers wanted to give up reference to mind and just study behavior, matched by a "general drift" in the same direction in human psychology. This drift, Angell pointed out, is "not deliberate" and is thus likely to be "substantial and enduring."

Moreover, there were many flourishing fields concerned with human beings in which introspection offered "no adequate approach": social psychology, racial psychology, sociology, economics, development, individual differences and others. The tendency to eliminate introspection is not just a product of new topics like the above, but is aided by functional psychology, which studies response more than conscious content.

Angell was not willing to completely abandon introspection. While it could no longer be psychology's premier method, it retained an important role in providing data not otherwise obtainable. It would be a "crowning absurdity," Angell said, for the new behavioral psychology to deny any significance to the "chief distinction" of human nature—mind. There was another danger in a behavioral psychology, Angell warned. By concentrating on behavior, psychologists would trespass on the territory of another science, biology; and thus there was a risk that psychology might be "swallowed up" by biology, or might become a mere vassal to biology as its "overlord."

Still, there was no mistaking Angell's message. Psychology was now the study of behavior. It was a natural science closely allied to biology, forsaking its philosophical roots. Its methods were now objective, introspection serving pragmatically when needed, but no longer at the center of the field. Concern with consciousness as such had been replaced by concern with the explanation, prediction, and control of behavior. The psychology viewed with such horror by Warner Fite had arrived.

BIBLIOGRAPHY

A general overview of the period is given by John L. Thomas in his contribution to Bailyn et al. *The great republic* (Boston: Little, Brown, 1977), "Nationalizing the republic." The standard history of the transformation of America at the turn of the century is Robert Wiebe, *The search for order 1877–1920* (New York: Hill and Wang, 1967). Daniel Boorstin concludes his history of the United States in *The Americans: The democratic experience* (New York: Vintage, 1974), which provides a wonderfully readable, even entertaining, account of twentieth-century America, entirely dispensing with political and military history. There are several good histories of Progressivism: Richard Hofstadter, *The age of reform* (New York: Vintage, 1975), Eric Goldman, *Rendezvous with destiny* (New York: Vintage, Rev. ed. 1975), and two books by David Noble, *The paradox of Progressive thought* (Minneapolis, Minn: University of Minnesota Press), and *The Progressive mind* (Minneapolis, Minn: Burgess, Rev. ed. 1981). Works that concentrate on intellectual and social aspects of our period include Henry F. May, *The end of American innocence* (Chicago: Quadrangle, 1964), and Morton White, *Social thought in America* (London: Oxford University Press, 1976), and *Science and sentiment in America* (London: Oxford University Press, 1972).

Dewey's philosophy is central to the thought of the first part of the twentieth century. Two useful accounts of his intellectual development are Morton G. White, *The origin of Dewey's instrumentalism* (New York: Octagon, 1964) and the chapter on Dewey in E. Flower and M. Murphey, *A history of philosophy in America* (New York: Capricorn, 1977). Dewey was the leading educational philosopher in this period, which witnessed far-ranging debate about the nature and aims of education, as schools were refashioned to meet the needs of a mass, industrialized society. Merle Curti, *The social ideas of American educators* (Paterson, N.J.: Littlefield, Adams, Rev. ed. 1965) summarizes the views not only of Dewey, but of James and Thorndike, to mention only the psychologists. Curti's book was originally published in 1931, and reflects an apparently socialist point of view that leads to much criticism of everyone but Dewey for putting too much emphasis on the individual.

There are three important book-length studies of psychology in this period. Brian Mackenzie, *Behaviorism and the limits of scientific method* (London: Routledge and Kegan Paul, 1977) ties behaviorism closely to positivism, as did the first edition of the present text, and to the problem of animal mind. John M. O'Donnell's *The origins of behaviorism: American psychology 1870–1920* (New York: New York University Press, 1985) was published after the above chapter was written, but he also argues that behaviorism emerged gradually and inevitably out of American realist, new, and functional psychology. Reba N. Soffer's *Ethics and society in England: The revolution in the social sciences 1870–1914* (Berkeley, Calif.: University of California Press, 1978) covers England for the same period we've covered America, and relates similar developments there to the British intellectual climate, claiming, contrary to the thesis I argued, that a "revolution" took place during these years.

A valuable source for the history of psychology from its founding days onward is the continuing series called *A history of psychology in autobiography*. The first three volumes, which cover the period here, were edited by Carl Murchison and published by Clark University Press. Since then subsequent volumes have been published under varying editorship and by different publishers.

Perhaps because of their tenuous status as scientists, psychologists were acutely conscious of the history of their discipline in its early years, and often wrote historical summaries of even recent developments. Edward Franklin Buchner wrote several such reviews, including an annual piece in *Psychological Bulletin* from 1904 to 1912 called "Progress in psychology," and two general accounts, "Ten years of American psychology" (*Science*, 1903, *18*, 193–204) and "A quarter century of psychology in America" (*American Journal of Psychology*, 1903, *13*, 666–680). Another general summary from the same period is James Mark Baldwin, "A sketch of the history of psychology" (*Psychological Review*, 1905, *12*, 144–145). Christian Ruckmich, "The history and status of psychology in the United States" (*American Journal of Psychology*, 1912, *23*, 517–531) is a valuable institutional history, including not only accounts of the founding of laboratories and so on, but a comparative economic analysis of the status within universities of psychology compared with other disciplines. Another institutional history, by a participant, is J. M. Cattell, "Early psychological laboratories" (*Science*, 1928, *67*, 543–548).

Perhaps the final confrontation between the old psychology and the new occurred on April 27, 1895 at the Massachusetts Schoolmaster's Club, when Larkin Dunton and W. T. Harris, educators in the old mold, confronted Hugo Münsterberg and G. Stanley Hall, new psychologists. The encounter was published as *The old psychology and the new* (Boston: New England Publishing Co., 1895).

The writings of, and some contemporary comments on, the pragmatist philosophers Peirce, James, and Dewey have been collected by Amelie Rorty, *Pragmatic philosophy* (Garden City, N.Y.: Doubleday), and H. Standish Thayer, *Pragmatism: The classic writings* (New York: Mentor, 1970). Bruce Kuklick's *Rise of American philosophy* (New Haven: Yale University Press, 1977) traces the development of pragmatism and sets it against a larger framework. Dewey's major psychological papers have been gathered up by Joseph Ratner, *John Dewey: Philosophy, psychology, and social practice* (New York: Capricorn, 1965).

The presidential addresses of the presidents of the APA have been summarized, and the more important ones reprinted, in Ernest R. Hilgard, *American psychology in historical perspective* (Washington, D.C.: American Psychological Association).

In addition to the referenced works, students interested in animal psychology, Thorndike, and Pavlov may wish to consult the following. B. P. Babkin has written a biography of Pavlov (Chicago: University of Chicago Press, 1949); his experimental research program is detailed in *Conditioned reflexes*, available as a reprint paperback from Dover (New York, 1960). Thorndike's application of his learning theory may be found in his *Educational psychology* (New York: Arno, 1964), the brief edition of which appeared almost simultaneously with Watson's behaviorism (1914). Watson wrote two popular articles for *Harper's Magazine* (1909, *120*, 346–353, and 1912, *124*, 376–382), which, while they offer few clues to his incipient behaviorism, are good accounts of early twentieth-century animal psychology. A fine history of animal psychology is given by Robert Boakes *From Darwin to behaviorism: Psychology and the minds of animals* (New York: Cambridge University Press, 1984). Thomas Cadwallader, "Neglected aspects of the evolution of American comparative and animal psychology" (in G. Greenberg and E. Tobach, Eds. *Behavioral evolution and integrative levels*, Hillsdale, N.J.: Erlbaum, 1984) concentrates on the American scene.

There are two good places to enter the consciousness debate. The debate grew so important that the American Philosophical Association decided to devote its 1912 convention to the problem. To prepare for the meeting, the association appointed a committee to summarize the main points of the debate and to draw up a bibliography. Their report appears in *The Journal of Philosophy*, 1911, *8*, 701–708. The debate continued in philosophy past 1912, and eventually inspired an excellent treatment of the problem of consciousness, including views and issues not treated in the text, by Charles Morris, *Six theories of mind* (Chicago: University of Chicago Press, 1932). Between these two, every aspect of the debate is covered, and all the relevant literature cited, with the exception (for some unknown reason) of the papers of Edgar Singer. His key paper was "Mind as an observable object" (*Journal of Philosophy*, 1911, *8*, 180–186), followed up in the same place with two replies the next year, "Consciousness and behavior" (*Journal of Philosophy*, 1912, *9*, 15–19), and "On mind as observable object" (*Journal of Philosophy*, 1912, *9*, 206–214).

REFERENCES

Angell, J. R. (1903a) A preliminary study of the localization of sound. *Psychological Review 10:* 1–18.

Angell, J. R. (1903b) The relation of structural and functional psychology to philosophy. *Philosophical Review 12:* 243–271.

Angell, J. R. (1907) The province of functional psychology. *Psychological Review 14:* 61–91.

Angell, J. R. (1911) Usages of the terms mind, consciousness, and soul. *Psychological Bulletin 8:* 46–47.

Angell, J. R. (1913) Behavior as a category of psychology. *Psychological Review 20:* 255–270.

Arnold, Felix (1905) Psychological standpoints. *Psychological Bulletin 2:* 369–373.

Baldwin, J. M. (1895) *Mental development in the child and the race*. New York: Macmillan.

Bartlett, F. C. (1932) *Remembering*. Cambridge, England: Cambridge University Press.

Bawden, H. H. (1903) The functional theory of parallelism. *Philosophical Review 12:* 299–319.

Bawden, H. H. (1904) The meaning of the psychical in functional psychology. *Philosophical Review 13:* 298–319.

Bawden, H. H. (1910) Mind as a category of psychology. *Psychological Bulletin 7:* 221–225.

Bernard, L. L. (1911) *The transition to an objective standard of social control*. Chicago: University of Chicago Press.

Bolton, T. (1902) A biological view of perception. *Psychological Review 9:* 537–548.

Boorstin, D. J. (1974) *The Americans: The democratic experience*. New York: Vintage Books.

Bryan, W. L. and Harter, N. (1897) Studies in the psychology of the telegraphic language. *Psychological Review 4:* 27–53.

Calkins, M. W. (1906) A reconciliation between structural and functional psychology. *Psychological Review 13:* 61–81.

Cattell, J. M. (1896) Address of the president. *Psychological Review 3:* 134–148.

Cattell, J. M. (1904) The conceptions and methods of psychology. *Popular Science Monthly 66:* 176–186

Danziger, K. (1979) The social origins of modern psychology. In A. Buss (Ed.) *Psychology in social context*. New York: Irvington.

Dewey, J. (1896) The reflex-arc concept in psychology. *Psychological Review 3:* 357–370.

Dewey, J. (1900) Psychology and social practice. *Psychological Review 7:* 105–124.

Dewey, J. (1957) *Reconstruction in philosophy*. Boston: Beacon.

Ebbinghaus, H. (1885/1964) *Memory*. New York: Dover.

Fite, W. (1913) The science of man. *The Nation 96* (April 10): 368–370.

Frost, E. P. (1912) Can biology and physiology dispense with consciousness? *Psychological Review 3:* 246–252.

Haggerty, M. E. (1911) The nineteenth annual meeting of the A.P.A. *Journal of Philosophy 8:* 204–217.

Hale, M. (1980) *Human science and social order*. Philadelphia: Temple University Press.

Herrnstein, R. and Boring, E. eds. (1965) *A source book in the history of psychology*. Cambridge: Harvard University Press.

James, W. (1892) A plea for psychology as a natural science. *Philosophical Review 1:* 146–153.

James, W. (1904) Does "consciousness" exist? *Journal of Philosophy 1:* 477–491.

James, W. (1907/1955) *Pragmatism*. New York: Meridian.

Jastrow, J. (1901) Some currents and undercurrents in psychology. *Psychological Review 8:* 1–26.

Joncich, G. (1968) *The sane positivist: A biography of E. L. Thorndike*. Middletown, Conn.: Wesleyan University Press.

Judd, C. H. (1910) *Psychology: General introduction*. New York: Scribner's.

Köhler, W. (1925) *The mentality of apes*. New York: Harcourt Brace.

Kuklick, B. (1977) *The rise of American philosophy*. New Haven: Yale University Press.

Ladd, G. T. (1892) Psychology as a so-called "natural science." *Philosophical Review 1:* 24–53.

McDougall, W. (1912) *Psychology: The study of behaviour*. New York: Holt.

Mills, W. (1899) The nature of animal intelligence. *Psychological Review 6:* 262–274.

Mills, W. (1904) Some aspects of the development of comparative psychology. *Science 19:* 745–757.

Parmelee, M. (1913) *The science of human behavior*. New York: Macmillan.

Pavlov, I. P. (1957) *Experimental psychology and other essays*. New York: Philosophical Library.

Sanford, E. C. (1903) Psychology and physics. *Psychological Review 10:* 105–119.

Sechenov, I. M. (1863/1965) *Reflexes of the brain.* Reprinted in Herrnstein and Boring (1965).

Sechenov, I. M. (1973) *Biographical sketch and essays.* New York: Arno.

Swartz, C. K. (1908) The scientific association of Johns Hopkins University. *Science 28:* 814–815.

Thilly, F. (1905) Review of Angell's psychology. *Philosophical Review 14:* 481–487.

Thorndike, E. L. (1898a) Review of Evans' "Evolution, ethics and animal psychology." *Psychological Review 5:* 229–230.

Thorndike, E. L. (1911/1965) *Animal intelligence.* New York: Hafner.

Thorndike, E. L. (1929/1968) *Human learning.* New York: Johnson Reprint Corporation.

Titchener, E. B. (1898b) Postulates of a structural psychology. *Philosophical Review 7:* 449–465.

Turner, F. M. (1974) *Between science and religion.* New Haven: Yale University Press.

Ward, J. (1904) The present problems of general psychology. *Philosophical Review 13:* 603–621.

Ward, J. (1920) *Psychological principles.* Cambridge, England: Cambridge University Press.

Watson, J. B. (1907) Comparative psychology. *Psychological Bulletin 4:* 288–302.

Watson, J. B. (1909) A point of view in comparative psychology. *Psychological Bulletin 6:* 57–58.

Wozniak, R. (1982) Metaphysics and science, reason and reality: The intellectual origins of genetic epistemology. In J. Broughton and D. Freeman Noir (Eds.) *The cognitive developmental psychology of James Mark Baldwin.* (Hillsdale, N.J.: Ablex).

Yerkes, R. (1905a) Animal psychology and the criterion of the psychic. *Journal of Philosophy 2:* 141–149.

Yerkes, R. (1905b) Review of Claparede, "Is comparative psychology legitimate?" *Journal of Philosophy 2:* 527–528.

CHAPTER 11

Psychology Takes Off

The Behaviorist Era (1913–1950)

DEVELOPING BEHAVIORALISM (1913–1930)
    Behaviorism Proclaimed
    The Initial Response (1913–1918)
    Behaviorism Defined (1919–1930)
MAJOR FORMULATIONS OF BEHAVIORALISM (1930–1950)
    Psychology and the Science of Science
    Edward Chace Tolman's Purposive Behaviorism
    Clark Leonard Hull's Mechanistic Behaviorism
    Tolman vs. Hull
CONCLUSION: WE'RE ALL BEHAVIORISTS NOW

In the years encompassing World War I and leading up to World War II, psychology experienced tremendous growth. The numbers of psychologists grew dramatically, their work took them increasingly into applied areas little known to the academic founders of psychology, and psychology enjoyed popularity with ordinary people—even if it did not always command their respect. Within the field the chief developments are the rise of applied psychology, especially mental testing, and the triumph of behavioralism as the psychology of the twentieth century.

DEVELOPING BEHAVIORALISM (1913–1930)

Behaviorism Proclaimed

John Broadus Watson (1878–1958) was a young, ambitious animal psychologist who, as we saw in the last chapter, had by 1908 defined a purely objective, nonmentalistic approach to animal psychology, shortly after graduating from the University of Chicago and taking a position at Johns Hopkins University. In his autobiography he says that he had broached the idea of a purely objective human psychology to his teachers during his days as a graduate student at Chicago, but that his proposals were greeted with such horror that he kept his own counsel. After establishing himself as a leading animal psychologist in his own right, he felt emboldened to expand publicly the scope of his objective psychology. On February 13, 1913, he began a series of lectures on animal psychology at Columbia University with a lecture on "Psychology as the Behaviorist Views It." Encouraged by the editor of *Psychological Review,* Howard Warren (who for some time had been trying to get Watson to publish his new view of psychology), Watson published his lecture; in 1943 a group of eminent psychologists rated this paper as the most important one ever published in the *Review*.

From the paper's aggressive tone it was clear that Watson was issuing a manifesto for a new kind of psychology: behaviorism. In those years manifestos were rather more common than they are today. For example, in Watson's year of 1913 modern art came to America in the notorious Armory Show, a kind of manifesto in paint for modernism. Modern artists also issued written manifestos for various modernist movements, such as futurism and dadaism. Watson's manifesto for behaviorism shared the goals of these modernist manifestos: to repudiate the past and set out, however incoherently, a vision of life as it might be. Watson began with a ringing definition of psychology as it might be:

> Psychology as the behaviorist views it is a purely objective branch of natural science. Its theoretical goal is the prediction and control of behavior. Introspection forms no essential part of its methods, nor is the scientific value of its data dependent on the readiness with which they lend themselves to interpretation in terms of consciousness. The behaviorist, in his efforts to get a unitary scheme of animal response, recognizes no dividing line between man and brute. The behavior of man, with all of its refinement and complexity, forms only a part of the behaviorist's total scheme of investigation.

In the tradition of modernist manifestos Watson went on to repudiate psychology as it had been. Watson refused to see any difference between structuralism and functionalism. Both of them adopted the traditional definition of psychology as "the science of the phenomena of consciousness," and both of them used the traditional "esoteric" method of introspection. However, psychology so conceived had "failed to make its place in the world as an undisputed natural science." As an animal psychologist, Watson felt especially constrained by mentalism. There seemed to be little room for animal work, as animals were unable to introspect, forcing psychologists to "construct" conscious contents for them on analogy to the psychologists' own minds. Moreover, traditional psychology was anthropocentric, respecting the findings of animal psychology only insofar as they bore upon questions of human psychology. Watson found this situation intolerable, and aimed at reversing the traditional priorities. In 1908 he had declared the autonomy of animal psychology as the study of animal behavior; now he proposed to use "human beings as subjects and to employ methods of investigation which are exactly comparable to those now employed in animal work." Earlier comparative psychologists had warned that we should not anthropomorphize about animals; Watson urged psychologists not to anthropomorphize about human beings.

Watson faulted introspection on empirical, philosophical, and practical grounds. Empirically, it simply failed to define questions it could convincingly answer. There was as yet no answer even to the most basic question of the psychology of consciousness, how many sensations there are and the number of their attributes. Watson saw no end to a sterile discussion: "I firmly believe that, unless the introspective method is discarded, psychology will still be divided on the question as to whether auditory sensations have the quality of 'extension' . . . and upon many hundreds of other [questions] of like character."

Watson's second ground for rejecting introspection was philosophical: It was not like the methods of natural science, and therefore it was not a scientific method at all. In the natural sciences, good techniques provide "reproducible results," and then, when these are not forthcoming, "the attack is made upon the experimental conditions" until reliable results are obtained. In mentalistic psychology, however, we must study the private world of an observer's consciousness. This means that instead of attacking experimental conditions when results are unclear, psychologists attack the introspective observer, saying, "Your introspection is poor" or "untrained." Watson's point seemed to be that the results of introspective psychology possess a personal element not found in the natural sciences; this contention forms the basis for methodological behaviorism.

Finally, introspection failed practical tests. In the laboratory it demanded that animal psychologists find some behavioral criterion of consciousness, an issue we know involved Watson, as he reviewed the issue several times for the *Psychological Bulletin*. But he now argued that consciousness was irrelevant to animal work: "One can assume either the presence or absence of consciousness anywhere in the phylogenetic scale without affecting the problems of behavior one jot or one tittle." Experiments are in fact designed to find out what an animal will do in some novel circumstance, and its behavior is then observed; only later must the researcher attempt the "absurd," reconstructing the animal's mind as it behaved. But Watson pointed out that reconstructing the animal's consciousness added nothing at all to what had already been accomplished in the observation of behavior. In society, introspective psychology was likewise irrelevant, offering no solutions to the problems facing people in modern life. Indeed, Watson reports that it was his feeling that mentalistic psychology had "no realm of application" that early made him "dissatisfied" with it. So it is not surprising to find that the one area of existing psychology Watson praised was applied psychology: educational psychology, psychopharmacology, mental testing, psychopathology, and legal and advertising psychology. These fields were "most flourishing" because they were "less dependent on introspection." Sounding a key theme of Progressivism and of behavioralism to come, Watson lauded these "truly scientific" psychologies because they "are in search of broad generalizations which will lead to the control of human behavior."

On Watson's account, then, introspective psychology had nothing to recommend it and much to condemn it. "[P]sychology must discard all reference to consciousness." Psychology must now be defined as the science of behavior, and "never use the terms consciousness, mental states, mind, content, introspectively verifiable, imagery and the like. . . . It can be done in terms of stimulus and response, in terms of habit formation, habit integrations and the like. Furthermore, I believe that it is really worthwhile to make this attempt now."

The "starting point" of Watson's new psychology would be the "fact that organisms, man and animal alike, do adjust themselves to their environment"; that is, psychology would be the study of adjustive behavior, not conscious content. Description of behavior would lead to the prediction of behavior in terms of stimulus and response: "In a system of psychology completely worked out, given the response the stimuli can be predicted [Watson meant *retrodicted*]; given the stimuli the response can be predicted." Ultimately, Watson aimed to "learn general and particular methods by which I may control behavior." Once control techniques become available, the leaders of society will be able to "utilize our data in a practical way." While Watson did not cite Auguste Comte, his program for behaviorism—describe, predict, and control observable behavior—was clearly in the positivist tradition. The only acceptable form of explanation for both Comte and Watson was "explanation in physico-chemical terms."

The methods by which we are to achieve psychology's new goals are left rather vague, as Watson was later to admit (Watson 1916a). The only thing made really clear about behavioral methodology in the manifesto is that under behaviorism, work "on the human being will be comparable directly with the work upon animals," because behaviorists "care as little about [a human subject's] 'conscious processes' during the conduct of the experiment as we care about such processes in the rat." He gives a few examples of how sensation and memory might be behavioristically investigated, but they are not very convincing and would soon be replaced by Pavlov's conditioned reflex method.

Watson does say some startling things about human thinking. He asserts that thinking does not involve the brain—there are no "centrally initiated processes"—but consists in "faint reinstatement of . . . muscular acts," specifically "motor habits in the larynx." "In other words, wherever there are thought processes there are faint contractions of the systems of musculature involved in the overt exercise of the customary act, and especially in the still finer systems of musculature involved in speech. . . . [I]magery becomes a mental luxury (even if it really exists) without any functional significance whatever." While Watson's claims may outrage the lay reader, we should see that his conclusions are the logical outcome of the motor theory of consciousness (McComas 1916). On the motor theory, conscious content simply reflects without affecting stimulus-response connections; Watson is simply pointing out that since mental content has "no functional significance," there's no point in studying it save accumulated prejudice: "[O]ur minds have been warped by fifty odd years which have been devoted to the study of states of consciousness." Peripheralism had been gaining force as a doctrine in psychology since at least the time of Sechenov, and Waton's version of it would be found in the most influential and important forms of behavioralism until the coming of cognitive science in the 1960s.

In another Columbia lecture, "Image and Affection in Behavior," also published in 1913, Watson continued his assault on mental content. He considers, and rejects, the formula of methodological behaviorism, the view that "I care not what goes on in [a person's] so called mind" as long as his behavior is predictable. But for Watson, methodological behaviorism is a "partial defeat" he found unacceptable, preferring instead "to attack." He reiterated his view that "there are no centrally initiated processes." Instead, thinking is just "implicit behavior" that sometimes occurs between a stimulus and the resulting "explicit behavior." Most implicit behavior, he hypothesizes, occurs in the larynx, and is open to observation, though the technique of such observation had not been developed. The important point for Watson is that there are no functional mental processes playing causal roles in determining behavior. There are only chains of behavior, some of which are difficult to observe. Should this be true—and Watson applies his thesis to both mental images and experienced emotions, as the title states—no part of psychology could escape the behaviorist's scheme, for mind would be shown to be behavior; the behaviorist would concede no subject to the mentalist. Finally, Watson suggests a theme that would emerge more vividly in his later writings, and that shows how his behaviorism was part of a larger revolt against the cultural past, not simply a revolt against a failed introspective psychology. Watson claims that allegiance to mentalistic psychology is at root clinging to religion in a scientific age that has made religion obsolete. Those who believe that there are centrally initiated processes—that is, behaviors begun by the brain and not by some outside stimulus—really believe in the soul. Watson said that since we know nothing about the cortex, it is easy to attribute the functions of the soul to the cortex: Both are unknown mysteries. Watson's position was extremely radical: Not only did the soul not exist, neither did the cortex as anything other than a relay station connecting stimulus and response; both soul and brain could be ignored in the description, prediction, and control of behavior.

The Initial Response (1913–1918)

How did psychologists receive Watson's manifesto? One might expect that behaviorism would become the rallying cry of younger psychologists and the object of denunciation by their elders. In fact, when later Watson's manifesto took its revered place as the starting point of behaviorism, it was thought to have been received in just such fashions. However, as Samelson (1981) has shown, published responses to "Psychology as the Behaviorist Views It" were both remarkably few and remarkably restrained.

There were a few responses in 1913 itself. Watson's teacher, Angell, added some references to behaviorism in the published version of "Behavior as a Category of Psychology." He said he was "heartily sympathetic" to behaviorism, and recognized it as a logical development of his own emphasis on behavior. Nevertheless, he did not think that introspection could ever be entirely eliminated from psychology, if only as providing useful reports on the processes connecting stimulus and response; Watson himself admitted such use of introspection, but called it the "language method." Angell bid behaviorism "Godspeed" but counseled it to "forego the excesses of youth," which, like most counsel to youth, went unheeded.

Without actually citing Watson, M. E. Haggerty agreed that the emerging laws of learning, or habit formation, reduced behavior to "physical terms," so there was no "longer any need to invoke ghosts in the form of consciousness" to explain thinking. Robert Yerkes criticized Watson for "throwing overboard" the method of self-observation that set psychology off from biology; under behaviorism psychology would be "merely a fragment of physiology." The philosopher Henry Marshall was afraid that psychology might be "evaporating." He observed the behavioral *Zeitgeist* of which behaviorism was the latest manifestation, and concluded that it contained much of value, but that to identify behavior study with psychology was an "astounding confusion of thought," since consciousness remained to be investigated whatever the achievements of behaviorism. Mary Calkins, who had earlier proposed her self-psychology as a compromise between structural and functional psychology, now proposed it as a mediator between behaviorism and mentalism. Like most of the other commentators, she agreed with much of Watson's critique of structuralism and applauded the study of behavior; but she nevertheless found introspection to be the indispensable, if sometimes troublesome, method of psychology.

The other commentaries on behaviorism in the years before World War I took much the same line as these initial responses: The deficiencies of structuralism were acknowledged, the virtues of studying behavior were conceded, but introspection was nevertheless defended as the *sine qua non* of psychology. The study of behavior was just biology; psychology, to retain its identity, had to remain introspective. A. H. Jones (1915) spoke for many when he wrote, "We may rest assured then, that whatever else psychology may be, it is at least a doctrine of awareness. To deny this . . . is to pour out the baby with the bath." Titchener (1914) also saw behavior study as biology rather than psychology. Since the facts of consciousness exist, he said, they can be studied, and such is the task of psychology. While behaviorism might accomplish much, since it was not psychology at all, it posed no threat to introspective psychology. One of the few substantive criticisms of Watson's behaviorism was offered by H. C. McComas (1916), who correctly saw it as a natural consequence of the motor theory of consciousness. McComas showed that Watson's identification of thinking with laryngeal movements stood falsified: Some people had already lost their larynxes due to disease, without thereby losing the ability to think.

With the exception of McComas's paper, however, reactions to behaviorism in the prewar years tended to assert the same thing: That, while behavior study was valuable, it was really a form of biology rather than psychology, because psychology was by definition the study of consciousness, and must, perforce, use introspection as its method. While these critics' position was not unreasonable, they seemed not to notice that Watson might succeed in fundamentally redefining psychology altogether. As we have seen, Watson was riding the crest of behavioralism, and if enough psychologists adopted his definition of their field, it would as a matter of historical fact cease to be the study of the mind, and would become the study of behavior. While his radical peripheralism might not be accepted, behavioralism would be, and behaviorism would be its name.

Watson, of course, did not remain silent while his views were debated. He was chosen by a nominating committee and ratified by the members of the APA to be the president for 1916. In his presidential address he tried to fill the most conspicuous gap in behaviorism: the method and theory by which it would study and explain behavior. Watson had tried for some years to show that thinking was just implicit speech, but had failed. So he turned to the work of Karl Lashley, a student in Watson's laboratory, who had been replicating and extending Pavlov's conditioning techniques. Watson now presented the conditioned reflex work as the substance of behaviorism: Pavlov's method applied to humans would be behaviorism's tool of investigation, while the conditioned reflex theory would provide the basis for the prediction and control of behavior in animals and people. Watson's address set out in detail how the conditioned reflex method could be applied to both humans and animals, providing an objective substitute for introspection. Nor was Watson loath to apply the theory outside the laboratory. In another 1916 paper Watson argued that neuroses were just "habit disturbances," most usually "disturbances of speech functions." We see again that Watson's program was not merely scientific but social; even as he was first learning about and investigating conditioned reflexes he was prepared to assert that speech, and thus neurotic symptoms, were just conditioned reflexes, poor behavior adjustments that could, in turn, be corrected by the application of behavior principles.

We have noted various reactions to Watson's manifesto. However, apart from about a dozen papers, few psychologists or philosophers wrote about it. The reason is not far to seek. A manifesto is a work of rhetoric, and when we separate Watson's rhetoric from his substantive proposals we find that he said little that was new, but said it in especially angry tones. In the last chapter we showed that the behavioral approach had overcome psychology slowly and almost unnoticed in the years after 1892. What Watson did was to give behavioralism an aggressive voice, and to give it a name that stuck—"behaviorism," however misleading that name has since become. In its time, then, his manifesto merited little attention. Older psychologists had already admitted that psychology needed to pay attention to behavior—after all, it was they who had moved the field toward behavioralism—but remained concerned to preserve the traditional mission of psychology, the study of consciousness. Younger psychologists of Watson's generation had already accepted behavioralism, and so accepted his broad position without any sense of excitement, even if they might reject his extreme peripheralism. So no one was either outraged or inspired by Watson's manifesto of psychological modernism, for they had learned to live with modernism or were already practicing it. Watson created no revolution, but he did make clear that psychology was no longer the science of consciousness. "Psychology as the Behaviorist Views It" simply marks the moment when behavioralism became ascendant and created for later behavioralists a useful "myth of origin." It provided for them a secure anchoring point in the history of psychology, and a justification for the abandonment of an introspective method they found boring and sterile. But all of these things would have happened had Watson never become a psychologist.

Behaviorism Defined (1919–1930)

Along with the rest of psychology, the discussion of behaviorism was interrupted by World War I. As we shall see, psychology was much changed by its involvement with the war; when psychologists resumed their consideration of behaviorism, the grounds of the discussion were quite different than they had been before the war. The value of objective psychology had been proved by the tests psychologists had devised to classify soldiers, and that success had brought psychology before a wider audience. After the war the question was no longer whether behaviorism was legitimate, but what form behaviorism should take. In the 1920s psychologists attempted to define behaviorism; but, as we shall see, they failed to make of it a coherent movement, much less a Kuhnian paradigm.

As early as 1922 it was clear that psychologists were having trouble understanding behaviorism, or formulating it in any widely agreeable way. Walter Hunter, a sympathizer of Watson's, wrote "An Open Letter to the Anti-behaviorists." He thought behaviorism was exactly what Watson preached, the definition of psychology as the study of "stimulus and response relations." He viewed the various "new formulas" for behaviorism that by then had been offered as "illegitimate offspring" making it difficult for psychologists to see what behaviorism was. Later he (Hunter 1925) would try to finesse the issue by defining a new science, "anthroponomy," the science of human behavior. But Hunter's new science never caught on, leaving psychologists to redefine psychology in some new, "behavioristic" way.

Some of them, most notably Albert P. Weiss (for example, 1924) and Zing Yang Kuo (1928), attempted to formulate behaviorism as Watson had, only more precisely. Kuo defined behaviorism as "a science of mechanics dealing with the mechanical movements of . . . organisms," and held "the duty of the behaviorist is to describe behavior in exactly the same way as the physicist describes the movements of a machine." This mechanistic, physiologically reductionist psychology, modern inheritor of La Mettrie, was most clearly and comprehensively set out by Karl Lashley (1890–1958), the student with whom Watson had studied the conditional reflex in animals and humans.

Lashley wrote that behaviorism had become "an accredited system of psychology," but that in its emphasis on "experimental method" had failed to give any satisfactory "systematic formulation" of its views. In light of behaviorism's being "so great a departure from tradition in psychology," a clearer formulation of behaviorism was needed. Heretofore, Lashley claimed, three forms of behaviorism had been advanced. The first two were scarcely distinguishable as forms of "methodological behaviorism." They allowed that "facts of conscious experience exist but are unsuited to any form of scientific treatment." It had been, according to Lashley, the beginning point of Watson's own behaviorism, but ultimately proved unsatisfying because it conceded too much to introspective psychology. Precisely because it acknowledged the "facts of consciousness," methodological behaviorism admitted that it could never be a complete psychology and had to concede a science, or at least a study, of mind alongside the science of behavior. Opposed to methodological behaviorism was "strict behaviorism" (or, as Wheeler [1923] named it, radical behaviorism), whose "extreme" view was that "the supposedly unique facts of consciousness do not exist." Such a view seems at first sight implausible, and Lashley conceded that it had not been put forward with any convincing arguments. Lashley made his own view plain:

> Let me cast off the lion's skin. My quarrel with behaviorism is not that it has gone too far, but that it has hesitated . . . that it has failed to develop its premises to their logical conclusion. To me the essence of behaviorism is the belief that the study of man will reveal nothing except what is adequately describable in the concepts of mechanics and chemistry. . . . I believe that it is possible to construct a physiological psychology which will meet the dualist on his own ground . . . and show that [his] data can be embodied in a mechanistic system. . . . Its physiological account of behavior will also be a complete and adequate account of all the phenomena of consciousness . . . demanding that all psychological data, however obtained, shall be subjected to physical or physiological interpretation.

Ultimately, Lashley says, the choice between behaviorism and traditional psychology comes down to a choice between two "incompatible" world views, "scientific versus humanistic." It has been demanded of psychology heretofore that "it must leave room for human ideals and aspirations." But "other sciences have escaped this thralldom," and so must psychology escape from "metaphysics and values" and "mystical obscurantism" by turning to physiology. In physiology it can find principles of explanation that will make of psychology a natural science, value-free, capable of addressing its "most important problems," its "most interesting and vital questions, the problems of human conduct." It will then be able to recapture the "problems of everyday life" from "sociology, education, and psychiatry," the applied fields ignored by introspective psychology. Lashley's formula for psychology is clearly La Mettrie's: the mechanistic, physiological explanation of behavior and consciousness. It is also clearly in the tradition of Comte's positivism. It preaches a scientistic imperialism against the humanities and questions of value, setting up instead a value-free technology claiming to solve human problems. Lashley, Weiss, Kuo, and Watson attempted to define behaviorism quite narrowly, almost dismantling psychology as an independent discipline. Other psychologists and philosophical observers of psychology thought their conception too narrow, and defined a more inclusive behavioristic psychology.

The neorealist philosopher Perry (1921) saw behaviorism as nothing new, but "simply a return to the original Aristotelian view that mind and body are related as activity and organ." Adopting behaviorism did not mean denying that mind has a role in behavior. On the contrary, "If you are a behaviorist you regard the mind as something that *intervenes*" in determining behavior, and behaviorism rescues mind from the parallelistic impotence imposed on it by introspective psychology. On the other hand the neorealist Stephen Pepper (1923), who had studied with Perry at Harvard, while similarly refusing to identify Watson's behaviorism as *the* behaviorism, nonetheless flatly contradicted Perry: For Pepper, the central contention of behaviorism was that consciousness plays no causal role in determining behavior, and that behaviorism's destiny was to bring psychology into "connection with the rest of the natural sciences." Jastrow (1927), who had been around since the beginning of psychology in America, saw nothing new in behaviorism, calling James, Peirce, and Hall "behaviorists." Psychology as the study of behavior was part of the "reconstruction" of psychology that had been taking place for the previous fifty years. It was a mistake, Jastrow argued, to confuse Watson's "radical" behaviorism with the more general and moderate behaviorism held by most American psychologists.

When we set side by side the views of Lashley, Perry, Pepper, and Jastrow, it becomes clear that "behaviorism" was a term of infinite elasticity. It might signify physiological reductionism, or just the study of behavior by objective means; it might mean a significant break with the past, or it might be very old; it might mean seeing mind as a causal actor in determining behavior, or it might mean the denial of mind as causal agent. Woodworth (1924) was clearly correct when he wrote that there is no "one great inclusive enterprise" binding together the various claimants to the title "behaviorism." Woodworth saw behaviorism's "essential program" as "behavior study, behavior concepts, laws of behavior, control of behavior," not the "neuromechanistic interpretation" of psychology associated with Watson. Woodworth observes that psychology had begun as the nonintrospective study of reaction times, memory, and psychophysics, but had been sidetracked in its development as a science by Titchener, Kulpe, and others around 1900. Behaviorism—

or, as we have defined it here, behavioralism—was a program for psychology, not a new method. Scientific psychology was bound to become behavioralistic; Watson had wrought nothing new.

One point of note arises in several of the papers advocating behaviorism, connecting behavioralism with its past in functionalism and its future in cognitive science: James's "automatic sweetheart." In contrasting behaviorism with humanism, Lashley noted that "the final objection to behaviorism is that it just fails to express the vital, personal quality of experience," an objection "quite evident in James's arguments concerning the "automatic sweetheart." Hunter (1923) likewise considered James's possible objection to behaviorism: It claims one's beloved is an automaton, and can one truly love a machine? With Lashley, who said descriptions of experience "belong to art, not science," Hunter dismissed worries about whether one could love, or be loved by, a machine as concerned only with the "aesthetic satisfaction" of the belief, not its scientific truth. B. H. Bode (1918) treated the problem more fully, defending the behaviorist point of view. Bode argued that upon reflection, there is no meaningful difference between a human sweetheart and a mechanical one, because no behavioral difference between them could be discerned:

> If there is no [objectively observable] difference, then the consciousness of the spiritually animated maiden plainly makes no difference in the behavior; it is a mere concomitant or epiphenomenon . . . mechanism becomes the last word of explanation, and the mystery of the eternally feminine takes on much the same quality as the mystery of higher mathematics.

Finally, a critic of behaviorism, William McDougall, put the issue in the most up-to-date terms. The term "robot" had just been coined by Carel Capek in his science fiction play *R. U. R.*, Rossum's Universal Robots. MacDougall (1925) saw the critical question framed by behaviorism as "Men or robots?" Behaviorism rested on the claim that human beings are just machines—robots—but that claim was unproved. In Woodworth's opinion it remained to be determined that robots could do anything human beings can do.

The concern over James's automatic, or robot, sweetheart raises the central problem of scientific psychology in the twentieth century: Can human beings be consistently conceived of as machines? This question transcends all the systems of psychology since James's (or even La Mettrie's) time, as it ties together functionalism, realism, behaviorism, and cognitive psychology. Following the development of computers in World War II, one of their creators would pose James's question in more intellectual terms: Can a machine be said to think if you can talk to it and be fooled into believing you are talking to another person? And A. M. Turing, followed by many cognitive psychologists, would give Bode's answer: If you can't tell it's just a machine, then we're just machines, too. The prospect of the automatic sweetheart filled some psychologists with excitement, but others, such as James, with revulsion. Lashley was very likely right when he saw the battle over behaviorism not just as a battle between different ways of doing psychology, but as a much deeper battle between "mechanistic explanation and finalistic valuation," between a view of human beings as robots, or as actors with purposes, values, hopes, fears, and loves.

Following World War II, in which he served unhappily in the Army working up tests for aviators, Watson moved his research and his advocacy for behaviorism in a new direction. He now intensively pursued a human psychology based on the conditioned reflex by investigating the acquisition of reflexes in infants. Watson believed that nature endowed human beings with very few unconditioned reflexes, so that the complex behavior of adults might be explained as simply the acquisition of conditioned reflexes over years of Pavlovian conditioning. Contrary to eugenicists and their followers, who believed that people inherit a great deal of their intellect, personality, and morality, Watson (1925) asserted that "there is no such thing as inheritance of *capacity, talent, temperament, mental constitution and characteristics.*" For example, Watson denied that human hand preference was innate. He could find no structural differences between babies' left and right hands and arms, nor were the different hands endowed with different strengths. So although he remained puzzled by the fact that most people were right-handed, he put the cause of it down to social training, and said there would be no harm in trying to turn apparently left-handed children into right-handers. Nothing could better demonstrate Watson's radical peripheralism: Since he could find no peripheral differences between the hands' strength and structure, there could be, he concluded, no biological basis to handedness. He completely ignored the "mysterious" (Watson 1913b) cortex of the brain, seeing it as no more than a relay station for neural impulses. We now know that the left and right hemispheres of the human brain have very different functions, and that differences between right- and left-handers are determined there. To attempt to change a natural left-hander into a right-hander is to impose a very trying task, one well calculated to upset and make feel inferior the left-handed child.

In any event, to establish the truth of his equally radical environmentalism— "Give me a dozen healthy infants . . . and my own specified world to bring them up in and I'll guarantee to take any one at random and train him to become any type of specialist I might select—doctor, lawyer, artist, merchant-chief, and, yes, even beggar-man and thief" (Watson 1930)—Watson turned to the nursery to show that humans are so much plastic material waiting to be molded by society. The most famous of his studies with infants is "Conditioned Emotional Reactions" (Watson and Rayner 1920). Watson carried out an experiment on an infant known as "Albert B." designed to show that people are born with only a few "instincts"—fear, rage, and sexual response—and that all other emotions are conditioned versions of these unconditioned ones. As his US to produce fear (UR), Watson chose a loud noise, the sound of a large metal bar being struck by a hammer; this stimulus had been determined to be one of the few that would scare little Albert. He paired the noise with a CS, a rat whom Albert had liked to pet. Now, however, when Albert touched the rat, Watson struck the bar; after seven such pairings the child showed fear of the rat alone. Watson claimed to have established a "conditioned emotional reaction," and asserted that his experimental arrangement was the prototype of emotional learning by a normal human in the normal human environment. Watson thought to have demonstrated that the rich emotional life of the adult human being was at bottom no more than a large number of conditioned responses built up over years of human development. We should point out that Watson's claims are dubious and his ethics in this experiment questionable (Samelson 1980); furthermore, the experiment is often misdescribed by secondary sources (Harris 1979). Watson was, at least, consistent. He fell in love with graduate student collaborator Rosalie Rayner—entailing a scandal that cost him his job at Johns Hopkins in 1920—and wrote to her that "every cell I have is yours singly and collectively," and that all his emotional responses "are positive and towards you," "likewise each and every heart response" (Cohen 1979).

Watson had always been willing to write about psychology for a popular audience. After 1920, following his expulsion from academia, he became the first modern popular psychologist (Buckley 1984), writing, for example, a series of articles on human psychology from the behaviorist perspective in *Harper's* from 1926 to 1928. There, Watson began by laying out behaviorism as the scientific replacement for mentalistic psychology and for psychoanalysis, which had earlier captured the popular mind. According to Watson, psychoanalysis had "too little science—real science" to long command serious attention, while the traditional psychology of consciousness "never had any right to be called a science." As he often did in his popular writings, Watson connected mentalistic psychology with religion, asserting that "mind and consciousness" were but "carryovers from the church dogma of the middle ages." The mind, or soul, was, according to Watson, one of the mysteries by whose invocation "churchmen—all medicine men in fact— have kept the public under control." Psychoanalysis was just "a substitution of demonology for science," and through such "solid walls of religious protection" science was "blasting" a new path.

Watson defied the mentalist to "prove" that "there is such a thing as consciousness." To the assertion by a mentalist that he had a mental life, Watson simply replied, "I have only your unverified and unsupported word that you have" images and sensations. So the concepts of mentalism remained "mythological, the figments of the psychologist's terminology." In place of the fantastic, secretly religious, traditional mentalistic psychology, behaviorism substituted a positivistic, scientific psychology of description, prediction, and control of behavior. Watson said that behavioral psychology began with the observation of the behavior of our fellows, and issued, suitably codified by science, in "a new weapon for controlling the individual." The social use of behavioral science was made clear by Watson: "[We] can build any man, starting at birth, into any kind of social or a-social being upon order." Elsewhere (Watson 1930) Watson said, "It is a part of the behaviorist's scientific job to be able to state what the human machine is good for and to render serviceable predictions about its future capacities whenever society needs such information." Very much in the tradition of Comte's positivism, Watson's behaviorism rejected religion and the moral control of behavior, and aimed to replace these with science and the technological control of behavior through behavioral psychology. Behaviorism was well prepared to mesh with Progressivism. Because of Progressivism's interest in establishing rational control over society through scientific means, Progressive politicians and apologists found an ally in behaviorism, which seemed to promise exactly the technology Progressivism needed to replace the outworn authority of tradition.

MAJOR FORMULATIONS OF BEHAVIORALISM (1930–1950)

By 1930 behavioralism was well established as the dominant viewpoint in experimental psychology. Watson's usage had triumphed, and psychologists called the new viewpoint "behaviorism," while recognizing that behaviorism took many forms (Williams 1931). The stage was set for psychologists to create specific theories for predicting and explaining behavior within the new viewpoint of behavioralism. The central problem they addressed in the coming decades would be learning (McGeoch 1931). Functionalism had taken the ability to learn to be the criterion of animal mind, and the development of behavioralism had only magnified its importance. Learning was the process by which animals and humans adjusted to the environment, by which they were educated, and by which they might be changed in the interest of social control or therapy. So it is not surprising that what would later be regarded as the Golden Age of Theory in psychology—the years 1930 to 1950—would be golden only for theories of learning, rather than perception, thinking, group dynamics, or anything else.

The other major development of these decades in experimental psychology was psychologists' increasing self-consciousness about proper scientific method. Psychologists, as we have often noted, have always felt uncertain about the scientific status of their *soi-disant* "natural science" and have consequently been eager to find some methodological recipe to follow by which they could infallibly make psychology a science. Watson had, in denouncing mentalism, seen its irredeemable flaw to be the "unscientific" method of introspecting, and had proclaimed psychology's scientific salvation to be objective method, taken over from animal study. Watson's message struck home, but his own recipe was too vague and confused to provide anything more than an attitude. In the 1930s psychologists became aware of a very specific, prestigious recipe, logical positivism, for making science. The positivist's philosophy of science codified what psychologists already wanted to do; so they accepted the recipe and determined the goals and language of psychology for decades to come. At the same time, their own original ideas were molded so subtly by logical positivism that only now can we see the molding process at work.

Psychology and the Science of Science

We have already remarked how behavioralism reflected the image of science drawn by Comtean positivism: Its goal was the description, prediction, and control of behavior, and its techniques were to be put to use as tools of social control in a rationally managed society. The early, simple positivism of Comte and Mach had changed, however. By the early twentieth century it was clear that positivism's extreme emphasis on talking about only what could be directly observed, excluding from science concepts such as "atom" and "electron," could not be sustained. Physicists and chemists found that their theories could not dispense with such terms, and their research results confirmed for them, albeit indirectly, the reality of atoms and electrons (Holton 1978). So positivism changed, and its adherents found a way to admit into science terms apparently referring to unobserved entities, without giving up the basic positivist desire to expunge metaphysics from human, or at least scientific, discourse.

This new positivism came to be called logical positivism, because it wedded the positivist's commitment to empiricism to the logical apparatus of modern formal logic. Logical positivism was a complex and changing movement directed by many hands, but its basic idea was simple: Science had proven to be humankind's most powerful means of understanding reality, of producing knowledge, so that the task of epistemology should be to explicate and formalize the scientific method, making it available to new disciplines and improving its practice among working scientists. Thus the logical positivists purported to provide a formal recipe for doing science, offering exactly what psychologists thought they needed. Logical positivism began with a small circle of philosophers in Vienna just after World War I, but soon became a worldwide movement aimed at the unification of science in one grand scheme of investigation orchestrated by the positivists themselves. Logical positivism had many aspects, but two have proved especially important to psychologists looking for the "scientific way," and were adopted as talismans of scientific virtue in the 1930s: formal axiomatization of theories, and the operational definition of theoretical terms.

Scientific language, the logical positivists explained, contained two kinds of terms. Most basic were *observation terms,* which referred to directly observable properties of nature: redness, length, weight, time durations, and so on. The older positivism had stressed observation, and had insisted that science should contain only observation terms. Logical positivists agreed that observations provided the bedrock of science, but recognized that theoretical terms were necessary parts of scientific vocabulary, providing explanations in addition to descriptions of natural phenomena. Science simply could not do without terms such as "force," "mass," "field," and "electron." The problem, though, was how to admit science's theoretical vocabulary as legitimate, while excluding metaphysical and religious nonsense. The solution the logical positivists arrived at was to closely tie theoretical terms to bedrock observation terms, thereby guaranteeing their meaningfulness.

The logical positivists argued that the meaning of a theoretical term should be understood to consist in procedures linking it to observation terms. So, for example, "mass" would be defined as an object's weight at sea level. A term that could not be so defined could be dismissed as metaphysical nonsense. Such definitions were called "operational definitions," following the usage of Percy Bridgman, a physicist who had independently proposed the same idea in 1927.

The logical positivists also claimed that scientific theories consisted of theoretical axioms relating theoretical terms to one another. For example, a central axiom of Newtonian physics was "force equals mass times acceleration," or "$F = M \times A$" This theoretical sentence expresses a putative scientific law, and may be tested by deriving predictions from it. Since each term has an operational definition, it is possible to take an operational measure of the mass of an object, accelerate it to a measurable speed, and then measure the resulting force generated by the object. Should the predicted force correspond to the measured force in the experiment, the axiom would be confirmed; should the values disagree, the axiom would be disconfirmed and would need to be revised. On the logical positivist account of theories, theories explained because they could predict. To explain an event was to show that it could have been predicted from the preceding circumstances combined with some scientific "covering law." So to explain why a vase broke when it was dropped on the floor, one would show that given the weight of the vase (operationally defined mass) and the height it was dropped from (operationally defined acceleration in earth gravity), the resulting force would be sufficient to crack the vase's porcelain structure.

Logical positivism formalized the ideas of the earlier Comtean and Machian positivists. For both, observation yielded unquestioned truth—both forms of positivism were empiricist. The laws of science were no more than summary statements of experiences: Theoretical axioms were complex summaries of the interactions of several theoretical variables, each of which was in turn wholly defined in terms of observations. To the logical positivist it did not matter if there were atoms or forces in reality; what counted was whether or not such concepts could be systematically related to observations. Logical positivists were thus, for all their apparently tough-minded insistence on only believing what one observes, really romantic idealists (Brush 1980), for whom ideas—sensations, observation terms— were the only ultimate reality. Nevertheless, logical positivism seemed to offer a specific recipe for doing science in any field of study: First, operationally define one's theoretical terms, be they "mass" or "hunger"; second, state one's theory as a set of theoretical axioms from which predictions could be drawn; third, carry out experiments to test the predictions, using operational definitions to link theory and observations; and finally revise one's theory as observations warrant.

Because the logical positivists had studied science and set out their findings in explicit logical form, S. S. Stevens (1939), the psychologist who brought operational definition to psychology (Stevens 1935a,b), called it "the Science of Science," which promised to at last make of psychology "an undisputed natural science" (as Watson had wished), and to unify it with the other sciences in the logical positivists' scheme for the "unity of science." Operationism was exciting to psychologists because it promised to settle once and for all fruitless disputes about psychological terminology: What does "mind" mean? "Imageless thought"? "Id"? As Stevens (1935a) put it, operationism was "the revolution that will put an end to the possibility of revolution." Operationism claimed that terms that could not be operationally defined were scientifically meaningless, while scientific terms could be given operational definitions everyone could agree on. Moreover, operationism's revolution ratified behaviorism's claim to be the only scientific psychology, because only behaviorism was compatible with operationism's demand that theoretical terms be defined by linking them to observation terms (Stevens 1939). In psychology this meant that theoretical terms could not refer to mental entities, but only to classes of behavior. Hence mentalistic psychology was unscientific, and had to be replaced by behaviorism.

By the end of the 1930s, operationism was entrenched dogma in psychology. Sigmund Koch—by 1950 an apostate from the operationist faith—wrote in his 1939 doctoral thesis that "almost every psychology sophomore knows it is bad form if reference to 'definition' is not qualified by the adjective 'operational.' " In operationism lay psychology's scientific salvation: "Hitch the constructs appearing in your postulates to a field of scientific fact [via operational definition], and only then do you get a scientific theory" (Koch 1941).

At a loftier professional level, the president of the APA agreed with Koch. John F. Dashiell (1939) observed that philosophy and psychology were coming together again, not to have philosophers set psychologists' agenda—from that tyranny psychology had won "emancipation"—but to work out science's proper methods. Foremost in the "rapprochement" of philosophy and psychology were two ideas of the logical positivists. The first was operationism; the other was the demand that scientific theories be collections of mathematically stated axioms. Dashiell commended one psychologist for meeting this second requirement: In "the same positivistic vein [as operationism] Hull is urging us to look to the systematic character of our thinking" by producing a rigorous, axiomatic theory. Dashiell's admiration of Clark L. Hull as the foremost logical positivist among psychologists was, as we will see, wrong. Hull was a mechanist and a realist, believing in the physiological reality of his theoretical terms. However, Dashiell's opinion became later psychologists' myth, a comforting belief that although the specifics of their theories were mistaken, Hull and E. C. Tolman had set psychology firmly on the path toward science as the logical positivists had defined it. The true natures of their theories of learning were obscured for decades, not only from the understanding of psychologists generally, but even from the understanding of Hull and Tolman themselves. Regardless of its flaws and its distorting effect on the independent ideas of Hull and Tolman, there can be no doubt that logical positivism became psychology's official philosophy of science until at least the 1960s.

Edward Chace Tolman's Purposive Behaviorism

Although it was seldom acknowledged, behaviorism's central problem was to account for mental phenomena without invoking the mind. More liberal behavioralists might—and would eventually—leave mind in psychology as an unseen, but nevertheless causal, agent that determines behavior. But at least in its early days, and in its continuing radical strain, behaviorism has aimed to oust mind from psychology. Watson, Lashley, and the other reductive, or physiological, behaviorists tried to do so by claiming that consciousness, purpose, and cognition were myths, so that the task of psychology was to describe experience and behavior as products of the mechanistic operation of the nervous system. The motor theory of consciousness could be used to good effect in such arguments, as showing that conscious contents were just sensations of bodily movements, reporting, but not causing, behavior.

Bearing a B.S. in electrochemistry, E. C. Tolman (1886–1959) arrived at Harvard in 1911 to undertake graduate study in philosophy and psychology, settling on the latter as most in tune with his capacities and interests. There he studied with the leading philosophers and psychologists of the day, Perry and Holt, Münsterberg and Yerkes. For a time, reading E. B. Titchener "almost sold [him] on structuralistic introspection," but he noticed in his courses with Münsterberg that although Münsterberg "made little opening speeches to the effect that *the* method in psychology was *introspection*," the work in his laboratory was "primarily objective in nature" and that little use could be made of introspective results in writing up experimental papers. So reading Watson's *Behavior* in Yerkes's comparative psychology course came "as a tremendous stimulus and relief" for showing that "objective measurement of behavior, not introspection, was the true method of psychology." Tolman's years at Harvard were also the great years of neorealism, just then being promulgated by Perry and Holt.

Neorealism provided the foundation for Tolman's approach to the problem of mind as he developed it after taking a position at the University of California at Berkeley in 1918. Evidence for mind was of two sorts: introspective awareness of consciousness, and the apparent intelligence and purposefulness of others' behavior. Following Perry, Tolman found Watson's "muscle-twitchism" (Tolman 1959) too simple and crude to account for either kind of evidence. Neorealism implied that there was no such thing as introspection, since there were no mental objects to observe; in the neorealist view "introspection" was only an artificially close scrutiny of objects in one's environment, in which one reported their sensory attributes in great detail. Tolman allied this analysis with the motor theory of consciousness, arguing that introspection of internal states such as emotions was just the "back action" of behavior on awareness (Tolman 1923). In either event, introspection was of no special importance to scientific psychology; in saying this, Tolman's "New Formula for Behaviorism" (Tolman 1922) was a methodological behaviorism, conceding that awareness existed, but ruling its results out of science's court.

Similarly, evidence of intelligent purpose in behavior could be handled from the neorealist perspective. The leading purposive psychology of the day was William McDougall's "hormic" psychology. In "Behaviorism and Purpose" (1925) Tolman criticized McDougall for handling purpose in the traditional Cartesian way: McDougall, "being a mentalist, merely *infers* purpose from [the persistance of] behavior, while we, being behaviorists, *identify* purpose with" persistance toward a goal. Following Perry and Holt, Tolman held that "purpose . . . is an objective aspect of behavior" that an observer directly perceives; it is not an inference *from* observed behavior. Tolman subjected memory to the same analysis, at once recalling the Scottish realists and anticipating B. F. Skinner: "Memory, like purpose, may be conceived . . . as a purely empirical aspect of behavior." To say that one "remembers" a nonpresent object, X, is just to say that one's current behavior is "causally dependent" on X.

In summary, then, Tolman proposed a behaviorism that excised mind and consciousness from psychology as Watson wanted to do, but that would retain purpose and cognition, not as powers of a mysterious "mind" inferred from behavior, but as objective, observable aspects of behavior itself. In another contrast to Watson, Tolman's behaviorism was "molar" rather than "molecular" (Tolman 1926, 1935). In Watson's molecular view behavior was defined as muscular responses caused by triggering stimuli, so that the appropriate strategy to adopt in predicting and controlling behavior was to analyze complex behaviors into their smallest muscular components, which in turn could be understood physiologically. Tolman, viewing behavior as ineliminably purposive, studied whole, integrated, *molar* acts.

For example, according to a molecularist, a subject who has learned to withdraw her finger from an electrode when a warning signal precedes shock has learned a specific conditioned muscular reflex; according to a molar behaviorist she has learned a global avoidance response. Now turn the subject's hand over, so that the same reflex would drive her finger into the electrode; the Watsonian predicts just that—a new molecular reflex will have to be learned, while Tolman predicts that the subject will immediately avoid the shock with an untrained withdrawal movement based on having learned a molar response of shock-avoidance (Wickens 1938; the results supported Tolman, unsurprisingly).

At the same time that he was treating purpose and cognition from a neorealist perspective, Tolman hinted at a different, more traditionally mentalistic approach to the problem they presented; this approach served Tolman well following the demise of neorealism in the 1920s, and is fundamental to cognitive science today. In an early paper Tolman (1920) wrote that thoughts "can be conceived from an objective point of view as consisting in internal presentations to the organism" of stimuli not now present. Later, right alongside arguments that cognitions are "immanent" in behavior and not inferred, Tolman (1926) speaks of consciousness as providing "representations" that guide behavior. To speak of cognitions and thoughts as internal representations of the world playing a causal role in determining behavior breaks with both neorealism and behaviorism: with neorealism because representations are inferred like Lockean ideas; with behaviorism because something mental is given a place among the causes of behavior. As Tolman developed his system he relied more and more on the concept of representation, as we shall see, becoming an inferential behavioralist committed to the real existence of mind.

In 1934 Tolman traveled to Vienna, where he came under the influence of the logical positivists, particularly Rudolf Carnap, the leader of the Vienna Circle. In Carnap's treatment of psychology, the traditional terms of mentalistic folk psychology should be understood as referring not to mental objects, but to physicochemical processes in the body. So, for example, the meaning of the statement "Fred is excited" derives from the glandular, muscular, and other bodily processes that produce excitement; Carnap's analysis is a version of the motor theory of consciousness. While awaiting the full reduction of mental terms to their true physiological referents, we must, Carnap held, compromise on a sort of behaviorism. Since we do not know the physicochemical referent of "excitement," we should understand "excitement" to refer to the behaviors that lead one to attribute excitement to someone else; this compromise is acceptable, since the behaviors are "detectors" of the unknown, underlying physiology. In the long run we should be able to eliminate behaviorism and understand mentalistic language in purely physiological terms. Carnap did recognize that in addition to its referential function, language may serve an expressive function; if I say "I feel pain," I am not just referring to some physical process within my body, I am expressing anguish. According to Carnap, the expressive function of language lies outside scientific explication, and is the subject of poetry, fiction, and, more generally, art.

Carnap's psychology was not incompatible with Tolman's independently developed views, but it did give Tolman a new way to articulate his behaviorism, within a philosophy of science daily growing in prestige and influence. Soon after his return, Tolman reformulated his purposive behaviorism in logical positivist language. Scientific psychology, Tolman (1935) wrote, "seeks . . . the objectively statable laws and processes governing behavior." Descriptions of "immediate experience . . . may be left to the arts and to metaphysics." Tolman was now able to be quite precise about behaviorism's research program. Behavior was to be regarded as a dependent variable, caused by environmental and internal (but not mental) independent variables. The ultimate goal of behaviorism, then, is "to write the form of the function f which connects the dependent variable [behavior] . . . to the independent variables— stimulus, heredity, training, and physiological" states such as hunger. Since this goal is too ambitious to be reached all at once, behaviorists introduce intervening variables that connect independent and dependent variables, providing equations that allow one to predict behavior given values of the independent variables. Molar behaviorism defines independent variables "macroscopically" as purposes and cognitions defined as characteristics of behavior, but eventually molecular behaviorism will be able to explain molar independent variables "in detailed neurological and glandular terms."

Tolman (1936) expanded these remarks and redefined his behaviorism as "operational behaviorism." Operational behaviorism is cast in the mold of "the general positivistic attitude now being taken by many modern physicists and philosophers." The adjective "operational" reflects two features of his behaviorism, Tolman explained. First, it defines its intervening variables "operationally" as demanded by modern logical positivism; second, it emphasizes the fact that behavior is "essentially an activity whereby the organism . . . operates on its environment." There are "two main principles" of operational behaviorism. First, "it asserts that the ultimate interest of psychology is solely the prediction and control of behavior." Second, this interest is to be achieved by a functional analysis of behavior in which "psychological concepts . . . may be conceived as objectively defined intervening variables . . . defined wholly operationally."

In these two papers Tolman has set out clearly and forcefully the classical program of methodological behaviorism as defined under the influence of logical positivism. However, we should observe that Tolman did not get his conception of psychology from the logical positivists. Their philosophy of science meshed with what Tolman already thought and practiced, providing at most a sophisticated and prestigious justification for his own conceptions; his terms independent, dependent, and intervening variable are enduring contributions to psychological language. More important, Tolman seems quickly to have shed his operationism for psychological realism. According to operationism, theoretical terms do not refer to anything at all, but are simply convenient ways of summarizing observations. So the definition of a hungry rat's intention would be its visibly persistent orientation toward the goal box in a maze. However, in his later writings (for example, Tolman 1948) Tolman speaks of cognitions, at least, as psychologically real entities, not just as shorthand descriptions of behavior. So "cognitive maps" are representations of the environment that a rat or person consults to guide intelligent behavior toward a goal. In the years after his return to Vienna, Tolman did not teach or even especially discuss logical positivism (Smith 1986). It is therefore possible that his 1935 and 1936 papers, although widely read expositions of methodological behaviorism, never represented Tolman's real conception of psychology.

Finally, it is interesting to note that Tolman sometimes seemed to be fumbling for a conception of psychology that was not quite available—namely, the computational conception of cognitive science. In 1920 Tolman rejected the "slot machine" view of organisms associated with Watson. In this view the organism was a machine in which any given stimulus elicited some reflexive response, just as putting a coin in the slot of a vending machine produces a fixed product. Rather, Tolman would prefer to think of an organism as "a complex machine capable of various adjustments such that, when one adjustment was in force," a given stimulus would produce one response, while under a different internal adjustment, the same stimulus would call out a different response. Internal adjustments would be caused either by external stimuli or by "automatic changes within the organism." The model Tolman wished for in 1920 was the computer, whose responses to input depend on its programming and its internal state. Similarly, Tolman anticipated the information-processing account of mind when in 1948 he described the mind as "a central control room" in which "incoming impulses are usually worked over and elaborated . . . into a cognitivelike map of the environment."

Clark Leonard Hull's Mechanistic Behaviorism

Clark Leonard Hull (1884–1952), like so many people born in the nineteenth century, lost his religious faith as a teenager and struggled ever afterward for a substitute faith. Hull found his in mathematics and science. Just as Thomas Hobbes had been inspired by reading the book of Euclid, so Hull could say that "the study of geometry proved to be the most important event of my intellectual life." Hull also concluded, as had Hobbes, that one should conceive of thinking, reasoning, and other cognitive powers, including learning, as quite mechanical in nature, and capable of being described and understood through the elegant precision of mathematics. His infatuation with mathematics led him first to seek a career as a mining engineer, but an attack of polio forced him to make new plans. He toyed with the idea of being a minister in the Unitarian church—"a free, godless religion"—but "the prospect of attending an endless succession of ladies' teas" led him to abandon that calling. He sought "a field allied to philosophy in the sense of involving theory," which was so new that he might quickly "find recognition," and that would engage his penchant for machinery by allowing him "to design and work with automatic apparatus." Psychology met "this unique set of requirements," and Hull set out to "deliberately make a bid for a certain place in the history of science." He began by studying James's *Principles*, at first by having his mother read to him during his convalescence. Hull spent his undergraduate years at the University of Michigan, where for a course in logic he built a machine for displaying the logic of syllogisms. Turned down for graduate study by Yale—where he eventually spent most of his professional career—and Cornell, Hull took his Ph.D. from the University of Wisconsin.

Hull eventually made his mark in psychology by his theory and research on learning, and his first investigations presage the influential Hull of the 1930s. As an undergraduate he studied learning in the insane, and attempted to formulate mathematically precise laws to account for how they form associations (Hull 1917). His doctoral dissertation concerned concept formation, and again was very quantitative (Hull 1920). However, due to a series of accidents, Hull spent the next few years doing research in unrelated areas: hypnosis (an "unscientific" field, which Hull tried to improve using "quantitative methodology"); the effects of tobacco on behavior (for which Hull designed a machine through which people could smoke without inhaling tobacco's chemicals); and aptitude testing. In connection with the last, Hull designed a machine for calculating the correlations between the scores of the various tests in a test battery. Doing so confirmed for him the idea that thinking was a mechanical process that might be simulated by an actual machine; Pascal had been horrified by the same insight, but Hull found in it a hypothesis on which to work.

Like every psychologist, Hull had to grapple with Watson's behaviorism. At first, although he sympathized with Watson's attacks on introspection and call for objectivity, Hull was put off by Watson's dogmatism, and by "the semi-fanatical ardor with which some young people would espouse the Watsonian cause with . . . a fanaticism more characteristic of religion than of science." Taking up an interest in Gestalt psychology, Hull as a young professor at Wisconsin managed to get Kurt Koffka to visit for a year. However, Koffka's "strikingly negative" attitude toward Watson paradoxically convinced Hull "not that the Gestalt view was sound" but that Watson's behaviorism needed improvement along the mathematical lines Hull was already inclined to follow: "Instead of converting me to *Gestalttheorie*, [I experienced] a belated conversion to a kind of neo-behaviorism—a behaviorism mainly concerned with the determination of the quantitative laws of behavior and their deductive systematization." In 1929 Hull moved to Yale University, where he embarked on a most influential career as the preeminent experimental psychologist of his day.

Hull's program had two components. First, as we have seen, Hull was fascinated by machinery and was convinced that machines could think, so he attempted to build machines capable of learning and thinking. The first description of such a machine came in 1929, representing, as he put it, "a direct implication of the mechanistic tendency of modern psychology. Learning and thought are here conceived as by no means necessarily a function of living protoplasm than is serial locomotion" (Hull and Baernstein 1929). The other component of Hull's theoretical ambition represented a continuation of the geometric spirit of Hobbes and the associationism of Hume, whom Hull thought of as the first behaviorist. Around 1930, Hull says, "I came to the definite conclusion . . . that psychology is a true natural science'' whose task is the discovery of ''laws expressible quantitatively by means of a moderate number of ordinary equations'' from which individual and group behaviors may be deduced as consequences. Given Hull's mechanistic and mathematical interests, it is unsurprising to learn that he contracted a bad case of physics envy, and fancied himself the Newton of behavior. In the mid-1920s he read Newton's *Principia,* and it became a sort of bible for him (Smith 1986). He assigned portions of it to his seminars, and placed it on his desk between himself and visitors; it represented for him the very pinnacle of scientific achievement, and he strove to emulate his hero.

The goals of building intelligent machines and of formalizing psychology according to a mathematical system were not incompatible; Newtonians had conceived of the physical universe as a machine governed by precise mathematical laws: Hull simply aimed to do the same thing for allegedly mental phenomena and behavior. During the early 1930s Hull pursued both formal theory and learning machines in tandem, publishing increasingly mathematical treatments of complex behaviors such as the acquisition and assembling of simple S-R habits, and promising the production of ''psychic machines'' capable of thought and useful as industrial robots (Hull 1930a,b, 1931, 1934, 1935). However, as the 1930s wore on, Hull's psychic machines played a less and less prominent place in his work. It appears that he feared that his preoccupation with intelligent machines would appear ''grotesque'' to outsiders, and that his work on them would be suppressed, as university authorities had suppressed his earlier work on hypnosis (Smith 1986). At the same time, like Tolman and most other psychologists, Hull came under the influence of logical positivism. Its insistence on formalism and the reduction of the mental to the physical was quite consistent with Hull's own philosophy of science, so that he found increased emphasis on formal, mathematical theory to be most useful as ''propaganda'' by which to advance his cause (Smith 1986).

Hull's turn from the pursuit of psychic machines and formal theories to the exclusive pursuit of the latter may be conveniently dated to 1936, the year in which he was president of the APA, and he described in his presidential address his ambitions for theoretical psychology. In his talk Hull tackled the central problem of behaviorism: accounting for mind. He noted the same outward sign of mind as Tolman did: purposive, persistent behavior in the striving for goals. However, he proposed to account for them in a completely different way, as the outcome of mechanistic, lawful, principles of behavior: ''The complex forms of purposive behavior [will] be found to derive from . . . the basic entities of theoretical physics, such as electrons and protons.'' Hull recognized that traditionally such a mechanistic position had been only philosophical, and he proposed to make it scientific by applying what he took to be scientific procedure. Science, Hull stated, consisted of a set of ''explicitly stated postulates'' (as did Euclid's geometry) from which, ''by the most rigorous logic,'' predictions about actual behaviors would be deduced. Just as Newton had derived the motions of the planets from a small set of physical laws, so Hull proposed to predict the motions of organisms from a (rather larger) set of behavioral laws set forth in his paper. The virtue of the scientific method, Hull claimed, was that its predictions could be precisely tested against observations, while the nebulous claims of philosophy, whether idealistic or materialistic, could not be.

Using his set of proposed postulates, Hull tried to show that purposive behavior could be accounted for mechanistically. Finally, he asked, ''But what of consciousness?'' and in answering this question articulated his own version of methodological behaviorism. Psychology could dispense with consciousness, Hull said, "for the simple reason that no theorem has been found as yet whose deduction would be facilitated in any way by including" a postulate referring to consciousness. "Moreover, we have been quite unable to find any other scientific system of behavior which . . . has found consciousness necessary" to deduce behavior. As did Tolman, Hull set conscious experience, the original subject matter of psychology, outside the bounds of psychology as behaviorists viewed it. Hull, like Watson, attributed continued interest in consciousness among psychologists to "the perseverative influences of medieval theology," claiming that "psychology in its basic principles is to a considerable degree in the thrall of the middle ages, and that, in particular, our prevailing systematic outlook in the matter of consciousness is largely medieval." But, concluded Hull, "fortunately the means of our salvation is clear and obvious. As ever, it lies in the application of scientific procedures. . . . For us to apply the methodology, it is necessary only to throw off the shackles of a lifeless tradition."

Reference to purposive robots was relegated to a footnote in which Hull mentioned "a kind of experimental shortcut to the determination of the ultimate nature of adaptive behavior." If one could build "from inorganic materials . . . a mechanism which would display" the adaptive behaviors derived from his postulates, then "it would be possible to say with assurance and a clear conscience that such adaptive behavior may be 'reached' by purely physical means." During his actual presentation to the APA, Hull demonstrated for the audience one of his learning machines, and they were deeply impressed by its performance (Chapanis 1961). Since Hull rarely mentioned his "psychic machines" again, his statement of the central thesis of cognitive science has gone unnoticed, or has been dismissed as peripheral to Hull's thinking. In fact, it is obvious that mechanical simulation of thought was central to Hull's thinking, and gave rise to the formal theory for which he became famous and through which he became influential

We have already seen how in the mid-1930s Tolman began to articulate his psychology with the terminology of logical positivism; the same happened to Hull. After 1937 he identified his system with "logical empiricism" and applauded the "uniting" of American behavior theory with Viennese logical positivism, which was producing "in America a behavioral discipline which will be a full-blown natural science" (Hull 1943a). From then on, Hull bent his efforts to the creation of a formal, deductive, quantitative theory of learning and largely left his psychic machines behind, though they continued to play a heuristic, unpublished role in Hull's thinking (Smith 1986). Adoption of positivist language obscured Hull's realism, as it did Tolman's. Hull, of course, did not believe in purposes and cognitions, as Tolman did, but he was a realist in believing that the postulates of his theories described actual neurophysiological states and processes in the nervous systems of living organisms, human or animal.

He set forth his postulate systems in a series of books. The first was *Mathematico-Deductive Theory of Rote Learning* (Hull et al 1940), which offered a mathematical treatment of human verbal learning. The book was praised as "giving a foretaste of what psychology will be like when it reaches systematic, quantitative, precision" (Hilgard 1940). The rote learning theory was a "dress rehearsal" for his major work, *Principles of Behavior* (Hull 1943b), the expression of "the behavior system . . . which I had gradually been developing throughout my academic life," and which had formed the basis of his APA presidential address. Upon publication, the *Psychological Bulletin* accorded it a "special review" in which *Principles of*

Behavior was praised as "one of the most important books published in psychology in the twentieth century (Koch 1944)." The book promised to unify all of psychology under the S-R formulation, and to perform needed "radical surgery" on the "withering *corpus* of social science," saving it for real science. Hull revised his system twice more (Hull 1951, 1952), but it was *Principles* that fulfilled his ambition of making a permanent name for himself in the history of psychology.

Tolman vs. Hull

Tolman's purposive behaviorism inevitably came into conflict with Hull's mechanistic behaviorism. Tolman always believed that purpose and cognition were real, although his conception of their reality changed over time. Hull, on the other hand, sought to explain purpose and cognition as the result of mindless mechanical processes describable in logico-mathematical equations. During the 1930s and 1940s Tolman and Hull engaged in a sort of intellectual tennis match: Tolman would attempt to demonstrate that purpose and cognition were real, while Hull and his followers patched up the theory or tried to show that Tolman's demonstrations were flawed.

Let us consider an example of an experiment that contrasts the cognitive and S-R views. It was actually reported in 1930 (Tolman 1932), well before the Hull-Tolman debates really got underway, but it is a simpler version of more complex experiments described in Tolman's "Cognitive Maps in Rats and Men" (1948), meant to differentially support Tolman's theory. The maze is shown in Figure 11-1. Rats were familiarized with the entire maze by forcing them to run each path in early training. Having learned the maze, a rat coming out of the start box into the choice point must pick one of the paths. How does he do this?

A Hullian analysis may be sketched. The choice point presents stimuli (S) to which three responses (Rs) corresponding to each path have been conditioned during initial training. For a variety of reasons, most obviously the different amounts of running that must be done in each alley, Path 1 is preferred to Path 2, which is preferred to Path 3. That is, connection $S \rightarrow R_1$ is stronger than $S \rightarrow R_2$, which is stronger than $S \rightarrow R_3$. Such a state of affairs may be notated

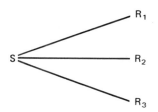

This is called a *divergent habit family hierarchy*. Now, should a block be placed at Point 1, the rat will run into it, back up, and choose Path 2. The connection $S \rightarrow R_1$ is weakened by the block, so that $S \rightarrow R_2$ becomes stronger and is acted on. On the other hand, if the second block is placed, the rat will retreat to the choice point and again choose Path 2 as $S \rightarrow R_1$ is again blocked, and $S \rightarrow R_2$ becomes stronger. However, the block will be met again, $S \rightarrow R_2$ will weaken, and finally $S \rightarrow R_3$ will be strongest and Path 3 will be chosen. This is the Hullian prediction.

Tolman denied that what is learned is a set of responses triggered to differing degrees by the stimuli at the choice point. Instead, he held that the rat learns a

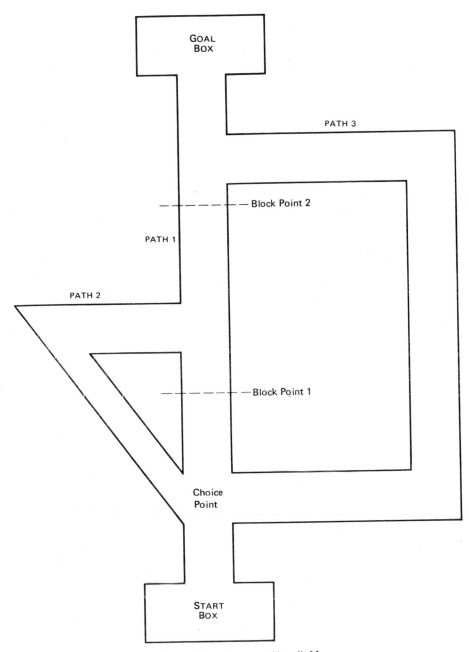

FIGURE 11-1. Tolman-Honzik Maze

mental map of the maze that guides its behavior. According to this view, the rat encountering the first block will turn around and choose Path 2, as in the S-R account, because Path 2 is shorter than 3. However, if it encounters Block 2, the rat will know that the same block will cut off Path 2 as well as Path 1. Therefore the rat will show "insight": It will return and choose Path 3, ignoring Path 2 altogether. A map displays all aspects of the environment, and is more informative than a set of S-R connections. The results of the experiment supported Tolman's cognitive theory of learning over Hull's S-R account.

While Hull and Tolman differed sharply on their specific accounts of behavior, we should not forget that they shared important assumptions and goals. Both Tolman and Hull wanted to write scientific theories of learning and behavior applying to at least all mammals, including human beings. They pursued their mutual goal by experimenting on and theorizing about rats, assuming that any difference between rat and human was trivial, and that results from laboratories represented naturalistic behavior as well; they followed Herbert Spencer's formula for psychology. Both Tolman and Hull rejected consciousness as the subject matter of psychology, and took the description, prediction, and control of behavior as psychology's task; they were behavioralists, specifically, methodological behaviorists. Finally, both were influenced by, and seemed to endorse, logical positivism.

Psychologists have tended to assume (as in the first edition of this book) that Tolman and Hull were slavish adherents of logical positivism, and that they personally set the positivist style of modern psychology. However, such a judgment does them a disservice, obscures their independence, and depreciates their creativity. Tolman and Hull reached their conceptions of science, psychology, and behavior quite independently of logical positivism. When they encountered logical positivism in the 1930s, each found he could use this prestigious philosophy to more powerfully state his own ideas; but we must not forget that their ideas were their own. Unfortunately, because they did adopt positivist language and because positivism quickly came to be psychologists' philosophy of science, the real programs of Tolman and Hull were obscured or forgotten, resulting in some fruitless controversies in the 1950s, as we shall see in Chapter 13.

While both Tolman and Hull were honored and influential, there is no doubt that Hull was very much more influential than Tolman. At Berkeley, Tolman filled students with enthusiasm for psychology and a healthy disrespect for scientific pomposity. He wrote lively papers and took a zestful approach to science, saying that "in the end, the only sure criterion is to have fun. And I have had fun" (Tolman 1959). He was never a systematic theorist, and had finally to confess to being a "crypto-phenomenologist" who designed his experiments by imagining what he would do if he were a rat, being gratified to find that rats were as clever and commonsensical as he was, being no machines. Unfortunately, this all meant that while Tolman could inspire students, he could not teach them a systematic viewpoint with which to evangelize psychology. Tolman had no disciples.

Hull, however, did. Instead of valuing having fun, Hull valued the long, arduous labor of constructing postulates and deriving theorems from them. Though tedious, this gave Hull an explicit set of ideas with which to infect his students for spreading throughout the discipline. Moreover, Hull's institutional situation was ideal for building discipleship. Besides the department of psychology at Yale, Hull had the Institute of Human Relations (IHR) there, which attracted bright minds from many disciplines eager to learn the rigors of science for application to their fields and to the problems of the world. We will later see how social learning theory emerged from Hull's seminars at the IHR. Hull found someone to continue his program in Kenneth Spence (1907–1967). Spence collaborated on Hull's great books, continued his rigorous theorizing into the 1950s, created a truly positivist version of neobehaviorism, and trained many leading experimental psychologists of the 1950s and 1960s: Hull's intellectual grandchildren. And, of course, Hull's rigorous theoretical system, pristinely mechanistic and eschewing any mysticism about purpose and cognition, were perfectly in tune with the naturalistic-positivistic *Zeitgeist* of American psychology after World War I.

Studies during the 1950s therefore consistently found Hull's impact on psychology to be much greater than Tolman's. For example, as late as the 1960s, a study of which psychologists were most often cited in the leading journals of psychology (Myers 1970) found that the most-cited psychologist was Kenneth Spence, with Hull himself at eighth place. This is especially remarkable considering that Hull had been dead since 1952, and that his theory had been subjected to scathing criticism since the early 1950s. Despite the fact that many psychologists saw a cognitive "revolution" taking place in the 1960s, E. C. Tolman, the purposive, cognitive behaviorist, did not place in the top thirty.

CONCLUSION: WE'RE ALL BEHAVIORISTS NOW

Hull's colleague Kenneth Spence observed in 1948 that few psychologists "ever seem to think of themselves, or explicitly refer to themselves as behaviorists," because behaviorism was "a very general point of view which has come to be accepted by almost all psychologists." Spence noted one exception to his conclusion: Tolman protested perhaps too much that he was a good behaviorist. Spence also recognized that behaviorism took many forms, so that the term "behaviorism" was rather slippery. Still, behaviorism had made progress, Spence thought, because all the neobehaviorisms sharply separated themselves from Watson's early, rather crude formulation of classical behaviorism. Spence tried to tidy up the Babel of behaviorisms by formulating a behaviorist metaphysics along logical positivist lines. He hoped to create a common creed on which all behaviorists might agree. As we shall see in Chapter 13, his hope was misplaced, as the Tolmanians refused to assent.

On the horizon of experimental psychology lay a newly formulated radical behaviorism that after World War II would challenge and then replace all other behaviorisms. B. F. Skinner, a writer turned psychologist, had begun in 1931 to work out a behaviorism in the radical spirit of Watson, but with a new set of technical concepts. Skinner's influence lay in the future, when after the war psychologists would again lose confidence in their enterprise and begin to look for a new Newton. Before the war, however, Skinner was not taken too seriously. E. R. Hilgard (1939) said of Skinner's first major theoretical statement, *Behavior of Organisms,* that its narrow conception of psychology would greatly limit its influence.

During the years when academic psychologists came to accept behavioralism as the only legitimate approach to the problems of scientific psychology, other psychologists were beginning to tackle the problems of society. Psychology experienced its greatest growth not in experimental psychology, but in applied psychology.

Note: The bibliographies for Chapters 11 and 12 have been combined following Chapter 12.

REFERENCES

Angell, J. R. (1913) Behavior as a category of psychology. *Psychological Review 20:* 255–270.

Bode, B. H. (1918) Consciousness as behavior. *Journal of Philosophy 15:* 449–453.

Bridgman, P. (1927) *The logic of modern physics.* New York: Macmillan.

Brush, S. G. (1980) The chimerical cat: Philosophy of quantum mechanics historical perspective. *Social Studies of Science 10:* 394–447.

Buckley, K. (1984) *Mechanical man: John B. Watson and the beginnings of behaviorism.* Westport, Conn.: Guildford Press.

Calkins, M. W. (1913) Psychology and the behaviorist. *Psychological Bulletin 10:* 288–291.

Chapanis, A. (1961) Men, machines and models. *American Psychologist 16:* 113–131.

Cohen, D. B. (1979) *J. B. Watson: The founder of behaviorism.* London: Routledge and Kegan Paul.

Dashiell, J. F. (1939) Some rapprochements in contemporary psychology. *Psychological Bulletin 36:* 1–24.

Haggerty, M. E. (1913) The laws of learning. *Psychological Review 20:* 411–422.

Harris, B. (1979) Whatever happened to Little Albert? *American Psychologist 34:* 151–160.

Hilgard, E. R. (1939) Review of B. F. Skinner, *Behavior of organisms. Psychological Bulletin 36:* 121–124.

Hilgard, E. R. (1940) Review of Hull et al. *Psychological Bulletin 37:* 808–815.

Holton, G. (1978) *The scientific imagination: Case studies.* Cambridge, England: Cambridge University Press.

Hull, C. (1917) The formation and retention of associations among the insane. *American Journal of Psychology 28:* 419–435.

Hull, C. (1920) *Quantitative aspects of the evolution of concepts.* Psychological Monographs 28, no. 123.

Hull, C. (1930a) Simple trial and error learning: A study in psychological theory. *Psychological Review 37:* 241–256.

Hull, C. (1930b) Knowledge and purpose as habit mechanisms. *Psychological Review, 37:* 511–525.

Hull, C. (1931) Goal attraction and directing ideas conceived as habit phenomena. *Psychological Review 38:* 487–506.

Hull, C. (1934) The concept of the habit-family-hierarchy in maze learning. *Psychological Review 41:* 33–54 and 131–152.

Hull, C. (1935) The conflicting psychologies of learning: A way out. *Psychological Review 42:* 491–516.

Hull, C. (1937) Mind, mechanism and adaptive behavior. *Psychological Review 44:* 1–32.

Hull, C. (1938) The goal-gradient hypothesis applied to some ''field-force'' problems in the behavior of young children. *Psychological Review 45:* 271–300.

Hull, C. (1943a) The problem of intervening variables in molar behavior theory. *Psychological Review 50:* 273–288.

Hull, C. (1943b) *Principles of behavior.* New York: Appleton-Century-Crofts.

Hull, C. (1951) *Essentials of behavior.* New Haven: Yale University Press.

Hull, C. (1952) *A behavior system.* New Haven: Yale University Press.

Hull, C. and Baernstein, H. (1929) A mechanical parallel to the conditioned reflex. *Science 70:* 14–15.

Hull, C., Hovland, C., Ross, R., Hall, M., Perkins, D., and Fitch, F. (1940) *Mathe-*

matico-deductive theory of rote learning: A study in scientific methodology. New Haven: Yale University Press.

Hull, C. (1952) Clark L. Hull. In E. G. Boring, H. S. Langfeld, H. Werner, and R. M. Yerkes (Eds.) *A history of psychology in autobiography*. V. 4. Worcester, Mass.: Clark University Press.

Hunter, W. S. (1922) An open letter to the anti-behaviorists. *Journal of Philosophy 19:* 307–308.

Hunter, W. S. (1923) Review of A. A. Roback, "Behaviorism and psychology." *American Journal of Psychology 34:* 464–467.

Hunter, W. S. (1925) Psychology and anthroponomy. In C. Murchison (Ed.) *Psychologies of 1925.* Worcester, Mass.: Clark University Press.

Jastrow, J. (1927) The reconstruction of psychology. *Psychological Review 34:* 169–195.

Jones, A. H. (1915) The method of psychology. *Journal of Philosophy 12:* 462–471.

Koch, S. (1941) The logical character of the motivation concept. *Psychological Review 48:* 15–38 and 127–154.

Koch, S. (1944) Hull's *Principles of behavior*: A special review. *Psychological Bulletin 41:* 269–286.

Kuo, Z. Y. (1928) The fundamental error of the concept of purpose and the trial and error fallacy. *Psychological Review 35:* 414–433.

Langfeld, H. S. (1943) Fifty years of the *Psychological Review. Psychological Review 50:* 143–155.

Lashley, K. S. (1923) The behavioristic interpretation of consciousness. *Psychological Review 30* 1: 237–272, 1: 329–353.

MacDougall, R. (1925) Men or robots? In C. Murchison (Ed.) *Psychologies of 1925.* Worcester, Mass.: Clark University Press.

McComas, H. C. (1916) Extravagances in the motor theory of consciousness. *Psychological Review 23:* 397–406.

McGeoch, J. A. (1931) The acquisition of skill. *Psychological Bulletin 28:* 413–466.

Myers, C. R. (1970) Journal citations and scientific eminence in psychology. *American Psychologist 25:* 1041–1048.

Pepper, S. (1923) Misconceptions regarding behaviorism. *Journal of Philosophy 20:* 242–245.

Perry, R. B. (1921) A behavioristic view of purpose. *Journal of Philosophy 18:* 85–105.

Samelson, F. (1980) J. B. Watson's Little Albert, Cyril Burt's twins, and the need for a critical science. *American Psychologist 35:* 619–625.

Samelson F. (1981) Struggle for scientific authority: The reception of Watson's behaviorism, 1913–1920. *Journal of the History of the Behavioral Sciences 17:* 399–425.

Skinner, B. F. (1938) *Behavior of organisms*. New York: Appleton-Century-Crofts.

Smith, L. J. (1986) *Behaviorism and logical positivism: A revised account of the alliance.* Stanford, Calif.: Stanford University Press.

Spence, K. (1948) Postulates and methods of "behaviorism." *Psychological Review 55:* 67–78.

Stevens, S. S. (1935a) The operational basis of psychology. *American Journal of Psychology 43:* 323–330.

Stevens, S. S. (1935b) The operational definition of psychological concepts. *Psychological Review 42:* 517–527.

Stevens, S. S. (1939) Psychology and the science of science. *Psychological Bulletin 36:* 221–263.

Titchener, E. B. (1914) On "Psychology as the behaviorist views it." *Proceedings of the American Philosophical Society 53:* 1–17.

Tolman, E. (1920) Instinct and purpose. *Psychological Review 27:* 217–233.

Tolman, E. (1922) A new formula for behaviorism. *Psychological Review 29:* 44–53.

Tolman, E. (1923) A behavioristic account of the emotions. *Psychological Review 30:* 217–227.

Tolman, E. (1925) Behaviorism and purpose. *Journal of Philosophy 22:* 36–41.

Tolman, E. (1926) A behavioristic theory of ideas. *Psychological Review 33:* 352–369.

Tolman, E. (1935) Psychology vs. immediate experience. *Philosophy of Science.* Reprinted in Tolman (1951/1966).

Tolman, E. (1932) *Purposive behavior in animals and men.* New York: Century.

Tolman, E. (1936) Operational behaviorism and current trends in psychology. In Tolman (1951/1966).

Tolman, E. (1948) Cognitive maps in rats and men. *Psychological Review 55:* 189–209.

Tolman, E. (1951/1966) *Behavior and psychological man.* Berkeley: University of California Press.

Tolman, E. (1952) Edward Chace Tolman. In E. G. Boring, H. S. Langfeld, H. Werner, and R. M. Yerkes (Eds.) *A history of psychology in autobiography.* V. 4. Worcester, Mass.: Clark University Press.

Tolman, E. (1959) Principles of purposive behaviorism. In S. Koch (Ed.) *Psychology: A study of a science.* V. 2. New York: McGraw-Hill.

Warren, H. (1938) Howard C. Warren. In C. Murchison (Ed.) *A History of psychology in autobiography.* V. 1. Worcester, Mass.: Clark University Press.

Watson, J. B. (1913a) Psychology as the behaviorist views it. *Psychological Review 20:* 158–177.

Watson, J. B. (1913b) Image and affection in behavior. *Journal of Philosophy 10:* 421–428.

Watson, J. B. (1916a) The place of the conditioned reflex in psychology. *Psychological Review 23:* 89–116.

Watson, J. B. (1916b) Behavior and the concept of mental disease. *Journal of Philosophy 13:* 589–597.

Watson, J. B. (1930) *Behaviorism.* New York: Norton.

Watson, J. B. and Rayner, R. (1920) Conditioned emotional reactions. *Journal of Experimental Psychology 10:* 421–428.

Weiss, A. P. (1924) Behaviorism and behavior. *Psychological Review 31:* 1 :32–50, 2 :118–149.

Wheeler, R. W. (1923) Introspection and behavior. *Psychological Review 30:* 103–115.

Wickens, D. D. (1938) The transference of conditioned extinction from one muscle group to the antagonistic muscle group. *Journal of Experimental Psychology 22:* 101–123.

Williams, K. (1931) Five behaviorisms. *American Journal of Psychology 43:* 337–361.

Woodworth, R. S. (1924) Four varieties of behaviorism. *Psychological Review 31:* 257–264.

Yerkes, R. M. (1913) Comparative psychology: A question of definition. *Journal of Philosophy 10:* 581–582.

CHAPTER 12

Psychology Takes Off

Psychology and Society (1913–1950)

APPLIED PSYCHOLOGY (1896–1916)
PSYCHOLOGISTS IN PROFESSIONAL CONTROVERSY (1917–1940)
    Psychologists in the Great War
    Psychologists at Work
    Professional Psychologists Assert Themselves
PSYCHOLOGISTS IN SOCIAL CONTROVERSY (1917–1940)
    Is America Safe for Democracy? Impact of Army
    Intelligence Testing
    Making America Safe for Democracy: Immigration Control
    and Eugenics
    Flaming Youth and the Reconstruction of the Family
    When Psychology Was King
PSYCHOLOGY TRANSFORMED (1940–1950)
    In the Crucible of War: Psychology Reunified
    Redefining Clinical Psychology
    Psychology Fails to Get a Slice of the Big Science Pie
CONCLUSION
    Psychologists Look Ahead to the Psychological Society
    Values and Adjustment

Entrance into World War I marked the end of two decades of profound social change, transforming the United States from a rural country of island communities into an industrialized, urbanized nation of everywhere communities. The United States became a great power that could project military might across the Atlantic Ocean, and decide the outcome of a European war. Progressive politicians saw in the war a welcome chance to achieve their goals of social control, creating a unified, patriotic, efficient nation out of the mass of immigrants and scattered groups created by industrialization. Led by President Wilson, they also saw a chance to bring Progressive, rational control to the whole world. As one Progressive exclaimed, "Long live social control; social control, not only to enable us to meet the rigorous demands of the war, but also as a foundation for the peace and brotherhood that is to come."

But the Great War to End All Wars frustrated and then shattered the Progressives' dreams. The government created bureaucracies whose watchword was efficiency and whose aims were standardization and centralization, but they accomplished nothing. The horrors of the war, in which many European villages lost their entire male populations for a few feet of foreign soil, brought Americans face to face with the irrational, and left many Europeans with lifelong depression and pessimism. After the war the victorious powers fell to dividing up the spoils of war like vultures, and Wilson became little more than a pathetic idealist ignored at Versailles and then at home, unable to bring America into his League of Nations World War I did nothing but lay the groundwork for World War II.

The pessimistic, darkly expectant mood of the era was captured in 1920 by William Butler Yeats in the poem "The Second Coming"*:

> Turning and turning in the widening gyre
> The falcon cannot hear the falconer:
> Things fall apart; the centre cannot hold;
> Mere anarchy is loosed upon the world,
> The blood-dimmed tide is loosed, and everywhere
> The ceremony of innocence is drowned;
> The best lack all conviction, while the worst
> Are full of passionate intensity.
> Surely some revelation is at hand;
> Sure the Second Coming is at hand.
> The Second Coming! Hardly are those words out
> When a vast image out of "Spiritus Mundi"
> Troubles my sight: somewhere in sands of the desert
> A shape with lion body and the head of a man,
> A gaze blank and pitiless as the sun,
> Is moving its slow thighs, while all about it
> Reel shadows of the indignant desert birds.
> The darkness drops again; but now I know
> That twenty centuries of stony sleep
> Were vexed to nightmare by a rocking cradle,

*Reprinted with permission of Macmillan Publishing Co., Inc., from *Collected Poems* by William Butler Yeats. Copyright 1924 by Macmillan Publishing Co., Inc., renewed 1952 by Bertha Georgie Yeats.

And what rought beast, its hour come round at last,
Slouches towards Bethlehem to be born?

Intellectuals and social and political leaders learned the lesson that reason was not enough to achieve social control. In the aftermath of war the lesson was underlined by the revolt of the Flaming Youth of the 1920s and the seeming breakdown of the families that had raised them. Convinced of the wisdom of science, however—for scientism still ran strong in America—American leaders turned to social science, especially psychology, to solve the problems of the postwar world, to give them the tools by which to manage the irrational masses, to reshape the family and the workplace. As Philip Rieff put it, the Middle Ages, with faith in God, ruled through the church; the progressive nineteenth century, with faith in reason, ruled through the legislature; the twentieth century, with faith in science tempered by recognition of the irrational, rules through the hospital. In the twentieth century, then, psychology would become one of the most important institutions in society; no wonder that psychologists' ideas became more widely applied, the latest scientific marvel read by leaders for clues to social control, and by the masses for insights into the springs of their own behavior.

APPLIED PSYCHOLOGY
(1896–1916)

In 1892 William James wrote, "The kind of psychology which could cure a case of melancholy, or charm a chronic insane delusion away, ought certainly to be preferred to the most seraphic insight into the nature of the soul." James identified a tension in modern psychology—especially modern American psychology—that has steadily increased throughout the twentieth century: the tension between the psychologist as scientist and the psychologist as practitioner of a craft. The tension has been most evident in the history of the American Psychological Association (APA), founded in 1892. It was founded to advance the cause of psychology as science, but very quickly its members turned to the application of their science, and the APA found itself embroiled in largely unwanted problems concerned with defining and regulating the practice of psychology as a technological profession. There was, however, especially in America, no going back on the development of professional applied psychology: Psychology's social circumstances and the ideology of pragmatism and functionalism required it.

In nineteenth-century Germany the academicians who controlled the gates of admission to the great universities had needed to be convinced of psychology's legitimacy as a discipline. Their leading academicians were the philosophers; and in their Mandarin culture, pure knowledge was valued above technology. Naturally, Wundt and the other German psychologists founded a discipline strictly devoted to "seraphic insights into the nature of the soul." In the United States things were very different. American universities were not institutions controlled by a few academicians working for the central state, but were a variegated collection of public and private schools subject more to local whim than central control. As de Tocqueville observed, Americans valued what brought practical success, and sought social and personal improvement rather than pure knowledge. So the tribunal that would pass on psychology's worthiness in America was composed of practical men of business and industry interested in techniques of social control. Naturally, then, psychologists came to stress the social and personal utility of their discipline instead of its refined scientific character.

As with phrenology, American psychology wanted to be recognized as a science, but especially as a science with practical aims. On the occasion of the twenty-fifth anniversary of the APA John Dewey (1917) denounced the concept, characteristic of Gall or Wundt, of the mind as a creation of nature existing before society. By placing mind beyond society's control, such a view acted as a bastion of political conservatism, Dewey held. He offered his pragmaticist conception of mind as a social creation as the proper foundation for experimental psychology. Since in Dewey's view mind was created by society, it could be deliberately molded by society, and psychology, the science of the mind, could take as its goal social control, the scientific management of society. Such a psychology would fall in with Progressivism and give American psychology the social utility Wundt's psychology lacked.

American psychologists thus offered a science with pragmatic "cash value." Pragmatism demanded that ideas become true by making a difference to human conduct; so, to be true, psychological ideas would have to show that they did matter to individuals and society. Functionalism argued that the role of mind was to adjust the behavior of the individual organism to the environment. Naturally, then, psychologists would come to be interested in how the process of adjustment played itself out in American life, and would then move to improve the process of adjustment to make it more efficient and to repair the process of adjustment when it went awry. Since adjustment was the great function of mind, every sphere of human life was opened to the psychological technologist: the child's adjustment to the family; parents' adjustments to their children and to each other; the worker's adjustment to the workplace; the soldier's adjustment to the army; and so on through every aspect of personality and behavior: No aspect of life would finally escape the clinical gaze of professional psychologists.

Interest in these matters appeared as soon as psychology reached America. Central to the first applications of psychology was Cattell's invention of the "mental test" in 1890. At the Columbian Exposition of 1893, psychology came to the public's attention when they entered an exhibit and took psychological tests. The first "psychological clinic" was opened in 1896 by Lightner Witmer, and many others sprang up in the ensuing years. These clinics used tests to diagnose children with school problems, but generally offered no treatment. A related development was the child guidance clinic; the first such clinic was attached to a juvenile court in Chicago in 1909. There, psychologist Grace Fernald gave tests to children brought before the court. The earliest tests used with retarded children were "tests" made up using the brass instruments of the psychological laboratory, but these were soon replaced by the more sophisticated Binet test. The center of this activity was the Vineland Training School opened in 1905; its director, Henry Goddard, introduced the Binet test to the United States. In 1908 the mental hygiene movement got started with a book by a former mental patient, *A Mind That Found Itself*, endorsed by William James himself. The aim of the mental hygienists was the prevention of psychological problems, and it provided a further impetus to the child guidance clinics, which began to look for problems before they developed. At the McLean Hospital, mental patients were tested and became subjects of investigations by psychologists. Finally, psychology was applied to business and industry, first to advertising by Walter Dill Scott, who gave a talk on the psychology of advertising in 1901, becoming eventually professor of advertising at Northwestern University in 1915. In the same year psychologists began to use tests to pick workers for particular jobs.

Just before the United States entered World War I, then, psychologists were actively applying their ideas and techniques—especially tests—to a wide range of social problems. Their efforts, however, were scattered and small scale. When the war came, psychologists enlisted to apply themselves to a truly massive task: the evaluation of men for fitness to serve in the U.S. Army. One year later psychology had become a permanent part of the intellectual landscape of American life, and its terminology had become part of the American vocabulary.

PSYCHOLOGISTS IN PROFESSIONAL CONTROVERSY (1917–1940)

Psychologists in the Great War

Psychologists, like Progressives, saw the Great War as an opportunity—an opportunity to show that psychology had come of age as a science and could be put to service. The organizer of psychology's efforts to serve the nation at war was Robert Yerkes, the comparative psychologist. With pride he explained in his presidential address to the APA just months after the war began, how:

> In this country, for the first time in the history of our science, a general organization in the interests of certain ideal and practical aims has been effected. Today, American psychology is placing a highly trained and eager personnel at the service of our military organizations. We are acting not individually but collectively on the basis of common training and common faith in the practical value of our work.

Just as Progressives used the war to unify the country, Yerkes exhorted psychologists to "act unitedly in the interests of defense," bringing psychologists together "as a professional group in a nation-wide effort to render our professional training serviceable."

On April 6, 1917, only two days after the United States declared war, Yerkes seized the opportunity of a meeting of Titchener's "Experimentalists" to organize psychology's war efforts. Following a whirlwind of activity by Yerkes and some others—including a trip to Canada to see what Canadian psychologists were doing in their war—the APA formed twelve committees concerned with different aspects of the war, ranging from acoustic problems to recreation. Few young male psychologists were left uninvolved; but in this war, unlike the next, only two committees really accomplished anything: Walter Dill Scott's committee on motivation, which became the Committee on Classification of Personnel of the War Department, and Yerkes's own committee on the psychological examination of recruits, which concentrated on the problem of eliminating the "mentally unfit" from the U.S. Army. There was considerable tension between Yerkes and Scott from the outset. Yerkes came from experimental psychology and brought research interests to the job of testing recruits, hoping to gather data on intelligence as well as serve the needs of the military. Scott's background was industrial psychology, and he brought a practical, management perspective to military testing, aiming above all at practical

FIGURE 12-1 That psychological examination, 1918. In retrospect we can see that the Army tests of intelligence were absurd. This cartoon, from *The Camp Sherman News,* reprinted in *Psychological Bulletin,* 1919, expresses the ordinary soldier's experience of the tests. Groups of men were assembled in rooms, given pencils and response sheets, had to obey shouted orders to do unfamiliar things, and to answer strange questions. The test items that the unfortunate recruit in the cartoon has to answer are but slight exaggerations of the real items. Stephen Jay Gould gave the Beta test to Harvard undergraduates, following the exact procedures used in the war, and found that although most students did well, a few barely made "C"

results, not scientific results. At the wartime organizational meeting of the APA at the Walton Hotel in Philadelphia, Scott said that he "became so enraged at [Yerkes's] points of view that I expressed myself very clearly and left the [APA] council" (von Mayrhauser 1985). Scott believed Yerkes to be making a power play to advance his own interests in psychology, and accused Yerkes of concealing self-interest behind sham patriotism. The upshot of the quarrel was that Yerkes and Scott went their own ways in applying tests to the examination of recruits. Yerkes (who had always wanted to be a doctor) set up under the Surgeon General's office in the Sanitary Corps, and Scott under the Adjutant General's office.

Insofar as concrete results welcomed and used by the military were concerned, Scott's committee was the more effective of the two. Drawing on his work in personnel psychology at the Carnegie Institute of Technology, Scott developed a rating scale for selecting officers. By himself, Scott convinced the Army of the scale's utility, and was allowed to form his War Department committee, which quickly became involved in the more massive undertaking of assigning the "right man to the right job" in the Army. By the end of the war Scott's committee had grown from 20 to over 175 members, had classified nearly 3,500,000 men, and developed proficiency tests for 83 military jobs. Scott was awarded a Distinguished Service Medal for his work.

Yerkes's committee did virtually nothing for the Army—he won no medal—but it did a great deal to advance professional psychology. In this respect their most obvious achievement was to invent the group test of intelligence. Heretofore intelligence tests, the most important of which was Binet's, had been administered to individual subjects by clinical psychologists. Obviously, individual tests could not be administered to millions of draftees, so in May 1918 Yerkes assembled leading test psychologists at the Vineland Training School to write an intelligence test that could be given to groups of men in brief periods of time. Initially, Yerkes believed that group tests of intelligence were unscientific, introducing uncontrolled factors into the test situation, and wanted to test each recruit individually; but associates of Scott's at Vineland persuaded him that individual testing was just impossible under the circumstances (von Mayrhauser 1985). Yerkes's group designed two tests, the Army Alpha test for literate recruits, and the Army Beta test for presumed illiterates who did badly on the Alpha. Recruits were graded on a letter scale from A to E, just like in school; "A" men were likely officers, "D" and "E" men were the unfit (see Figure 12-1).

Overcoming considerable skepticism, and following a trial period of testing at one camp, in December 1917 the Army approved general testing of all recruits. Throughout the war Yerkes's work was met with hostility and indifference by Army officers who saw Yerkes's psychologists as meddlers having no business in the Army, and by Army psychiatrists who feared psychologists might assume some of their roles within the military. Nevertheless, 1,175,000 men were tested before the program was ended in January 1919. With the invention of the group test, Yerkes and his colleagues had invented a tool that greatly expanded the potential scope of

---

level. Gould's students, of course, were greatly experienced with standardized tests, in contrast with raw draftees under great stress, many of whom had little or no education. One can only imagine how puzzled and confused the average testee was, and sympathize with the hapless soldier at Camp Sherman.

psychologists' activities, and multiplied by many times the numbers of Americans that might be scrutinized by the profession.

In concluding his presidential address Yerkes "looked ahead and attempted to prophesy future needs" for psychology. "The obvious and significant trend of our psychological military work is toward service . . . the demand for psychologists and psychological service promises, or threatens, to be overwhelmingly great." Yerkes foresaw better than he knew; while speaking only of psychological service in the military, Yerkes's words describe the most important change in institutional psychology in the twentieth century. Before the war applied psychologists had worked in relative obscurity in isolated settings around the country; during the war they touched millions of lives in a self-conscious, organized professional effort to apply psychology to a pressing social need; after the war psychology was famous, and applied psychology grew by leaps and bounds, concerning itself with the "menace of the feebleminded," with immigrants, with troubled children, with industrial workers, with advertising, with problems of the American family. Applied psychology had arrived as an important actor on the American social scene, and its influence has never ceased to grow in the seventy years since Yerkes called psychologists to military service.

Psychologists at Work

Aside from advertising psychology, which affects everyone with a radio or TV, more people have been affected by industrial psychology—the applications of psychology to business management—than by any other branch of applied psychology. As we have seen, the beginnings of industrial psychology lay before the war; but as with the rest of applied psychology, its efflorescence occurred after the war.

The goal of Progressives, in business as in government, was efficiency, and the path to efficiency in every case was thought to be through science. The first exponent of scientific management in business was Frederick Taylor (1856–1915), who developed his ideas around the turn of the century, and published them in *Principles of Scientific Management* in 1911. Taylor studied industrial workers at work and analyzed their jobs into mechanical routines that could be performed efficiently by anyone, not just by the masters of a craft. In essence Taylor turned human workers into robots, mindlessly but efficiently repeating routinized movements. Taylor was not a psychologist, and the shortcoming of his system was that it managed jobs, not people, overlooking the worker's subjective experience of work and the impact of the worker's happiness on productivity. Nevertheless, Taylor's goal was that of scientific psychology: "[U]nder scientific management arbitrary power, arbitrary dictation ceases; and every single subject, large and small, becomes the question for scientific investigation, for reduction to law." And when these laws were understood, they could be applied in the pursuit of greater industrial efficiency.

Gradually, managers recognized that it was not enough to manage jobs; efficiency and profits could be improved only if workers were managed as people with feelings and emotional attachments to their work. After the war, in the wake of psychologists' apparent success with the large-scale personnel problems posed by the Army, industrial psychology became increasingly popular in American business. Perhaps the most influential piece of research demonstrating the usefulness of applying psychology to industry—management via feelings—was carried out in the early 1920s by a group of social scientists led by psychologist Elton Mayo at the Hawthorne plant of the Western Electric Company.

The "Hawthorne Effect" is one of the best known of psychological results, and seemed to demonstrate the importance of subjective factors in determining a worker's industrial efficiency. While the experiments carried out were complex, the results from the relay assembly room are central to defining the Hawthorne Effect. A group of female workers assembling telephone relays were chosen for experimentation. The scientists manipulated nearly every aspect of the work situation, from the schedule of rest pauses to the amount of lighting, and found that virtually everything They did increased productivity, even when a manipulation meant returning to the old way of doing things. The researchers concluded that the increases in productivity were caused not by changes to the workplace, but by the activity of the researchers themselves. They felt that the workers were impressed by the fact that management cared about their welfare, and the workers' improved feelings about their jobs and about the company translated into improved output. Following a Populist line of thought already articulated by John Dewey's prescriptions for education, Mayo thought that because of industrialization, workers had become alienated from society, having lost the intimate ties of preindustrial life that bound people together in the insular communities of the past. Unlike the nostalgic Populists, however, Mayo, like Dewey, saw that the agrarian world was irretrievably lost, and urged business to fill the void by creating communities of workers who found meaning in their work. Various measures were instituted to meet workers' apparent emotional needs; one of the first and most obviously psychological was the creation of "personnel counseling." Workers with complaints about their jobs or about how they were treated by their employers could go to psychologically trained peer counselors to whom they could relate their frustrations and dissatisfactions. Such programs slowly grew in numbers over the following decades.

Recently, the Hawthorne results have been reanalyzed, resulting in the disconcerting finding that the Hawthorne Effect is a myth (Bramel and Friend 1981). There is no firm evidence that the workers in the relay room ever felt better about the company as a result of the experiments, and much evidence to suggest that the workers regarded the psychologists as company spies. The improved productivity of the relay assembly team is easily explained as a result of the replacement, in the middle of the experiment, of a disgruntled, not very productive worker by an enthusiastic, productive worker. More broadly, a radical critique of industrial psychology (Baritz 1960, Bramel and Friend 1981) argues that industrial psychology produces happy robots, but robots nonetheless. Mayo's personnel counselors were to "help people think in such a way that they would be happier with their jobs"; one counselor reported being trained to "deal with attitudes toward problems, not the problems themselves" (Baritz 1960). By using psychological manipulation, managers could deflect workers' concerns from objective working conditions, including wages, and turn them instead to preoccupations with feelings, to their adjustment to the work situation. Workers would still carry out the robotic routines laid down by Taylor, but would do so in a happier frame of mind, prone to interpret discontent as a sign of poor psychological adjustment rather than as a sign that something was really wrong at work.

Professional Psychologists Assert Themselves

After the war psychologists in increasing numbers began practicing applied psychology. At the time it was called, inappropriately, "clinical" psychology, because of its roots in Witmer's psychological "clinic." In fact, the "clinical" psychology of these years bore little resemblance to today's clinical psychology. The term has come to mean primarily the practice of psychotherapy by psychologists, but before World War II "clinical" psychology had mostly to do with giving tests to various populations: children, soldiers, workers, and mental patients, and occasional individual clients.

In any event, "clinical" psychologists rarely performed research, and were often employed outside universities, working for companies or on their own as psychological consultants. The old guard of scientific psychologists who had founded the APA, for all their apparent commitment to useful psychology, were made uncomfortable by the increasing numbers of "clinical" psychologists. The APA, after all, had been founded to "advance psychology as a science," and it was not at all clear that clinicians were advancing scientific psychology, because they did no research. Moreover, clinicians were predominantly women, and male psychologists had a hard time taking women seriously as anything more than psychological dilettantes.

During the 1920s and 1930s the APA vacillated in its treatment of applied psychologists. Entry to the association had for some time depended on having published articles in scientific journals; then a class of associate members was created for the nonscientists, who enjoyed only limited participation in the association. These "clinical" psychologists, whose numbers rapidly swelled, naturally resented their second-class status. During the same period the APA recognized that, as the official organization of psychologists, it bore some responsibility for assuring the competence of practicing psychologists, being deeply concerned about charlatans and frauds passing themselves off as genuine psychologists, and tarnishing the honor of the science in the eyes of the public. So for a time the APA issued certificates, badges of authenticity, to applied—or, as they were officially called, "consulting"—psychologists. The experiment was short-lived, however. Few psychologists bothered to apply for the certificates. The academicians of the APA also were unwilling to exert themselves to attain the proper ends of professionalization by enforcing standards and taking legal action against psychological frauds.

Gradually, applied psychologists got fed up with the APA. They realized that their interest, the creation of a socially accepted and defined practice of psychology on a par with physicians, lawyers, engineers, and other professional practitioners of a craft, could not be realized in an association devoted exclusively to psychology as an academically based science. As early as 1917 applied psychologists tried to form their own association, but the enterprise was controversial and died when the APA agreed to the creation of a clinical section within the association. In 1930 a group of applied psychologists in New York formed a national organization, the Association of Consulting Psychologists (ACP). The ACP pressed states (beginning with New York) to establish legal standards for the definition of "psychologist," wrote a set of ethical guidelines for the practice of psychology, and began its own journal, the *Journal of Consulting Psychology,* in 1937. Despite pleas by professional psychologists for the APA to get involved in defining and setting standards for practitioners of the psychological craft (for example, Poffenberger 1936), the association continued to fail them. So in 1938 the unhappy psychologists of the clinical section of the APA left the parent organization, and joined with the ACP to create the American Association for Applied Psychology (AAAP).

During the years between world wars, applied psychologists groped for an identity distinct from traditional, scientific psychology. The interests of academic and professional psychologists were different and to some extent incompatible—the advancement of research versus the advancement of the legal and social status of clinicians. Academic psychologists feared—and still fear—the growing numbers of applied psychologists, worrying that they might lose control of the association they founded. Yet the applied psychologists remained inextricably linked to academic psychology. They received their training in university departments of psychology, and traded on the claim of psychology to be a scientific discipline. So, while applied psychologists established a professional identity by founding the AAAP, the absolute divorce of scientific and applied psychology could be only temporary.

PSYCHOLOGISTS IN SOCIAL CONTROVERSY (1917–1940)

As psychologists began to concern themselves with the problems of American society, they naturally became involved in wider social, political, and intellectual controversies outside academia. Three issues attracted attention more than others: the apparently depressing picture of American intelligence revealed by the Army intelligence tests; the revival of eugenics, caused in part by the test results; and the need to rethink the functions of the family, caused by the revolt of the Flaming Youth of the 1920s. Finally, all this public attention turned psychology into something of a popular fad in the dozen years following the Great War.

Is America Safe for Democracy? Impact of Army Intelligence Testing

Progressives believed with E. L. Thorndike (1920) that "in the long run it has paid the masses to be ruled by intelligence." But the results of the Army Alpha and Beta tests suggested that there were alarmingly few intelligent Americans—"A" men, and rather too many feebleminded Americans—"D" and "E" men. Yerkes's massive report on the results of the Army tests recorded a mean American mental age of 13.08. Terman's work on translating and standardizing the Binet test had set the "normal" average intelligence at a mental age of 16. Henry Goddard had coined the term "moron" to denote anyone with a mental age of less than 13, so that nearly half of the drafted white men (47.3 percent) would have to be considered morons. Performance by recent immigrant groups and blacks was even worse. Yerkes (1923) told readers of *Atlantic Monthly* that "racial" differences in intelligence were quite real. Children from the older immigrant stock did quite well on the Army tests. Draftees of English descent ranked first, followed by the Dutch, Danish, Scots, and Germans. Descendants of later-arriving immigrants did badly. The bottom of the distribution of intelligence (excluding blacks) were Turks, Greeks, Russians, Italians, and Poles. At the very bottom were blacks, with a mental age on the Army tests of just 10.41.

The results appalled people who agreed with Galton that intelligence is innate. In his book's title psychologist William McDougall (1921) asked, *Is America Safe for Democracy?* and argued that unless action were taken, the answer was no: "Our civilization, by reason of its increasing complexity, is making constantly increasing demands upon the quality of its bearers; the qualities of those bearers are diminishing or deteriorating, rather than improving." Henry Goddard, who had helped construct the Army tests, concluded that "the average man can manage his affairs with only a moderate degree of prudence, can earn only a very modest living, and is vastly better off when following direction than when trying to plan for himself'' (Gould 1981). The Galtonian alarmists were convinced that individual and racial differences were genetic in origin and consequently incapable of being erased by education. For example, Yerkes (1923) noted that blacks living in Northern states outscored Southern blacks by a wide margin, but claimed that this was because smarter blacks had moved North, leaving the feebleminded behind. He could, of course, have noted that blacks were more likely to receive an education in the North than in the South, but he did not even consider such a possibility.

There were critics of the tests and their alleged results, but for a long time the critics were ignored. The most insightful critic was the political writer Walter Lippman, who published a devastating critique of the alarmist interpretation of the Army results in the *New Republic* in 1922 and 1923 (reprinted in Block and Dworkin 1976). Lippman argued that the average American cannot have a below-average intelligence. Terman's figure of a ''normal'' mental age of 16 was based on a reference norm of a few hundred schoolchildren in California; the Army results were based on over 100,000 recruits. Therefore it was more logical to conclude that the Army results represented average American intelligence than to stick with the California sample and absurdly conclude that the American average was below average. Moreover, the classification of men into A, B, C, D, and E categories was essentially arbitrary, reflecting the needs of the Army, not raw intelligence. For example, the alarmists were alarmed that only 5 percent of the recruits were ''A'' men; but Lippman pointed out that the tests were constructed so that only 5 percent *could* be ''A'' men, since the Army wanted to send 5 percent of the recruits to Officer Training School. Had the Army only wanted half the number of officers, the tests would have been designed to yield 2.5 percent ''A'' men, and the alarmists would have been even more alarmed. In short, Lippman showed, there wasn't anything in the Army results to get excited about. But despite Lippman's cautions, many people did get excited about the Army tests. The Galtonian alarmists pressed for political action to do something about the supposed ''menace of the feeble-minded,'' and as we shall shortly see, they got it.

Another and more enduring legacy of the Army tests was the enhanced status given to mental tests by their application to war work. Lewis Terman, whose interest in human measurement had begun at age ten when his ''bumps'' were read by an itinerant phrenologist, was elected president of the APA, and in his presidential address (Terman 1924) argued that mental tests were equal to experiments in scientific value, and that moreover they were capable of addressing ''one of the most important [issues] humanity faces,'' the relative contributions of nature and nurture to intelligence. Later, Terman (1930) predicted the widespread use of tests in schools, in vocational and educational guidance, in industry, politics and law, and even in ''matrimonial clinics,'' where tests would be given to couples before they decided to wed. The goals of the phrenological Fowlers would be realized in Terman's world. Another leading test psychologist, Charles Spearman, grandiosely described the results from intelligence tests as having supplied the ''long missing genuinely scientific foundation for psychology, . . . so that it can henceforward take its due place along with the other solidly founded sciences, even physics itself'' (quoted by Gould 1981). Test psychologists were as prone to physics envy as experimental psychologists.

Terman's vision appeared to be well on its way to fulfillment. In his report on the Army results, Yerkes spoke of ''the steady stream of requests from commercial concerns, educational institutions, and individuals for the use of army methods of psychological examining or for the adaptation of such methods to special needs'' (quoted in Gould 1981). With Terman, Yerkes foresaw a bright future for applied psychology based on mental tests. He (Yerkes 1923) called psychologists to answer the "need for knowledge of man [which] has increased markedly in our times." Since "man is just as measurable as a bar or a . . . machine," psychologists would find that "more aspects of man will become measurable . . . more social values appraisable," resulting in psychological "human engineering." In the "not remote future" applied psychology would be as precise and effective as applied physics. The goals of Progressive social control would have been reached with the tools of psychology.

Making America Safe for Democracy
Immigration Control and Eugenics

> We can have almost any kind of a race of human beings we want. We can have a race that is beautiful or ugly, wise or foolish, strong or weak, moral or immoral.
>
> This is not a mere fancy. It is as certain as any social fact. The whole question lies in what we can induce people to *want*. Greece wanted beautiful women and got them. Rome did the same thing. The Dark Ages wanted ugly men and women and got them. . . . We want ugly women in America and we are getting them in millions. For nearly a generation . . . three or four shiploads have been landing at Ellis Island every week. If they are allowed to breed the future "typical American," then the typical future American is going to be as devoid of personal beauty as this vast mass of humanity, the majority of which has never learned to love or understand woman's beauty nor man's nobility of form. And the moment we lose beauty we lose intelligence. . . . Every high period of intellectual splendor has been characterized by "fair women and brave men." The nobility of any civilization can, to a considerable extent, be measured by the beauty of its women and the physical perfection of its men. . . .
>
> [N]o man can travel over America and not be impressed with the association between a high type of womanly beauty and a high type of art and culture. . . .
>
> As I have said, it is all a question of ideals. We can breed the race forward or backward, up or down.
>
> Albert Edward Wiggam,
> *The Fruit of the Family Tree*

Galtonians regarded the recent immigrant and the black as Prospero regarded Caliban in Shakespeare's *The Tempest:* as "a devil, a born devil, on whose nature, nurture can never stick." The Army tests demonstrated their irredeemable stupidity, fixed in the genes, which no amount of education could improve. Since education was helpless to improve the intelligence, morality, and beauty of Americans, they concluded, something would have to be done about the stupid, the immoral, and the ugly, were America not to commit "race suicide." Specifically, according to Galtonians, inferior stock would have to be prevented from immigrating to America, and those Americans already here but cursed with stupidity or immorality would have to be prevented from breeding. Galtonians sought, therefore, to restrict immigration to what they regarded as the better sort of people, and to implement negative eugenics, the prevention from reproduction of the worst sort of people.

While only occasionally leaders in the politics of immigration and eugenics, psychologists played an important role in support of Galtonian aims.

The worst Galtonians were outright racists. Their leader was Madison Grant, author of *The Passing of the Great Race.* He divided the supposed "races" of Europe into the Nordic, Alpine, and Mediterranean, the first of which, blond and Protestant, were self-reliant heroes more intelligent and resourceful than other races. The Nordics, Grant and his followers said, had founded the United States, but were in danger of being swamped by the recent influx of immigrants from other racial groups. Yerkes (1923) himself endorsed Grant's fantastic racism, calling for selective immigration laws designed to keep out the non-Nordics, and so fend off the "menace of race deterioration" in the United States. Yerkes wrote the forward for psychologist Carl Brigham's *A Study of American Intelligence,* which used the Army results to show that due to immigration—and, worse, "the most sinister development in the history of the continent, the importation of the negro"—that "the decline of American intelligence will be . . . rapid . . . [unless] public action can be aroused to prevent it. There is no reason why legal steps should not be taken which would insure a continuously progressive upward evolution. . . . Immigration should not only be restrictive but highly selective" (Gould 1981).

Galtonians pressed for action from Congress to stanch the flow of inferior types of people in the United States. Broughton Brandenburg, president of the National Institute of Immigration, testified, "It is not vainglory when we say that we have bred more than sixty million of the finest people the world has ever seen. Today, there is to surpass us, none. Therefore any race that we admit to our body social is certain to be more or less inferior" (Haller 1963). The most effective propagandist for the Galtonian, racist view of immigrants was A. E. Wiggam, author of *The New Decalogue of Science* and *The Fruit of the Family Tree,* quoted above. Following Galton, Wiggam preached race improvement as almost a religious duty, and his popular books spread his pseudoscientific gospel to thousands of readers. The passage quoted above reveals the crass racism and intellectual snobbery pervading the whole Galtonian movement in the United States. Wiggam's cant and humbug derive not from Darwin or Mendel, but from blind prejudice. In a scientistic age bigotry adopts the language of science, since the language of heresy will no longer do.

The Galtonian arguments were fallacious and Brigham recanted in 1930, acknowledging the worthlessness of the Army data. Nevertheless, in 1924 Congress passed an immigration restriction act—only recently altered—that limited the number of future immigrants to a formula based on the number of immigrants from each country in 1890, before the flow of non-"Nordic" immigrants increased. Racism won a great battle in a nation that 148 years before had pledged its sacred honor to the thesis that "all men are created equal." No longer would the poor huddled masses yearning to breathe free—Polish or Italian, Mexican or Vietnamese—find free entry into the land of the free.

But what could be done about the "cacogenic"—genetically undesirable— people already in the United States? The Army tests did much to further the cause of eugenics in the United States. British eugenics, as we saw in Chapter 9, was concerned with class rather than race, with positive rather than negative eugenics, and had no real success in obtaining eugenics legislation. American eugenics, however, was obsessed with race, proposed aggressive programs of negative eugenics, and was remarkably successful at getting them written into law.

Eugenics in the United States began just after the Civil War. At John

Humphrey Noyes's Oneida Community, one of several socialist-Utopian "heavens on earth" created in the nineteenth century, a program called "stirpiculture" was begun in 1869. Based on Noyes's interpretations of Darwin and Galton, the program involved planned matings between the most "spiritually advanced" members of the community; not surprisingly, Noyes fathered more stirpiculture babies than anyone else (Walters 1978). In the 1890s the sexual reformer and feminist Victoria Woodhull preached that the goal of the emancipation of women and sexual education was "the scientific propagation of the human race."

Noyes and Woodhull followed Galton in advancing voluntary positive eugenics as the best application of evolution to human betterment. The turn to negative eugenics and to compulsory control of so-called cacogenic people began with the biologist Charles Davenport. With money from the Carnegie Institution he established a laboratory at Cold Spring Harbor, New York, in 1904, which, with the addition of his Eugenics Records Office, became the center of American eugenics. Davenport was determined to "annihilate the hideous serpent of hopelessly vicious protoplasm" (quoted in Freeman 1983), and popularized his views with *Eugenics: The Science of Human Improvement by Better Breeding* (1910) and *Heredity in Relation to Eugenics* (1911). Davenport believed that alcoholism, feeblemindedness, and other traits were based on simple genetic mechanisms, and that they in turn caused ills such as pauperism and prostitution. Prostitutes, for example, were morons who were unable to inhibit the brain center for "innate eroticism," so turned to a life of sex. Committed to a belief that various ethnic groups were biologically distinct races, Davenport's writings are full of derogatory ethnic stereotypes supposedly rooted in the genes: Italians were given to "crimes of personal violence," Hebrews were given to "thieving." Davenport claimed that if immigration from Southeastern Europe were not halted, future Americans would be "darker . . . smaller . . . and more given to crimes of larceny, kidnapping, assault, murder, rape, and sex-immorality." Davenport wanted to place "human matings . . . upon the same high plane as that of horse breeding."

The leading eugenicist among psychologists was Henry Goddard, superintendent of the Vineland, New Jersey, Training School for Feeble-Minded Boys and Girls. Galton had drawn up family trees of illustrious men and women; with help from Davenport's Eugenics Records Office, Goddard drew up a family tree of stupidity, vice, and crime, *The Kallikak Family: A Study in the Heredity of Feeblemindedness*. Goddard presented the Kallikaks as the "wild men to today," possessing "low intellect but strong physiques." To support his description Goddard included photographs of Kallikaks doctored to make them look subhuman and sinister (Gould 1981). Like Davenport, Goddard believed that "the chief determiner of human conduct is a unitary mental process which we call intelligence . . . which is inborn . . . [and] but little affected by any later influences" (quoted by Gould 1981). Goddard held that "the idiot is not our greatest problem. He is indeed loathsome," but he is unlikely to reproduce on his own, so "it is the moron type that makes for us our great problem." Precisely because these "high grade defectives" can pass for normal, getting married and having families, Goddard feared their influence on American intelligence. Their numbers would swamp the relatively few offspring of the well-to-do, natural American aristocracy.

Davenport, Goddard, and other Galtonian alarmists proposed various eugenics programs. One was education, aimed to promote positive eugenics. For example, in the 1920s state fairs featured Fitter Families contests, sometimes in a "human stock" show, while eugenicists set up charts and posters showing the laws of inheritance and their application to humans. Some eugenicists favored contraception as a means of controlling cacogenics, but others feared it would promote licentiousness and be used mainly by intelligent people able to make plans, that is, the sort of people who should breed more, not less. McDougall (1921) wanted to encourage the fit to breed by them government subsidies to support their children. Goddard favored the segregation of morons, idiots, and imbeciles in institutions like his own, where they could live out happy lives in a setting suited to their feeble-mindedness, barred only from having children.

The solution favored by Davenport and most other eugenicists was compulsory sterilization of the cacogenic. Voluntary methods were likely to fail, they feared, and permanent institutionalization was rather expensive. Sterilization was a one-time procedure that guaranteed nonreproduction of the unfit at small cost to the state. Sterilizations without legal backing had begun before the turn of the century in the Midwest; H. C. Sharp invented the vasectomy and performed hundreds on mental defectives in Indiana. Compulsory sterilization laws had also been introduced before the Great War. The first legislature to consider one was Michigan's, in 1897, but it failed to pass. In 1907 Indiana passed the first sterilization law, but it was overturned by the state supreme court in 1921, and was replaced with an acceptable law in 1923. After the war, state after state passed compulsory sterilization laws, until by 1932 over 12,000 people had been sterilized in thirty states, 7,500 of them in California. The conditions warranting sterilization ranged from feeblemindedness (the most common ground) to epilepsy, rape, "moral degeneracy," prostitution, and being a drunkard or "drug fiend."

The constitutionality of the compulsory sterilization laws was upheld with but one dissenting vote by the U.S. Supreme Court in 1927 in the case of *Buck* v. *Bell,* arising in the state of Virginia, second to California in the number of sterilizations performed. Carrie Buck was a black "feebleminded" girl living in the state colony for the feebleminded, who bore an allegedly feebleminded daughter out of wedlock. She was sterilized by court order, and then sued the state of Virginia. The majority opinion was written by Oliver Wendell Holmes, a justice noted for his sympathy with Progressivism and willingness to listen to expert scientific opinion in deciding cases. He wrote, "It is better for all the world, if instead of waiting to execute degenerate offspring for crime, or to let them starve for their imbecility, society can prevent those who are manifestly unfit from continuing their kind. . . . Three generations of imbeciles are enough" (Landman 1932).

There were critics of eugenics and especially of human sterilization. Humanists such as G. K. Chesterton denounced eugenics as a pernicious offspring of scientism, reaching toward "the secret and sacred places of personal freedom, where no sane man ever dreamed of seeing it." Catholics condemned eugenics for "a complete return to the life of the beast," seeing people as primarily animals to be improved by animal means, rather than as spiritual beings to be improved by virtue. Leading biologists, including most notably those who synthesized Darwin and Mendel, condemned eugenics as biologically stupid. For example, since 90 percent of all subnormally intelligent children are born to normal parents, sterilizing the subnormal would have little effect on national intelligence or the rate at which subnormal children were born. Moreover, the "feebleminded" could have normal children. Carrie Buck's child, initially called feebleminded, proved later to be normal, even bright. Civil libertarians such as Clarence Darrow denounced eugenic sterilization as a means by which "those in power would inevitably direct human breeding in their own interests." In the social sciences the attack on eugenics was led by anthropologist Franz Boas and his followers. Boas argued that differences between human groups were not biological but cultural in origin, and taught the "psychic unity of mankind." His teachings inspired psychologist Otto Klineberg to empirically test eugenicists' claims. He traveled to Europe and tested pure Nordics, Alpines, and Mediterraneans, finding no differences in intelligence. In the United States he showed that Northern blacks did better on intelligence tests by virtue of getting more schooling, not because they were more intelligent. In 1928 Goddard changed his mind, arguing that "feeble-mindedness is *not incurable*" and that they "do not generally need to be segregated in institutions" (Gould 1981).

By 1930 eugenics was dying. Thomas Garth (1930), reviewing "Race Psychology" for the *Psychological Bulletin,* concluded that the hypothesis that races differ on intelligence and other measures "is no nearer being established than it was five years ago. In fact, many psychologists seem practically ready for another, the hypothesis of racial equality." The leading spokesmen for eugenics among psychologists, Brigham and Goddard, had taken back their racist views. The Third International Conference of Eugenics attracted fewer than one hundred people. But what finally killed eugenics was not criticism but embarrassment. Inspired by the success of eugenic laws in the United States, the Nazis began to carry out eugenic programs in deadly earnest. Beginning in 1933, Hitler instituted compulsory sterilization laws that applied to anyone, institutionalized or not, who carried some allegedly genetic defect. Doctors had to report such people to Hereditary Health Courts, which by 1936 had ordered a quarter-million sterilizations. The Nazis instituted McDougall's plan, subsidizing third and fourth children of the Aryan elite, and providing S.S. mothers, married or not, with spas at which to bear their superior children. In 1936 marriages between Aryans and Jews were forbidden. In 1939 inmates of asylums with certain diseases began to be killed by state order, including all Jews, regardless of their mental condition. At first the Nazis' victims were shot; later they were taken to "showers" where they were gassed. The final solution to the Nazis' eugenics desires was of course the Holocaust, in which 6 million Jews perished by order of the state. The Nazis enacted the final, logical conclusion of negative eugenics, and Americans, sickened by the results, simply ceased to preach and enforce negative eugenics. Many of the laws remained on the books, however. It was not until 1981 that Virginia amended its eugenics laws, following the revelation of state hospital records detailing the many instances of court-ordered sterilization. Moreover, eugenics continues as genetic counseling, in which bearers of genetically based diseases, such as sickle-cell anemia, are encouraged not to have children, or to do so under medical supervision, so that amniocentesis can be used to diagnose any undesirable condition, permitting abortion of "unfit" human beings.

Flaming Youth and the Reconstruction of the Family

I learned to my astonishment that I had been involved in a momentous debauch; the campus reeked of a scandal so sulphurous it hung over our beanies for the rest of the academic year. In blazing scareheads the Hearst Boston *American* tore the veil from the excesses tolerated at Brown University dances. At these hops, it thundered, were displayed a depravity and libertinism that would have sickened Petronius, made Messalina hang her head in shame. It portrayed girls educated at the best finishing schools, crazed with alcohol and inflamed by ragtime, oscillating cheek to cheek with young ne'er-do-wells in raccoon coats and derbies. Keyed up by savage jungle rhythms, the *abandonnes* would then reel out to roadsters parked on Waterman Street, where frat pins were traded for kisses under cover of darkness. . . . [T]he writer put all his metaphors into one basket and called upon outraged society to apply the brakes, hold its horses, and retrieve errant youth from under the wheels of the juggernaut.

> S. J. Perelman
> "Sodom in the Suburbs"

Youth was in revolt during the 1920s—it was the Jazz Age and the day of the flapper—and, of course the older generation, led by Hearst leader writers, were aghast. Youth seemed to embody the chaos of modernism described by Yeats's "Second Coming." Confused and bewildered, the parents of the 1920s *Flaming Youth*—the title of a best-selling novel pandering to parents' fears, and object of Perelman's satiric pen—tried to understand what had gone wrong with their children; and, more important, they tried to learn what to do about it. The apparent crisis of the family and its youth created an opportunity for social scientists, including psychologists, to extend the realm of their concern, and of scientific social control, from the public arena of politics and business into the intimate circle of the family.

As social scientists saw it, families as traditionally conceived and organized were out of date in the modern world. Families had been economic units, in which father, mother, and child had distinct and productive roles to play. In the industrialized world, however, work was leaving the home, so that individuals, not families, were the economic units. Children should not be permitted to work, since they needed to be in school learning the values and habits of urbanized American society. Women were "following their work out of the home" to factories and businesses. The labor of men was likewise apart from the home, being just an eight-hour job, not a way of life. The family was no longer a socially functional unit. Progressive Deweyites considered the family selfish because a parent's concern was for his or her own child, whereas in the modern, urban world it was necessary to be equally concerned with all children. The crisis of Flaming Youth was but a symptom, social scientists said, of a deeper social crisis.

The family would have to be remade, then, by professional social scientists bringing their expertise to bear on problems of family adjustment. Raising children could no longer be thought of as something anyone could do without help. The state, through professional social scientists, was to have the leading role in child rearing. As one reformer wrote, "The state is but the coordinated parentage of childhood . . . compel[ling] co-partnership, co-operation, corporate life and conscience" (Fass 1977). In a phrase, motherhood must become "mothercraft," a profession requiring education and training. Making a profession of raising children advanced the cause of professional social science, providing an ideology that justified intervening in family life with "expert" advice not possessed by ordinary people.

Since the traditional family's role as economic unit no longer existed, social scientists had to provide the new family with a new function: "The distinguishing feature of the new family will be affection. The new family will be more difficult, maintaining higher standards that test character more severely, but will offer richer fruit for the satisfying of human needs." "It does not seem probable that the family will recover the functions it has lost. But even if the family doesn't produce thread and cloth and soap and medicine and food, it can still produce happiness." In the view of reformers, the function of the family was to produce emotional adjustment to modern life. The modern parent, then, was to become something of a psychotherapist, monitoring children's emotional states and intervening when necessary to adjust their states of mind. The ideas of parent as professional and the family as the producer of emotional happiness mutually reinforced one another. Parents would need, at the very least, training in their new therapeutic roles, and would probably also need a cadre of experts to call on for advice, and to fall back on when acute difficulties arose. Applied psychologists would naturally find a fertile field for professional application of psychology to child rearing, child guidance, and child psychotherapy.

Meanwhile, youth were constructing a new set of values and a new social control system for themselves. As parents lost control of their children, youth found in the culture of their peers a new center for life apart from the family. Youth set their own values, their own style, their own goals. Central to the youth culture of the 1920s was having a "good personality," learning to be "well rounded," and fitting in with other youth. Youth valued self-expression and sociability, attending to personal satisfaction instead of the production of objective accomplishments. Groups such as fraternities and sororities enforced conformity to the new rules of personality with therapeutic tricks of their own. Deviant youth were forced to participate in "truth sessions" in which their "objectionable traits" and weaknesses were identified and analyzed. Then the offender would make amends, since "the fraternity's group consciousness is the strongest thing. One doing wrong not only disgraces oneself but his fraternity group" (Fass 1977).

Parents and youth, then, were not so far apart, despite the ravings of Hearst's leader writers. Both were being remade by the "triumph of the therapeutic," the modern tendency to define life in psychological terms. Parents were learning that their function was therapeutic, producing emotionally well-adjusted children. The youth culture similarly valued emotional adjustment, and tried to achieve it through therapeutic techniques of its own. The central values of the twentieth century were formed during the 1920s: being true to one's "real" self, expressing one's "deepest" feelings, "sharing" one's personality with a larger group.

Just as the new family and the youth culture were struggling toward a redefinition of life as centered on self, not accomplishment, an anthropologist and psychologist, Margaret Mead, came back from the South Seas bearing witness to an idyllic society in which people had little work to do and led peaceful lives of perfect adjustment, harmony, and sexual fulfillment. As in the Enlightenment, when philosophes had felt themselves emerging from centuries of religious repression, there was a longing for the free and easy life—especially the sexual life—apparently to be found in Tahiti. Committed to environmentalism, the philosophes had thought that Tahitian paradise could be constructed in Europe through social engineering. As twentieth-century intellectuals reacted against Victorian sexual morality and the excesses of eugenics, they felt themselves on the verge of a "new Enlightenment" or, as Watson put it, of a "social Renaissance, a preparation for a change in mores" (Freeman 1983). So they fastened on Margaret Mead's *Coming of Age in Samoa* as the philosophes had on *Voyage to Bougainvillea:* "Somewhere in each of us, hidden among our more obscure desires and our impulses of escape, is a palm fringed South Seas island . . . a langorous atmosphere promising freedom and irresponsibility. . . . Thither we run to find love which is free, easy and satisfying" (Freeman 1983).

Margaret Mead was a young psychologist and anthropologist who studied under the founder of modern American anthropology, Franz Boas, whose opposition to eugenics we have already noted. Boas and his followers were convinced, with John Dewey, that human nature was, in Dewey's words, a "formless void of impulses" shaped by society into a personality. They agreed with Dewey that mind was a social construction owing nothing to nature and everything to culture. Similarly, culture was just "personality writ large," according to Ruth Benedict, another student of Boas: Personality, being entirely shaped by culture, imaged culture in the historical individual, and culture, the molder of personality, was the personality of a society. If eugenicists went to one extreme, denying nurture any influence over nature, Boasians went to the other, regarding culture as "some kind of mechanical press into which most individuals were poured to be molded." Agreeing with Watson at his most extreme, Mead wrote how the "almost unbelievably malleable" raw material of human nature was "moulded into shape by culture."

Mead traveled to American Samoa, conducted (rather sloppy) fieldwork, and returned with a description of a society that at once seemed to support the Deweyite and Boasian conception of an infinitely plastic human nature, and to offer the ideal form of the happy society, in which people experienced "perfect adjustment" to their surroundings, their society, and to each other. Mead limned a society that knew no Flaming Youth in stressful revolt against their parents, a society with no aggression, no war, no hostility, no deep attachment between parent and child, husband and wife, no competition, a society in which parents were ashamed of the outstanding child, and proud of the slowest, who set the pace for the development of every other child. Most alluring was the idea that the Samoans, far from regarding sex as a sin, thought sexual relations "the pastime *par excellence,* a "fine art," making "sex [into] play, permissible in all hetero- and homosexual expression, with any sort of variation as an artistic addition." The Samoan avoidance of strong feelings and deep attachments extended to love: "Love between the sexes is a light and pleasant dance. . . . Samoans condone light love-affairs, but repudiate acts of passionate choice, and have no real place for anyone who would permanently continue . . . to prefer one woman or one man." Samoans regarded jealousy as a sin, and did not regard adultery as very serious, Mead reported. Before marriage, Mead said, adolescents experienced a free and easy promiscuity, each boy and girl engaging in many light sexual dalliances of no deep moment. There were no Flaming Youth because what Flaming Youth wanted, condemned by fuddy-duddy Hearst writers, was approved, even encouraged by Samoan society. Samoans also lived the superficial lives of conformity to the group and average well-roundedness that Flaming Youth defined as its norm. Putting it in scientistic terms, one commentator on Mead's book remarked on "the innocent, strangely impersonal, naively mechanistic-behavioristic sexing of the light-hearted youths of far-off Samoa."

Mead's Samoans promised to resolve the nature-nurture disputes of the 1920s against the eugenicists and in favor of the Boasians. Mead's work also lifted up a vision of a new Utopia of sexual freedom and perfect happiness, a vision that outraged Hearst's Boston *American* but became the foundation for the *Playboy* philosophy. Finally, it gave psychologists the central role in constructing the new society. Commenting upon the work of Boas and his students, Bertrand Russell, who had earlier endorsed Watson's behaviorism, asserted that "the scientific psychologist, if allowed a free run with children" could "manipulate human nature" as freely as physical scientists manipulated nature. Psychologists and other social scientists could ask, even dream, no more than this: to be the architects of a new

Western civilization, well adjusted and harmonious, emotionally open and sexually liberated, warm and supporting and not in neurotic pursuit of excellence. Mead's Samoa, a culture entirely outside the traditions of the West, became the social scientists' Holy Grail, a blueprint for them to follow in constructing the New Man of Deweyite, Progressive idealism.

The reality behind the Flaming Youth and Samoan society was different, however, from both the Hearst writer's ravings and Mead's more prosaic depictions. Perelman's "orgy" was in fact "decorous to the point of torpor": "I spent the evening buffeting about the stag line, prayerfully beseeching the underclassmen I knew for permission to cut in on their women . . . [frequently] retiring to a cloakroom with several other blades and choking down a minute quantity of gin, warmed to body heat, from a pocket flask. Altogether, it was a strikingly commonplace experience, and I got to bed without contusions. . . ." Derek Freeman (1983) has shown that Samoa, far from being the sexual paradise described by Mead, was obsessed with virginity, and rife with rape, aggression, competition, and deep human feelings.

When Psychology Was King

The psychology of introspection held no fascination for the ordinary American. Margaret Floy Washburn, a student of Titchener's, described in her APA presidential address (1922) the reaction of an intelligent janitor to her psychological laboratory: "This is queer place. It somehow gives you the impression that the thing can't be done." By the 1920s, however, psychology had gone behavioral and was proving—in industry, in schools and courts, and in war—that psychology could be done. Contemporary observers remarked on the tremendous popularity of psychology with the public. The first historian of the 1920s, Frederick Lewis Allen (1931), wrote, "Of all the sciences it was the youngest and least scientific which most captivated the general public and had the most disintegrating effect upon religious faith. Psychology was king. . . . [O]ne had only to read the newspapers to be told with complete assurance that psychology held the key to the problems of waywardness, divorce, and crime." Grace Adams, another student of Titchener's, who had abandoned psychology for journalism and who had become quite critical of psychology, called the period from 1919 to 1929 the "Period of the Psyche." Humorist Stephan Leacock wrote in 1923 of how "a great wave of mind culture has swept over the community."

Psychology achieved its special place in public attention because of the intersection of the revolution in morals led by Flaming Youth (Ostrander 1968) with the final triumph of scientism. "The word science," Allen said, "had become a shibboleth. To preface a statement with 'Science teaches us' was enough to silence argument." Religion seemed on the verge of destruction. Liberal theologian Harry Emerson Fosdick wrote, "Men of faith might claim for their positions ancient tradition, practical usefulness, and spiritual desirability, but one query could prick all such bubbles: Is it scientific?" (Allen 1931). The faithful responded in two ways: Modernists such as Fosdick strove to reconcile science with the Bible; fundamentalists (the word was coined by a Baptist editor in July 1920) strove to subordinate science, especially Darwinism, to the Bible. Many other people, of course, simply lost all faith. Watson, for example, had been raised as a strict Baptist in Greenville, South Carolina, and had [like 71 percent of early behaviorists (Birnbaum 1964)] chosen the ministry as his vocation, only to give it up on his mother's death. In graduate school he had a nervous breakdown and abandoned religion completely.

Science undermined religion; scientism bid to replace it. The Flaming Youth of the 1920s were the first generation of Americans to be raised in the urban, industrial, everywhere communities of twentieth-century life. Cut off from the traditional religious values of the vanishing island communities, they turned to modern science for instruction in morals and rules of behavior. Postwar psychology, no longer preoccupied with socially sterile introspection, was the obvious science to which to turn for guidance concerning living one's life and getting ahead in business and politics.

Popular psychology simultaneously accomplished two apparently contradictory things. It provided people with a sense of liberation from the outdated religious morality of the past; this use was stressed by Flaming Youth and their sympathizers yearning for the sexual freedom of a tropical isle. At the same time it provided new, putatively scientific techniques for social control; this use was stressed by Progressives. As one popularizer, Abram Lipsky, wrote in *Man the Puppet: The Art of Controlling Minds:* "We are at last on the track of psychological laws for controlling the minds of our fellow men" (Burnham 1968). Ultimately, the liberating and controlling effects of psychology were not at odds. While Flaming Youth liberated themselves from old values, they chose new, psychological ones, and psychological techniques of control were used to enforce them.

The first wave of popular psychology, and what the general public thought of as the "new psychology" (Burnham 1968), was Freudianism, used to dissolve Victorian morals. Under the microscope of psychoanalysis traditional morals were found to be neurosis-breeding repressions of healthy biological needs, primarily sex. Youth concluded (falsely) from psychoanalytic doctrine that, "The first requirement for mental health is an uninhibited sex life. As Oscar Wilde wisely counseled, ' Never resist temptation!' " (Graves and Hodge 1940). Lady Betty Balfour, addressing the Conference of the British Educational Association in 1921, expressed the popular view of proper Freudian child rearing: She was "not sure that the moral attitude was not responsible for all the crime in the world." Children, vulgar Freudians believed, should be reared with few inhibitions, so they might grow up unrepressed, happy, and carefree like Mead's notional Samoans.

The second wave of popular psychology in the 1920s was behaviorism, which the general public sometimes confused with psychoanalysis. Robert Graves and Alan Hodge, literate observers of the English scene, nevertheless described psychoanalysts as viewing people as "behaviouristic animals." The leading popularizer of behaviorism was Watson himself. He had turned to psychoanalysis in the wake of his nervous breakdown and, while impressed with Freud's biological emphasis, came to regard analytic psychology as "a substitution of demonology for science." The "unconscious" of psychoanalysis was a fiction, Watson held, representing no more than the fact that we do not verbalize all the influences on our behavior. If we do not talk about stimuli, we are not aware of them and so call them unconscious according to Freudian jargon, but there is no mysterious inner realm of mind whence come hidden impulses (Watson 1926c). According to Watson, there was "too little science—real science—in Freud's psychology" for it to be useful or enduring, and he offered behaviorism as the new claimant for popular attention (Watson 1926a).

Watson described behaviorism as representing "a real renaissance in psychology," overthrowing introspective psychology and substituting science in its place. Watson consistently linked introspective psychology to religion and railed against both. Behaviorists "threw out the concepts of mind and of consciousness, calling them carryovers from the church dogma of the Middle Ages. . . . Consciousness [is] just a masquerade for the soul" (Watson 1926a). "Churchmen—all medicine men in fact—have kept the public under control" by making the public believe in unobserved mysteries such as the soul; science, says Watson the philosophe, is "blasting" through the "solid wall of religious protection" (1926b). Having disposed of the traditional past, both social and psychological, Watson offered strong opinions and advice on the issues of the day.

Watson attacked eugenics. Belief in human instincts, he wrote, has been "strengthened in the popular view by the propaganda of the eugenists," whose programs for selective breeding are "more dangerous than Bolshevism." Watson maintained that there are no inferior races. Taking note of American racism, Watson said that Negroes had not been allowed to develop properly, so that even if a Negro were given a million dollars a year and sent to Harvard, white society would be able to make him feel inferior anyway (1927b). A human being, Watson told readers of *Harper's,* is "a lowly piece of protoplasm, ready to be shaped . . . crying to be whipped into shape" (1927b) and promised that the behaviorist "can build any man, starting at birth, into any kind of social or asocial being upon order" (1926a).

Since there were no human instincts, and human beings could be built to order, Watson naturally had much advice to give to parents eager for scientific child-rearing techniques. Watson took a strong line, denying any influence of heredity on personality and maintaining that, "The home is responsible for what the child becomes" (1926a). Homemaking, including child rearing and sexual technique, should become a profession for which girls ought to be trained. Their training would brook no nonsense about loving children, cuddling them, or putting up with their infantile demands. Watson viewed the traditional family (and the new affectionate family of other family reformers) with scorn. According to Watson, a mother lavishes affection on children out of a misplaced "sex-seeking response." Her own sexuality is "starved," so she turns to cuddling and kissing her child; hence the need for training in sex.

Watson's advice (Watson 1928b) on how to raise children is brutally behavioristic:

> There is a sensible way of treating children. Treat them as though they were young adults. Dress them, bathe them with care and circumspection. Let your behavior always be objective and kindly firm. Never hug and kiss them, never let them sit in your lap. If you must, kiss them once on the forehead when they say good night. Shake hands with them in the morning. . . . Try it out. . . . You will be utterly ashamed of the mawkish, sentimental way you have been handling it. . . .
>
> Nest habits, which come from coddling, are really pernicious evils. The boys or girls who have nest habits deeply imbedded suffer torture when they have to leave home to go into business, to enter school, to get married. . . . Inability to break nest habits is probably our most prolific source of divorce and marital disagreements. . . .
>
> In conclusion won't you then remember when you are tempted to pet your child that mother love is a dangerous instrument? An instrument which may inflict a never

healing wound, a wound which may make infancy unhappy, adolescence a nightmare, an instrument which may wreck your adult son or daughter's vocational future and their chances for marital happiness.

Watson's book (written with the assistance of Rosalie Rayner Watson, his second wife) *Psychological Care of Infant and Child,* from which the above quotations are taken, sold quite well. Even Carl Rogers, founder of client-centered therapy and later a leader of humanistic psychology, tried to raise his first child "by the book of Watson." Occasionally, Watson so despaired of the ability of a mother to raise a happy child—he dedicated the child-care book to the first mother to do so—that he advocated taking children away from their parents to be raised by professionals in a creche (Harris and Morawski 1979), the solution proposed by Skinner in his utopian novel *Walden II.*

"The behaviorist, then," wrote Watson (1928a), "has given society . . . a new weapon for controlling the individual." "If it is demanded by society that a given line of conduct is desireable, the psychologist should be able with some certainty to arrange the situation or factors which will lead the individual most quickly and with the least expenditure of effort to perform that task." In his second career as an advertising executive, Watson had an opportunity to demonstrate the power of behavioral social control by manipulating consumers. Expelled from academia for his affair with and subsequent marriage to Rosalie Rayner, Watson was hired by the J. Walter Thompson advertising agency, which was looking for the scientific principles that would control the minds of men and women.

Central to Watson's schemes for social control was using the word as a whip to the human emotions. In evangelical preaching words were used as whips to stir up hearers into an emotional conversion experience that would move them to Christ. To give a famous Puritan example, Jonathan Edwards's sermon, "Sinners in the Hands of an Angry God," which described people as suspended over hellfire like a spider on a single, silken thread, was constructed to appeal to his parishioners' hearts, not to their intellects. Watson was named after, and taught the views of, John Albert Broadus, a leading Baptist evangelist. Broadus taught that reason was not a secure base for morals, so that preaching had to exploit fear and anger as the emotional bases of the habits of good Christian living, and praised Edwards's sermon. In "The Heart or the Intellect" Watson (1928a) described the need to condition the emotions in order to effect social control. The head, Watson said, cannot control the guts, making imperative the use of classical conditioning techniques to build in the habits demanded by modern society.

As evangelists had stressed fear in the training of children, so Watson's child-rearing advice always ran to the punitive. He said that people don't use their talents to the full because they have not been pushed hard enough: "The stuff [talent] is there crying out to be whipped into shape. It is a cry for getting some kind of shock or punishment . . . which will force us to develop to the limits of our capabilities" (Watson 1927b). He repeatedly held up Little Albert B. (Albert Broadus?) (Creelan 1974) as a model of proper emotional training. In adult humans, language could be used as Edwards and Broadus used it, to manipulate emotions in order to bring about some desired behavior. For example, in setting up an advertising campaign for baby powder, Watson used statements by medical experts to make mothers feel anxious about their infant's health and uncertain about their own competence to look after their child's hygiene. Feelings of anxiety and insecurity would then make mothers more likely to purchase a product endorsed by experts. At the same time, though Watson may not have meant to teach this message, his advertising made parents feel more dependent on experts to teach them how to raise their children. In this way, advertising helped to reinforce social scientists' message that society needed professional social scientists to solve its problems.

It is not surprising, then, that Progressives embraced Watson's behaviorism. In the New York *Herald Tribune* Stuart Chase, who later coined the phrase "New Deal," exclaimed that Watson's *Behaviorism* was perhaps "the most important book ever written. One stands for an instant blinded with a great hope" (quoted by Birnbaum 1955). As Watson (1928a) had said, behaviorism gave society "a new weapon for controlling the individual" and Progressives were eager to wield it in pursuit of their dreams of social control. Watson, they thought, had correctly described the laws of conditioning governing the masses of humankind. Progressives, however, were pleased to place themselves among the "very few" individuals endowed with "creative intelligence," exempt from the laws of conditioning, and able to use them as tools to escape "the voice of the herd" and to manage the herd toward Progressive ends. The "great hope" of Progressivism was always that an elite of scientific managers might be empowered to run society, and behaviorism seemed to provide exactly the techniques Progressives needed to control the behavior, if not the minds, of men. Watson himself, it should be said, did not fall in with the Progressives' schemes. He insisted that the laws of conditioning applied to everyone, whether or not their ancestors had come over on the Mayflower, and that anyone could be trained to use behavioral techniques for self-control or the control of others (Birnbaum 1964).

While Watson's popularized behaviorism was welcomed by many, others found it disturbing or shallow. Joseph Jastrow (1929) felt that psychology was degraded by Watson's popularization of himself in magazines and newspapers. What was valuable in behaviorism—the study of behavior—"will survive the 'strange interlude' of . . . behaviorism" and Watson's public antics. Grace Adams ridiculed Watson's behaviorism for sharing "most of the appealing points of psychoanalysis with few of its tedious difficulties," the resulting shallow system being "a cheering doctrine, surely—direct, objective, and completely American." Warner Fite (1918), already depressed by the experimental psychology of 1912, regarded behaviorism as the logical end product of scientism, or, as he put it, in "behavioristic psychology we behold the perfected beauty of the scientific prepossession." According to behaviorists, "Mind, in the sense of an inner, personal, spiritual experience, must be laid away, along with the immortal soul, among the discarded superstitions of an unscientific past. . . . According to them, your behavior is simply and solely what other persons are able to observe; and how you look, not to yourself, but to the world—that is all there is of *you*." Lumping together the effects of psychoanalysis and behaviorism, Fite foresaw the psychological society of the later twentieth century: "Doubtless the time is coming, before we are through with the [scientific] prepossession, when all domestic and social intercourse will be made luminous and transparent by the presence of expert psychologists. In those fair days social intercourse will be untroubled by falsehood or insincerity, or even by genial exaggeration."

By 1930 the fad for psychology had run its course. After the crash of 1929, the popular press had more pressing economic matters to consider, and the volume of pieces written on psychology diminished noticeably. Grace Adams hoped that its influence was finished, but in fact psychology was only in retrenchment (Sokal 1983). Psychology continued to grow and expand its areas of application throughout the 1930s, albeit at a slower rate than in the glory years after World War I. Its reemergence on the popular stage awaited another cue of war.

PSYCHOLOGY TRANSFORMED (1940–1950)

As it had just twenty-four years earlier, world war would profoundly affect psychology. The Great War to End All Wars had transformed a tiny, obscure academic discipline into an ambitious, visible profession. World War II provided an even greater opportunity for psychologists to act together in pursuit of social good and their own professional interests. Along the way the war caused psychology to grow at a faster rate than ever, to reunify into a single academic-applied profession, and to invent a new professional role—the psychotherapist—which quickly threatened to become the role that defined American psychologists. After the war ended psychology fought unsuccessfully to be included among the sciences supported by federal research money. As a profession, however, psychology was more successful. The government found itself in need of mental health professionals, and embarked on a program to recruit and train a new psychological profession, requiring that psychology define itself anew and set standards for its practitioners.

In the Crucible of War: Psychology Reunified

In the 1930s, as we have seen, psychology was racked by deep divisions. Professional psychologists had formed their own organization, the American Association of Applied Psychologists (AAAP), breaking with the APA in 1938. Another dissident group was the Society for the Psychological Study of Social Issues (SPSSI), formed by left-wing psychologists in 1936. Although affiliated with the APA, SPSSI psychologists aimed, in contrast to the traditional academicians of the APA, to use psychology to advance their political views. For example, SPSSI psychologists marched in New York's May Day parade carrying banners that read "Adjustment comes with jobs" (it was the depth of the Depression) and "Fascism is the world's worst behavior problem!" (Napoli 1981). The older APA, devoted as it was to pure research and scholarly detachment, had a hard time finding a place for either the AAAP or SPSSI.

However, it seemed to many psychologists, such as Robert Yerkes and Ernest Hilgard, that the institutional divisions within psychology could and should be overcome. After all, the professionals of the AAAP received their educations in academic departments of psychology, and it was the scientific principles of psychology that SPSSI wished to apply to pressing social problems. So, in the years following the break between the AAAP and the APA, informal negotiations were carried on with the aim of reunifying psychologists under a single banner.

The process was greatly accelerated by the coming of World War II. In 1940, even before the United States entered the war, the APA had assembled an Emergency Committee to plan for the inevitable involvement of the United States and its psychologists in the global conflict; in 1941, several months before the Japanese attack on Pearl Harbor, the *Psychological Bulletin* devoted a whole issue to "Military Psychology." In the same year the APA moved to remove the greatest bar to full participation by applied psychologists in the association. At the annual meeting of the APA in September, the requirement that a prospective member have published research beyond the dissertation was replaced with a requirement that to join the APA one had to present either publications or a record of five years' "contribution" to psychology as an associate, the class of membership to which AAAP psychologists had belonged.

Once the war began, changes came at a faster pace. The annual meetings were abandoned in response to government calls to conserve vital fuels. A Committee on Psychology and War was formed, planning not only for war activities by psychologists, but for a significant postwar social role for psychology as well. The committee noted that in view of the coming world conflict psychology should be unified, as it had been in the last war, and to this end it proposed creation of a "general headquarters" for psychology. Such headquarters came into existence as the Office of Psychological Personnel (OPP) located in Washington, D.C.

Creation of the OPP as a "general headquarters" for psychology was a major event in the history of institutional psychology in the United States. Prior to 1941 the APA had no permanent central office: The APA was located in the professorial offices of whomever was its secretary in a given year. The OPP, however, became the central office of the American Psychological Association, located in Washington—fount of funding and locus of lobbying—ever since. Psychologists at the OPP saw an opportunity both to reunify psychology and to advance psychology's role in American society. Leonard Carmichael (1942), psychology's representative on the National Research Council, wrote that "this office [the OPP] may well mark the initiation of a central agency for psychologists which will have an important and growing effect upon the psychological profession." The head of the OPP, Stuart Henderson Britt (1943), defined the job of the OPP as more than doing useful war work, serving in addition "*the advancement of psychology as a profession*" (italics in original) and promoting "sound public relations for psychology."

There was much war work to be done. Psychologists were in great demand by the military. Uniquely among the social sciences, psychology was listed as a "critical profession" by the War Department. A survey of psychologists in December 1942, just one year after Pearl Harbor, turned up 3,918 psychologists (not all of them APA members), of whom about 25 percent were engaged full time in war-related activities. Many other psychologists served the war effort indirectly. E. G. Boring, for example, wrote a text on military psychology called *Psychology for the Fighting Man*, which in turn became a textbook used at West Point (Gilgen 1982). As in World War I, psychologists served in many specialized capacities, ranging from test administration to studying the psychological demands made on human performance by new and sophisticated weapons, to the biological control of guided missiles. The war made human relations in industry more important, emphasizing the role of the psychologist in efficient industrial management. Industry faced two problems psychologists could help solve. Producing war materiel required vastly increased rates of production, while at the same time regular factory workers were drafted into the military, being replaced with new, inexperienced workers, especially women, who began for the first time to enter the work force in large numbers. The War Production Board, alarmed by problems of low productivity, absenteeism, and high turnover, appointed an interdisciplinary team headed by Elton Mayo to apply social science techniques to retaining workers and improving their productivity. The business community came to recognize that "the era of human relations'' was at hand, since "the factors that 'make a man tick' can be described and analyzed with much of the precision that would go into the dies for . . . a Sherman tank" (Baritz 1960).

Even as the war raged, psychologists prepared for the postwar world by setting their own house in order. The Emergency Committee set up the Intersociety Constitutional Convention, a meeting of representatives of the APA, the AAAP, SPSSI, and other psychological groups, such as the National Council of Women Psychologists. The convention created a new APA along federal lines. The "new" APA was to be an organization of autonomous divisions representing the various interest groups within psychology. New bylaws were written including, in addition to the APA's traditional purpose as the advancement of psychology as a science, the advancement of psychology "as a profession, and as a means of promoting human welfare." Robert Yerkes, who did more than anyone else to create the new APA, laid out the goals of the organization to the convention: "The world crisis has created a unique opportunity for wisely planned and well directed professional activities. In the world that is to be, psychology will play a significant role, if psychologists can only unite in making their visions realities" (paraphrased by Anderson 1943). In the gloomiest year of the war, psychologists began to glimpse a rosy future.

In 1944 the memberships of the APA and AAAP were polled to ratify the new bylaws. In the APA members—the traditional academic psychologists—approved the new APA by 324 votes to 103 (out of 858 eligible voters), while among the associates (likely members of the AAAP) the vote was 973 to 143 in favor (out of 3,806 eligible to vote). While the endorsement of the new APA, especially among its traditional members, was short of ringing, nevertheless the new bylaws were approved. The OPP became the office of the executive secretary of the APA, now permanently housed in Washington. A new journal, *The American Psychologist,* was created to serve as the voice of the new united psychology.

In this new APA there was a young and growing segment, almost entirely new: the clinical psychologist as psychotherapist.

Redefining Clinical Psychology

"It seems as if the ivory tower had literally been blown out from under psychology" (Darley and Wolfle 1946). Before the war psychology had been controlled by the academicians of the APA, despite complaints from and concessions to the AAAP. The war, however, drastically altered the social role of psychologists, and the balance of political power in psychology, primarily by inventing a new role for applied psychologists to fill in quickly growing numbers. During the 1930s applied psychologists continued as they had in the 1920s, serving primarily as testers, evaluating employees, juvenile offenders, troubled children, and people seeking guidance about their intelligence or personality. However, the war created a pressing demand for a new kind of service from psychologists: psychotherapy, previously the preserve of psychiatrists.

Of all the varied jobs psychologists performed in wartime the most common one, as in World War I, was testing—testing of recruits to determine for what military job they were most suited or testing soldiers returning from the front to determine if they needed psychotherapy. As late as 1944 Robert Sears could describe the role of the military psychologist in these traditional terms. However, the soldiers returning from the front needed more psychological services than anyone had anticipated or the existing psychiatric corps could provide. By the end of the war, of 74,000 hospitalized veterans, about 44,000 were hospitalized for psychiatric reasons. Psychologists had heretofore performed diagnostic duties as part of military medical teams, but faced with the overwhelming need to provide psychotherapy, psychologists—however ill-trained—began to serve as therapists, too. Even experimental psychologists were pressed into service as therapists. For example, Howard Kendler, fresh from Kenneth Spence's rigorously experimental program at the University of Iowa, wound up doing therapy at Walter Reed Army Hospital in Washington.

As the war wound down it became clear that the desperate need for psychological services among veterans would continue. In addition to the hospitalized veterans, "normal" veterans experienced numerous adjustment difficulties. At the very least, men who had been wrenched from their prewar jobs, towns, and families desired counseling about how to make new lives in the postwar world; 65 percent to 80 percent of returning servicemen reported interest in such advice (Rogers 1944). Others suffered from the World War II equivalent of the posttraumatic stress syndrome of the Vietnam veterans of the 1970s. Secretary of War Stimson wrote in his diary about "a rather appalling analysis of what our infantrymen are confronting in the present war by way of psychosis. The Surgeon General tells us the spread of psychological breakdown is alarming and that it will affect every infantryman, no matter how good and strong" (Doherty 1985). Upon return to the United States veterans felt a "sense of strangeness about civilian life," were often bitter about how little people at home appreciated the horrors of combat, and experienced restlessness, disturbed sleep, excessive emotionality, and marital and family disturbances. Finally, many veterans were handicapped by wounds, and needed psychological as well as physical therapy (Rogers 1944).

The Veterans Administration (VA) acted to provide the services veterans needed. To meet the need for vocational guidance, the VA established guidance centers at universities, where GIs were receiving college educations paid for by the GI bill. Psychologists working at these counseling centers continued the development of prewar applied psychology on a larger scale than before, and their activities by and large define the job of today's counseling psychologist. More disturbed veterans, especially those in VA hospitals, needed more than simple advice; and the VA set out to define a new mental health professional, the clinical psychologist, who could provide psychotherapy to the thousands of veterans who needed it. In 1946 the VA set up training programs at major universities to turn out clinical psychologists whose job would be therapy as well as diagnosis. Because it was the largest employer of clinical psychologists, the VA did much to define the job of the clinical psychologist and how he or she would be trained.

Spurred by the VA, the newly reunified APA, now fully emerged from the ruined ivory tower of academe, undertook the tasks it had avoided for decades, defining the professional psychologist and setting up standards for his or her training. These tasks have not proved easy, and to this day there is widespread disagreement among psychologists about the proper nature of training for the professional psychologist. Since World War II the APA has established many panels and commissions to look into the matter, but no proposal has satisfied everyone, and controversy about the nature of clinical psychology has been chronic.

The most obvious model of professional training was rejected by the committees appointed after the war to set up professional training in psychology. Typically, schools that train the practitioners of a craft are separate from the scientific discipline to which they are related. Thus physicians are trained in medical schools, not biology departments, and chemical engineers are trained in engineering schools, not chemistry departments. Of course, physicians are not ignorant of biology and chemical engineers are not ignorant of chemistry, but their schooling in basic science is considered quite distinct from their training in the crafts to which they aspire. Psychologists, however, needed to separate themselves from their very close rivals, the psychiatrists, who from the first appearance of "clinical" psychology before World War I had feared that psychologists might usurp their therapeutic duties. So, rather than define themselves as merely practitioners of a craft springing from science, as physicians had, clinical psychologists decided to define themselves as *scientist-practitioners*. That is, graduate students training to become clinical psychologists were to be taught to be scientists first—carrying out research in scientific psychology—and professionals—practitioners of a craft—second. It was as if physicians were to be trained first as biologists and only secondarily as healers. The appeal of the scheme was that it preserved for clinicians the prestige of being scientists while allowing them to fill the many jobs the VA had open for psychotherapists (Murdock and Leahey 1986). The model of the clinical psychologist as scientist/professional was enshrined by the Boulder Conference of 1949. As we shall see in future chapters, the Boulder model has not been without its detractors, and periodically the APA has been called upon to rethink its approach to professional training. Additionally, from the very first (for example, Peatman 1949) academic psychologists have been afraid that their discipline would be taken over by professionals, and they would become the second-class citizens of the APA.

Whatever the trials and tribulations surrounding the redefinition of clinical psychology, it grew rapidly, becoming in the public mind the primary function of the psychologist. In 1954, during the annual meeting of the APA, Jacob Cohen and G. D. Wiebe asked the citizens of New York who "the people with the badges" were. Of the interviewees, 32 percent correctly identified them as psychologists, though almost as many, 25 percent, thought they were psychiatrists. When asked what the people with the badges did, 71 percent said it was psychotherapy, work scarcely done by psychologists before 1944; 24 percent said "teachers," leaving 6 percent "other." The founders of the APA had prided themselves on being scientists, and had formed their organization to advance the cause of psychology as a science. By 1954, just sixty-two years later, scientific psychology had largely ceased to exist in the public mind, replaced by an applied discipline with, given what even the best scientific minds in psychology—Hull, Tolman, Thorndike, Watson—had accomplished, a remarkably shallow foundation.

Psychology Fails to Get a Slice of the Big Science Pie

Allied victory in World War II depended in many respects on the successful employment of science, primarily physics, in the pursuit of war aims. During the war federal spending on scientific research and development went from $48 million to $500 million, from an 18 percent share in overall research spending to 83 percent. When the war ended politicians and scientists recognized that the national interest demanded continued federal support of science, and that control of research monies should not remain a monopoly of the military. Congress, of course, never allocates money without debate, and controversy over the proposed vehicles by which research dollars would be allocated centered on two problems concerning who would be eligible to apply for it.

The first problem has rarely concerned psychology, but is important to understanding how research funds are doled out in the modern era of Big Science, in which huge amounts of money can be awarded to only a few of the investigators who would like to have their research supported. The problem is this: Should money only be given to the best scientists, or should it be parceled out on some other basis, perhaps allocating a certain amount of funds for each state? Progressive, New Deal politicians such as Wisconsin Senator Robert La Follette pushed the latter scheme, but were defeated by elitists in the scientific ranks and their conservative political allies who saw to it that applications for research money would be strictly competitive. As the system has evolved, most research money is "won" by a few elite institutions of higher education, while researchers at universities of lesser prestige are pressured to compete for grants they are in little position to gain. Universities value their scientists winning grants because they get "overhead money"—money ostensibly to be spent on electricity, janitors, and other laboratory maintenance—which they in fact spend for new buildings, to hire more staff, to purchase copiers, and many other things they would not otherwise be able to afford. In this system of grants, scientists are not employees of their university; rather they are its means of support. Scientists, in turn, are compelled to direct their research not to the problems they think are important, but to those the federal funding agencies think are important. Thus scientists spend much of their time and talent trying to second-guess bureaucrats, who themselves are implementing vague congressional directives.

Of direct importance to psychology was whether or not the funding agency to be created, the National Science Foundation (NSF), should support research in the social sciences. Old Progressives and New Deal liberals included a Division of the Social Sciences in the original NSF bill, but it was opposed by natural scientists and conservative legislators. A leading supporter of the original bill, Senator J. William Fulbright of Arkansas, argued that the social sciences should be included because they "could lead us to an understanding of the principles of human relationships which might enable us to live together without fighting recurrent wars." Opponents argued that "there is not anything that leads more readily to isms and quackeries than so-called studies in social science unless there is eternal vigilance to protect."

In debate, even Senator Fulbright found little good to say about social science, conceding that "there are many crackpots in the field, just as there were in the field of medicine in the days of witchcraft." He was unable to give an adequate definition of social science, and wound up quoting a natural scientist who said that "I would not call it a science. What is commonly called social science is one individual or group of individuals telling another group how they should live." In a letter to Congress leading physical scientists opposed the Division of Social Science. The original bill mollified them by including special controls "to prevent the Division of Social Sciences getting out of hand," as Fulbright put it on the floor of the Senate. He also said, "It would surprise me very much if the social sciences' division got anything at all" because the NSF board would be dominated by physical scientists. The upshot of the debate was a vote of 46 to 26 senators to remove the Division of Social Sciences. As sciences, the social sciences did not command universal respect (social scientists might feel that with a friend like Fulbright they did not need enemies), however much their concrete services, such as counseling, psychotherapy, and personnel management, might be needed.

While the government was not yet sympathetic to supporting psychology and the other social sciences, a new foundation, the Ford Foundation, was. For decades private research foundations, most notably the Rockefeller Foundation, had made modest grants to support social science. After the war the Ford Foundation was established as the world's largest, and it decided to fund the behavioral sciences—it has been said that John Dewey coined the term, but the Ford Foundation minted it—in a big way. The foundation staff saw behavioral sciences as the bright hope for the future, because they might be used to end war and ameliorate human suffering, and they proposed to use Ford's immense resources to give "an equal place in society" "for the study of man as the study of the atom." At the top levels of the foundation the staff's proposal met the same kind of resistance found in the Senate. The president, Paul Hoffman, said that social science was "a good field to waste billions," and his adviser, Robert Maynard Hutchins, president of the University of Chicago, said that the social science research he had seen—and Chicago had the first school of social science—"scared the hell out of me." Nevertheless, the Ford staff, led by lawyer Rowman Gaither, who had helped start the Rand Corporation, pushed ahead with their ambitious plan and got it approved. At first the foundation tried to give the money away as grants; but since this didn't get rid of the money fast enough, and took it out of their control, they set up the Center for Advanced Studies in the Behavioral Sciences in California. This center was a place where elite social scientists could go for a few years at a time and freed from academic pressures pursue theorizing and research in a congenial climate, sharing their ideas with colleagues from every field.

CONCLUSION

Psychologists Look Ahead to the Psychological Society

By the end of the war it was clear to psychologists that their ivory tower had indeed been destroyed. Psychology's links to its ancient roots in philosophy—to "long-haired" philosophers (Morgan 1947)—were irrevocably severed, and for the good of psychology according to the newest generation of American psychologists. At an APA symposium on "Psychology and Post-War Problems," H. H. Remmers observed, but did not mourn, psychology's loss of its "philosophical inheritance":

> Our philosophical inheritance has unfortunately not been an unmixed blessing. Deriving from that relatively sterile branch of philosophy known as epistemology and nurtured by a rationalistic science which tended to exalt thought at the expense of action and theory over practice, psychology has too frequently ensconced itself in the ivory tower from which pedants descended upon occasion to proffer pearls of wisdom, objectivity, and logical consistency to their charges without too much concern about the nutritional adequacy of such a diet.

Clifford T. Morgan made the same point more bluntly at a 1947 conference on "Current Trends in Psychology" by observing that, "Biggest of them all is that in the past thirty years psychology has shortened its hair, left its alleged ivory tower, and gone to work." Clearly, the world in the making demanded that psychologists be concerned less with abstruse, almost metaphysical, questions inherited from philosophy, and be concerned more with questions about how to achieve human happiness.

Psychologists entered their brave new world with anxious hope. Wayne Dennis, speaking at the Current Trends conference, proclaimed that "Psychology today has unlimited potentialities" [sic]. At the same time he worried that psychology had not yet achieved the "prestige and respect" needed to earn a "successful existence as a profession. We cannot function effectively as advisers and consultants, or as researchers in human behavior, without holding the confidence and good opinion of a considerable part of the population." His worries were not misplaced, as the Senate's debate on the Division of Social Sciences in the NSF demonstrates. Dennis spoke for many when he advocated further professionalization of psychology as the means of achieving public respect. Psychologists, he said, should set their own house in order, tighten requirements for training in psychology, persecute pseudo-psychologists, and establish certification and state licensing standards for professional psychologists.

Despite such temporary worries, psychologists saw for themselves a secure and powerful place in the postwar world. Remmers, reflecting the views of many psychologists, defined psychology's new, postphilosophical job: "Psychology in common with all science must have as its fundamental aim the service of society by positive contributions to the good life . . . knowledge for knowledge's sake is at best a by-product, an esthetic luxury." In colleges, psychology should be "placed on a par with the other sciences," and its role should be to teach the undergraduate how "to assess himself and his place in society." More broadly, psychology should help construct a "science of values" and learn to use "journalism, radio, and in the near future, television" to achieve "culture control." Psychology should be more widely used in industry, education—"the most important branch of applied psychology"—gerontology, child rearing, and the solution of social problems such as racism. Remmers failed only to mention psychological psychotherapy among the potential contributions of psychology to human happiness. Psychologists were at last prepared to give people what William James had hoped for in 1892: a "psychological science that will teach them how to *act*."

Values and Adjustment

There was an unremarked irony in psychology's postwar position. The old psychology of Scottish common-sense philosophy had proudly taken as its ultimate mission the training and justification of Christian religious values. The new psychology of brass-instrument experiments had, in challenging the old psychology, proudly cast off moral, especially religious, values in the name of science. With scientism becoming the new religion of the modern age, however, by 1944 Remmers could envision psychology as a "science of values." Psychology had come full circle—from serving the Christian God and teaching his values, to becoming itself, as John Burnham (1968) put it, a "*deus ex clinica*" representing the values of scientism.

What were the new values? Sometimes psychology seemed, in keeping with the value-free pose of science, only to offer tools for social control. Watson, for example, saw conditioning as a technique by which psychology might inculcate society's values, whatever they might be, in its citizens. As Remmers put it, the "good life" to be furthered by psychology was "the homeostasis of society"; psychology would keep people from unpleasantly rocking the boat. Watson, Remmers, and other control-minded psychologists would have agreed with the motto of the 1933 World's Fair: "Science Finds, Industry Adopts, Man Conforms" (Glassberg 1985). Emphasis on techniques of social control is symptomatic of the psychology of adaptation's deep relationship with political Progressivism, and laid applied psychologists open to Randolph Bourne's criticism of Progressive politicians. Once a Progressive himself, Bourne came to realize that Progressives held no clear values of their own: "They have, in short, no clear philosophy of life except that of intelligent service. They are vague as to what kind of society they want, or what kind of society America needs, but they are equipped with all the administrative attitudes and talents to attain it" (Abrahams 1985).

On the other hand psychology sometimes held up a positive value of its own, the cult of the self. Psychology's object of study and concern is the individual human being, and its central value became encouraging the never-ending growth of individuals. As Dewey had said, "Growth itself is the only moral end." The contradiction between pretending to have no values and holding the value of individual growth was not noticed by American psychologists because their central value was so American as to be transparent. From the time of de Tocqueville Americans had sought self-improvement more than anything else. Continuing growth and development seems as natural and necessary to Americans as God-centered stasis, the never-changing ideal divine order, had seemed to Europeans of the Middle Ages. In our world of self-made individuals, psychological techniques that fostered continual growth and change appeared value-free: What American society and psychology wanted was individualism.

However, the value of individualism had undergone important change since the nineteenth century. *Character* was the concept by which people understood the individual in the nineteenth century. Emerson defined character as "moral order through the medium of individual nature," and the adjectives used to describe character included duty, work, golden deeds, honor, integrity, and manhood. In his or her character, then, a person had a certain relationship, good or evil, to an encompassing and transcendent moral order. Aspiring to good character demanded self-discipline and self-sacrifice; popular psychologists such as the phrenologists offered guides to the diagnosis of one's own and others' character, and gave advice on how to improve one's character. In the twentieth century, however, the moral concept of *character* began to be replaced by the narcissistic concept of *personality,* and self-sacrifice began to be replaced by self-realization. The adjectives used to describe personality were not moral: fascinating, stunning, magnetic, masterful, dominant, forceful. Having a good personality demanded no conformity to moral order, but instead fulfilled the desires of the self and achieved power over others. Character was good or bad; personality was famous or infamous. Psychologists, having shed the religious values that defined character, aided the birth of personality. Self-growth meant realizing one's potential, not living up to impersonal moral ideals—and potential, that which has not yet become actual, can be bad as often as good. Some potential is for doing bad things. Developing everyone's full potential, then, can be bad for society. Thus psychology's cultivation of individual growth was at odds with its claim to provide society with tools of social control.

This same essentially moral conflict exists between the psychology of developing potential and the most important concept of the psychology of adaptation, adjustment. Everything in twentieth-century psychology has revolved around the concept of adjustment. In experimental psychology, psychologists of learning studied how the mind, and, later, behavior, adjusted the individual organism to the demands of its environment. In applied psychology, psychologists developed tools to measure a person's adjustment to his or her circumstances, and should the adjustment be found wanting, tools to bring the child, worker, soldier, or neurotic back into harmony with society. In the psychological conception, sin was replaced with behavior deviation and absolute morality was replaced with statistical morality (Boorstin 1973). In more religious times one had a problem if one offended a moral norm standing outside himself and society; now one had a problem if one offended society's averages as determined by statistical research. In theory, psychology placed itself on the side of individual expression, no matter how eccentric. In practice, by offering tools for social control and by stressing adjustment, it placed itself on the side of conformity.

A new Hellenistic Age was in the making. In the first Hellenistic Age the natural sciences flourished at Alexandria, supported by the state. People's first desire was personal happiness—*ataraxia*—and they sought out teachers who promised a recipe by which one might find freedom from disturbance. In the modern Hellenistic Age the natural sciences would again flourish with government support. People's first desire would again be personal happiness—adjustment—and they would seek out psychologists for recipes by which they might find fulfillment, sex, and the right job, things without which the modern person would be greatly disturbed. In both Hellenistic Ages there remained a deep hunger for more transcendent truths, but in neither were they forthcoming.

BIBLIOGRAPHY

For a general account of American history for the years 1912 to 1950 see John L. Thomas, "Nationalizing the republic" (for the period 1912–1920) and Robert H. Wiebe, "Modernizing the republic" (for the period 1920 and after), both in Bernard Bailyn et al., *The Great Republic* (Boston: Little, Brown, 1977). For a general account of the period with an emphasis on social history, including shrewd observations on the role of the social sciences as shapers of modern morality, see Daniel Boorstin (1973); for an emphasis on politics see Eric F. Goldman, *Rendezvous with destiny: A history of modern American reform*, 3d ed. (New York: Vintage, 1977).

The period between the wars has been studied a great deal, with emphasis on the 1920s. The first book on the 1920s was Allen (1931); for a more recent interpretation see Geoffrey Perrett, *America in the twenties: A history* (New York: Touchstone, 1982). Ostrander (1968) provides a brief account of changes in morals in the 1920s. For American religion during these years see George M. Marsden, *Fundamentalism and American culture: The shaping of twentieth century evangelicalism 1870–1925* (Oxford: Oxford University Press, 1980). Graves and Hodge (1940) provide a wonderfully well-written account of the British scene between the wars.

Several important studies of the social movements are discussed in Chapters 11 and 12. On eugenics the standard history is sure to become Daniel J. Kevles, "Annals of eugenics: A secular faith," which appeared in *The New Yorker*, October 8, 15, 22, and 29, 1984, and as a book, *In the name of eugenics: Genetics and the uses of human heredity* (New York: Knopf, 1985); quotations in the eugenics section are from Kevles unless otherwise noted. Gould (1981) contains useful accounts of American hereditarian attitudes, as well as a critique of intelligence testing and an account of immigration restriction upon which I relied and borrowed quotations. On the sterilization movement the indispensable first source is Landman (1932), which contains valuable detail on sterilization legislation and court decisions. Landman was sympathetic to the ideals of the negative eugenicists, but quite critical of their practices. For the applications of social science to industry and other social problems see

Baritz (1960), who focuses on industrial social science, and Napoli (1981), who discusses applied psychology in all its varied roles. On Flaming Youth see Fass (1977), from whom the quotations in the text are drawn, who presents the problems of youth in the 1920s from the perspectives of the youth themselves, popular commentators, and social scientists. A related source is Christopher Lasch's *Haven in a heartless world: The family besieged* (New York: Basic Books, 1977), which concentrates on social scientists' views of the family. An excellent book that touches on many subjects, including American hereditarianism, the reaction against it by American social scientists, and changing conceptions of the ideal family is Derek Freeman (1983), who dismantles Margaret Mead's romantically naive portrait of the Samoans, first by setting it in its historical context, and then by contrasting it to his own more intimate and prolonged fieldwork. My account of the change from "character" to "personality" is based on Warren I. Susman, " 'Personality' and the making of twentieth-century culture," in J. Higham and P. Conkin, eds., *New directions in American intellectual history* (Baltimore: Johns Hopkins University Press, 1979). Finally, the situation of American science after World War II may be found in Daniel J. Kevles, *The physicists: The history of a scientific community in America* (New York: Knopf, 1978); while Kevles obviously concentrates on physics, he provides a general account of the controversy surrounding creation of the NSF.

Moving on to works specifically on psychology, Sokal (1983) and Burnham (1968) offer good broad accounts of psychology in the 1920s, focusing on psychology's social relations, especially in the case of Burnham. For the period after World War II, with some prewar background, consult Gilgen (1982). On behaviorism in particular see Birnbaum's works (1955, 1964) as well as David Bakan, "Behaviorism and American urbanization," *Journal of the History of the Behavioral Sciences* (1966, 2: 5–28); John C. Burnham, "On the origins of behaviorism," *Journal of the History of the Behavioral Sciences* (1968, 4: 143–152); and Paul Creelan (1974). For the application of intelligence tests to World War I recruits, see Daniel J. Kevles, "Testing the Army's intelligence: Psychologists and the military in World War II, *Journal of American History* (1968, 55: 565–581); and Franz Samelson, "Putting psychology on the map: Ideology and intelligence testing," in Allan R. Buss, ed., *Psychology in social context* (New York: Irvington, 1979), who draws on archival sources to demonstrate how psychologists were affected by the social and political context of the World War I and postwar years. The sources and results of the clash between Yerkes and Scott are told by von Mayrhauser (1985), part of his forthcoming doctoral dissertation at the University of Chicago. There are several useful histories of clinical psychology. The broadest is John M. Reisman, *The development of clinical psychology* (New York: Appleton-Century-Crofts, 1966). More attention to professional issues is provided by Robert I. Watson, "A brief history of clinical psychology," *Psychological Bulletin* (1953, 50: 321–346); and Virginia Staudt Sexton, "Clinical psychology: An historical survey," *Genetic Psychology Monographs* (1965, 72: 401–434). An insider's account of the growth of clinical psychology during and immediately after World War II is given by E. Lowell Kelly, "Clinical psychology," in Dennis (1947). A brief overview of clinical psychology training issues is found in Leonard Blank, "Clinical psychology training, 1945–1962: Conferences and issues," in Leonard Blank and Henry David, eds., *Sourcebook for training in clinical psychology* (New York: Springer, 1964).

Psychologists themselves have provided periodic treatments of their immediate history. For the period in question, the broadest and most detailed treatment is given by Jerome S. Bruner and Gordon W. Allport, "Fifty years of change in American psychology," *Psychological Bulletin* (1940, 37: 757–776), which provided the basis for Allport's APA presidential address, "The psychologist's frame of reference" *Psychological Bulletin* (1940, 37: 1–28). Earlier relevant surveys include Robert Davis and Silas E. Gould, "Changing tendencies in general psychology," *Psychological Review* (1929, 36: 320–331); Florence L. Goodenough, "Trends in modern psychology," *Psychological Bulletin* (1934, 31: 81–97); and Herbert S. Langfeld, "Fifty volumes of the Psychological Review," *Psychological Review* (1943, 50: 143–155). Later accounts looking back to the period in question are Kenneth E.

Clark, "The APA study of psychologists," *American Psychologist* (1954, *9:* 117–120); W. A. Kaess and W. A. Bousfield, "Citation of authorities in textbooks," *American Psychologist* (1954, *9:* 144–148); Russell Becker, "Outstanding contributors to psychology," *American Psychologist* (1959, *14:* 297–298); and Kenneth Wurtz, "A survey of important psychological books," *American Psychologist* (1961, *16:* 192–194).

The narrative account of psychology's preparation for and participation in World War II, including reunification of the APA and AAAP and planning for psychology's postwar role, is based on careful reading of all the *Psychological Bulletins* for the relevant years. The reference to Carmichael (1942) is to his oral report to the meeting of the APA council (the association did not meet because of the war) in New York on September 3, 1942, beginning in the *Bulletin* at page 713.

Finally, a contemporary account of psychology's place in the postwar competition for research funds is given by Robert Leeper "An analysis of science legislation in the last Congress," *American Psychologist* (1947, *2:* 127–135). For the debate in the Senate itself, see the *Congressional Record;* Leeper's page references to the *Record* are unaccountably mistaken: One should look up bill S-1805 in the Index for 1946; the quotations in the text are from p. 8048, while other brief considerations on the social sciences may be found throughout the entire, oft-interrupted, debate. My account of the founding of the Ford Foundation and its interest in behavioral science is based on an Invited Address to Cheiron, the Society for the History of the Behavioral Sciences, June 13, 1985, by Arnold Thackray, "Inventing behavioral science."

REFERENCES

Abrahams, E. (1985) Founding father of the New Republic. Review of D. W. Levy, Herbert Croly of the *New Republic: The life and thought of an American Progressive*. Washington Post Book World, Sunday, May 12: 7.

Adams, G. (1934) The rise and fall of psychology. *Atlantic Monthly 153:* 82–90.

Allen, F. L. (1931) *Only yesterday: An informal history of the 1920's*. New York: Harper & Row.

Anderson, J. E. (1943) Outcomes of the Intersociety Constitutional Convention. *Psychological Bulletin 40:* 585–588.

Baritz, L. J. (1960) *The servants of power: A history of the use of social science in American industry*. Middletown, Connecticut: Westleyan University Press.

Birnbaum, L. T. (1955) Behaviorism in the 1920's. *American Quarterly 7:* 15–30.

Birnbaum, L. T. (1964) Behaviorism: John Broadus Watson and American Social Thought 1913–1933. Unpublished doctoral dissertation, University of California, Berkeley.

Block, N. J. and Dworkin, G. (Eds.) (1976) *The I.Q. controversy: Critical readings*. New York: Pantheon.

Boorstin, D. J. (1973) *The Americans: The democratic experience*. New York: Vintage.

Braeman, J., Bremner, R. H., and Brody, D. (Eds.) (1968) *Change and continuity in twentieth-century America: The 1920's*. Columbus, Ohio: Ohio State University Press.

Bramel, D. and Friend, R. (1981) Hawthorne, the myth of the docile worker, and class bias in American psychology. *American Psychologist 36:* 867–878.

Britt, S. H. (1943) The Office of Psychological Personnel—Report for the second six months. *Psychological Bulletin 40:* 436–446.

Buckley, K. W. (1982) The selling of a psychologist: John Broadus Watson and the application of behavioral techniques to advertising. *Journal of the History of the Behavioral Sciences 18:* 207–221.

Burnham, J. C. (1968) The new psychology: From narcissism to social control. In J. Braeman et al. (1968).

Cohen, J. and Wiebe, G. D. (1955) Who are these people? *American Psychologist 10:* 84–85.

Creelan, P. G. (1974) Watsonian behaviorism and the Calvinist conscience. *Journal of the History of the Behavioral Sciences, 10:* 95–118.

Darley, J. and Wolfle, D. (1946) Can we meet the formidable demand for psychological services? *American Psychologist 1:* 179–180.

Dennis, W. (1947) Psychology as a profession. In W. Dennis (1947).

Dennis, W. (Ed.) (1947) *Current trends in psychology.* Pittsburgh: University of Pittsburgh Press.

Dewey, J. (1917) The need for social psychology. *Psychological Review 24:* 266–277.

Doherty, J. C. (1985) World War II through an Indochina looking glass. *Wall Street Journal,* April 30, 1985: 30.

Fass, P. (1977) *The damned and the beautiful: American youth in the 1920's.* Oxford: Oxford University Press.

Fite, W. (1918) The human soul and the scientific prepossession. *Atlantic Monthly 122:* 796–804.

Freeman, D. (1983) *Margaret Mead and Samoa: The making and unmaking of an anthropological myth.* Cambridge: Harvard University Press.

Garth, T. R. (1930) A review of race psychology. *Psychological Bulletin 27:* 329–356.

Gilgen, A. R. (1982) *American psychology since World War II: A profile of the discipline.* Westport, Connecticut: Greenwood Press.

Glassberg, D. (1985) Social science at the Chicago World's Fair of 1933–34. Paper presented at the annual meeting of Cheiron, the Society for the History of the Behavioral Sciences, Philadelphia, June 15.

Gould, S. J. (1981) *The mismeasure of man.* New York: W. W. Norton.

Graves, R. and Hodge, A. (1940) *The long week-end: A social history of Britain 1918–1939.* New York: W. W. Norton.

Haller, M. (1963) *Eugenics: Hereditarian attitudes in American thought.* New Brunswick, New Jersey: Rutgers University Press.

Harris, B. and Morawski, J. (1979) John B. Watson's predictions for 1979. Paper presented at the 50th annual meeting of the Eastern Psychological Association, Philadelphia, April 1979.

Jastrow, J. (1929) Review of J. B. Watson, *Ways of behaviorism, psychological care of infant and child, battle of behaviorism. Science 69* (April 26): 455–457.

Landman, J. H. (1932) *Human sterilization: The history of the sexual sterilization movement.* New York: Macmillan.

Leacock, S. (1923) A manual of the new mentality. *Harper's Magazine 148:* 471–480.

McDougall, W. (1921) *Is America safe for democracy?* New York: Scribner's. Reprint ed. New York: Arno Press, 1977.

Morgan, C. T. (1947) Human engineering. In W. Dennis (1947).

Murdock, N. and Leahey, T. H. (1986, April) Scientism and status: The Boulder model. Paper presented at the annual meeting of the Eastern Psychological Association, New York.

Napoli, D. S. (1981) *Architects of adjustment: The history of the psychological profession in the United States.* Port Washington, New York: Kennikat Press.

Ostrander, G. M. (1968) The revolution in morals. In J. Braeman et al. (1968).

Peatman, J. G. (1949) How scientific and how professional is the American Psychological Association? *American Psychologist 4:* 486–489.

Perelman, S. J. (1958) Sodom in the suburbs. In S. J. Perelman, *The most of S. J. Perelman.* New York: Simon and Schuster.

Poffenberger, A. T. (1936) Psychology and life. *Psychological Review 43:* 9–31.

Remmers, H. H. (1944) Psychology—Some unfinished business. *Psychological Bulletin 41:* 713–724.

Rogers, C. (1944) Psychological adjustments of discharged service personnel. *Psychological Bulletin 41:* 689–696.

Sears, R. R. (1944) Clinical psychology in the military services. *Psychological Bulletin 41:* 502–509.

Sokal, M. M. (1983) James McKeen Cattell and American psychology in the 1920's. In Josef Brozek (Ed.) *Explorations in the history of psychology in the United States.* Lewisburg, Pennsylvania: Bucknell University Press.

Terman, L. M. (1924) The mental test as a psychological method. *Psychological Review 31:* 93–117.

Terman, L. M. (1930) Lewis M. Terman. In C. Murchison (Ed.) *A history of psychology in autobiography.* V. 2. Worcester, Massachusetts: Clark University Press.

Thorndike, E. L. (1920) Intelligence and its uses. *Harper's Magazine 140:* 227–235.

von Mayrhauser, R. T. (1985) Walking out at the Walton: Psychological disunity and the origins of group testing in early World War I. Paper presented at the annual meeting of Cheiron, the Society for the History of the Behavioral Sciences, Philadelphia, June 14.

Walters, R. G. (1978) *American Reformers 1815–1860.* New York: Hill and Wang.

Washburn, M. F. (1922) Introspection as an objective method. *Psychological Review 29:* 89–112.

Watson, J. B. (1926a) What is behaviorism? *Harper's Magazine 152:* 723–729.

Watson, J. B. (1926b) How we think: A behaviorist's view. *Harper's Magazine 153:* 40–45.

Watson, J. B. (1926c) Memory as the behaviorist sees it. *Harper's Magazine 153:* 244–250.

Watson, J. B. (1927a) The myth of the unconscious. *Harper's Magazine 155:* 502–508.

Waston, J. B. (1927b) The behaviorist looks at the instincts. *Harper's Magazine 155:* 228–235.

Watson, J. B. (1928a) The heart or the intellect. *Harper's Magazine 156:* 345–352.

Watson, J. B. (1928b) *Psychological care of infant and child.* New York: W. W. Norton.

Wiggam, A. E. (1924) *The fruit of the family tree.* Indianapolis, Indiana: Bobbs-Merrill.

Yerkes, R. M. (1918) Psychology in relation to the war. *Psychological Review 25:* 85–115.

Yerkes, R. M. (1923) Testing the human mind. *Atlantic Monthly 131:* 358–370.

World War II transformed psychology from a relatively staid science to a profession increasingly concerned with human welfare. Clinical psychology as we know it today—doing psychotherapy—was created by the need for psychological services for returning war veterans. Psychology experienced explosive growth after the war, especially in its applied branches. Scientific psychology grew, too, but at a much slower pace. Growth led to fragmentation. Psychologists divided along professional lines into clinicians, counselors, industrial psychologists, experimental psychologists, and others. Theoretically, the divisions of the past continued and new ones were invented. Radical behaviorism was added to the behaviorisms of the 1930s and 1940s. Mediational behaviorism developed out of Hullian behaviorism. Cognitive psychology began in the 1950s and matured into cognitive science in the 1970s.

Psychology has become a major institution in modern American life. It is accepted in every college and university as a popular study. Psychologists work in business and industry, and troubled people consult psychologists for help with their problems. Psychological language has become part of everyday life. Some critics say that ours has become the psychological society. Psychology's tremendous growth and increasing influence, along with changes in scientific behavioral psychology, will occupy us in the last three chapters of this book.

CHAPTER 13

Eclectic Psychology (1950–1958)

TROUBLES WITH BEHAVIORISM (1950–1954)
　Philosophical Behaviorism
　Are Theories of Learning Adequate?
ARE THEORIES OF LEARNING NECESSARY? RADICAL BEHAVIORISM (1938–1958)
　Radical Behaviorism
　The Experimental Analysis of Behavior
　Interpreting Human Behavior
THE ROOTS OF COGNITIVE SCIENCE (1943–1958)
　Informal Behaviorism
　Early Cognitive Theories
　Artificial Intelligence
PSYCHOLOGY AND SOCIETY (1950–1958)

Following the crises and turmoil of the war years, psychology settled into comfortable eclecticism. Psychologists were all behavioralists now, and different behavioral theories existed side by side in relative peace. The various species of self-styled behaviorism included common-sense theories about attitudes and beliefs in social psychology, and "behaviorist" and nonbehaviorist theories of cognition. While much theoretical debate existed among the various positions, there was relatively little of the stridency that had marked the birth of behaviorism. Three important developments took place in the harmonious environment of eclectic psychology. First was the growing influence of B. F. Skinner's radical behaviorism in experimental psychology and then in its application to human thought and behavior. The second major development, which occurred primarily outside psychology, was the founding of the field of artificial intelligence. This field eventually gave birth to cognitive psychology, cognitive science, and a renaissance in the philosophy of mind. Finally, clinical and applied psychology continued to grow, threatening to turn the APA into more of a professional trade organization than a scientific association. With this came the laying of the first barely visible foundations of the psychological society of the 1970s and 1980s.

TROUBLES WITH BEHAVIORISM (1950–1954)

The most consciously troubled area in psychology after the war was the core of traditional scientific psychology, experimental psychology, which by 1950 meant primarily the study of learning. Sigmund Koch, already becoming an effective gadfly to the pretensions of scientific psychology, wrote in 1951 that "psychology seems now to have entered an era of total disorientation." In another 1951 paper Koch asserted that, "Since the end of the World War II, psychology has been in a long and intensifying crisis   its core seems to be disaffection from the theory of the recent past. Never before had it seemed so evident that the development of a science is not an automatic forward movement. . . ." Koch located two causes of the "crisis" in experimental psychology, one internal and one external. Within experimental psychology, Koch saw a decade-long stagnation in the development of the prewar theoretical systems of learning theory. Outside, clinical and applied psychology were bidding for "social recognition" by abandoning theory for useful practices so they could take on "social responsibilities." In the rush toward social usefulness theoretical psychologists had become depressed and were looking for a "new wave" to excite them again.

Koch was not a cranky prophet alone in his dissatisfaction with the state of experimental psychology, for signs of dissatisfaction abounded. In 1951 Karl Lashley, at one time Watson's student, attacked the standard S-R chaining theory of complex behaviors, originally proposed by Watson himself. Lashley argued on physiological grounds that chaining was impossible because of the relatively slow transmission of nervous impulses from receptor to brain and back to effector. Lashley proposed instead that organisms possess central planning functions that coordinate sets of actions as large units, not as chains. Lashley specifically argued that language was organized this way, raising a problem that would increasingly bedevil behaviorism. On another front in 1950 Frank Beach, a student of animal behavior, decried experimental psychologists' increasing preoccupation with rat learning. He questioned whether psychologists were interested in a general science of behavior or in only one topic, learning, in only one species, the Norway rat. Without studies of other behaviors and species, he argued, the generality of laboratory findings must remain suspect. He also pointed out the existence of species-specific behaviors such as imprinting that are not the exclusive result of either learning or instinct. Such behaviors escape all existing learning theories, which sharply divide the learned from the unlearned and then study only the latter. Problems of comparative psychology would increasingly plague the psychology of learning in the 1950s and the 1960s.

Philosophical Behaviorism

Psychological behaviorism arose out of the problems of animal psychology and in revolt against introspective mentalism. Consequently, behavioristic psychologists never addressed one of the more obvious difficulties that might be raised against their movement—namely, that ordinary people believe they possess mental processes and consciousness. There exists a folk psychology of mind that deserves attention from any psychological program departing from it. It may fairly be asked why, if there are no mental processes—as behaviorists seem to maintain—ordinary language is so rich in descriptions of mind and consciousness? Philosophical behaviorists addressed the problem of reinterpreting common-sense mentalistic psychology into acceptable "scientific" behavioristic terms as part of their more general program of linking claims about unobservables with observables.

As it is usually presented, philosophical or "logical behaviorism is a semantic theory about what mental terms mean. The basic idea is that attributing a mental state (say thirst) to an organism is the same as saying that the organism is disposed to behave in a certain way (for example to drink if there is water available)" (Fodor 1981). According to logical behaviorists, when we attribute a mental statement to a person, we're really just describing their actual or likely behavior in a given circumstance, not some inner mental state. In principle, then, it would be possible to eliminate mentalistic concepts from everyday psychology and replace them with concepts referring only to behavior. As stated, logical behaviorism is rather implausible. For example, according to logical behaviorism, to believe that ice on a lake is too thin for skating must mean that one is disposed not to skate on the ice and to say to others that they ought not skate on the lake. However, things are not so simple. If you see someone you thoroughly dislike about to skate out on the ice, you may say nothing, hoping that your enemy will fall through the ice and look a fool. Should you harbor real malice toward the skater—if, for example, he is blackmailing you—you may say nothing, hoping he will drown; indeed, you may direct him to the weakest ice. So the mental statement "believing the ice is thin" cannot be simply and directly translated into a behavioral disposition, because how one is disposed to behave depends on other beliefs that turn on still others—for example, that the skater *is* the blackmailer—making any direct equation of mental state and behavioral disposition impossible.

The difficulties of logical behaviorism are relevant to experimental psychology because its doctrines are the application of operationism to ordinary psychological terms. For logical behaviorism's equation of mental state and behavior or behavioral disposition provides operational definitions of "belief," "hope," "fear," "being in pain," and so on. The example of the thin ice shows that one cannot give an operational definition of "believing the ice is thin," and failure to "operationalize" so simple and straightforward a concept casts doubt on the whole enterprise of operationism in psychology. The British philosopher G. E. Moore, following Ludwig Wittgenstein, refuted the logical behaviorist, operationist treatment of mental terms more bluntly: "When we pity a man for having toothache, we are not pitying him for putting his hand to his cheek" (Luckhardt 1983).

Logical behaviorism is so obviously false that it makes an admirable straw man for philosophers of other dispositions, but it is not clear that anyone has actually held the position just sketched. It is typically attributed to Rudolph Carnap, Gilbert Ryle, and Ludwig Wittgenstein, but in fact these philosophers held different and more interesting views on the nature of mentalistic folk psychology. We discussed Carnap's "behaviorism" in Chapter 11 in connection with E. C. Tolman, who was for a time under Carnap's influence. Carnap came closest to holding the position of logical behaviorism, but we should bear in mind that for him it was just a temporary way station on the road to interpreting mentalistic language as talk about brain states. As we shall see in Chapter 15, Carnap's physicalistic view is fraught with difficulties; but it is possible to separate the idea that mental terms refer to behavioral dispositions from the idea that they refer to brain states.

In *The Concept of Mind* (1949) English philosopher Gilbert Ryle attacked what he called (in a now famous phrase) "the dogma of the Ghost in the Machine" begun by Descartes. Descartes defined two worlds—one material and including the body, the other mental, a ghostly inner stage on which private mental events took place. Ryle accused Descartes of making a huge "category mistake," treating mind as if it were a distinct thing opposed to the body and somehow lying behind behavior. Here is an example of a category mistake: A person is taken on a tour of Oxford University and sees its college buildings, its library, its deans, its professors, and its students. At the end of the day the visitor asks, "You've showed me all these things, but where is the university?" The mistake is in supposing that since there is a name "Oxford University," it must apply to some object separate from the buildings and so on, yet be like them in being a thing. So Ryle claimed that Cartesian dualism is a category mistake. Cartesians describe behaviors with "mental" predicates such as "intelligent," "hopeful," "sincere," "disingenuous," and then assume that there must be a mental thing behind the behaviors that makes them intelligent, hopeful, sincere, or disingenuous. Here, says Ryle, lies the mistake, because the behaviors *themselves* are intelligent, hopeful, sincere, or disingenuous; no inner ghost is needed to make them so. Moreover, inventing the Ghost in the Machine accomplishes nothing, because if there were an inner ghost, we would still have to explain why its operations are intelligent, hopeful, sincere, or disingenuous. Is there a Ghost in the Ghost? And a Ghost in the Ghost in the Ghost? The Ghost in the Machine, far from explaining mental life, vastly complicates our efforts to understand it.

So far one might, as Ryle feared, put him down as a behaviorist claiming that mind *is* only behavior. But Ryle held that there is indeed more to mental predicates than simple descriptions of behavior. For example, when we say birds are "migrating" we see them flying south, and a behaviorist might say that "migration" is just "flying-south behavior." However, as Ryle pointed out, to say that birds are "migrating" is to say much more than that they are flying south since the term "migration" implies a whole story about why they are flying south, how they will return later, how it happens every year, and theories about how they navigate. So to say birds are "migrating" goes *beyond* saying that they are flying south, but it does not go *behind* saying that they are flying south. Similarly, to say a behavior is "intelligent" does more than simply describe some behavior, since it brings in the various criteria we have for saying a course of action is intelligent—for example, that it is appropriate to the situation, and it is likely to be successful. But saying a person is acting intelligently does not go behind the behavior to some ghostly inner calculations that make it intelligent, however much it goes beyond a behaviorist's description of what the person is doing. While Ryle rejected dualism, and while his analysis of mind had some similarities to behaviorism, it was rather different from either psychological behaviorism or logical, philosophical behaviorism.

A difficult and subtle analysis of ordinary psychological language was made by the Viennese (later British) philosopher Ludwig Wittgenstein. Wittgenstein argued that Cartesian philosophers had led people to believe that there are mental objects (for example, sensations) and mental processes (for example, memory), whereas in fact there are neither. As an example of a mental object, consider *pain*. Quite clearly, the behaviorist is wrong in asserting that pain is behavior. The behaviorist error is in thinking that first- and third-person uses of "pain" are symmetrical. If we see someone moaning and holding his head, we say, "He is in pain"; but I do not say, "I am in pain" because I observe myself moaning and holding my head, as strict operationism requires. So the sentence "I am in pain" does not describe behavior; nor, held Wittgenstein, does it describe some inner object. An object can be known, so we can say true things about it—for example, "I know this book, *Wittgenstein,* costs $5.95." But a statement of knowledge only makes sense if we can doubt it, that is, if some other state of affairs may be true than the one we think. So one can sensibly say, "I don't know if *Wittgenstein* costs $5.95." Now, "I know I'm in pain" seems to make sense and point to an inner object of description, but the statement "I don't know that I'm in pain" is simply nonsense; of course, one can have experienced bodily damage and not feel pain, but one cannot meaningfully say, "I don't know if I'm in pain." Another problem with thinking of pain as an object concerns how pains are located. Should I hold a piece of candy between my fingers and then put my fingers in my mouth, we would agree that the candy is in my mouth as well as my hand. But suppose I have a pain in my finger, and put my finger in my mouth. Is the pain *in* my mouth? It seems odd to say so; pains are therefore not assigned location as we assign locations to ordinary objects. Wittgenstein concluded that pain is not some inner object that we know at all, and that statements about pain (or joy, or ecstasy) are not descriptions of anything. Rather they are expressions. Moaning expresses pain, it does not describe pain. Wittgenstein maintained that sentences such as "I am in pain" are learned linguistic equivalents of moaning, expressing but not describing the state of pain. Pain is perfectly real; it is not, however, a ghostly mental object.

Luckhardt (1983) introduces a useful analogy to clarify Wittgenstein's point. A painting expresses an artist's conception through the physical medium of paint on canvas. We find it beautiful (or ugly) as we interpret it. Behaviorists are like paint salesmen, who point out that since the painting is made of paint, its beauty is identical with the arrangements of the paints on the canvas. However, this is obviously absurd, since a painting venerated for its beauty among academic painters and audiences in 1875 is likely to be considered tacky kitsch by modernists and their audience. Beauty depends on an interpretation of paint on canvas and is not identical with it. The painting is, again, a physical expression by an artist that is in turn interpreted by its viewers. So "I am in pain," like moans and grimaces, is a physical expression by a person that must be interpreted by those who hear it.

Likewise, mental processes do not consist in any*thing,* either, argued Wittgenstein. Consider memory. Obviously, we remember things all the time, but is there an inner mental process of remembering common to all acts of memory? Wittgenstein thought not. Malcolm (1970) gives the following example: Several hours after you put your keys in the kitchen drawer, you are asked, "Where did you put the keys?" You may remember in any of several ways:

1. Nothing occurs to you, then you mentally retrace your steps earlier in the day and have an image of putting them in the drawer, and say, "I left them in the kitchen drawer."
2. Nothing occurs to you. You have no images, but ask yourself "Where did I put them?" then exclaim, "The kitchen drawer!' "
3. The question is asked while you are deep in conversation with another person. Without interrupting your talk, you point to the kitchen drawer.
4. You are asked while writing a letter. Saying nothing you walk over to the drawer, reach in, and hand over the keys, all the while composing the next sentence in the letter.
5. Without any hesitation or doubt you answer directly, "I put them in the kitchen drawer."

In every case you remembered where the keys were, but each case is quite unlike the others. The behaviors are different, so there is no essential behavioral process of remembering; there is no uniform mental accompaniment to the act of remembering, so there is no essential mental process of remembering; and since there is no common behavior or conscious experience, there is no essential physiological process of remembering. In each case there is behavior, there are mental events, and there are physiological processes, but no one of them is the same, so there is no uniform *process* of memory. We group these events together under "memory" not because of some essential defining feature of each episode, the way we define "electrons" in terms of uniform defining features, but because they share what Wittgenstein called a "family resemblance." The members of a family resemble one another, but there is no single feature all members possess. Two brothers may share similar noses, a father and son similar ears, two cousins similar hair, but there is no essential defining feature shared by all. Wittgenstein argued that terms referring to mental processes are all family-resemblance terms, having no defining essence that can be captured. "Remembering," "thinking," "intending" are not processes, but human abilities. To the Wittgensteinian the Würzburg psychologists' efforts to lay bare the processes of thinking had to end in failure, for there are no processes of thought to be found. Thinking, like remembering, is just something people *do* (Malcolm 1970).

If Wittgenstein is right, the consequences for psychology are profound. Wittgenstein (1953) had a poor opinion of psychology: "The confusion and barrenness of psychology is not to be explained by calling it a 'young science. . . .' For in psychology there are experimental methods and *conceptual confusion.* . . ." Psychology's conceptual confusion is to think there are mental objects and mental processes when there are not, and then to seek for explanations of the fictitious objects and processes.

> I have been trying in all this to remove the temptation to think that there "*must* be" a mental process of thinking, hoping, wishing, believing, etc., independent of the process of expressing a thought, a hope, a wish, etc. . . . If we scrutinize the usages which we make of "thinking," "meaning," "wishing," etc., going through this process rids us of the temptation to look for a peculiar act of thinking, independent of

the act of expressing our thoughts, and stowed away in some particular medium.''
(Wittgenstein 1958)

Wittgenstein's point here is related to Ryle's: There is nothing behind our acts; there is no Ghost in the Machine. Behind the point about psychology there is a broader point about science: Explanations stop somewhere (Malcolm 1970). It is no good asking a physicist why an object once set in motion will travel in a straight line forever unless acted on by another force, because this is a basic assumption that allows physics to explain other things. No one has seen an object move that way and the only apparently undisturbed objects we can observe moving, the planets, move (roughly) in circles; indeed, the ancients assumed that an object in space set in motion would naturally move in a circle. Similarly, a physicist cannot explain why quarks have the properties they do, only how, given those properties, their behavior can be explained. Psychologists have all along supposed that thinking, memory, wishing, and so on required explanations, but Ryle, and especially Wittgenstein, claim that they do not. They are human abilities, and thinking, remembering, and wishing are things we just *do* without there being some ''inside story,'' mental or physiological, although they are not just behaviors, either. Psychologists went wrong when they framed their question as, ''What is the process of thinking?'' naturally coming up with theories about mental processes. As Wittgenstein remarks, ''We talk of processes and states and leave their nature undecided. Sometimes perhaps we shall know more about them—we think. But that is just what commits us to a particular way of looking at the matter. For we have a definite concept of what it means to learn to know a process better. The decisive movement in the conjuring trick has been made, and it was the very one that we thought quite innocent'' (Wittgenstein 1953).

To Wittgenstein, we cannot scientifically explain behavior, but we can understand it. To understand people's behavior, and the expressions of their thoughts, we must take into consideration what Wittgenstein called human ''forms of life.'' ''What has to be accepted, the given, is—so one could say—*forms of life*'' (Wittgenstein 1958). In discussing Luckhardt's painting metaphor we pointed out that the beauty of a painting lies in its interpretation. How we interpret the painting depends on the immediate and overall context in which we meet it. The gallery-goer may have read art history and criticism, and this knowledge will shape her appreciation of the picture. She will see Frank Stella's latest canvas against the background of Stella's previous work, the works by other artists arranged in the show, and by knowledge of the history, ambitions, and techniques of modern and postmodern painting. Simply as paint on canvas the painting has no meaning and is neither beautiful nor ugly; it takes on meaning only in the eye of an interpretive viewer. All this context is a ''form of life,'' the form of life of modernism and postmodernism in the arts. Observe that a person who knows nothing of modernism is likely to find a Stella work literally without meaning, because that person does not participate in the appropriate form of life. Should he take modern art history classes, he can learn a new form of life and the painting will become meaningful.

Wittgenstein's point is that human action is only meaningful within the setting of a form of life. An untutored Westerner is likely to find practices of another culture, or another historical time, without meaning in the same way the naive gallery-goer finds the Stella painting meaningless. The reverse is true: Some African tribesmen came to a city for the first time and were deeply shocked when in a tall building they saw two men go into a box and emerge a few seconds later as three women. (They saw an elevator.) If Wittgenstein's claim is correct, then not only can psychology not be a science because there are no mental processes and objects for it to study and explain, but psychology and the other social sciences cannot be sciences because their are no historically permanent and cross-culturally universal principles for understanding human thought and behavior. Psychology, he says, should give up the "craving for generality" and "the contemptuous attitude to the particular case" it has picked up from natural science (Wittgenstein 1953), and accept the modest goal of explicating forms of life and explaining particular human actions within their historically given forms of life.

Are Theories of Learning Adequate?

Hull and Tolman were not professionally raised on logical positivism and operationism, but the succeeding generation of experimental psychologists, coming into professional maturity after World War II, was. Many of the new generation believed with Sigmund Koch that the theoretical debates of the 1930s and 1940s had led nowhere, that the problems of the psychology of learning—the heart of the adjustment process—were not being solved. So in the later 1940s and through the early 1950s theoretical psychologists engaged in earnest self-scrutiny, applying the tools of logical positivism and operationism to developing tactics of theory construction in psychology, and applying the criteria of positivism and operationism to the theories of Hull and Tolman.

Central to much of the metatheoretical discussion of the period was the status of what Tolman had called "intervening variables," the theoretical concepts such as cognitive map and habit strength that Hull and Tolman employed to explain behavior. The terms of the debate were framed in 1948 by Kenneth MacCorquodale and Paul Meehl, who distinguished between intervening variables and "hypothetical constructs." While meant to be a dimension along which psychological concepts might be arrayed, in practice their distinction was used dichotomously, and theoretical analysts tended to write about intervening variables *vs.* hypothetical constructs. Intervening variables were concepts defined purely operationally, as mere shorthand descriptions for experimental procedures or measurements. Hypothetical constructs on the other hand possessed, perhaps in addition to operational meaning, "surplus meaning" over and above procedures and measurements. It was usually argued that hypothetical constructs were temporary expedients aiding creativity in the early stages of scientific development. Failure to "purify" hypothetical constructs into intervening variables was described as a "practice that cannot be scientifically defended," since "valid intervening variables . . . are the only kinds of constructs admissible in sound scientific theory" (Marx 1951).

No one was very clear on what the surplus meaning of hypothetical constructs consisted in. Sometimes it seemed to mean no more than the idiosyncratic associations its proposer might have for it (Kendler 1952); sometimes it seemed to refer to hypothetical neural mechanisms thought to underlie behavior (Marx 1951); and sometimes it seemed to consist in reference to more abstract models of behavior (Tolman 1949). Whatever surplus meaning was, however, everyone save Tolman and his associates (Tolman 1949, Krech 1949) agreed that it was bad, and should be purged from psychological theory as soon as possible.

An important and illustrative example of the fight over the meaning and status of hypothetical constructs is the controversy between Tolmanians and neo-Hullians over what is learned, which had continued since the 1930s. Neo-Hullians maintained that when an animal learns, for example, how to run a maze, it has learned a series of responses to be executed at different points in the maze. Tolmanians continued to maintain that the animal learns a cognitive map representation of the maze. A huge number of experiments had been done to resolve these two points of view, but by 1950 no progress had been made in determining which was correct. In 1952 Howard Kendler, a student of Spence's, argued that the dispute between Tolmanians and neo-Hullians was a pseudodispute. Applying operational criteria, Kendler tried to show that there was no real difference between the two camps. Since "the only meaning possessed by . . . intervening variables is their relationship to both independent and dependent variables," any theory of learning is only about responses to given choice points in a maze. Kendler accused the Tolmanians of committing "the fallacy of reification" by believing that cognitive maps are more than shorthand descriptions of maze behavior. Since theoretical concepts must be defined operationally—in terms of behaviors occurring under specified conditions—differences between Hull's and Tolman's positions were no more than differences "between personal thought processes leading to the invention of theoretical constructs."

Kendler's very influential paper illustrates how logical positivism and operationism blinded psychologists of the period to other ways of doing science, even when those other ways were practiced by dominant figures such as Hull and Tolman. Hull and Tolman were both *realists;* that is, they believed their constructs referred to some real object or process occurring within living organisms. In Hull's case these processes were physiological; but Kendler dismissed Hull's commitment to the physiological reality of his concepts as an "individual's intuitive conception," not to be mixed up with the operational definition of the concepts, which alone are scientifically meaningful. With respect to Tolman, Kendler entirely failed to consider that Tolman's constructs might refer to *psychologically* real entities. Kendler, advocate of operationism and the pure intervening variable, was a nominalist, defining terms only in terms of their use, failing to see that theoretical constructs might refer to something besides behavior. Tolman's colleague Benbow Ritchie (1952) tried to point out Kendler's mistake, but the tide of operationism was too strong. Psychologists by and large accepted Kendler's judgment that there was no real difference between Hull and Tolman, and went on to other things.

Kendler's paper also reaffirms that operationism is a species of idealism rather than materialistic realism. Notice that intervening variables do not actually intervene. As just "shorthand descriptions" they have no reality in the organism, and so play no causal role in intervening between stimulus and response. Intervening variables do no more than organize the scientist's experience of others' behavior. Thus direct experience is, for operationism, the ultimate reality, and operationism is therefore a form of idealism.

At the Dartmouth Conference on Learning Theory held in 1950, the new generation of learning theorists evaluated learning theories in the light of the logical positivism they assumed, and thought their teachers had accepted. Hull's theory, as the one they believed most closely shared their positivist standards of theory construction, came in for the most devastating criticism. Sigmund Koch, the author of the report on Hull, said, "We have done what may be construed as a nasty thing. We have proceeded on a literal interpretation of some such proposition as: 'Hull has put forward a hypothetico-deductive theory of behavior.'" Proceeding on that interpretation, Koch showed that, judged by positivistic criteria, Hull's enterprise was a total failure. Koch's rhetoric was damning: Hull's theory suffered from "horrible indeterminacy" and "manifold inadequacies" in the definition of its independent variables; it was "empirically empty" and a "pseudoquantitative system"; and it failed to progress from the 1943 formulation to the ones of the early 1950s: "It may be said with confidence that with respect to most of the issues considered . . . there has been no evidence of constructive advance since 1943." The other theories, including those of Tolman, B. F. Skinner, Kurt Lewin (a Gestalt psychologist), and Edwin R. Guthrie (another behaviorist), were variously criticized for failure to meet positivist criteria for good theory.

Clearly, the older theories of learning were not adequate, at least as judged by the standards of logical positivism. But were the logical positivist's standards necessarily right? At Dartmouth it was noticed that B. F. Skinner's brand of behaviorism failed to live up to logical positivistic principles because it did not try to. Skinner had set his own standards of theoretical adequacy, and judged by them his theory did well. Perhaps, then, change was called for in psychologists' goals, rather than in their continued pursuit of goals set by abstract philosophy. Were theories of learning needed at all?

ARE THEORIES OF LEARNING NECESSARY? RADICAL BEHAVIORISM (1938–1958)

Radical Behaviorism

> Define
> And thus expunge
> The *ought*
> The *should*
> * * *
> Truth's to be sought
> In *Does* and *Doesn't*

> B. F. Skinner, *For Ivor Richards* (1971)

By far the best known and most influential of all the major behaviorists is Burrhus Frederick Skinner (born 1904), whose radical behaviorism, if accepted, would constitute a momentous revolution in humanity's understanding of the human self, demanding as it does no less than the complete rejection of the entire intellectual psychological tradition nurtured in philosophy that we have considered in this book. It would replace this tradition with a scientific psychology grounded in neo-Darwinian evolutionary theory, which looks outside humans for the causes of behavior. Every psychological thinker we have considered, from Thales to Wundt, even to Hull and Tolman, intended psychology to be an explication of internal processes, however conceived—processes that produce behavior or conscious phenomena. Skinner follows Watson in placing responsibility for behavior squarely in the environment, however. A person does not act at the behest of moral values, the "ought" and "should," the highest guides to action for Plato. For Skinner, people deserve neither praise nor blame for anything they "do" or "don't." The environment controls behavior so that both good and evil, if such exist, reside there, not in the person. To paraphrase Shakespeare's Julius Caesar: "The fault, dear Brutus, lies in our contingencies of reinforcement, not ourselves."

The heart of radical behaviorism may best be approached by looking at Skinner's attitude to Freud in his paper "A Critique of Psychoanalytic Concepts and Theories." For Skinner, Freud's great discovery was that much human behavior has unconscious causes. However, to Skinner Freud's great mistake was in inventing a mental apparatus–id, ego, superego—and its attendant mental processes to explain human behavior. Skinner believed that the lesson taught by the unconscious is that mental states are simply irrelevant to behavior. We may observe that a student shows a neurotic subservience to her teachers. The Freudian might explain this by asserting that the student's father was a punitive perfectionist who demanded obedience, and that his child incorporated a stern father image that now affects the student's behavior in the presence of authority figures. Skinner would allow us to explain the current servility by reference to punishments at the hand of a punitive father, but he would insist that the link be direct. The student cowers now because as a child she received punishment from a similar person, not because there is any mental image within her of her father. For Skinner, the inference to an unconscious father image explains nothing that cannot be explained by simply referring current behavior to the consequences of past behavior. The mental link adds nothing to an account of behavior, according to Skinner, and in fact complicates matters by requiring that the mental link itself be explained. Skinner has extended this criticism of mental entities to encompass all traditional psychologies, rejecting equally the superego, apperception, habit strength, and cognitive maps. All are unnecessary steps in the explanation of behavior.

Skinner's rejection of mental or hypothetical entities as unnecessary fictions is similar to Aristotle's rejection of Plato's Forms. Aristotle argued that the Forms were unseen, fictitious entities introduced into the universe to explain those things that could be seen, but which really add nothing to our understanding of the observable world and which themselves require explaining. Similar, too, was Ockham's rejection of the doctrine of mental faculties. That we remember does not imply the existence of an unobservable faculty of memory. Ockham pointed out that remembering is a mental *act,* not a faculty. Skinner holds that remembering is simply an act, without any reference to mind at all. In Skinner's case, as in Aristotle's and Ockham's, the desire is to simplify our understanding of nature and of the human as a natural creature by eliminating anything not absolutely necessary to scientific explanation, especially any reference to hypothetical, unobservable entities. Aristotle did away with the Forms, Ockham the faculties, and Skinner the mind.

Although radical behaviorism represents a sharp break with any traditional psychology, whether scientific or common sense, its intellectual heritage can be located. It stands clearly in the empiricist camp, especially with radical empiricism from Ockham to Francis Bacon to Hume to Mach. As a young man, Skinner read Bacon's works, and he often refers favorably to the great inductivist. Like Bacon, Skinner believes that truth is to be found in observations themselves, in "does" and "doesn't," rather than in our interpretations of our observations. Skinner's first psychological paper was an application of Mach's radical descriptive positivism to the concept of the reflex. Skinner concluded that a reflex is not an entity inside an animal, but merely a convenient descriptive term for a regular correlation between stimulus and response. This presages his rejection of all hypothetical entities.

Skinner's account of behavior is also heir to Darwin's analysis of evolution, as Skinner himself often suggests, although until recently he considered only the individual evolutionary question. Darwin argued that species constantly produce variant traits and that nature acts on these traits to select those that contribute to survival, eliminating those that do not. Similarly, for Skinner an organism is constantly producing variant forms of behavior. Some of these acts lead to favorable consequences—are reinforced—while others do not. Those that do are strengthened, for they contribute to the organism's survival and are learned. Those that are not reinforced are not learned and disappear from the organism's repertoire, just as weak species become extinct. Both Skinner's analysis of behavior and his values are Darwinian, as we shall see.

Like many innovative scientific thinkers, Skinner received little early training in his discipline. He took his undergraduate degree in English at Hamilton College, intending to be a writer, studying no psychology. However, a biology teacher called his attention to works by Pavlov and the mechanist physiologist Jacques Loeb. The former taught him a concern for the total behavior of an organism, and the latter impressed him with the possibility of careful, rigorous, scientific research on behavior. He learned of Watson's behaviorism from some articles by Bertrand Russell on Watson, whom Skinner then read. After failing to become a writer, Skinner turned to psychology filled with the spirit of Watsonian behaviorism. He initiated a systematic research program on a new kind of behavior, the operant.

The Experimental Analysis of Behavior

The basic goal guiding Skinner's scientific work is stated in his first psychological paper and was inspired by the success of Pavlov's work with conditioned reflexes. Wrote Skinner in "The Concept of the Reflex" (1931), "Given a particular part of the behavior of an organism hitherto regarded as unpredictable (and probably, as a consequence, assigned to non-physical factors), the investigator seeks out the antecedent changes with which the activity is correlated and establishes the conditions of the correlation." The goal of psychology is to analyze behavior by locating the specific determinants of specific behaviors, and to establish the exact nature of the relationship between antecedent influence and subsequent behavior. The best way to do this is by experiment, for only in an experiment can all the factors affecting behavior be systematically controlled. Skinner thus calls his science "the experimental analysis of behavior."

A behavior is explained within this system when the investigator knows all the influences of which the behavior is a function. We may refer to the antecedent influences acting on a behavior as *independent variables,* and the behavior that is a function of them we may call the *dependent variable.* The organism can then be thought of as a *locus of variables.* It is a place where independent variables act together to produce a behavior. There is no mental activity that interevenes between independent and dependent variables, and traditional references to mental entities may be eliminated when independent variables have been understood. Skinner assumes that physiology will ultimately be able to detail the physical mechanisms controlling behavior, but that analysis of behavior in terms of functional relationships among variables is completely independent of physiology. The functions will remain even when the underlying physiological mechanisms are understood.

Thus far, Skinner's account closely follows Mach. Scientific explanation is nothing more than an accurate and precise description of the relationship between observable variables; for Skinner these are environmental variables and behavior variables. Just as Mach sought to exorcise "metaphysical" reference to unobserved causal links in physics, so Skinner sought to exorcise "metaphysical" reference to causal mental links in psychology. In his early work Skinner emphasized the descriptive nature of his work, and it is still sometimes called *descriptive behaviorism*. We may note here the mirror-image nature of Skinnerian and Titchenerian psychology. Titchener also followed Mach by seeking only to correlate variables analyzed within an experimental framework, but of course he wanted a description of consciousness, not behavior. Skinner sometimes concedes the possibility of such a study, but dismisses it as irrelevant to the study of behavior as Titchener had dismissed the study of behavior as irrelevant to the psychology of consciousness.

What separates Titchener and Skinner, besides their subject matters, is the importance of control for Skinner. Skinner is Watsonian in wanting not just to describe behavior but to control it. In fact, for Skinner control is the ultimate test of the scientific adequacy of observationally determined functions between antecedent variables and behavior variables. Prediction alone is insufficient, for prediction may result from the correlation of two variables causally dependent on a third, but not on each other. For example, children's toe size and weight will correlate very highly: the bigger a child's toe, the heavier he or she is likely to be. However, toe size does not "cause" weight, or vice versa, for both depend on physical growth, which causes changes in both variables. According to Skinner an investigator can only be said to have explained a behavior when in addition to being able to predict its occurrence he can also *influence* its occurrence through the manipulation of independent variables. Thus an adequate experimental analysis of behavior implies a technology of behavior, wherein behavior may be engineered for specific purposes, such as teaching. Titchener always vehemently rejected technology as a goal for psychology, but it is a concern of Skinner's that became increasingly pronounced after World War II.

The experimental analysis of behavior is without doubt the closest psychology has come to a normal science research program. It began with Skinner's first psychological book, *The Behavior of Organisms* (1938). This work contains most of the important concepts of the experimental analysis of behavior, and Skinner wrote in 1977 that *The Behavior of Organisms* "has long been out of date . . . but I am continually surprised at how little of the book is actually wrong or no longer relevant." We would expect this in a document that defines a successful paradigm and research program: It laid out the "hard core" of the program, as well as some specific hypotheses in the "protective belt." What is out of date are only the latter; the hard core remains relevant.

In *Behavior of Organisms* Skinner distinguished two kinds of learned behavior, each of which had been studied before but not clearly differentiated. The first category Skinner called *respondent* behavior, or learning, studied by Pavlov. This category is properly called *reflex* behavior, for a respondent is a behavior *elicited* by a definite stimulus, whether unconditioned or conditioned. It loosely corresponds to "involuntary" behavior, such as the salivary responses studied by Pavlov. The second category Skinner called *operant* behavior or learning, which corresponds loosely to "voluntary" behavior. Operant behavior cannot be elicited, but is simply emitted from time to time. However, an operant's probability of occurrence may be raised if its emission is followed by an event called a *reinforcer;* after reinforcement it will be more likely to occur again in similar circumstances. Thorndike's puzzle boxes define an operant learning situation: the imprisoned cat emits a variety of behaviors; one of which, such as pressing a lever, leads to escape, which is *reinforcing*. With the cat placed back in the box, the probability of the correct response is now higher than before; the operant response, lever-pressing, has been strengthened. These three things—the setting in which the behavior occurs (the puzzle box), the reinforced response (lever-pressing), and the reinforcer (escape)—collectively define the *contingencies of reinforcement*. The experimental analysis of behavior consists of the systematic description of contingencies of reinforcement as they occur in all forms of animal or human behavior.

These contingencies are analyzed in Darwinian fashion. Emitted behavior is parallel to random variation in species' traits. Reinforcement from the environment follows some operants and not others; the former are strengthened and the latter are extinguished. The environment's selection pressures select favorable responses through the process of operant learning, just as successful species flourish while others become extinct. Skinner considers the experimental analysis of behavior to be part of biology, concerned with explaining an individual's behavior as the product of the environment resulting from a process analogous to that which produces species. There is no room in either discipline for vitalism, mind, or teleology. All behavior, whether learned or unlearned, is a product of an individual's reinforcement history or his genetic make up. Behavior is never a product of intention or will.

Skinner's definition of the operant and its controlling contingencies distinguishes him from other behaviorists in three frequently misunderstood ways. First, operant responses are never elicited. Suppose we train a rat to press a lever in a Skinner box (or "experimental space," as Skinner would call it), reinforcing the bar press only when a certain light is on above the bar. The rat will soon come to bar-press whenever the light comes on. It may appear that the stimulus of the light elicits the response—but according to Skinner, this is not so. It merely sets the occasion for reinforcement. It enables the organism to discriminate a reinforcing situation from a nonreinforcing situation, and is thus called a *discriminative stimulus*. It does not elicit bar-pressing as an unconditioned stimulus or a conditioned stimulus elicited salivation in Pavlov's dogs. Thus Skinner denies that he is an S-R psychologist, for that formula implies a reflexive link between a response and some stimulus, a link that exists only for respondents. Watson adhered to the S-R formula, for he applied the classical conditioning paradigm to all behavior. The spirit of radical behaviorism is so clearly Watsonian that many critics mistake Watson's analysis of behavior for Skinner's.

There is a second way in which Skinner is not an S-R psychologist. He says that the organism may be affected by controlling variables that need not be considered stimuli. This is clearest with respect to motivation. Motivation was seen by Hullians and Freudians as a matter of drive-stimulus reduction: Food deprivation leads to unpleasant stimuli associated with the hunger drive, and the organism acts to reduce them. Skinner sees no reason for the drive-stimuli. They are examples of mentalistic thinking that may be eliminated by directly linking food deprivation to change in behavior. Depriving an organism of food is an observable procedure that will affect an organism's behavior in lawful ways, and there is no gain in speaking of "drives" or their associated stimuli. A measurable variable, although not conceived in stimulus terms, may be causally linked to changes in observable behavior. The organism is truly a locus of variables, and whether or not the variables are stimuli of which the organism is aware is irrelevant, which renders the S-R formulation less applicable to Skinner.

The third important aspect of the operant concerns the definition. Behavior for Skinner is merely movement in space. This definition recalls Democritus's statement, "Only atoms and the void exist in reality," but Skinner is careful not to define operants as simple movements. To begin with, an operant is not a response; it is a class of responses. The cat in the puzzle box may press the escape lever in different ways on different trials. Each is a different *response* in that its form is different at each occurrence, but all are members of the same *operant,* for each response is controlled by the same contingencies of reinforcement. Whether the cat butts the lever with its head or pushes it with its paw is unimportant—both are the same operant. Similarly, two otherwise identical movements may be instances of different operants if they are controlled by different contingencies. You may raise your hand to pledge allegiance to the flag, to swear to tell the truth in court, or to wave to a friend. The movements may be the same in each case, but each is a different operant, for the setting and reinforcement (the contingencies of reinforcement) are different in each case. This proves to be especially important in explaining verbal behavior: "Sock" is at least two operants controlled either by (a) a soft foot covering or (b) a punch in the nose. Earlier behaviorists such as Hull tried to define responses in purely physical terms as movements and were criticized for ignoring the meaning of behavior. A word, it was argued, is more than a puff of air; it has meaning. Skinner agrees, but places meaning in the contingencies of reinforcement, not the speaker's mind.

These are the most important theoretical ideas that guide the experimental analysis of behavior. When Skinner asked "Are theories of learning necessary?" and answered "No," he did not intend to eschew all theory. What he rejected was theory that refers to the unobserved hypothetical entities he considers fictions, be they ego, cognitive map, or apperception. He did accept theory in the Machian sense as being a summary of the ways in which observable variables correlate, but no more. But Skinner is additionally guided by theoretical assumptions at the level of the disciplinary matrix, and it is those we have just reviewed.

Skinner also defined an innovative and radical methodology, or shared exemplar, in his *Behavior of Organisms.* First, he chose an experimental situation that preserved the fluidity of behavior, refusing to chop it up into arbitrary and artificial "trials." An organism is placed in a space and reinforced for some behavior that it may make at any time. The behavior may be closely observed as it continuously changes over time, not as it abruptly changes with each trial. Second, the experimenter seeks to exert maximal control over the organism's environment, so that the experimenter may manipulate, or hold constant, independent variables and so directly observe how they change behavior. Third, a very simple, yet somewhat artificial response is chosen for study. In Skinner's own work this has typically been either a rat pressing a lever or a pigeon pecking a key to obtain food or water. Choosing such an operant makes each response unambiguous, easily observed, and easily counted by machines to produce a cumulative record of responses. Finally, Skinner defined rate of responding as the basic datum of analysis. It is easily quantified; it is appealing as a measure of response probability; and it has been found to vary in lawful ways with changes in independent variables. Such a simple experimental situation stands in contrast to the relative lack of control found in Thorndike's puzzle boxes or Hull's and Tolman's mazes. The situation is capable of defining precise puzzles for the investigator, since it imposes so much control on the organism. The investigator need only draw on previous research to select what variables to manipulate and observe their effects on response rate. There is minimal ambiguity about what to manipulate or measure. Skinner provided a well-defined exemplar shared by all who practice the experimental analysis of behavior.

A final methodological point also sets Skinner apart from the other behaviorists. Skinner completely dispenses with statistics or statistically dictated experimental design. He believes statistics are necessary only for those who infer an inner state from behavior. Such researchers see actual behavior as indirect measures of the inner state, contaminated by "noise," and thus they must run many subjects and treat data statistically to get measures of this hypothetical state. Skinner studies behavior itself, so there can be no "noise." All behavior is to be explained; none may be explained away as irrelevant or as "error variance." His experimental paradigm gives such clear-cut results and allows such control that "noise" does not occur. As a result, those who practice the experimental analysis of behavior run only a few subjects (often for long periods) and do not use statistics. The statistics are unnecessary, for one can see in graphic records of behavior how response rate changes as variables are altered; no inference is necessary.

The research that results from these guiding assumptions has a clear normal science cast. Skinner asserts that his and his followers' research tests no hypotheses but simply extends the experimental analysis of behavior piece by piece into new territory. For Kuhn, the puzzle-solving rather than hypothesis-testing character of normal science is one of its defining features, for normal science research extends the paradigm rather than tests it. The appeal of well-defined normal science is attested by the fact that the experimental analysis of behavior has many practitioners, so many that it has its own division in the APA.

Skinner has his own clear picture of the experimental analysis of behavior's paradigm. In commenting on graduate training Skinner remarks that his students would be ignorant of learning theory, cognitive psychology, and most of sensory psychology or mental measurement. On the methodological side they would "never see a memory drum" (Evans 1968). Scientific training such as this would surely produce the Kuhnian normal scientist we described in Chapter 1. (Interestingly, such a training program was instituted for a while at Columbia University after World War II [Krantz 1973].)

It should be noted that the practice of a unique normal science within the larger body of psychology exacts a price. The experimental analysts have established their own journals, one in 1958 (*Journal of the Experimental Analysis of Behavior*), and one in 1967 (*Journal of Applied Behavioral Analysis*). A study of citations in articles appearing in the first has shown that from 1958 to 1969 writers in *JEAB* cited their own journal more and more, and others less and less, indicating a growing isolation of the experimental analysis of behavior from psychology as a whole (Krantz 1973). The establishment of their own division in the APA underscores this isolation. Like Freud, Skinner undoubtedly views this isolation with equanimity, for he, just as Freud, feels he is on the correct track toward a scientific psychology while everyone else remains trapped in the prescientific past.

Interpreting Human Behavior

In his *Behavior of Organisms* Skinner carefully articulated his experimental analysis of behavior as a paradigm for animal research. In the 1950s, while other behaviorists were liberalizing their brands of behaviorism, Skinner began to extend his radical behaviorism to human behavior without changing any of his fundamental concepts. Skinner viewed human behavior as animal behavior not significantly different from the behavior of the rats and pigeons he had studied in the laboratory.

His most important undertaking was to interpret language within the framework of radical behaviorism. As a would-be writer Skinner was naturally interested in language, and some of his earliest, albeit unpublished research was on speech perception. His ideas on language were set forth in a series of lectures at Harvard University and then in a book, *Verbal Behavior* (1957). At the same time, Skinner was also concerned with using his radical behaviorism and experimental analysis of behavior as bases for the construction of a Utopian society and the reconstruction of existing society. His first extended treatment of these problems came in *Walden II* (1948) and *Science and Human Behavior* (1953).

Although "most of the experimental work responsible for the advance of the experimental analysis of behavior has been carried out on other species . . . the results have proved to be surprisingly free of species restrictions . . . and its methods can be extended to human behavior without serious modification." So writes Skinner in what he considers his most important work, *Verbal Behavior*. The final goal of the experimental analysis of behavior is a science of human behavior using the same principles first applied to animals. Extension of his analysis to human behavior increasingly preoccupied Skinner after World War II.

The scope and nature of the extension is well conveyed in an interesting paper, "A Lecture in 'Having' a Poem," about how he came to write his only published poem, partially quoted above. In this paper he draws an analogy between "having a baby" and "having a poem": "A person produces a poem and a woman produces a baby, and we call the person a poet and the woman a mother. Both are essential as loci in which vestiges of the past come together in certain combinations." Just as a mother makes no positive contribution to the creation of the baby she carries, so "the act of composition is no more an act of creation than 'having' the bits and pieces" that form the poem. In such case something new is created, but there is no creator. Again we see the hand of Darwin: A baby is a random combination of genes that may be selected for survival or may die. A poem is a collection of bits and pieces of verbal behavior, some of which are selected, some of which are rejected, for appearance in the poem. As Darwin showed that no divine Mind was necessary to explain the production and evolution of natural species, so Skinner seeks to show that no human mind is necessary for the production of verbal behavior or language, man's unique possession according to Descartes.

His argument is worked out in most detail in *Verbal Behavior,* which appeared in 1957. It is a complex and subtle book that defies easy summary. Only a few salient points may be discussed here. It is a work of interpretation only. Skinner reported no experiments, and sought only to establish the plausibility of applying his analysis to language, not its reality. Further, to say he is analyzing language is misleading; the title of his book is *Verbal Behavior,* behavior whose reinforcement is mediated by other persons. The definition includes an animal behaving under the control of an experimenter, who together form a "genuine verbal community." It excludes the listener in a verbal interchange, except insofar as the listener reinforces speech (for example, by replies or compliance with demands) or acts as a discriminative stimulus (one speaks differently to one's best friend and to one's teacher). The definition makes no reference to the process of communication we usually assume takes place during speech. Skinner's account may be contrasted with that of Wundt, who excluded animals from consideration, examined the linguistic processes of both speaker and listener, and attempted to describe the communication of a *Gesamtvorstellung* from the mind of a speaker to the mind of a hearer.

Nevertheless, *Verbal Behavior* is basically about what we ordinarily consider language, or more accurately speech, for Skinner analyzed only real utterances spoken in analyzable environments, not the hypothetical abstract entity "language." Skinner introduced a number of technical concepts in his discussion of verbal behavior. To show the flavor of his analysis, we will briefly discuss his concept of the "tact," because it corresponds roughly to the problem of universals, and because Skinner considers it the most important verbal operant.

We apply the three-term set of contingencies of reinforcement, stimulus, response, and reinforcement. A *tact* is a verbal *operant response* under the *stimulus control* of some part of the physical environment, and correct use of tacts is reinforced by the verbal community. So a child is reinforced by parents for emitting the sound "doll" in the presence of a doll (Skinner 1957). Such an operant "makes contact with" the physical environment and is called a *tact*. Skinner reduced the traditional notion of reference or naming to a functional relationship between a response, its discriminative stimuli, and its reinforcer. The situation is exactly analogous to the functional relation holding between a rat's bar-press in a Skinner box, the discriminative stimulus that sets the occasion for the response, and the food that reinforces it. Skinner's analysis of the tact is a straightforward extension of the experimental analysis of behavior paradigm to a novel situation.

Skinner extended his analysis to metaphor, metonymy, and the subtleties of "tact" behavior, but we need not pursue them. The essential extension of the paradigm has been shown. Two points deserve further comment. First, Skinner's analysis of the tact is the purest nominalism ever proposed by anyone tackling the problem of universals. A noun is now indeed no more than a puff of air emitted under certain definable contingencies of reinforcement. There is no Platonic Form of cat, no Aristotelian essence of catness, no Ockhamist mental concept of Cat, only a certain verbal habit. Skinner pursues Hume's reduction of knowledge to habit to its final end, substituting purely behavioral for mental habits. The essence of "cat" is no more than the contingencies of reinforcement governing its utterance.

The second point raises an important general aspect about Skinner's treatment of human behavior, his notion of private stimuli. Skinner believes that earlier behaviorists (he calls them methodological behaviorists) such as Tolman and Hull were wrong to exclude private events (such as mental images, toothaches) from behaviorism simply because such events are unobservable. Skinner holds that part of each person's environment includes the world inside her or his skin, those stimuli to which the person has privileged access. Such stimuli may be private but they can control behavior and so must be included in any behaviorist analysis of human behavior. Many verbal statements are under such control, including complex tacts. For example: "My tooth aches" is a kind of tacting response controlled by a certain kind of painful inner stimulation.

This simple analysis implies a momentous conclusion. For how do we come to be able to make such statements as the private tact? Skinner's answer is that the verbal community has trained us to observe our private stimuli by reinforcing utterances that refer to them. It is useful for parents to know what is distressing a child, so they attempt to teach a child self-reporting verbal behaviors. "My tooth aches" indicates a visit to the dentist, not the podiatrist. Such responses thus have Darwinian survival value. It is these self-observed private stimuli that constitute consciousness. It therefore follows that human consciousness is a product of the reinforcing practices of a verbal community. A person raised by a community that did not reinforce self-description would not be conscious in anything but the sense of being awake. The person would have no self-consciousness.

Self-description also allows Skinner to explain apparently purposive verbal behaviors without reference to intention or purpose. For example, "I am looking for my glasses" seems to describe my intentions, but Skinner (1957) argues: "Such behavior must be regarded as equivalent to *When I have behaved in this way in the past, I have found my glasses and have then stopped behaving in this way.*" Intention is a mentalistic term Skinner has reduced to the physicalistic description of one's bodily state.

The last topic discussed in *Verbal Behavior* is thinking, the most apparently mental of all human activities. Skinner continued, however, to exorcise mentalism by arguing that "thought is simply *behavior.*" Skinner rejected Watson's view that thinking is subvocal behavior, for much covert behavior is not verbal, yet can still control overt behavior in a way characteristic of "thinking": *I think I shall be going* can be translated *I find myself going,*" a reference to self-observed, but nonverbal stimuli.

The simplicity of Skinner's argument is hard to grasp. Once one denies the existence of the mind, as Skinner does, all that is left is behavior, so thinking must be behavior under the control of the contingencies of reinforcement. The thought of B. F. Skinner is, in his terms, simply "the sum total of his responses to the complex world in which he lived." "Thought" is simply a tact that we have learned to apply to certain forms of behavior, a tact Skinner would ask us to unlearn, or at least not teach to our children. For Skinner does not merely wish to describe behavior, human or animal, he wants to control it, control being a fundamental part of the experimental analysis of behavior. Skinner believes that current control of human behavior, based as it is on mental fictions, is ineffective at best and harmful at worst.

During World War II, Skinner worked on a behavioral guidance system for air-to-surface missiles called "Project Orcon" for *Or*ganic *Con*trol. He trained pigeons to peck at a projected image of the target that the missile they were imprisoned in was to seek out. Their pecking operated controls on the missile so that it followed its target until it struck the target, destroying target and pigeons alike. Skinner achieved such complete control of the pigeons' behavior that they could carry out the most difficult tracking maneuvers during simulated attacks. The work impressed him with the possibility of a thorough control of any organism's behavior. Skinner's superiors found the project implausible, and no pigeon-guided missiles ever flew. Shortly afterward, however, Skinner wrote his most widely read book, *Walden II,* a utopian novel based on the principles of the experimental analysis of behavior.

In the book, two characters represent Skinner: Frazier (an experimental psychologist and founder of Walden II, an experimental utopian community) and Burris (a skeptical visitor ultimately won over to membership in Walden II). Near the end Frazier speaks to Burris: "I've had only one idea in my life—a true *idée fixe.* . . . The idea of having my own way. 'Control' expresses it, I think. The control of human behavior, Burris." Frazier goes on to describe Walden II as the final laboratory and proving ground of the experimental analysis of behavior: "Nothing short of Walden II will suffice." Finally Frazier exclaims: "Well, what do you say to the design of personalities? the control of temperament? Give me the specifications and I'll give you the man! . . . Think of the possibilities! A society in which there is no failure, no boredom, no duplication of effort. . . . Let us control the lives of our children and see what we can make of them."

We have met the *idée fixe* of control before in the history of behaviorism. Frazier's claim to custom-make personalities recalls Watson's claim to custom-make the careers of infants. We have seen how important the desire for social control in Progressivism was to the favorable reaction to Watson's behaviorism. Skinner is heir to the Progressive desire to scientifically control human lives in the interest of society, more specifically the survival of society, the ultimate Darwinian and Skinnerian value. He is also heir, and consciously so, to the tradition of Enlightenment optimism about human progress. Skinner asks us, in an otherwise disillusioned age, not to give up Rousseau's utopian dream, but to build a Utopia on the principles of the experimental analysis of behavior. If pigeons' behavior can be controlled so that the birds guide missiles to their death, so a human being, whose behavior is likewise determined, can be controlled to be happy, productive, and to feel free and dignified. *Walden II* was Skinner's first attempt to describe his vision.

THE ROOTS OF COGNITIVE SCIENCE (1943–1958)

While Skinner's radical behaviorism continued the Watsonian tradition of rejecting all inner causes of behavior, behaviorists, with Hull and Tolman, did not. After World War II one class of inner cause, cognitive processes, received increasing attention. Psychologists treated cognition from a variety of perspectives, including neo-Hullian "liberalized" or informal behaviorism, and a diverse range of eclectic accounts American and European. In the long run the most important approach to cognition grew out of mathematics and electrical engineering, and had little or nothing to do with psychology and its problems. This was the creation of the field of *artificial intelligence* by the invention of the modern digital computer during World War II.

Informal Behaviorism

Few behavioralists were willing to agree with Skinner that organisms were "empty," that it was illegitimate to postulate, as Hull had, mechanisms taking place within the organism linking together stimulus and response. As Charles Osgood (born 1916) put it, "Most contemporary behaviorists [can] be characterized as 'frustrated empty boxers'" (Osgood 1956). They were aware of the pitfalls of "junkshop psychology," in which mental faculties or entities were multiplied as fast as the behaviors to be explained. Yet they increasingly believed that behavior, especially "the phenomena of meaning and intention, so obviously displayed in human language behavior, entirely escape the single-stage conception" of blackbox S-R psychology (Osgood 1957). It was obvious to psychologists concerned with the human higher mental processes that people possess "symbolic processes," the ability to represent the world internally, and that human responses were controlled by these symbols, instead of being directly controlled by external stimulation. Their problem was avoiding "junkshop psychology": "What is the least amount of additional baggage needed to handle symbolic processes?" (Osgood 1956).

They solved it by building on Hull's concept of the "pure stimulus act," turning it into the concept of two-stage mediational S-R theory. Hull had proposed that some behaviors exist only to stimulate some further response by the organism. If you ask people to describe how they tie their shoes, for example, they will typically go through the finger motions of shoe-tying while verbally describing what they are doing. Such behavior is an example of Hull's "pure stimulus act." It is not too hard to imagine these acts occurring internally, without any outward show. For example, if asked, "How many windows do you have at home?" you will likely walk through a mental house and count the windows. Such processes *mediate* between external stimuli and our responses to them. The neo-Hullian psychologists conceived of human symbolic processes as internal continuations of S-R chains:

$$S \longrightarrow \{r \longrightarrow s\} \longrightarrow R$$

An external stimulus elicits an internal mediating response, which in turn has internal stimulus properties; and it is these internal stimuli, rather than external ones, that actually elicit overt behavior. "The great advantage of this solution is that, since each stage is an S-R process, we can simply transfer all the conceptual machinery of single-stage S-R psychology into this new model without new postulation" (Osgood 1956). So cognitive processes could be admitted into the body of behavior theory without giving up any of the rigor of the S-R formulation, and without inventing any uniquely human mental processes. Behavior could still be explained in terms of S-R behavior chains, except that now some of the chains took place invisibly within the organism. Behavioralists now had a language with which to discuss meaning, language, memory, problem solving, and other behaviors apparently beyond the reach of radical behaviorism.

The approach defined by Osgood had many inventors and practitioners. Osgood applied it to language with especial reference to the problem of meaning, which he tried to measure behaviorally with his semantic differential scale. Irving Maltzman (for example, 1955) and Albert Goss (for example, 1961) applied it to problem solving and concept formation. The broadest program of human psychology in the liberalized vein was social learning theory, led by Neal Miller (born 1909). Miller and others at Hull's Institute for Human Relations at Yale tried to construct a psychology that would do justice to Freud's insights into the human condition, but remain within the objective realm of S-R psychology. They downplayed the axioms and quantification of Hull's animal work in order to incorporate humans within the S-R framework, and added in mediation as a way of talking about mental life in terms more precise than Freud's. Miller's 1959 description of his brand of behaviorism, including the whole neo-Hullian mediational camp, as "liberalized S-R theory" is apt. Social learning theorists did not abandon S-R theory, they only loosened its restrictions in order to be able to encompass human language, culture, and psychotherapy.

An outstanding example of the ability of mediational theory to assimilate human symbolic processes into the S-R framework was Howard and Tracy Kendler's work on reversal shift learning. Their teacher, Kenneth Spence, had worked out an impressive theory of discrimination learning in animals, assuming them to do no more than associate external stimuli to overt responses, what Osgood called single-stage S-R learning. However, as more complex forms of discrimination experiments were tried on animals and humans, some peculiar things began to happen.

Consider the discrimination problem pictured in Figure 13-1. We may require an organism to discriminate the stimuli shown under Preshift Training, rewarding

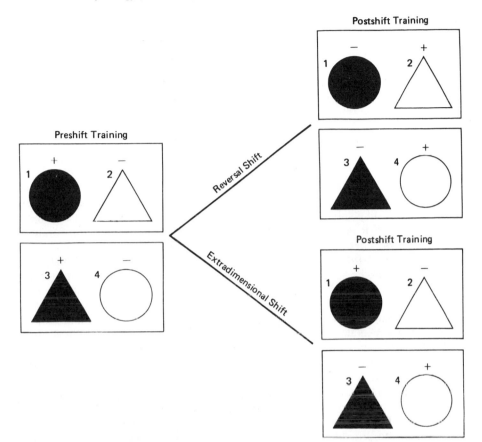

FIGURE 13-1   Discrimination shift learning paradigm involving a comparison between a reversal (RS) and extradimensional shift (EDS). For each pair of discriminanda, plus indicates reinforcement; minus indicates nonreinforcement. A counterbalanced design is conventionally used so that each cue (*black, white, circle,* and *triangle*) is correct for one-fourth of the subjects during both the preshift and postshift problems. (Adapted from Kendler and Kendler 1975.)

responses (say, bar-pressing) only to the stimuli marked ''+'' and not those marked ''−''. Soon the organism will only press the bar when + stimuli are present and not otherwise. This is so far only simple discrimination learning as described in the last chapter. After this initial learning, we then change the contingencies of reinforcement as shown under Postshift Training in one of two ways, each without informing the organism of the change, but simply requiring a new discrimination to be learned. In either case the reinforced responses are marked +, the nonreinforced ones marked −. The point of the experiment is to find out which kind of shift in contingencies will be more easily learned.

According to Hull's theory, as modified by Spence, what the learner acquires during preshift training is a set of S-R associations. The learner must learn to bar-press (R) to stimuli 1 and 3, but not to bar-press (−R) to stimuli 2 and 4. Four S-R habits are learned: (1) $S_1 \rightarrow R$; (2) $S_2 \rightarrow -R$; (3) $S_3 \rightarrow R$; (4) $S_4 \rightarrow -R$. Given these four habits, a learner should find the extradimensional shift easier. For in an extradimensional shift two habits are still correct, (1) $S_1 \rightarrow R$ and (2) $S_2 \rightarrow -R$, while two habits must be unlearned and replaced: (3) $S_3 \rightarrow R$ is incorrect and must be replaced by $S_3 \rightarrow -R$, and (4) $S_4 \rightarrow -R$ is incorrect and must be replaced by $S_4 \rightarrow R$. In a reversal shift, however, all the earlier habits must be unlearned and replaced with new ones.

Research on this problem began during World War II and revealed an interesting pattern. Animals in a discrimination shift procedure behaved as predicted by the simple S-R model, finding extradimensional shifts easier than reversal shifts. However, college students responded to the shifts in the opposite way, preferring reversal to extradimensional shifts. Further, when children were the subjects, it was found that the younger the child, the more he or she behaved according to S-R theory, that is, like animals. These findings present an anomaly for Hullian theory. Hull's laws of S-R learning are found not to be the same across different species or even across members of the same species at different ages.

In the mid-1950s Howard Kendler proposed a "mediational" analysis of these findings in the spirit of informal behaviorism's moderate centralism. Kendler suggested that the single-stage S-R laws applied to animal learning, but that humans possess central and developing cognitive processes—including most importantly language—that modify the laws of learning. These central responses *mediate* between environmental stimuli and overt response. According to this model an environmental stimulus elicits a central, covert symbolic response: $S \rightarrow r$. This central response has covert stimulus properties: $r \rightarrow s$. These stimulus properties then control overt behavior: $s \rightarrow R$. Thus any cognitively mediated behavior is an associative chain of stimulus-response events, some of which are symbolic: $S \rightarrow r \rightarrow s \rightarrow R$. This scheme is in full accord with Miller's working assumption that central responses ($r \rightarrow s$) obey the same behavioral laws as overt responses ($S \rightarrow R$). According to informal behaviorism the brain functions like the body, only covertly.

The mediational apparatus may be used to explain the apparently anomalous behavior of the college students. The adult subject makes a mediational response (r) to the stimuli to be discriminated. We may regard theses responses as implicit labels for the stimuli that categorize them according to the two stimulus dimensions defining the four stimuli. In Figure 13-1 two dimensions, brightness and shape, define the stimuli. The subject learns to make the mediational response "brightness" to the stimuli, because this is the dimension relevant to the preshift training where black figures are reinforced and white ones are not. The mediational association $r_{brightness} - s_{brightness}$ controls the terminal overt response: to press the lever when black stimuli are present. We may write what is learned as follows in S-R language.

$$S \rightarrow r \xrightarrow[\text{brightness}]{} s \xrightarrow[\text{brightness}]{} R \text{ black (press lever)}$$

What happens after each possible shift? In the reversal shift, brightness is still the relevant stimulus dimension, so the mediational response is correct, and all the subject must learn is a new terminal response, pressing the lever when the white stimuli are present:

$$S \rightarrow r \xrightarrow[\text{brightness}]{} s \xrightarrow[\text{brightness}]{} R_{\text{white (press lever)}}$$

However, when the shift is extradimensional, the terminal responses are wrong and the mediational response is wrong. Brightness is no longer the relevant stimulus dimension; shape is, so the subject must learn the S-R chain.

$$S \longrightarrow r_{shape} \longrightarrow s_{shape} \longrightarrow R_{circle} \text{ (press lever).}$$

There is more to learn in the extradimensional shift case, and so it naturally takes longer.

The Kendlers' analysis of discrimination shift learning is an example of a paradigm successfully responding to anomalous findings. However, the Kendlers and Miller did not leave the paradigm intact, for strong versions of peripheralism and phylogenetic continuity had to be modified to accommodate the demands of the higher mental processes of human beings. We must recognize, however, that these changes were not revolutionary. As Miller states, S-R theory was liberalized; it was not overthrown. Later on, some would look back and see shift learning as a crisis-inducing anomaly, but it was not. The Kendlers successfully met its challenge within a modified S-R pattern.

So mediation theory proved capable of handling a troublesome finding. The cost was giving up a unified account of animal and human learning, but the gain was making minimal concessions to human mental capacities. In line with the old Spencerian paradigm, human beings were not qualitatively different from animals, only quantitatively so. All learning was learning by S R association (Osgood 1956), but human learning involved internal associations as well as external ones.

While it was a major—perhaps the major—theoretical position in the 1950s, mediational behaviorism proved to be a bridge linking the inferential behavioralism of the 1930s and 1940s to the inferential behavioralism of the 1980s: cognitive psychology. The diagrams of mediational processes quickly became incredibly cumbersome (see, for example, the Osgood papers already cited). More important, there was no very good reason to think of processes one couldn't see anyway as little chains of r's and s's. The mediationalists' commitment to internalizing S-R language resulted primarily from their desire to preserve rigor and avoid the apparent unscientific character of "junkshop psychology." In essence, they lacked any other language with which to discuss the mental processes in a clear and disciplined fashion, and took the only course they saw open to them. However, when a new language of power, rigor, and precision came along—the language of computer programming—it proved easy for mediational psychologists to abandon their r-s life raft for the ocean liner of information processing.

Early Cognitive Theories

Not all psychologists interested in cognition worked within the framework of neo-Hullian mediational psychology. In Europe cognitive development had been studied by the Swiss psychologist Jean Piaget (1896–1981) since the 1920s. In the United States social psychologists had gradually abandoned the concept of the group mind in the first decades of the twentieth century, gradually defining it as it is today, as the study of people in groups. During the war social psychologists had been concerned to study attitudes, how persuasion and propaganda changes attitudes, and the relation of attitudes to personality. After the war social psychologists continued to develop theories about how people form, integrate, and act on beliefs. Finally, Jerome Bruner studied how personality dynamics shape people's perceptions of the world, and how people solve complex problems.

Genetic Epistemology

Although European psychology in the early twentieth century was quiescent, it was by no means extinct. Piaget was a most important European psychologist. Piaget, like Freud and Wundt before him, had begun with purely biological interests, but eventually found himself practicing an innovative psychology. In Piaget's case the influences that drew him away from biology were threefold. First, he maintained a strong interest in the questions of epistemology, although he believed traditional philosophies to be too speculative and unscientific. Second, he experienced psychoanalysis with one of Freud's pupils, and studied with Jung's mentor, Bleuler, at Zurich. Third, he worked with Alfred Binet's collaborator, Theophile Simon, administering intelligence tests to children. Out of this eclectic background Piaget formulated a unique cognitive psychology. The traditional problems of epistemology are important: What is knowledge, and what are people that they may have knowledge? To Piaget, these questions should admit of a scientific answer based on sound theory and empirical research. In particular, Piaget felt it should be possible to trace the psychological growth of knowledge in children as they grow up by studying their reactions to intellectual situations, as in intelligence tests, followed up by probing questions as in psychoanalysis. Finally, Piaget's biological orientation shines through in his conception of knowledge as a set of cognitive structures that enable a child to adapt to the environment. Piaget calls his field of study *genetic epistemology,* the study of the origins of knowledge in child development.

As one would expect with a European psychologist, Piaget shows strong Kantian influences. The titles of many of his works are the names of Kant's transcendental categories: *The Child's Conception of Space, The Child's Conception of Number, The Child's Conception of Time,* and many more. In other ways, too, Piaget is distinctly European. Like Wundt, Piaget is interested in the general human mind, which Piaget calls the *epistemic subject,* not in individuals or their unique lives. Also like Wundt, Piaget is less interested in applied aspects of his work than are Americans, although he has written on education. The question of whether training can accelerate the course of cognitive growth Piaget calls "The American Question," for it is not asked in Europe. In true pragmatic fashion Americans want to know how to get knowledge faster and more efficiently.

Piaget began his studies of children's knowledge in the 1920s, but—after a brief flurry of interest—his work was largely ignored in the United States. It was only in the 1960s that his work was rediscovered, in a context to be discussed in the next chapter. From 1930 to 1960 Piaget's thought was clearly out of step with American behaviorism, and his works consequently went largely unread and untranslated.

The details of Piaget's theory are complex, but Piaget is no behaviorist. Genetic epistemology is concerned with human knowledge, not human behavior, and Piaget's theory explicitly attempts to characterize the mental structures that guide a child's knowledge of the world. Furthermore he rejects associationism and atomism in favor of *structuralism,* a European philosophy that explains human behavior by reference to unobserved, abstract, mathematically describable structures.

During his long intellectual lifetime Piaget systematically pursued his own research program, paying only occasional attention to behaviorism. Thus, although he was little read before 1960, Piaget and his genetic epistemology constituted a sophisticated alternative to behaviorism ready to be picked up when behaviorism faltered. After 1960, as young psychologists became disenchanted with behaviorism, Piaget would be increasingly read, translated, and researched by students of cognitive development.

Social Psychology

Social psychology is the study of the person as a social being, and so has roots going back to the Greek political thinkers and to Hobbes's first political science. We have said little about it before because as a field it is exceedingly eclectic, unified by no coherent vision of humanity. It draws our attention now because during the 1940s and 1950s it continued to employ mental concepts of a common-sense sort. We will briefly consider one theory widely influential in the 1950s and early 1960s, Leon Festinger's theory of cognitive dissonance.

Festinger's theory is about a person's beliefs and their interaction. He holds that beliefs may agree with one another, or they may clash. When beliefs clash they induce an unpleasant state called *cognitive dissonance,* which the person tries to reduce. For example, a nonsmoker who is persuaded that cigarettes cause lung cancer will feel no dissonance, for her or his belief that smoking causes cancer agrees with and supports her or his refusal to smoke. However, a smoker who comes to believe smoking causes cancer will feel cognitive dissonance, for the decision to smoke clashes with this new belief. The smoker will act to reduce the dissonance, perhaps by giving up smoking. However, it is quite common to manage dissonance in other ways. For example, a smoker may simply avoid antismoking information in order to avoid dissonance.

Festinger's theory provoked much research. One classic study appears to challenge the law of effect. Festinger and a collaborator, J. Merrill Carlsmith, devised some extremely boring tasks for subjects to perform, such as turning screws for a long time. Then the experimenter got the subject to agree to tell a waiting subject that the task was fun. Some subjects were paid $20 for telling the lie; others were paid only $1. According to the theory, the $20 subjects should feel no dissonance: The large payment justified their little lie. However, the $1 subjects should feel dissonance: They were telling a lie for a paltry sum. One way to resolve this dissonance would be to convince ones self that the task was in fact fun, for if one believed this, telling another subject that it was fun would be no lie. After the whole experiment was over, another experimenter interviewed the subjects and discovered that the $1 subjects voted the task significantly more enjoyable than the $20 subjects, as Festinger's theory predicted. The finding appears inconsistent with the law of effect, for we might expect that a $20 reward for saying the experiment was fun would change one's report about the enjoyability of the experiment more than a $1 reward.

What is most important about the theory of cognitive dissonance for our purposes is that it is a cognitive theory—a theory about mental entities, in this case about a person's beliefs. It is not an informal behaviorist theory, for Festinger did not conceive of beliefs as mediating responses, but, in common-sense terms, as beliefs that control behavior. The theory of cognitive dissonance and other cognitive theories in social psychology constitute a vigorous cognitive psychology outside the

orbit of strict behaviorism. Festinger's 1957 book, *A Theory of Cognitive Dissonance,* makes no reference to behaviorist ideas. Social psychologists rarely challenged behaviorism, but their field was an alternative to it.

The "New Look in Perception"

Shortly after the war a new approach to the study of perception arose. Dubbed
the "New Look" in perception, it was led by Jerome S. Bruner (born 1915). The
New Look arose from an attempt to unify several different areas of psychology—
perception, personality, and social psychology—and from a desire to refute the
prevalent conception going back at least to Hume and strongly present in S-R
behavior theory, that perception was a passive process by which a stimulus impressed (Hume's term) itself on the perceiver. Bruner and his colleagues proposed a
view of perception in which the perceiver takes an active role, rather than being a
passive register of sense data. Bruner and others did a variety of studies to support
the idea that a perceiver's personality and social background play a role in affecting
what the perceiver sees. The most famous and controversial of these studies concern
perceptual defense, and raise the possibility of subliminal perception. Bruner and
others in the New Look movement presented words to subjects for brief intervals, as
had Wundt in his studies of the span of consciousness. However, these modern
researchers varied the emotional content of the words: some were ordinary or
"neutral" words, others were obscene or "taboo" words. Bruner and his associates found that longer exposures are required for a subject to recognize a taboo word
than to recognize a neutral word. It appears that subjects somehow unconsciously
perceive the negative emotional content of a taboo word and then attempt to repress
its entry into awareness. Subjects will see the word only when the exposure is so
long that they cannot help seeing it.

Research on perceptual defense was extremely controversial for many years,
some psychologists arguing that subjects see taboo words as quickly as neutral
words, falsely denying the experience as long as possible to avoid embarrassment.
The controversy grew heated and has never been fully resolved. What is significant
for us is that the New Look in perception analyzed perception as an active mental
process involving both conscious and unconscious mental activities intervening
between a sensation and a person's response to it. The idea of perceptual defense is
much closer to psychoanalysis than to behaviorism, a fact in part responsible for the
controversy surrounding Bruner's findings. In any event, the New Look was a
cognitive alternative to behaviorism.

A Study of Thinking

Concern with perception and his demonstrations that mind and personality
actively shape it led Bruner to a study of the old "higher mental processes"
(Bruner, Goodnow, and Austin 1956). While he was not a mediational theorist, and
placed his own theorizing in the psychodynamic tradition, Bruner linked his own
interest in cognitive processes to the new mediational S-R theories, and identified a
"revival" "in interest in and investigation of the cognitive processes." In the
landmark book *A Study of Thinking,* Bruner investigated how people form concepts
and categorize new stimuli as members of different conceptual categories. Bruner
and his colleagues presented subjects with arrays of geometrical figures defined

along many dimensions: shape, size, color, and the like. The subject was then asked to figure out what concept the experimenter had in mind by choosing, or being presented with, examples and nonexamples of the experimenter's concept. For example, the concept to be discovered might be "all red triangles," and the experimenter might begin by pointing out to the subject a large red triangle as an example of the concept. The subject would then choose other stimuli from the array and be told whether each was or was not a member of the concept class. For example, if the subject chose a large red square, the subject would be told "No"; and if the subject chose a small red triangle, he or she would be told "Yes." The subject would choose instances until he or she was prepared to guess the definition of the experimenter's concept.

Bruner, Goodnow, and Austin did not view the process of concept learning in terms of learning implicit mediational responses, although some informal behaviorists did. Rather, they looked on concept formation as an active, not reactive, process in which the subject's choices are guided by some strategy constructed to solve the problem. Again, the details of the theory are not important for our purposes. What is important is the mentalistic nature of Bruner's theory. The subject is not seen as a passive connector between S and R or even as linking S-r-s-R, or as a locus of variables. Instead, concept formation is an active intellectual process in which a subject constructs and follows certain strategies and decision procedures that guide (or fail to guide) the subject to the correct concept.

The investigations and theories of the mediational behaviorialists, Piaget, Festinger, and Bruner demonstrate psychologists' revived interest in human cognitive processes following the war. However, while these research programs were vigorous, their theories were due to be assimilated and eclipsed by a different kind of cognitive psychology, whose roots and conceptions lie almost entirely outside the field of psychology altogether. For during World War II there appeared the thinking machine.

Artificial Intelligence

Ever since Descartes, philosophers of the mind and psychologists had been attracted and repelled by the similarity of man and machine. Descartes thought that all human cognitive processes save thinking were carried out by the machinery of the nervous system, and based his divisions of man vs. brute and mind vs. body on his conviction. Pascal feared that Descartes was wrong, since it seemed to him his calculator could think, and turned to the human heart and its faith in God to separate man from machine. Hobbes and La Mettrie embraced, and de Sade reveled in, the idea that people are no more than animal-machines, alarming the romantics who, with Pascal, sought the secret essence of humanity in feeling rather than intellect. Leibniz dreamed of a universal thinking machine, and the English engineer Charles Babbage tried to build one. William James worried about his automatic sweetheart, concluding that a machine could not feel and so could not be human. Watson, with Hobbes and La Mettrie, proclaimed that man is but a machine, and that human salvation lay in accepting that reality and engineering a perfect future, limned by Skinner in *Walden II*. Science fiction writers and filmmakers began to explore the differences, if any, between human and machine in *Rossum's Universal Robots* and *Metropolis*. But no one had yet built a machine that anyone could even hope would emulate human thinking. Until World War II.

Since the time of Newton the trend of science has been the mechanization of the world picture. As we have seen, in the twentieth century psychologists had wrestled with the refuge of teleology, purposive behavior. Hull tried to give a mechanical account of purpose; Tolman first left it in behavior as an observable, later putting it in the organism's cognitive map room; and Skinner tried to dissolve purposes into environmental control of behavior. None of these attempts to deal with purpose is entirely convincing, but for present purposes Tolman's failure is the most revealing. Tolman could be fairly criticized for committing the Cartesian category mistake and building a homunculus (or, in the case of a rat, a ratunculus) into a person's head, and explaining that person's behavior as the outcome of the homunculus's decision making. For a map implies a map reader; there really was a Ghost in Tolman's machine. Psychologists seemed to be on the horns of a trilemma: (1) They could try to explain purposive behavior by reference to inner events, as Tolman did; but this risked inventing a mythical inner Ghost whose behavior was as mysterious as the outer behavior one wanted to explain to begin with. (2) They could try to explain away behavior as purely mechanical, as Hull had, or as subtle and mislabled environmental control of behavior, as Skinner did; but, while suitably scientific and tough minded, this seemed to deny the obvious fact that behavior is goal directed. (3) Or, following Brentano and Wittgenstein they could accept purpose as the irreducible bedrock of human action, neither requiring nor needing explanation; but this denied that psychology could be a science of the same sort as physics, a conclusion unthinkable to psychologists in the grip of physics envy.

Out of scientific work in World War II came the modern high-speed digital computer, bringing with it concepts that made the first alternative more attractive than it had ever been, because they seemed to offer a way around the bogey of the Ghost in the Machine. The most important of these concepts were the idea of *informational feedback* and the concept of the computer *program*. The importance of feedback was grasped immediately; the importance of the idea of programming took longer to be realized, but eventually gave rise to a new solution to the mind-body problem called *functionalism*. What made the concepts of feedback and programming impressive, even commanding, was their association with real machines that seemed to think.

Given the contemporary rivalry between information-processing psychology and radical behaviorism, there is irony in the fact that the concept of feedback, and hence modern cognitive psychology, arose out of the same war problem that Skinner had worked on in his Pelican project. Project ORCON had aimed at the ORganic CONtrol of missiles. Mathematicians and computer scientists aimed at the mechanical control of missiles and other weapons, inventing the modern digital computer. In 1943 three researchers described the concept of informational feedback that lay behind their solution to guiding devices to targets: They showed how purpose and mechanism were not incompatible. As a fact, feedback had been used by engineers since at least the eighteenth century. The achievement of Rosenblueth, Wiener, and Bigelow (1966) was making feedback a scientific concept and describing it in general terms. A good example of a system using feedback is a thermostat and a furnace. You give the thermostat a goal when you set the temperature at which you want to keep your house. The thermostat contains a thermometer that measures the house temperature, and when the temperature falls below the set temperature, it turns on the furnace. As the furnace warms the room, the thermometer registers the change, and turns the furnace off when the correct temperature is reached. Here is a feedback loop of information: The thermostat is sensitive to the state of the room, and based on the information received by its thermometer takes action. The action in turn changes the state of the room, which feeds back to the thermostat, changing its behavior, which in turns influences the room temperature, and so on in an endless cycle.

In a simple way the thermostat and the furnace constitute a purposive organism. Their goal is to maintain a constant temperature, and they are able to respond appropriately to changes in the environment. And there is, of course, no Ghost in the Thermostat. In older times there would have been a servant who read a thermometer and stoked the furnace when necessary; but he has been replaced by a mere machine, and a simple one at that. The promise of the concept of feedback is that it might be possible to analyze all purposive behavior as instances of feedback: The organism has some goal (for example, to get food), is able to measure its distance from the goal (for example, it's at the other end of the maze), and behave so as to reduce and finally eliminate that distance. The Ghost in the Machine, or Tolman's cognitive map reader, could be replaced by complex feedback loops. Practically, too, servants and industrial workers might be replaced by machines capable of doing what before only people could do.

So, machines could be purposive. Were they then intelligent, or at least capable of becoming intelligent? Could they emulate human intelligence? Whether computers were or could be intelligent became the central question of cognitive science, and the question was raised in its modern form by the brilliant mathematician A. M. Turing, who had contributed much to the theory of computers during the war. In 1950 Turing published a paper in *Mind*, "Computing Machinery and Intelligence," that defined the field of artificial intelligence and established the program of cognitive science. "I propose to consider the question, Can machines think?" Turing began. Since the meaning of "think" was so terribly unclear, Turing proposed to set his question more concretely "in terms of a game which we call the 'imitation game.'" Imagine an interrogator talking via computer terminal to two respondents, another human and a computer, without knowing which is which. The game consists in asking questions designed to tell which respondent is the human and which is the computer. Turing proposed that we consider a computer intelligent when it can fool the interrogator into thinking it is the human being. Turing's imitation game has since become known as the Turing Test, and is widely taken to be the criterion of artificial intelligence (AI). Workers in the field of AI aim to create machines that can perform many of the same tasks previously done only by people, ranging from playing chess to assembling automobiles to exploring the surface of Mars.

We have already seen that some psychologists, most notably Hull, had tried to construct learning machines. There were naturally some psychologists, therefore, who were drawn to the computer for a model of learning and purposive behavior. In conversation with Harvard psychologist E. G. Boring, Norbert Wiener asked what the human brain could do that electronic computers could not, moving Boring (1946) to ask the same question as Turing: What would a robot have to do to be called intelligent? After reviewing human intellectual faculties and psychologists' early attempts to mimic them with machines, Boring formulated his own version of the Turing Test: "Certainly a robot whom you could not distinguish from another student would be an extremely convincing demonstration of the mechanical nature of man and the unity of science." For Boring, a thinking robot could carry much metaphysical baggage, since it would vindicate La Mettrie's declaration that man is a machine, and promised to secure psychology a place among the natural sciences. Boring's hopes have become the expectations of contemporary cognitive scientists.

In the early 1950s various attempts were made to create electronic or other mechanical models of learning and other cognitive processes. The English psychologist J. A. Deutsch (1953) built an "electro-mechanical model . . . capable of learning mazes and discrimination . . . [and insightful] reasoning." Similar models were discussed by L. Benjamin Wyckhoff (1954) and James Miller (1955). Slack (1955) used the similarities between feedback and Dewey's reflex arc to attack Hullian S-R theory. Another English psychologist, Donald Broadbent (1957), proposed a mechanical model of attention and short-term memory in terms of balls being dropped into a Y-shaped tube representing various sensory "channels" of information. Broadbent argued that psychologists should think of the input to the senses not as stimuli but as *information*. Information-processing concepts were applied to human attention and memory by George Miller in a now classic paper, "The Magical Number Seven, Plus or Minus Two: Some Limits on Our Capacity for Processing Information" (1956). Miller was moving away from an electic behaviorist position on human learning, and would emerge as one of the leaders of cognitive psychology in the 1960s. In the 1956 paper Miller drew attention to limitations on human attention and memory, and set the stage for the first massive wave of research in information-processing psychology, which concentrated on attention and short-term memory.

In all of these early papers attempting to apply computer concepts to psychology there was some confusion about what was actually doing the thinking. Encouraged by the popular phrase for the computer, "electronic brain," there was a strong tendency to think that it was the electronic device itself that was thinking, and that psychologists should look for parallels between the structure of the human brain and the structure of electronic computers. For example, James Miller (1955) envisioned a "comparative psychology . . . dealing not with animals but with electronic models," since the actions of computers are "in many interesting ways like living behavior." However, the identification of neural and electronic circuitry was much too simple. As Turing said in his 1951 paper, computers are general-purpose machines (the theoretically ideal general-purpose computer is called a *Turing machine*). The actual electronic architecture of a computer is unimportant, because what makes a computer behave as it does is its *program,* and the same program may be run on physically different machines and different programs run on the same machine. Turing pointed out that a man in a room with an infinite supply of paper and a rulebook for transforming input symbols into output symbols could be regarded as a computer; in such circumstance his behavior would be controlled only trivially by his neurology, since his answers to questions would be dictated by the rulebook, and if one changed the rulebook, his behavior would change. The distinction of computer and program was crucial to cognitive psychology, for it meant that cognitive psychology was not neurology, and that cognitive theories of human thinking should talk about the human mind—that is, the human program—rather than the human brain. A correct cognitive theory would be implemented by the human brain and could be run on a properly programmed computer, but the theory would be in the program, not in the brain or the computer.

What began to emerge in the 1950s was a new conception of the human being as machine, and a new language in which to formulate theories about cognitive processes. People could be described, it seemed, as general-purpose computing devices, born with certain hardware and programmed by experience and socialization to behave in certain ways. The goal of psychology would be the specification of how human beings process information; the concepts of stimulus and response would be replaced by the concepts of information input and output, and theories about mediating r-s chains would be replaced by theories about internal computations and computational states. This new conception of psychology was clearly stated by Allan Newell, J. C. Shaw, and Herbert Simon in 1958, in "Elements of a Theory of Problem Solving." Since the early 1950s they had been at work on writing programs that would solve problems, beginning with a program that proved mathematical theorems, the Logic Theorist, and moving onto a more powerful program, the General Problem Solver (GPS). They had previously published their work primarily in computer engineering journals, but writing now in *Psychological Review* they defined the new cognitive approach to psychology:

> The heart of [our] approach is describing the behavior of the system by a well-specified program, defined in terms of elementary information processes. . . .
> Once the program has been specified, we proceed exactly as we do with traditional mathematical systems. We attempt to deduce general properties of the system from the program (the equations); we compare the behavior predicted from the program (from the equations) with actual behavior observed . . . [and] we modify the program when modification is required to fit the facts.

Newell, Shaw, and Simon claimed special virtues for their approach to psychological theorizing. Computers are "capable of realizing programs" making possible very precise predictions about behavior. Additionally, in order to actually run on a computer, programs must provide "a very concrete specification of [internal] processes" ensuring that theories be precise, never vague and merely verbal. The Logic Theorist and the General Problem Solver represent, Newell, Shaw, and Simon conclude, "a thoroughly operational theory of human problem solving."

Newell, Shaw, and Simon make stronger claims for their problem-solving programs than Turing made for his hypothetical AI program. Researchers in artificial intelligence wanted to write programs that would behave like people without necessarily thinking like people. So, for example, they write chess-playing programs that play chess but use the brute-force number-crunching ability of supercomputers to evaluate thousands of moves before choosing one, rather than trying to imitate the human chess master who evaluates many fewer alternatives, but does so more cleverly. Newell, Shaw, and Simon, however, moved from artificial intelligence to *computer simulation* in claiming that not only did their programs solve problems, but that they solved problems in the same way human beings did. In a computer simulation of chess (of which there are a few) the programmer would try to write a program whose computational steps are the same as those of a human master chess player. The distinction of AI and computer simulation is important because pure AI is not psychology. Efforts in AI may be psychologically instructive for suggesting the kinds of cognitive resources humans must possess to achieve intelligence, but specifying how people actually behave intelligently requires more.

While apparently breaking with the past in giving up altogether on S-R theory of any form, GPS is really a continuation of the Hullian impulse in psychology. Like Hull, Newell, Shaw, and Simon want a theory that is fundamentally mathematical, precise, and well specified, that can predict behavior in detail as deductions from the theory, and that is thoroughly operational. The theory of the General Problem Solver hews to the ideal of Newton's *Principia Mathematica* as much as Hull could have wished, and Hull could have fairly seen the implementation of the program on a computer as justification and fulfillment of his own preoccupation with building a learning machine. Newell, Shaw, and Simon are simply bringing to the Hullian impulse much better tools with which to theorize, and a much richer language in which to frame behavioralist theories. Computers were invented by electrical engineers and mathematicians, not psychologists; the concept of programming general-purpose machines was mathematician John von Neuman's and Turing's, not any psychologist's; Newell, Shaw, and Simon were from Carnegie-Mellon University, a university outside the circle of leading academic universities at which behaviorism held sway, and closely connected with business, industry, and engineering; and Simon was more an economist than psychologist, winning the Nobel Prize for economics in 1978, for his theory of "satisficing" (for example, Simon 1956). Their work, like that of Broadbent, Miller, and the other pioneers in cognitive science, assimilated a powerful tool invented outside psychology to the central program of behavioralism: the description, prediction, and control of human behavior.

PSYCHOLOGY AND SOCIETY (1950–1958)

American psychologists—and by the 1950s psychology had become an American science (Reisman 1966)—entered the 1950s with a confidence in the future shared by most other Americans. The war had ended, the Depression was only an unpleasant memory, the economy and the population were booming. To Fillmore Sanford (1951), secretary of the APA, the future of psychology lay with professional psychology, and that future was bright indeed, because a new era dawned, "the age of the psychological man":

> Our society appears peculiarly willing to adopt psychological ways of thinking and to accept the results of psychological research. American people seem to have a strong and conscious need for the sorts of professional services psychologists are . . . equipped to give. . . . [T]he age of the psychological man is upon us, and . . . psychologists must accept responsibility not only for having spread the arrival of this age but for guiding its future course. Whether we like it or not, our society is tending more and more to think in terms of the concepts and methods spawned and nurtured by psychologists. And whether we like it or not, psychologists will continue to be a consequential factor in the making of social decisions and in the structuring of our culture.

Sanford argued that psychologists had an unprecedented opportunity to "create a profession the like of which has never before been seen, either in form or content . . . the first *deliberately designed* profession in history."

By every quantitative measure, Sanford's optimism was justified. Membership in the APA grew from 7,250 in 1950 to 16,644 in 1959; the most rapid growth occurred in the applied divisions, and psychologists, by establishing various boards and committees within the APA, did deliberately design their profession, as Fillmore hoped. Despite skirmishes with the other APA, the American Psychiatric Association (which was loath to give up its monopoly on mental health care and opposed the legal recognition of clinical psychology), states began to pass certification and licensing laws covering applied, primarily clinical and counseling, psychologists, defining them legally and, of course, acknowledging them as legitimate

professionals (Reisman 1966). Psychology in industry prospered as industry prospered, business people recognizing that "we need not 'change human nature,' we
need only to learn to control and to use it" (Baritz 1960). Popular magazine articles
on psychology began to appear regularly, often telling people how to choose genuine clinical psychologists from psychological frauds. Psychologists basked in the
favorable series on psychology appearing in *Life* by Ernest Havemann in 1957: they
gave him an award for his series.

Certain troublesome divisions remained, however. Within psychology, traditional experimental and theoretical psychologists were becoming unhappy with the
increasing numbers and influence of applied psychologists. In 1957 a committee of
the Division of Experimental Psychology polled their membership's attitudes to the
APA. They found that although 55 percent approved of the APA, 30 percent were
opposed to it; and they noted a growing, though still minority, desire for the
experimentalists to secede from the APA (Farber 1957). The first claims were made
that clinical psychologists (and psychiatrists) could effectively neither diagnose
(Meehl 1954) nor treat (Eysenck 1952) their patients. Divided among themselves,
psychologists were also divided from the mainstream of American thought in the
1950s. Surveying the social attitudes of twenty-seven leading psychologists, Keehn
(1955) found that they were far more liberal than the country as a whole. Compared
to most Americans, psychologists were nonreligious or even antireligious (denying
that God exists, that survival of bodily death occurs, and that people need religion),
were opposed to the death penalty, believed that criminals should be cured rather
than punished, and supported easier divorce laws.

Amid the prosperity and general good feelings of the 1950s there was a small
but growing disturbing current, felt faintly within psychology itself and more
strongly in the larger American culture: an unhappiness with the ethos and ethic of
adjustment. Robert Creegan (1953) wrote in *American Psychologist* that "the job of
psychology is to criticize and improve the social order   rather than to adjust
passively . . . [and] grow fat." Sociologist C. Wright Mills deplored the application of psychology to industrial social control "in the movement from authority to
manipulation, power shifts from the visible to the invisible, from the known to the
anonymous. And with rising material standards exploitation becomes less material
and more psychological" (Baritz 1960). Psychoanalyst Robert Lindner (1953) attacked the ideology of adjustment as a dangerous "lie" that had reduced human
beings to a "pitiful" state, and threatened "to send the species into the evolutionary shadows." Lindner blamed psychiatry and clinical psychology for preserving
the myth of adjustment by regarding neurotics and other unhappy humans as "sick"
when in fact, according to Lindner, they were in healthy but misdirected rebellion
against a stifling culture of conformity. The goal of therapy, Lindner wrote, should
not be conforming the patient to sick society but working "to transform the negative
protest and rebellion of the patient into positive expression of the rebellious urge."

Outside psychology rebellion against adjustment was more widespread and
grew with the decade. In sociology David Riesman's *The Lonely Crowd* (1950) and
William H. Whyte's *The Organization Man* (1956) dissected and attacked the
American culture of conformity. In politics Peter Viereck praised *The Unadjusted
Man: A New Hero for America*. Novels such as J. D. Salinger's *Catcher in the Rye*
(1951), Sloan Wilson's *The Man in the Grey Flannel Suit* (1955), and Jack Kerouac's *On the Road* (1957) expressed the unhappiness of people caught in a grey
world of adaptation and conformity, yearning for lives less constrained and more
emotional. The movie *Rebel Without a Cause* portrayed the tragic fate of one whose

anxiety and unhappiness found no constructive purpose. And the fierce, restless energy of the young—whose numbers were growing rapidly—exploded in music, in rock and roll, the only creative outlet it could find.

At the end of the decade sociologist Daniel Bell wrote about the exhaustion of ideas during the 1950s. The beliefs of the past were no longer acceptable to young thinkers, and the middle way of adjustment was "not for [them]; it is without passion and deadening." Bell identified a "search for a cause" moved by "a deep, desperate, almost pathetic anger." The world, to many young minds, was grey and unexciting. In psychology eclecticism could be boring, for there were no issues to fight over, no battles to be fought as before, when psychology had begun, or when functionalist battled structuralist, and behaviorist battled introspectionist. Psychology was thriving, but to no clear end, apparently happy in its work of adjustment.

All this was about to change.

BIBLIOGRAPHY

Accessible discussions of logical behaviorism may be found in Fodor (1981); Arnold S. Kaufman, "Behaviorism," *Encyclopedia of the social sciences,* V. 1 (New York: Macmillan, 1967, 268–273); Arnold B. Levison, ed., *Knowledge and society: An introduction to the philosophy of the social sciences* (Indianapolis: Bobbs-Merrill, 1974), Ch. VI; and Norman Malcolm, *Problems of mind: Descartes to Wittgenstein* (New York: Harper Torchbooks, 1971), Ch. III. Ryle's *Concept of mind* (1949) is well written, even witty, and quite readable even by someone with no previous knowledge of philosophy. Wittgenstein, on the other hand, is a notoriously difficult philosopher to understand. For our present purposes, his most important works are *The blue and brown books* (1958), a published version of Cambridge lectures delivered in 1933 and 1934, which formed the preliminary studies for the posthumously published *Philosophical investigations* (1953). Wittgenstein wrote in a sort of dialogue style, arguing with an unnamed interlocutor, and, like Plato, tended to develop arguments by indirection rather than outright statement. Further difficulty understanding his philosophy arises from the fact that in an important sense he had nothing positive to say, aiming like Socrates at clearing up misconceptions instead of offering his own. As Malcolm (1971) put it, "Philosophical work of the right sort merely unties knots in our understanding. The result is not a theory but simply—no knots!" So one should not tackle Wittgenstein without guidance. The best book-length introduction is Anthony Kenny's *Wittgenstein* (Cambridge: Harvard University Press, 1973). The best treatment of Wittgenstein's philosophy of mind is Malcolm (1970). Luckhardt (1983) is also helpful and clear, especially concerning Wittgenstein's attitude to behaviorism.

Papers expounding the positivistic view of psychological theory construction nearly filled the pages of the *Psychological Review* in the late 1940s and early 1950s. Some of them, including Kendler's, are collected in Melvin Marx, ed., *Theories in contemporary psychology* (New York: Macmillan, 1963). A witty reply to Kendler from the realist perspective was given by Tolman's colleague Benbow F. Ritchie, "The circumnavigation of cognition," *Psychological Review* (1953, *60:* 216–221). Ritchie likens Kendler to an operationist geographer who defines problems of navigation purely in terms of the procedures for getting from one point to another on the earth's surface, thereby dismissing the dispute between the "flat-earth theorists" and the "ball theorists" as a pseudoissue, since both theories are operationally reducible to statements about movement on the earth's surface, rendering irrelevant any "surplus meaning" concerning the shape of the earth. The "what is learned" debate has been insightfully studied by philosopher Ron Amundson "Psychology and epistemology: The place versus response controversy," *Cognition* (1985, *20:* 127–155). If you are interested in the many experiments done concerning "what is learned," you should consult reviews found under the heading "Learning" in the *Annual review of psychology,* which began publication in 1950. Also useful is Ernest R. Hilgard's (later coauthored by Gordon Bower) text, *Theories of learning,* whose first edition appeared in 1948 (New York: Appleton-Century-Crofts). For an account of the broader issues raised by operationism, see Thomas H. Leahey, "Operationism and ideology," *Journal of Mind and Behavior* (1983, *4:* 81–90).

The works of B. F. Skinner are fully listed in the references. The best single book of Skinner's to read is *Science and human behavior* (New York: Macmillan, 1953), because there he discusses his philosophy of science, explains his scientific work, and goes on to criticize society in light of his conclusions, offering behaviorist remedies for social ills. He has just completed his autobiography, in three volumes, all published by Knopf (New York): *Particulars of my life* (1976), *The shaping of a behaviorist* (1979), and *A matter of consequences* (1983). Richard Evans has conducted two interviews with Skinner. *B. F. Skinner: The man and his ideas* (New York: Dutton, 1968) provides a good introduction to Skinner and *A dialogue with B. F. Skinner* (New York: Praeger, 1981) provides an update. Paul Sagal discusses *Skinner's philosophy* (Washington, D.C.: University Press of America, 1981). Some of Skinner's most recent works are cited in Chapter Fifteen.

Miller (1959) provides a good general introduction to informal, "liberalized" behavioralism, although he focuses on his own research and neglects the many other mediational behaviorists, such as Osgood, who were important figures in the 1950s. Miller and his associates, particularly John Dollard, developed their social learning theory over many years and in many publications, beginning with John Dollard, Leonard Doob, Neal Miller, O. Hobart Mowrer, and Robert Sears, *Frustration and aggression* (New Haven: Yale University Press, 1939). Their most important books were Neal Miller and John Dollard, *Social learning and imitation* (New Haven: Yale University Press, 1941); and John Dollard and Neal Miller, *Personality and psychotherapy* (New York: McGraw-Hill, 1950). As the title of the last book implies, Miller and Dollard were pioneers in behavioral psychotherapy, and an excellent summary of their therapeutic methods and comparison with other systems may be found in Donald H. Ford and Hugh B. Urban, *Systems of psychotherapy: A comparative study* (New York: McGraw-Hill, 1963). The Kendlers presented their mediational theory of reversal shift learning in many publications, but the classic paper was Howard Kendler and Tracy Kendler, "Vertical and horizontal processes in problem solving," *Psychological Review* (1962, *69:* 1–16). Their cited 1975 paper provides a retrospective on their work, and shows how it turned gradually into information-processing psychology.

Jerome Bruner and George S. Klein provide an account of the beginnings and guiding concepts of the New Look in perception in "The functions of perceiving: New Look retrospect," in B. Kaplan and S. Wapner, eds., *Perspectives in psychological theory: Essays in honor of Heinz Werner* (New York: International Universities Press, 1960). Jean Piaget wrote many books, most of them very difficult. A comprehensive statement of his theory for the period in question in his *The psychology of intelligence* (Totowa, New Jersey: Rowman & Littlefield, 1948). Piaget's *Six psychological studies* (New York: Random House, 1964) collects some of his more accessible papers. Secondary sources include Alfred Baldwin, *Theories of child development,* 2d ed. (New York: John Wiley, 1980); John Flavell, *The developmental psychology of Jean Piaget* (New York: van Nostrand, 1963); Herbert Ginsberg and Sylvia Opper, *Piaget's theory of intellectual development* (Englewood Cliffs, New Jersey: Prentice-Hall, 1969); and Thomas H. Leahey and Richard J. Harris, *Human learning* (Englewood Cliffs, New Jersey: Prentice-Hall, 1985). Finally, Howard Gruber and Jacques Voneche have compiled *The essential Piaget* (New York: Basic Books, 1977), a comprehensive anthology of extracts from all Piaget's major works, including some rare adolescent pieces, and have added their own penetrating commentary. Later chapters will include references to later works by Piaget and critical secondary sources.

Borings (1946) is the first paper I know of to address the meaning of the World War II computer revolution for psychology, and it includes a comprehensive listing of the prewar mechanical models, including Hull's. Broadbent (1958) is useful for comparing information-processing and S-R theories. Finally, a book that doesn't fit well anywhere but that documents the revival of interest in cognition in the early 1950s is Bruner et al. (1957), a collection of papers given at the University of Colorado Symposium on Cognition in 1955. The meeting was attended by leading psychologists of cognition, including mediation theory (Charles Osgood), social psychology (Fritz Heider), psychoanalysis (David Rapaport), and Bruner himself. Only one approach was missing: artificial intelligence. Its omission demonstrates that the computer revolution had not yet hit psychology, and demonstrates how the field of AI developed entirely separately from the psychology of thinking.

A brief survey of general historical developments during the 1950s may be found in the relevant sections of Bernard Bailyn, David Davis, David Donald, John Thomas, Robert Wiebe, and Gordon Wood, *The great republic* (Boston: Little, Brown, 1977). Emphasis on the social, cultural, and intellectual history of the period is in Jeffery Hart, *When the going was good: American life in the fifties* (New York: Crown, 1982). For psychology in the 1950s see Reisman (1966) and Albert R. Gilgen, *American psychology since World War II: A profile of the discipline* (Westport, Connecticut: Greenwood Press, 1982). If one is interested in the conflict between the two APAs, psychological and psychiatric, one should read the professional journal of the APA, the *American Psychologist*. The year of maximum conflict appears to have been 1953, when the journal was filled with articles, letters, and notes on the struggle of psychologists to win legal approval of their profession over the protests of the psychiatrists. Lindner's work (1953) should be regarded as a symptom of some psychologists' unhappiness with the ideology of adjustment rather than as offering a sound set of analyses or arguments in itself. It depends on a dubious reading of Freud and Darwin, advocates negative eugenics, and is, in general, rather hysterical in its treatment of modern life.

REFERENCES

Baritz, L. J. (1960) *The servants of power: A history of the use of social science in American industry*. Middletown, Connecticut: Wesleyan University Press.

Beach, F. A. (1950) The snark was a boojum. *American Psychologist 5:* 115–124.

Bell, D. (1960) *The end of ideology: On the exhaustion of political ideas in the fifties*. Glencoe, Illinois: The Free Press.

Boring, E. G. (1946) Mind and mechanism. *American Journal of Psychology 59:* 173–192.

Broadbent, D. E. (1957) A mechanical model for human attention and immediate memory. *Psychological Review 64:* 205–215.

Broadbent, D. E. (1958) *Perception and communication*. New York: Pergamon Press.

Bruner, J. S., Brunswik, E., Festinger, E., Heider, F., Muenzinger, K. F., Osgood, C. E., and Rapaport, D. (1957) *Contemporary approaches to cognition*. Cambridge, England: Cambridge University Press.

Bruner, J. S., Goodnow, J., and Austin, G. (1956) *A study of thinking*. New York: John Wiley.

Creegan, R. (1953) Psychologist, know thyself. *American Psychologist 8:* 52–53.

Deutsch, J. A. (1953) A new type of behavior theory. *British Journal of Psychology 44:* 304–318.

Estes, W., Koch, S., MacCorquodale, K., Meehl, K., Mueller, C., Schoenfeld, W., and Verplanck, W. (1954) *Modern learning theory*. New York: Appleton-Century-Crofts.

Evans, R. I. (1968) *B. F. Skinner: The man and his ideas*. New York: Dutton.

Eysenck, H. J. (1952) The effects of psychotherapy: An evaluation. *Journal of Consulting Psychology 16:* 322–324.

Farber, I. E. (1957) The division of experimental psychology and the APA. *American Psychologist 12:* 200–202.

Festinger, L. (1957) *A theory of cognitive dissonance*. Stanford: Stanford University Press.

Festinger, L. and Carlsmith, J. M. (1959) Cognitive consequences of forced compliance. *Journal of Abnormal and Social Psychology 58:* 203–210.

Fodor, J. A. (1981) The mind-body problem. *Scientific American 244:* 114–122.

Goss, A. E. (1961) Verbal mediating responses and concept formation. *Psychological Review 68:* 248–274.

Keehn, J. D. (1955) The expressed social attitudes of leading psychologists. *American Psychologist 10:* 208–210.

Kendler, H. H. (1952) "What is learned?"—A theoretical blind alley. *Psychological Review 59:* 269–277.

Kendler, H. H. and Kendler, T. (1975) From discrimination learning to cognitive development: A neobehavioristic odyssey. In W. K. Estes (Ed.), *Handbook of learning and cognitive processes.* V. 1. Hillsdale, New Jersey: Erlbaum.

Koch, S. (1951a) The current status of motivational psychology. *Psychological Review 58:* 147–154.

Koch, S. (1951b) Theoretical psychology 1950: An overview. *Psychological Review 58:* 295–301.

Krantz, D. L. (1973) Schools and systems: The mutual isolation of operant and non-operant psychology. In M. Henle, J. Jaynes, and J. Sullivan (Eds.), *Historical conceptions of psychology.* New York: Springer.

Krech, D. (1949) Notes toward a psychological theory. *Journal of Personality 18:* 66–87.

Lashley, K. S. (1951) The problem of serial order in behavior. In L. A. Jeffress (Ed.), *Cerebral mechanisms in behavior.* New York: John Wiley.

Lindner, R. F. (1953) *Prescription for rebellion.* London: Victor Gollancz.

Luckhardt, C. G. (1983) Wittgenstein and behaviorism. *Synthese 56:* 319–338.

MacCorquodale, K. and Meehl, P. E. (1948) On a distinction between hypothetical constructs and intervening variables. *Psychological Review 55:* 95–107.

Malcolm, N. (1970) Wittgenstein on the nature of mind. American Philosophical Quarterly Monograph Series, Monograph 4: 9–29.

Maltzman, I. (1955) Thinking: From a behavioristic point of view. *Psychological Review 62:* 275–286.

Marx, M. (1951) Intervening variable or hypothetical construct? *Psychological Review 58:* 235–247.

Meehl, P. E. (1954) *Clinical vs. statistical prediction: A theoretical analysis and review of the evidence.* Minneapolis: University of Minnesota Press.

Miller, G. A. (1956) The magical number seven, plus or minus two: Some limits on our capacity for processing information. *Psychological Review 63:* 81–97.

Miller, J. G. (1955) Toward a general theory for the behavioral sciences. *American Psychologist 10:* 513–531.

Miller, N. (1959) Liberalization of basic S-R concepts. In S. Koch (Ed.), *Psychology: Study of a science.* V. 2. New York: McGraw-Hill.

Newell, A., Shaw, J. C., and Simon, H. A. (1958) Elements of a theory of problem solving. *Psychological Review 65:* 151–166.

Osgood, C. E. (1956) Behavior theory and the social sciences. *Behavioral Science 1:* 167–185.

Osgood, C. E. (1957) A behavioristic analysis of perception and language as cognitive phenomena. In Bruner et al. (1957).

Reisman, J. M. (1966) *The development of clinical psychology.* New York: Appleton-Century-Crofts.

Ritchie, B. F. (1953) The circumnavigation of cognition. *Psychological Review 60:* 216–221.

Rosenblueth, A., Wiener, N., and Bigelow, J. (1966) Behavior, purpose, and teleology (1943). Reprinted in J. V. Canfield (Ed.), *Purpose in nature.* Englewood Cliffs, New Jersey: Prentice-Hall.

Ryle, G. (1949) *The concept of mind.* New York: Barnes & Noble.

Sanford, F. H. (1951) Across the secretary's desk: Notes on the future of psychology as a profession. *American Psychologist 6:* 74–76.

Simon, H. A. (1956) Rational choice and the structure of the environment. *Psychological Review 63:* 129–138.

Skinner, B. F. (1931) The concept of reflex in the description of behavior. *Journal of General Psychology 5:* 427–458.
Skinner, B. F. (1938) *The behavior of organisms.* Englewood Cliffs, New Jersey: Prentice-Hall.
Skinner, B. F. (1948) *Walden II.* New York: Macmillan.
Skinner, B. F. (1953) *Science and human behavior.* New York: Macmillan.
Skinner, B. F. (1954) A critique of psychoanalytic concepts and theories. Reprinted in *Cumulative Record.* 3rd ed. Englewood Cliffs, New Jersey: Prentice-Hall, 1972.
Skinner, B. F. (1957) *Verbal behavior.* Englewood Cliffs, New Jersey: Prentice-Hall.
Skinner, B. F. (1971) A lecture on having a poem. Reprinted in *Cumulative Record.* 3rd ed. Englewood Cliffs, New Jersey: Prentice-Hall, 1972.
Skinner, B. F. (1977) Herrnstein and the evolution of behaviorism. *American Psychologist 32:* 1006–1012.
Slack, C. W. (1955) Feedback theory and the reflex-arc concept. *Psychological Review 62:* 263–267.
Tolman, E. C. (1949) Discussion. *Journal of Personality 18:* 48–50.
Turing, A. M. (1950) Computing machinery and intelligence. *Mind 59:* 433–460.
Viereck, P. (1956) *The unadjusted man: A new hero for modern America.* New York: Capricorn Books.
Wittgenstein, L. (1953) *Philosophical investigations.* 3d ed. New York: Macmillan.
Wittgenstein, L. (1958) *The blue and brown books.* New York: Harper Colophon.
Wyckoff, L. B. (1954) A mathematical model and an electronic model for learning. *Psychological Review 61:* 89–97.

CHAPTER 14

Years of Turmoil (1958–1968)

CHALLENGES TO BEHAVIORISM
   Humanistic Psychology
   Cartesian Linguistics
EROSION OF THE FOUNDATIONS
   The Disappearance of Positivism
   Constraints on Animal Learning
   Awareness and Human Learning
COGNITIVE PSYCHOLOGY ASSERTS ITSELF
   The New Structuralism
   The New Mentalism
   Man the Machine: Information Processing
PSYCHOLOGY AND SOCIETY
   Funding Social Science
   Professional Psychology
   Values
CONCLUSION: REVOLT BUT NO REVOLUTION
   From Yippie to Yuppie
   From Mediation to Information Processing

By the mid-1950s behavioralism had settled down into a comfortable eclecticism. Skinnerians, neo-Hullians, and broadly cognitive theorists lived together with disagreement but without serious division. The situation was reminiscent of the years just before World War I, when functionalists, Titchenerians, Wundtians, and others lived together in relative harmony as the new psychologists. In 1913 Watson shattered the atmosphere of eclectic harmony, even though he did not really alter the behavioralistic direction American psychology was already taking. Nevertheless, in his wake there was a period of stress and self-inspection. Psychologists grappled with the challenge of behaviorism, and came to a conscious redefinition of their field by the 1930s. Similarly, in the late 1950s angry voices challenged the eclectic status quo, and set off a new period of self-examination and inflamed rhetoric. Whether or not psychology was taken in a revolutionary direction after 1960 any more than it was after 1913 is a question to which we will have to return.

CHALLENGES TO BEHAVIORISM

Humanistic Psychology

Although humanistic psychology did not take off until the late 1950s, its immediate historical roots lay in the post–World War II period. Its most important founders are Carl Rogers (born 1902) and Abraham Maslow (1908–1970). While both were initially attracted to behaviorism, both became aware of its limitations and staked out similar alternatives. Rogers developed his *client-centered psychotherapy* in the 1940s, and used it with soldiers returning to the United States. Client-centered psychotherapy is a phenomenologically oriented technique in which the therapist tries to enter into the world view of the client, and help the client work through his or her problems so as to live the life the client most deeply desires. Rogers's client-centered therapy offered a significant alternative to the psychoanalytic methods used by psychiatrists, and thus played an important role in the establishment of clinical and counseling psychology in the postwar period. Because of his emphasis on empathic understanding, Rogers came into conflict with behaviorism, which treated human beings just as it treated animals—as machines whose behavior could be predicted and controlled, without any attention being paid to subjective consciousness. In 1956 Rogers and Skinner began a series of debates about the relative adequacy of their points of view (Rogers and Skinner 1956). Phenomenological psychology is especially appealing to the clinician, for the clinician's stock in trade is empathy, and phenomenology is the study of subjective experience. Rogers distinguishes three modes of knowledge. The first is the objective mode, in which we seek to understand the world as an object. The second and third modes of knowing are subjective. One is each person's own subjective knowledge of personal conscious experience, including each person's intentions and sense of freedom. The other mode of subjective knowledge is the attempt to understand another person's subjective inner world. The clinician, of course, must master this last mode of knowing, for in Roger's view it is only by understanding the client's personal world and subjective self that the clinician can hope to help the client. Rogers believes that personal beliefs, values, and intentions control behavior. He hopes that psychology will find systematic ways to know the personal experience of other people, for then therapy will be greatly enhanced.

Rogers argues that behaviorism limits itself exclusively to the objective mode of knowledge and so constrains psychology within a particular set of allowable techniques and theories. It treats human beings exclusively as objects, not as experiencing subjects in their own right. In specific contradistinction to Skinner, Rogers puts great emphasis on each person's experienced freedom, rejecting Skinner's purely physical causality. Wrote Rogers (1964): "The experiencing of choice, of freedom of choice . . . is not only a profound truth, but is a very important element in therapy." As a scientist he accepts determinism, but as a therapist he accepts freedom: the two "exist in different dimensions."

Abraham Maslow was humanistic psychology's leading theorist and organizer. Beginning as an experimental animal psychologist, he turned his attention to the problem of creativity in art and science. He studied creative people and concluded that they were actuated by needs dormant and unrealized in the mass of humanity. He called these people self-actualizers because they made real—actualized—their human creative powers, in contrast to most people, who work only to satisfy their animal needs for food, shelter, and safety. Maslow concluded that creative geniuses were not special human beings, but that everyone possessed latent creative talents that could be realized if it were not for socially imposed inhibitions. Maslow's and Rogers's views come together in that they both sought ways to jolt people from comfortable but stultifying psychological ruts, and move them to realize their full potential as human beings.

In 1954 Maslow created a mailing list for "people who are interested in the scientific study of creativity, love, higher values, autonomy, growth, self-actualization, basic need gratification, etc." (Sutich and Vich 1969). The number of people on Maslow's mailing list grew quickly, and by 1957 it became clear that more formal means of communication and organization were needed. So Maslow and his followers launched the *Journal of Humanistic Psychology* in 1961 and the Association for Humanistic Psychology in 1963.

Humanistic psychologists deserve the name because, in agreement with the ancient Greek humanists, they believe that "the values which are to guide human action must be found within the nature of human and natural reality itself" (Maslow 1973). But humanistic psychologists could not accept the naturalistic values of the behaviorists. Behaviorists treated human beings as things, failing to appreciate their subjectivity, consciousness, and free will. In the view of humanistic psychologists behaviorists were not so much wrong as misguided. Behaviorists applied a perfectly valid mode of knowledge—Rogers's objective mode—to human beings, who could only be partially encompassed by this mode of knowing, by ordinary science. Most especially, humanistic psychologists were distressed by behaviorists' rejection of human free will and autonomy. Where Hull, "a near saint of pre-breakthrough [that is, prehumanistic] psychology" treated human beings as robots, humanistic psychologists proclaimed that "Man is aware. . . . Man has choice. . . . Man is intentional" (Bugental 1964).

Humanistic psychologists thus sought not to overthrow behaviorists (first-force psychology), or psychoanalysts (second-force psychology), but to build on their mistakes and go beyond them. "I interpret this third psychology [humanistic psychology] to include the first and second psychologies. . . . I am Freudian and I am behavioristic and I am humanistic" (Maslow 1973). Humanistic psychology, then, while offering a critique of and an alternative to behaviorism, tended still to live with the eclectic spirit of the 1950s. While it thought behaviorism was limited, it thought behaviorism nevertheless valid within its domain, and humanistic psychologists sought to add to behaviorism an appreciation of human consciousness that would round out the scientific picture of human psychology. A more strident, consciously revolutionary voice came from outside psychology, from the field of linguistics.

Cartesian Linguistics

If anyone played Watson to the eclectic peace of the 1950s it was the linguist Avram Noam Chomsky (born 1928). Chomsky was radical in both politics and linguistics, the study of language. In politics Chomsky was an early and outspoken critic of the war in Vietnam, and of the United States' support of Israel in the Middle East. In linguistics Chomsky revived what he took to be Descartes's rationalistic program, proposing highly formal accounts of language as the organ by which reason expresses itself, and resurrecting the notion of innate ideas. Because Chomsky regarded language as a uniquely human, rational possession, he was brought into conflict with behavioral treatments of language.

The Attack on Verbal Behavior

Since the time of Descartes language has been seen as a special problem for any mechanistic psychology. Hull's student Spence suspected that language might render inapplicable to human laws of learning derived from animals. In 1955 the informal behaviorist Osgood referred to the problems of meaning and perception as the "Waterloo of contemporary behaviorism," and in response attempted to provide a mediational theory of language, applicable only to human beings (Osgood 1957). The philosopher Norman Malcolm (1964), sympathetic to behaviorism, regards language as "an essential difference between man and the lower animals."

B. F. Skinner, however, was a dissenter from the Cartesian view, shared in part even by fellow behaviorists. The whole point of *Verbal Behavior* was to show that language, while it is a complex behavior, could be explained by reference to only the principles of behavior formulated from animal studies. Skinner therefore denied that there is anything special about language, or verbal behavior, or that there is any fundamental difference between humans and the lower animals. Somewhat as the empiricist Hume raised Kant from his dogmatic slumbers to a defense of the transcendental mind, Skinner's Humean treatment of language roused a rationalist counterattack that said behaviorism was not merely limited, but completely wrong. Further, a rationalist account of language was offered in its place. In the next section we will look at the new psycholinguistics; here we will summarize the rationalist attack on *Verbal Behavior*.

In 1959 the journal *Language* carried a lengthy review of Skinner's *Verbal Behavior* by a young and obscure linguist named Noam Chomsky. In his view he was attacking not only Skinner's work, but empiricist ideas in linguistics, psychology, and philosophy generally. Chomsky regarded Skinner's book as a "*reductio ad absurdum* of behaviorist assumptions," and wanted to show it up as pure "mythology" (Jakobovits and Miron 1967). These are the words of an angry revolutionary, and Chomsky's review is perhaps the single most influential psychological paper published since Watson's behaviorist manifesto of 1913.

Chomsky's basic criticism of Skinner's book was that it is an exercise in equivocation. Skinner's fundamental technical terms—stimulus, response, reinforcement, and so on—are well defined in animal learning experiments, but cannot be extended to human behavior without serious modification, as Skinner claims. Chomsky argued that if one attempts to use Skinner's terms in rigorous technical senses, they can be shown not to apply to language, while if the terms are metaphorically extended, they become so vague as to be no improvement on traditional linguistic notions. Chomsky systematically attacked each of Skinner's concepts, but we will consider only two examples: his analysis of stimulus and reinforcement.

Obviously, to any behaviorist proper definitions of the stimuli that control behavior are important. The difficulty of defining "stimulus," however, is a notorious one for behaviorism, noted by Thorndike and even some behaviorists. Are stimuli to be defined in purely physical terms, independent of behavior, or in terms of their effects on behavior? If we accept the former definition, then behavior looks unlawful, for very few stimuli in a situation ever affect behavior. While if we accept the latter definition, behavior is lawful by definition, for then the behaviorist only considers those stimuli that do systematically determine behavior. Chomsky raised this problem and others specific to Skinner's *Verbal Behavior*. First, Chomsky pointed out that to say each bit of verbal behavior is under stimulus control is scientifically empty; for given any respone, we can always find *some* relevant stimulus. A person looks at a painting and says "It's by Rembrandt, isn't it?" Skinner would assert that certain subtle properties of the painting determine the response. Yet the person could have said: "How much did it cost?" "It clashes with the wallpaper," "You've hung it too high," "It's hideous!" "I have one just like it at home," "It's forged," and so on, virtually *ad infinitum*. No matter what is said, *some* property could be found that "controls" the behavior. Chomsky argued that there is no prediction of behavior, and certainly no serious control, in this circumstance. Skinner's system is not the scientific advance toward the prediction and control of behavior it pretends to be.

Chomsky also pointed out that Skinner's definition of stimulus becomes hopelessly vague and metaphorical at a great remove from the rigorous laboratory environment. Skinner speaks of "remote stimulus control," in which the stimulus need not impinge on the speaker at all, as when a recalled diplomat describes a foreign situation. Skinner says the suffix "-ed" is controlled by the "subtle property of stimuli we speak of as action in the past." What physical dimensions define "things in the past"? Chomsky argued that Skinner's usage here is not remotely related to his usage in his bar-pressing experiments, and that Skinner has said nothing new about the supposed "stimulus control" of verbal behavior.

Chomsky next considered reinforcement, another term easily defined in the usual operant learning experiment in terms of delivered food or water. Chomsky argued that Skinner's application of the term to verbal behavior is again vague and metaphorical. Consider Skinner's notion of automatic self-reinforcement. Talking to oneself is said to be automatically self-reinforcing: That is why one does it. Similarly, thinking is also said to be behavior that automatically affects the behaver and is therefore reinforcing. Also consider what we might call remote reinforcement: A writer shunned in his own time may be reinforced by expecting fame to come much later. Chomsky argued (1959) that "the notion of reinforcement has totally lost whatever meaning it may ever have had. . . . A person can be reinforced though he emits no response at all [thinking], and the reinforcing 'stimulus' need not impinge on the 'reinforced person' [remote reinforcement] or need not even exist [an unpopular author who remains unpopular]."

Chomsky also criticized the behaviorist view of language acquisition and sketched his own position on that and other matters. We shall consider the positive side of Cartesian linguistics in the next chapter. Here, the important thing to note is Chomsky's revolutionary attitude. He is not prepared to accept Skinner's *Verbal Behavior* as a plausible scientific hypothesis. It is clear that he regards *Verbal Behavior* as hopelessly muddled and fundamentally wrong. His acute and unrelenting criticism, coupled with his own positive program, are aimed at the overthrow of behaviorist psychology, not its liberalization as called for by Miller, or its transcendence as called for by Rogers. For Chomsky, behaviorism cannot be built upon, cannot be transcended; it can only be replaced. Just as Watson's polemic inaugurated a profound change in psychology by arguing the overthrow of functionalism and structuralism, so Chomsky's biting review touched off crisis and revolt.

Adult Language

Noam Chomsky did not merely criticize B. F. Skinner's *Verbal Behavior,* he proposed his own highly sophisticated analysis of language, especially syntax. He created a new formal method, called *transformational grammar,* for describing a language's grammatical structure. Since transformational grammar is enormously complex, involving formal logic and abstract mathematics, we will only summarize Chomsky's general points.

Chomsky's central insight is that language is creative. Aside from clichés and television reruns, every sentence you speak is new. Every human being, in every act of language, is creating new responses and understanding new stimuli. Chomsky believes no behaviorist approach to language can cope with its endless creativity and flexibility. He argues that creativity can only be understood by recognizing that language is a rule-governed system. As part of their mental processes, persons possess a set of grammatical rules that allow them to generate new sentences by appropriately combining linguistic elements. Each person can thus generate an infinity of sentences by repeated application of the rules of grammar, just as a person can generate numbers infinitely by repeated application of the rules of arithmetic. Chomsky argues that human language will not be understood until psychology describes the rules of grammar, the mental structures that underlie speaking and hearing. A superficial behaviorist approach, which studies only speech and hearing but neglects the inner rules that govern speech and hearing, is necessarily inadequate.

Like Wundt, Chomsky distinguishes inner and outer language phenomena, but he calls them deep and surface structures. The distinction may be exemplified in the following sentences: (1) John is easy to please; (2) John is eager to please. If we diagram the grammar of these sentences, we will discover they are identical: Subject + verb + predicate adjective + infinitive phrase. However, this analysis is of surface structure only, and is false to the deeper logical structure of the sentences. This may be shown by applying the same grammatical operation to the two supposedly identical sentences, by moving "to please" to the front of each sentence. This generates: (1) To please John is easy, and (2) To please John is eager. The first is still an acceptable sentence; the latter is not. We must conclude that the sentences are not grammatically the same. The sentences differ in logical deep structure. In sentence 2, John is the grammatical subject of the sentence, and its logical subject as well: John does the pleasing. However, in sentence 1, John is the grammatical subject but the logical object: John receives pleasing from someone else. The sentences have identical surface grammatical structure, but different deep structures. The reverse relationship may also hold. "The boy hit the ball" and "The ball was hit by the boy" have different surface structures, but the same deep structure, for they mean the same thing. Chomsky believes that behaviorism has limited itself to studying surface structures and cannot handle these deeper relationships.

Chomsky poses other problems for the behaviorist approach. Consider sentences such as: (3) The rabbit is ready to eat; (4) The shooting of the hunters was terrible; and (5) They are cooking apples. Each of these sentences has two meanings. Sentence 3 might be spoken by a chef or a pet owner. Sentence 4 either says the hunters were shot or they made a lot of noise. Sentence 5 either says those apples are to be cooked with, or those people are cooking apples. In each case one may respond in two very different ways to identical stimuli, depending on how one analyzes the sentences grammatically. Different analyses produce different meanings. Chomsky argues that when one hears a sentence one analyzes it using grammatical rules, and that this is an act of *mind*. To study and describe only behavior is inadequate for a scientific understanding of language. Just as theory in physics refers to unobservable entities such as the quark and abstract properties such as a quark's "charm" or "color," so theory in psychology should refer to unobservable mental structures to explain observable behavior.

Chomsky's ideas were enormously influential on psycholinguistics, rapidly and completely eclipsing behaviorist approaches, whether mediational or Skinnerian. Many psychologists became convinced that their behaviorist views were wrong and committed themselves to a renewed study of language along Chomskian lines. Chomsky's technical system, described in *Syntactic Structures* (which appeared in 1957, the year of *Verbal Behavior*), provided a new paradigm around which to design research. Study after study was done, so that in only a few years Chomsky's ideas had generated much more empirical research than had Skinner's. Chomsky's impact is nicely described by George Miller. In the 1950s Miller had adhered to a behaviorist picture of language, but personal contact with Chomsky convinced him the old paradigm had to be abandoned. By 1962 he could write, "In the course of my work I seem to have become a very old-fashioned kind of psychologist. I now believe that mind is something more than a four letter, Anglo-Saxon word—human minds exist, and it is our job as psychologists to study them." The mind, exorcized by Watson in 1913, had returned to psychology, brought back by an outsider, Noam Chomsky.

Language Acquisition

Chomsky places himself with rationalism, something quite unusual for an American thinker. He considered his critique of *Verbal Behavior* to be an attack on the inadequacy of any empiricist account of language. Chomsky's rationalism is nowhere more evident than in his theory of language acquisition. Like Descartes, Chomsky views language as the human's unique possession, setting us off sharply from other animals. Like Plato, Descartes, and Leibniz, Chomsky argues that some knowledge—specifically for Chomsky knowledge of language—is at least in part innate.

Chomsky distinguishes linguistic competence from performance. Competence is a person's knowledge of the rules of language; performance is the person's actual use of those rules in speaking or hearing. Performance is only an indirect and often imperfect reflection of competence, as anyone knows who has read unedited transcripts of speech. People have limited memories; they are distractable; they change their minds and so change their grammar in midstream. Those and other nonlinguistic factors help determine language performance. However, each person possesses a sophisticated and unconscious knowledge of the rules of grammar, and this competence seems to be the same for all native speakers of a given language. Where does competence come from?

Chomsky argues that much of it is innate. Competence is not taught. An immigrant's child, for example, easily picks up English on the street, and studies of parent-child interaction show parents to be more interested in the truth of what their three- or four-year-old says than in its grammatical form. Since performance only indirectly reflects competence, and since grammatical rules are unobservable, children might be expected to have a hard time figuring out what the rules are—that is, acquiring their competence—which they have largely done by age five. Chomsky believes that this achievement is possible only if each child is born with a general knowledge of what human language is like and of what is relevant and what not. This point is reinforced by the existence of linguistic universals, features of language found in all known languages. Chomsky says they exist because they reflect innate linguistic structures. Chomsky is not arguing that the Chinese child innately knows Chinese, or that the French child innately knows French, but that each human child comes equipped with biologically given structures that make it possible for the child to learn any human language simply by being exposed to it.

We will find a similar situation in Marler's ethological studies of birdsong learning. Baby birds are equipped with brain structures that enable them to learn their species calls. These structures tell the chick what is birdsong and what isn't, and which birdsongs to learn (its own species'). Marler himself has suggested a similarity between birdsong acquisition and language acquisition. Both sets of communication abilities are functionally important for the organism's survival, for without language one cannot be a part of human society. Therefore natural selection will have favored the development of biological processes that support language or birdsong acquisition.

As with adult language, Cartesian linguistics has generated enormous amounts of research. Under the behaviorist paradigm studies of language learning had largely been word counts, focusing on what seemed to be the elementary response units strung together by S-R chaining. After Chomsky's proposal, studies of language acquisition became much more numerous, with independent investigators examining child syntax, often reporting almost identical data and writing identical grammars. Unsuspected regularities in child behavior were found only because Chomsky's grammatical system made them significant; they had gone unnoticed by behaviorist researchers. Studies of language acquisition in different cultures were undertaken for the first time, discovering that the early stages of language learning are the same everywhere. All these findings support Chomsky's nativist proposal.

There was also another kind of research performed in an interesting echo of the empiricist response to Descartes's nativism. Investigators now proposed to carry out La Mettrie's old idea of teaching language to an ape. Several such programs began in the 1960s, the most successful being the attempt to teach sign language to chimpanzees. Whether or not any of the linguistic monkeys possess something equivalent to human language is still controversial, although it is clear that they can communicate with their keepers. But as with La Mettrie, the goal has been to show that human language is not as unique as Descartes or Chomsky believed, and that it can be learned like any other nonnative behavior.

Unfortunately, La Mettrie's logic is faulty. The fact that a bird fancier can learn birdcalls does not demonstrate that birds do not have innate mechanisms that underlie their own language learning. Similarly, the fact that a chimpanzee can be taught language abilities after prolonged and intensive instruction does not show that the human child in a natural setting learns language without applying innate mechanisms. What happens in the wild may be quite different from what happens in an artificial laboratory setting.

EROSION OF THE FOUNDATIONS

Just as humanistic psychologists were challenging behaviorism's dominance in their own way, some of the fundamental working assumptions of behaviorism, and even of behavioralism, were coming into question. Combined with the attacks of critics, doubts thrown on these assumptions helped open the door for the formulation of new theories, some in the tradition of behavioralism, some more radical.

The Disappearance of Positivism

In the 1930s logical positivism had provided a philosophical justification for behaviorism, helping to redefine psychology as the study of behavior rather than mind. Positivism modified at least the formulation of the leading learning theories of the era, and completely captured the allegiance of young experimental psychologists who hitched their stars to operationism, using it as an analytical tool to define which problems were worth studying and which were blind alleys.

However, the methodological view of science became increasingly suspect in the late 1950s and beyond. Since its founding, logical positivism had undergone continuous change that took it further and further away from the simple logical positivism of the 1920s. For example, in the 1930s it was recognized that theoretical terms cannot be neatly linked to observations by the single step of operational definition, a fact some psychologists acknowledged without abandoning the jargon of operationism. Younger philosophers, though, were less inclined to accept the positivist paradigm even in principle, so that during the 1960s, the movement became moribund. It began to be called "the Received View," like a dead theology, and a symposium on "The Legacy of Logical Positivism" was published in 1969.

Although many criticisms of "the Received View" were offered, perhaps the most fundamental was that its explication of scientific practice was false. Historically oriented philosophers of science, such as Thomas Kuhn, Stephen Toulmin, and N. R. Hanson, showed that the supposed objectivity of science was a myth. In Chapter 1 we discussed how science is a human enterprise in which researchers see what they expect to see, investigate some problems and not others as defined by unconscious paradigms, respond to current intellectual demands, and suppress novelty. Positivism's postmortem dissection of science as a logically coherent system consisting of axioms, theorems, predictions, and verifications distorts and falsifies science as a lively, fallible human enterprise.

If positivism is false even as a reconstruction of physics, what kind of guide can it offer to a young science such as psychology? Behaviorism to a large degree proceeded on the premise that the positivist analysis of science was correct, and adopted methods and theories consistent with positivism's precepts. If the analysis is wrong, can the science be right? The crises of behaviorism, especially the learning theory crisis of 1950, can be seen as an empirical refutation of logical positivism.

Kuhn's views have themselves become popular with many psychologists. As cognitive psychology seemed to replace behaviorism in the later 1960s, references to scientific revolutions and paradigm clashes abounded. Kuhn's doctrines seemed to justify a revolutionary attitude: Behaviorism must be overthrown, it cannot be reformed. Many psychologists adopted a kind of scientific revolutionary radical chic paralleling the widespread revolutionary radical political chic of the 1960s. Using *The Structure of Scientific Revolutions* to justify a scientific revolution raises an interesting problem in social psychology. Can the perception of revolution be a self-fulfilling prophecy? Would there have been a revolution against behaviorism without Kuhn's book? Or, more subtly, could belief in Kuhn's ideas have created the appearance of revolution where there was really only conceptual evolution?

We shall return to these questions at the end of the chapter, when we again ask, "Was there a revolution?" What is important at present for the fate of behaviorism was that by the later 1960s few, if any, philosophers of science believed positivism to be a credible philosophy of science. Many rejected the social psychological approach of Kuhn, but it was clear that positivism was no longer a viable alternative. Positivism had simply disappeared, and along with it, behaviorism's philosophical foundation.

Constraints on Animal Learning

At the other end from philosophy, behaviorism was anchored by empirical studies of animal behavior. Watson began his career as an animal psychologist, and Tolman, Hull, and Skinner rarely studied human behavior, preferring the more controlled situations that could be imposed on animals. Animal experiments were expected to yield general behavioral laws applicable to a wide range of species, including humans, with little or no modification. Tolman spoke of cognitive maps in rats and persons, Hull of the general laws of mammalian behavior, and Skinner of the extension of animal principles to verbal behavior. It was believed that the principles that emerged from artificially controlled experiments would illuminate the ways in which all organisms learn regardless of evolutionary conditioning. The assumption of generality was crucial to the behaviorist program, for if laws of learning are species-specific, studies of animal behavior are pointless for understanding humanity.

Evidence accumulated in the 1960s, however, that the laws of learning uncovered with rats and pigeons are not general, and that serious constraints exist on what and how an animal learns, constraints dictated by the animal's evolutionary history. This evidence came both from psychology and other disciplines. On the one hand psychologists discovered anomalies in the application of learning laws in a variety of situations, while on the other hand ethologists demonstrated the importance of innate factors in understanding an animal's behavior in the natural environment its ancestors evolved in.

In developing the pigeon-guided missile, Skinner worked with a young psychologist, Keller Breland, who was so impressed by the possibilities of behavior control that he and his wife became professional animal trainers. As Skinner put it in 1959: "Behavior could be shaped up according to specifications and maintained indefinitely almost at will . . . Keller Breland is now specializing in the production of behavior as a saleable commodity." Skinner's claim for Breland resembles Frazier's boast in *Walden II* of being able to produce human personalities to order.

However, in the course of their extensive experience in training many species to perform unusual behaviors, the Brelands found instances in which animals did not perform as they should. In 1961 they reported their difficulties in a paper whose title, "The Misbehavior of Organisms," puns on Skinner's first book, *The Behavior of Organisms*. For example, they tried to teach pigs to carry wooden coins and deposit them in a piggy bank. Although they could teach behaviors, the Brelands found that the behavior degenerated in pig after pig. The animals would eventually pick up the coin, drop it on the ground and root it, rather than deposit it in the bank. The Brelands report that they found many instances of animals "trapped by strong instinctive behaviors" that overwhelm learned behaviors. Pigs naturally root for their food, and so they come to root the coins that they have been trained to collect to get food reinforcers. Breland and Breland (1972) conclude that psychologists should examine "the hidden assumptions which led most disastrously to these breakdowns" in the general laws of learning proposed by behaviorism. They are clearly questioning behaviorism's paradigmatic assumptions in the light of experimental anomalies.

They identified three such assumptions: "That the animal . . . [is] a virtual *tabula rasa,* that species differences are insignificant, and that all responses are about equally conditionable to all stimuli." These assumptions are fundamental to empiricism, and statements of them have been made by the major behaviorists. Although limits on these assumptions had been suggested before, the Brelands' paper seemed to open the floodgates to discoveries of more anomalies under more controlled conditions.

We may mention one such line of research, conducted by John Garcia and his associates. Garcia was a student of Krechevsky, Tolman's major pupil. Garcia studied what he called "conditioned nausea," a form of classical conditioning. Standard empiricist assumptions, enunciated by Pavlov, held that any stimulus could act as a conditioned stimulus, which through conditioning could elicit any response as a conditioned response. More informally, any stimulus could be conditioned to elicit any response. Empirical studies further indicated that conditioned stimulus and unconditioned stimulus had to be paired within about a half-second of each other for learning to take place.

Using a variety of methods, Garcia let rats drink a novel-tasting liquid, and then made the rats sick over an hour later. The question was whether rats would learn to avoid the place they were sick, the unconditioned stimulus immediately connected with their sickness, or the solution they drank, although it was remote in time from the unconditioned response. The latter uniformly occurred. The usual laws of classical conditioning did not hold. Garcia argued that rats know instinctively that nausea must be due to something they ate, not stimuli present at the time of sickness. This makes good evolutionary sense, for sickness in the wild is more likely to be caused by drinking tainted water than by the bush under which a rat was sitting when it felt sick. Connecting taste with sickness is more biologically adaptive than connecting it with visual or auditory stimuli. It appears, therefore, that evolution constrains what stimuli may be associated with what responses.

Garcia's research was initially greeted with extreme skepticism and was refused publication in the major journal devoted to animal behavior. However, studies by other researchers demonstrated for many behaviors that an animal's evolutionary inheritance places distinct limits on what it can learn. Garcia's studies are now considered classics.

Meanwhile, ethologically oriented biologists had maintained a tradition of studying animals' natural behaviors in their evolutionary context. Ethologists stressed the role of instinct in determining behavior, and this tradition never adopted the *tabula rasa* assumptions of behaviorism. Their work, therefore, provided further anomalies for empiricism. For example, Peter Marler and his colleagues have intensively investigated birdsong learning over many years. Song is functionally important to birds in their natural environments, for many birds use distinct calls to establish territories, attract mates, and warn of danger, all abilities vital to the survival of their species. What Marler found is that some bird species for whom song has functional significance come programmed to learn their own species calls. Birds who hear no song when young grow up without song, so extreme nativism is ruled out. But birds exposed to songs of other species do not learn these songs, even though the songs are within their vocal range. Birds learn their species' songs only when exposed to them as youngsters. This indicates that birds are born with the innate ability to attend to and learn only certain sounds. Again, this makes good evolutionary sense, for a bird that learned to sing the wrong songs, or imitate the sounds of passing cars, would be unable to mate and have offspring. Since adult birds do not teach their young to sing, young birds must have native mechanisms that direct their learning to the appropriate sounds.

Often ethological work presented many instances of natural learning being determined by animals' genetic makeup, casting further doubt on the validity of empiricism and on the belief that the laws of learning discovered in the laboratory could be extended across species without serious modification.

In 1961 the Brelands stated that ethological work had done more to further understanding of animal behavior than behaviorist laboratory studies. By the 1970s animal psychologists were proclaiming that a revolution had occurred in which the old paradigm was shattered (Bolles 1975). Although such an assessment is premature, the existence of books and symposia in the 1970s on constraints on learning indicated that the field of animal learning was in crisis, that the old security of the rat lab and the anchor of general learning laws were gone.

This particular crisis reveals an interesting fact about the influence of Darwin on American psychology. Both functionalists and behaviorists viewed mind and behavior as adpative processes, adjusting the organism to its environment. We have seen that Skinner's analysis of learning is squarely and consciously based on an extension of natural selection. Yet behaviorism adopted the empiricist assumptions of the *tabula rasa* and species-general laws of learning and ignored the contribution of evolution to behavior. This was the product of another behaviorist assumption, peripheralism. Behaviorists of course recognized that a dog cannot respond to a tone it cannot hear; nor can it learn to fly. These constraints, however, are only on the organism's peripheral sensory and motor abilities. Since behaviorism denied that central processes exist, it could not recognize evolutionary limits on them. Therefore it had to assume that as long as an organism could sense a stimulus, it could be associated with any response it could physically make.

However, many of the anomalies uncovered by researchers such as the Brelands, Garcia, and Marler seem to involve either tastes or sights or sounds an animal can sense, yet Garcia showed that rats are predisposed to link only certain stimuli and responses, and Marler showed that birds do not learn other species' songs they hear and could physically produce. Both findings seem to indicate some central control over learning—central control that is at least partly determined by heredity.

Therefore, although behaviorism, following functionalism, adopted the theory of natural selection as a conceptual tool, it denied the biological implications of evolution because it denied centralism. Peripheralism is a central assumption of behaviorism, the study of observable behavior, and it supported other paradigmatic assumptions. The assumptions of the disciplinary matrix interlocked to produce the expectation of general laws of learning.

We may note, finally, that behaviorism's extreme empiricism denied already established constraints on learning. For example, Thorndike himself found great differences in how easily cats learned to escape from different puzzle boxes. In particular, they had a difficult time learning to lick their paws in order to escape. Such a behavior is not naturally connected to escape, and so cats were slow to discover the connection. Similarly, early students of animal behavior from Darwin to the ethologists had described biologically determined behavior patterns. All of this is consistent with the extension of a normal science paradigm. Certain anomalies are quietly ignored or put down to bad method (for example, the anecdotal method) until they become too serious to ignore, as they did in the 1960s in animal learning.

Awareness and Human Learning

Logical positivism and the assumption that the laws of learning discoverable with rats and pigeons were applicable without serious exception to all other species, including human beings, were fundamental assumptions of the behaviorist form of behavioralism that had been formulated in the 1930s. Behavioralism rested on a different assumption, that consciousness was of marginal importance in explaining behavior, including human behavior. The motor theory of consciousness and neo-realist theories of consciousness viewed consciousness as an epiphenomenon that might at best report some of the determiners of behavior—and not do that very well—but played no role in the actual determination of behavior. Münsterberg, Dewey, and the functionalists placed the determinants of behavior in the environment and in physiological processes, seeing consciousness as merely floating over brain and body, reporting what it saw. Psychology, then, became the study of behavior, not consciousness, although consciousness might be consulted for its occasionally apt insights on why its owner behaved as he or she did. Within this broad framework behaviorists developed their research programs, using positivism to buttress the behavioralist disdain for consciousness, and turning to rigorous, experimental study of animal learning to find the answer to behavioralism's basic question, What causes behavior?

In its behaviorist form the causal impotence of consciousness was asserted by the doctrine of the automatic action of reinforcers. The doctrine was contained in Thorndike's Law of Effect in the phrase "stamped in": Reward automatically "stamps in" an S-R connection; it does not lead consciousness to a conclusion upon which action is taken. In 1961 the automatic action of reinforcers was forcefully and dogmatically stated by Leo Postman and Julius Sassenrath: "It is an outmoded and an unnecessary assumption that the modification of behavior must be preceded by a correct understanding of the environmental contingencies." While a subject might report contingencies accurately, this only meant that consciousness had observed the causes of the changed behavior, not that consciousness had itself caused behavior to change.

Some experiments seemed to support the view. For example, Greenspoon (1955) was interested in nondirective psychotherapy, in which the therapist merely says "um-hum" periodically during a session. From the behaviorist perspective this situation could be analyzed as a learning situation. The patient emits behaviors, some of which are reinforced by "um-hum." Therefore the patient should come to talk about those things that are reinforced, and not others. Greenspoon took this hypothesis to the laboratory. Subjects were brought to an experimental room and induced to say words. Whenever the subject said a plural noun, the experimenter said "um-hum." After a while extinction was begun; the experimenter said nothing. At the end of the session the subject was asked to explain what had been going on. Only ten of seventy-five subjects could do so and, interestingly, Greenspoon excluded their data from analysis. His results showed that production of plural nouns increased during training and then decreased during extinction—exactly as operant theory predicts—and in the apparent absence of awareness of the connection between plural nouns and reinforcement. Experiments similar to Greenspoon's found similar results.

In the 1960s, however, various researchers disenchanted with behaviorism, and often under Chomsky's influence, challenged the validity of the "Greenspoon effect," or learning without awareness. They argued that Greenspoon's method was inadequate. The questions probing awareness were vague, and they were asked only after extinction, by which time subjects who had been aware of the response-reinforcement contingency could have concluded they had been wrong. Replication of the Greenspoon procedure showed that many subjects held technically incorrect hypotheses that nevertheless led to correct responses. For example, a subject might say "apples" and "pears" and be reinforced, concluding that fruit names were being reinforced. The subject would continue to say fruit names and be rewarded, yet when the subject told the hypothesis to the experimenter, the subject would be called "unaware."

Even behaviorists started turning up anomalies. A paper in the 1961 *Journal of Experimental Analysis of Behavior* found that student experimenters told that "um-hum" would increase the reinforced behavior reported such results, while those told that "um-hum" would lower the reinforced operant reported exactly that! Further, interviews showed that most student experimenters had made up their data. Finally, graduate students, rigorously trained to follow Greenspoon's procedure, completely failed to modify their subjects' behavior.

Those who doubted the automatic action of reinforcers carried out extensive experiments to show the necessity of awareness to human learning. One extensive research program was conducted by Don E. Dulany, who constructed a sophisticated axiomatic theory about types of awareness and their effects on behavior. His experiments seemed to show that only subjects aware of the contingencies of reinforcement could learn, and that subjects' confidence in their hypotheses was systematically related to their overt behavior.

By 1966 the area of verbal behavior was in a state of crisis that called for another symposium. The organizers of the meeting had optimistically hoped that they could gather psychologists from different backgrounds together to work out a unified S-R theory of verbal behavior. They called together mediationists such as Howard Kendler, workers in the Ebbinghaus verbal learning tradition, colleagues of

Noam Chomsky, and rebellious thinkers such as Dulany. Instead of unanimity the symposium discovered dissent and disenchantment, ranging from mild displeasure with the current state of verbal learning to a formal proof of the inadequacy of the S-R paradigm's theories of language. In closing the book, the editors cited Kuhn, identifying behaviorism as a paradigm in crisis (Dixon and Horton 1968). The last sentence in the book is: "To us, it appears that a revolution is certainly in the making."

Another Kuhnian point was made by a later writer, William Brewer. As with the anomalies in animal learning, it turns out that evidence against the automatic action of reinforcers existed from early days of the behaviorist paradigm. In an extensive review of the literature going back to 1919, Brewer found that the vast majority of findings indicated that awareness of the contingencies of reinforcement was necessary for human learning. This conclusion holds over a wide range of human behavior from the verbal response studies by Greenspoon and Dulany down to apparently involuntary responses such as the galvanic skin response. As we saw with animal learning, anomalies turned up but were ignored until there was some reason to notice them. Brewer concluded his paper, "There is no convincing evidence for operant or classical conditioning in adult humans" by writing: "S-R psychology has been subjected to powerful attacks from outside of psychology by Chomsky. It now appears that one need not use the abstract phenomenon of language to pull the house down. The conditioning curves of learning were the foundation upon which S-R psychology was built. Now it seems obvious that that foundation was one of sand."

Brewer did not observe, however, that demonstrations that human behavior was under conscious control challenged more than S-R or radical behaviorism. Such demonstrations strike to the core of behavioralism, for they contradict the motor theory of consciousness and make consciousness an autonomous and effective actor in the world (Collier 1964). Should Brewer's position stand up, it would follow that consciousness deserved far more attention than it had gotten since 1900, and that some form of mentalistic psychology might emerge with a real claim to scientific legitimacy.

COGNITIVE PSYCHOLOGY ASSERTS ITSELF

Because of the attacks on behaviorism and the weakening of its supporting assumptions, cognitive psychology, which had never disappeared, was reinvigorated and attracted more attention and adherents than ever before. Precisely because the situation in experimental psychology was confused and in great flux, several forms of cognitive psychology emerged and vied for center stage. The three most important were structuralism, mentalism, and information processing. The first two were associated with the more radical cognitive psychologists, who sought a clear break with the past in American psychology; structuralism in particular looked to European psychology and continental European philosophical traditions in philosophy, though mentalism also found historical roots in psychology's European past. Information-processing psychology was more conservative. While it rejected behaviorism, it nevertheless remained within the behavioralistic tradition of American psychology in the twentieth century. It adopted and adapted the approaches and procedures of artificial intelligence and cognitive simulation to forge a new language in which to cast psychological models from which behavior might be predicted and controlled.

The New Structuralism

The first form of cognitive psychology to emerge was structuralism. This was not a continuation of Titchener's system, with which it shares nothing but the name, but was an independent movement of continental European origin. Structuralism hopes to be a unifying paradigm for all the social sciences, and its adherents range from philosophers to anthropologists. Structuralists believe that any human behavior pattern, whether individual or social, is to be explained by reference to abstract structures, frequently believed to be logical or mathematical in nature. In the realm of social behavior the leading exponent of structuralism is Claude Levi-Strauss, who seeks to explain everything from a culture's myths to its cooking practices by describing a small set of logical structures that underlie these myths and cooking practices.

In psychology the leading structuralist was Jean Piaget. Piaget was originally trained as a biologist, but his interests shifted to epistemology, to which field he applied his scientific method. He criticized philosophers for remaining content with armchair speculations about the growth of knowledge when the questions of epistemology could be empirically investigated. Genetic epistemology was his attempt to chart the development of knowledge in children. Piaget divided the growth of intellect into four stages, in each of which occurs a distinct kind of intelligence. Piaget believed intelligence does not grow quantitatively, but undergoes widespread qualitative metamorphosis, so that the five-year-old not only knows less than the twelve-year-old, but also thinks in a different way. Piaget traced these different kinds of intelligence, or ways of knowing the world, to changes in the logical structure of the child's mind. Piaget attempted to describe the thinking of each stage by constructing highly abstract and formal logical models of the mental structures he believed guide intelligent behavior.

Some other psychologists are at least partially structuralists. It is sometimes held that Freud was a structuralist because he attempted to describe the structure of personality, but he lived long before the movement became self-conscious. Noam Chomsky may be regarded as a structuralist for trying to explain language in terms of its formal grammatical structure. In this Chomsky follows the lead of the French linguist Ferdinand de Saussurre (1857–1913), who many think provided the inspiration for structuralism as a movement.

Structuralism has had enormous influence in continental European philosophy, literary criticism, and social science, including psychology. The leading exponents of structuralism, Levi-Strauss, Michel Foucault, and Piaget were French-speaking, and carried on the Platonic-Cartesian rationalist attempt to describe the transcendent human mind. Piaget, for example, limited his interest to "the epistemic subject," the person as abstract knower. He disclaimed all interest in the "completely American" topic of individual differences. Also, like Wundt, he cared little for application. He spoke humorously of "the American question," a question never asked of him in Europe, namely, how can the stages of intellectual development be accelerated by training? Piaget felt it was best not to try, preferring to let natural development take its course.

As one might expect, given the European rationalist background of structuralism, its impact on American psychology has been limited. Americans have paid great attention to Piaget since 1960, and his theory has generated a good deal of research. However, few American psychologists have adopted his structuralism. His logical models are generally viewed as too abstruse and far removed from behavior to be of any value. Americans are impressed by his findings, but frequently explain them in other terms. Additionally, Americans are interested in individual differences and the effects of experience or training on cognitive development and do not care greatly about Piaget's idealized "epistemic subject." As happened with Wundt, Americans have taken what they value from a rationalist psychology, but have remained securely empiricists.

Chomsky's transformational grammar has suffered a similar fate. After an initial flurry of interest, psychologists came to feel that Chomsky's formal grammar, like Piaget's logical models, had little psychological reality, but merely gave overly complex formal descriptions of behavior. His nativist theory of language acquisition also gained initial acceptance, to be followed only by retreat to more empiricist accounts. After 1956 psycholinguists were prepared to declare themselves separate from, and perhaps superior to, formal linguists.

The New Mentalism

As the dominance of behaviorism weakened and alternatives such as structuralism and information-processing psychology were being explored, a small group of cognitive psychologists influenced by old-fashioned mentalism has arisen. Psychologists of this extremely loose camp have resurrected some very old theory and research, as two examples will show.

The Würzburg psychologists did experiments on the memorization of proverbs, which showed that people frequently remember not what a proverb says, but what it means. In recent research William F. Brewer has replicated the Würzburg finding with ordinary sentences. For example, when they read "The bullet struck the bull's-eye," most people later recall "The bullet hit the bull's-eye." More strikingly, "The absent-minded professor didn't have his car keys" is often "recalled" as "The absent-minded professor forgot his car keys." Brewer argues that subjects store in memory not a string of word concepts but the global idea described by a sentence. When the idea is recalled, the idea may be expressed differently, as in the first sentence. Sometimes the stored idea is not exactly what was said, as the second sentence shows. Brewer's ideas are partially based on Wundt's similar analysis of language, in which complex ideas, *Gesamtvorstellungen*, are spoken and reconstructed, sometimes incorrectly, by the hearer. Practical implications of the theory have also been explored. Jurors, for example, may recall not what a witness actually said, but rather recall their own reconstructions of what the witness meant and so distort the findings of a court.

Another example of new mentalism is the work of John C. Bransford and his colleagues. They have constructed paragraphs describing such processes as washing clothes in terms so vague that the hearer cannot tell what the passage is about unless told. The passages are not gibberish; each sentence is grammatical and each word meaningful, but the whole paragraph is ambiguous. Bransford has found that subjects who hear the passage without knowing the topic remember almost nothing, while those who are told the topic show good recall. To explain these results, Bransford calls on Bartlett's old idea of the *schema*, a central idea around which memory is organized. Bransford believes his findings challenge the more associative information-processing view of memory as structured concept modes. According to the information-processing account, a person who does not know the topic should be able to store each concept word and its associated material and so remember the passage. The results, however, show that this is not the case. Bransford argues that cognitive psychologists should include nonassociative factors such as the schema in their studies of memory.

Like the Gestalt psychologists, proponents of mentalism find themselves with some interesting demonstrations and provocative ideas, but with no acceptable paradigm to give them structure. The mentalists are a small and eclectic group, swamped, to their dissatisfaction, by the larger information-processing school.

Man the Machine: Information Processing

In 1957 Herbert Simon, coauthor of the General Problem Solver (GPS), prophesied "that within ten years most theories in psychology will take the form of computer programs . . ." (Dreyfus 1972). But GPS exerted little influence on the psychology of problem solving during the 1960s. In 1963 Donald W. Taylor reviewed the research area of thinking and concluded that while computer simulation of thinking shows "the most promise" of any theory, "this promise, however, remains to be justified." Three years later Davis (1966) surveyed the field of human problem solving and concluded, "There is a striking unanimity in recent theoretical orientations to human thinking and problem solving . . . that associational behavioral laws established in comparatively simple classical conditioning and instrumental conditioning situations apply to complex human learning"; Davis relegated GPS to one of three other minor theories of problem solving. Ulric Neisser, in his influential text *Cognitive Psychology* (1967), dismissed computer models of thinking as "simplistic" and not "satisfactory from the psychological point of view." On the tenth anniversary of his prediction, Simon and his colleagues quietly abandoned GPS (Dreyfus 1972).

Yet it was acknowledged by everyone, including its opponents, that cognitive psychology was booming during the 1960s. In 1960 Donald Hebb, one of psychology's recognized leaders, called for the "Second American Revolution" (the first was behaviorism): "The serious analytical study of the thought processes cannot be postponed any longer." In 1964 Robert R. Holt said that "cognitive psychology has enjoyed a remarkable boom." The boom extended even to clinical psychology, as Louis Breger and James McGaugh (1965) argued for replacing behavioristic psychotherapy with therapy based on information-processing concepts. By 1967 Neisser could write that "A generation ago a book like this one would have needed at least a chapter of self-defense against the behaviorist position. Today, happily, the climate of opinion has changed and little or no defense is necessary."

Attempts to turn psychology into a branch of computer science had failed, but had brought about a renaissance in cognitive psychology as psychologists accepted "the familiar parallel between man and computer" (Neisser 1967). It was easy to think of people as information-processing devices that receive input from the environment (perception), process that information (thinking), and act upon decisions reached (behavior). While attempts to write running programs to emulate thought seemed rather boring to psychologists, the general image of human beings as information processors was immensely exciting. So while Simon was wrong in predicting that psychological theories would be written as computer programs, the broader vision of artificial intelligence and computer simulation had triumphed by 1967, having far more influence than either of its rivals, structuralism and mentalism.

The reason for the simultaneous failure of computer programs to become the new wave in psychological theory and the success of the general information-processing perspective may be found by continuing the quotations from Hebb and Neisser. Hebb: "The serious analytical study of the thought processes cannot be postponed any longer. . . . The mediational postulate . . . is a powerful tool, and the time has come to use it." Neisser: "Today, the climate of opinion is changed and little or no defense is necessary. Indeed, stimulus-response theorists themselves are inventing hypothetical mechanisms with vigor and enthusiasm and only faint twinges of conscience. The basic reason for studying the cognitive processes has become as clear as the reason for studying anything else: because they are there."

It is important to remember the large community of psychologists who fell into the mediational tradition of psychology, whether neo-Hullian or neo-Tolmanian. These psychologists already accepted the idea of processes intervening between stimulus and response, and had throughout the 1950s "invented hypothetical mechanisms," mostly in the form of mediating r-s links holding together observable S-R connections. During the 1950s neobehaviorist human psychology flourished (Cofer 1978). Ebbinghaus's study of memory had been revived in the field called "verbal learning," and, independently of computer science, verbal learning psychologists had begun by 1958 to distinguish between short term and long-term memory. The field of psycholinguistics—an interdisciplinary combination of linguistics and psychology—had begun in the early 1950s under the auspices of the Social Science Research Council. The Office of Naval Research had since the end of World War II funded conferences on verbal learning, memory, and verbal behavior. A Group for the Study of Verbal Behavior was organized in 1957. It began, like Maslow's humanistic psychologists, as a mailing list; it became, again like the humanists, a journal, the *Journal of Verbal Learning and Verbal Behavior*, in 1962.

These groups were interconnected, and all the psychologists involved with verbal behavior and thinking took the mediational version of S-R theory for granted. For example, in psycholinguistics the "grammars [of the pre-Chomsky linguists] and mediation theory were seen to be variations of the same line of thought" (Jenkins 1968). While as late as 1963 Jenkins (Gough and Jenkins 1963) could discuss "Verbal Learning and Psycholinguistics" in purely mediational terms, it was clear by 1968 that Chomsky had "dynamited the structure [of mediational psycholinguistics] at the linguistic end" (Jenkins 1968). Chomsky convinced these psychologists that their S-R theories, even including mediation, were inadequate to explain human language. So they looked for a new language in which to theorize about mental processes, and were naturally drawn to the language of the computer, information processing. The "S" of the S-r-s-R formula could become "input," the "R" could become "output," and the "r-s" could become "processing." Moreover, information-processing language could be used, even without writing computer programs, as a "global framework within which precisely stated models could be constructed for many different . . . phenomena and could be tested in quantitative fashion" (Shiffrin 1977). Shiffrin is describing the landmark paper of the information-processing, non-computer-programming tradition, "Human Memory: A Proposed System and Its Control Processes" (Atkinson and Shiffrin 1968), from which virtually all later accounts of information processing descend.

Information-processing language gave mediational psychologists exactly what they needed. It was rigorous, up to date, and at least as quantitative as Hull's old theory, without having to make the implausible assumption that the processes linking stimulus and response were just the same as single-stage learning processes in animals. Psychologists could now talk about "coding," "search sets," "retrieval," "pattern recognition," and other information structures and operations with every expectation that they were constructing scientific theories. Information-processing psychology met psychologists' physics envy better than Hull's had, for information-processing psychologists could always point to computers as the working embodiment of their theories. The theories might not *be* computer programs, but they were *like* computer programs in regarding thinking as the formal processing of stored information. Thus, while information-processing theories were independent of computational theories in artificial intelligence, they were conceptually parasitic on them, and cognitive psychologists hoped that at some future point their theories would be programs. Simon's prophecy failed, but his dream remained.

PSYCHOLOGY AND SOCIETY

Funding Social Science

The political relations of the social sciences, including psychology, went from disaster to apparent triumph during the 1960s. The disaster was Project Camelot, the largest social science project ever conceived, under which the United States Army, together with the CIA and other intelligence agencies, gave up to $6 million to social scientists at home and abroad to pinpoint potential political trouble spots (for example, incipient guerrilla wars) and to use social scientific expertise to formulate remedies (for example, counterinsurgency actions). However, when in 1965 Project Camelot ceased to be secret, social science was thrown under a cloud. Foreign governments viewed Project Camelot as American meddling in their internal affairs. Their complaints led to a congressional investigation and to the termination of Project Camelot in July 1965. The image of social science was tarnished because social scientists participating in Project Camelot appeared to be tools of the American government rather than disinterested investigators of social phenomena.

However, out of the Camelot debacle social science was able to finally break through to a place at the federal research grant trough. As, in the mid-1960s, American cities exploded with race riots and street crime, and President Lyndon Johnson launched the War on Poverty, congressmen were moved to ask if social science could do something about race hatred, poverty, crime, and other social problems. Psychologist Dael Wolfle, an experienced observer of relations between science and government, wrote in *Science* in 1966 that "a call for large scale support of the social sciences was a recurring theme of the 25–27 January meeting of the House of Representatives Committee on Science and Technology." Wolfle thought that the time "may be ripe for special support of the social sciences," especially in view of recent advances in "quantitative and experimental methodology," so that "within a reasonable time, these disciplines can offer substantially increased help in meeting pressing social problems." As late as 1966, out of $5.5 billion spent by the federal government on scientific research, only $221 million (less than 5 percent) went to social science; but by 1967 the mood in Congress "was to do something generous for the social sciences" (Greenberg 1967).

What Congress would do, however, remained unclear (Carter 1966, Greenberg 1967). In the Senate liberal Democrats were eager to give social scientists money, and to make them into social planners. Fred Harris, perhaps the most liberal person in the Senate and soon to attempt a (doomed) run for the Democratic presidential nomination in 1968, introduced bill S. 836 to the 90th Congress, authorizing the establishment of a National Social Science Foundation (NSSF) modeled on the National Science Foundation (NSF). Walter Mondale, heir to Hubert Humphrey's liberal Democratic mantle, introduced S. 843, the "Full Opportunity and Social Accounting Act," whose leading provision was the establishment in the president's executive office of a "Council of Social Advisers" who would carry out the "social accounting," using their presumed expertise to advise the president on the social consequences of government's action and to rationally plan America's future. In the House, Emilio Q. Daddario proposed a more conservative way to "do something generous for the social sciences" by rewriting the charter of the NSF. The NSF had been mandated to support the natural sciences, but had been permitted to support "other sciences" as well, and had in fact given small amounts to support social science ($16 million in 1966 [Carter 1966]). Daddario's bill, H.R. 5404, charged the NSF to support social as well as natural science, and to include social scientists on its governing body.

Organized psychology paid great attention to the Senate bills. *American Psychologist,* the official organ of the APA, devoted a special issue to the Harris and Mondale proposals; and Arthur Brayfield, executive secretary of the APA, submitted a long statement to Congress in support of S. 836. However, individual psychologists and other social scientists had mixed reactions to the proposal to set up an NSSF. On the positive side an NSSF would give social scientists a federal funding source under their own control, and would acknowledge their importance to the country, enhancing their social prestige. On the negative side an NSSF might create a social science ghetto, stigmatizing social science by the act of setting it off from the "real sciences" in the NSF, and might at the same time give social science too much visibility; Project Camelot had given social scientists more publicity and controversy than they were prepared to handle. Among the psychologists who testified before Harris's committee considering the NSSF bill, two (Brayfield and Ross Stagner) were enthusiastic, two (Rensis Likert and Robert R. Sears) supported it with reservation, and one (Herbert Simon) opposed it. Wolfle, in an editorial in *Science* (1966), supported Simon's position. There was one point of loud universal agreement among all witnesses: Social science deserved a lot more federal money than it was getting; Sears, for example, said that regardless of what agency gave it, social science funding should go up "many times" the current level.

Social scientists got their money, but did not get the NSSF or the "Council of Social Advisers." Mondale's bill, like his 1984 candidacy for president, went nowhere. Harris's bill never got out of committee. Daddario, however, got his bill to rewrite the NSF charter through the House and enlisted the support of liberal Senator Edward Kennedy, who drafted a revised version of the new NSF bill accepted by Daddario, passed by the Senate, and finally signed into law by President Johnson on July 18, 1968, as Public Law 90-407. The NSF, wanting to keep its control over American science and therefore ready as always to respond to the desires of Congress (the director, Leland J. Haworth, had assured Harris that the NSF *wanted* to support social science), promised to infuse new funds into social science. While psychologists might still suffer physics envy, hoping for federal grants took away some of the sting.

As it turned out, psychology gained nothing from the NSF's increased funding of social sciences. From 1966 to 1976 NSF spending on social sciences except psychology rose 138 percent, while spending on psychology *declined* 12 percent. Moreover, not only did NSF continue to spend more on the natural sciences than the social sciences, the rate at which spending on the natural sciences increased was faster than the increase on the social sciences; for example, spending on physics and chemistry, the most traditional fields of natural science, rose 176 percent between 1966 and 1976. Why psychology fared so poorly remains unclear (Kiesler 1977).

Professional Psychology

In contrast to experimental psychology, where an exciting change from behaviorism to cognitive psychology seemed to be taking place, during the decade 1958 to 1968 professional psychology seemed to be adrift. As Nevitt Sanford (1965) wrote, "Psychology is really in the doldrums right now. . . . The revolution in psychology that occurred during World War II . . . has been over for some time."

There was no doubt that while psychology was growing faster than any other profession (Garfield 1966), clinical and applied psychology were growing even faster. At the 1963 meeting of the APA there were 670 openings in clinical psychology for only 123 applicants (Schofield 1966). The membership in the academic divisions of the APA had grown at a 54 percent rate between 1948 and 1960, while the professional divisions had grown at a 149 percent rate and the mixed academic/professional divisions had grown 176 percent (Tryon 1963). The relative success of the professional as opposed to the traditional scientific branches of psychology led to increased tension between the two classes of psychologists (Shakow 1965; Chein 1966, who coined the labels "scientist" and "practitioner" for the two sides in what he saw as an "irrational" and "destructive" division among psychologists). Echoing the debates of the 1930s, Leonard Small (1963) said that the greatest task facing psychology was "to obtain recognition for its competence," and hinted that if the APA did not assist professional psychologists in achieving this, they would organize separately.

However, while professional psychology was experiencing tremendous growth, professional psychologists were still somewhat uncertain as to their social and scientific roles. The Boulder Conference on clinical psychology had said that clinical psychologists were supposed to be both scientists and practitioners, but it was becoming obvious that few clinicians were becoming scientists, opting instead for the private or institutionalized practice of psychotherapy (for example, Blank and David 1963; Shakow 1965; Garfield 1966; Hoch, Ross, and Winder 1966). The Boulder model was increasingly challenged, and psychologists began to think about training psychologists purely as professionals, along the lines of physicians' training (Hoch, Ross, and Winder 1966), and to reflect on their aims as both scientists and professionals (Clark 1967).

Amid all this self-searching, professional psychologists had reason to worry about their public image. The use of psychological tests in education, business, industry, and government had mushroomed since World War II, including not just intelligence tests, but instruments designed to measure personality traits and social attitudes. Many people began to feel that these tests—inquiring as they often did into sexuality, parent-child relations, and other sensitive areas—were invasions of privacy, products of the morbid curiosity of psychologists and susceptible to abuse by employers, government, or anyone looking for tools of social control. In 1963 psychologists were upset by the popularity of *The Brain Watchers,* a book by journalist Martin Gross, which assailed the use of personality and social tests by government and industry. The antitest movement culminated in 1965, when some school systems burned the results of personality tests administered to children, and Congress investigated the use of personality tests by the federal government to screen possible employees, resulting in restrictions on their use. By 1967 psychologists were probably not surprised to learn that their prestige was pretty low. When parents were asked which of six professions they would most like their child to enter, they ranked them as follows, from most preferred to least: surgeon, engineer, lawyer, psychiatrist, dentist, psychologist. Most galling was the finding that parents preferred the clinical psychologist's archenemy, the psychiatrist, by 54 percent to 26 percent (Thumin and Zebelman 1967).

Values

In 1960 psychiatrist Thomas Szasz began an effective assault on the entire mental health establishment by analyzing *The Myth of Mental Illness* (Szasz 1960a,b). Szasz pointed out that the concept of mental illness was a metaphor based on the concept of physical illness, a bad metaphor with pernicious consequences. Szasz's analysis draws upon Ryle's analysis of the concept of mind. Ryle had argued that the mind was a myth, the myth of the Ghost in the Machine. Szasz simply drew attention to the conclusion that if there is no Ghost in the human machine, the Ghost—the mind—can hardly become ill. Just as we (falsely) attribute behaviors to an inner Ghost who causes them, so, Szasz said, when we find behaviors annoying we think the Ghost must be sick, and invent the (false) concept of mental illness: "Those who suffer from and complain of their own behavior are usually classified as 'neurotic'; those whose behavior makes others suffer, and about whom others complain, are usually classified as 'psychotic.'" So, according to Szasz, "Mental illness is not something a person has [he has no inner, sick Ghost], but is something he does or is."

Belief in mental illness has evil consequences, Szasz thought. To begin with, psychiatric diagnoses are stigmatizing labels that ape the categories of physical illness, but in reality function to give political power to psychiatrists and their allies in mental health. People labeled "mentally ill" can be deprived of their freedom and locked up for indeterminate periods of time, though they may have committed no crime; and while locked up can be given drugs against their will, something that may not be done even to convicted felons in prison: "There is no medical, moral, or legal justification for involuntary psychiatric interventions. They are crimes against humanity." In a deeper sense the concept of mental illness undermines human freedom, belief in moral responsibility, and the legal notions of guilt and innocence deriving from human freedom and moral responsibility. Instead of treating a human being who may have offended us or committed a crime as an autonomous agent, we treat him or her as a diseased thing with no will. Because the myth of mental illness is a conspiracy of kindness—we would like to excuse and help people who have done wrong—a person categorized as mentally ill, and therefore not responsible for his or her behavior, will likely come to accept his or her supposed helplessness, ceasing to view himself or herself as a morally free actor. And by contagion, as science sees all action as determined beyond self-control, everyone may cease to believe in freedom and moral responsibility. Hence the myth of mental illness strikes at the very heart of Western civilization, committed as it is to human freedom and responsibility for one's actions.

Szasz is not saying that everything called "mental illness" is a fiction, only that the concept of "mental illness" itself is a fiction. It is obviously possible for a brain to be diseased and cause bizarre thoughts and antisocial behavior. However, in such a case there is no mental illness at all, but a genuine bodily disease. But, Szasz held, most of what are called "mental illnesses" are "problems of living," not true diseases. Problems of living are quite real, of course, and a person suffering from them may need professional help working them out, so that psychiatry and clinical psychology are legitimate professions: "Psychotherapy is an effective method of helping people—not to recover from an 'illness,' but rather to learn about themselves, others, and life." Conceived medically, psychiatry is a "pseudoscience"; conceived educationally, it is a worthy vocation.

Szasz's ideas were, and remain, highly controversial. To orthodox psychiatrists and clinical psychologists he is a dangerous heretic whose "nihilistic and cruel philosophies . . . read well and offer little except justification for neglect" of the mentally ill (Penn 1985). But to others his ideas are attractive, offering an alternative conception of human suffering that does not needlessly turn an agent into a patient. Szasz and his followers in the "antipsychiatry movement," as it is sometimes called, have had some success in changing the legal procedures by which people can be involuntarily committed to mental hospitals. In many states such commitments are now hedged about with legal safeguards; no longer is it possible in most places to carry off someone to the local mental ward merely on the say-so of a single psychiatrist, as it was in 1960 when Szasz wrote.

As American society became more troubled in the 1960s, by the struggle for civil rights, by riots and crime, and above all by the Vietnam war and the controversies attending upon it, the value of adaptation—conformity—was decisively rejected by increasing numbers of Americans. The roots of the discontent lay in the 1950s, as we have seen, but in the 1960s criticism of conformity became more open and widespread.

In social science, for example, Snell and Gail J. Putney attacked conformity in *The Adjusted American: Normal Neuroses in the Individual and Society* (1964). In *Civilization and Its Discontents* Freud had argued that civilized people are necessarily a little neurotic, the psychological price paid for civilization, so that psychoanalysis could do no more than reduce neuroses to ordinary unhappiness. According to Putney and Putney, however, "normal neuroses" are not just ordinary unhappiness but are real neuroses that can and ought to be cured. Adjusted Americans, the Putneys said, have learned to conform to a cultural pattern that deceives them about what their real needs are. Because "normalcy . . .[is] the kind of sickness or crippling or stunting that we share with everybody else and therefore don't notice" (Maslow 1973), adjusted Americans are ignorant of their deepest yearnings and try to satisfy culturally prescribed rather than real human needs, consequently experiencing frustration and pervasive anxiety. The Putneys rejected the value of adjustment, replacing it with the value of "autonomy, [meaning] the capacity of the individual to make valid choices of his behavior in the light of his needs." Maslow (1961) thought that such views were held by most psychologists: "I would say that in the last ten years, most if not all theorists in psychology have become antiadjustment," and he endorsed the value of autonomy—self-actualization—as a replacement for adjustment.

Autonomy could be gained, humanistic psychologists said, through psychotherapy. Chief exponent of this view was Carl Rogers. His client-centered psycho-therapy tried to take clients on their own terms and lead them not to adjustment to the regnant norms of society, but to insights into their real needs, and thence to an ability to meet them. A client who had been through successful psychotherapy became a Heraclitean human. By the end of successful client-centered therapy, Rogers (1958) said, "The person becomes a unity, a flow of motion . . . he has become an integrated process of changingness." Rogers's therapy centered on feelings. The person who came for help, the client (like Szasz, Rogers rejected the metaphor of mental illness and refused to call those he helped "patients"), suffered above all from inability to properly experience and fully express his or her feelings. The therapist worked with the client to open up and experience feelings fully and directly, and to share these feelings with the therapist. So the "flow of motion" within the healthy human was most importantly a flow of feelings immediately and fully experienced. In the Rogerian conception, then, the unhealthy individual was one who controlled and withheld feelings; the healthy person—Maslow's self-actualizer—was one who spontaneously experienced the emotions of each moment and expressed emotions freely and directly.

Rogers, Maslow, and the other humanistic psychologists proposed the new values of growth and authenticity for Western civilization. Values concern how one should live one's life, and what one should treasure in life. Humanistic psychol-ogists proposed that one should never become settled in one's ways, but instead be always in flux: the Heraclitean human. They taught that one should treasure feel-ings. Both values derive from psychotherapy as Rogers practiced it.

The value humanistic psychologists called "growth" was the openness to change Rogers hoped to bring about in his clients. A therapist naturally wants to change the client because, after all, the client has come seeking help to improve his or her life. Humanistic psychotherapists make change a basic human value, the goal of all living, whether within or without therapy. Humanistic psychologists agreed with Dewey that "growth itself is the only moral end."

The other new value—authenticity—concerned the open expression of feel-ings characteristic of the person who had been through Rogerian therapy. Maslow (1973) defined authenticity as "allowing your behavior and your speech to be the true and spontaneous expression of your inner feelings." Traditionally, people had been taught to control their feelings and to be careful in how they expressed them. Proper behavior in business and among acquaintances—manners—depended on not expressing one's immediate feelings, and on telling little lies that oiled public social intercourse. Only with one's most intimate circle was free, private, emotional expression allowed, and even then only within civilized bounds. But humanistic psychologists opposed manners with authenticity, teaching that emotional control and deceptive emotional expression—Maslow called it "phoniness"—were psy-chological evils, and that people should be open, frank, and honest with each other, baring their souls to any and all as they might with a psychotherapist. Hypocrisy was regarded as a sin, and the ideal life was modeled on psychotherapy: The good person (Maslow, 1973) was unencumbered by hangups, experienced emotions deeply, and freely shared feelings with others.

Humanistic psychologists were clear that they were at war with traditional Western civilization and were trying to make a moral as well as a psychological revolution. Maslow (1967) denounced being polite about the drinks served at a party as "the usual kind of phoniness we all engage in" and proclaimed that "the English language is rotten for good people." Rogers (1968) closed an article on

"Interpersonal Relationships: USA 2000" by quoting "the new student morality" as propounded at Antioch College: [We deny] "that nonaffective modes of human intercourse, mediated by decency of manners, constitute an acceptable pattern of human relations."

Rogers's ideas were, of course, not new in Western civilization. Valuing emotional feeling, trusting intuition, and questioning the authority of reason can be traced back through the romantics to the Christian mystics, and to the cynics and skeptics of the Hellenistic Age. Rogers, Maslow, and the others, however, gave expression to these ideas within the context of a science, psychology, speaking with the authority of science. The humanistic psychologists' prescription for *ataraxia*—feeling and sharing—began to be put into practice in the modern Hellenistic Age. As the troubles of civilization mounted, ordinary life became intolerable for many; and as people had in the ancient Hellenistic world, they sought for new forms of happiness outside the accepted bounds of culture.

Humanistic psychology, a product of the modern Academy, advocated a modern form of skepticism. Maslow (1962) describes the "innocent cognition" of the self-actualized person this way:

> If one expects nothing, if one has no anticipations or apprehensions, if in a sense there is no future . . . there can be no surprise, no disappointment. One thing is as likely as another to happen. . . . And no prediction means no worry, no anxiety, no apprehension, no foreboding. . . . This is all related to my conception of the creative personality as one who is totally here-now, one who lives without the future or the past.

Maslow here captures the recipe for *ataraxia* of the Hellenistic skeptics, to form no generalizations, and hence be undisturbed by what happens. The humanistic self-actualizer, like the ancient skeptic, accepts what is without disturbance, "goes with the flow," and is carried without trouble down the constantly flowing stream of change of modern American life.

A much more visible manifestation of the new Hellenism were the hippies, who, like the ancient cynics, dropped out of the conventional society they scorned and rejected. Like humanistic psychologists they were at war with their culture, distrusted reason, and valued feeling, but carried their anti-intellectualism and contempt for manners to greater extremes, attempting to actually live lives that were Heraclitean flows of feeling, unconstrained by intellect or manners. It began around 1964 and quickly became a powerful cultural movement, described variously as "a red warning light for the American way of life," "a quietness, an interest—something good," or "dangerously deluded dropouts" (Jones 1967). To explore and express their feelings hippies turned to drugs. Few had heard of Carl Rogers or Abraham Maslow, though the hippies shared their values; but they had heard of another psychologist, Timothy Leary. Leary was a young, ambitious, and successful Harvard psychologist whose personal problems drove him inward, to his feelings. He began to use drugs, at first peyote and then LSD, on himself and others to attain the Heraclitean state of being, the "integrated process of changingness" open to new experience and intensely aware of every feeling. The hippies followed Leary into the "psychedelic," mind-expanding world, using drugs (as had Coleridge and other young romantics) to erase individual discursive consciousness (Kant's *Verstand*) and replace it with rushes of emotion, strange hallucinations, and alleged cosmic, transcendental insights (*Vernunft*). For the hippies, as for the post-

Kantian idealists, the ultimate reality was mental, not physical; and they believed drugs would open the "doors of perception" to the greater, spiritual world of mind. Even without drugs, hippies and humanistic psychologists were not quite of this world. In a letter Maslow wrote, "I live so much in my private world of Platonic essences . . . that I only *appear* to others to be living in the world" (Geiger 1973).

By 1968 the hippie movement, and the associated movement of protest against the war in Vietnam, was at its height. The Age of Aquarius was at hand, an age of skepticism and cynicism—the new Hellenistic Age—which we have not yet passed through.

CONCLUSION: REVOLT BUT NO REVOLUTION

Satirist Tom Lehrer once described Gilbert and Sullivan's famous patter songs as "full of sound and fury, signifying absolutely nothing." The 1960s were full of sound and fury, and 1968 was perhaps the worst year of all: the assassinations of Martin Luther King and Robert F. Kennedy, violent eruptions from the ghettos of every major American city, the growing antiwar movement. Never were the words of Yeats's "Second Coming" more true: Things seemed to be falling apart, America's youth lacked all conviction—the hippies dropped out of "straight" society—or were full of passionate intensity against their parents and their nation—the Weather Underground wanted to overthrow the government with bombs and terrorism. Many citizens wondered what rough beast was slouching toward Bethlehem to be born. In its "Prairie Fire Manifesto" the Weather Underground proclaimed, "We live in a whirlwind; nonetheless, time is on the side of the guerrillas." In psychology the humanistic psychologists were at war with the culture of intellect, siding with and inspiring the hippies and their political wing, the Yippies, while cognitive psychologists cried for a Kuhnian revolution against Hull, Spence, and Skinner. But was there anything more to the 1960s than sound and fury?

No.

From Yippie to Yuppie

While humanistic psychology fancied that it offered a radical critique of modern American society, it was at heart profoundly conservative, even reactionary. In his concept of self-actualization Maslow did no more than refurbish—tarnish might be a better word—Aristotle's *scala naturae* with modern psychological jargon. In its cultivation of feeling and intuition, humanistic psychology harked back to the romantic rejection of the scientific revolution, but was never honest enough to say so. Humanistic psychologists, including Maslow and Rogers, always counted themselves scientists, ignoring the deep conflict between science's commitment to natural law and determinism and their own commitment to the primacy of human purpose. Humanistic psychology is therefore a sort of fraud trading on the good name of science to push ideas entirely at variance with modern science. In the nineteenth century Dilthey and others of the authentic romantic tradition offered reasons for setting the human sciences—the *Geisteswissenschaften*—apart from physics, chemistry, and the other *Naturwissenschaften*, but humanistic psychologists could only offer barely articulate protests against scientistic imperialism. If a case is to be made against the natural scientific, reductionistic image of human beings, it must come from a different, more intelligent, source.

Similarly, the hippies and their followers, far from providing a radical critique of "Amerika," as they were wont to spell it, embodied every contradiction of the American past. They worshiped simple, pre-urban lives, yet mostly lived in cities (which were more tolerant of deviance than small towns) and focused their lives on drugs and electronic music, products of the industrial world they feigned to reject. With the humanistic psychologists they valued feelings and openness to new experience, echoing the romantic poet Blake's cry, "God save us from single vision and Newton's sleep." As humanistic psychology failed to displace behavioralism, so did the hippie movement fail to overthrow straight society. In 1967 a theologian at the University of Chicago said that the hippies "reveal the exhaustion of a tradition: Western, production-oriented, problem-solving, goal-oriented and compulsive in its way of thinking" (Jones 1967). As late as 1986, during the second term of the Reagan administration, in the years of the compulsively fit, compulsively successful Yuppies, it was obvious that problem solving and goal achievement were not exhausted. In 1967 the Eastern imports American feared were Zen, Buddhism, and the Maharishi Mahesh Yogi; today they are Nissans, Sonys, and Fujis. All that remains of the humanistic revolt is "feeling good about yourself."

Nor were the hippies and the humanistic psychologists the great nonconformists they made themselves out to be. The hippies lived strange lives, but they demanded conformity to their nonconformism. For them the great sin was to be "straight," to hold to the values of one's parents and one's natal culture, to work hard, to achieve, to be emotionally "closed." A song by a pioneer rock band, Crosby, Stills, Nash, and Young, depicts a member of the counterculture resisting the temptation to cut his hair. Humanistic psychologists did not shed adaptation as a virtue. Maslow (1961) described his utopia, Eupsychia, as a place where "there would be no need to hang onto the past—people would happily adapt to changing conditions." The great therapeutic breakthrough of the humanistic psychologists was the encounter group, in which people supposedly learned to be open and authentic. As Rogers describes it, members were coerced into being authentic:

> As time goes on the group finds it unbearable that any member should live behind a mask or a front. The polite words, the intellectual understanding of each other and relationships, the smooth coin of tact and cover-up . . . are just not good enough. . . . Gently at times, almost savagely at others, the group *demands* that the individual be himself, that his current feelings not be hidden, that he remove the mask of ordinary social intercourse. (Zilbergeld 1983)

Humanistic psychologists, like the hippies, did not really question the value of adaptation and social control; they just wanted to change the standards to which people had to adapt.

From Mediation to Information Processing

By 1968 it was clear that of the three claimants to cognitive psychology, the most influential and widely held was information-processing psychology. And by 1968 it was becoming clear that just as humanistic psychology and the counterculture represented no radical break with the past, information-processing psychology was a continuation of behavioralism, not its revolutionary replacement. There was to be sure revolutionary sound and fury in the 1960s, supported by citations of Kuhn's *Structure of Scientific Revolutions* (for example, Palermo 1971); but closer examination of the leading ideas of the information-processing psychologists reveals that they were not about to become mentalists.

Despite the fact that he wrote about "Imagery: The Return of the Ostracized," Robert R. Holt (1964) unwittingly linked the new cognitive psychology to its behavioralist forebearers. He acknowledged that the concept of mediation had already brought cognitive concepts into behaviorism, and set out the goal of cognitive psychology in terms Hull could have endorsed: constructing "a detailed working model of the behaving organism." Indeed, for Holt an attractive feature of information-processing models was precisely that with them one could "construct models of the pyschic apparatus in which there can be processing of information without consciousness." Marvin Minsky (1968), the leader of artificial intelligence at MIT, was eager to show that AI could find "mechanistic interpretations of those mentalistic notions that have real value," thereby dismissing mentalism as prescientific.

Herbert Simon, one of the founders of modern information-processing psychology, betrays the continuity of information processing with behavioralism, and even its affinity with behaviorism, very well in his *Sciences of the Artificial* (1969) writing, "*A man, viewed as a behaving system, is quite simple. The apparent complexity of his behavior over time is largely a reflection of the complexity of the environment in which he finds himself.*" Simon, like Skinner, views human beings as largely the products of the environment that shapes them, since they themselves are simple. In the same work Simon follows Watson in dismissing the validity of mental images, reducing them to lists of facts and sensory properties associatively organized. Simon also argues that complex behaviors are assemblages of simpler behaviors. Information-processing psychologists share many important behaviorist assumptions: atomism, associationism, and empiricism. On the philosophical side information processing espouses materialism, holding that there is no independent Cartesian soul, and positivism, continuing to insist on operationalizing all theoretical terms (Simon 1969). Proponents of this position are made uncomfortable by Chomsky's nativism and his abstract analysis of language. They believe his linguistics confuses formal logical description of grammar with the concrete psychological processes that in fact produce grammatical speech.

Information-processing psychologists reject peripheralism. They believe complex processes intervene between stimulus (input) and response (output). Unlike Watson or Skinner, information-processing cognitive psychologists are willing to infer central mental processes from observable behavior. However, although peripheralism was part of Watson's and Skinner's behaviorisms, it was not shared by Hull, Tolman, or informal behaviorism. The information-processing adherents do not believe central processes are covert versions of S-R associations, but their theory is not far removed from Hull's or Tolman's, except in complexity and sophistication.

Information-processing psychology is a form of behavioralism. It represents a continuing conceptual evolution in the psychology of adaptation, for it views cognitive processes as adaptive behavioral functions, and is in a sense a reassertion of earlier American functionalism. The functionalists saw the mind as adaptive, but were trapped by the limited metaphysics of the nineteenth century into espousing at the same time a strict mind-body parallelism, engendering a conflict exploited by Watson in establishing behaviorism. The cybernetic analysis of purpose, and its mechanical realization in the computer, however, vindicated the functionalist attitude by showing that purpose and cognition were not necessarily mysterious, and need not involve dualism.

Watson's and Skinner's behaviorisms were extreme statements of the psychology of adaptation that attempted to circumnavigate the inaccessible—and therefore potentially mythical—reaches of the human mind. The information-processing view follows the steps of William James, Hull, and Tolman in seeing, beneath behavior, processes to be investigated and explained. Behaviorism was one response by the psychology of adaptation to crisis; information processing is another, but in both we see a deeper continuity under the superficial changes. Perhaps to those involved, the revolt against S-R psychology is a scientific revolution; but viewed against the broader framework of history, the revolt is a period of rapid evolutionary change, not a revolutionary jump.

BIBLIOGRAPHY

For histories of humanistic psychology see Anthony J. Sutich, "Introduction," *Journal of Humanistic Psychology* (1961, *1:* vii–ix); and Sutich and Vich (1969). There are two good collections of articles from the various facets of humanistic psychology: James F. T. Bugental, *Challenges of humanistic psychology* (New York: McGraw-Hill, 1967); and Sutich and Vich (1969). Rogers (1964) is considered by humanistic psychologists to be a representative work (Sutich and Vich 1969); and Maslow (1973) offers a varied selection of his papers.

The most accessible of Noam Chomsky's books is *Language and mind,* enlarged ed. (New York: Harcourt Brace Jovanovich, 1972).

For constraints on animal learning, see Seligman and Hager (1972), who reprint the most important papers of the period and add useful commentary. Garcia discusses the troubles he had publishing his taste-aversion work in "Tilting at the papermills of academe," *American Psychologist* (1981, *36:* 149–158). The occasion of the address is ironic, since it was given upon Garcia's acceptance of a prestigious APA award for his initially rejected work. A similar experience of frustration followed by fame is reported by a pair of other taste-aversion researchers, Paul Rozin and James Kalat, "This week's citation classic: Specific hungers and poison avoidance as adaptive specializations of learning," *Psychological Review* (1971, *78:* 459–486), "*Current Contents; Social and Behavioral Sciences* (August 4, 1980, *31:* 14).

Without question, the best guide to the awareness and learning literature is Brewer (1974).

Collections of the leading research in artificial intelligence and computer simulation for both ends of our period are available in E. A. Feigenbaum and J. Feldman, eds., *Computers and thought* (New York: McGraw-Hill, 1963); and M. Minsky, ed., *Semantic information processing* (Cambridge: MIT Press, 1968); Feigenbaum and Feldman also reprint Turing's classic paper. Hubert L. Dreyfus (1972) provides a history and penetrating critique of work in AI and computer simulation. Cofer (1978) is a valuable history of the activities of the mediational behaviorists from World War II to 1962. Neisser's *Cognitive psychology* (1967) is viewed by many psychologists as having created cognitive psychology in its modern form.

A complete autopsy of Project Camelot and the ensuing political fallout may be found in a special issue of *American Psychologist* (1966, *21,* no. 5, May). Good accounts of the maneuvering around the founding of an NSSF as opposed to including social science in the NSF are given by Carter (1966) and Greenberg (1967). The *American Psychologist* special issue on the Harris and Mondale bills was 1967, *22* (no. 11, November). It reprints both bills, articles by their sponsors (Mondale's has the earnest but mushy and soporific qualities of his presidential campaign speeches), and the testimony given before the committees considering each bill. Digests of the testimony on the NSSF bill may be found in *Transaction* (1968, *5,* no. 1 January–February: 54–76). For the legislative histories of the bill, the place to go is the *Congressional Record* for the 90th Congress, Session 2. Mondale's bill is introduced and never heard from again. Harris's bill was discussed on the floor of the Senate, mostly by a cosponsor, Senator Ralph Yarborough, but otherwise languished in committee. Representative Daddario's bill to revise the NSF is fully discussed in an excellent but anonymously written report entered in the *Record* on pages 14889–14895, including complete background on the establishment of the NSF, a legislative history of Daddario's bill, and an accounting of all the changes to NSF that it made. It is interesting to observe the support of liberal Democrats for social science. Charles G. McClintock and Charles B. Spaulding, "Political affiliation of academically affiliated psychologists," *American Psychologist* (1965, *20:* 211–221), showed that until after World War II psychologists had voted with the rest of the public—Republican before F.D.R. and Democratic afterward—but they had, unlike the rest of the voting populace, continued to become more Democratic after the war. In the 1952 and 1956 elections American voters as a whole had supported the liberal and rather intellectual Adlai Stevenson against Eisenhower by only 44 percent and 42 percent, while psychologists had voted for Stevenson by margins of 63 percent and 68 percent. By 1960 a bare majority of voters voted for John Kennedy, while 79 percent of psychologists did so. Psychologists, like their supporters in the Senate, were more liberal than the country as a whole, and social scientists benefited greatly from the rise of political liberalism from 1965 to 1980.

In 1963 *American Psychologist* (*18*) devoted two special issues to the problems of clinical psychology, no. 6 (June) and no. 9 (September). Alarm over Martin Gross's *The brain watchers* is found in various "Comments" in the August (no. 8) issue of the same year. Political controversies over the use and abuse of tests led to a special issue devoted to "Testing and public policy" in 1965 (*20,* [no. 11, November]). The whole fuss was humorously captured by satirist Art Buchwald in a column published in the *Washington Post* (Sunday, June 20, 1965), in which he made up his own personality test. Since 1965 Buchwald's test has been widely circulated among psychologists, many of whom are ignorant of its origin.

Szasz's views were first presented in his book (Szasz 1960a) and elaborated in many books and articles since. While Ryle's *Concept of mind* is in Szasz's bibliography, he does not in fact derive his own argument from Ryle; nevertheless, the affinity of the two analyses is clear. For a contemporary "straight" view of the hippie movement, see Jones (1967). However, the movement is best appreciated through its art and music, of which the most lasting has proved to be the music: the Grateful Dead and the Jefferson Airplane in particular made records still likely to be accessible. Also illuminating is the New Journalism that came out of and at first depended on the movement. My own favorites are Tom Wolfe's *The electric Kool-Aid acid test* (New York: Bantam, 1968) and anything by Hunter S. Thompson, but most relevantly *Fear and loathing in Las Vegas: A savage journey into the heart of the American dream* (New York: Popular Library, 1971). Wolfe's book is especially interesting in the present context, as it centered on the quintessential hippie group, the Merry Pranksters of Ken Kesey, author of a brilliant antipsychiatric novel, *One flew over the cuckoo's nest* (New York: New American Library, 1963). Wolfe became the outstanding observer of the new psychological Hellenistic Age.

REFERENCES

Atkinson, R. M. and Shiffrin, R. M. (1968) Human memory: A proposed system and its control processes. *Psychology of Learning and Motivation 2:* 89–195. Reprinted in Bower (1977).

Beach, F. (1960) Experimental investigations of species-specific behavior. *American Psychologist 15:* 1–18.

Blank, L. and David, H. (1963) The crisis in clinical psychology training. *American Psychologist 18:* 216–219.

Bolles, R. C. (1975) Learning, motivation, and cognition. In W. K. Estes, ed., *Handbook of learning and the cognitive processes.* V. 1. Hillsdale, New Jersey: Erlbaum.

Bower, G., ed. (1977) *Human memory: Basic processes.* New York: Academic.

Breger, L. and McGaugh, J. L. (1965) Critique and reformulation of "learning-theory" approaches to psychotherapy and neurosis. *Psychological Bulletin 63:* 338–358.

Breland, K. and Breland, M. (1961) The misbehavior of organisms. *American Psychologist 16:* 681–684. Reprinted in Seligman and Hager (1972).

Brewer, W. F. (1974) There is no convincing evidence for operant or classical conditioning in normal, adult, human beings. In W. Weimer and D. Palermo, eds., *Cognition and the symbolic processes.* Hillsdale, New Jersey: Erlbaum.

Bugental, J. F. T. (1964) The third force in psychology. *Journal of Humanistic Psychology 4:* 19–26.

Carter, L. J. (1966) Social sciences: Where do they fit in the politics of science? *Science 154:* 488–491.

Chein, I. (1966) Some sources of divisiveness among psychologists. *American Psychologist 21:* 333–342.

Chomsky, N. (1957) *Syntactic structures.* The Hague: Mouton.

Chomsky, N. (1959) Review of B. F. Skinner's *Verbal behavior. Language 35:* 26–58. Reprinted in Jakobovits and Miron (1967).

Chomsky, N. (1966) *Cartesian linguistics.* New York: Harper & Row.

Clark, K. (1967) The scientific and professional aims of psychology. *American Psychologist 22:* 49–76.

Cofer, C. N. (1978) Origins of the *Journal of Verbal Learning and Verbal Behavior. Journal of Verbal Learning and Verbal Behavior 17:* 113–126.

Collier, R. (1964) Selected implications from a dynamic regulatory theory of consciousness. *American Psychologist 19:* 265–269.

Davis, G. (1966) Current status of research and theory in human problem solving. *Psychological Bulletin 66:* 36–54.

Dixon, T. R. and Horton, D. C., eds. (1968) *Verbal behavior and general behavior theory.* Englewood Cliffs, New Jersey: Prentice-Hall.

Dreyfus, H. L. (1972) *What computers can't do: A critique of artificial reason.* New York: Harper & Row.

Garfield, S. L. (1966) Clinical psychology and the search for identity. *American Psychologist 21:* 343–352.

Geiger, H. (1973) Introduction: A. H. Maslow. In Maslow (1973).

Gough, P. B. and Jenkins, J. J. (1963) Verbal learning and psycholinguistics. In Marx (1963).

Greenberg, D. S. (1967) Social sciences: Progress slow on House and Senate bills. *Science 157:* 660–662.

Greenspoon, J. (1955) The reinforcing effect of two spoken sounds on the frequency of two behaviors. *American Journal of Psychology 68:* 409–416.

Hebb, D. O. (1960) The second American Revolution. *American Psychologist 15:* 735–745.

Hoch, E., Ross, A. O., and Winder, C. L. (1966) Conference on the professional preparation of clinical psychologists. *American Psychologist 21:* 42–51.

Holt, R. R. (1964) Imagery: The return of the ostracized. *American Psychologist 19:* 254–264.

Jakobovits, L. and Miron, M., eds. (1967) *Readings in the psychology of language.* Englewood Cliffs, New Jersey: Prentice-Hall.

Jenkins, J. J. (1968) The challenge to psychological theorists. In Dixon and Horton (1968).

Jones, R. (1967) Youth: The hippies. *Time,* July 7: 18–22.

Kiesler, S. B. (1977) Research funding for psychology. *American Psychologist 32:* 23–32.

Malcolm, N. (1964) Behaviorism as a philosophy of psychology. In T. W. Wann, ed. (1964).

Marx, M., ed. (1963) *Theories in contemporary psychology.* New York: Macmillan.

Maslow, A. (1961) Eupsychia—The good society. *Journal of Humanistic Psychology 1:* 1–11.

Maslow, A. (1962) Notes on being-psychology. *Journal of Humanistic Psychology 2:* 47–71.

Maslow, A. (1967) Self-actualization and beyond. In J. F. T. Bugental, ed., *Challenges of humanistic psychology.* New York: McGraw-Hill.

Maslow, A. (1973) *The farther reaches of human nature.* New York: Viking/Esalen.

Miller, G. (1962) Some psychological studies of grammar. *American Psychologist 17:* 748–762. Reprinted in Jakobovits and Miron (1967).

Minsky, M. (1968) Introduction. In M. Minsky, ed., *Semantic information processing.* Cambridge: MIT Press.

Neisser, U. (1967) *Cognitive psychology.* New York: Appleton-Century-Crofts.

Osgood, C. (1957) A behaviorist analysis of perception and language as cognitive phenomena. In J. Bruner et al., *Contemporary approaches to cognition.* Cambridge: Harvard University Press.

Palermo, D. (1971) Is a scientific revolution taking place in psychology? *Science Studies 1:* 135–155.

Penn, I. N. (1985) The reality of mental illness (letter to the editor). *The Wall Street Journal,* June 24: 33.

Postman, L. and Sassenrath, J. (1961) The automatic action of verbal rewards and punishments. *Journal of General Psychology 65:* 109–136.

Putney, S. and Putney, G. J. (1964) *The adjusted American: Normal neuroses in the individual and society.* New York: Harper Colophon.

Rogers, C. R. (1958) A process conception of psychotherapy. *American Psychologist 13:* 142–149.

Rogers, C. R. (1964) Toward a science of the person. In T. W. Wann, ed. (1964).

Rogers, C. R. (1968) Interpersonal relationships: U.S.A. 2000. *Journal of Applied Behavioral Science 4:* 265–280.

Rogers, C. R., and Skinner, B. F. (1956) Some issues concerning the control of human behavior: A symposium. *Science 124:* 1057–1065.

Sanford, N. (1965) Will psychologists study human problems? *American Psychologist 20:* 192–198.

Schofield, W. (1966) Clinical and counseling psychology: Some perspectives. *American Psychologist 21:* 122–131.

Seligman, M. E. P. and Hager, J. L., eds. (1972) *Biological boundaries of learning.* New York: Appleton-Century-Crofts.

Shakow, D. (1965) Seventeen years later: Clinical psychology in the light of the 1947 committee on training in clinical psychology report. *American Psychologist 20:* 353–367.

Shiffrin, R. M. (1977) Commentary on "Human memory: A proposed system and its control processes." In Bower (1977).

Simon, H. (1969) *The sciences of the artificial.* Cambridge: MIT Press.

Small, L. (1963) Toward professional clinical psychology. *American Psychologist 18:* 558–562.

Sutich, A. J. and Vich, M. A. (1969) Introduction. In A. J. Sutich and M. A. Vich, eds., *Readings in humanistic psychology.* New York: The Free Press.

Szasz, T. S. (1960a) *The myth of mental illness.* New York: Harper Perennial Library. Rev. ed. 1974.

Szasz, T. S. (1960b) The myth of mental illness. *American Psychologist 15:* 113–119.

Taylor, D. W. (1963) Thinking. In Marx (1963).

Thumin, F. J. and Zebelman, M. (1967) Psychology and psychiatry: A study of public image. *American Psychologist 22:* 282–286.

Tryon, R. C. (1963) Psychology in flux: The academic-professional bipolarity. *American Psychologist 18:* 134–143.

Wann, T. W., ed. (1964) *Behaviorism and phenomenology: Contrasting bases for modern psychology.* Chicago: Chicago University Press.

Wolfle, D. (1966a) Social problems and social science. *Science 151:* 1177.

Wolfle, D. (1966b) Government support for social science. *Science 153:* 485.

Zilbergeld, B. (1983) *The shrinking of America: Myths of psychological change.* Boston: Little, Brown.

CHAPTER 15

Contemporary Psychology

COGNITIVE SCIENCE
The Triumph of Information Processing
The New Functionalism
DOUBTS ABOUT COGNITIVE SCIENCE
Is Information Processing a Paradigm?
Was There a Revolution?
Is the Turing Test Valid?
Is Formalism Plausible?
Conclusion
THE STRANGE DEATH OF RADICAL BEHAVIORISM
Beyond Freedom and Dignity
Critique of Cognitive Science
CHALLENGES TO SCIENTIFIC PSYCHOLOGY
From Psychology's Occult Doubles
From Biology
From the Humanities
PSYCHOLOGY AND SOCIETY
Giving Psychology Away
Clinical Psychology
The Turn to Service
CONCLUSION: THE PSYCHOLOGICAL SOCIETY

COGNITIVE SCIENCE

The Triumph of Information Processing

During the 1960s and early 1970s information-processing theory gradually replaced mediational theory as the language of cognitive psychology. By 1974 the venerable *Journal of Experimental Psychology* contained articles by proponents of only two theoretical orientations, information processing and radical behaviorism, the former substantially outnumbering the latter. In 1975 the journal was divided into four separate journals, two concerned with human experimental psychology, one with animal psychology, and one with long, theoretical-experimental papers; and the human journals were controlled by the information-processing point of view. During the same years information-processing psychologists launched their own journals, including *Cognitive Psychology* (1970), and *Cognition* (1972); and the new cognitive view spread to other areas of psychology, including social psychology (Mischel and Mischel 1976), social learning theory (Bandura 1974), developmental psychology (Farnham-Diggory 1972), animal psychology (Hulse, Fowler, and Honig 1978), psychoanalysis (Wegman 1984), and psychotherapy (Mahoney 1977; Meichenbaum 1977; founding of the journal *Cognitive Therapy and Research* [1977]), and even philosophy of science (Rubinstein 1984). Mediational behaviorism ceased to exist, and the radical behaviorists were confined to a sort of publications ghetto comprising three journals: *Journal of the Experimental Analysis of Behavior, Journal of Applied Behavior Analysis,* and *Behaviorism.*

The fields of artificial intelligence and computer simulation began to merge in the late 1970s into a new field distinct from psychology, called *cognitive science.* Cognitive scientists launched their own journal, *Cognitive Science,* in 1977, and held their first international conference a year later (Simon 1980). Cognitive science defined itself as the science of what George Miller named *informavores* (Pylyshyn 1984). The idea was that all information-processing systems—whether made of flesh and blood, like human beings, or silicon and metal, like computers, or of whatever materials might be invented or discovered—operated according to the same principles and therefore constituted a single field of study, cognitive science, "converging around the information processing paradigm" (Simon 1980).

The proponents of cognitive science were confident that their position was secure as the only respectable scientific game in town. Herbert Simon (1980), writing about the behavioral and social sciences for the centenary issue of *Science* declared that "Over the past quarter-century, no development in the social sciences has been more radical than the revolution—often referred to as the information processing revolution—in our way of understanding the processes of human thinking." Simon dismissed behaviorism as "confining" and "preoccupied with laboratory rats" and praised information-processing theory for helping psychology achieve "a new sophistication" and for creating a "general paradigm, the information processing paradigm," which preserved behaviorism's "operationality" while surpassing it "in precision and rigor."

As defined by Simon, the "long-run strategy" of human cognitive science had two goals, each of which is reductionistic in its own way. First, "human complex performance"—the old " 'higher mental processes' "—would be connected with "the basic elementary information processes and their organization." In other words, cognitive science, like behaviorism, aimed to show that complex behavior could be reduced to assemblages of simpler behaviors. Second, "we cannot be satisfied with our explanations of human thinking until we can specify the neural substrates for the elementary information processes of the human symbol system." In other words, like the strict behaviorism of Karl Lashley and A. P. Weiss, cognitive science aimed to show that human thinking could be reduced to neurophysiology.

In 1979 Lachman, Lachman, and Butterfield attempted in their often-cited *Cognitive Psychology and Information Processing* to describe information-processing cognitive psychology as a Kuhnian paradigm. They claimed that around 1970 information-processing psychology had become "the dominant paradigm in cognition, and cognitive psychology now appears to be in a state of normal science." They defined cognitive psychology in terms of the computer metaphor discussed in the last chapter: Cognitive psychology is about "how people take in information, how they recode and remember it, how they make decisions, how they transform their internal knowledge states, and how they translate these states into behavioral outputs. The analogy is important. It makes a difference whether a scientist thinks of humans as if they were laboratory animals or as if they were computers." Our choices seem to rest entirely between viewing people as rats or as computers; we may not think of them as human beings. Behavioralism began when psychologists refused to anthropomorphize human beings; the information-processing "paradigm" wants to "computermorphize" human beings.

In discussing an example of "cognitive behavior" [sic], Lachman, Lachman, and Butterfield presuppose that people *must* process information, thereby legitimating information-processing psychology's answers to questions about why people behave as they do. When you drive a car you *must* "perceive each familiar landmark anew each time," "have represented the landmark's appearance in your memory," "match up your current perception of the landmark to its stored representation," and so on, though "decid[ing] repeatedly when to shift gears" and where to park. Wittgenstein pointed out that how we frame questions about human behavior determines a great deal—probably more than the empirical facts—about the answers we get from our investigations. Lachman, Lachman, and Butterfield's analysis of driving is a splendid example of this process at work; when they say we *must* do the things they claim—even if they are out of awareness, as Lachman, Lachman, and Butterfield concede—information-processing psychology is forced on us, and the only possible answers to the question of how we drive or do anything else become information-processing ones. The form of the question dictates the answer.

Lachman, Lachman, and Butterfield's explication of the information-processing "paradigm" makes clear that information-processing psychology is a form of behavioralism with strong affinity to all but radical behaviorism. Speaking of "cognitive behavior," for example, shows that information processing is the latest form of behavioralism. Their dismissal of introspection as "unreliable and impoverished" and their evaluation of mentalistic introspective psychology as having "reached a dead end" by 1913 are consistent with behavioral views on the psychology of consciousness. They identify the study of consciousness with the study of attention as a stage in information processing, a narrow view of consciousness that Wundt would have rejected. Lachman, Lachman, and Butterfield themselves recognize that information processing took over much from neobehaviorism: nomothetic explanation, empiricism, focus on the laboratory, operationism, and "the rational canons of natural science." In short, though Lachman, Lachman, and Butterfield specifically deny it, information processing adopted a modified logical positivism from neobehaviorism. This becomes clearest at the end of the book, when the authors become confused about the existence of the information processes they have discussed for five hundred pages. They would clearly like to assert that information processes are real processes that actually take place inside an organism. Yet these processes are generally observable to neither the person who is having them nor to a neuroscientist watching the brain. Information-processing psychology is then forced to define its theoretical terms operationally: "Flowcharts, in a way, have the same status for us that operational definition had for our predecessors." But, as we learned from Howard Kendler's operational analysis of the "What is learned?" controversy of the 1950s, operationism is antirealistic, treating theoretical terms simply as convenient fictions. The tension between realism and operationalism is manifest in the last pages of *Cognitive Psychology and Information Processing,* but its authors do not seem to feel it, lamely concluding that it is too early to tell if human information processes are real or not.

The convergence of artificial intelligence and cognitive psychology into the field of cognitive science, and the grandiose claims of cognitive scientists, already stated by Simon, one of the first cognitive psychologists, are repeated by the Research Briefing Panel on Cognitive Science and Artificial Intelligence (Estes and Newell 1983). According to the panel, cognitive science addresses a "great scientific mystery, on a par with understanding the evolution of the universe, the origin of life, or the nature of elementary particles," and is "advancing our understanding of the nature of mind and the nature of intelligence on a scale that is proving revolutionary."

An important part of the optimism of cognitive scientists, and the conceptual basis of the merger of cognitive psychology and artificial intelligence, was the computer metaphor of mind:body::program:computer, known as *functionalism.* For it is functionalism that allows cognitive scientists to regard people and computers as essentially similar, despite their material differences.

The New Functionalism

The basis thesis of functionalism derives from the activity of computer programming. Suppose I write a simple program for balancing my checkbook, in a programming language such as BASIC. The program will specify a set of *computational functions:* retrieving my old balance from memory, subtracting checks written, adding deposits made, and comparing our results to the bank's. Ignoring minor formatting differences, I can enter and run this program on many different machines: an Apple, an Atari, an IBM PC, an IBM Sierra mainframe, an Amdahl mainframe, and so on. In each case the same computational functions will be carried out, although the physical processes by which each computer will perform them will be different, because the internal structure of each machine is different.

To be able to predict, control, and explain the behavior of a computer, it is unnecessary to know anything at all about the electronic processes involved; all one needs to understand is the higher-level computational functions in the system. I am composing these words on a program called AppleWorks, and because I understand the programmed functions of AppleWorks I can use AppleWorks effectively—that is, I can predict, control, and explain my computer's behavior. I know absolutely nothing about the lower-level computational functions that compose higher-level functions such as moving paragraphs about, nor do I know anything about how my

Apple's hardware works; but such knowledge is not necessary to use any properly programmed computer.

Functionalism simply extends the separation of program and computer to include human beings. Computers use hardware to carry out computational functions, so functionalism concludes that people use "wetware" to do the same things. When I balance my checkbook by hand, I carry out exactly the same functions as my BASIC computer program does. My nervous system and my Apple's microchip are materially different, but we instantiate the same program as we each do my accounts. So, functionalism concludes, my mind is a set of computational functions that runs my body in exactly the same way that a computer program is a set of computational functions that controls a computer: My mind *is* a running program. In this way psychologists can hope to predict, control, and explain human behavior by understanding the human "program" and without understanding the nervous system and brain. Cognitive psychologists are thus like computer programmers asked to study an alien computer. They dare not fool with the machine's wiring, so they attempt to understand its program by experimenting with its input-output functions.

Behind functionalism is an important assumption. A computer program can be written to carry out any activity that can be completely described as a set of formal rules. Balancing a checkbook can be described as a formal procedure in which certain rules are applied to various numerical quantities. The claim that a computer can do activity X assumes that X is a formalizable task. To claim that a computer can play chess assumes that chess is a formal rule-governed activity. And likewise with composing music, deciding whether or not to have an abortion, getting married, deciding to get married, playing poker, seducing an attractive person. If a computer is to do any of these things, or to imitate how people do them (obviously a computer can't get married—yet), it must be the case that each activity can be formalized as a precise set of rules that can be captured in the computational functions of a program.

The attraction of functionalism and information processing is that they offer a solution to the behaviorist's problem: how to explain the intentionality of behavior without any residue of teleology. Within behavioralism there were two basic approaches. Pure mechanists such as Hull tried to describe humans and animals as machines that blindly responded to whatever stimuli they happened to encounter. E. C. Tolman, after abandoning his early realism, opted for a representational strategy: Organisms build up representations of their world that they use to guide overt behavior. Each strategy was flawed and finally failed. Tolman was able to show, contrary to Hull, that animals do not simply respond to their environment. Rather they learn about it, and base their behavior on more than just the currently operative stimuli, using representations stored away from earlier experience as well. Tolman's approach, however, ran into the homunculus problem: He implicitly postulated a little rat in the head of a real rat, who read the cognitive map and pulled the levers of behavior. In short, he created a Ghost in the Machine, failing to explain purpose and pushing the problem into the mysterious Ghost. The mediational neo-Hullians tried to combine Hull's mechanistic S-R theory with Tolman's intuitively plausible representationalism by regarding mediating r-s mechanisms as representations, an interpretation countenanced by Hull's concept of the "pure stimulus act." But the mediational compromise rested on the counterintuitive notion that the brain's r-s connections follow exactly the same laws as overt S-R connections

Functionalism preserves the virtues of Hull's and Tolman's approaches while seeming to avoid their vices by invoking the sophisticated processes of computer programs instead of little r-s links. Computers carry out their computational functions upon internal representations; in the checkbook example the program directs the computer to manipulate representations of my previous balance, my checks, my deposits, and so on. Yet my Apple contains no little accountant bent over ledger books doing arithmetic: There is no ghostly accountant in the machine. Rather, the machine applies precisely stated formal rules to the representations, carrying out the computations in a completely mechanistic fashion. From the perspective of functionalism, both Hull and Tolman were right, but it remained for the computational approach to put their insights together. Hull was right that organisms are machines; Tolman was right that organisms build up representations from experience. According to functionalism, computer programs apply Hullian mechanistic rules to Tolmanian representations, and, if functionalism is correct, so do living organisms.

As Lachman, Lachman, and Butterfield state, "Information processing psychology is fundamentally committed to the concept of representation." Brentano recognized that intentionality is the criterion of mentality. Mental states such as beliefs possess "aboutness": They refer to something beyond themselves, which neurons cannot do. Tolmanian representations possess intentionality: A cognitive map is about, is a representation of, a maze. What kinds of representations do computers use?

Although the concept of representation seems easy, it is fraught with difficulty, as Wittgenstein pointed out. Suppose I draw a stick figure, like so:

What does it represent? At first glance you might take it to be a man walking with a walking stick. But I might be using it to represent a fencer standing at rest, or to show how one ought to walk with a walking stick, or a man walking backward with a stick, or a woman walking with a stick, or many other things. Another example: No matter how much you might look like a portrait of Henry VIII, it remains a representation of Henry, not of you. Of course, I might use it to represent you if someone asks what you look like and you are not around. So representations don't represent by virtue of their appearance. Exactly what does make a representation a representation is a matter of debate, but functionalism has a distinctive strategy for handling the problem.

Any representation has both semantics and syntax. The semantics of a representation is its meaning; its syntax is its form. If I write the word DESK, its meaning (semantics) lies in its reference to certain items of furniture, and its syntax is the actual structure and arrangement of the letters D, E, S, and K. From a scientific, materialistic standpoint, the mysterious thing about representations is their meaning, their intentionality; that was the original point of Brentano's concept of intentionality, showing that meaning could not be reduced to physical processes. But, as remarked above, the goal of functionalism is to unmystify intentionality, bringing behavior and mental processes within the scope of mechanistic science. It tries to do this by reducing semantics to syntax.

When I typed DESK a moment ago, did the computer understand its meaning? No; it treated those letters purely syntactically, storing them as a set of 0's and 1's in its binary machine language. However, I can ask AppleWorks to do what appear to be intelligent things, couchable in mentalistic language, with the word DESK. So I can ask it to find every occurrence of DESK in a given file, and it will find both occurrences of DESK and of "desk." I could ask it to substitute CHAIR for every occurrence of DESK. If I had the word DESK in a dictionary database, I could ask for the meaning of DESK and I would be told. Yet although the computer could do all these things with the word DESK, it could not be said to possess the semantic component of DESK. For in every case the computer would operate by looking for the unique machine code of 0's and 1's into which it coded DESK, and then carrying out my specified operation on that register. The computer operates only on the syntax of a representation, although its behavior may be consistent with its knowing the meaning of the representation. Although from its behavior it may seem to know the semantic meaning of DESK, all it really knows is the syntax of 0's.

Another way of expressing this difficult but important point is to borrow some terminology from Daniel Dennett (1978), one of the creators of functionalism. When we play chess with a computer we are likely to treat it as a human being, attributing to it mental dispositions: It *tries* to develop its queen early, it *wants* to capture my queen's pawn, it's *afraid* I will seize control of the center of the board. Dennett calls this adopting the *intentional stance*. We naturally adopt the intentional stance toward people, sometimes toward animals, and toward machines in certain cases. But what is going on inside the computer is not intentional at all. The layout of the pieces on the chessboard is represented internally as a complex pattern of 0's and 1's in the computer's working memory. Then the computer finds a rule that applies to the current pattern and executes the rule, changing the content of a memory register, which is displayed on a video screen as the move of a chess piece. Next an input command—your chess move—alters the pattern of 0's and 1's, and the computer again applies the applicable rule to the new pattern, and so on. The program does not *try, want,* or *fear,* it simply carries out formal computations on patterns of 0's and 1's, and you regard that as intentional behavior.

In an interview with Jonathan Miller, Dennett (1983) summarizes the computational approach to intentionality this way (the dialogue is somewhat compressed):

> The basic idea is that you start at the top with your whole intelligent being, with all its beliefs and desires and expectations and fears—all its information. Then you say: "How is all that going to be represented in there?" You break the whole system down into subsystems, little homunculi. Each one is a specialist, each one does a little bit of the work. Out of their cooperative endeavors emerge the whole activities of the whole system.
>
> But isn't this another way of being unscientifically mentalistic?
>
> Yes, you do replace the little man in the brain with a committee, but the saving grace is that the members of the committee are stupider than the whole. The subsystems don't individually reproduce the talents of the whole. That would lead you to an infinite regress. Instead you have each subsystem doing a part; each is less intelligent, knows less, believes less. The representations are themselves less representational, so you don't need an inner eye to observe them; you can get away with some sort of inner process which "accesses" them in some attenuated sense.

So while we attribute intentionality to the chess-playing computer, in fact it is only a collection of nonintentional, stupid subsystems carrying out blind computations on syntactically defined representations, following mechanistic rules.

Where does this leave people? Margaret Boden, a popularizer and philosophical exponent of AI, thinks it leaves people as they are; she sees AI as entirely compatible with humanistic treatments of people as creators and users of meaning (Boden 1977, 1979). Other philosophers, however, take the computational metaphor more seriously, and reach a different conclusion. Stephen Stich (1983) has forcefully argued that the only scientifically acceptable theories in human cognitive psychology will eventually have to be syntactic theories, which treat human information processing just like a computer's, as mechanical computation on syntactically defined representations. Dennett (1978) tries to straddle these two views, acknowledging that in science we must ultimately treat people as machines, but that the "folk psychology" of belief and desire may be retained as an instrumental calculus for everyday use. Stich replies that, in the end, scientific truth must prevail as it always has: "The general conception of the cosmos embedded in the folk wisdom of the West was utterly and thoroughly mistaken. . . . Nor is there any reason to think that ancient camel drivers would have greater insight or better luck when the structure at hand was the structure of their own minds rather than the structure of matter or of the cosmos." This is the attitude of scientistic imperialism: "If our science is inconsistent with the folk precepts that define who and what we are, then we are in for rough times. One or the other will have to go." "Deprived of its empirical underpinnings, our age old conception of the universe within will crumble just as certainly as the venerable conception of the external universe crumbled during the Renaissance." Stich finds the prospect cheering.

It is well to take the computational argument seriously. Although (as Lachman, Lachman, and Butterfield [1979] point out) most cognitive psychologists use information-processing as a language and do not write computer programs, still the final "cash value," to use William James's phrase, of information processing lies in the promise to turn information-processing theory into computational theory. As Ulric Neisser (1984), a frequent critic of information processing, nevertheless admits, "Models that actually run on real computers are more convincing than models that exist only as hypotheses on paper." The inspiring thing to psychologists about artificial intelligence was, as George Miller (1983) says, that when behaviorists said that talk of mind was "moonshine," cognitive psychologists could point to AI: "It can't be moonshine if I can build one."

Moreover, cognitive science draws its scientific respectability from the promise of writing computational theories. In a briefing for federal officials such as the president's science adviser, the Research Briefing Panel on Cognitive Science and Artificial Intelligence wrote:

> The hypothesis that links artificial intelligence and human cognition together, providing the frame within which scientific inquiry proceeds, holds that all intelligence, including human intelligence, arises from the ability to use symbols. By symbols, we mean physical symbol systems, noted above, as first understood in computer science. Without this stipulation the hypothesis would constitute only another version of the long-held view that symbols are important in human mental life. But with the notions of symbol and symbol system firmly connected to the physical world via the realization in computers, the hypothesis anchors the study of all the higher processes of mind to the same scientific world of mechanism as all other natural sciences. (Estes and Newell 1983)

In their briefing the panel works hard to establish the scientific status of cognitive science—the briefing very soberly presents cognitive science as serious basic science—and the claim that "symbolic behavior can be realized in a physical system" distances cognitive science from psychology's unscientific moonshine by pushing it toward physics and Newtonian mechanism. Clark Hull made the same move, but lacked the means to convincingly turn his theories into working machines.

Ultimately, information-processing theories must be turned into formal computational theories, because if they are not there will be no more reason to think of people as computers than as animals. And perhaps a good deal less. After all, computers are composed of silicon and metal, humans and animals are made of flesh and blood; computers are designed and manufactured, humans and animals evolved; computer minds spring into full-blown existence when the machine is started, humans and animals develop from infancy to adulthood; computers do not actively interact with the world through bodies, humans and animals do. On a less physical level, computers have no society, no culture, nor do they live in groups; humans and some animals live in groups, and only humans live in culture, a world they themselves create. The similarity of human and computer is really rather slight, and we should worry if it is the only game in town. Lachman, Lachman, and Butterfield say that it matters which analogy we follow, animal or computer. The analogy does, indeed, matter. But which analogy is right? Is either?

DOUBTS ABOUT COGNITIVE SCIENCE

When in 1957 Herbert Simon prophesied that by 1967 psychological theories would be written as computer programs, he also foresaw that "within ten years a digital computer will be the world's chess champion" and that "within ten years a digital computer will discover and prove an important new mathematical theorem." In 1965 Simon predicted that "machines will be capable, within 20 years, of doing any work that a man can do" (Dreyfus 1972). In 1986 none of Simon's forecasts had come to pass. More important, some psychologists and philosophers had begun to wonder if they *could* come to pass. The issue is not Simon's credibility as a prophet—others in artificial intelligence made similar claims (Dreyfus 1972)—but the credibility of the information-processing, computational approach to psychology. For if it should turn out that computers in principle cannot do "any work that a man can do," then treating people as computers would be bad psychological theory.

In 1981 James J. Jenkins, who had experienced the transition from mediational behaviorism to information processing, asserted that "there is a malaise in cognitive psychology, a concern with trivia, a lack of direction." He asked, and seemed to answer in the negative, "Is the field advancing as we feel sciences are supposed to advance? . . . Is the field developing and deepening our understanding of cognitive principles, processes, or facts that can contribute to the solution of real problems and generate answers to relevant questions?" While Jenkins did not doubt that "human beings are universal machines" and was able to find "some [better] directions for cognitive psychology," he pictured a field adrift. In the same year the editors of *Cognition,* then celebrating its tenth birthday, fretted that "in cognitive psychology, progress is [not] obvious," that since 1971 there had been in the field no "major development," that "little has really changed" (Mehler and Franck 1981).

Even more dissatisfied with the state of cognitive psychology was Ulric Neisser, the man who had helped establish it and the information-processing approach in his *Cognitive Psychology* of 1967. In 1976 he wrote a new text, *Cognition and Reality,* which "destroyed my reputation as a mainstream cognitive psychologist" (Goleman 1983). In the new book Neisser said, "The actual development of cognitive psychology in the last few years has been disappointingly narrow," wondered "whether its overall direction is genuinely productive," and said he had come to "realize that the notion of *information processing* deserves a closer examination." Neisser began to argue that cognitive psychology should "take a more 'realistic' turn." Subsequently, Neisser's unhappiness with cognitive psychology has not diminished: "The upshot of so much effort has been disappointing. There is little sense of progress" (Neisser 1982). The "information processing approach remains somehow unsatisfying as an account of human nature" (Neisser 1984). Neisser urges that the information-processing approach be replaced with an "ecological approach" that studies cognition in natural contexts instead of in the narrow confines of experiments invented to meet the needs of the laboratory.

While such disgruntled views may not be typical of cognitive psychologists, Jenkins, Mehler, Franck, and Neisser are acknowledged leaders in the field, and their unhappiness is surely a symptom of something wrong. But what?

Is Information Processing a Paradigm?

In their eagerness to rebel against behaviorism, cognitive psychologists embraced Thomas Kuhn's analysis of science, and rushed to proclaim information processing a new scientific "paradigm" for psychology (for example, Lachman, Lachman, and Butterfield 1979). However, most "Kuhnian" analyses of psychology tended to overlook an important component, perhaps the most important component, of a paradigm as described by Kuhn. Kuhn claimed that a paradigm has two parts, the disciplinary matrix, a set of philosophical assumptions, and the shared exemplar, a visibly successful research achievement providing a model for investigations of nature conducted within the paradigm. Psychologists' analyses of information processing and its rivals focused on the rather nebulous disciplinary matrix and neglected the shared exemplar (again see Lachman, Lachman, and Butterfield 1979; for a recent example see Brewer and Nakamura 1984).

But, as Kuhn recognized, much—perhaps most—of a paradigm's puzzle-solving power derives from the shared exemplar, because it defines the puzzles. Pavlov's research program furnishes an instructive example. While Pavlov clearly had philosophical assumptions about psychology, more important to the brilliance of his research was his *experimental* paradigm, the shared exemplar of all classical conditioning research: pairing US with CS. Pavlov's experimental setup allowed him to pose concrete, answerable questions, such as, What happens if I alter the temporal relationship of US and CS? Or if there is more than one CS? Or if I present CS without US? No matter what one's philosophical prejudices, one cannot do research without a concrete model, and a scientific community's research cannot accumulate toward a common goal without a *shared* exemplar.

Perhaps cognitive psychologists neglect the shared exemplar because information-processing psychology does not offer one. The first to identify the problem (though without the Kuhnian terminology) was Allen Newell (1973) of the original Newell, Shaw, and Simon GPS team. Newell's paper was one of the first to express unhappiness with information processing, and is often cited by other dissidents. In commenting on the papers at a cognitive psychology symposium, Newell said that "half of me is half distressed and half confused. Half of me is quite content and clear on where we are going." Newell's happy half applauded the fine technical achievements of the research presented at the symposium. The distressed half looked at all the fine research at hand, anticipated more fine research yet to come, but asked, "*Where will psychology then be? Will we have achieved a science of man adequate in power and commensurate with his complexity?*" The problem Newell saw was that cognitive psychologists were investigating a myriad of specific phenomena—he listed fifty-nine, and implied there were more—but that it was impossible to "put them all together." As he tried to put them all together "[i]t became less and less clear to me that all these papers were cumulating."

While cognitive psychologists share the disciplinary matrix of information processing, they have no shared exemplar around which to organize their collective research, so that the papers cannot accumulate. Nor is there reason to think things have changed since 1973. Both Jenkins (1981) and Neisser (1982) echo Newell's complaint.

Lack of a shared exemplar affects theory construction. Because each cognitive scientist is concerned with his or her own phenomenon, small-scale theories of specific tasks proliferate, while the goal of constructing a general cognitive theory is neglected. Jenkins (1981) complains that these small theoretical models are "not models of the mind, but rather models of the task being performed by the subjects." Precisely because human beings have such general and flexible intelligence, when they are asked to do a laboratory task they take on the characteristics of the task, so that a theoretical model of subjects' behavior reflects the demands of the task, and captures no general aspect of mental functioning.

The task-modeling approach is encouraged by the computational metaphor of artificial intelligence. In AI a programmer who wants a computer to accomplish some task examines the task very closely and writes a program that allows the computer to succeed. Workers in cognitive psychology seem to do the same thing: They analyze a task and ask what a person (rather than the AI programmer's computer) must be doing to solve the task. In AI the approach poses no problems, because the programmer's goal is simply to write a successful program. In cognitive psychology, however, the goal ought to be different: to discover how people do in fact accomplish what they do. Focusing on the task in an AI manner leads psychologists to study what information processing says people must logically be doing and may obscure what they really are doing.

A further obstacle to theorizing in information-processing psychology is that its disciplinary matrix, to continue using Kuhn's terms, is too vague and ill-defined to demand rigorous theorizing. This is especially true when information processing is used as a metaphor without specific commitment to producing a computational version of a theory. About all the information-processing metaphor says is that people take in input, represent and process it internally, and produce output. Since the constraints of the approach are so vague, it is little wonder that cognitive psychologists analyze and theorize about tasks rather than people; at least a task specifies and constrains how one should theorize and for what one should account. As a result there is no shared agreement on the enterprise of cognitive psychology. Speaking of memory, the most widely investigated of the cognitive processes, Endel Tulving (1979), one of the field's leaders, argued that, "After a hundred years of laboratory-based study of memory, we still do not seem to possess any concepts that the majority of workers would consider important or necessary.'' Tulving's contention is supported by the findings of White (1985). White examined seven leading textbooks in cognitive psychology and found widespread disagreement on important ideas. Of 3,246 publications cited in all the books, only 19 (0.6 percent) were cited by every author. Only 146 (4.5 percent) were cited in as many as three texts. Examination of the texts' content showed that few phenomena were discussed in all of them, and that even frequently occurring concepts were often discussed under different names.

Clearly, despite claims to the contrary from Lachman, Lachman, and Butterfield (1979) and others, information-processing psychology is not a Kuhnian paradigm. There is no widely shared exemplar or even set of exemplars. There is no tightly woven disciplinary matrix of pretheoretical assumptions constraining the forms theories take. Information processing is, as Lachman, Lachman, and Butterfield say, a metaphor; but it is no more than that. The metaphor of information processing provides only an *approach* to psychology within the behavioralist tradition.

Was There a Revolution?

Like the citizens of the United States, France, and the Soviet Union, cognitive scientists share a myth of revolutionary origin. Proponents of information processing believe that information processing constitutes a Kuhnian paradigm, that behaviorism constituted another, and that in the 1960s a Kuhnian scientific revolution occurred during which information processing overthrew behaviorism. We have already learned that neither information processing nor behaviorism were paradigms, so it is reasonable to doubt if there was a revolution. Information processing is best viewed as the latest form of behavioralism, with strong affinities to historical forms of behaviorism. Mentalism was the study of conscious experience as such; behavioralism is the study of behavior: What attitude does information processing take to consciousness and introspection?

In an influential paper on the introspectability of information processes, Richard E. Nisbett and Timothy Wilson (1977) describe the characteristic information-processing account of consciousness: ''It is the *result* of thinking, not the process of thinking, that appears spontaneously in consciousness'' (Miller 1962). Nisbett and Wilson then elaborate on the information-processing view, reviewing evidence ''consistent with the most pessimistic view concerning people's ability to report accurately about their cognitive processes.'' They conclude that people have ''little or no direct introspective access to higher order cognitive processes,'' and that when people are asked to describe the processes that caused their behavior ''they do not do so on the basis of any true introspection. Instead, their reports are based on a priori, implicit, causal theories,'' that is, on folk theories about their behavior. Reports will be true when folk theories are true, false when folk theories are false; but in any case it is not from introspection of information processes that people derive accounts of their own behavior.

Wundt would not have been surprised at Nisbett and Wilson's findings, because their experiments were quite like those of the Würzburg psychologists whose work Wundt denounced. In both the Nisbett-Wilson and Würzburg experiments people performed some more or less complex task and were then asked why they behaved as they did. For example, after performing the task of choosing the best pantyhose from a display, subjects talked about superior color and texture. In fact, each pair of pantyhose was identical; subjects tended overwhelmingly to choose the rightmost pair. Wundt was quite aware, and argued in his critique of the Würzburg school's experiments, that this sort of retrospective accounting of mental process can yield no scientific data.

The real issue lying between Wundt and Nisbett and Wilson shows that it is not their respective evaluations of Würzburg-type experiments that has changed, but rather the meaning they give their interpretations. Nisbett and Wilson do not doubt that their subjects knew what was going on in consciousness during the experiments, but argue that conscious content did not reflect underlying cognitive processes. Thus for them verbal reports of consciousness may be safely ignored in explaining behavior. In other words, Nisbett and Wilson are behavioralists whose scientific aim is the prediction and control of behavior. Like Ralph Barton Perry, they argue that while one knows more about oneself than anyone else, one's mind is nevertheless in principle open to complete scrutiny from outside. Wundt, however, was a mentalist. What bothered him about the Würzburg results was that their descriptions of conscious content were so variable. He had no interest in behavior; for him the subject matter of psychology was conscious experience in itself and for itself, without regard to how it predicted or explained behavior. Nisbett and Wilson have no interest in consciousness unless it helps them predict, explain, and control behavior; when they find it cannot, they throw it out altogether.

Nisbett and Wilson's analysis has not escaped criticism, but the critics still operate within the framework of behavioralism. Nisbett and Wilson concluded that introspective reports "may have little value" in trying to construct cognitive explanations of behavior. Critics tend to argue that Nisbett and Wilson's conclusion is just a little too bleak: Sometimes people's introspective reports have scientific value. The most important of the more optimistic accounts of verbal reports was that of K. Anders Ericsson and Herbert Simon (1980). Ericsson and Simon began by stating information-processing psychology's goal in a way that would have cheered Clark Hull or John Watson: "We would like to have processing models so explicit that they could actually produce the predicted behavior from the information in the stimulus." In their account of information processing one frequently important stage of processing involves placing material in short-term memory (STM), either during processing as a way station or at the end of processing when a response is produced. "Within the context of this general model, verbalization processes produce (externalize) information that is in STM." Thus, under the right conditions (typically violated in the Nisbett and Wilson studies), verbal reports of information-processing activity can be accurate, as reports of one stage of information processing.

The Ericsson and Simon view of introspection differs only in emphasis from Nisbett and Wilson and from behaviorism. Nisbett and Wilson think that verbal reports of cognitive processes are only very rarely accurate; Ericsson and Simon think that they are accurate about certain aspects of information processes, but certainly not all. Nisbett and Wilson implicitly urge that verbal reports be entirely discarded from cognitive science; Ericsson and Simon argue that when used properly, as "subject behavior," they may be of service to the cognitive scientist, which view seems to have become the consensus (Klatzky 1984). Ericsson and Simon recognize that their account is not very different from Watson's. Watson abjured introspection, but thought that having subjects talk aloud while solving problems might reveal their thought processes, and Ericsson and Simon agree. Since Watson believed thinking was talking to yourself, talking aloud would, by definition, reveal thought. Ericsson and Simon, however, regard thinking as unconscious data processing, so their use of talking is more confused and confusing than Watson's. Nevertheless the point stands: The information-processing account of awareness is little different from the behaviorist account.

Behavioralists wanted to predict, control, and explain behavior. Some behavioralists were willing to theorize about processes linking environment and behavior, and to use verbal reports as evidence concerning mediating processes. Other behavioralists rejected inner processes (radical behaviorism), and some rejected introspective reports (methodological behaviorism). Information-processing cognitive scientists are not radical behaviorists, since they are happy to theorize about mediating processes, but they disagree about how useful verbal reports are in finding out about them. Neither behaviorism nor information-processing psychology is interested in consciousness for its own sake: Both are forms of behavioralism.

Exactly what is it, from the information-processing standpoint, that subjects are supposed to detect by introspection? It is admitted that subjects know of what they are conscious, and no one claims that people might introspect the states of their brain, Of what then are they supposed to be aware? Nisbett and Wilson quote a researcher who said, "I don't remember any subject who ever described anything like the process of [cognitive] dissonance reduction that we knew to have occurred." Wittgenstein observed much of what Nisbett and Wilson observed: When people remember something—where they left their keys, for example—the conscious processes they experience are infinitely different from case to case. He concluded from this that there was no process called "memory." Information-processing psychologists find the same thing, and conclude that people do not know the unconscious process called "memory." The information-processing view rests on an assumption: There are processes that *must* have occurred, whether or not anyone observed them. Yet these processes, at least for the most part, do not occur in consciousness, where they might be observed, nor would one see them if one opened up the brain—"dissonance reduction" is not a brain process. While Wittgenstein's conclusion that there are no cognitive processes may seem strange, the information-processing view is also strange, perhaps stranger. They assert that there *must be* information processes taking place in people who are not aware of them, processes that cannot be observed by a neuroscientist. Instead of taking people's inability to report these processes as evidence that they do not exist, as Wittgenstein did, information-processing psychologists impugn people's awareness of the reasons for their actions. Like the angels of Neoplatonic Christianity, information processes *must* exist, whether anyone sees them or not.

Here we again see the AI model of cognitive psychology at work. Cognitive psychologists take a task and analyze it from the information-processing perspective, working out what a computer program would have to do to accomplish it. Then they assume that something very similar *must* be happening in humans doing the same task. Should subjects verbally report similar processes, cognitive psychologists will be pleased at the support for their model. Should subjects report something different, it does not matter, because subjects do not always understand their own minds. In either event, the logical analysis of the task dictates the psychological theory, just as it does in AI. What subjects say will be taken seriously only when it supports the model, and can be dismissed as erroneous folk theorizing when it does not.

These considerations return us to a problem that troubled Lachman, Lachman, and Butterfield (1979). Do the information processes postulated by cognitive psychology really occur in human thinking, or are they only convenient fictions that help cognitive scientists predict, control, and explain behavior? If information processes are neither consciously experienced events nor brain events, it becomes difficult to say what they might be other than theoretical conveniences. Some cognitive scientists, most notably John Anderson (1978, 1981), have concluded that radical behaviorism is correct in claiming that there is no way of knowing what processes take place between stimulus and response. Since more than one information-processing model is compatible with any set of behavioral data, and since the processes may not be directly observed, there is no sure way of deciding between competing models. In other words, there is no point in claiming psychological reality for any information-processing model. Theoretical models are useful insofar as they help predict, describe, and control human behavior: "Lack of unique identifiability [of one model of behavior over another] is no reason not to postulate internal structure and representation. . . . [G]o ahead and get on with the business of science: Postulate some set of internal structures and processes that are consistent with the data and don't worry about unique identifiability" (Anderson 1981). While Anderson's views are not typical of cognitive scientists (see Hayes-Roth 1979; Pylyshyn 1979), they do reveal the difficulties of postulating information processes that are neither introspectible conscious contents nor identifiable brain states.

The debate over the psychological reality of information processes repeats the "What is learned?" debate among behaviorists of the 1950s. Then, too, there were realist theorists such as Tolman and Hull, asserting the reality of cognitive maps and habit strengths. And there were also nominalists such as Howard Kendler, asserting that theoretical terms must be regarded as useful fictions only. In its attitudes to consciousness, introspection, and verbal reports, and in its theoretical debates, information-processing psychology is updated, high-tech behavioralism, differing from behaviorism only in theoretical language, not in substance. Information pro cessing psychologists would have little trouble subscribing to the creed of behaviorism laid out by John B. Watson in the first paragraph of his 1913 behaviorist manifesto.

Cognitive scientists believe in a revolution because it provides them with an origin myth, an account of their beginnings that helps legitimize their practice of science (Brush 1974). Kuhn provided the language of paradigm and revolution, Chomsky provided the angry voice crying for change, and the sound and fury of the alienated 1960s provided an exciting backdrop for the shift from mediational behaviorism to information processing. But there was no revolution: Behavioralism continued with a new language, a new model, and new concerns directed to its familiar end: the description, prediction, and control of behavior (Leahey 1981).

Myths of revolution usually turn out on close examination to be misleadingly simple. The revolution of the thirteen colonies against England was mainly an assertion of traditional English liberties, not a revolution at all. The French Revolution begun in the name of Reason drowned in blood and unleashed Napoleon on Europe. The Russian Revolution traded Oriental despotism for totalitarian tyranny. The cognitive revolution was an illusion.

Is the Turing Test Valid?

Imagine that you are seated at a table in an empty room. On the table before you are a book and a supply of paper, and in the wall in front of the table are two slots. Into the left-hand slot come pieces of paper on which are written Chinese characters. You know nothing about Chinese. When you receive a slip of paper, you examine the string of symbols on it and find the corresponding string in the book. The book tells you to copy out a new set of Chinese figures on one of your pieces of paper and pass it out the right-hand slot. You can do this for any string of characters that comes in the left slot. Unknown to you, Chinese psychologists on the other side of the wall are feeding into the left slot Chinese stories followed by questions about the stories, and they receive answers out of the other slot. From their point of view the machine beyond the wall understands Chinese, because they are able to carry on a conversation with the machine, receiving plausible answers to their questions. They conclude that the machine beyond the wall understands Chinese and has passed the Turing test.

Of course, you know that you understand nothing—you are just writing down one set of meaningless squiggles by instructed response to another set of meaningless squiggles. John Searle (1980), whose thought experiment this is, points out that you are functioning in the "Chinese Room" exactly as a computer functions. The computer accepts machine code input (patterns of 0's and 1's), applies syntactic rules to transform these representations into new representations (new patterns of 0's and 1's), and generates output. It is the computer user alone who calls what the computer is doing "understanding stories," "playing chess," "simulating an atomic strike," or whatever, just as it is the Chinese psychologists who say that the room "understands Chinese." Searle's argument shows that the Turing test is not an adequate measure of intelligence, because the Chinese Room passes the Turing test without understanding anything, and its mode of operation is exactly the same as a computer's.

Searle goes on to point out an important peculiarity about cognitive simulation compared to other kinds of simulation. Meterologists construct computer simulations of hurricanes, economists of U.S. foreign trade activity, and biologists of photosynthesis. But their computers do not develop 100 mph winds, multibillion-dollar trade deficits, or convert light into oxygen. Yet cognitive scientists claim that when and if they simulate intelligence—that is, a program passes the Turing test—their machine will *really be* intelligent. In other fields simulation and real achievement are kept separate, and Searle regards it as absurd to ignore the distinction in cognitive science.

Searle distinguishes between *weak AI* and *strong AI*. Weak AI would be maintaining the distinction between simulation and achievement, and using computers as other scientists do, as wonderfully convenient calculating devices with which to use and check theories. Strong AI is the claim—refuted by the Chinese Room thought experiment—that simulation of intelligence *is* intelligence. Searle believes that strong AI can never succeed, for the same reason that a computer cannot perform photosynthesis: It's made out of the wrong materials. In Searle's view it is the natural biological function of certain plant structures to photosynthesize, and it is the natural biological function of brains to think and understand. Machines have no natural biological functions and so can neither photosynthesize nor understand. Computers may provide tools to help investigate photosynthesis and understanding, but they cannot, Searle concludes, ever actually do either one. Searle's argument is similar to a point made by Leibniz:

> And supposing there were a machine, so constructed as to think, feel, and have perception, it might be conceived as increased in size, while keeping the same proportions, so that one might go into it as into a mill. That being so, we should, on

examining its interior, find only parts which work one upon another, and never anything by which to explain a perception. (Gunderson 1984)

Is Formalism Plausible?

There is in cognitive science no small amount of scientistic hubris. According to the Briefing Panel of Cognitive Science, because computers engage in *"symbolic behavior"* (precisely what Searle's argument denies), "we ourselves can program computers to deal with many things—anything to which we set our mind." (The panel has apparently forgotten the grandiose claims made in the 1950s that never came to fruition.) Hidden underneath the panel's claim is the assumption of *formalism*. Computers can do anything that can be written as a computer program, and the panel, following Simon in claiming that computers can be programmed to do "anything a man can do," "anything to which we set our mind," implicitly asserts that anything people do is a formal procedure. Formalism in psychology represents the final development of the mechanization of the world picture. Just as physical science succeeded by analyzing nature as a machine, cognitive science hopes to succeed by analyzing human beings as machines (Dreyfus 1972). However, Searle's Chinese Room already challenges mechanistic formalism by showing that formal processing of symbols does not yield understanding of language. Other challenges have also arisen, the greatest of which is the *frame problem,* because it challenges not only the ability of computers to imitate human intelligence, but the very possibility of achieving machine intelligence at all.

Daniel Dennett (1984) asks us to consider the following story:

Once upon a time there was a robot, named R_1 by its creators. Its only task was to fend for itself. One day its designers arranged for it learn that its spare battery, its precious energy supply, was locked in a room with a time bomb set to go off soon. R_1 located the room, and the key to the door, and formulated a plan to rescue its battery. There was a wagon in the room, and the battery was on the wagon, and R_1 hypothesized that a certain action which it called PULLOUT (WAGON, ROOM) would result in the battery being removed from the room. Straightaway it acted, and did succeed in getting the battery out of the room before the bomb went off. Unfortunately, however, the bomb was also on the wagon. R_1 *knew* that the bomb was on the wagon in the room, but didn't realize that pulling the wagon would bring the bomb out along with the battery. Poor R_1 had missed that obvious implication of its planned act.

Back to the drawing board. "The solution is obvious," said the designers. "Our next robot must be made to recognize not just the intended implications of its act, but also the implications about their side effects, by deducing these implications from the descriptions it uses in formulating its plans." They called their next model the robot-deducer, R_1D_1. They placed R_1D_1 in much the same predicament that R_1 had succumbed to, and as it too hit upon the idea of PULLOUT (WAGON, ROOM) it began, as designed, to consider the implications of such a course of action. It had just finished deducing that pulling the wagon out of the room would not change the color of the room's walls, and was embarking on a proof of the further implication that pulling the wagon out would cause its wheels to turn more revolutions than there were wheels on the wagon—when the bomb exploded.

Back to the drawing board. "We must teach it the difference between relevant implications and irrelevant implications," said the designers, "and teach it to ignore the irrelevant ones." So they developed a method of tagging implications as either relevant or irrelevant to the project at hand, and installed the method in their next model, the robot-relevant-deducer, or R_2D_1 for short. When they subjected R_2D_1 to the test that had so unequivocally selected its ancestors for extinction, they were surprised to see it sitting, Hamlet-like, outside the room containing the ticking bomb, the native hue of its resolution sicklied o'er with the pale cast of thought, as Shakespeare (and more recently Fodor) has aptly put it. ''Do something!'' they yelled at it. ''I am,'' it retorted. ''I'm busily ignoring some thousands of implications I have determined to be irrelevant. Just as soon as I find an irrelevant implication, I put it on the list of those I must ignore, and . . .'' the bomb went off.

R1 and his descendants are caught in the frame problem. How is it possible to formalize human knowledge and problem-solving skills as a set of computerized rules? It is quite obvious that people do not do what the R robots do: Somehow we just solve problems rapidly and with little conscious thought, just as the Würzburg psychologists discovered. If we did work the ways the Rs did, we, like they, would have died long ago. Rather than working computationally, humans seem to work intuitively: Solutions to problems just occur to us without thinking; adaptive behaviors happen without thought. We do not have to think to ignore all the absurdities that $R_2 D_1$ had to work at ignoring, because the absurd and irrelevant implications of our behavior just do not occur to us. But a computer, being a formal system, must work out all the implications of its acts and then ignore them.

Empirical evidence also implies that people's behavior is not formalizable. Hubert Dreyfus's study of expert performance—for example, flying fighter planes—shows that only novices apply rules to guide their behavior, while experts just fly (Rose 1985). Eleanor Rosch's (1977) studies of human concepts show that they are not based on tidy, computerlike lists of defining attributes, but are centered on stereotypical prototypes surrounded by fuzzy boundaries. Consider, for example, the problem of differentiating between *glass, cup,* and *mug* (Leahey and Harris 1985). Each term conjures up an ideal prototype, but setting the boundaries between them is problematic. The prototype of the cup has a handle on it, but we call paper cups *cups,* not glasses. One might say it's because they are not made of glass, but would one call a glass something that is shaped like a teacup but is made of glass? If mugs have handles but are thicker than cups, is there a minimum thickness a cup must have to become a mug? Does the name of the moment depend on what a vessel holds? Is a paper cup filled with beer a ''cup of beer''? If we fill a typical glass with coffee, do we call it a ''glass of coffee'' as we offer it to a visitor? If we fill a mug with water, is it a ''mug of water''? Our intuitions are troubled by these borderline cases, suggesting that we do not use formal rules to distinguish between *glass, cup,* and *mug.* If such homely concepts cannot be formalized, it is wildly improbable that computers can be programmed to do anything we set our minds to, including morality, justice, politics, art, drama, poetry, or even the everyday encounters of social life.

Conclusion

Increasingly, workers in cognitive science acknowledge limitations on their achievements, and shy away from the pretensions of the past (Waldrop 1984; Rose 1985). Most believe that in time the A1 approach to cognition will be vindicated: There will be intelligent machines and human behavior will be explicable in terms of computational information processing. But even these scaled-down ambitions are best regarded as hopes. If Dreyfus, Searle, and other critics of cognitive science are correct, human beings will remain exceptions to the mechanized world picture.

THE STRANGE DEATH OF
RADICAL BEHAVIORISM

While it is true that radical behaviorism has been somewhat ghettoized, it would be false to assert, as many have, that it is dead. For the radical behaviorists' ghetto is lively indeed. They have their own successful journals, as noted earlier; their own division within the APA (Division 25); and their own society, the Association for Behavior Analysis, which runs a fourth journal, *The Behavior Analyst*. Radical behaviorists continue to pursue their own research, to develop the conceptual foundations of their discipline, to grapple with cognitive science, and to offer proposals for remaking society.

Beyond Freedom and Dignity

In *Walden II* and *Science and Human Behavior* Skinner first described his ideal society and its rationale. Against the backdrop of the 1960s Skinner returned to the problems of society, and again offered radical behaviorism and its technology of behavior as cures for the ills of the modern world. During the 1970s and 1980s Skinner became preoccupied with spreading his social message, in talk after talk (for example, Skinner 1985b) and at greatest length in his book *Beyond Freedom and Dignity*. Skinner argues that it is a great mistake to assume, as everyone does, that people possess free will, and hence moral responsibility and dignity; most psychologists assume, as Skinner does, that humans are not free—after all, cognitive scientists think men are machines—but few of them talk about (at least in public, as Skinner does) the ethical consequences of determinism. Nor is Skinner depressed by determinism, because he finds in the technology of behavior ways to improve human life, and attacks those who stand in the way of its use.

The consequences of a rigorous determinism for understanding human nature are profound. In general, our own experience and the teachings of our culture tell us there is free will, although from time to time philosophers such as Spinoza have argued otherwise. It appears that one chooses to lift one's arm, that one chooses a profession, that one chooses for whom to vote. To accept a rigorous determinism and apply it to one's own behavior is extremely difficult, requiring the overthrow of a lifetime's habits of thought. Yet such a revolution is required when Skinner asks that we give up the traditional notions of freedom and dignity.

As early as his first paper (1931) Skinner wrote of the *"preconceptions of freedom"* that hinder the scientific understanding of behavior. Skinner assumes that all behavior is determined, and that consequently a notion such as freedom is nonsense. In his view a desire for freedom is always a response to punishment. Skinner draws an important distinction between positive reinforcement and punishment. Positive reinforcement effectively controls behavior without undesirable consequences, since it lets you do essentially what you want. Punishment, on the other hand, is generally ineffective and produces unfortunate side effects, since organisms react emotionally to punishment. Organisms seek to avoid—that is, to be free from—punishment, but do not avoid positive reinforcement, which is by definition desirable. Historically, governments have tried to control behavior through punishment. One is told what *not* to do, not what to do. As an emotional reaction to punishment, a "literature of freedom" has grown up demanding freedom from punishment, but which has also fostered a belief in freedom as a characteristic of life, a false belief according to the scientific assumption of determinism. Now that the early aims of the literature of freedom have been attained in constitutions and so forth, the illusory notion of freedom stands in the way of further progress, for it rails against the control of behavior by positive reinforcement as well as by punishment.

Skinner argues that if humanistic goals, the goals of human happiness, are to be reached, it will be done only by controlling behavior through positive reinforcement, for scientific control is more efficient than the haphazard control exerted by the current social environment. It is important to remember again that Skinner assumes all behavior is always completely determined, that there is never freedom of choice. Therefore he proposes that we substitute deliberate, systematic control for inefficient control. If the goal is happiness, it will be reached faster if we apply methodical control, and this cannot be done without first abandoning belief in freedom, which prohibits such control.

The concept of dignity depends on belief in free will. We believe that one deserves praise for freely chosen good acts, and deserves blame for freely chosen wrong acts. However, Skinner, like Spinoza, argues that both praise and blame are equally irrational, since all behavior is determined for Skinner by the contingencies of reinforcement, not by an individual's free will. We do not blame the rain for getting us wet or praise the sun for warming our skin (although ancient religions did); we accept each as a natural occurrence beyond the will of any person. Skinner asks us to view human behavior as we have other natural phenomena, not religiously, but scientifically, recalling Watson's linkage of religion and mentalism. The poet is not to be praised for "having a poem," for the poet is merely the site at which external variables operate. The rapist is not to be blamed for "having a rape," for the rapist, too, is a locus of variables that converge on an act society condemns. Desirable behaviors are to be strengthened by positive reinforcement, while undesirable behaviors will not be learned, at least in a properly engineered society such as Walden II. Both freedom and dignity are outmoded concepts, inconsistent with scientific determinism, which stand in the way of an effective control of human behavior.

To what end are we to be controlled? Skinner's answer is Darwinian. A culture is an experiment in survival, just as a species is an experiment in survival. The ultimate biological value is survival, for the "good" species is the one that survives. Similarly, the "good" society will be the one that survives. Skinner argues that the chances our society will survive will be greatly enhanced should it adopt the methods of the experimental analysis of behavior in pursuit of life, liberty, and the pursuit of happiness. Scientific control is our surest guarantee against both unhappiness and extinction. The technology of behavior must be used, Skinner argues, if humanity is to survive. The old mentalistic scheme of freedom and dignity is outmoded and must be replaced by his science of behavior. Skinner wrote (1971): "The ease with which mentalistic explanations can be invented on the spot is perhaps the best gauge of how little attention we should pay to them. . . . It is science or nothing."

Skinner stands clearly in the tradition of those who would improve humans by improving their environment. He feels an affinity for Jean-Jacques Rousseau, who, although he believed humans are free, located their faults in the environment: "Man is born free but he is everywhere in chains." In *Emile* Rousseau proposes that a teacher's student will be happiest if the student feels free, but is kept under the teacher's subtle control. Skinner's *Walden II* is a Rousseauian Utopia. Control is benign and hidden, so feelings of freedom and dignity remain, even though they have no referents beyond those feelings.

Skinner is, finally, a humanist in the tradition of the Sophists. Science exists to serve human happiness, not such transcendent Platonic ends as Reason and Truth. For Skinner, the human being, at least as scientifically understood, is the measure of all things. Reason and logic are arbitrary verbal behaviors whose truth lies only in the contingencies of reinforcement, not in a realm of Ideas. Freedom and dignity are verbal operants, not linguistic expressions of enduring values. The crisis Skinner sets for the modern person is the crisis set for ancient Greeks by the Sophists, and by the Marquis de Sade for eighteenth-century Europeans. Is there anything of value in human affairs beyond feelings, if freedom and dignity mean nothing else? To what can we cling if all tradition is thrown into doubt, if the old center cannot hold? Skinner answers: "the experimental analysis of behavior." He says, "I am all for *feelings* of causal adequacy as I am for feelings of freedom and dignity. I want people to be adequate, unhampered, successful, and aware of the fact that they are so, and I have suggested ways in which that may be brought about—by changing their environment" (Skinner 1984a).

Critique of Cognitive Science

Skinner, of course, has always been critical of theories referring to unobserved internal states that cause behavior. Although Skinner has always scorned cognitive science as a "magical term" (1984a) whose popularity "is largely due to the freedom to use a lay vocabulary, not the discovery of an alternative science of comparable rigor to the experimental analysis of behavior" (1984b), until recently he has not responded to it in detail (see, for example, Skinner 1974). However, he has now (Skinner 1985a) accused it of many shortcomings.

Skinner accuses cognitive science of reviving and resting upon two (to him) obnoxious doctrines: the copy theory of perception—cognitive science's central concept of mental representations; and the common-sense idea that mental states cause behavior—the concept of the inner person. Against representations Skinner reasserts his familiar perceptual realism: "What is seen is [a] presentation, not a representation" of an object. Skinner goes on to reject the idea that representations are "stored" in a "memory" from which they are "retrieved." Skinner says these notions depend on a misleading analogy to physical records:

> When physical records are stored, the records continue to exist until they are retrieved, but is that true when people "process information"? A storage battery would be a better model of a behaving organism. We put electricity into a battery and take it out when needed, *but there is no electricity in the battery*. When we "put electricity in," we change the battery, and it is a changed battery that "puts out electricity" when tapped. Organisms do not acquire behavior as a kind of possession; they simply come to behave in various ways. The behavior is not in them at any time.

Skinner here in his own way states a criticism of information-processing theory that we have met before: Exactly where does information processing take place? We observe and respond to the environment, we have sensations and thoughts in consciousness, and neuroscientists will one day be able to observe the brain processes behind thought and behavior; but the information-processing psychologists have invented a nonphysical, fictitious level of discourse between consciousness and the brain. If there are no representations, and no storage and retrieval of representations, then there is no information processing and no inner person making decisions on the basis of stored representations. Skinner (1984b) simply denies the validity of the human-computer analogy: "Information processing was devised for, and is useful for formulating, systems which are not analogous to the human organism."

Skinner accuses cognitive science of being bad science, and at the same time shows that he is less scientistic than they. He says, "We need a language of feelings and states of mind in our daily lives. It is the language of literature and most of philosophy. Clinical psychologists use it to learn many things about the histories of their clients that they could not discover any other way." But Skinner insists such mental talk has no place in a *science* of behavior. Skinner concludes with strong language:

> *I accuse* cognitive scientists of misusing the metaphor of storage. . . .
>
> *I accuse* cognitive scientists of speculating about internal processes . . . they have no appropriate means of observation. . . .
>
> *I accuse* cognitive scientists of emasculating the experimental analysis of behavior. . . .
>
> *I accuse* cognitive scientists of reviving a theory in which feelings and states of mind . . . are taken as the causes of behavior. . . .
>
> *I accuse* cognitive scientists, as I would psychoanalysts, . . . of inventing explanatory systems which are admired for a profundity which is more properly called inaccessibility.
>
> *I accuse* cognitive scientists of relaxing standards of definition and logical thinking and releasing a flood of speculation . . . inimical to science.

Finally, Skinner cries out against radical behaviorism's confinement to a ghetto: "Let us bring behaviorism back from the Devil's island to which it was transported for a crime it never committed, and let psychology become once again a behavioral science."

Skinner's plea may be answered, for there appear to be grounds for reconciliation between one form of cognitive science, Neisser's (1984) "ecological psychology," and radical behaviorism. Like the radical behaviorist the "ecological cognitive psychologist [begins] . . . with a careful description of the environment and people's ordinary activities within it." Like the radical behaviorist, the ecological cognitive scientist "tak[es] the environment seriously." Like the radical behaviorist, "ecological psychologists are generally reluctant to construct models or to postulate hypothetical mental events." Like the radical behaviorist, the ecological psychologist believes that "introspection does not reveal [the] structures" in the environment to which people respond. Neisser does not discuss the parallels between his description of ecological psychology and radical behaviorism, but they are there.

CHALLENGES TO SCIENTIFIC PSYCHOLOGY

From Psychology's Occult Doubles

One of psychology's leaders in the first decades of the twentieth century, Joseph Jastrow, was annoyed by being constantly asked about psychic phenomena, and by the implicit confusion between psychology and psychical research. Today psychologists are still embarrassed by their links to "occult" disciplines and marginal sciences. Part of the embarrassment stems from psychology's social success. People today look to psychology for advice on all sorts of personal and social problems, so that some practitioners of occult crafts have come to cast their work in a psychological mold. Astrology, for example, is often defended as a means of reading character and a source of advice in love and business, rather than as a prophetic science, its original claim. The clichéd opening line, "What's your sign?" is based on the notion that people born under certain signs have certain personalities and will get along well or ill with those born under certain other signs. There is nothing to the claim, but there is a strong parallel to psychological tests that purport to reveal character and suggest interpersonal strategies. In fact, *Teacher* magazine carried an article in 1978 suggesting that pupils be grouped by astrological sign, a purpose for which psychological tests had long been used. In supermarket tabloids "spiritual healers" and "advisers" tout themselves as counselor on "love, health, alcohol, business," subjects shared with professional psychologists and psychiatrists.

Experimental psychologists, too, have their occult doubles in the field of psychical research, whose newer name, parapsychology, helps tie the fields together in the public mind. Like experimental psychologists, parapsychologists have their own journals and associations. Their work sometimes appears on the program of APA meetings under the auspices of the Division of Humanistic Psychology, and parapsychologists are active in the new transpersonal psychology movement, which bills itself as a "fourth force" in psychology, going beyond humanism to a more cosmic, transcendental psychology. At the time I am writing this, the transpersonal psychologists have gathered enough signatures within the APA to request recognition as a new division, Division 45.

Mainstream psychologists have a problem differentiating themselves from what they regard as pseudosciences without seeming dogmatically intolerant. Scientifically minded psychologists, which includes not only experimentalists but the vast majority of professional psychologists, try to separate themselves from pseudoscience on formal methodological grounds. However, as we saw in Chapter 1, formal "demarcation criteria" do not work very well. The rejection of parapsychology and, *a fortiori,* spiritualism and astrology, rests on their violation of the substantive content of science, not violation of it methods. For parapsychologists do in fact follow the methodological canons of science. They conduct carefully controlled research, they use statistics, they are on the watch for fraud, they replicate their studies more than mainstream psychologists do, and they are outraged when such hard work fails to gain them recognition as scientists.

Occult science has failed to gain scientific recognition because it does not fit in with the content of science. To begin with, psychologists have a hard enough time explaining how people understand natural language, so they get annoyed when parapsychologists badger them about telepathy and clairvoyance. To borrow Kuhnian language, a scientific community recognizes as scientists those who might be able to contribute to solving current puzzles, and it dismisses researchers concerned with bizarre anomalies as cranks. It might turn out in the future that the cranks were on to something, but scientific research is an orderly process focused on current problems, not speculative possibilities. An instructive parallel occurred in the flurry of interest a few years ago in the claim by a science journalist that a human being had been cloned. Biologists dismissed the assertion as wild and ludicrous—not because a human could not in principle be cloned, but rather because it was absurd to attempt it now, and regarded anyone trying for a human clone as a crank.

Scientists accept only their own breed of science as scientific. Method will not save your reputation if your topic of research does not come within the boundaries currently accepted by science.

The real problem with parapsychology is that it violates the oldest and deepest of science's substantive commitments, the commitment to naturalism, to explain happenings in the universe in natural terms. The founders of psychical research and parapsychology were frank in challenging naturalism by hoping to turn the scientific method against scientific content. They hoped to prove with statistics and experiment that spiritual powers and spiritual life existed, that life continued after death. But science in the twentieth century is firmly committed to naturalism and materialism. Naturalism is science's central dogma, without which it could not function, and anyone who challenges this dogma has little hope of gaining a hearing from science.

Some parapsychologists have attempted to steer around these objections by dropping the quasi-religious claims that animated the psychical researchers and by adopting up-to-date scientific vocabulary. Thus some parapsychologists try to explain psychical wonders in the Alice-in-Wonderland terms of modern quantum physics, while others cast their research and theories in information-processing terms. Their attempt to finally naturalize the supernatural seems to have little chance of success, but it is instructive to ask what would happen if they did succeed. Parapsychology might gain the ear of science, but it would very likely lose the ear of the public. Science has been accepted by many as a substitute religion—but most still want religion, even under the parapsychological guise of science. In a world where religion falls back on "creationist science" to defend faith, which is by definition unscientific, all the borderlines are fuzzy indeed.

Ordinary people do not go to spiritualistic séances, write to psychic advisers, and read astrology books to learn about information-processing mechanisms and ESP (Tart 1978). They want some sense of how to live their lives. For many more moderns than Frederic Myers the Old World sustenance of traditional religion fails to sustain faith in the age of science: of nuclear war, the space shuttle, and the ironies of doctors heroically struggling to perform *in utero* surgery on one fetus only to abort another of the same age. Science has accomplished so much it seems natural to turn to it for answers to ancient moral and religious questions. But it cannot give them. Science gives us the techniques to diagnose fetal abnormalities, and even ways to operate on some of them before the baby is born; it gives us ways to abort fetuses early and late. But it is helpless to tell us which choice to make, to tell us when the fetus becomes a human being, to decide between right and wrong.

Psychology, more than any science, occupies treacherous ground between *is* and *ought*. Physical science reveals the workings of impersonal nature; and while it can harm and benefit humankind, it is unreasonable to ask that its laws tell us how to use them. Yet psychology is the science of human behavior. It purports to reveal the springs of human action, and consequently it seems on the surface not unreasonable to ask it how to act, how to make sense of our lives. Certainly, psychology writers from Aristotle to Bentham to Skinner have moved from science to morality, pretending to describe the perfect, scientifically engineered community and to prescribe the laws of the land as dictated by human nature. But this urge to ask a science for moral guidance is not legitimate. Operant psychology may help me control my child's behavior, but it cannot tell me how she should behave. Cognitive psychology may help me construct lessons that my students remember, but it cannot tell me what my students should learn. Science deals with facts, not morals.

Occult psychology—parapsychology, spiritualism, astrology—is the clearest manifestation of the confusion of science and values that pervades all of psychology. Each occult system takes on the trappings of science in order to borrow its authority and uses that authority to promote various moral and religious values. Practitioners of occult psychology have not been loath to satisfy humankind's spiritual needs. Practitioners of mainstream psychology, however much they try to distance themselves from their occult doubles, have also not been loath to prescribe to troubled humans: in clinical and counseling practices, in industrial psychology, in advertising psychology. We see, then, that psychology, whether mainstream or occult, has been used to meet human needs that science cannot meet. People need to know how they ought to act—they need ethics and morality. People need to find meaning in their lives—they need a form of life, a structure within which to live. Science can meet neither need, and the deepest fraud of psychology's occult doubles is pretending that science can do so. Mainstream psychology itself sits awkwardly astride science and morality. Psychology calls itself a science, yet, with its occult neighbors, it is tempted to become a new religion (Albee 1977a). Psychological science, like any science, may encompass means, but it can never encompass ends.

From Biology

Depression is the most common psychological disorder of our time (Klerman 1979). It has long been treated by psychotherapy, but it now seems likely that long-term, nonsituational depression, called *endogenous* depression, is caused by deficiencies in the brain of certain neurotransmitters (Snyder 1980), not by early childhood experiences or any other psychological cause. People who suffer from endogenous depression can be effectively treated with antidepressant drugs: After a few weeks, they stop feeling depressed. Therefore it may be that "much of the by now entrenched psychodynamic theory is irrelevant or misleading," that treating biological depression psychologically is "tragic . . . since a large fraction of the 30,000 suicides a year in the United States are probably committed by people with [endogenous] depressions" (Wender and Klein 1981). Faced with this challenge to their practice, clinical psychologists respond by asserting that psychotherapy may nevertheless be useful in helping depressives (and others with biochemical disorders), even if they are also treated with drugs (Peele 1981). Nevertheless, a challenge remains: A psychological state, depression, has been shown to have a biological cause. A piece of psychology has been reduced to biology. Perhaps psychology will be "cannibilized" by biology, as biologist E. O. Wilson (1975) has predicted.

Reductionism

The idea that one science can reduce another derives from the positivist notion, now called the "unity of science" (Putnam 1982), that all the sciences can be arranged in a hierarchy from highest to lowest, with each science reducible to a more basic science, until we arrive at physics, the most basic science. According to this theory, psychology is more basic than sociology, and can reduce its social concepts to psychological concepts of individual behavior. Psychology's concepts and laws of individual behavior can in turn be reduced to the concepts and laws of neurophysiology, which describes the functioning of individuals' bodies. It has become generally agreed that such reduction is implausible. Functionalists, for example, argue that mental states are defined by what they do—their function—rather than by the material that performs the function. Thus two people might be engaging in the psychological function of "thinking of Paris," but it is highly unlikely that exactly the same cells in their brains are firing.

The clearest refutation of unity-of-science reductionism comes from Donald Davidson's (1980) "anomalous monism." Davidson rejects Cartesian or religious dualism, but defends a form of materialism in which the psychological concepts of folk psychology cannot be reduced to the laws of neurophysiology even though every mental event is identical with some brain event. If we accept materialism, then we accept that every mental event is also a brain event. However, for psychology to be reduced to neurophysiology, it must be the case that psychological concepts, not just psychological events, must correspond to neurophysiological concepts. When we explain a person's speech or actions psychologically, we do so against a background of assumed beliefs and desires. Most important, we assume that a person is rational, that his or her beliefs are reasonably coherent and consistent. If a man says things that are blatantly contradictory, if his actions are inconsistent with his beliefs, we conclude that he is irrational, give up trying to explain his behavior psychologically, and may banish him from human society. Davidson concludes: "But in inferring this system [of interconnected beliefs and desires] from the evidence, we necessarily impose conditions of coherence, rationality and consistency. These conditions have no echo in physical theory, which is why we can look for no more than rough correlations between psychological and physical phenomena." In short, there is no danger that neurophysiology can reduce psychology. Psychological theory is autonomous.

Sociobiology

E. O. Wilson, who said that biology would "cannibalize" psychology (and all the social sciences), had in mind as the cannibal the division of biology he named sociobiology. Sociobiology is the study of the biological basis of social behavior, and represents the application of the neo-Darwinian theory of evolution to behavior. The basic idea of sociobiology is that behavioral traits as well as morphology are shaped by natural selection. Since aggression, group living, cooperation, parenting, and sexual behavior help determine whether an animal succeeds or fails in growing up and having offspring, it seems highly probable that evolution has shaped these social behaviors in different ways in different species in different ecological circumstances. Work on the evolutionary, biological basis of social behavior in animals was well advanced when Wilson summarized it in his text *Sociobiology* in 1975. The book became the center of a ferocious and often bitter controversy when in his last chapter Wilson speculatively extended his biological perspective to human beings, claiming that social science and psychology would disappear into biology.

A few psychologists found Wilson's ideas stimulating (for example, Campbell 1975), but naturally most were alarmed (among them Wispé and Thompson 1976; Wyers et al. 1980). The field most likely to be absorbed into sociobiology was the study of animal behavior, and while many psychologists resist it (Wyers et al. 1980), there are signs that absorption is taking place (Fox 1983). The field of comparative psychology had been in crisis for some time (Hodos and Campbell 1969; Lockard 1971; Wasserman 1981; Gottlieb 1984), seeming not to have progressed since the time of Beach's 1950 critique (Lown 1975; Porter, Johnson, and Granger 1981), and so could be revitalized and redirected by the fresh approach of sociobiology.

The alarm of human psychologists was based on a misunderstanding of evolutionary biological explanations. Their deep misunderstanding of sociobiology was visually portrayed on the cover of *Time* for August 1, 1977: "Why you do what you do: SOCIOBIOLOGY: A new theory of behavior." The cover showed a young man and woman in a partial embrace; their expressions were blank and their limbs were connected to strings that rose out of the picture into the hands of an unseen puppeteer, presumably their genes. Human psychologists feared that sociobiology might displace psychology as an account of human behavior. So, for example, a sociobiologist might explain that Bill Smith cheated on his wife because mammalian males have a desire for sexual variety. However, contrary to the claims of some sociobiologists themselves, sociobiology does not and cannot explain individual behavior, which is the province of psychology. Sociobiology can explain why the members of a species have certain dispositions, why they find some things easy to learn and others hard to learn. To continue the example, males have a disposition toward sexual variety because males can fertilize many females, and if they do so they will achieve evolutionary success, having many offspring. Females are less disposed to sexual variety because the number of offspring they can have is much smaller, so that they are better off concentrating on one fit male, rather than risking pregnancy by unknown males of questionable fitness. Thus sociobiology may explain why Bill Smith feels a desire for sex with women other than his wife—but no more. A man may feel such desire, but refuse to act on it because he believes adultery to be immoral; in a different culture polygyny may be normal, so Bill could take a new wife without qualms. Thus how an individual behaves is not determined by biology, but by the forces of his or her own individual life, including learning, culture, and moral beliefs. Psychology is the study of the individual and, while it can learn about human dispositions from evolutionary biology, the explanation of human action remains its exclusive preserve. Sociobiology is an insightful colleague, but it is a toothless cannibal.

Conclusion

Psychology is not about to be devoured by either neurophysiology or sociobiology. However, considerations from each context suggest a different and, to some, more disturbing conclusion. Perhaps psychology cannot be a science at all.

Paul and Patricia Churchland (for example, Churchland 1985) have argued that neurophysiology will replace and eliminate rather than reduce psychology. From their perspective Davidson's anomalous monism provides no defense against their claims, but instead supports them (Rosenberg 1983, 1984). The Churchlands claim that folk psychology, and along with it all forms of intentional, representational psychology such as functionalism, are scientifically false in the same way that Ptolemaic astronomy was false. The failure of psychological concepts to map onto neurophysiology shows that psychological concepts are false, and so they must be replaced by neurophysiological ones. Anomalous monism admits that every mental event is identical with some brain event, claiming only that psychology organizes its talk about mental events in ways irreducible to physical science. The Churchlands urge us to drop psychology altogether, and talk only about brain events and the laws of neurophysiology. Precisely *because* "considerations of rationality, coherence and consistency . . . have no echo in physical theory," they should be eliminated.

The Churchlands' crusade represents scientism at its imperialistic worst. They (like Stephan Stich) want people to give up talking about hopes, beliefs, desires, and so on merely because such concepts have no place in science. But their view is like the paint salesman's view of art. Obviously, the aesthetic properties of a painting depend upon the physical qualities of its paint, and equally clearly they are logically independent of the paint's physical properties. Eliminative materialism is like saying that because we cannot map the aesthetic properties of paintings onto the physical qualities of the paint, we should give up aesthetics. If humans adopt the eliminative view, they will have to give up a lot: law (there is no physical difference between murder in self-defense and murder for gain); morality (whether a fetus should be aborted does not depend on physical properties); fiction (Shakespeare and Dickens make constant reference to intentions, beliefs, and so on—even "Dallas" could not be understood neurophysiologically); politics (science cannot tell fascism from freedom), and, of course, everyday loves, hopes, fears, expectations, and interests.

The eliminativist views folk and intentional psychology as scientific theories and then regards them as false. The lesson to learn from this controversy is that folk psychology is no more a science than aesthetic theory is. Intentional psychology is not autonomous science, it is not a science at all, and as such is quite ineliminable. The Churchlands may be right that scientific psychology will one day be purely neurophysiological. It is clear, however, that no human form of life can be built on physical science alone, precisely because science cannot tell right from wrong; and making that distinction, and making meaningful sense of life, is the essence of being human.

Related considerations from sociobiology reinforce the conclusion that human psychology is not and cannot be a science (Rosenberg 1980; Hull 1984; Leahey 1982, 1984). Science searches for exceptionless general laws that apply to spatiotemporally unrestricted objects. So physics is not about our solar system, but about stars and planets anywhere and everywhere. It is about quarks and leptons, not chairs and books, though these are made of quarks and leptons. Chairs and books are not suited to scientific laws because they are spatiotemporally local, products of a particular culture in a particular time, and science is universal, applying to all times and places. Of course we can talk intelligibly about furniture, but such talk is not science. There is a craft, and even a practice, of furniture design and making, but a craft is not a science.

From the standpoint of evolution, species are not spatiotemporally unrestricted, and so cannot fit into scientific laws. Every species is an individual, a product of a particular history, inhabiting a particular ecological niche. The laws of evolutionary biology apply across species: They should apply to any self-replicating organism anywhere, any time. So just as there cannot be scientific laws about just our sun or just our moon, there cannot be laws about particular species. Of course, there will be disciplined studies of the sun and the moon, of gerbils and dolphins, but these studies will produce facts about individual things and species, not general laws. But if there is no science of gerbils or dolphins, because they are individuals rather than general entities, so there is also no science of *Homo sapiens*. Psychology is a disciplined study of one species, but it will produce no spatiotemporally unrestricted laws, and so cannot be a science.

In 1671 Elizabeth Knapp was declared a witch (Demos 1982). A psychologist reading about her would conclude that she suffered from catatonic schizophrenia: She was alternately sane and insane, and when insane would hold fixed poses and experience hallucinations and delusions. It is quite likely that a tendency to schizophrenia is a genetic, inherited disposition. A biologist, then, could explain her disease from the standpoint of evolution and genetics, and from the standpoint of neuroscience, but he or she could not tell the whole story. Even if one inherits a tendency to schizophrenia, certain individual experiences are required to cause the disease to actually manifest itself, and personal learning is the province of the psychologist. Moreover, Elizabeth Knapp's hallucinations and delusions centered on the devil: She seemed to see him, to speak in his voice, and she claimed to have signed a compact to serve him. The content of her hallucinations and delusions was determined by her culture, not by the abnormal state of her brain. A modern schizophrenic would be more likely to hallucinate space aliens and have delusions about the CIA. Neuroscience says that Elizabeth Knapp and a modern schizophrenic suffer from the same brain disease, and so cannot explain why Elizabeth saw the devil while moderns see Martians. History, social science, and psychology can, and only they can. Physical science can explain, predict, and control the natural world, including the world of our bodies. Humans, however, live not just in the physical world, but "in a world we ourselves create." Our forms of life lie beyond science, but not beyond disciplined inquiry.

From the Humanities

Psychology and the other social sciences are, of course, not the only disciplines concerned with human beings. There are also the humanities. While the humanities are often honored, the honor generally takes the form of lip service rather than sincere respect. In the modern world science and technology are revered, and whatever does not fit their mold is deemed eccentric—interesting, perhaps, but decidedly second-rate. Psychologists are not the only people to suffer from physics envy. Hence, since the time of August Comte and John Stuart Mill, psychologists have acted on the assumption that, to quote Mill, "The backward state of the Moral Sciences [today's social sciences] can only be remedied by applying to them the methods of Physical Science, duly extended and generalized." After a hundred years of psychological physics envy, however, it is not at all clear that Mill was right. As Johann Herder said in the seventeenth century, "We live in a world we ourselves create," so the study of the human world—the object of the humanities—should be very different from the study of the physical world. The case of Elizabeth Knapp brings the point home. We may know all there is to know about the genetics and biochemistry of schizophrenia, and be able to cure it with sophisticated drugs, but to sympathize with her, to *understand* her predicament and what it meant to her and her neighbors, requires different tools than science can give us. It requires *hermeneutics*.

Hermeneutics traditionally denotes the field of biblical exegesis: closely examining a text of the Bible and interpreting its meaning. Broadly speaking, it is what is done in the humanities. An English literary critic takes the text of *Macbeth* and tries to set forth and discuss its meaning—for Shakespeare, for Shakespeare's audience, for us, his modern audience. The critic does not care about the causal processes in William Shakespeare that caused him to write *Macbeth;* instead he or she tries to grasp the human meaning of the play. A historian considering the case of Elizabeth Knapp does much the same thing. He or she may find useful the scientific hypothesis that schizophrenia is a brain disease, but the historical interest lies in understanding what Elizabeth Knapp and her contemporaries made of her condition. Doing this requires not science, but understanding and the ability to enter into the worldview of another place and time, making rational sense of it, a sense that can then be set down for the historian's readers.

It is possible to regard psychology from a hermeneutical rather than a scientific standpoint. Take, for example, Freud's theory of dreams. One might regard it as a scientific account of how dreams come about in the night: Repressed ideas, released from the shackles of repression, filter up toward consciousness and are reworked as they go by dreamwork into a disguised form suitable for conscious expression. In this scientific account of dreams it ought ideally to be possible to follow the moment-by-moment construction of a dream from repressed impulse in the brain stem to conscious experience in the visual and auditory centers of the cerebral hemispheres.

But the title of Freud's book was *Die Traumdeutung,* "The Meaning of Dreams," or, as usually translated, "The Interpretation of Dreams." If one disregards the theory of his last chapter, one finds that Freud treated dreams primarily as texts to be interpreted: He practiced hermeneutics. Like the critic studying *Macbeth,* Freud took a dream as a text, a meaningful expression of a person's unconscious neurotic problems. Used as a text examined for meaning, it is irrelevant if the dream was produced as the scientific theory describes, and the process of creation can be ignored much as the critic ignores the process by which Shakespeare wrote *Macbeth.* Working together, therapist and client can recover the underlying meaning of the dream, and in so doing reveal something important about the client, and, they hope, relieve him or her of neurotic misery.

It is possible to take hermeneutics as a model for psychology and the social sciences. For we may regard not just dreams but all of behavior as texts to be scrutinized for meaning. Their meaning derives from the form of life we share as human beings in a historical culture—the historian and anthropologist deal with alien forms of life—and the job of the psychologist from the hermeneutical point of view is to *make sense* of human life in this time and place rather than to predict, control, and scientifically explain it. The hermeneuticist practices *Geisteswissenschaft*—human science—rather than *Naturwissenschaft.* As the word "science" is used today, hermeneutics is no science because it does not aim at universal exceptionless causal laws. Because we live in a scientistic age, labeling something "unscientific" seems to consign it to a junk heap of useless and pointless oddities. If we can free ourselves from physics worship and scientism, however, we can see hermeneutics as only different from science, and value it on its own terms. Moreover, hermeneutics concerns itself with human life: with right and wrong, with love and hate, with what it means to be human rather than animal, and this concern is not obviously inferior to science.

PSYCHOLOGY AND SOCIETY

Giving Psychology Away

Against the background of turmoil and alienation of the late 1960s, psychology experienced an outbreak of "relevance" in 1969 (Kessel 1980). Psychologists fretted that they were not doing enough to solve the problems of society. The most widely cited expression of psychologists' impulse to social relevance was George Miller's 1969 presidential address to the APA, in which he stated, "I can imagine nothing we could do that would be more relevant to human welfare, and nothing that could pose a greater challenge to the next generation of psychologists, than to discover how best to give psychology away." Miller asserted that "scientific psychology is one of the most potentially revolutionary intellectual enterprises conceived by the mind of man. If we were ever to achieve substantial progress toward our stated aim—toward the understanding, prediction, and control of mental and behavioral phenomena—the implications for every aspect of society would make brave men tremble." However, Miller said, despite continuous work by applied psychologists, on the whole psychologists "have been less effective than we might have been" in providing "intellectual leadership in the search for new and better personal and social relationships." In considering how to give psychology away, Miller rejected behavioral technology for psychology's playing a part in a broad mutation of human and social values: "I believe that the real impact of psychology will be felt not through . . . technological products . . . but through its effects on the public at large, through a new and different public conception of what is humanly possible and what is humanly desirable." Miller called for "a peaceful revolution based on a new conception of human nature" based on edcuation: "Our scientific results will have to be instilled in the public consciousness in a practical and usable form."

Miller was riding the crest of the wave of public interest in psychology. In 1967 *Psychology Today* began publishing, and in 1969 *Time* inaugurated its "Behavior" department, so psychology was being almost given away in the popular media. Psychologists pushed social relevance as never before. The theme of the 1969 APA meeting was "Psychology and the Problems of Society," and the pages of *American Psychologist* began to fill with articles and notes on student activism, psychology's duty to social responsibility, and hip references to Bob Dylan, the musical poet of youth rebellion.

Not all psychologists eschewed psychological technology in solving social problems. Two years after Miller, Kenneth Clark (1971), in his APA presidential address, argued that political leaders should have "imposed" on them the "requirement" that "they accept and use the earliest perfected form of psychotechnological, biochemical intervention which would assure their positive use of power." In an article in *Psychology Today* psychologist James McConnel proclaimed, "Somehow we've got to learn to *force* people to love one another, to *force* them to want to behave properly. I speak of psychological force." The technology was available, McConnel opined, by which society can "gain almost absolute control over an individual's behavior. . . . We should reshape our society so that we all would be trained from birth to want to do what society wants us to do." McConnel concluded, "Today's behavioral psychologists are the architects and engineers of the Brave New World."

McConnel was not alone in his eagerness to take over and reshape traditional social functions. Harriet Rheingold (1973) urged the creation of a new psychological profession, the "Scientists of [Child] Rearing" that "must be accepted as the highest in the land." Furthermore, "parents must be taught how to rear their children," and, like clinical psychologists themselves, "parents to be must be certified." Along similar lines, Craig T. Raimey (1974) called for organized psychology to push for "the establishment of adequate services to the children of this nation." Psychological professionals would play many roles in Raimey's utopian scheme, functioning on local advisory councils, in coordinating agencies, as referral resources, and above all in schools, which would play the central role in screening, assessing, and treating unfortunate children.

Ironically, the problems that psychology sought to cure in society erupted in the APA. A ferocious debate started in the 1970s about the social value, if any, of standardized tests, especially I.Q. tests. It had long been known that black children did much worse than white children on I.Q. tests. Arthur Jensen (1969) started an uproar when, in a seeming return to old eugenic positions, he argued that the difference was genetic; blacks were inherently inferior to whites, so that the Great Society's compensatory education programs were doomed to failure. Debate between Jensen, his critics, and supporters raged for several years. At the 1968 APA convention the Black Psychological Association presented a petition calling for a moratorium on the use of I.Q. tests in schools, alleging widespread abuse, specifically that tests participated in the oppression of black children by relegating them to low achievement school tracks. The APA responded in typical academic-bureaucratic fashion: It appointed a committee. In 1975 it published its report (Cleary, Humphries, Kendrick, and Wesman 1975). It predictably concluded in standard academic-bureaucratic fashion that while tests might be abused, they were basically sound.

The committee's finding was unsatisfactory to black psychologists. Speaking as chair of the Association of Black Psychologists, George D. Jackson (1975) called the report "blatantly racist" and concluded that "we need *more* than a moratorium now—we need government intervention and strict legal sanctions." The debate over testing has continued ever since, and in fact a few school systems have seriously curtailed the use of tests to track students. Nevertheless, there remains irony in organized psychology's inability to happily resolve problems very similar to those of the society it presumed to scientifically revolutionize.

Some Americans, especially conservative ones, did not want what psychologists were giving away. In a widely quoted speech, then Vice President Spiro Agnew (1972) blasted psychologists, especially B. F. Skinner and Kenneth Clark, for proposing "radical surgery on the nation's psyche." Agnew quoted John Stuart Mill, "Whatever crushes individuality is despotism" and added, "we are contending with a new kind of despotism." Conservative columnist John Lofton (1972) contributed to a special issue of *American Psychologist* concerned with the serious overproduction and underemployment of Ph.D. psychologists. From some man-in-the-street interviews, Lofton concluded that the public believed, "The tight market for Ph.D's is a good thing. There are too many people with a lot of knowledge about unimportant things." People were unsympathetic to psychology, Lofton said, because they were concerned about abuses of behavior-modification technology and tests, and felt traditional American resentment of "lordly Ph.D's, of whatever stripe." Academic psychology, including cognitive psychology, has been similarly castigated from outside: "The discipline continues to traffic in two kinds of propositions: those that are true but self-evident and those that are true but uninteresting. . . . [On] almost any issue that might be considered important for human existence . . . it offers pitifully little that rises above the banal" (Robinson 1983).

Ten years after Miller's address, a symposium was held to see what progress had been made in giving psychology away. Most of the reports were rather gloomy; even the optimists thought little had been accomplished. Two authors were especially scathing. Sigmund Koch (1980) tore Miller's speech apart, revealing its fatuities, flabby thinking, and self-contradictions. He argued that, if anything, psychology was being given away too well in pop psychotherapy and a flood of self-help books. Koch said, "In sum, I believe the most charitable thing we can do is not to give psychology away, but to take it back." Michael Scriven (1980), a philosopher turned program evaluator, issued psychology a failing report card. Psychology failed for being ahistorical, for not applying to itself the standards it applied to others, for fancying itself value-free, and for continuing indulgence in the Newtonian fantasy. George Miller, who was there to introduce Koch and Scriven, was depressed: "Two men who I admire enormously have just destroyed my life."

Clinical Psychology

Clinical psychology was invented just after World War II. By 1968 there were twelve thousand clinical psychologists in the world, and their ranks had swelled to over forty thousand by 1983—the overwhelming majority was located in the United States (Zilbergeld 1983). Although there was some concern that such rapid growth might be eroding the quality of therapists in training (Strupp 1976), clinical psychologists could hardly doubt that theirs was a growth field. Nevertheless, clinical psychologists were not completely happy.

To begin with, the question of how best to train clinical psychologists would not go away. The 1950 Boulder model had laid down that clinical psychologists were to be trained as scientific psychologists first and as professional service providers second. However, it was clear that the Boulder model was honored more in the breach than in the observance. By and large, clinical students wanted to help people and learn how to practice therapy, and regarded the scientific part of their training as a boring chore. Some clinical psychologists welcomed the seeming death of the Boulder model. George W. Albee (1970), for example, argued that it had been a mistake for clinical psychologists to model themselves on physicians to begin with, when in fact they should be agents of widespread social change. Other clinicians, of course, defended the Boulder model (for example, Shakow 1976). Faced with change that seemed to be slipping out of organized psychology's control, the APA set up another conference on clinical training.

This one met in Colorado, too, at the resort of Vail in 1973. Despite dissension, it endorsed something that Boulder and other training conferences had rejected, the recognition of a new degree in cinical psychology, the Psy. D., for professionally oriented students. The Psy. D. program would reduce the scientific demands made on students in training, and would frankly mint practitioners rather than academicians (Strockler 1975). Naturally, the proposals proved controversial; some clinicians welcomed the idea (Peterson 1976), while others (Perry 1979) denounced the Psy. D. and a related development, the establishment of "free-standing" professional schools, so-called because they were not affiliated with a university.

Another problem that would not go away was clinical psychology's status anxiety. On the one hand mainstream clinical psychologists wanted to assert their superiority over the growing horde of therapy providers who did not hold a Ph.D. or were not trained in psychology, such as clinical social workers, marriage counselors, and psychiatric nurses. The most psychologists could do about them was to keep out of the APA anyone without a Ph.D. On the other hand clinical psychologists wanted to assert their virtual equality with psychiatrists, who felt disdain for clinical psychologists. Seymour Post (1985) called clinical psychologists and anyone else without an M.D. "barefoot doctors of mental health." "Amazingly,"

Post went on, "this group of laymen is now clamoring for all the privileges of being a physician, including the right to admit patients to hospitals under their direct management. . . ." Worse, "patients come to them with symptoms as they would to a general physician or internist. They are not competent to play such a role. Malpractice is the rule."

Naturally, psychologists resent such attitudes. Whatever the merits of Post's arguments, however, it is certainly true that clinical psychologists were clamoring, at least on their own behalf, for something approaching the legal status of psychiatrists. Clinical psychologists had won the right to be licensed by the state, despite some well-placed misgivings about whether licenses really served the public interest as opposed to the private interests of psychologists (Gross 1978). On the other hand, when a hospital accreditation committee restricted clinical psychologists to hospital practice under an M.D., clinical psychologists were outraged (Dörken and Morrison 1976). The biggest dispute between clinical psychology and psychiatry, however, naturally involved money.

Who should pay for psychotherapy? Although the obvious answer is the client or patient, most medical treatment today is paid for by insurance companies or the government, and questions arise about whether or not psychotherapy should be included in third-party payment plans. A few psychiatrists and clinical psychologists (such as Albee 1977b) agree with Szasz that there is no such thing as mental illness, and logically conclude that psychotherapy is not really therapy, and so should not be covered under third-party payment schemes. Medical therapy for actual disorders of the nervous system (such as endogenous depression) would be covered. In practice, however, most therapists recognize that if psychotherapy costs had to be born by clients, their practices would bring in a lot less income. Psychiatrists and clinical psychologists therefore agree that third parties should pay for psychotherapy, but they disagree bitterly about who should *be* paid.

For many years, much to the resentment of clinical psychologists, insurance companies agreed with psychiatrists that only M.D.'s should be paid for medical procedures, and, with certain special limitations that did not apply to organic diseases, they covered psychotherapy only if performed by a psychiatrist. Clinical psychologists rightly viewed this as a monopoly, and pressed for "freedom of choice" legislation in the states that would force insurance companies to pay clinical psychologists, too. Of course, psychologists wanted to share the monopoly, not destroy it outright. Already faced with rising costs, insurance companies allied with psychiatry to resist the encroachments of psychology and filed suit (the test case arose in Virginia) alleging improper interference with the practice of medicine and business. Ultimately, freedom of choice laws were upheld in the courts, but the battle was long, and fueled the long-standing hostility between the APA and the "other" APA, the American Psychiatric Association. The battle was refought in a new arena during the late 1970s and early 1980s, when the federal government considered passing national health insurance; but Reagan's budget reduction programs rendered the issue moot.

The squabble over insurance raised a nasty question embarrassing to psychiatrist and clinical psychologist alike: Does psychotherapy *work?* Private and public health plans do not pay for quackery, so treatments must be proven safe and effective. The first person actually to investigate the outcomes of psychotherapy was the English psychologist Hans J. Eysenck in 1952. He concluded that getting therapy was no better than just waiting for therapy for the same period of time—the "cure" rate for spontaneous remission was as good as for therapy. This implies that psychotherapy is a fraud. Since then, psychotherapists have challenged Eysenck's conclusion, and hundreds of psychotherapy outcome studies have been done. Naturally, mainstream clinical psychologists eagerly argue that psychotherapy, or at least their kind of psychotherapy, is effective, but the evidence is at best extremely mixed. There is a consensus that psychotherapy is probably better than doing nothing for a psychological problem, although the magnitude of improvement is not very great. However, many studies have concluded that professional psychotherapy with a trained therapist may be no more beneficial than amateur therapy or self-help (Prioleau, Murdock, and Brody 1983; Zilbergeld 1983). It is also not clear if psychotherapy is safe. Zilbergeld (1983) quotes estimates that most clinicians are not competent, and describes numerous cases of people made worse by therapy.

In terms of numbers of practitioners and patients, clinical psychology is a success. But it remains riven by doubts about its identity, its status, and its effectiveness. Carl Rogers, who is the founder of clinical psychology if anyone is, has said, "Therapists are not in agreement as to their goals or aims. . . . They are not in agreement as to what constitutes a successful outcome of their work. They cannot agree as to what constitutes a failure. It seems as though the field is completely chaotic and divided" (Zilbergeld 1983).

The Turn to Service

Although Sigmund Koch and Michael Scriven complained about the quality of the psychology that was being given away, psychologists generally seemed to be heeding George Miller's appeal to get involved with the problems of society. For as the 1970s wore on psychologists were less likely to be found in the haunts of scientific psychology's founders, the classroom and the laboratory, than in settings where they provided services. One of the major changes in the United States in the 1960s and 1970s was the change from a primarily industrial-productive economy to a service-information economy. Between 1960 and 1979 the total U.S. labor force grew by 45 percent, while the service sector grew by 69 percent. The greatest growth occurred in the social sciences, whose ranks grew by an incredible 495 percent; psychology grew by 435 percent.

Increasingly, psychologists were choosing specialties outside the old core area of experimental psychology. Between 1966 and 1980 the increase of new Ph.D.'s in experimental psychology averaged only 1.4 percent per year (the slowest growth of all specialty areas), while growth in applied areas was much greater: For example, clinical psychology grew about 8.1 percent per year, counseling 12.9 percent, and school psychology 17.8 percent. By 1980 applied psychologists made up about 61 percent of all doctoral psychologists, while traditional experimentalists constituted but 13.5 percent. And new psychologists were choosing to work outside academia. In 1967 61.9 percent of new doctoral psychologists took work in colleges or universities; by 1981 the figure was down to 32.6 percent. The most rapidly growing employment setting was self-employment, as a privately practicing clinician or consultant. Self-employed psychologists were not even counted before 1970. In 1970 only 1.3 percent of new doctoral psychologists chose self-employment, but by 1981 6.9 percent did so. Other rapidly growing employment settings were government, business, and nonprofit institutions. Even psychologists trained in research specialties were increasingly likely to be employed outside academic settings, although often nonacademic employment was forced on them by the limited number of university and college jobs. In 1975 68.9 percent of new research specialty doctoral psychologists went into academic settings; in 1980 only 51.7 percent did so, for an average annual decline of 8 percent. There were offsetting increases in employment outside academia, so that there were few actually unemployed psychology Ph.D.'s.

Psychologists by 1985 could be found virtually everywhere, touching millions of lives. At the Educational Testing Service, psychologists continued to refine the Scholastic Aptitude Test (SAT), familiar to virtually every reader of this book, and pushed testing into new areas. You cannot become a golf pro without taking a multiple choice ETS test (Owen 1985). At the Stanford Research Institute, psychologists and others worked on an ambitious marketing program, the Values and Lifestyle Program (VALS). VALS used a technique called "psychographics" to break American consumers into several well-defined groups, such as "I-Am-Mes," "Belongers," and "Achievers." Companies and advertising agencies paid for VALS profiles to target their products to the most receptive groups and tune their pitches to the psychological makeup of their audiences (Atlas 1984). Clinical psychologists, despite some official misgivings from the APA, were running radio call-in shows on which people could air their problems and seek advice and comfort from a psychologist (Rice 1981). Such shows started locally, but by 1985 a nationwide radio network, Talk Radio, devoted at least six hours a day to the "psych jockeys." People were bringing their troubles to psychologists as never before: Between 1957 and 1976 the percentage of Americans who had consulted a mental health professional rose from 4 percent to 14 percent; among the college-educated, the change was from 9 percent to 21 percent. In fact, the number of people exposed to therapeutic techniques is very much greater, since many self-help organizations, such as those for losing weight and stopping smoking, use such techniques (Zilbergeld 1983). Finally, bookshops have Psychology sections mostly filled with self-help psychology books, and we can add to these most of the books in the Family Life sections concerning sex, intimacy, and child rearing.

By 1985 psychologists were everywhere, and were taking themselves seriously as a social force. Charles Kiesler (1979), executive officer of the APA, wrote: "I see psychology, then, as a national force for the future: as a knowledgeable force on scientific issues, on the delivery of human services, and on various human concerns about which we know something."

CONCLUSION: THE PSYCHOLOGICAL SOCIETY

Ever since its beginnings in ancient Greece, psychology has perched awkwardly astride the dividing line between science and morals, between what is—how human beings really are—and what ought to be—how human beings should behave. Natural science can rest content with describing nature as it is, giving humans power for good or evil. The other social disciplines, or *Geisteswissenschaften,* describe what human beings have made of themselves across cultures and throughout history. Psychology, however, shares the Neoplatonic tragedy of humankind. People are at once animals, part of the natural world, and, in a sense, divine makers of social worlds, and psychology must come to grips with "man the animal" and "man the creator" of forms of life. Psychology is perennially torn apart by its conflicting obligations, tempted on the one hand by the Newtonian dream of a natural science of humankind, yet likewise tempted to build a better form of life, to remake society in its own image.

Through it all, psychology has remained the study of the individual human being. The human species is studied by biology; human society is studied by sociology and anthropology. In our own time psychology, as the avowed science of the individual person, has come to replace traditional ways of moralizing about human action, and to replace them with its own perspective centered on the self and on feelings. In Platonism and traditional religion the rules by which people live their lives have been thought to come from outside, from a transcendent realm of the Good or from the transcendent world of God. However, as religious and metaphysical traditions have been eroded by mechanistic science, people have turned to science for moral guidance, and this has led them, inevitably, to psychology, the science of individual action. It is quite natural, then, that as transcendental norms fade they should be replaced by scientific ones, and the priest or shaman be replaced by the clinical psychologist. Psychology, as the study of the individual, must then decree that the rules by which we should live life come from within each one of us, rather than from outside, and that these new rules can be discovered by looking within ourselves, by finding out how we really feel about things. In our psychological society we are told to buy products because if we do we will "feel good" about them, and, even more important, about ourselves. Similarly, we are encouraged to share our feelings freely with others—whether they want to hear them or not—because only in this way, psychology says, can we become real human beings.

Psychology, however much behaviorists and cognitive scientists might object, teaches introspection as the final judge of right and wrong, and encourages people to undertake an inward journey in search of introspective certainty concerning our real feelings and our supposed secret selves. In the United States, at least, psychology has become a new religion establishing an inner quest for self where before there had been an outer quest for God. The most acute observer of modern America, Tom Wolfe (1977), described the psychological society this way: Americans "plunged straight toward what has become the alchemical dream of the Me Decade. The old alchemical dream was changing base metals into gold. The new alchemical dream is: changing one's personality—remaking, remodeling, elevating, and polishing one's very *self* . . . and observing, studying, and doting on it. (Me!)" (ellipses in original). The Me Decade, the Me Society, is the nearly inevitable result of scientism and psychology. If there is no transcendent truth outside nature, and if psychology is the science of the individual, then the only proper guide to life must come from scientific psychology, and that entails looking within for truth that cannot come from without.

For good or ill, we human beings of the West, especially the United States, live in a psychological society. We are raised according to the findings of child psychologists, and raise our children following the newer findings of child psychologists. In business we turn to psychologists to manage workers and help us sell our products; as consumers we are vulnerable to appeals crafted by psychologists. When we fall in love we find ourselves in a "relationship" to be scrutinized in terms of our feelings, and if we find trouble doing that, we phone or visit a psychologist to help us out. We have come to believe the Deweyan notion that there are no fixed rules, that growth is the only moral end. Since there are no outside goals to aim for, only inner ones, only growth and constant change are left to measure our self-worth and our love for each other. As Woody Allen, neurotic spokesman for the psychological society, complains in *Annie Hall,* "A relationship, I think, is like a shark; it has to constantly move forward or it dies."

BIBLIOGRAPHY

The literature on cognitive science is vast. A excellent introduction to AI is John Haugeland, *Artificial Intelligence: The very idea* (Cambridge: MIT Press/Bradford). The easiest introduction to functionalism is Jerry Fodor, "The mind body problem," *Scientific American* (1981, *244* [no. 1, January]: 114–123). In addition to the works described in the bibliography to the last chapter, there are two useful anthologies on foundations and criticisms of cognitive science. They are John Haugeland, ed., *Mind design* (Cambridge: Bradford/MIT, 1981); and Douglas R. Hofstadter and Daniel C. Dennett, eds., *The mind's eye* (New York: Basic, 1981). The latter book is edited by two defenders of formalistic AI, and although they reprint papers critical of cognitive science, such as Searle (1980, also reprinted by Haugeland), they try to defend the AI approach throughout their commentary. It is therefore useful to also read Searle's review of *The mind's eye* in the *New York Review of Books,* April 29, 1982. Waldrop (1984) provides a readable account of some of the latest work in AI. Owen J. Flanagan, *The science of the mind* (Cambridge: MIT Press, 1984), canvasses the field of cognitive psychology, including Freud, James, and Piaget, as well as information processing. There are two kinds of information processing: serial processing, in which processing steps are carried out one at a time, and parallel processing, in which many steps are carried out at once. For a variety of reasons existing computers, and hence existing cognitive science models of intelligence, are based on concepts of serial processing. However, some workers in AI have moved away from building machines with powerful, fast, serial central processors, to building large arrays of much simpler processors interconnected in parallel. Because this is how the brain is set up—neurons are simple but multiply connected to many other neurons—it is possible that the parallel processing machines will shed new light on human thinking. However, because the work is in its infancy, its promise and implications are unclear. For an accessible introduction to this new line of AI work, see "Seeking the mind in the pathways of the machine," *The Economist* (29 June–5 July, 1985). An outstanding book on the promise and the limits of AI, including its moral implications, is Joseph Weizenbaum, *Computer power and human reason* (San Francisco: W. H. Freeman, 1976). Weizenbaum is an eminent MIT computer scientist who has become revolted by what he regards as "obscene" uses of computers, for example, to do psychotherapy. Finally, while there is no historical connection between modern functionalism and earlier functionalism, there are interesting parallels. For example, John Dewey, in "The realism of pragmatism," *Journal of Philosophy* (1905, *2:* 324–327), describes his instrumentalism as a representational theory of mind.

There is a great deal of current work on consciousness. For the information-processing view see Klatzky (1985), and George Mandler (in press), "Consciousness: Its function and construction," in *Cognitive psychology: A survey of cognitive science* (Hillsdale, New Jersey: Erlbaum); for the transpersonal psychology view see Ronald S. Valle and Rolf von Eckatsberg, eds., *The metaphors of consciousness* (New York: Plenum, 1981); for a variety of scientific approaches see Kenneth Pope and Jerome Singer, eds., *The stream of consciousness* (New York: Plenum, 1978). Don Dulany and his associates at the University of Illinois, Champaign, are carrying out systematic research on the conscious control of behavior; see, for example, Dulany, Richard A. Carlson, and Gerald A. Dewey, "A case of syntactical learning and judgment: How conscious and how abstract?" *Journal of Experimental Psychology: General* (1984, *113:* 541–555). The article by Nisbett and Wilson (1977) provoked many replies, rebuttals, and elaborations. The only review of the literature I know of is an excellent but unpublished one by William Faw, "What does it mean to say 'People have little awareness of the nature or even existence of the cognitive processes that mediate judgments, inferences, and the products of complex social behavior'?: A study of the Nisbett and Wilson anti-introspection debate.'' Two replies to Nisbett and Wilson I find especially interesting: John G. Adair and Barry Spinner, ''Subject's access to cognitive processes: Demand characteristics and verbal report,'' *Journal for the Theory of Social Behavior* (1981, *11:* 31–52); and John Sabini and Maury Silver, ''Introspection and causal accounts,'' *Journal of Personality and Social Psychology* (1981, *40:* 171–179).

A truly excellent way to understand radical behaviorism and its relations to critics and rival views, especially cognitive science, is to read a special issue of *The Behavioral and Brain Sciences* (1984, *7* [no. 4, December]) devoted to the ''Canonical Papers of B. F. Skinner.'' The issue reprints Skinner's most important papers, and follows them with critical commentary from dozens of philosophers and scientists, followed in turn by Skinner's replies. It should be pointed out that radical behaviorism is no longer Skinner's monopoly, and that others who call themselves behaviorists today formulate the field with different emphases. For instructive examples, see Willard F. Day, ''Contemporary behaviorism and the concept of intention,'' in William J. Arnold, ed., *Nebraska symposium on motivation 1975 (Vol. 23): Conceptual foundations of psychology* (Lincoln: University of Nebraska Press, 1976); Charles P. Shimp, ''Cognition, behavior, and the experimental analysis of behavior,'' *Journal of the Experimental Analysis of Behavior* (1984, *42:* 407–420); or Gerald E. Zuriff, *Behaviorism: A conceptual reconstruction* (New York: Columbia University Press, 1985).

For psychology's occult doubles see Thomas H. Leahey and Grace Evans Leahey, *Psychology's occult doubles: Psychology and the problem of pseudoscience* (Chicago: Nelson Hall, 1983); and Thomas H. Leahey and Grace Evans Leahey, ''Occult muddles: Essay review of recent books on the occult,'' *Journal of the History of the Behavioral Sciences,* in press, 1986.

The references in the text provide a survey of reductionism. For sociobiology, there are many points of entry. Leahey and Harris (1985) have a one-chapter treatment of sociobiology. David Barash offers the best book-length treatments, including his text *Sociobiology and behavior,* 2d. ed. (New York: Elsevier, 1982) and his book on human sociobiology, *The whisperings within* (New York, Penguin, 1979). Michael Ruse, *Sociobiology: Sense or nonsense?* (Dordrecht, Holland: D. Reidel, 1979) is a wise introduction to and balanced evaluation of the field.

Hermeneutics is a sprawling, diverse field with many practitioners. It is primarily a European movement, though recently much interest has been shown in American philosophical and psychological circles. One way to begin to understand hermeneutics is through sources that explicitly contrast it with more familiar ways of thinking. The last part of Dreyfus (1972) contrasts European phenomenology, a branch of hermeneutics, with AI. Kenneth J. Gergen has recently criticized social psychology for not being a science, and his alternative ''social constructionism,'' although not explicitly hermeneutic, is closely related. His most famous paper, which provoked both interest and outrage in social psychology, was ''Social psychology as history,'' *Journal of Personality and Social Psychology* (1973, *26:* 309–320), expanded into a book, *Toward transformation in social knowledge* (New York: Springer-Verlag, 1982). His ideas have been vehemently rejected by mainstream social psychologists. Barry Schlenker reasserted the Newtonian values of the profession in his reply to Gergen's paper, ''Social psychology and science,'' *Journal of Personality and Social Psychology* (1974, *29:* 1–15). The editors of the *Personality and Social Psychology Bulletin* organized a symposium around the Gergen-Schlenker exchange, including new statements by the combatants, and it may be found in *Personality and Social Psychology Bulletin* (1976, *2:* 371–444). Using a lively dialogue form, Gary Gutting contrasts hermeneutics with positivism and mainstream philosophy of science in ''Paradigms and hermeneutics, A dialogue on Kuhn, Rorty, and the social sciences,'' *American Philosophical Quarterly* (1984, *21:* 1–15). The reference to Rorty is to philosopher Richard Rorty, who has incorporated hermeneutics into a reinvigorated pragmatism that has stirred up the same sort of storm in philosophy that Gergen did in social psychology. He analyzes and rejects traditional philosophy and introduces hermeneutics in *Philosophy and the mirror of nature* (Princeton: Princeton University Press, 1980); he develops his new view in *Consequences of pragmatism* (Minneapolis: University of Minnesota Press, 1982), which is briefly summarized in "The fate of philosophy," *The New Republic* (1982, *187,* [no. 16, October 18]: 28–34). Several books about hermeneutics have been published, but the one I have found to be the clearest is Roy J. Howard, *Three faces of hermeneutics: An introduction to current theories of understanding* (Berkeley: University of California Press, 1982); Howard's book is especially helpful because he connects hermeneutics to English-speaking philosophy, particularly to the followers of Wittgenstein.

The references provide a survey of works on the applications of psychology. On the fuss over insurance, see three special issues of *American Psychologist* devoted to the topic, September 1977 and August 1983, in the "Psychology in the Public Forum" section, and February 1986. The literature evaluating psychotherapy is vast, difficult, and treacherous. Probably the best place to enter the literature is Prioleau, Murdock, and Brody (1983). They do a good job of discussing the complex issues involved in evaluating therapy outcomes, the "Peer Commentary" section gives ample voice to critics who disagree with the article's contention that therapy is ineffective, and the reference section lists all the important works. Zilbergeld (1983) also discusses this literature, more readably but less precisely. See also J. Berman and N. Norton, "Does professional training make a therapist more effective?" *Psychological Bulletin* (1985, *98:* 401–407).

The statistics in the "Turn to Service" section are drawn from Georgine M. Pion and Mark W. Lipsey, "Psychology and society: The challenge of change," *American Psychologist* (1984, *39:* 739–754). David Owen's book on the SAT (1985) should be read by everyone who has taken the SAT or is a parent of someone who will take the SAT. Owen really does "rip the lid" off an incredibly corrupt institution that serves no ends but its own and does significant social harm. Anyone who reads the book will agree with Jonathan Yardley of the *Washington Post* that the SAT "is a scam," and with Owen's conclusion that ETS should be abolished.

The outstanding impressionistic portrait of the psychological society is Wolfe (1977). Another, more sardonic, tourist is Shiva Naipul, who reports in "The pursuit of wholiness," *Harper's* (April 1981: 20–27). The most scientific survey of the psychological society comes from pollster Daniel Yankelovich, "New rules in American life: Searching for self-fulfillment in a world turned upside down," *Psychology Today* (April 1981, 35–91). The term "psychological society" seems to have been coined by writer Martin L. Gross, *The psychological society: A critical analysis of psychiatry, psychotherapy, and the psychological revolution* (New York: Touchstone, 1978). Gross's book is quite good, if a little heavy-handed at times. Two related books are Peter Schrag, *Mind control* (New York: Delta, 1978), which is positively Orwellian in tone; and R. D. Rosen, *Psychobabble* (New York: Avon, 1979), which provides a witty tour of various pop psychotherapies. Several broad critiques of the psychological society exist, and I will mention only those I find especially useful. First, there is an excellent but often overlooked book by Daniel Boorstin, *The image: A guide to pseudo-events in America* (New York: Harper Colophon, 1964). The first book I know of to specifically address psychology's contribution to a new moral order was Phillip Rieff, *The triumph of the therapeutic* (New York: Harper & Row, 1966). Concern with the psychological society and the therapeutic sensibility grew more intense in the 1970s, producing Richard Sennett, *The fall of public man* (New York: Vintage, 1976), my own favorite of these books; and Christopher Lasch, *The culture of narcissism* (New York: W. W. Norton, 1979), which has probably had the greatest impact. An excellent book, which focuses closely on the therapeutic sensibility encouraged by clinical psychology and psychiatry, is Zilbergeld (1983), with the unforgettable title *The shrinking of America.* Two related books bear mention. First is Alasdair MacIntyre, *After virtue: A study in moral theory* (Notre Dame: University of Notre Dame Press, 1981), who takes a long view of the turn from exterior to interior standards of morality, extending back to the prephilosophic Greeks. The best actual antidote to the language of feelings is Miss Manners: Judith Martin, *Miss Manners' guide to excruciatingly correct behavior* (New York: Warner Books, 1982).

REFERENCES

Agnew, S. (1972) Agnew's blast at behaviorism. *Psychology Today 5* (no 8, January): 4, 84, 87.

Albee, G. W. (1970) The uncertain future of clinical psychology. *American Psychologist 25:* 1071–1080.

Albee, G. W. (1977a) The protestant ethic, sex, and psychotherapy. *American Psychologist 32:* 150–161.

Albee, G. W. (1977b) Does including psychotherapy in health insurance represent a subsidy to the rich from the poor? *American Psychologist 32:* 719–721.

Anderson, J. R. (1978) Arguments concerning representations for mental imagery. *Psychological Review 85:* 249–277.

Anderson, J. R. (1981) Concepts, propositions, and schemata: What are the cognitive units? In Flowers (1981).

Atlas, J. (1984) Beyond demographics. *Atlantic Monthly* (October): 49–58.

Bandura, A. (1974) Behavior theory and the models of man. *American Psychologist 29:* 859–869.

Boden, M. (1977) *Artificial intelligence and the nature of man.* New York: Basic Books.

Boden, M. (1979) The computational metaphor in psychology. In N. Bolton, ed., *Philosophical problems in psychology.* London: Methuen.

Brewer, W. F. and Nakamura, G. V. (1984) The nature and functions of schemas. In R. S. Wyer and T. K. Srull, eds., *Handbook of social cognition.* Hillsdale, New Jersey: Erlbaum.

Brush, S. G. (1974) Should the history of science be rated 'X'? *Science 183:* 1164–1172.

Campbell, D. T. (1975) On the conflicts between biological and social evolution and between psychology and moral tradition. *American Psychologist 30:* 1103–1126.

Churchland, P. (1985) *Matter and consciousness.* Cambridge: MIT/Bradford.

Clark, K. (1971) The pathos of power: A psychological perspective. *American Psychologist 26:* 1047–1057.

Cleary, T., Humphries, L., Kendrick, S., and Wesman, A. (1975) Educational uses of tests with disadvantaged students. *American Psychologist 30:* 15–91.

Davidson, D. (1980) *Essays on actions and events.* Oxford: Clarendon Press.

Demos, J. P. (1982) *Entertaining Satan: Witchcraft and the culture of early New England.* New York: Oxford University Press.

Dennett, D. (1978) *Brainstorms.* Cambridge: MIT/Bradford.

Dennett, D. (1983) Artificial intelligence and the strategies of psychological investigation. In Miller (1983).

Dennett, D. (1984) Cognitive wheels: The frame problem of AI. In Hookway (1984).

Dörken, H. and Morrison, D. (1976) JCAH standards for accreditation of psychiatric facilities: Implications for the practice of clinical psychology. *American Psychologist 31:* 774–784.

Dreyfus, H. (1972) *What computers can't do: A critque of artifical reason.* New York: Harper & Row.

Ericsson, K. A. and Simon, H. (1980) Verbal reports as data. *Psychological Review 87:* 215–251.

Estes, W. K. and Newell, A. (Co-chairs) (1983) Report of the Research Briefing Panel on Cognitive Science and Artificial Intelligence. In *Research Briefings 1983.* Washington, D.C.: National Academy Press.

Eysenck, H. J. (1952) The effects of psychotherapy: An evaluation. *Journal of Consulting Psychology 16:* 319–324.

Farnham-Diggory, S., ed. (1972) *Information processing in children.* New York: Academic Press.

Flowers, J. H. (1981) *Nebraska symposium on motivation 1980 (V. 28): Cognitive processes.* Lincoln: University of Nebraska Press.

Fox, J. (1983) Debate on learning theory is shifting. *Science 222:* 1219–1222.

Goleman, D. (1983) A conversation with Ulric Neisser. *Psychology Today 17* (no. 5, May): 54–62.

Gottlieb, G. (1984) Evolutionary trends and evolutionary origins: Relevance to theory in comparative psychology. *Psychological Review 91:* 448–456.

Gross, S. J. (1978) The myth of professional licensing. *American Psychologist, 33:* 1009–1016.

Gunderson, K. (1984) Leibnizian privacy and Skinnerian privacy. *The Behavioral and Brain Sciences 7:* 628–629.

Hayes-Roth, F. (1979) Distinguishing theories of representation. *Psychological Review 86:* 376–382.

Hodos, W. and Campbell, C. B. G. (1969) Scala naturae: Why there is no theory in comparative psychology. *Psychological Review 76:* 337–350.

Hookway, C., ed. (1984) *Minds, machines, and programs.* New York: Cambridge University Press.

Hull, D. L. (1984) Historical entities and historical narratives. In Hookway (1984).

Hulse, S., Fowler, H., and Honig, W., eds. (1978) *Cognitive processes in animal behavior.* Hillsdale, New Jersey: Erlbaum.

Jackson, G. D. (1975) On the report of the ad hoc committee on educational uses of tests with disadvantaged students. Another psychological view from the Association of Black Psychologists. *American Psychologist 30:* 88–93.

Jenkins, J. J. (1981) Can we find a fruitful cognitive psychology? In J. H. Flowers (1981).

Jensen, A. (1969) How much can we boost I.Q. and scholastic achievement? *Harvard Educational Review 39:* 1–123.

Kasschau, R. A. and Kessel, F. S., eds. (1980) *Psychology and society: In search of symbiosis.* New York: Holt, Rinehart & Winston.

Kessel, F. S. (1980) Psychology and society: In search of symbiosis. Introduction to the symposium. In Kasschau and Kessel (1980).

Kiesler, C. A. (1979) Report of the Executive Officer 1978. *American Psychologist 34:* 455–462.

Klatzky, R. (1984) *Memory and awareness: An information-processing perspective.* San Francisco: W. H. Freeman.

Klerman, G. L. (1979) The age of melancholy? *Psychology Today 12* (no. 11, April): 36–42, 88.

Koch, S. (1980) Psychology and its human clientele: Beneficiaries or victims? In Kasschau and Kessel (1980).

Lachman, R., Lachman, J., and Butterfield, E. (1979) *Cognitive psychology and information processing.* Hillsdale, New Jersey: Erlbaum.

Leahey, T. H. (1981) The revolution never happened: Information processing is behaviorism. Paper presented at the 52nd annual meeting of the Eastern Psychological Association, New York, New York, April 23.

Leahey, T. H. (1982) Will psychology disappear? The new prospects for reductionism. Paper presented at the annual meeting of the Eastern Psychological Association, Baltimore, Maryland, April.

Leahey, T. H. (1984) Evolution, history and cognitive science: Psychology without science or science without psychology. Paper presented at the annual meeting of the Eastern Psychological Association, Baltimore, Maryland, April.

Leahey, T. H. and Harris, R. J. (1985) *Human learning.* Englewood Cliffs, New Jersey: Prentice-Hall.

Lockard, R. B. (1971) Reflections of the fall of comparative psychology: Is there a lesson for us all? *American Psychologist 26:* 168–179.

Lofton, J. (1972) Psychology's manpower: A perspective from the public at large. *American Psychologist 27:* 364–366.

Lown, B. A. (1975) Comparative psychology 25 years after. *American Psychologist 30:* 858–859.

Mahoney, M. J. (1977) Reflections on the cognitive-learning trend in psychotherapy. *American Psychologist 32:* 5–13.

McConnell, J. V. (1970) Criminals can be brainwashed—Now. *Psychology Today 3* (no. 11, April): 14–18, 74.

Mehler, J. and Franck, S. (1981) Editorial. *Cognition 10:* 1–5.

Meichenbaum D. (1977) *Cognitive behavior modification: An integrative approach.* New York: Plenum.

Miller, G. A. (1972) *Psychology: The science of mental life.* New York: Harper & Row.

Miller, G. A. (1983) The background to modern cognitive psychology. In J. Miller (1983).

Miller, J. (1983) *States of mind.* New York: Pantheon.

Mischel, W. and Mischel, H. (1976) A cognitive social learning approach to morality and self-regulation. In T. Lickona, ed., *Moral development and behavior.* New York: Holt, Rinehart & Winston.

Neisser, U. (1976) *Cognition and reality.* San Francisco: W. H. Freeman.

Neisser, U. (1982) Preface; Memory: What are the important questions? In U. Neisser, ed., *Memory observed: Remembering in natural contexts.* San Francisco: W. H. Freeman.

Neisser, U. (1984) Toward an ecologically oriented cognitive science. In T. M. Schlecter and M. P. Toglia, eds., *New directions in cognitive science.* Norwood, New Jersey: Ablex.

Newell, A. (1973) You can't play 20 questions with nature and win. In W. G. Chase, ed., *Visual information processing.* New York: Academic Press.

Nisbett, R. E. and Wilson, T. D. (1977) Telling more than we can know: Verbal reports on mental processes. *Psychological Review 84:* 231–259.

Owen, D. (1985) *None of the above: Behind the myth of scholastic aptitude.* Boston: Houghton Mifflin.

Peele, S. (1981) Reductionism in the psychology of the eighties: Can biochemistry eliminate addiction, mental illness, and pain? *American Psychologist 36:* 807–818.

Perry, N. J. (1979) Why clinical psychology does not need alternative training models. *American Psychologist 34:* 603–611.

Peterson, D. R. (1976) Need for the Doctor of Psychology degree in professional psychology. *American Psychologist 31:* 792–798.

Porter, J., Johnson, S., and Granger, R. G. (1981) The snark is still a boojum. *Comparative Psychology Newsletter 1* (no. 5, December): 1–3.

Post, S. C. (1985) Beware the 'Barefoot doctors of mental health.' *The Wall Street Journal,* Thursday, July 25: 21.

Prioleau, L., Murdock, M., and Brody, N. (1983) An analysis of psychotherapy versus placebo studies. *The Behavioral and Brain Sciences 6:* 275–310.

Putnam, H. (1982) Reductionism and the nature of psychology. *Cognition 2:* 131–146.

Pylyshyn, Z. W. (1979) Validating computational models: A critique of Anderson's indeterminacy claim. *Psychological Review 86:* 383–405.

Pylyshyn, Z. W. (1984) *Computation and cognition: Toward a foundation for cognitive science.* Cambridge: MIT/Bradford.

Raimey, C. T. (1974) Children and public policy: A role for psychologists. *American Psychologist 29:* 14–18.

Rheingold, H. (1973) To rear a child. *American Psychologist 28:* 42–46.

Rice, B. (1981) Call-in therapy: Reach out and shrink someone. *Psychology Today,* December: 39–44, 87–91.

Robinson, P. (1983) Psychology's scrambled egos. *Washington Post Book World, 13* (no. 28, July 10): 5, 7.

Rosch, E. (1977) Human categorization. In N. Warren, ed., *Studies in cross-cultural psychology.* London: Academic Press.

Rose, F. (1985) The black knight of AI. *Science 85,* March: 46–51.

Rosenberg, A. (1980) *Sociobiology and the preemption of social science.* Baltimore: Johns Hopkins University Press.

Rosenberg, A. (1983) Content and consciousness versus the intentional stance. *The Behavioral and Brain Sciences 3:* 375–376.

Rosenberg, A. (1984) Davidson's unintended attack on psychology. Paper presented at the Conference on the Philosophy of Donald Davidson, New Brunswick, New Jersey, May 1.

Rubinstein, R. A. (1984) *Science as a cognitive process.* Philadelphia: University of Pennsylvania Press.

Scriven, M. (1980) An evaluation of psychology. In Kasschau and Kessel (1980).

Searle, J. (1980) Minds, brains, and programs. *The Behavioral and Brain Sciences 3:* 417–424.

Shakow, D. (1976) What is clinical psychology? *American Psychologist 31:* 553–560.

Simon, H. (1980) The social and behavioral sciences. *Science 209:* 72–78.

Skinner, B. F. (1931) The concept of reflex in the description of behavior. *Journal of General Psychology 5:* 427–458.

Skinner, B. F. (1972) *Beyond freedom and dignity.* New York: Knopf.

Skinner, B. F. (1974) *About behaviorism.* New York: Knopf.

Skinner, B. F. (1984a) Some consequences of selection. *The Behavioral and Brain Sciences 7:* 502–510.

Skinner, B. F. (1984b) Representations and misrepresentations. *The Behavioral and Brain Sciences 7:* 655–667.

Skinner, B. F. (1985a) Cognitive science and behaviorism. *British Journal of Psychology:* in press.

Skinner, B. F. (1985b) What is wrong with everyday life in the Western world? Paper presented at the annual meeting of the American Psychological Association, Los Angeles, California, August 26.

Snyder, S. H. (1980) *Biological aspects of mental disorder.* New York: Oxford University Press.

Stich, S. P. (1983) *From folk psychology to cognitive science: The case against belief.* Cambridge: MIT/Bradford.

Strickler, G. (1975) On professional schools and professional degrees. *American Psychologist 31:* 1062–1066.

Strupp, H. (1976) Clinical psychology, irrationalism, and the erosion of excellence. *American Psychologist 31:* 561–571.

Tart, C. (1978) Information processing mechanisms and ESP. Invited address presented at the annual meeting of the American Psychological Association, Toronto, Canada, August 31.

Tulving, E. (1979) Memory research: What kind of progress? In L. G. Nilsson, ed., *Perspectives on memory research.* Hillsdale, New Jersey: Erlbaum.

Waldrop, M. M. (1984) The necessity of knowledge. *Science 223:* 1279–1282.

Wasserman, E. A. (1981) Comparative psychology returns. *Journal of the Experimental Analysis of Behavior 35:* 243–257.

Wegman, C. (1984) *Psychoanalysis and cognitive psychology.* New York: Academic Press.

Wender, P. H. and Klein, D. F. (1981) The promise of biological psychiatry. *Psychology Today 15* (no. 2, February): 25–41.

White, M. G. (1985) On the status of cognitive psychology. *American Psychologist 40:* 116–119.

Wilson, E. O. (1975) *Sociobiology: The new synthesis.* Cambridge: Harvard University Press.

Wispé, L. G. and Thompson, J. N., eds. (1976) The war between the words: Biological vs. social evolution and some related issues. *American Psychologist 31:* 341–384.

Wolfe, T. (1977) The Me Decade and the third great awakening. In T. Wolfe, *Mauve gloves and madmen, clutter and vine.* New York: Bantam Books.

Wyers, E. J., et al. (11) (1980) The sociobiological challenge to psychology: On the proposal to "cannibalize" comparative psychology. *American Psychologist 35:* 955–979

Zilbergeld, B. (1983) *The shrinking of America: Myths of psychological change.* Boston: Little, Brown.

Index

Abelard, Peter, 67, 69;
—voluntaristic ethics of, 69
act psychology, Brentano, 278
Action Theory, Munsterberg, 268–70, 272
actuality/potentiality, Leibniz on, 102
Adams, Grace, 353, 349
adaptation, 114 (*See also* psychology of adaptation); psychology of, Galton's, 239–40;
psychology of, Spencer's, 239–40; Watson on, 303
Adjusted American (Putney & Putney), 432
adjustment, ethic of, 403
Adler, Alfred, psychoanalysis, 227
advertising, 332–33
Age of Reason, 103, 114, 124, 286
aggression, Lorenz on, 233
Agnew, Spiro, 474
AI, 371, 397–402, 427, 437, 453, 456, 460;
See also artificial intelligence
Albigensianism, women in, 68
alchemy, 78, 90
Alcmaeon, 39
Alexander the Great, 52–53
Allen, Woody, shark, 479–80
Ambrose, St., 54
American revolution, 134
analysis of history, Carlyle's, 30; Hegel's, 30;
Marx's, 30; *Zeitgeist*, 30
analysis of science, biological, 25; Dewey's, 24;
Holton's, 6, 8, 21; James's, 24; Kuhn's, 12–20; Lakatos's, 8, 19–20; Mayr's, 25–27; J. S. Mill's, 24–25; mathematics and, 77; Newton and, 24–5; naturalistic, 11–18;
Newtonian fantasy and, 24–5; pragmatic, 24–5; Putnam's, 22; physics envy and, 24–5;
Popper's, 20–1; realistic, 22; Suppe's, 6,

Toulmin's, 3, 18–20; themata and, 19–20;
Weltanschauung, 11–12
Anaximander, 38
Anderson, John, 457
Angel, J. R., 194, 287; on consciousness, 293–5, 305; on functionalism, 272, 267–8; on introspection, 295
Animal Education (Watson), 287–8
animal intelligence, Descartes on, 95–96;
Thorndike on, 280–1
animal learning, 125
animal magnetism (mesmerism), 155
animal mind, 286–7
animal psychology, 280–7; Morgan on, 241;
Romanes on, 241–2
animal spirits, 84
Anna O., Freud and, 215
Annie Hall, shark, 480
anomalous monism, 468, 469
Anthropology (Kant), 119–20
anxiety, 404
APA, 201, 277, 293, 320, 321, 331–3, 358, 385, 402–3, 430, 465, 473; clinicians in, 475–7; professionalization of, 260–3; race controversy in, 474–5; reunified, 354–39; rift in, 338–9; U.S. army and, 333–5
apperception, Leibniz, 103
Aquinas, St. Thomas, 67, 70–5, 77, 81–2, 235;
on god, 72; on mind, 72; on the soul, 72; on women, 67, Bertrand Russell on, 72, 120
Aristotle, 23–5, 47–52, 62–6, 70–3, 90, 95, 121, 126, 147–8, 253, 380, 435, 466; *De Anima*, 49; dualism, 49; empiricism, 71–3;
epistemology, 47–8; four causes, theory of, 48–9; on god, 48–9; on imagination, 51–2;
on motivation, 52; on memory, 51–2; on

489

Aristotle (*cont.*)
    mind, 51; potentiality and actuality, theory
    of, 48–9; philosophy of science, 448–9; scala
    natura, theory of, 48–9; on soul, 49–50; on
    sense perception, 50
artificial intelligence, 371, 397–402, 424; *See
    also* AI
associationism, 112, 126, 130, 141–4, 175,
    184–5, 198, 243, 394; Hartley's theory of,
    121–123
astrology, 465
astronomy, 161–162
atomic theory, 21–22
atomism, 26, 40–1, 125, 184–5, 195, 279; De-
    mocritus's theory of, 40–2
Augustine, St., 54–55, 61, 64, 67, 77, 81–2,
    93
authenticity, 433, 436
automatic sweetheart (James), 290–1, 309
autonomy, 432–3
Autrecourt, 108

Bacon, Francis, 81, 84, 90, 108, 149, 380
Bacon, Roger, 77–78
Bain, Alexander, 169, 182, 235, 238; founds
    Mind, 165–7
Bartlett, Frederick, schema theory of, 279
Baumer, Franklin, 139
Bawden, H. Heath, 276, 278
Beach, Frank, on species-specific behavior,
    371–72
Beattie, James, 115
Bechterev, V. M., 284
Behavior of Organisms (Skinner), 382, 385
behavior, biological determinism and, 419–21;
    experimental analysis of, 381–5; *See also*
    Skinner, B. F.
behavioralism, 257–367, 293–5,417, 421, 447,
    456–7; defined, 259–60; S-R, 390–93
behaviorism, 91–92, 201, 228, 236, 243, 253,
    257, 425, 444–5; defined, 306–11; informal,
    372–4; logical, 372–4; mechanistic, 318–22;
    meta-physical, 260; methodological, 260,
    315; operational, 316; radical, 423, 456, 464;
    radical, Skinner's, 249–9, 325, 379–89 (*See
    also,* Skinner, B. F.); troubled, 371–7; Wat-
    son founds, 287–8
Bell, Charles, 164
Bentham, Jeremy, 142–144, 172, 466
Berkeley, George, Bishop, 97–8, 108–110,
    112, 120, 126, 144, 200, 246, 251–2; ideal-
    ism of, 109–10; on perception, 109–10
Bernard, Claude, 145–146
Bernard, St., 62
Bernheim, Hippolyte, 156
Bessel, F. W., 161
Beyond Freedom and Dignity (Skinner), 461–3
Beyond the Pleasure Principle (Freud), 222–4
Bible, 62, 151–2, 349
Binet, Alfred, 332; imageless thought, 192
Blake, William, 139

Boas, Franz, 345, 348
Boden, Margaret, 450
Bonaventure, St., 70–71
Boring, E. G., 162, 399
Boulder model, 430, 475
Braid, James, hypnotism, 155–156
Brainwatchers (Gross), 431
Bransford, John C., 425–6
Breland and Breland, 419–20
Breland, Keller, 418–21
Brentano, Franz, 115, 196, 199, 292, 398, 448;
    act psychology of, 278; intentionality, theory
    of, 199
Breuer, Joseph, 214–16
Brewer, William, 423, 425
Broadbent, Donald, 400
Broca, Pierre Paul, 164
Brown, Norman O., 226
Brown, Thomas, 122–123, 142
Bruner, Jerome, 394–6
Bruno, Giordano, 81
Bryan, William Jennings, 151–152, 262
Buchner, E. F., 277, 287
Buck, Carrie, eugenics, 344
Buridan, Jean, 78
Burke, Edmund, 141
Burnham, John, 361
Burtt, E. A., 92
Butterfield, Herbert, 88

Cabala, influence on Freud, 210
Cabanis, Pierre, 172
cacogenic, eugenics, 342
Calkins, Mary, 277; self-psychology of, 305
Campanella, Tomasso, 92
Carlyle, Thomas, 141, 144, 171; analysis of
    history, 30
Carmina Burana, love, 68
Carnap, Rudolph, 316, 373; on language, 317
Cartesian linguistics, 414, 416
Cartesianism, 92–6, 103–4, 139, 147, 169,
    398, 437, 468
castration complex, Freud's theory of, 222
Catcher in the Rye, 403
Cattell, James McKeen, 252, 262, 268, 273,
    332
causation, 112–113
Chain of Being, scala natura, 148
Charcot, Jean Martin, Freud and, 213–14; hyp-
    notism of, 156
Chesterton, G. K., on scientism, 344
childrearing, 473–4; Freudians, vulgar, on, 340;
    Watson on, 350–4
Chinese Room (Searle), 457–8, 459
Chomsky, Noam, 169, 412–17, 422, 424–5,
    427
Christians, god of, 54–5, 61–3, 76
Christianity, early, 46, 54–55; evangelical,
    243–44
Churchland, P. and P., 469–70
Cioffi, Frank, 227; seduction scenes, 211–12

civilization, Freud on, 222, 225–6
Civilization and its Discontents (Freud) 226,
  432
Clark, Kenneth, 473, 474
classical conditioning, (Pavlov), 280, 283–6
client-centered therapy, 410
cognitive dissonance, 395–6
cognitive map, 398, 447; Tolman on, 179
cognitive psychology, 179; *See also* cognitive
  science
cognitive science, 450, 459; Skinner on, 463–4
Combe, George, 247
computer models, 446–451; Tolman's, 317
computer programs, 427
computer simulation, 401–2
Comte, Auguste, 144–146, 147, 311–13, 471
Conan Doyle, Sir Arthur, falsificationism, 8
conceptualism, 75
Condillac, Etienne Bonnot de, 126–127, 130,
  132, 156–7, 166
conditioning, evolutionary, 418; Skinner on,
  359; Watson on, 310
congress, funding of science, 359
consciousness, 199–202, 250–1, 253, 260, 271,
  275–6, 288–92, 423; Angell on, 293–5, 305;
  Freud on, 209, 219; Frost on, 294; Tolman
  on, 316; Yerkes on, 287
Copernicus, Nicholas, 81, 90, 207
creationist science, oxymoronic nature of, 466
criteria of the psychic, Yerkes' review of,
  286–7
cynicism, 434
Cynics, 53

d'Holbach, Paul, 126
Dartmouth Conference on Learning Theory,
  378–79
Darwin, Charles, 26–27, 83, 114, 123, 126,
  139–42, 166, 172–3, 207, 234, 236–68,
  273, 275, 381, 386, 421, 462; Descent of
  Man, 237–8; Origin of Species, 147–53, 237
Darwin, Erasmus, Zoonomia, 149
Darwinian revolution, 149–153
Dashiell, John F., 314
Davenport, Charles, founds eugenics, 343–44
Davidson, Donald, 468
De Anima (Aristotle), 49
de Magnete (Gilbert), 84
de Tocqueville, Alexis, 245
death instincts (Freud), 223
Democritus, atomism of, 40–42
Dennett, Daniel, 449–50, 459–60
dependent variables, defined, 381
Descartes, René, 79, 82, 91–6, 99–100, 102–9,
  124–5, 132, 133, 184, 286, 373–74, 397,
  415, 416, 424; on animal intelligence, 95–6,
  286, 289; on god, 93–4; Kant and, 119;
  Locke and, 96–8; on mind, 95; on soul, 95
Descent of Man (Darwin), 237–8
determinism, 461–2
Deutsch, J. A., 400

development, Plato on, 46
Dewey, John, 287, 332, 337, 348, 400, 479;
  analysis of science, 24; environmentalism of,
  265; instrumentalism, theory of, 292–3; Progressivism and, 262–6; pragmatism of, 263–
  6; reflex arc, critique of, 270–1, 274–5
Diderot, Denis, 126
Diogenes, 53
disciplinary matrix (Kuhn), 12
Donders, F. C., mental chronometry, 162, 192
dreams, Freud on, 218–20
Dreyfus, Hubert, 460
dualism, 92–6, 102, 121–2, 125, 169, 468; Aristotle on, 49; Plato's, 51; Ryle on, 373–4,
  376
Dulany, Don E., 422–3
Dunlap, Knight, introspection, critique of, 294

Ebbinghaus, Hermann, 279–80, 422–3
education, Plato on, 46
Edwards, Jonathan, 245–46, 352
ego, Freud on, 218, 223–5
Ehrenfels, Christian, 195
Einstein, Albert, logical positivism, critique of,
  6–7
Emile (Rousseau), 133, 462
Empedocles, 40–41
empiricism, 28, 40, 71–8, 96–8, 102, 109–18,
  124, 127–8, 130, 133, 144–6, 156–7, 170,
  182, 251–3, 267–8, 380, 420; Aristotle's,
  71–3; Locke's, 96–8; radical, 289
Enlightenment, 77, 100–1, 103–4, 108, 123–4,
  129, 130–5, 139, 141–2, 148, 152, 171, 181
Enlightenment, new, 347
environmentalism, 379–80; Dewey's, 265
Epictetus, 53
Epicureans, 125
Epicurus, 53
erotogenic zones, Freud on, 222
Esdaile, James, 155
ESP, 17, 466
Essay on Man (Pope), 134–5
ether, 154
ethology, 420–1
Euclid, 99, 318, 320
eugenics, 341–45; Buck, Carrie, 344;
  cacogenics, 342; contraception and, 343;
  Davenport founds, 343–4; Galton on, 239,
  343; genetic counseling as, 345; Nazis and,
  345; sterilization practices in, 334; Wiggam,
  341, 342
Eupsychia (Maslow), 435
evangelical preaching, influence on Watson,
  349, 352
evolution, 147–149, 234
existentialism, 100, 128
Eysenck, Hans J., 476

faculty psychology, 116, 95, 126–7, 251–2;
  Christian, 70–3, Ibn Sīnā's, 61–7; Kant on,
  119; Puritan, 245–7

falsificationism, 7–11; Popper's, 6–7
family, social science on, 346–49
Fechner, Gustav Theodore, 162, 168, 172; psychophysics, 192; unconscious, 208–9
feedback, 398
Festinger, Leon, 395–6
Fichte, Johann, 120, 182
field theory, Gestalt, 201
fin de siècle, nineteenth century, 139, 153
finalism, 125
Fite, Warner, 259–60, 295
fixity of species, 148–149
Flourens, Jean-Pierre-Marie, 163–165
Ford Foundation, funding of social science, 360
formalism, 459
Forms, (Plato), 43–4, 53–4, 67, 73–4, 76, 83–84, 94
Foucault, Michel, 424
foundational philosophy, Rorty's critique of, 5
four causes, Aristotle on, 48–49
Fowler, O. and L., 247
frame problem, fatal nature of, 459–60
Frances, St. of Assisi, 69
Freeman, Derek, Samoa revisited, 348
Freud, Sigmund, 26, 83, 103–4, 128, 141, 146, 148, 154, 156, 159, 172–3, 200, 207–32, 234, 385, 432, 472; Beyond the Pleasure Principle, 222–4; Civilization and its Discontents, 226; Future of an Illusion, 225–6; on instincts, 209–12, 223; Interpretation of Dreams, 214–20; mentalism, 207–28; Oedipus complex, 212–3; 219–20; 222; perversions, 221; Project for a Scientific Psychology, 217–8, 222; pornography, Victorian, 210; on religion, 225–6; repression, 209, 213, 218, 221; Studies in Hysteria, 215–6; sexuality, Victorian, 212–3, 220–2; seduction mistake, 211–12; Three Essays on the Theory of Sexuality, 220–2; unconscious, theories of, 208–9, 224–5; Wundt and, 213, 217–8; Watson and, 340; women, Victorian, 212–3
Freudians, vulgar, on childrearing, 340
Fromm, Erich, 147
Frost, Elliot, on consciousness, 294
functional psychology, 271–4, 312, 331, 398, 420, 437–8, 467–9; Angell's, 272, 276–8; instrumentalism and, 292; James's, 268; Titchener on, 272–4
functionalism, new, 446–51
funding, of psychology, 428–30; Congress and, 359; Ford Founation and, 360
Future of an Illusion (Freud), 225–6

Galen, 65–66
Galileo, 77–8, 81, 84, 90–2,1 94, 133
Gall, Franz Joseph, 156–158, 163–6, 234, 247
Galton, Francis, 238–40; adaptation, psychology of, 239–40; on eugenics, 239, 343
Garcia, John, 419–20
Gassendi, Pierre, 125

Gassner, Johann, 154
General Problem Solver, 401–2, 426, 452–3
genetic counseling, as eugenics, 345
genetic epistemology, 394–5, 424
genetics, Mendel invents, 150
Gestalt, 195–198, 200–2, 234, 319, 426
Gestalt psychology, 426; isomorphism, 198; Lewin, 379; phi phenomenon, 196; *See also* Koffka, Kurt; Kohler, Wolfgang; or Wertheimer, Max
Ghost in the Machine, 373, 447–8
Gilbert, William, de Magnete, 84
god, 103–104, 103–4, 108–10, 116, 124, 127–8, 131, 134, 144, 147–9, 151, 171–2, 244, 247, 248, 252, 397, 479
god, Aristotle on, 48–49; Aquinas on, 72; Christian, 61–3, 76; Descartes on, 93–4; Freud on, 225–6; Kant on, 118; Leibniz on, 102; Newton on, 91; Plotinus on, 53–4; Spinoza on, 100–1; Spencer on, 235; *See also* gods
Goddard, Henry, 332; on Kallikaks, 343, 345; testing and, 339–41
gods, Christian, 54–55; Jewish, 54; Mithraist, 54; Olympian, 54; Roman, 54
Gottfried von Strasbourg, Tristan and Isolde, 68
GPS, see General Problem Solver
Grant, Madison, racism of, 342
Great Man view of history, Carlyle's, 30
Greenspoon effect, 422–3
Gross, Martin, 431
Grosseteste, Robert, 77–78
Guthrie, Edwin R., 379

habit, 110–114
Haggerty, M. E., on consciousness, 293
Hall, G. Stanley, 250; and James, 252
Hamlet, Freud on, 220
Hamlet, (Shakespeare), 79, 82
Hanson, N. R., 417
Hartley, David, 142, 156, 167; associationism, 121–3
Hartmann, Eduard von, on the unconscious, 208
Hawthorne Effect (Mayo), 336–37
Hebb, Donald, 426
hedonism, 41–2, 127–8, 173, 173
Hegel, G. W. F., 120, 170, 171, 246; analysis of history, 30; idealism, 267
Hellenistic Age, 52–3; new, 363, 434
Helmholtz, Hermann von, 161–162, 170, 173, 179–81, 283
Helvetius, Claude, 127–128
Heraclitus, 39–42, 147–9, 266–7, 268
Herbart, Johann Friedrich, 168–169; Freud and, 224; on the unconscious, 208
Herder, Johann Gottfried, 130–133, 141, 172, 181, 187
hermeneutics, 83, 471–2
Hickock, Laurens Perseus, 246
hierarchy of theories (Suppes), 10
Hilgard, E. R., 325

Hinkley, John, 28
history, analyses of, see analysis of history
hippies, 434–5
Hobbes, Thomas, 103, 112, 318, 319, 395,
397; Freud and, 226; Leviathan, 98–100; on
natural law, 99–100; on the state, 99
Holmes, Oliver Wendell, 247–8
Holmes, Sherlock, falsificationism, 8
Holt, E. B., 289, 315; specific response, doctrine of, 290
Holton, Gerald, analysis of science, 6, 8, 21
Homer, 35
hormic psychology (McDougall), 316
Houdini, Harry, 159–160, 247
Hull, Clark L., 314–5, 377–9, 384–5, 389–93,
398, 400–2, 411–12, 418, 427, 435, 437–8,
447–8, 451, 455, 457; behaviorism, mecha-
nistic, of, 318–22; Institute of Human
Relations (Yale) and, 324–5
Human Learning (Thorndike), 282–3
Human Understanding (Toulmin), 18–24
humanism, 79–83
humanistic psychology, see psychology,
humanistic
Hume, David, 108, 110–116, 117–8, 121–3,
130, 134, 142, 144, 167, 246, 251–2, 319–
20, 380, 412
Hunter, Walter, 307
Husserl, Edward, phenomenology of, 199
Hutcheson, Francis, 110
Huxley, Thomas Henry, 149, 152–153, 158–9,
171
hypnotism, Braid on, 155–156; Charcot on,
156; Freud and, 215–6; hysteria and, 156;
mesmerism and, 153–6; Nancy school of,
156; Salpetriere school of, 156
hysteria, 214–6; Freud on, 219, 224–5; hypnotism and, 156

I. Q. tests, 474
Ibn Rushd, 63, 67
Ibn Sīnā, 64–67, 70–2; faculty psychology of,
64–7; on imagination, 65; on memory, 65; on
the soul, 64–7
idealism, 168, 172, 120, 378; Berkeley's, 109–
110; Hegel's, 267
Iliad, 35
imageless thought, 192–199
imagination, Aristotle on, 51–52; Ibn Sīnā on,
65
immigrants, control of, 381; testing of, 339–41
independent variables, defined, 381
individualism, 133; love and, 68–9; mysticism
and, 69
information processing, 400–1, 426; Tolman
and, 317; triumph of, 444–6
innate ideas, 115–116; Locke on, 97; Plato on,
46; See also nativism
instincts, Freud's theory of, 209–12, 223
Institute of Human Relations (Yale), 324–25

instrumentalism, Dewey's, 292–3; in functionalism, 292
intelligence tests, racism in, 339–41
intentionality, 115
intentionality (Brentano), 199
Interpretation of Dreams (Freud), 214, 218–20,
472
introspection, 93, 110, 119, 179, 185, 260,
287, 319, 445, 455–6; Angell on, 295; Dunlap on, 294; Kant on, 119; Kulpe on, 191–2,
195; mentalism and, 193; Watson on, 302;
Wundt on, 185
introspectionism, 349
Islam, 62–67
isomorphism, Gestalt concept of, 198

Jackson, George D., 474
James, William, 55, 146, 153, 167, 169, 172,
182, 200, 207, 252–3, 257, 259, 262, 264,
273, 275–6, 278–81, 288–9, 331, 332, 397,
438, 450; analysis of science, 24; automatic
sweetheart, 290–1; functionalism of, 268;
Pragmatism, 266–8; pragmatism of, 249–50,
288; Principles of Psychology, 249–50, 250–
1, 266, 268–72
Jastrow, Joseph, 464; pragmatism and, 249, 308
Jenkins, James J., 451–3
Jensen, Arthur, 474
Jerome, St., 55; on women, 67–68
Jews, 82, 345; Freud and, 213–4; medieval,
62–3
Johnson, Lyndon, 428–9
Judd, C. H., 294
Julius Caesar (Shakespeare), 380
Jung, Karl, psychoanalysis of, 227

Kallikaks (Goddard), 343, 345
Kant, Immanuel, 77, 108, 110, 114, 117–21,
123, 130, 139, 162, 168, 178, 246, 248, 412;
Anthropology, 119–20; Descartes and, 119;
faculty psychology of, 119; Freud and, 217–
8; on god, 118; on introspection, 119; on the
soul, 119; Transcendental Ego, concept of,
119–20
Kendler, Howard, 422–3, 446; 390–3; logical
positivism and, 378
Kendler, Tracy, 390–3
Kepler, Johannes, 84, 94, 133
Kerouac, Jack, 403
Kiesler, Charles, 478
King, Martin Luther, Jr., 435
Klineberg, Otto, 345
Knapp, Elizabeth, witch, 471–2
Koch, Sigmund, 314, 322, 371, 474–5; on
positivism, 378–9
Koffka, Kurt, 196, 201, 319
Kohler, Wolfgang, 196, 199, 201–2, 280–1
Kraepelin, Emil, 186
Krechevsky, I., 419
Kuhn, 90, 104, 207, 307, 305, 417–8, 423,
435, 445, 452–4; analysis of science, 12–18,

Kuhn (*cont.*)
19, 20; disciplinary matrix, 15–16; normal
science, 15–16; paradigm, 12–18; shared exemplars, 12–13; Structure of Scientific
Revolutions, 12
Kulpe, Oswald, 200, 308–9; on introspection,
191–192, 195
Kuo, Zing Yang, 307

L'Homme Machine (La Mettrie), 126
La Mettrie, Julien Offroy de, 125–128, 286,
308–9, 397, 399, 416–7; L'Homme Ma-
chine, 126; vitalism, 125–6
Lachman, Lachman, and Butterfield, 445–6,
448, 450–1, 454
Ladd, G. T., 252, 266
Lafayette, Marquis de, 154
Lakatos, Imre, analysis of science, 8, 19–21,
285
Lamarck, J. -B., 148, 151, 173, 234–8
language, acquisition of, 415–17; adult, 414–5;
Carnap on, 317; Skinner on, 384, 386–9;
Wundt on, 187–8; *See also* Chomsky, Noam
Lashley, Karl, 371, 445; on behaviorism, 307;
Law of effect (Thorndike), 421
Leahey and Leahey, on pseudoscience, 7
learning, Plato, 46; animal, constraints on, 418–
21; Hull on, 320–23; human, 421–3; operant,
382; Tolman on, 322–3; Watson on, 310–11
Leary, Timothy, 434–5
Leibniz, Gottfried Wilhelm, 101–103, 117,
121–2, 167, 185–6, 172, 395, 415, 458; ap-
perception, 103; attention, 103; causes, final,
102; development, 102; Freud and, 224; on
god, 102; on mind, 102; on memory, 103;
parallelism, mind/body, 102; on perception,
102–3; on the soul, 103; unconsciousness in,
208–9
Leonardo da Vinci, 79, 81
Lévi-Strauss, Claude, 424
Lewin, Kurt, 198, 379
libido (Freud), 208
Liebault, A. A., 156
Lindner, Robert, 403
Lippman, Walter, on testing, 340
Little Albert (Watson), 310
Locke, John, 96–98, 103, 108, 110, 112, 115,
124, 126, 134, 139, 182, 245; Descartes and,
96–8; empiricism of, 96–8; on innate ideas,
97; on mind, 96–8; on nativism, 97
Lofton, John, 474
Logic Theorist, 401
logical positivism, 5–6, 24–5, 321, 324, 417–
8, 421; demise of, 378–9; Einstein on, 6–7;
Kendler and, 378; operationism of, 312–15;
See also operationism, positivism
Lorenz, Konrad, on aggression, 223
Lotze, Hermann, 169, 172, 183
love, Carmina Burana on, 68; Gottfried von
Strasbourg on, 68; individualism and, 68–9

Luckhardt, Grant, 374
Luther, Martin, 81–82

Macbeth (Shakespeare), 82
Mach, Ernst, 146, 312, 313, 380
Machiavelli, 79
Magendie, Francois, 164
Maimonides, 63
Maine de Biran, Francois-Pierre, 166–167,
171–2
Malcolm, Norman, 375–76
Malthus, Thomas, 150–151
mandarins, Chinese, 37; German, 182
Marcus Aurelius, 53
market research, 478
Marler, Peter, 416
Marshall, Henry, 305
Marx, Karl, 147, 206, 207, 132; analysis of his-
tory, 30
Maskelyne, John, 159–160
Maslow, Abraham, 410–12, 432–6
materialism, 127–128, 158–60
Mayer, A. M., imageless thought, 192, 194
Mayo, Elton, Hawthorne Effect, 336–37; indus-
trial psychology and, 355–6
Mayr, Ernst, analysis of science, 25–27
McComas, H. C., on the motor theory of con-
sciousness, 305
McConnel, James, 473
McCosh, James, 252
McDougall, William, 294, 309; hormic psychol-
ogy, 316; racism in, 339, 345
Mead, Margaret, Samoa, views of, 347–49
mechanism, 84, 90, 103, 124–125, 147, 149,
153, 318–22, 397–8, 447, 451, 459
mediational S-R theory, 392–3
Meinong, Alexius, 195
memory, 455–6, 375; Aristotle on, 51–2; Ibn
Sīnā on, 65; Leibniz on, 103
Mendel, Gregor, genetics of, 150
mental chronometry, Donder's, 162, 192
mental hygiene, 332
mentalism, 259–60, 277–8, 312, 332, 423,
425–6; Freud's, 207–8; introspection and,
193; Watson on, 311
Mesmer, Franz Anton, 153–156
mesmerism, 153–156; animal magnetism, 155;
hypnotism, 153–6
Metaphysical Club, 247–9, 253
microcosm/macrocosm, 83–84
Mill, James, 122, 143, 189, 195, 471; tinkertoy
theory of, 143
Mill, John Stuart, 143–5, 182, 185, 195, 471;
analysis of science, 24–5
Miller, George, 450
Mills, C. Wright, 403
Mills, Wesley, 280
mind, 288, 420, 423, 431–2; Aquinas on, 72;
Aristotle on, 51; Bain on, 165–7; behaviorism, logical, on, 372–4; Descartes on, 95;

mind (*cont.*)
  Hume on, 111; Locke on, 96–8; Leibniz on, 102; Ockham on, 74–7; rediscovered, 395–7; Skinner on, 380, 386
Minsky, Marvin, 437
Misbehavior of Organisms (Breland & Breland), 419
misogyny, 67–68
Mithraism, 54
molar theory, Tolman's, 316
molecularism, 316
Mondale, Walter, 429
Montaigne, Michel de, 79, 82–84
Morgan's canon, animal psychology, 241
Morgan, C. Lloyd, on animal psychology, 241
Morgan, Clifford T., 360–61
Moses, model for Freud, 227
motor theory of consciousness, 268–72, 423, 305
MTC, see Motor Theory of Consciousness
Müller, Johannes, 165–166, 179
Musterberg, Hugo, 259, 289, 315, 421; Action Theory of, 268–70, 272
Myer, Max, 294
Myers, Frederic, 159–160, 172, 466
mysticism, individualism and, 69
myth of mental illness, 431–2

Nancy, school of hypnotism, 156
nativism, 102, 115–6, 416–9; Locke on, 97; Plato on, 46; *See also* Descartes; Chomsky, Noam
natural law, 103, 152; Hobbes on, 99–100
natural selection, 149–153
naturalism, 73, 77, 123–9, 152, 159, 171, 466; and science, 11–18
Nature, 99, 103, 134, 115
nature/nurture debate, 416–17
Nazis, 63, 200, 234; eugenics of, 345; Freud and, 213–4
Neisser, Ulric, 426–7, 464
neobehaviorism, 446
neoHullians, 378–93
neoPlatonism, 40, 54, 61–4, 67, 69, 70–73, 84, 90
neorealism, 289–92, 315
Neumann, John von, 402
neurophysiology, 467–71
neuroses, Freud on, 221; Watson on, 306
New Look in perception, 396
Newell, Allen, 401–2, 452–4
Newell, Shaw, & Simon, 452–3; *See also* GPS
Newton, Isaac, 4, 77, 84, 90, 94–5, 103–4, 108, 112, 121, 124, 125, 126, 130, 133–4, 139, 142, 144, 154, 162, 313, 320, 397, 401–2, 451; analysis of science, 24–5; on god, 91
Newtonian fantasy, psychologist's, 24–25
Nicholas of Autrecourt, 76–78

Nietzsche, Friedrich, influence on Freud, 210
Noble Savage, 103, 133
nominalism, 75–76
normal science (Kuhn), 15–16
noumena (Kant), 117–118
Noyes, John Humphrey, leader of Oneida, 343
NSF, 361, 429

occasionalism, 102
Ockham, William of, 74–79, 108, 380; on mind and soul, 74–77
Odyssey (Homer), 35
Oedipus complex (Freud), 212–13, 219–20, 222, 224
Ogden, R. M., on imageless thought, 193
On the Road (Kerouac), 403
Oneida community (Noyes), 343
operant conditioning, Skinner on, 383; Thorndike, E. L. on, 280–3
operationism, 312–5, 377, 445; *See also* logical positivism, 445
ordinary language philosophy, 374–7, 425
Oresme, Nicholas, 78
orgy, boring, Perelman, S. J. describes, 345–46, 349
Origin of Species (Darwin), 147–153, 237
Orth, J., on imageless thought, 192–194
Osgood, Charles, 389–90, 393

paradigm (Kuhn), 12–18, 445, 452–4; Skinner's, 385
parallelism, 121–122; Leibniz on, 102
parapsychology, 465, 467
Parmenides, 39–40, 93
Pascal, Blaise, 391, Pensées, 100 101
Pavlov, I. P., 294, 310, 381–2, 419, 452; classical conditioning, 280, 283–6; conditioned response, concept of, 285; Lashley and, 306; Watson and, 303
Pearson, Karl, 239–40
Peirce, C. S., pragmatism of, 247–9, 267
penis envy, Freud on, 222
Pensées (Pascal), 100–101
perception, 110, 115, 253, 396; Berkeley on, 109–10
perceptual defense, 396
Perelman, S. J., attends orgy, boring, 345–46, 349
peripheralism, 420–1, 437; Sechenov's, 304; Watson's, 303–5
Perry, Ralph Barton, 289–90, 308, 455
perversions, Freud on, 221
petite perception (Leibniz), 102 103
Petrarch, Francesco, 79–80
phenomena (Kant), 117–118
phenomenology, 195; Husserl's, 199
phi phenomenon, Gestalt, 196
philosophers, 31, 124, 126, 129, 139, 244, 347
phrenology, 153, 156–8, 163–4, 234–7, 247; as pseudoscience, 7

physics, 22–23
physics envy, psychologists', 24–5
Piaget, Jean, 47, 102, 169, 393–5, 397, 424
Pico della Mirandola, 79–80
Plato, 38–49, 73–4, 92–95, 121, 147, 156,
  182, 267, 379, 415, 424, 435; associationism
  in, 46, 52; dualism, 51; on development, 46;
  Forms, doctrine of, 53–4, 67; innate ideas in,
  46; on learning, 46; on reincarnation, 46; on
  the soul, 45; Timaeus, 45, 63
Platonism, 69, 73, 77, 78, 81, 91, 129–30,
  138, 479; Christian, 54–5
pleasure principle (Freud), 217
Plotinus, on god, 53–4
Pope, Alexander, Essay on Man, 134–5
Popper, Karl, 37; analysis of science, 20–21;
  falsificationism, 6–7
pornography, Victorian, influence on Freud,
  210
positivism, 29, 144–146, 181, 311–15, 377,
  417–8, 437; failings of, 9–11; Koch and,
  378–9; See also logical positivism
potentiality and actuality, Aristotle on, 48–49
pragmatism, 181, 248, 331, 332; analysis of
  science, 24–5; Dewey's, 263–6; James's,
  249–51, 266–8, 288; Jastrow's, 249, 308;
  Peirce's, 247–9, 267
preconscious (Freud), 209
Priestly, Joseph, 122
Principles of Psychology (James), 247–8, 250–
  1, 266, 268–72, 319
professionalization, of APA, 260–3
program, computer, 398, 400, 446–51
Progressivism, 311, 330–3, 336, 341, 363;
  Dewey and, 262–6; Watson, and 353, 359
Project for a Scientific Psychology (Freud),
  217–18, 222
Project Camelot, 428
Project Orcon, 388, 398
Protagoras, 42
pseudoscience, 7, 16; ESP as, 17; Leahey &
  Leahey on, 7; phrenology as, 7
psychical research, 158–160
psychoanalysis, 403; Adler and, 227; Jung and,
  227; See also Freud, Sigmund
psycholinguistics, 427
psychology, applied, 331–3, 338, 358; clinical,
  337, 356–8, 475–7; cognitive, 393–402,
  423–6, 436–8, 444, 453–4, 463–4, 466,
  451–2; ecological, 464; humanistic, 411,
  417, 432–6, 437–8, 465; industrial, 336–7;
  information processing, 400–1; Mayo on,
  355–56; occult doubles of, 464–7; operant,
  466; purposive, 316; Rogers's, 352; social,
  395–6
psychophysics (Fechner), 192
psychotherapy, 422, 430, 476–7
purposive machines, 398–9
Putney, Snell and Gail J., 432
Pythagoras, 38–39

quantum physics, 466
quantum theory, 22–23

R2-D2, ancestors of, blown up, 459–60
racism, 340–3; Grant's, 342; intelligence tests
  and, 339–41; McDougall's, 339, 345
Raimey, Craig T., 473–4
rationalism, 39–40, 55, 92–6, 130, 139, 182,
  200, 267–8, 415, 425–5
Rayner, Rosalie, Watson and, 310
realism, 75–76, 288–9, 378; analysis of science, 22
Rebel Without a Cause, 403–4
reductionism, 444–5, 467–8
reflex arc, Dewey on, 270–1, 274, 27
Reflexes of the Brain (Sechenov), 283–4, 286
Reid, Thomas, 98, 108, 114–7, 117–8, 121–3,
  195, 244, 251–3
reincarnation, Plato, 46
religion, Freud, 225–26
Remmers, H. H., 360
representation, concept of, 450, 459
repression (Freud), 209, 213, 218, 221
revolution, cognitive, 454–7
Rheingold, Harriet, 473–4
Rieff, Phillip, 331
Riegel, Klaus, 147
Riesman, David, 403
robots, 397
Rogers, Carl, 433–6, 477; and psychology, humanistic, 352
Romanes, George John, on animal psychology,
  241–42
romantic love, 68
romanticism, 122, 130–1, 135–42, 148, 200–
  243
Rome, 53; fall of, 55, 59–61
Rorty, Richard, foundational philosophy, cri-
  tique of, 5
Rosch, Eleanor, 460
Rosenblueth, Wiener, and Bigelow, 398
Rousseau, Jean-Jacques, 462; Emile, 133; social
  contract, 103, 132–3
Royce, Josiah, 291
Russell, Bertrand, 381; on Aquinas, 72, 120; on
  behaviorism, 348–9
Ryle, Gilbert, 373–74, 376

S-R theory, 383, 389–93, 396–7, 416, 421–3,
  427, 437–8, 447–8
Sade, The Marquis de, 128–129, 160
Salinger, J. D., 403
Salpetriere, school of hypnotism, 156
Samoa, Mead's views of, 347–49
Samoa Revisited (Freeman), 348
Sanford, E. C., 286
Sanford, Fillmore, 402
Sanford, Neville, 430
Sartre, Jean-Paul, 100

scala natura, 435; Aristotle, 48–9; Chain of Being and, 148
schema theory, Bartlett, Frederick, 279
schizophrenia, Wundt on, 186
scholasticism, 90, 92
Schopenhauer, Arthur, 120, 141, 172; on Will, 209
science, analysis of; see analysis of science
scientism, 77, 152, 349; Chesterton on, 344
Scott, Walter Dill, 332–35
Scottish philosophers, 108, 114–7, 244, 249, 251–2, 361
Searle, John, 458–9, 460
Sebright, John, 149
Sechenov, I. M., peripheralism of, 304; Reflexes of the Brain, 283–4, 286
seduction mistake, Cioffi on, 211–12; Freud's, 211–2
self-psychology (Calkins), 305
Selz, Otto, 195
sensationism, 156–157; Titchener's, 190–1
sexuality, Victorian, Freud on, 212–13, 220–21
Shakespeare, Hamlet, 82, 460; Julius Caesar, 380; Macbeth, 82; Tempest, 341
shared exemplar (Kuhn), 12–13
Sharp, H. C., inventor of the vasectomy, 344
Siger of Brabant, 76–77
Simon, Herbert, 401–2, 428, 437, 444–5, 451
Singer, Edgar A., 289–91
skepticism, 98, 114, 435
Skeptics, 53
Skinner, B. F., 26, 83, 110, 126, 133, 146, 152–3, 191, 259, 294, 371, 379, 397–8, 410–21, 435, 437–8, 461–3, 466, 474; behaviorism, radical, 248–9, 325, 379–89; on mind, 380; on the reflex, 380
Small, Leonard, 430
Smith, Adam, 123
Social Contract (Rousseau), 103, 132–3
Social Darwinism, 236–37
sociobiology, 468–70
Socrates, 42–3
sophism, 41–2, 43, 92–3
soul, 437; Aristotle on, 49–50; Aquinas on, 72; Descartes on, 95; Ibn Sīnā on, 64–7; Kant on, 119; Leibniz on, 103; medieval philosophy on, 69; Ockham on, 75; Plato on, 45; Singer on, 291; Watson on, 304
species-specific behavior, 371–72
specific response, Holt's doctrine of, 290
Spence, Kenneth, 325, 357, 391–2, 435
Spencer, Herbert, 152, 182, 235–7, 235, 324; on adaptation, psychology of, 239–40; on god, 235; social Darwinism of, 236–7
Spinoza, Baruch, 82, 102, 112, 121, 462; on god, 100–101; on the state, 100–1
spiritualism, 158–160, 153, 467
Spurzheim, Johann Caspar, 158
sterilization, eugenics and, 334
Stevens, S. S., 314

Stewart, Dugald, 115–7, 122–3, 252
Stich, Steven, 470
Stoicism, 53–54; Freud and, 228
structuralism, 110, 277–8, 394, 423–5
Structure of Scientific Revolutions (Kuhn), 12
Studies in Hysteria (Freud), 215–16
sublimation (Freud), 222
superego (Freud), 225–26
Suppe, Frederick, analysis of science, 6, 11–2, 19, 22
Suppes, Patrick, hierarchy of theories, 10
Szasz, Thomas, 431–2

tabula rasa, 141, 173, 234, 419–20
Taine, Hippolyte-Adolphe, 167–168, 169
Transcendentalism, 246
Taylor, Donald W., 426
Taylor, Frederick, 336–37
teleology, 48–9; Leibniz on, 102
Tempest (Shakespeare), 341
Tennyson, Alfred Lord, 149
Terman, Lewis, testing, 340–41
Tertullian, 62
testing, 332, 334–36, 430–1, 478; evils of, 339–41; Goddard and, 339–41; of immigrants, 339–41; I.Q., 474; Lippman on, 340; Terman on, 340–1
Tetens, Johann Nikolaus, 130
Thales, 37–8
themata, in analysis of science, 19–20
Thilly, Frank, 276
thinking, Wurzburg School on, 191–195
Thomasius, Christian, 129–130
Thoreau, Henry David, 243
Thorndike, E. L., 197–198, 286, 384–5, 421; Animal Intelligence, 281–2; Human Learning, 282–3; operant conditioning, study of, 280–3; on punishment, 282
Three Essays on the Theory of Sexuality (Freud), 220–2
Timaeus, (Plato), 45, 63
tinker-toy theory of the mind, 143, 184, 195
Titchener, E. B., 91, 98, 110, 115, 146, 179, 183, 188–191, 193, 195, 199–201, 305, 308–9, 315, 333, 349, 382, 410, 424–5; on functionalism, 272–4; sensationism of, 190–1; Wundt and, 188–9
Tocqueville, Alexis de, 264–5
Tolman, E. C., 201, 289, 314–18, 321, 373, 377–9, 384–5, 389, 398, 418, 427, 457, 289; cognitive map concept, 322; computer model and, 317; on consciousness, 316; information processing and, 317; molar behaviorism of, 316
Toulmin, Stephen, analysis of science, 18–24, 417; Human Understanding, 18–24
Tracy, Destutt de, 166
Transcendental Ego (Kant), 119–120
transformational grammar, 414
Tristan and Isolde, 68

Tulving, Endel, 453–4
Turing, A. M., 399, 402
Turing machine, 400
Turing test, 399, 457–8

U. S. Army, APA and, 333–35
unconscious, 159–60, 172, 177; dynamic, 209;
Fechner on, 208–9; Freud on, 208–9, 224–5;
Hartmann on, 208; Herbart on, 208; Leibniz
on, 208–9
universals, 74

VA hospitals, 357
VALS, 478
vasectomy (Sharp), 344
Verbal Behavior (Skinner), 386–8, 412–15
Vesalius, 66
Vico, Giambattista, 130–131, 172, 187
Viereck, Peter, 403
Vietnam War, 432, 435
Virgin Mary, 68
vitalism, 141, 148; La Mettrie's, 125–6
Völkerpsychologie, 184, 187, 191
Voltaire, 124, 126
voluntarism, 141
voluntaristic ethics, Abelard's, 69

Walden II, 386, 388–9, 397, 419, 461–2
Wallace, Alfred Russel, 151, 160
Ward, James, 169, 278–9
Washburn, Margaret Floy, 349
Washington, George, 154
Watson, John B., 122, 201, 243, 257, 292,
294, 301–4, 315, 316, 318, 319, 348–9,
379, 382, 389, 473–8, 455–7, 462; Animal
Education, 287–8; on adaptation, 303; be-
haviorism of, 193, 287–8; Comte and, 303;
on childrearing, 350–4; on conditioning,
310–11; evangelical preaching, influence on,
349, 352; Freud and, 340; on introspection,
302; Little Albert, study of, 310; on mental-
ism, 311; on neuroses, 306; Pavlov and, 303;
Progressivism and, 353, 359; peripheralism
of, 303–5; Rayner and, 310; on the soul, 304
Watt, Henry J., 194
Weber, E. H., 163
Weiss, Albert P., 307–8, 445
Weltanschauung analysis of science, 11–12
Wertheimer, Max, 196–197
Wheeler, W. M., 228

Whyte, William, 403
Wiebe, G. D., 358
Wiggam, A. E., eugenics of, 341, 342
Wilberforce, William, 151–2
Will, Schopenhauer on, 209
Wilson, E. O., 454, 467–9
Wilson, Woodrow, 330
witchcraft, 471–2
Witmer, Lightner, 332, 337–8
Wittgenstein, Ludwig, 374–7, 398, 448, 456
Wolfe, Tom, 479
Wolff, Christian, 130
Wolfle, Dael, 428
women, Aquinas on, 67; Albigensianism and,
68; Boccaccio on, 68; St. Jerome on, 67–8;
romantic love and, 68; Victorian, Freud on,
212–3
Woodhull, Victoria, 343
Woodworth, Robert, 308–9; on imageless
thought, 192, 294
Wordsworth, William, 144
World War I, 257, 333
World War II, 257, 354–56, 369, 382, 385–6,
388, 393, 397
Wright, Chauncey, 248
Wundt, Wilhelm, 4, 26, 91, 102–3, 115, 120,
129–32, 141, 144, 146, 148, 163, 167, 172–
3, 177, 179–89, 196, 197, 199–201, 207,
234, 238, 239, 249, 250, 252, 257, 259,
260, 262, 268–9, 272, 279, 332, 386–7,
396, 410, 414, 424, 455; Freud and, 213,
217–8; on introspection, 185; on language,
187–8; on schizophrenia, 186; Titchener and,
188–9; on Wurzburg school, 191–3
Wurzburg school, 278, 425, 454–5; studies of
thinking, 191–5; Wundt criticizes, 191–3
Wyckhoff, L. B., 400

Xenophanes, 38

Yeats, William Butler, 332–1, 346
Yerkes, Robert, 293, 305, 333–5, 339–41; re-
views criteria of mind, 286–7
Youth, 1950s, 403–4
Youth, 1960s, 434–5
Youth, Flaming, 339, 349–50

Zeitgeist analysis of history, 30
Zeno, 53
Zoonomia (Darwin), 149